꿈이당

꿈 꾸어라!
이 루어라!
당 신 뜻대로!

KB004972

경찰대학 영어

유형별 기출문제 총정리

특수대학 입학시험 연구회 편

나는 똑똑한 것이 아니라
단지 문제를 더 오래 연구할 뿐이다.

– 알버트 아인슈타인

성과를 내려는 사람들은 수없이 많습니다.
하지만 마음만으로 원하는 결과를 얻을 수 있는 것은 아닙니다.

어렵고 힘든 목표를 성취하려면 끈기 있는 자세가 필요합니다.
쉽게 단념하지 않고 견딜 때 노력이 결실을 맺을 수 있는 가능성이 열립니다.

재능이 부족하다고 도중에 멈춘다면 성공할 수 있는 기회도 주어지지 않습니다.
스스로 포기하기보다는 끈기를 가지고 노력하세요.

〈꿈이당〉은 수험생 여러분의 노력을 응원합니다.
〈꿈이당〉과 함께 합격의 그날까지 꾸준히 나아가시기 바랍니다.

씨마스

이 책의 구성과 특징

1 경찰대학 경쟁률 및 출제 경향

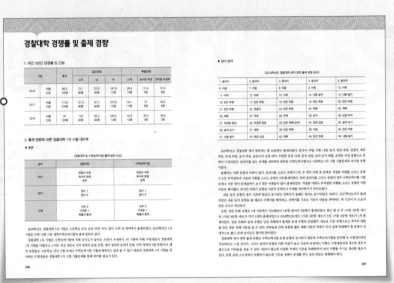

지난 3년간 경찰대학 경쟁률 및 국어·영어·수학 과목의 전반적인 출제 경향과 대비책, 2018학년도 영어 기출문제 분석표를 수록하였습니다.

2 경찰대학 영어 기출문제 Part별·유형별 출제 경향 분석

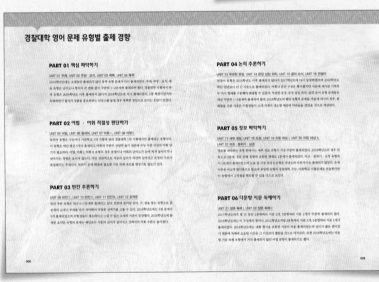

경찰대학 영어 기출문제를 23개의 유형으로 분류한 후 6개의 Part로 묶었습니다. 각 Part별·유형별 출제 경향을 분석하여 학습 방향을 잡을 수 있도록 하였습니다.

3 경찰대학 영어 문제 유형을 설명하는 Example

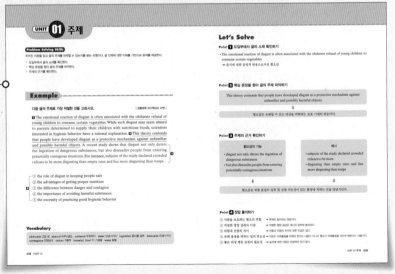

각 유형별 대표 기출문제를 선정하여 각 단원 맨 앞에 수록하였습니다. 해당 지문의 핵심 영단어 및 문제 해결 과정을 담아 수험생들이 스스로 풀이 과정을 점검해 볼 수 있도록 하였습니다.

4 경찰대학 기출문제를 수록한
Practice

각 유형별 경찰대학 영어 기출문제를 수록하였습니다. 수험생들은 해당 문제를 통해 경찰대학 영어 시험 유형에 익숙해질 수 있습니다.

5 동일 유형 사관학교 · 수능 기출문제를 수록한 More Practice

추가 연습이 가능하도록 각 유형별로 사관학교와 대학수학능력시험 기출문제를 수록하였습니다.

6 상세하고 정확한 해설

지문별 해석, 핵심 영단어, 정답 풀이 과정을 담은 해설집을 별도로 수록하였습니다.

목 차

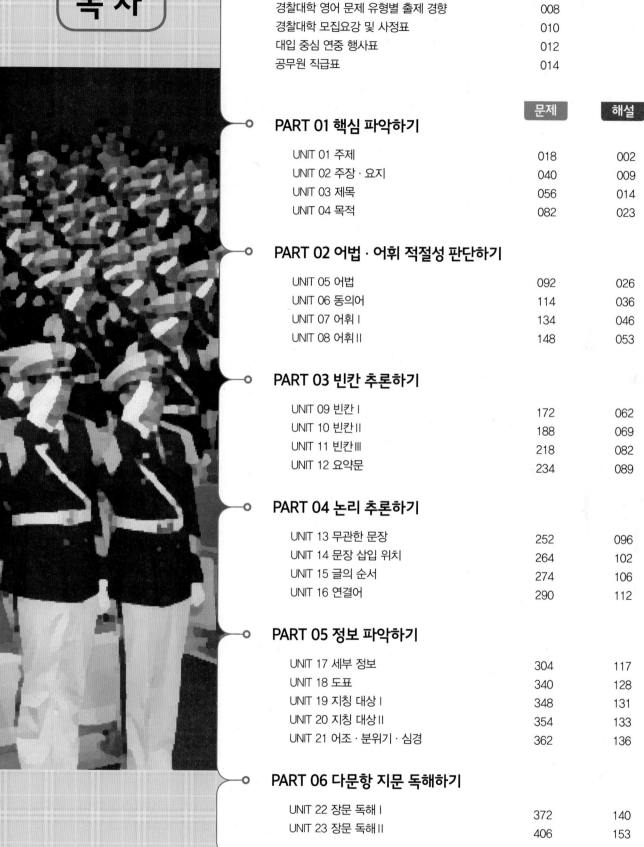

경찰대학 경쟁률 및 출제 경향

1. 최근 3년간 경쟁률 및 인원

구분		총계	일반전형			특별전형		
			소계	남	여	소계	농어촌 학생	한마음 무궁화
2018	비율	68.5	73.1	57.6	197.8	26.4	21.4	31.4
	인원	100명	90명	80명	10명	10명	5명	5명
2017	비율	113.6	121.5	97.2	315.8	43.1	37	49.2
	인원	100명	90명	80명	10명	10명	5명	5명
2016	비율	97	103	85.2	245.5	42.6	35.4	49.8
	인원	100명	90명	80명	10명	10명	5명	5명

2. 출제 경향에 따른 경찰대학 1차 시험 대비책

● 총론

〈경찰대학 및 수학능력시험 출제 범위 비교〉

영역	경찰대학	수학능력시험
국어	화법과 작문 독서와 문법 문학	화법과 작문 독서와 문법 문학
영어	영어 I 영어 II	영어 I 영어 II
수학	수학 II 미적분 I 확률과 통계	수학 II 미적분 I 확률과 통계

　　2018학년도 경찰대학 1차 시험은 고등학교 문과 교과 과정 국어, 영어, 수학 전 영역에서 출제되었다. 2019학년도 1차 시험은 수학 나형 기준 대학수학능력시험과 출제 범위가 같다.

　　경찰대학 1차 시험은 수학능력시험에 비해 난이도가 높다는 의견이 우세하다. 타 시험에 비해 수험생들이 경찰대학 1차 시험을 어렵다고 느끼는 주요 원인은 국어 영역의 문법 문항, 영어 영역의 동의어 문항, 수학 영역의 5점 문항이다. 해당 문항들은 고등학교 내신 시험 문제나 수학능력시험 기출문제에서는 쉽게 볼 수 없기 때문에 경찰대학 1차 시험을 준비하는 수험생들은 경찰대학 1차 시험 기출문제를 통해 대비할 필요가 있다.

● 영어 영역

〈2018학년도 경찰대학 영어 영역 출제 문항 분석〉

1. 동의어	2. 동의어	3. 동의어	4. 동의어	5. 동의어
6. 어법	7. 어법	8. 어법	9. 어휘	10. 어휘
11. 어휘	12. 어휘	13. 어휘	14. 내용 일치	15. 내용 일치
16. 빈칸 추론	17. 빈칸 추론	18. 빈칸 추론	19. 빈칸 추론	20. 빈칸 추론
21. 빈칸 추론	22. 연결어	23. 빈칸 추론	24. 제목	25. 제목
26. 제목	27. 주제	28. 주제	29. 요지	30. 심경 파악
31. 무관한 문장	32. 무관한 문장	33. 빈칸 추론(요약)	34. 문장 삽입	35. 글의 순서
36. 글의 순서	37. 제목	38. 빈칸 추론	39. 어법	40. 빈칸 추론
41. 내용 일치	42. 문장 삽입	43. 제목	44. 빈칸 추론	45. 내용 일치

2018학년도 경찰대학 영어 영역에는 총 45문항이 출제되었다. 동의어, 어법, 어휘, 내용 일치, 빈칸 추론, 연결어, 제목 추론, 주제 추론, 요지 추론, 글쓴이의 심경 파악, 무관한 문장 삭제, 문장 삽입, 글의 순서 배열, 요약문 작성 유형으로 문항이 구성되었다. 동의어를 묻는 문제를 제외하면 대부분 수학능력시험이나 사관학교 1차 시험 기출문제와 유사한 유형이었다.

올해에도 어휘 문항의 비중이 컸다. 동의어를 고르는 문항이 5개, 두 개의 어휘 중 문맥상 적절한 어휘를 고르는 문항이 2개, 부적절하게 사용된 어휘를 고르는 문항이 3개 출제되었다. 특히 동의어를 고르는 문항의 경우 수학능력시험 기출문제나 시중 영어 문제집에서 보기 힘든 어휘들이 많이 출제되었다. 적절한 어휘나 부적절한 어휘를 고르는 유형의 어휘 수준은 평이했다. 하지만 어휘가 포함된 지문의 문맥이나 주제를 파악하기가 까다로웠다.

내용 일치 유형의 경우 기존에 한글로 표기되던 선택지가 올해는 영어로 표기되었다. 따라서 2017학년도까지 출제되었던 내용 일치 문항을 풀 때보다 선택지를 해석하고, 선택지를 기초로 지문의 내용을 파악하는 데 시간이 더 소요되었을 것으로 예상된다.

또한, 장문 독해 유형은 4개 지문에서 지난해보다 1문항 줄어든 9문항이 출제되었다. 최근 몇 년 간 1지문 2문항 세트와 1지문 3문항 세트가 각각 2개씩 출제되었으나 2018학년도에는 1지문 2문항 세트가 3개, 1지문 3문항 세트가 1개 출제되었다. 장문 독해의 문제 유형은 단문 독해에서 출제된 문제 유형과 동일했다. 새로운 지문 유형으로는 부부의 대화를 담은 장문 독해 지문을 들 수 있다. 큰따옴표 안에 포함된 짧은 대화 지문의 비중이 커서 실제 독해해야 할 분량이 상대적으로 짧고 문제 난이도도 평이한 편이었다.

경찰대학 영어 영역 출제 유형은 수학능력시험 문제 유형과 유사하기 때문에 수학능력시험을 준비해 온 수험생이라면 익숙하다고 느낄 것이다. 그러나 동의어 문항의 어휘 수준이 높고 지문에 등장하는 어휘도 수험생들에게 생소한 경우가 많으므로 어려움을 겪을 수 있다. 따라서 평소에 다양한 주제의 지문을 독해하면서 낯선 어휘를 수시로 정리할 필요가 있다. 또한 실제 고사장에서 당황하지 않도록 시간을 정해서 문제를 푸는 실전 연습도 병행해야 한다.

경찰대학 영어 문제 유형별 출제 경향

PART 01 핵심 파악하기

UNIT 01 주제, UNIT 02 주장 · 요지, UNIT 03 제목, UNIT 04 목적

2018학년도에는 오랫동안 출제되지 않던 목적 유형 문제가 다시 출제되었다. 주제, 주장 · 요지, 제목 유형은 난이도나 형식의 큰 변화 없이 꾸준히 1~2문제씩 출제되어 왔다. 경찰대학 시험에서 목적 유형은 2009학년도 이후 출제되지 않다가 2018학년도에 다시 출제되었다. 2점 배점이었지만 독해하면서 필자가 상품을 홍보하려는 뉘앙스를 놓칠 경우 명백한 정답으로 보이는 오답이 있었다.

PART 02 어법 · 어휘 적절성 판단하기

UNIT 05 어법, UNIT 06 동의어, UNIT 07 어휘 I, UNIT 08 어휘 II

동의어 유형은 수능이나 사관학교 1차 시험과 달리 경찰대학 1차 시험에서만 출제되는 유형이다. 이 유형은 매년 평균 5개가 출제되고 어휘의 수준이 상당히 높기 대문에 수능 수준 이상의 어휘 암기가 필요하다. 어법, 어휘 I, 어휘 II 유형의 경우 문법이나 어휘의 난이도가 눈에 띄게 높아지거나 낮아지는 경향은 보이지 않는다. 다만 전반적으로 지문의 길이가 약간씩 길어지고 문장의 구조가 복잡해지는 추세이다. 따라서 문제 해결에 필요한 지문 독해 속도를 향상시킬 필요가 있다.

PART 03 빈칸 추론하기

UNIT 09 빈칸 I, UNIT 10 빈칸 II, UNIT 11 빈칸 III, UNIT 12 요약문

빈칸 추론 유형은 매년 6~7문제씩 출제되고 있다. 빈칸에 들어갈 단어, 구, 절을 찾는 유형으로 글 전체의 소재나 주제를 먼저 파악해야 적절한 선택지를 고를 수 있다. 2018학년도에는 3점 문제가 3개 출제되었으며 수험생들이 생소하다고 느낄 수 있는 소재의 지문이 등장했다. 2018학년도에 출제된 요약문 유형의 문제는 예년보다 지문의 길이가 길어지고 선택지의 어휘 수준도 높아졌다.

PART 04 논리 추론하기

UNIT 13 무관한 문장, UNIT 14 문장 삽입 위치, UNIT 15 글의 순서, UNIT 16 연결어

연결어 유형은 2013학년도 이후 출제되지 않다가 2017학년도에 다시 등장하였으며 2018학년도
에는 전년보다 더 긴 지문으로 출제되었다. 어휘나 문단 구성은 평이했지만 지문에 제시된 기억의
두 가지 형태를 구분해야 해결할 수 있었다. 무관한 문장, 문장 삽입 위치, 글의 순서 유형 문제들은
매년 꾸준히 1~2문제씩 출제되어 왔다. 2018학년도의 해당 유형의 문제들 가운데 의사의 의무, 판
례법을 다룬 지문은 수험생들이 소재 자체의 생소함 때문에 어려움을 겪었을 것으로 예상된다.

PART 05 정보 파악하기

UNIT 17 세부 정보, UNIT 18 도표, UNIT 19 지칭 대상 I, UNIT 20 지칭 대상 II,
UNIT 21 어조 · 분위기 · 심경

정보를 파악하는 유형 중에서는 세부 정보 유형이 가장 꾸준히 출제되었다. 2018학년도의 경우 단
독으로 2문제, 장문 독해 유형에 포함된 형태로 2문제가 출제되었다. 어조 · 분위기 · 심경 유형에
서 1문제가 출제되었으며 도표 및 지칭 대상 II 유형은 전년도와 마찬가지로 출제되지 않았다. 문제
수준은 비교적 평이하므로 평소에 동일한 유형의 경찰대학, 수능, 사관학교 기출문제로 연습한다면
이 유형에서 고득점을 획득할 수 있을 것으로 보인다.

PART 06 다문항 지문 독해하기

UNIT 21 장문 독해 I, UNIT 22 장문 독해II

2017학년도까지 몇 년 동안 2문항짜리 지문 2개, 3문항짜리 지문 2개가 꾸준히 출제되어 왔다.
2018학년도에는 이 구성에서 벗어나, 2012학년도처럼 2문항짜리 지문 3개, 3문항짜리 지문 1개가
출제되었다. 2018학년도에는 대화 형식을 포함한 지문이 처음 출제되었는데 길이가 짧은 편이었
기 때문에 독해에 소요된 시간은 그 이전보다 짧았을 것으로 여겨진다. 또한 2018학년도에는 다문
항 지문 독해 유형에서 거의 출제되지 않던 어법 문항이 출제되기도 했다.

경찰대학 모집요강 및 사정표

1. 전형 일정

구분		내용
원서 접수 (인터넷)	특별전형	5월 초 ~ 5월 중순
	일반전형	5월 중순 ~ 5월 말 ※ 특별전형 지원자는 일반전형으로 이중 지원 불가
1차 시험	시험 일자	7월 말(토) 08:30~13:30
	합격자 발표	8월 초
2차 시험	1차 합격자 서류 제출	1차 합격자 발표 시 ~ 8월 초
	신체검사	1차 합격자 발표 시 ~ 8월 말 ※ 경찰병원 및 경찰공무원 채용 신체검사 가능한 국·공립대학병원에서 개별 수검 후 인편 및 등기우편 제출(체력시험 당일 직접 제출도 가능)
	체력시험 인·적성검사	9월 중순 ※ 3일간 조를 나누어 시행(개인별 1일 소요, 식비 수험생 부담)
	자기소개서 제출	8월 말 ~ 9월 초 ※ 경찰대학 홈페이지 각종 서류양식 또는 원서접수 대행업체 다운로드 후 작성하여 자기소개서 파일 업로드
	면접시험	10월 중순 ※ 신체검사, 체력시험 합격자에 한해 진행(개인별 1일 소요, 식비 수험생 부담)
최종 사정	대학수학능력시험	시험 11월 중순 / 성적 발표 12월 초
	최종합격자 발표	12월 중순 경찰대학 홈페이지 발표 ※ 원서접수 대행업체 홈페이지에서 최종 합격/불합격 여부, 예비순위 확인 가능

2. 모집 인원

모집 인원 및 학과	일반전형	특별전형	
		농어촌학생	한마음 무궁화
100명 법학과/행정학과 각 50명(2학년 진학 시 결정)	90	5	5

3. 전형 기준

(1) 1차 시험

선발 인원	배점	과목	문항 수	시간	출제 범위
4배수	300점	국어	45	60분	화법과 작문, 독서와 문법, 문학 (※ 교육과정에 기초, 다양한 지문과 자료 활용)
		영어	45	60분	영어 Ⅰ, 영어 Ⅱ (※ 교육과정에 기초, 다양한 지문과 자료 활용)
		수학	25	80분	수학 Ⅱ, 미적분 Ⅰ, 확률과 통계

(2) 2차 시험

신체검사	체력시험	면접	비고
합 · 불	50점(5%) (1종목 이상 1점 불합격)	100점(10%) (인성 · 적격성 40, 창의성 · 논리성 30, 집단토론 30, 생활태도 감점 -10)	• 평가점수 60점 미만 불합격 • 인성 · 적격성 면접 평가 40점 만점 기준 4할(16점) 미만자는 전체 평가 점수 60점 이상이어도 불합격

(3) 기타

학교생활기록부	수학능력시험	비고
150점(15%)	500점(50%) 국수영 각 140, 탐구 80, 한국사 등급별 감점 반영	• 학생부 3학년 1학기까지 반영 • 영역별 가산점 없음

(4) 최종 사정

1차	2차	내신	수능	총점
200점	150점	150점	500점	1000점
총점 × 200/300	체력시험 50점 면접시험 100점	교과성적 135점 출석성적 15점	국영수 각 140점 탐구 80점 한국사 등급별 감점	

4. 2차 시험 면접평가 방법

항목	점수(100)	비고
인성 · 적격성 면접	40	• 평가점수 100 만점 기준 60점 미만 불합격 • 최종 사정 성적 환산 : (평가원점수 ÷ 2) + 50
창의성논리성 면접	30	
집단토론 면접	30	
생활태도 평가	감점제(최대 10점)	

5. 2차 시험 체력시험 내용

구분	진행 내용과 방법
신체검사	수검 후 서류 제출
체력시험	기준(1종목 이상 1점) 이하 불합격 5종목(달리기(100m · 1,000m), 윗몸일으키기, 좌우 악력, 팔굽혀펴기)
인적성검사	면접 자료로 활용
면접	신체검사, 체력시험 합격자를 조를 나누어 진행

※ 위 내용은 2019학년도 경찰대학 모집요강에 근거한 것입니다. 자세한 내용은 경찰대학 홈페이지를 참고하시기 바랍니다.

대입 중심 연중 행사표

월	일정(날짜,요일)	
	1, 2학년	3학년
3월	모의학력평가 대학별 선행학습영향평가보고서 발표 (31일 이전)	모의학력평가 대학별 선행학습 영향평가 보고서 발표 (31일 이전)
4월	2019학년도 대입전형 시행계획 발표 (5월 1일 이전) 중간고사	3학년 모의학력평가 대학 모의논술, 모의면접, 모의전형 일정 확인 중간고사
5월		대학별 수시 요강 발표(5월 초) 대학별 모의수능, 적성 실시
6월	모의학력평가	평가원 모의 대수능 경찰대학 원서접수(5월) 사관학교 원서접수(6월 말)
7월	기말고사	기말고사 사관학교 원서접수 마감(7월 초) 모의학력평가 경찰대학 1차 시험(7월 말) 사관학교 1차 시험(7월 말)
8월	2021학년도 대입전형 기본사항 발표 (9월 1일 이전)	경찰대학 1차 합격자 발표(8월 초) 사관학교 1차 합격자 발표(8월 초) 경찰대학 2차 시험(8~10월) 사관학교 2차 시험(8~9월) 대학수학능력시험 원서접수 시작(8월 말) 수시 학생부 기준일(8월 31일)
9월	중간고사 모의학력평가	중간고사 평가원 모의 대수능 대학별 정시 요강 발표(9월 초) 대학수학능력시험 원서접수 마감(9월 초) KAIST, DGIST, GIST, UNIST 원서접수(9월 초중) 수시모집 원서접수(4년제)(9월 중) 수시모집 원서접수(전문대학)(9월 중)

월		
10월		모의학력평가 해군사관학교 특별/수시 합격자 발표(10월 중) 육군사관학교 우선선발 합격자 발표(10월 중) 공군사관학교 최종 합격자 발표(10월 중)
11월	모의학력평가	수시 2차 접수기간(전문대학)(11월 초중) 대학수학능력시험 정시 학생부 기준일(11월 30일)
12월	기말고사(12월 말)	기말고사 수능 성적 발표(12월 초) 수시 합격자 발표 마감(4년제, 전문대학)(12월 중) 수시 합격자 등록기간(4년제, 전문대학공통)(12월 중) 수시 미등록 충원 등록 마감(4년제)(12월 말) 수시 충원 발표 등록(전문대학)(12월 말) 정시 원서접수(4년제)(12월 말~1월 초) 정시 원서접수(전문대학)(12월 말~1월 초) 경찰대학 최종 합격 발표(12월 중) 사관학교 최종 합격 발표(12월 중말)
1월		정시 원서접수 마감(4년제)(1월 초) 정시 원서접수 마감(전문대학)(1월 중) 정시 합격자 발표 마감(1월 말) 정시 합격자 등록기간(1월 말~2월초)
2월		정시 최초 합격자 발표(전문대학)(2월 초) 정시 미등록 충원 합격 등록 마감(4년제)(2월 초중) 정시 충원 합격자 발표 및 등록(전문대학)(2월 중) 추가모집 발표(2월 중) 추가모집 접수(2월 중말) 추가모집 발표(2월 말) 추가모집 합격자 등록기간(2월 말)

공무원 직급표

대우급수	행정부							
	일반	외교	초중등 교원	고등 교원	치안	교정	소방	군인
원수	대통령							
총리	국무총리							
부총리	감사원장							
장관	각부 장관 국정원장 교섭본부장	외통부 장관 특1급 외교관	교과부 장관					국방장관 대장 합참정/부의장 참모총장 군사령관
차관	국무총리실장 각부 차관 처장, 청장	외통부 차관	서울교육감	국립대 총장 대학 총장	치안총감	교정본부장	소방총감	국방차관
준차관	교육원장	특2급 외교관	교육감					중장 군작전사령관 해병대사령관
차관보	차관보	차관보			치안정감			중장 (군단장)
1급	관리관	대사				교정관리관	소방정감	소장
2급	이사관	공사 영사 총영사		30호봉 이상	치안감	교정이사관	소방감	준장
3급	부이사관	부영사 참사관 영사 대리		정교수 24~29 호봉	경무관	교정부이사관	소방준감	대령
4급	서기관	1등 서기관	교육연구관 24호봉 이상	부교수 17~23 호봉	총경	교정감 (서기관)	소방정	중령
5급	사무관	2등 서기관	교장 장학관 교감 18~23호봉	조교수 11~16 호봉	경정	교정관	소방령	소령
6급 갑	주사	3등 서기관	장학사 14~17호봉	9~10호봉	경감	교감	소방경	대위
6급 을	주사	3등 서기관	11~13호봉	7~8호봉	경위	교감	소방경	중위
7급	주사보		9~10호봉	6호봉 이하	경사	교위	소방위 소방장	소위/준위
8급	서기		4~8호봉		경장	교사	소방교	원사 상사 중사
9급	서기보		3호봉 이하		순경	교도	소방사	하사
의무복무	4등급 3등급 2등급 1등급				수경 상경 일경 이경	수교 상교 일교 이교	수방 상방 일방 이방	병장(수병) 상병 일병 이병

| | | | | 지방 행정 | | 입법부 | 사법부 | 공기업 | 기타 |
검찰	연구직	지도직	전문경력관	관선	자치				
						국회의장	헌재소장 대법원장 선관위원장		
						부의장			
검찰총장 (대검 검사장)					서울시장	상임위원장 원내대표 사무처장 국회의원	대법관 헌법재판관 행정처장 헌재사무처장	한국은행 총재	
고검 검사장				서울 부시장	광역시장 도지사	입법조사장 사무차장 입법차장	고법원장 지법원장 선관위원	사장 원장	
대검 차장검사				광역시 부시장 부지사		도서관장 예산정책처장	고법 부장판사 고법 부장판사	사장 원장 본부장	사기업사장 사기업본부장
지검 검사장 지검 차장검사				광역시도 실장	서울구청장 광역부시장				
				부시장 광역시도 국장	시장 구청장			본부장	사기업본부장
	연구관 23년 초과			관선구청장 부군수 국장	군수	관리관	관리관 11호봉 이상		
	19년 초과	지도관 19년 초과		읍면동장		이사관	이사관 8~10호봉	처장	전무이사
지검 부장검사	15년 초과	15년 초과		주사		부이사관	지법 부장판사 5~7호봉	실장	상무이사
부부장검사 평검사	8년 초과 전문의	8년 초과	가군 27호봉 이상	주사보		서기관	부부장판사 평판사 2~4호봉	국장	상무이사
사무관	연구관 이상 전문의	지도관 이상	가군 26호봉 이상	서기		사무관	사무관	부장 팀장 지방관장	사법연수원생 국법무관 부장 이사보
주사	연구사 5년 초과	지도사 10년 초과	나군 28호봉 이상	서기보		주사	주사	차장	
주사보	연구사 약사	지도사 5년 초과	나군 27호봉 이상			주사보	주사보	과장	
서기	간호사	지도사	다군 28호봉 이상			서기	서기	대리	
서기보			다군 27호봉 이상			서기보		사원	10급 기능직 공기업 주임

※ 이 표는 2015년 공무원 보수 등의 업무 지침인 '인사혁신처 예규 제5호' '호봉획정을 위한 상당계급 구분'을 참고하여 정리한 것입니다.

PART 01
핵심 파악하기

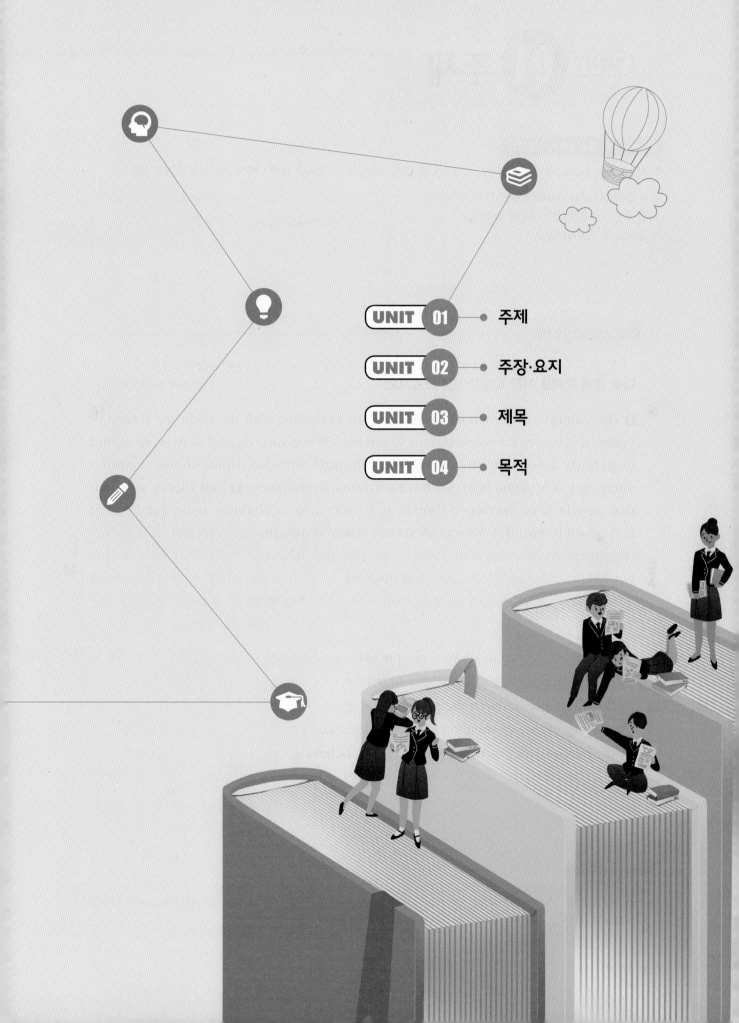

UNIT 01 주제

Problem Solving Skills

주어진 지문을 읽고 글의 주제를 파악할 수 있는지를 묻는 유형이다. 글 전체에 대한 이해를 기반으로 문제를 해결한다.

- 도입부에서 글의 소재를 확인한다.
- 핵심 문장을 찾아 글의 주제를 파악한다.
- 주제의 근거를 확인한다.

Example

다음 글의 주제로 가장 적절한 것을 고르시오. | 경찰대학 2017학년도 27번 |

❶ The emotional reaction of disgust is often associated with the obdurate refusal of young children to consume certain vegetables. While such disgust may seem absurd to parents determined to supply their children with nutritious foods, scientists interested in hygienic behavior have a rational explanation. ❷ This theory contends that people have developed disgust as a protective mechanism against unfamiliar and possibly harmful objects. A recent study shows that disgust not only deters the ingestion of dangerous substances, but also dissuades people from entering potentially contagious situations. For instance, subjects of the study declared crowded railcars to be more disgusting than empty ones and lice more disgusting than wasps. ❸

❹
① the role of disgust in keeping people safe
② the advantages of getting proper nutrition
③ the difference between danger and contagion
④ the importance of avoiding harmful substances
⑤ the necessity of practicing good hygienic behavior

Vocabulary

obdurate 고집 센 absurd 터무니없는 contend 주장하다 deter 단념시키다 ingestion 음식물 섭취 dissuade 단념시키다
contagious 전염성의 railcar 자동차 louse(pl. lice) 이, 기생충 wasp 말벌

Let's Solve

Point **1** 도입부에서 글의 소재 확인하기

- The emotional reaction of disgust is often associated with the obdurate refusal of young children to consume certain vegetables.

  → 음식에 대한 감정적 반응으로서의 혐오감

Point **2** 핵심 문장을 찾아 글의 주제 파악하기

> This theory contends that people have developed disgust as a protective mechanism against unfamiliar and possibly harmful objects.

> 혐오감은 유해할 수 있는 대상을 피하려는 보호 기제의 반응이다.

Point **3** 주제의 근거 확인하기

혐오감의 기능	예시
• disgust not only deters the ingestion of dangerous substances • but also dissuades people from entering potentially contagious situations	• subjects of the study declared crowded railcars to be more • disgusting than empty ones and lice more disgusting than wasps

> 혐오감은 위험 물질의 섭취 및 전염 가능성이 있는 환경에 처하는 것을 단념시킨다.

Point **4** 정답 풀이하기

① 사람을 보호하는 혐오의 역할 → 주제와 일치하는 정답이다.

② 적절한 영양 섭취의 이점 → 적절한 영양 공급은 예시의 일부에 불과하다.

③ 위험과 전염의 차이 → 위험과 전염의 차이에 대한 언급은 없다.

④ 유해 물질을 피하는 일의 중요성 → 지문은 유해물질을 피해야 한다는 내용이 아니라 혐오가 유해물질을 피하게 해준다는 내용이다.

⑤ 좋은 위생 행동 실천의 필요성 → 실천에 대한 내용은 언급되어 있지 않다.

01

다음 글의 주제로 가장 적절한 것을 고르시오.

| 경찰대학 2018학년도 26번 |

Catholicism held that the only God-given vocation was priesthood, but Protestants thought that people could be called to any of the secular crafts and trades. The belief that they were serving God encouraged them to work with religious fervor, leading them to produce more goods and make more money. Weber believed that the Protestant faith led inevitably to a capitalist economic society because it gave believers the chance to view the pursuit of profit as evidence of devotion, rather than of morally suspect motives such as greed and ambition. The idea of predestination also meant that believers need not worry about social inequalities and poverty, because material wealth was a sign of spiritual wealth.

① role of religion in creating social equality
② reasons for the rise of the Protestant faith
③ influence of Protestantism on economic ideals
④ importance of morality in economic activities
⑤ differences between Protestants and Catholics

다음 글의 주제로 가장 적절한 것을 고르시오.

Whether out of curiosity, vanity, or a motive as yet unexplored, people throughout the ages have wanted to see their own reflection. As early as 2500 B.C. the Egyptians had mirrors of highly polished metal, usually of bronze, occasionally of silver or gold. The first commercial glass mirrors were made in Venice in 1564; these were made of blown glass that was flattened and coated with an amalgam of mercury and tin. The Venetians proceeded to supply Europe with mirrors for centuries. It wasn't until 1840 that a German chemist named Justus Liebig came up with the method of silvering that we use today. By this technique, silver-ammonia compounds are subjected to the chemical action of a reducing agent, such as invert sugar, Rochelle salt, or formaldehyde, and the resulting metallic silver is spread evenly over the back of a smooth pane of plate glass.

① economic motivations behind the invention of the mirror
② outstanding achievements of German chemists
③ development of commercial glass mirror technology
④ human desires hidden in commercial glass mirrors
⑤ commonalities of ancient mirror technology in Europe

03

다음 글의 주제로 가장 적절한 것을 고르시오.

Success as a scientist is not simply a function of the quality of the ideas we hold in our heads, or of the data we hold in our hands, but also of the language we use to describe them. We all understand that "publish or perish" is real and dominates our professional lives. But "publish or perish" is about surviving, not succeeding. You don't succeed as a scientist by getting papers published. You succeed as a scientist by getting them cited. Having your work matter, matters. Success is defined not by the number of pages you have in print but by their influence. You succeed when your peers understand your work and use it to motivate their own.

① the enduring belief of 'the more writing, the better'
② the importance of influencing others in scientific writing
③ the necessity for pursuing research in unexplored areas
④ the favorable peer reviews needed for journal acceptance
⑤ the working ethics and strict quality control in publications

다음 글의 주제로 가장 적절한 것을 고르시오.

Music that was exciting to the contemporaries of Bach and Beethoven is still exciting, although we do not share their culture. The early Beatles' songs are still exciting although the Beatles have unfortunately broken up. Similarly, some Venda songs that must have been composed hundreds of years ago still excite me. Many of us are thrilled by Koto music from Japan, sitar music from India, Chopi xylophone music, and so on. I do not say that we receive music in exactly the same way as the players, but our own experiences suggest that there are some possibilities of cross-cultural communication. I am convinced that the explanation for this is to be found in the fact that at the level of deep structures in music there are elements that are common to the human psyche, although they may not appear in the surface structures.

① the potential of music to enrich culture
② the gradual divergence of music from culture
③ the ability of music to nourish the human psyche
④ the advantages of cross-cultural transmission of music
⑤ the universality of music that transcends time and culture

다음 글의 주제로 가장 적절한 것을 고르시오.

We often see stories of inspiring people and wonderful successes. Some of us put their pictures on our walls or clip notable quotes from them. But what does that do for us if the inspiring person has done things we will never or could never do? For many of us, the choice of a role model invites comparison, and if our abilities and outcomes do not measure up, the role model serves not as an inspiration but as a source of frustration and defeat. Choose as your role model someone who has accomplished something you can accomplish and something you want to accomplish. There is tremendous value in using co-workers or family members who you admire rather than famous athletes, leaders, or historical figures, who have experienced great successes but whose experience has less in common with yours.

① the success stories of a realistic role model
② the source of frustration in emulating a role model
③ the importance of selecting a reachable role model
④ the necessity for having an inspiring person around
⑤ the positive effects of imitating a person of high status

다음 글의 주제로 가장 적절한 것을 고르시오.

| 경찰대학 2015학년도 27번 |

Observational studies provide information as to some of the things mothers do around children, but little about their feelings, ideas and beliefs concerning children, child care and themselves. Mothers hold a range of views about children and parenting which are not necessarily in agreement with those of formal psychology and these may influence how they interact with their children. Some mothers find that being sensitive to their children does not come easily. This may be because they cannot relate easily to their children, because they are depressed or isolated, or because they do not believe that sensitivity is an important part of their relationship with the child. For some mothers there may be a mismatch between their behavior and feelings and those prescribed by psychological theories; and there may be conflict between their own needs and those of their children.

① reasons for mothers' negligence in child-rearing
② necessity to establish a philosophy of mothers' parenting
③ gaps between what mothers want and what their children want
④ psychological underpinnings of conflict between mothers and children
⑤ discrepancy in the concept of parenting between mothers and psychologists

다음 글의 주제로 가장 적절한 것을 고르시오.

| 경찰대학 2015학년도 28번 |

Alexander the Great launched Egypt's Greco-Roman period in 332 B.C. After conquering parts of western Asia, the Macedonian general was welcomed in Egypt by a people politically weary after several hundred years of unrest and occupation by outsiders. The mixing of Greek (and later Roman) influences with a still rich Egyptian culture helped set social and religious change spinning around the Mediterranean. In this newest period of vibrancy the Egyptians' styles of dress and sculpture worked their way to Greece and Rome, while Egyptian gods and demigods mingled with their counterparts in Greek and Roman mythology. The mother goddess Isis would eventually have temples built to her in the land of the Caesars, while many Greco-Roman gods and heroes would be honored in temples throughout Egypt.

① Egypt's social reform efforts during the Greco-Roman period
② political unrest in Egypt caused by Alexander the Great
③ cultural interchanges between Egypt and Greece/Rome
④ penetration of Egyptian lifestyles into the Greco-Roman world
⑤ Greek and Roman influences on Egyptian peasants' daily lives

08 다음 글의 주제로 가장 적절한 것을 고르시오.

The belief that optimism can keep you alive — or at least stave off cancer — gained traction after the release of a study on recovering breast-cancer patients in the Lancet medical journal in 1979. Since then, it has become a household idea that patients with a "fighting spirit" fare better than those with feelings of hopelessness. However, a few recent large-scale meta-analyses have found a lack of convincing evidence that optimism really extends the lives of cancer patients. Despite the lack of definitive data, the belief in the power of positive thinking has become so widespread that it might actually be doing harm. Cancer patients may feel inclined to act upbeat even when they are distraught, hide their despair instead of seeking solace or treatment, or blame themselves if their disease progresses.

① the dangers of hopelessness for cancer recovery
② the necessity of optimism for recovering patients
③ the downfalls of positive thinking for cancer patients
④ the importance of a sound doctor-patient relationship
⑤ the discovery of new preventative measures for cancer

다음 글의 주제로 가장 적절한 것을 고르시오.

| 경찰대학 2014학년도 27번 |

Aristarchus of the Aegean island of Samos first suggested that the earth and the other planets moved about the sun — an idea that was rejected by astronomers until Copernicus proposed it again 2,000 years later. After Copernicus, the Danish astronomer Tycho Brahe watched the motions of the planet Mars from his observatory on the Baltic island of Hveen; as a result Johannes Kepler was able to show that Mars and the earth and the other planets move in ellipses about the sun. Then Isaac Newton proposed his universal law of gravitation and laws of motion, and from these it was possible to derive an exact description of the entire solar system. This occupied the minds of some of the greatest scientists and mathematicians in the centuries that followed.

＊ellipse: 타원

① human endeavors to understand the solar system
② distortions of the solar system by ancient scientists
③ superstitions about the solar system in ancient times
④ history of pre-Newtonian physical laws and principles
⑤ some newly discovered information about planet movements

10

다음 글의 주제로 가장 적절한 것을 고르시오.

| 경찰대학 2013학년도 31번 |

There is consideration to which some advocates of freedom attach too little importance. In a community of children which is left without adult interference there is a tyranny of the stronger, which is likely to be far more brutal than most adult tyrannies. If two children, two or three years old, are left to play together, they will, after a few fights, discover which is bound to be the victor, and the other will then become a slave. Where the number of children is larger, one or two acquire complete mastery, and the others have far less liberty than they would have if the adults interfered to protect the weaker and less pugnacious. Consideration for others does not, with most children, arise spontaneously, but has to be taught, and can hardly be taught except by the exercise of authority. This is perhaps the most important argument against the abdication of the adults.

① the importance of freedom in child care
② understanding children's behaviors in various learning contexts
③ the relation of victors to slaves in a community of children
④ the necessity for adult interference in child care
⑤ various factors affecting children's leadership

The place of secondhand smoke in causing disease has been under study for years. A mid-sized city in a western state unexpectedly added to the data. Smoking in public and in workplaces was banned and six months later the ban was lifted. During the time that smoking was prohibited in public places, the rate of hospital admissions for heart attacks was 24. During the typical six-month period, the rate is 40 admissions. The researchers believed that the drop was evidence of the negative effects of secondhand smoke. Secondhand smoke contributes to heart attacks by elevating heart rate and decreasing the ability of blood vessels to dilate.

① effects of smoking in the workplace
② causes of heart attacks in mid-sized cities
③ the importance of a stress-free working environment
④ the relationship of secondhand smoke and heart attacks
⑤ the necessity of banning smoking in public and workplaces

12 다음 글의 주제로 가장 적절한 것을 고르시오.

The enormous outpouring of concern over juvenile delinquency in the 50's presented the movie industry with dangerous but lucrative possibilities. An aroused public of parents, youth-serving agencies, teachers, adolescents, and law enforcers constituted a huge potential audience for delinquency films at a time when general audiences for all films had declined. Yet this was a perilous subject to exploit, for public pressure on the film industry to set a wholesome example for youth remained unremitting. Moreover the accusation that mass culture caused delinquency was the focus of much contemporary attention. If the film industry approached the issue of delinquency, it had to proceed cautiously. It could not present delinquency favorably; hence all stories would have to be set in the moral firmament of the movie Code. Yet to be successful, films had to evoke sympathy from young people who were increasingly intrigued by the growing youth culture of which delinquency seemed to be one variant.

① the filming environments in the 50's
② challenges for the juvenile delinquency films in the 50's
③ the moral principles of juvenile delinquency films in the 50's
④ the rise and demise of juvenile delinquency films in the 50's
⑤ juvenile delinquency films as a lucrative business in the 50's

다음 글의 주제로 가장 적절한 것을 고르시오.

Some will say, so far so good. "We are mammal primates. But we have language, and the animals don't." By some definition perhaps they don't. But they do communicate extensively, and by call systems we are just beginning to grasp. It would be a mistake to think first language and then society. Language and culture emerge from our biological-social natural existence, animals that we were/are. Language is a mind-body system that co-evolved with our needs and nerves. Like imagination and the body, language rises unbidden. It is of a complexity that eludes our rational intellectual capacities. All attempts at scientific description of natural languages have fallen short of completeness, as the descriptive linguists readily confess, yet the child learns the mother tongue early and has virtually mastered it by six.

① 인간과 동물의 언어적 차이
② 인류의 정신문화가 반영된 언어
③ 동물 언어의 신경학적 접근 가능성
④ 언어 습득 과정에 대한 분석적 접근의 유용성
⑤ 생물학적 자연 상태와 연관된 인간 언어의 이해

14 다음 글의 주제로 가장 적절한 것을 고르시오.

| 경찰대학 2010학년도 26번 |

We know that what you eat, and don't eat, can affect your health. But is it possible, as the White Rabbit advised Alice, to "feed your head?" Is there such a thing as brain food? I'm convinced there is. The evidence for some foods, such as fish, is stronger than for others, like brightly colored vegetables. But none of those foods is bad for you, and they certainly won't make you any less smart. The reason fish is so good for the brain is the so-called omega-3 fatty acids it contains. Oily fish, like salmon, sardines, mackerel, and black cod, are the best sources of those special fats. One of the omega-3s — DHA — is the main constituent of cell membranes in the brain, and a deficiency of it can weaken the brain's architecture and leave it vulnerable to disease.

① how to keep brain active
② fish as a good diet for brain
③ vegetables containing omega-3
④ omega-3 as a good food for bones
⑤ amount of omega-3 for daily consumption

다음 글의 주제로 가장 적절한 것을 고르시오.

It may surprise you that many patients are reluctant to describe their symptoms to their physicians. But the situation is a common one. Many individuals believe that physicians are so skilled that they can easily identify a patient's problems through a thorough physical examination, the way a good mechanic can diagnose car problems. Moreover, physicians' relatively high social prestige and power may intimidate patients by making them feel that their problems are trivial and unimportant, or making them reluctant to volunteer information that might cast them in a bad light. Conversely, physicians may have difficulties encouraging their patients to provide the proper information. In many cases, physicians dominate an interview with questions of a technical nature, while patients attempt to communicate a personal sense of their illness and the impact it is having on their lives.

① miscommunication between physicians and patients
② physicians' skills to elicit patients' cooperation
③ the impact of physicians' power upon their patients
④ effective ways to diagnose patients' problems
⑤ technical questions used in interviews with patients

영국의 영화에 관한 다음 글의 주제로 가장 적절한 것을 고르시오. | 경찰대학 2010학년도 40번 |

The British government controlled all film-making during the Second World War and requested films which created positive accounts of the fighting forces. These films used a discourse of 'Britishness', constructing a notion of the 'British character' that implied that all people in Britain shared 'British' qualities. Characters in the 'forces' films were fair-minded and brave, but also had homely qualities like a sense of humour. 'Britain' and 'Britishness' were powerful discourses which encouraged people of different social classes and of the different cultures, regions and nations of Britain to believe that they were fighting for a common set of 'British' values.

① superiority of British films
② characters in the forces films
③ difficulties of film-making
④ films to educate soldiers
⑤ making films for unity

01 다음 글의 주제로 가장 적절한 것을 고르시오.

| 사관학교 2017학년도 31번 |

The seemingly simple question of "what defines a sport?" has been the subject of argument and conversation for years, among professional and armchair athletes alike. There seems to be no doubt that vigorous and highly competitive activities such as baseball, football, and soccer are truly "sports," but when the subject of other activities such as darts, chess, and shuffleboard is brought up we find ourselves at the heart of a controversy. If say, billiards, is not a sport, then what exactly is it? Those who would dispute that it is a sport would respond that it is a simple leisure activity. They would go on to claim a true sport first and foremost requires some form of physical exertion. More to the point, if a player does not break a sweat, what he or she plays is not a sport. Beyond that, more important criteria would be the need for decent hand-eye coordination and the ever-present possibility of sustaining injury. Billiards only fits one of those specifications (hand-eye coordination), so according to the doubters, it is not a real sport.

① leisure activities embedded in sports
② popularity of highly competitive activities
③ dispute over the defining criteria for sports
④ influence of sports on humans' mental health
⑤ characteristics that define billiards as a sport

다음 글의 주제로 가장 적절한 것을 고르시오.

Perhaps the most important dimension of the way that we think about ourselves is that of evaluation, that is our level of self-esteem. The degree to which we globally approve of ourselves has an impact on how we behave, particularly with other people. To a certain degree our evaluations of ourselves are dependent on comparisons with other people. For example, in judging specific abilities our judgements can really only be relative: the question of how good a tennis player/musician/cook one is can only be meaningful with reference to a scale derived from other people's performances. There is ample evidence that we look for opportunities to compare ourselves with relevant others. By *relevant* we mean others who are likely to be sufficiently close to us in terms of some overall scale for the comparison to be meaningful. For example, the local tennis club provides a more meaningful set of comparisons about our tennis skills than international championships would.

① damaging effects of over-focusing on competition
② role of relevant comparison in self-evaluation
③ importance of having high self-esteem
④ development of a competitive spirit
⑤ sports as a measure of self-worth

Twin sirens hide in the sea of history, tempting those seeking to understand and appreciate the past onto the reefs of misunderstanding and misinterpretation. These twin dangers are temporocentrism and ethnocentrism. Temporocentrism is the belief that your times are the best of all possible times. All other times are thus inferior. Ethnocentrism is the belief that your culture is the best of all possible cultures. All other cultures are thus inferior. Temporocentrism and ethnocentrism unite to cause individuals and cultures to judge all other individuals and cultures by the "superior" standards of their current culture. This leads to a total lack of perspective when dealing with past and/or foreign cultures and a resultant misunderstanding and misappreciation of them. Temporocentrism and ethnocentrism tempt moderns into unjustified criticisms of the peoples of the past.

① distinct differences in the ways of recording history
② universal features discovered in different cultures
③ historians' efforts to advocate their own culture
④ pros and cons of two cross-cultural perspectives
⑤ beliefs that cause biased interpretations of the past

다음 글의 주제로 가장 적절한 것을 고르시오.

The most normal and competent child encounters what seem like insurmountable problems in living. But by playing them out, he may become able to cope with them in a step-by-step process. He often does so in symbolic ways that are hard for even him to understand, as he is reacting to inner processes whose origin may be buried deep in his unconscious. This may result in play that makes little sense to us at the moment, since we do not know the purposes it serves. When there is no immediate danger, it is usually best to approve of the child's play without interfering. Efforts to assist him in his struggles, while well intentioned, may divert him from seeking and eventually finding the solution that will serve him best.

① dangers of playing violent games to mental health
② beneficial influence of playing outdoors in childhood
③ children's play as problem solving with minimal intervention
④ necessity of intervening in disputes between siblings
⑤ parental roles in children's physical development

Problem Solving Skills

주어진 지문을 읽고 글의 주장이나 요지를 고르는 유형이다. 주제 찾기와 유사한 유형으로, 주제문을 찾아 주장 또는 요지를 파악한다.

- 선택지를 통해 소재를 추측한다.
- 핵심 문장을 찾아 글의 주장 또는 요지를 파악한다.
- 주장 또는 요지를 뒷받침하는 필자의 생각을 확인한다.

Example

다음 글의 요지로 가장 적절한 것은?

| 경찰대학 2017학년도 29번 |

You don't have to go vegan, pledge allegiance to an exercise cult or become a full-time meditator to get the longevity benefits of healthy habits. ❷ The latest science is showing quite the opposite, in fact: that extending healthy life is attainable for many of us with just a few small changes that aren't especially hard to do — and won't make you miserable. Researchers have learned that logging hours at the gym cannot counteract the negative effects of sitting for long periods, for instance — but something as simple as fidgeting can. They've also discovered that cutting down on how much you eat doesn't have to be excruciating — and it can improve your chance for a longer life.

① Living a healthy lifestyle is easier said than done.
② Key changes in your diet can help you live longer.
③ Exercising is important for people with sedentary lifestyles.
④ Physical and mental well-being can be achieved with hard work.
⑤ Achieving longevity is not as difficult as one might imagine.

Vocabulary

vegan 채식주의자 pledge 서약하다 allegiance 충성 cult 예찬론자 meditator 명상가 longevity 장수 attainable 이룰 수 있는 log 기록하다 fidget 꼼지락거리다 excruciating 몹시 고통스러운, 극심한

Let's Solve

Point 1 선택지를 통해 소재 추측하기

healthy lifestyle, well-being, live longer, achieving longevity, sedentary lifestyles

건강한 삶과 생활 방식

Point 2 핵심 문장을 찾아 글의 요지 파악하기

• The latest science is showing quite the opposite, in fact: that extending healthy life is attainable for many of us with just a few small changes that aren't especially hard to do
  → 사소한 생활 습관의 변화만으로 건강한 삶을 얻을 수 있다

Point 3 요지를 뒷받침하는 필자의 생각 확인하기

You don't have to go vegan, pledge allegiance to an exercise cult or become a full-time meditator

something as simple as fidgeting can

cutting down on how much you eat doesn't have to be excruciating

사소한 생활 습관의 변화만으로 건강한 삶을 얻을 수 있다

Point 4 정답 풀이하기

① 건강한 생활방식을 실천하기보다 말하기가 쉽다.   → 요지와 배치된다.
② 식단의 주요 변화가 장수를 도울 것이다.   → 지엽적이다.
③ 운동은 앉아서 생활하는 사람들에게 중요하다.   → 지엽적이다.
④ 신체적이고 정신적인 건강은 열심히 운동해서 얻을 수 있다.   → 요지와 배치된다.
⑤ 장수하는 것은 생각보다 어렵지 않다.   → 요지와 일치한다.

01 다음 글의 요지로 가장 적절한 것은?

| 경찰대학 2018학년도 29번 |

You cannot buy happiness. You cannot go to the nearest grocery store and order a pound of happiness as you would a pound of butter. But, since happiness comes from within, you can secure a measure of happiness by your own acts. You can find that feeling of contentment by helping your less fortunate fellowmen. You can help those who, because of ill-fate, will not have a happy Christmas unless we share with them. During this season of peace and good will, let us not force those in need to look at happiness through our eyes. Rather, let us help them to see and find happiness through their own eyes. Let us not fail the less fortunate of the community.

① Measure your true happiness level by acts of good will.
② Catch the happiness virus in your local community.
③ Do not force your happy ways on your neighbors.
④ Exercise self-contentment to achieve mental well-being.
⑤ Find happiness by helping the needy around you.

다음 글의 요지로 가장 적절한 것은?

Recently I was reading about the endangered grizzly bears on the coast of British Columbia. The authors emphasized how the cubs were keen observers of their mothers' skills in searching for and consuming food. What the cubs learned by the mothers' modeling was a matter of life and death; without that knowledge the cubs probably would not survive. The same principle applies to us. How can we believe that when we live life like a rat race, our children somehow will not? That as we mindlessly acquire and consume, our children will somehow know moderation and meaning in their relationship to things? If I regularly cheat on little things — like not returning the extra change I receive at the counter, or pocketing found money without trying to find its owner — I am teaching that behavior to children.

[3점]

① Parents are spending more time reading books on wildlife.
② Mindful consumption lies at the center of being good parents.
③ Good parenting begins and ends with setting a good example.
④ Teaching good behavior to children outweighs earning money.
⑤ Children's behavior is subconsciously mirrored by their parents.

다음 글의 주장으로 가장 적절한 것은?

A lapse is a single event during which you take up an old behavior you've been trying to change. The key to overcoming lapses is to expect them on occasion just as traffic tie-ups and road construction may delay you on the highway. Think about the last time you embarked on a long road trip. Chances are you encountered something along the way that slowed you down — but you did not give up, turn the car around, and head home. You still reached your intended destination, though it may have taken you a little longer than expected. It's the same with personal change. Let's say you've been balancing your plate, adding more fruits and vegetables, but suddenly give in to the urge to eat a fast-food hamburger. You've just had a lapse.

[3점]

① You should remind yourself of the direction you'd like to be headed in.

② When you have an urge to resume an old habit, try to resist the urge.

③ Take a shortcut when your plan for change meets unforeseen delays.

④ Occasional deviations encountered on your way to change are not abnormal.

⑤ Seek support from those who are trying to change the same behavior as you are.

다음 글의 요지로 가장 적절한 것은?

In commercial society based upon exchange, every man "becomes in some measure a merchant." The pursuit of self-interest in the market, with its division of labor and his resulting dependence on others, leads him to adapt his behavior to the expectations of others. The market itself is therefore a disciplining institution. "The real and effectual discipline which is exercised over a workman, is not that of his corporation," Adam Smith wrote, "but that of his customers. It is the fear of losing their employment which restrains his frauds and corrects his negligence." In order to become successful in his economic exchanges with others, the individual is led to develop the moderate level of self-command which Smith calls "propriety." The character that the market promotes includes prudence and the ability to defer short-term gratification for long-term benefits.

① 시장에서의 개인의 경제 활동은 자기 훈육을 가져오게 된다.
② 개인의 이득 추구는 자기 조절에 의해 절제되어야 한다.
③ 노동자는 동료 노동자보다 고객에게 더 관심을 가져야 한다.
④ 개인은 지속적인 이득을 위해 즉각적인 만족을 희생해야 한다.
⑤ 시장에서의 개인 활동은 분업과 타인에의 의존을 바탕으로 한다.

Purported to treat a variety of ailments, from fevers to measles to epilepsy, rhinoceros horns have been prized ingredients in Chinese medicines for thousands of years. Sought after for their horns, white rhinos saw their population fall to 100 animals in South Africa by 1910. Today, despite a 1977 ban on the selling of rhino parts, Africa's rhinos once again are facing extinction. Since the ban has not been able to protect the rhinos from illegal poaching, ironically, legalizing a highly regulated trade in rhino horns can end up saving the animals. Rhino horns can be cut or shaved without injuring the animals, and they grow back. If tightly controlled by a single centralized organization, the current demand can be satisfied through legal horn cuttings, along with stockpiles of confiscated black-market horns and those collected from rhinos that die naturally.

① Rhino horns should be considered as an alternative to conventional medicine.
② Legalizing and regulating the trade of rhino horns can save the rhinos.
③ The government must strictly enforce the penalties of illegal poaching.
④ Confiscated black-market rhino horns need to be put to better use.
⑤ Cutting the horns of rhinos is inhumane and should be abolished.

다음 글의 주장으로 가장 적절한 것은?

If there is a garbage crisis, it is that we are treating garbage as an environmental threat and not as what it is: a manageable — though admittedly complex — civic issue. Although many old urban landfills are reaching their capacity, the reality is that there is — and always will be — plenty of room in this country for safe landfill. We've chosen to look at garbage not as a management issue, however, but as a moral crisis. The result is that recycling is now seen as an irreproachable virtue, beyond the scrutiny of cost-benefit analysis. But in the real world, the money municipalities spend on recycling is money that can't be spent on schools, libraries, health clinics, and police. In the real world, the sort of gigantic recycling programs that many cities and towns have embarked upon may not be the best use of scarce government funds.

① 쓰레기 매립지의 확대는 바람직하지 않다.
② 쓰레기 재활용은 도덕적 관점에서 접근해야 한다.
③ 쓰레기 재활용에는 충분한 사전 홍보가 선행되어야 한다.
④ 쓰레기 재활용에 쓰이는 과다한 정부 기금은 재고되어야 한다.
⑤ 쓰레기 재활용 프로그램은 공공기관부터 참여해야 한다.

다음 글의 요지로 가장 적절한 것은?

Scholars have often wondered exactly why the notion of unlimited progress by human beings took hold. The answer is to be found in their development of skill to secure the energy base. A gigantic, seemingly endless stock of solar energy — 3 billion years worth, to be precise — was there from the beginning. But we gradually have had all the energy we needed to replace the sun and would never again have to wait for nature to take its course. The concept of time, then, was changed: it became equivalent to a function of how fast we could harness the stored energy that lay deep in the coal seams and oil reservoirs. We could make the sun stay out twice as long if we chose, because we were dealing with the "stored sun" — sun that we could take out of the ground and manipulate at will. With these energy resources people became increasingly convinced that they were no longer dependent upon nature, and they could reorder the world to their own making.

① 대체 에너지 개발이 시급하다.
② 태양에너지는 언젠가 소멸할 것이다.
③ 문명의 발달은 무한히 지속될 수 있다.
④ 태양열 발전을 통해 환경 친화적 문명 발전을 이룰 수 있다.
⑤ 에너지 개발을 통하여 인간은 자연의 지배로부터 점차로 벗어났다.

다음 글에서 필자가 주장하는 바로 가장 적절한 것은? | 경찰대학 2011학년도 45번 |

Citizens ought to begin a movement, one that will take years, to inject the public trust notion into federal and state land and wildlife statutes. The responsible agencies are trustees, and the law ought to say so in forceful terms. What matters about the public trust doctrine is not just whether the courts will enforce it, but whether the trust can become a working part of federal and state policy. We must press the agencies to acknowledge the trusteeship and its high duties as a matter of administrative policy. Officials in the federal land agencies ought to say, with force and pride, "Yes, we are trustees of the nation's wonders." Those kinds of pronouncements will help set higher standards and create a climate for principled actions.

① 민간 기업에 야생지역 보호를 위탁해야 한다.
② 공공 기관의 야생지역 관리 정책은 재검토 되어야 한다.
③ 시민들이 직접 관리해야 야생지역이 효과적으로 보존될 수 있다.
④ 야생보호 시민운동이 제대로 진행될 수 있도록 공공기관이 지도해야 한다.
⑤ 야생지역 관리 임무가 자신에게 위탁된 것임을 관리기관이 자각하게 해야 한다.

다음 글의 주장으로 가장 적절한 것은?

Do we need recycling to save resources? No, not in the real world. The reason recycling is unprofitable is that most of the materials being recycled are either renewable paper from tree farms or cheap and plentiful glass from silica. Aluminium is profitable to recycle — and private concerns were already recycling it before the legislated mandates. Recycling is beginning to lose its halo as its costs become apparent and its effect on the volume of waste is found to be smaller than anticipated. Quotas and fines may force people to separate their trash, but they can't create industrial markets for the waste we recycle. Recycling can work, very effectively, on a region-by-region and commodity-by-commodity basis, but not on the level of government.

① Recycling on a government level may not work effectively.
② Recycling should be done by government mandates.
③ We should separate trash into different kinds.
④ We should not throw away garbage into nature.
⑤ Recycling is a profitable government project.

East Asia에 관한 다음 글의 요지로 가장 적절한 것은?

| 경찰대학 2010학년도 29번 |

The economic changes in East Asia are one of the most significant developments in the world in the second half of the 20th century. By the 1990s this economic development had generated expectations among many observers who saw East Asia linked together in ever-expanding commercial networks that would insure peace and harmony among nations. This optimism was, however, based on the highly dubious assumption that commercial interchange is invariably a force for peace. Such is not the case. Economic growth creates political instability within and between countries, altering the balance of power among them. Economic exchange brings people into contact, but it does not bring them into agreement.

① International politics causes economic depression.
② East Asia has constantly enjoyed economic growth.
③ Economic exchange does not bring peace necessarily.
④ Democracy of East Asian countries has improved a lot.
⑤ Economic development ensures international cooperation.

01 다음 글의 요지로 가장 적절한 것을 고르시오.

| 사관학교 2018학년도 28번 |

In everyday life, people are repeatedly exposed to different aspects of consumption. Advertising, traveling on a train, grocery shopping, watching television, listening to music, surfing the Internet, clothes shopping, and reading a book are all examples of things that people consume. Almost all behaviors that humans engage in are directly or indirectly linked to consumption. Even traditional holidays such as Christmas are these days mainly about consumption. What was originally a religious holiday has mainly been overtaken by aspects of consumption with the most typical example of this being Santa Claus delivering presents. Basically there is no way of escaping the fact that consumption is a part of humans' everyday lives. Hence, without studying how consumption affects individuals and groups, one can never truly say that we understand humans.

① 다양한 제품 개발로 소비 활동이 촉진될 수 있다.
② 개인의 선호에 따라 서로 다른 소비 양상이 나타난다.
③ 소비자는 자극적인 광고에 영향을 많이 받는 경향이 있다.
④ 인간을 이해하기 위해서는 소비에 대한 연구가 반드시 필요하다.
⑤ 크리스마스와 같은 종교적인 휴일에는 더 많은 소비가 발생한다.

다음 글의 요지로 가장 적절한 것을 고르시오.

Spatial cognition is a fundamental design requirement for every mobile species with a fixed territory or home base. And there is little doubt that it plays a central role in human thinking and reasoning. Indeed, the evidence for that centrality is all around us, in our language where spatial metaphors are used for many other domains and in the special role of place in memory. The idea that space is a fundamental intuition built into our nature goes back at least to Kant, and the idea that our perception of space is governed by cognitive universals informs much current cognitive science. But in some ways human spatial cognition is puzzling. First, it is unspectacular — we are not as a species, compared to bees or pigeons, bats or whales, particularly good at finding our way around. Second, human spatial cognition is obviously variable — hunters, sailors and taxi-drivers are in a different league from the ordinary city-dweller. This suggests that many aspects of effective spatial thinking depend on cultural factors, which in turn suggests limits to cognitive universals in this area.

[3점]

① 언어와 공간의 개념은 인간의 삶에서 상호 작용한다.
② 인간의 공간적 사고에는 인지적 보편성의 한계가 있다.
③ 인간의 공간적 사고는 시대와 문화를 초월하여 보편적이다.
④ 인간의 공간 인지 능력은 동물과 비교해서 뒤지지 않는다.
⑤ 인지과학은 공간 인지의 개념에 바탕을 두어야 한다.

03

다음 글의 요지로 가장 적절한 것은?

Many present efforts to guard and maintain human progress, to meet human needs, and to realize human ambitions are simply unsustainable — in both the rich and poor nations. They draw too heavily, too quickly, on already overdrawn environmental resource accounts to be affordable far into the future without bankrupting those accounts. They may show profit on the balance sheets of our generation, but our children will inherit the losses. We borrow environmental capital from future generations with no intention or prospect of repaying. They may blame us for our wasteful ways, but they can never collect on our debt to them. We act as we do because we can get away with it: future generations do not vote; they have no political or financial power; they cannot challenge our decisions.

① 환경 문제를 해결하기 위한 세대 간 협력이 중요하다.

② 인류의 발전은 다양한 환경 자원의 개발에 달려 있다.

③ 미래의 환경 문제에 대비한 국제사회의 공조가 필요하다.

④ 선진국들은 경제력을 기반으로 환경 자원을 선점하고 있다.

⑤ 현세대는 미래 세대에 대한 고려 없이 환경 자원을 남용하고 있다.

04 다음 글의 요지로 가장 적절한 것은?

One difference between winners and losers is how they handle losing. Even for the best companies and most accomplished professionals, long track records of success are punctuated by slips, slides, and mini-turnarounds. Even the team that wins the game might make mistakes and lag behind for part of it. That's why the ability to recover quickly is so important. Troubles are ubiquitous. Surprises can fall from the sky like volcanic ash and appear to change everything. That's why one prominent scholar said, "Anything can look like a failure in the middle." Thus, a key factor in high achievement is bouncing back from the low points.

① 경영의 전문화는 일류 기업의 조건이다.
② 위기 관리에는 전문가의 조언이 필요하다.
③ 합리적 소비는 필요와 욕구의 구분에서 비롯된다.
④ 폭넓은 인간 관계는 성공의 필수 요소이다.
⑤ 실패를 빨리 극복하는 것이 성공의 열쇠이다.

UNIT 03 제목

글의 내용에 적합한 제목을 찾는 유형이다. 선택지로 주어진 제목의 의미를 파악하고, 글 전체에 부합하는 선택지를 고른다.

- 도입부에서 글의 소재를 확인한다.
- 글의 요지를 파악한다.
- 소재와 관련된 글의 흐름을 파악한다.

Example

다음 글의 제목으로 가장 적절한 것을 고르시오.

| 경찰대학 2016학년도 25번 |

❶ The earliest Robin Hood ballad was printed in 1450, and it does not portray the dashing hero that we have come to know in popular culture. He was a yeoman, rough and cruel at times. The legend was more than likely based on a robber who kept the money he stole from the rich and occasionally helped the poor. He did not want to set up an ideal society in the forest. He and his men sought mainly to rectify social injustices and to live well. Robin Hood became so popular by the seventeenth century that people named places and ships after him. ❷ By the nineteenth century, many stories and songs had brought about major changes in the Robin Hood legend. His yeoman origins disappeared, and he increasingly became the heroic outlaw of Sherwood Forest who defended the rights of the poor.

① Robin Hood as a Robber
② Origins of Medieval Yeomen
③ Earlier Struggles of Robin Hood
④ Ideal Society in Sherwood Forest
⑤ Transformations in the Robin Hood Character

Vocabulary

ballad 민요, 이야기 portray 초상을 그리다, 묘사하다 dashing 늠름한 yeoman 자작농 cruel 잔혹한, 무자비한 occasionally 이따금, 때때로 rectify 수정하다, 교정하다

Let's Solve

Point 1 도입부에서 글의 소재 확인하기

• The earliest Robin Hood ballad was printed in 1450, and it does not portray the dashing hero that we have come to know in popular culture.

→ Robin Hood 캐릭터의 초기와 현재

Point 2 글의 요지 파악하기

• By the nineteenth century, many stories and songs had brought about major changes in the Robin Hood legend.

→ 19세기경 Robin Hood 전설에 변화가 일어남

Point 3 소재와 관련된 글의 흐름 파악하기

초기	19세기	현재
• a yeoman, rough and cruel at times. • a robber who kept the money he stole from the rich and occasionally helped the poor	major changes in the Robin Hood legend	the heroic outlaw of Sherwood Forest who defended the rights of the poor

Point 4 정답 풀이하기

① 강도로서의 Robin Hood
  → Robin Hood가 어떤 강도였는지는 글의 일부분에 해당하는 내용이다.

② 중세 자작농의 시초
  → 언급되어 있지 않다.

③ 초창기 Robin Hood의 고난
  → 언급되어 있지 않다.

④ Sherwood Forest의 이상적 사회
  → 초기와 달리 변화한 Robin Hood 캐릭터의 근거지가 Sherwood 숲이라는 언급이 있을 뿐 그곳의 이상적 사회에 대한 내용은 없다.

⑤ Robin Hood 캐릭터의 변화
  → 글 전체의 흐름을 대표하는 적절한 제목이다.

01 다음 글의 제목으로 가장 적절한 것을 고르시오.

| 경찰대학 2018학년도 24번 |

The center of mining and armor technology was Augsburg, in Germany, and that was no coincidence. Augsburg was near one of Europe's major deposits of iron ore, and the demand for metal from feudal states building forces of armored knights soon created a booming mining industry and an equally flourishing armorer business. To the annoyance of their customers throughout feudal Europe, the Germans charged sky-high prices, aware that those customers had no alternative: German armor was the best in the world, and if a customer didn't like the prices, he could sally forth on his next war with sticks and stones. Underwritten by these lavish profits, the German armorers could afford an extensive research and development effort. It resulted in stronger armor, for example, steel helmets with movable visors that covered the entire head.

① Farewell to Arms and Armors
② Past and Future of Armor Business
③ Stones vs. Steel: The Obvious Choice
④ Germany, the Hub of Armor Technology
⑤ High Quality and Low Prices: A Double-Edged Sword

다음 글의 제목으로 가장 적절한 것을 고르시오.

| 경찰대학 2018학년도 25번 |

Hate to haggle? You're not alone. A national survey found that just 48 percent of shoppers tried bargaining for a better deal on everyday goods and services in the past three years, down from 61 percent in 2007. But if you're chicken, you lose. Eighty-nine percent of those who haggled were rewarded at least once. Successful furniture hagglers saved $300 on average, as did those who questioned a health-related charge. Those who challenged their cell-phone plans saved $80. Clearly, people who don't haggle are leaving money on the table.

[3점]

① Can't Hurt to Ask
② ABCs of Haggling Better
③ Furniture Haggling Made Easy
④ Shopping Around: Reap the Rewards
⑤ Does Haggling Actually Inflate Prices?

다음 글의 제목으로 가장 적절한 것을 고르시오.

When you're carrying extra pounds, the extra expenses add up, starting with health care. In a 2013 Duke study, researchers tracked health care spending by body mass index (BMI) levels. The average annual cost for a person with a low BMI of 19 was $2,541. With a BMI of 25 — considered overweight — it was $2,893. At a BMI of 33, what's deemed obese, the costs topped $3,439. "The risk of illness starts increasing already from the lower end of 'normal weight,'" says lead researcher Truls Ostbye. The add-ons don't end at the doctor's office. A 2010 McKinsey study estimated that obese Americans spend an aggregate of $30 billion extra on clothes. It is also estimated that a 40-year-old obese man will pay twice as much for life insurance.

① Increasing Costs of Health Care
② Lose Weight, Lower Risk of Illness
③ The Price You Pay for Extra Pounds
④ Do Obese People Spend More on Clothes?
⑤ BMI: Not an Accurate Indicator of Weight

다음 글의 제목으로 가장 적절한 것을 고르시오.

Climbing the automobile ladder was hard work, and staying on top was even harder. Each year, employing the practice of perceived obsolescence, Chevrolet would roll out an entirely redesigned, and usually larger, model. A car that had been the height of fashion yesterday would look small, embarrassing, and worn-out tomorrow. As you would imagine, all of this provoked a good deal of anxiety from the bottom to the top of American society. Then in 1959, seemingly out of nowhere, simple full-page newspaper ads began to appear with an unadorned image of the Volkswagen Beetle and the headline "Think Small." The ad didn't say much more, except that the car was modest and efficient — it even called the Beetle a "flivver," contemporary slang for a piece of junk. People found the ads shockingly honest and hilarious, allowing them to publicly express an unnamed anxiety that marketers had been instilling in them for years. Will I make it to the top of the ladder? Who Cares?

[3점]

① Hard Economic Times: Think Small
② At the Top of the Automobile Ladder
③ New Ad: Step Down From Your Ladders
④ Does Your Car Represent Your Social Status?
⑤ International Automobile Warfare: Size Matters

다음 글의 제목으로 가장 적절한 것을 고르시오. | 경찰대학 2016학년도 26번 |

In one study a hundred men and women wore devices that took readings of their blood pressure whenever they interacted with someone. When they were with family or enjoyable friends, their blood pressure fell; these interactions were pleasant and soothing. When they were with someone who was troublesome, there was a rise. But the biggest jump came while they were with people they felt ambivalent about: an overbearing parent, a volatile romantic partner, or a competitive friend. A mercurial boss looms as the archetype, but this dynamic operates in all our relationships.

① High Blood Pressure: The Silent Assassin
② Uneasy Relationships: Your Body Doesn't Lie
③ Don't Be Bossed Around by Your Biorhythm
④ Can Health Monitoring Devices Save Your Life?
⑤ How Can You Deal with Uncomfortable Interactions?

06 다음 글의 제목으로 가장 적절한 것을 고르시오.

You must follow Cross-Continent Enterprise's (CCE) processes and adhere to the system of internal controls around supplier selection. Supplier selection should never be based on receipt of a gift, hospitality or payment. When supplier selection is a formal, structured invitation for the supply of products or services (often called a 'tender'), it is most important we maintain documentation supporting our internal controls. In the public sector, such a tender process may be required and determined in detail by law to ensure that such competition for the use of public money is open, fair and free from corruption. A tender process includes an invitation for other parties to make a proposal, on the understanding that any competition for the relevant contract must be conducted in response to the tender, no parties having the unfair advantage of separate, prior, closed-door negotiations for the contract where a bidding process is open to all qualified bidders and where the sealed bids are in the open for scrutiny and are chosen on the basis of price and quality.

① CCE's Regulations of the Supplier Selection Process
② Why Is Supplier Selection Important at CCE?
③ How to Boost Employee Morale of the Company
④ Legal Issues Surrounding the Tender Competition Process
⑤ Documentation Requirements in the Bidder Selection Process

다음 글의 제목으로 가장 적절한 것을 고르시오. | 경찰대학 2015학년도 26번 |

As light hits the Earth's atmosphere, the different colors react in different ways. Some of them get absorbed by the gas molecules while others do not. Most of the longer-wavelength colors (such as red and orange) pass straight through the atmosphere and are unaffected, while many of the shorter-wavelength colors (such as violet and blue) get absorbed by the gas molecules, because the wavelengths (i.e., the distance between the peaks of each wave) of these colors are similar in size to the diameter of an atom of oxygen. The gas molecules then radiate these colors and scatter them across the sky, causing the sky to appear blue.

① The Fate of Colors Destined by Wavelengths
② Science Behind the Science of Gas Molecules
③ The Nature of Light: The Longer, the Brighter
④ Gas Molecules vs. Wavelengths: Who Wins?
⑤ How Do Our Naked Eyes Perceive Colors?

다음 글의 제목으로 가장 적절한 것을 고르시오.

When billionaires turn to philanthropy after making their fortune, they often fund scholarships for poor students, work to improve health care, or contribute to the arts. Chang Yung-Fa's mission is nothing less than to "reorganize" social values. Five years ago he started a cartoon-illustrated magazine, *Morals*, that each month seeks to uplift people's sense of morality in Taiwan and around the world. Whether he's making money or giving away money, morality underpins much of what the 85-year-old Chang does. He believes that his Evergreen Group — which includes the world's fourth-largest container shipping company, hotels, EVA Airways and long-distance buses to the island's main airport — prospers largely because of congenial staff relations backed by the company culture of morality.

① Bothered Philanthropist in Taiwan
② Higher Morality, Greater Happiness
③ Instilling Morality in Taiwanese Companies
④ Entrepreneur Turned Morality Missionary
⑤ Business and Morality: Like Oil and Water

다음 글의 제목으로 가장 적절한 것을 고르시오.

| 경찰대학 2014학년도 25번 |

Perhaps the scientists most excited about reigniting the lunar program are not lunar specialists, but astronomers studying a wide range of subjects. Such scientists would like new missions to install a huge telescope with a diameter of 30 meters on the far side of the moon. Two things that a telescope needs for optimum operation are extreme cold and very little vibration. Temperatures on the moon can be as frigid as 200 degrees Celsius below zero in craters on the dark side. Because there is no seismic activity, the moon is a steady base. Permanent darkness means the telescope can be in constant use. Proponents claim that under these conditions a lunar-based telescope could accomplish as much in seventeen days as the replacement for the Hubble telescope will in ten years.

*seismic: 진동의 [3점]

① Lunar Program: Once in a Blue Moon
② The Case for a Lunar Space Observatory
③ Moon Exploration: One Small Step for Mankind
④ The New Hubble Telescope: Is It Worth It?
⑤ Lunar Specialists vs. General Astronomers

다음 글의 제목으로 가장 적절한 것을 고르시오.

| 경찰대학 2013학년도 28번 |

The amount of sunshine that reaches the Earth dropped by 10 percent between the early 1950s and the early 1990s. Scientists have found that the problem is not the sun. No instruments have recorded any dimming of the sun's rays. The problem appears to be between the Earth and the Sun. Pollution has gotten in the way. Particulates in pollution reflect sun back into outer space. Pollution also causes increased condensation in the air. This condensation forms thicker, darker clouds. To verify their theory, scientists point to areas with little or no pollution. Instruments in those places have shown sunshine as bright as ever.

① Let's Give the Sun a Vacation
② Sunshine: The More the Better
③ Pollution: An Unnatural Sunshade
④ How Can We Stop the Sun's Dimming?
⑤ Look for a Silver Lining in Every Cloud

다음 글의 제목으로 가장 적절한 것을 고르시오.

Walter Benjamin identifies traditional storytelling not only with the traveller, who returns from his wanderings with something to tell, but also with the preserver of local traditions, rooted in his native place. In the Middle Ages, these two types of storytelling interpenetrated because of the craft structure, whereby the resident master craftsman and the travelling journeyman came together in the workplace. But through the workings of "the secular productive forces of history," narrative has been taken from the realm of living speech. What stands in opposition to storytelling, what is in the process of replacing it entirely, is of course the novel, inseparably linked to the invention of printing and the notion of the book. The novelist is necessarily isolated, invisible, a hidden god who does not have the capacity to enter into colloquy with his fellow man, and thus cannot communicate that wisdom that is good counsel.

① Two Times, One Narrative
② Storytelling: Living Speech vs Dead Letters
③ A Solitary Hero in the Modern Narrative
④ The Decline of Storytelling, the Rise of the Novel
⑤ Craftsman and Journeyman: Two Sides of the Coin

다음 글의 제목으로 가장 적절한 것을 고르시오. | 경찰대학 2013학년도 30번 |

Modern psychology has been called "the science of the behavior of the college sophomore." During the 1960s and 1970s, several psychologists analyzed four journals in the field and found that 58 percent to 96 percent of the articles were based on studies with college students. More recently, I analyzed the articles in two of those journals in 1991 and found that 77 percent reported on research done with college students. Melvin Manis, a University of Michigan psychologist, who is also an editor of one of the journals studied, explains that convenience dictates the choice of subjects in other fields as well. "There's very little genetic research going on with elephants," he says. "Most of it is done with fruit flies, not only because they have short life spans but because they're much cheaper." That's fine if elephants and fruit flies have comparable genetic mechanisms. But do college students think, behave, and feel as their non-college peers do? Or, for that matter, as older adults do? The answer to both questions is "no."

① College Students: Now and Then
② Genetic Research: Smaller is Better?
③ Sampling Error in the Study of Psychology
④ College Students in Psychology: Too Many?
⑤ Thought Patterns of College Students and Older Adults

In India, the new year celebrations at the end of October focus on no one food but rather a balance of flavors, according to Julie Sahni, author of *Classic Indian Cooking. Appam*, a traditional cake made with rice flour, coconut, milk, and a kind of palm sap, is served along with a fudge called *barifi*. Both symbolize the wish for life to be lucky. But Sahni said other dishes, like mulligatawny soup (said to be good for a hangover) and green mango chutney, which is both sweet and hot, are served as well because a new year's feast must include tastes that are at once sweet, savory, sour, and hot. "The idea is to serve something that brings many flavors in your mouth, with the hope that life is going to bring many elements of pleasure and pain and you should take it all in good spirit," Sahni said.

① The Recipe of Traditional Indian Foods
② New Year Ceremonies in India
③ The Relation of Food to Health
④ The Elements of Pleasure and Pain in India
⑤ Food for Luck and Wisdom in India

다음 글의 제목으로 가장 적절한 것을 고르시오.

Mr. Halle acknowledged that it was difficult to get people to dig into their pockets to save some of life's more unpleasant varmints. "There are all sorts of species that we have a hard time finding arguments for," he said. "And one of the things that does environmentalists poor credit is to insist overly for any particular individual species. The millions that went into saving the California Condor, for example, as far as I'm concerned could have been better spent." Nevertheless, Mr. Halle said, genetic diversity is important and man ought to think carefully about the wider consequences before allowing any species to be endangered and die out. Everything, no matter how disgusting, is something else's lunch. As Jonathan Swift put it, "a flea hath smaller fleas that on him prey; and these have smaller still to bite them, and so proceed ad infinitum." Thus losing any plant or creature from what used to be called the Great Chain of Being can have all kinds of unforeseen effects.

① Various Kinds of Endangered Species
② How to Preserve the California Condor
③ Maintenance of Biological Diversity
④ Problems of Environmentalists' Approach
⑤ How to Save Unpleasant Animals

다음 글의 제목으로 가장 적절한 것을 고르시오. | 경찰대학 2011학년도 40번 |

While the students can decode and even become fluent oral readers, they do not truly comprehend the materials; they cannot read between the lines, infer meaning, or detect the author's bias, among other things. Reading is much more complex than simply mastering phonemic awareness and alphabet recognition. It is an incredibly complex psycholinguistic activity involving not only letter sounds, but also comprehension in all its facets, adjusting reading for varying purposes, literary appreciation, and most importantly, authentic and lifelong application. Plus, reading requires having a purpose for applying the skills. Am I reading this for pleasure or to prepare for a test, for example? Finally little of this complete knowledge will be engaged if the student is not interested, motivated, or enjoying the experience. Learning to read is hard work and takes energy and concentration. If it does not seem fun to children, it is difficult to sustain their interest.

① Reading as a Complex Activity Rather Than Just Decoding
② Keeping a Delicate Balance Between Coding and Decoding
③ Caught in a Trap While Reading Between the Lines
④ Experiential Approach to Teaching Reading Skills
⑤ Pleasure and Hardship of Learning Experience

다음 글의 제목으로 가장 적절한 것을 고르시오.　　| 경찰대학 2011학년도 41번 |

Gardens are short -lived in the chill of Flin Flon, a small mining town in Canada. But now residents of this mining town enjoy fresh fruits and roses year-round. The bounty grows 1,170 feet beneath the surface in what was a vacant chamber of a copper and zinc mine. The experiment was conceived by Wayne Fraser and Brent Zettle of Prairie Plant Systems Inc. to test the quality, yield, and cost of subterranean gardening. "The chamber is totally isolated from the surface, so the environment can be controlled cheaply and accurately," Zettle says. The mine installed high-intensity lights, a drip irrigation system, and computers. "Woody plants grow at a phenomenal rate," notes Zettle. Three months after planting, 80 rose plants produced 1,100 flowers, instead of the normal 700. The results are sold in local markets. Miners take great pride in their garden.

① A Shady Side of Mines
② Roses Bloom Deep in a Mine
③ A Heart Warmed in the Chill
④ A Miner's Love of Wild Flowers
⑤ A Prosperous Local Market for Miners

다음 글의 제목으로 가장 적절한 것을 고르시오.

Letters of recommendation are one of the least accurate forecasters of job performance. Some people even make recommendations that have an inverse relationship with the criterion; that is, if the applicant is recommended for hire, the company would do best to reject him or her! One of the biggest problems with letters of recommendation is their restricted range. As you might expect, almost all letters of recommendation are positive. Most often, the applicants themselves choose who will write the letters, so it isn't surprising that they pick people who will make them look good. Because of this restriction, the lack of predictive ability of the letter of recommendation is not unexpected.

① Defensible Strategies in Personnel Selection
② How to Write Good Letters of Recommendation
③ The Characteristics of Good Letters of Recommen-dation
④ Intentional Deception in Letters of Recommen-dation
⑤ The Limitations of Letters of Recommendation

다음 글의 제목으로 가장 적절한 것을 고르시오.

| 경찰대학 2010학년도 31번 |

Charlotte Church looks like a teenager, but she is far from average. She has an amazing voice. Her fans stand in lines for hours to get tickets for her concerts. Her singing career began when she performed on a TV show at the age of 11. The head of a record company was so impressed by her voice that he signed her up on the spot. Her first album rose to number one. She still attends school when she can. However, she is often away on tour for weeks at a time. She doesn't miss out on lessons, though, because she takes her own tutor with her! She spends three hours every morning with him. But how does she cope with this unusual way of life? She insists that she has the same friends as before. That may be true, but she can no longer go into town with them because everybody stops her to ask for her autograph. It seems that, like most stars, she must learn to put up with these restrictions.

① The Price of Fame
② A Teenage Star at Risk
③ A Teenager and Her Public Life
④ How Far can She Go from Here?
⑤ Hidden Attractions of a Superstar

다음 글의 제목으로 가장 적절한 것을 고르시오.

In the course of child rearing, nearly all parents believe they have stumbled upon certain "truths" about child development. Quite possibly their discoveries could be supported by a number of studies conducted by professionals in the field. The early physical development of children is an area in which systematic observations have provided a more or less standard profile. If a child's growth does not conform, it does not necessarily mean that there is something wrong; individual differences are expected to emerge. But within any given age group, children do seem to share certain abilities and to behave in many similar ways. Extreme differences between one's own child and other children of the same age may suggest problems in development. Standards of growth, therefore, provide parents with a way of knowing when to seek professional help and advice.

① What Causes Extreme Differences Among Children?
② Usefulness of the Standard Tracks of Early Development
③ Time to Seek Professional Advice for Newborn Babies
④ Moms' Concern About How Their Children Learn Language
⑤ Who Should Moms Talk to for Help with Their Children?

다음 글의 제목으로 가장 적절한 것은?

| 경찰대학 2009학년도 15번 |

A series of high-profile cases involving the loss of computer discs by Government departments has left many police forces having to rethink the way they carry confidential information. The City of London force believes it has already solved the problem with a clever piece of software that makes the system more secure without making it more complicated. *DeviceStick* allows officers to download information onto a specially-designed USB stick, which can only be accessed with the correct fingerprint and password. The system also allows the force to track who is accessing computer systems, and when. Gary Brailsford-Hart, head of information management at the City of London Police, said "it would be virtually impossible for anyone to access the information," in the event of a device being lost.

① Technology Developed by Police Forces
② Technology Designed for Accessing Information
③ Technology Used in the Fight Against Crime
④ Technology for Protecting Confidential Information
⑤ Technology for Preventing the Loss of Computer Discs

01 다음 글의 제목으로 가장 적절한 것을 고르시오.

| 사관학교 2018학년도 25번 |

People unconsciously signal that they are lying through inconsistencies in their nonverbal behavior. If you have ever caught someone in a lie, you might have noticed that statements made later in the conversation contradicted statements made at the beginning, or perhaps his or her gestures seemed to contradict the words being spoken. The person may have acted calm and aloof, but at the same time kept tapping his or her foot, playing with a button or piece of jewelry, and speaking with a higher pitch. Examinations of people's perceptions of courtroom testimony reveal that stereotypically deceptive behaviors don't necessarily trigger suspicion, but inconsistent nonverbal behaviors are frequently interpreted as deceptive regardless of the specific actions that are performed. Research has also shown that familiarity with a person's typical nonverbal behaviors makes it easier to detect deception. In particular, people are better able to tell whether a partner is telling the truth or lying when they have previous experience with that person's truthful behavior.

*aloof : 초연한, 무관심한

① Patterns of Behavior That Reveal Deception
② Psychological Factors That Lead to Deception
③ Common Characteristics of Nonverbal Messages
④ Developing a Strong Relationship Free of Deception
⑤ Inaccurate Assessments of People's Truth or Deception

다음 글의 제목으로 가장 적절한 것을 고르시오. | 사관학교 2015학년도 24번 |

We are accustomed to brushing our teeth every day. We know it to be a healthful ritual that preserves our teeth and gums and widens our smile. Its benefits are personal as well as social. But archaeologists working among the remains of eighteenth-century Annapolis — where a new class of people were eager for work — have suggested a new view of how and why we came to all this brushing and flossing and fussing. Mark Leone and his team of urban archaeologists found numerous toothbrushes under the streets of Annapolis. Eighteenth-century toothbrushes suggest a new emphasis on personal hygiene and the notion of the self-maintained individual. It's important: to have workers arrive on time and do a job, they have to develop discipline. So an industrial society emphasizes toothbrushes and a lot of other things like combs and clocks to help people make themselves orderly. Toothbrushes, it turns out, were instrumental in easing us into the Industrial Revolution.

① Annapolis: A Grand Archaeologist Attraction
② Appearance of "Toothbrush" in the English Language
③ Impact of the Toothbrush on the Dental Care Industry
④ Role of the Toothbrush in Developing an Industrial Workforce
⑤ Economic Changes Brought About by the Industrial Revolution

다음 글의 제목으로 가장 적절한 것은?

The names of pitches are associated with particular frequency values. Our current system is called A440 because the note we call 'A' that is in the middle of the piano keyboard has been fixed to have a frequency of 440 Hz. This is entirely arbitrary. We could fix 'A' at any frequency, such as 439 or 424; different standards were used in the time of Mozart than today. Some people claim that the precise frequencies affect the overall sound of a musical piece and the sound of instruments. Led Zeppelin, a band popular in the 70s, often tuned their instruments away from the modern A440 standard to give their music an uncommon sound, and perhaps to link it with the European children's folk songs that inspired many of their compositions. Many purists insist on hearing baroque music on period instruments, both because the instruments have a different sound and because they are designed to play the music in its original tuning standard, something that purists deem important.

① Should 'A' Always Be Tuned at 440 Hz?
② Arbitrary Tuning: A New Trend in Music
③ How to Correctly Measure Frequency Values
④ How Do Musicians Detect Pitch Differences?
⑤ Unstable Pitches: A Common Thread in Music

다음 글의 제목으로 가장 적절한 것은?

When we remark with surprise that someone "looks young" for his or her chronological age, we are observing that we all age biologically at different rates. Scientists have good evidence that this apparent difference is real. It is likely that age changes begin in different parts of the body at different times and that the rate of annual change varies among various cells, tissues, and organs, as well as from person to person. Unlike the passage of time, biological aging resists easy measurement. What we would like to have is one or a few measurable biological changes that mirror all other biological age changes without reference to the passage of time, so that we could say, for example, that someone who is chronologically eighty years old is biologically sixty years old. This kind of measurement would help explain why one eighty-year-old has so many more youthful qualities than does another eighty-year-old, who may be biologically eighty or even ninety years old.

① In Search of a Mirror Reflecting Biological Aging
② Reasons for Slow Aging in the Modern Era
③ A Few Tips to Guess Chronological Age
④ Secrets of Biological Aging Disclosed
⑤ Looking for the Fountain of Youth

Problem Solving Skills

글의 목적을 묻는 문제는 글을 쓴 직접적 이유가 무엇인지를 묻는 유형이다. 글의 세부사항을 구체적으로 이해하고 이를 통해 필자의 의도를 파악한다.

• 주요 어휘로 글의 소재를 파악한다.
• 글의 핵심이 되는 문장을 찾는다.
• 글의 세부 내용을 통해 글의 목적을 찾는다.

Example

다음 글의 목적으로 가장 적절한 것은?

| 경찰대학 2018학년도 28번 |

What could be more comforting than seeing your dog or cat curled up in blissful sleep? Both species spend almost half their day engaged in some form of sleep. But not all find it restful: older animals, those with muscular or joint issues, or very active dogs will often pace or relocate frequently. If your companion fits into one of these categories, he might benefit from a therapeutic bed. These specialized products offer support and comfort unlike regular beds or an impromptu sleeping spot. Regardless of age and health, a good bed promotes muscular-skeletal health and offers additional rejuvenating and healing benefits.

① to prevent domestic animal abuse
② to promote specialized pet furniture
③ to explain the benefits of good sleep
④ to inform pet owners of furniture hazards
⑤ to warn pet owners of poor pet sleep habits

Vocabulary

blissful 더없이 행복한 restful 편안한 pace 서성거리다 relocate 이동하다 therapeutic 치료법의 impromptu 즉흥적인
rejuvenate 활기를 되찾게 하다

Let's Solve

Point 1 주요 어휘로 소재 파악하기

> animals, dog, cat, sleep, restful, theraputic, support, comfort, health, healing, bed

⬇

> 동물들, 개, 고양이 + 잠자다, 편안한, 치료의, 지탱감, 편안함, 건강, 치유 + 침대

⬇

> 동물들을 위한 편안하고 지탱감 있는 침대

Point 2 글의 세부 내용을 통해 글의 목적 찾기

• your dog or cat curled up in blissful sleep • pace or relocate frequently ➡ he might benefit from a therapeutic bed	침대의 필요성

• These specialized products offer support and comfort	침대의 효용

✚

• a good bed promotes muscular-skeletal health • offers additional rejuvenating and healing benefits	효용의 구체적 예

⬇

> 동물의 건강한 수면에 전문화된 침대를 홍보하고 있다

Point 3 정답 풀이하기

① 가축 학대를 예방하기 위해
→ 동물 학대 및 그 예방에 대한 언급은 없다.

② 전문화된 애완동물 가구를 홍보하기 위해
→ 애완동물의 편안한 잠자리를 위한 치료 침대를 소개하는 글로, 직접적으로 제품의 장점을 언급하고 있다.

③ 좋은 수면의 이점을 설명하기 위해
→ 좋은 수면의 이점은 침대 구매를 독려하기 위해 언급되었다.

④ 애완동물 주인들에게 가구의 위험성을 알리기 위해
→ 가구의 위험성에 대한 언급은 없다.

⑤ 애완동물의 나쁜 수면 습관에 대해 주인들에게 경고하기 위해
→ 나쁜 수면 습관에 관한 언급은 침대 구매를 독려하기 위한 것이다.

01 다음 글의 목적으로 가장 적절한 것은?

경찰대학 2009학년도 36번

It is hard to build precise boundaries around periods in art history. But in the case of Cubism it is possible to say that the movement was ushered in by the *Demoiselles d'Avignon* conceived by Picasso towards the end of 1906 and abandoned in its present state during the course of the succeeding year. It is a disturbing and daring painting today. Sixty years ago, it must have seemed nothing short of incredible. It certainly dismayed and baffled even Picasso's warmest supporters. Braque, an intelligent and open-minded young painter, was frankly horrified when he first saw it. Yet some months later his great *Female Bathers* was to demonstrate that the *Demoiselles d'Avignon* had altered the entire course of his artistic evolution.

① 피카소의 파격적인 화풍 기술
② 저명한 화가들의 회화작품 비교
③ 화가들의 화풍이 바뀌는 이유 설명
④ 미술사에서의 입체파의 등장 소개
⑤ 브라크의 작품 "목욕하는 여인들" 평가

02

다음 글의 목적으로 가장 적절한 것은?

| 경찰대학 2008학년도 33번 |

This modern cowboy story is set in 1949. It follows three young men on a wild ride on horseback out of Texas and into northern Mexico. Their adventure takes them out of twentieth-century America and into a totally different world, where it is still possible to live with horses and nature. There are the bad guys and good guys, as in the classic films, but it is not just a rewriting of a John Wayne movie. The characters are convincing and the descriptions of the natural world are truly brilliant. The style is ambitious, and the masterful writing based on action-filled plot keeps our attention throughout. We hope the second volume will be as satisfying as this.

① To invite to the practice of storytelling
② To introduce a course on literature in college
③ To give information on famous western films
④ To advertise a new movie
⑤ To offer a review of a new book

03

다음 글의 목적으로 가장 적절한 것은?

| 경찰대학 2008학년도 34번 |

I have often wondered at the savagery and thoughtlessness with which our early settlers approached this rich continent. They came at it as though it were an enemy, which of course it was. They burned the forests and changed the rainfall; they swept the buffalo from the plains, blasted the streams, set fire to the grass, and ran a reckless scythe through the virgin and noble timber. Perhaps they felt that it was limitless and could never be exhausted and that a man could move on to new wonders endlessly. Certainly there are many examples to the contrary, but to a large extent the early people pillaged the country as though they hated it, as though they held it temporarily and might be driven off at any time.

① to explain the motives of the early settlement of America
② to describe how the settlements of early pioneers developed
③ to defend the way that early settlers exploited natural resources
④ to criticize early settlers' cruel treatment of Indians
⑤ to describe why and how early settlers destroyed their natural surroundings

01 다음 글을 쓴 목적으로 가장 적절한 것은?

| 사관학교 2012학년도 10번 |

Working in a large company such as this can be oddly isolating. If we were out in the field, like some of our fortunate colleagues, we would be active, meeting new people and moving around. However, for us office workers, we tend to just park our cars in the underground parkade, take an elevator to our floor and head to our little corners where we work the day away. The cafeteria may be a gathering place, but people tend to sit with those who work in the same office or on the same floor. I think a gym would provide an informal place which would bring together company personnel of all different departments and offices, of all different ages and backgrounds. If this idea were to be entertained, a suitable place to put it might be in the back room in the basement that is currently used for storage, or even in the 10th floor lounge which is rarely used. I believe such an investment would definitely be worth it, if not only for our health, also to help build company unity.

① 사무실 배정을 위한 아이디어를 모집하려고
② 직원들을 위한 체력단련장 신설을 제안하려고
③ 사무실 근무 직원의 하루 일과를 소개하려고
④ 사무실 칸막이 공사에 대한 반대의견을 밝히려고
⑤ 사내 친목 도모를 위한 점심 모임 참여를 독려하려고

다음 글을 쓴 목적으로 가장 적절한 것은?

As I mentioned at our last meeting, I would like you to conduct a one-month feasibility study on our proposal to extend our operations to include the Pacific Rim markets. If the results are positive, your report will go before the board of directors as we attempt to secure financing for this expansion. Since we are working under the current budget, your travel allowance will be tight. But I know you will make careful choices. I have included a copy of Neumann's Report on this matter. It is a bit out of date, but may still prove useful as a model. I look forward to weekly reports and, of course, to your final report, which is due no later than July 14th.

① to authorize a research project
② to ask for personal advice
③ to announce a special meeting
④ to make a formal invitation
⑤ to appreciate a financial donation

다음 글의 목적으로 가장 적절한 것은?

Want to improve your Korean writing? Writing is an essential tool that will help you adjust to Korean university life. The Ha-Rang Writing Center offers a free tutoring program open to all international students at our university. We encourage you to take advantage of this. The program has always been very popular among international students. Registration opens from November 28 for three days only. Once you are registered, we will match you with a perfect tutor and contact you to arrange your schedule. We are sure that you will be satisfied with our well-experienced tutors. Don't miss this great opportunity to improve your Korean writing. For more information, feel free to email Jiyung Yoon, HRWC Director, at jyoon@hrwc.org.

① 한국의 대학 생활과 관련한 유의 사항을 알리려고
② 한국어 글쓰기 강좌의 변경된 등록 절차를 공지하려고
③ 한국어 글쓰기 지도를 받을 외국인 학생을 모집하려고
④ 외국인 학생을 위한 글쓰기 센터 설립을 건의하려고
⑤ 한국어 글쓰기 지도 강사의 자격 요건을 안내하려고

다음 글의 목적으로 가장 적절한 것은?

Dear Coach Johnson,

My name is Christina Markle, Bradley Markle's mother. Bradley and I were thrilled to learn that you're holding your Gymnastics Summer Camp again this year. So I didn't hesitate to sign up and pay the non-refundable deposit for the second week program, which is from July 13 to 17. But today I remembered that our family is going to get back from a trip on July 13, and I'm afraid Bradley won't be able to make it on the very first day of the program. Rather than make him skip the day, I'd like to check to see if he could switch to the third week program. Please let us know if that's possible. Thank you.

Sincerely,

Christina Markle

① 캠프 참가를 위해 여행 일정을 조정하려고
② 캠프 참가 시기를 변경할 수 있는지 문의하려고
③ 캠프 등록 시 지불한 예치금 환불을 요구하려고
④ 캠프 일정이 분명하지 않은 것에 대해 항의하려고
⑤ 예약한 캠프 프로그램의 변경된 내용을 확인하려고

PART 02
어법 · 어휘 적절성 판단하기

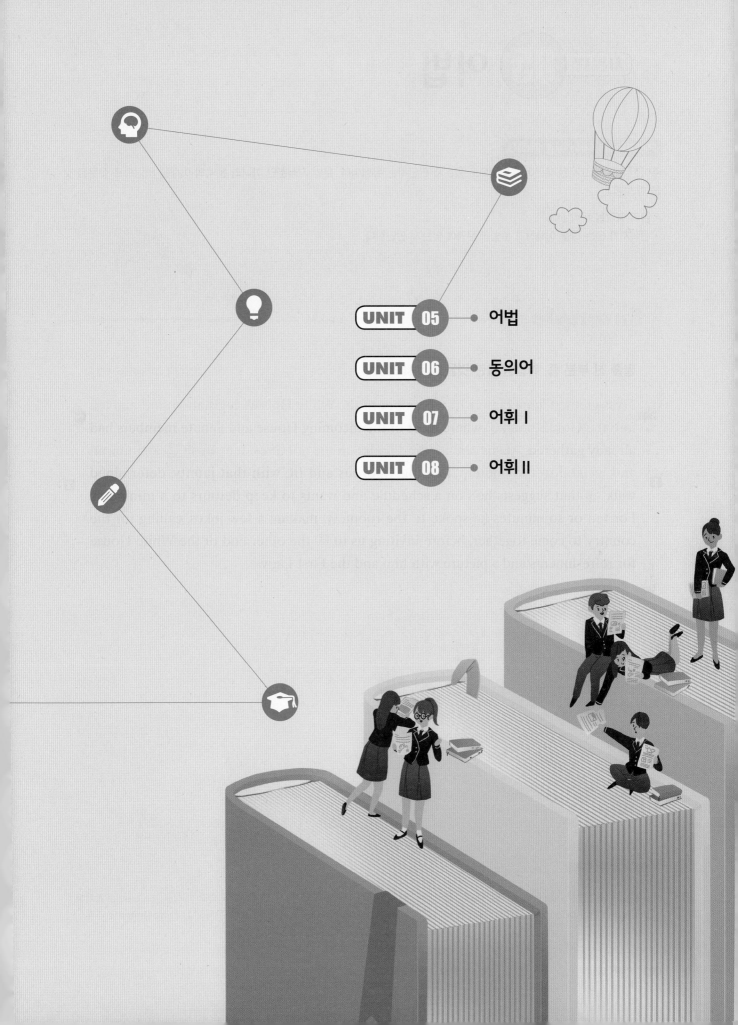

UNIT 05 어법

Problem Solving Skills

주어진 지문에 표시된 부분이 문법적으로 옳은지 판단하는 유형이다. 문법 지식뿐만 아니라 문맥의 이해를 바탕으로 잘못된 것을 가려낸다.

• 글의 맥락을 파악한다.
• 선택지가 묻는 바를 이해하고 문법과 문맥에 맞는지 판단한다.

Example

밑줄 친 부분 중, 어법상 틀린 것을 고르시오.　　　　　| 경찰대학 2018학년도 6번 |

I was greeted immediately by a member of the White House's legislative staff and led into the Gold Room, ① where most of the incoming House and Senate members had already gathered. At sixteen hundred hours on the dot, President Bush ② announced and walked to the podium, looking vigorous and fit, with that jaunty, determined walk ③ that suggests he's on a schedule and wants to keep detours to a minimum. For ten or so minutes he spoke to the room, ④ making a few jokes, calling for the country to come together, before inviting us to ⑤ the other end of the White House for refreshments and a picture with him and the First Lady.

Vocabulary

legislative 입법부 incoming 새로 당선된, 들어오는 House (미국 의회의) 하원 Senate (미국 의회의) 상원 on the dot 정각에
podium 지휘대 vigorous 활발한 jaunty 의기양양한 determined 단호한 detour 우회로, 우회하다 refreshments 다과

Let's Solve

Point **1** 글의 맥락 파악하기

> • I was greeted immediately by a member of the White House's legislative staff and led into the Gold Room
> • At sixteen hundred hours on the dot, President Bush ② <u>announced</u> and walked to the podium

> 글쓴이는 백악관에 초청 받아 Gold Room에 안내 받았고, 입장한 Bush 대통령의 연설을 들었다.

Point **2** 선택지가 묻는 바를 이해하고 문법과 문맥에 맞는지 판단하기

① where: 관계부사
→ 선택지 이하는 the Gold Room을 수식하는 역할을 한다. the Gold Room은 의미상 신임 상하원 의원들이 모인 곳이므로 선택지의 위치에는 in(전치사) + which(관계대명사) 또는 전치사의 의미를 포함하는 where(관계부사)가 오는 것이 적절하다.

② announced: 타동사 · 동사의 수동태
→ announce는 타동사이며, 해당 문장에서 announced의 형태로 과거시제 동사로 쓰였다. 타동사는 목적어를 필요로 하지만 해당 문장에서 announced의 목적어를 찾을 수 없으므로 부적절하다.
→ 문맥상 Bush 대통령이 누군가를 호명한 뒤 자신이 연단에 서는 것보다 누군가에 의해 Bush 대통령이 호명되어 연단에 서는 것이 자연스러우므로, was announced가 오는 것이 적절하다.

③ that: 관계대명사
→ 사물 선행사 jaunty, determined walk을 수식하는 관계대명사로는 that 또는 which가 올 수 있다.

④ making: 분사 구문 · 문장의 병렬구조
→ 본래 as he made a few jokes인 것이 접속사와 주어를 생략하면서 making으로 변한 분사구문으로, 뒤에 이어지는 calling과 병렬 구조를 이룬다.

⑤ the other: one – the other 표현
→ 둘 중에 하나는 one, 나머지 하나는 the other라고 표현하는데 문맥상 백악관의 반대편 끝으로 이동하는 것이므로, the other라고 하는 것이 적절하다.

01

다음 글의 밑줄 친 부분 중, 어법상 **틀린** 것을 고르시오. | 경찰대학 2018학년도 7번 |

San Francisco Giants pitcher Ryan Vogelsong and his wife, Nicole, watched the Fourth of July fireworks from their apartment's rooftop deck, which ① offers breathtaking views of landmarks such as the Bay Bridge, Alcatraz Island and Coit Tower. It was also there ② where they toasted with champagne his selection to the National League's All-Star team, the improbable high point — at least so far — of an itinerant career. The *San Francisco Chronicle* recently named him ③ as a candidate for the Cy Young Award. It ④ has been that kind of fairy-tale season for Vogelsong, 34, who has an 8-1 record and a 2.23 ERA for the defending World Series champs. Though his accomplishments this year overshadow anything Vogelsong has done before in baseball, they would not ⑤ be possible without the toils of an odyssey that has included stops in 10 minor league cities, plus San Francisco, Pittsburgh, Japan and Venezuela.

02

다음 글의 밑줄 친 부분 중, 어법상 **틀린** 것을 고르시오. | 경찰대학 2018학년도 8번 |

The absence of comparisons from the state of nature is crucial to Rousseau. By insisting that creatures who lived apart from sustained relationships could not yet ① have evolved the mind it takes to rank persons, Rousseau draws two great conclusions. First, natural inequalities — greater physical strength, better singing voice, or higher intelligence — come to matter only when a quality we happen to possess ② wins us respect, praise, worth, or value in the eyes of others. The second conclusion is ③ that natural man — and natural man alone — is honest. In society we are always concerned with ④ what others think of us; we are motivated to do what will win us honor and the respect of others. It gets to the point where my sense of myself is derived from the impressions other people ⑤ have me.

03

다음 글의 밑줄 친 부분 중, 어법상 틀린 것을 고르시오.

| 경찰대학 2017학년도 6번 |

An important interruption in the usual flow of energy apparently occurred millions of years ago when the growth of land plants and marine organisms ① exceeded the ability of decomposers to recycle them. The ② accumulating layers of energy-rich organic material were gradually turned into coal and oil by the pressure of the overlying earth. The energy stored in their molecular structure we can now ③ release by burning. And our modern civilization depends on immense amounts of energy from such fossil fuels ④ recovering from the earth. By burning fossil fuels, we are finally passing most of the stored energy on to the environment as heat. We are also passing back to the atmosphere—in a relatively very short time—large amounts of carbon dioxide that ⑤ had been removed from it slowly over millions of years.

04

다음 글의 밑줄 친 부분 중, 어법상 틀린 것을 고르시오.

| 경찰대학 2017학년도 7번 |

The earth has many resources of great importance to human life. Some are ① readily renewable, some are renewable only at great cost, and some are not renewable at all. The earth comprises a great variety of minerals, whose properties depend on the history of how they were formed as well as on the elements ② which they are composed. Their abundance ranges from rare to almost unlimited. But the difficulty of ③ extracting them from the environment is as important an issue as their abundance. A wide variety of minerals ④ are sources for essential industrial materials, such as iron, aluminum, magnesium, and copper. Many of the best sources are being depleted, making it more and more difficult and expensive ⑤ to obtain those minerals.

다음 글의 밑줄 친 부분 중, 어법상 틀린 것을 고르시오.

| 경찰대학 2017학년도 8번 |

On the European continent, Kant rejected the utilitarian defense of liberalism but put forward a compatible case for the autonomy that comes only to the person ① underline{free to choose} his own conception of the good life. J.S. Mill himself took inspiration from other German liberals, ② underline{being noted} in the frontispiece to *On Liberty* the work of a contemporary, Wilhelm von Humboldt. But this moment of convergence of German and Anglo-American liberalism was soon ③ underline{to pass}. With Hegel, and then Marx, German intellectual thought centrally explored the deficiencies in the ethic of individualism ④ underline{held} to characterize liberal societies. The transmission of ideas from Kant to Hegel to Marx is so dramatic as ⑤ underline{to rival} the initial flow of thought from Plato to Aristotle to Augustine.

[3점]

다음 글의 밑줄 친 부분 중, 어법상 틀린 것을 고르시오.

| 경찰대학 2016학년도 6번 |

I once lived in a coastal village of Papua New Guinea. Children there did not live with their own parents but moved from house to house ① underline{as} they wished. Ten-year-olds could ② underline{be seen} carrying babies or tending cooking fires. By fourteen they were doing adult work with confidence and pride. As the newest and most interesting thing in the village, I had a dozen or so kids ③ underline{sleeping} on my veranda. When tropical diarrhea struck in the small hours of the night, I had to pick my way out through a carpet of small brown bodies. It occurred to me ④ underline{what} this would be an easy place to be a parent, since the work and pleasure of parenting was shared by the whole village. In fact, any adult ⑤ underline{who} was present *was* a parent.

다음 글의 밑줄 친 부분 중, 어법상 틀린 것을 고르시오. | 경찰대학 2016학년도 7번 |

Born into great wealth but plunged into poverty as a teen, I grew up knowing more about the perils of losing success than the secrets of ① <u>attaining</u> it. Although my parents recovered after ② <u>being stripped</u> of everything in midlife, they never regained a prosperous mind-set. And I absorbed their fears ③ <u>more fully</u> than their successes. Those fears fueled my desire to be financially successful and ④ <u>was</u>, in part, what drove me to make a living out of teaching people how to achieve. I grew up to be a motivational speaker who inspired thousands of business executives and professional athletes ⑤ <u>to achieve</u> their goals using valuable principles of success.

다음 글의 밑줄 친 부분 중, 어법상 틀린 것을 고르시오. | 경찰대학 2016학년도 8번 |

There are numerous myths and legends associated with gems. Some tell of cursed stones; ① <u>others of</u> stones with special powers of healing, or that protect or give good luck to the wearer. Some of ② <u>the largest known</u> diamonds have legends associated with them that have been told and retold over centuries, and ③ <u>many now lost</u> are surrounded by tales of intrigue and murder. Some mines ④ <u>are thought to be cursed</u> — probably rumors spread by the mine owners to keep unwanted prospectors away. In Myanmar, for instance, where all gemstones belonged to the monarch, the belief that anyone who took a stone from a mine would be cursed ⑤ <u>may have deliberately cultivated</u> to curb losses of a valuable national asset.

[3점]

다음 글의 밑줄 친 부분 중, 어법상 틀린 것을 고르시오. | 경찰대학 2015학년도 6번 |

Bowling was very popular in the colonies. At first it was called ninepins. Ninepins was ① actually one of several bowling games played by the colonists. Another kind of bowling involved players rolling a larger ball and ② attempted to stop it as close as possible to a smaller ball resting on the green. The player ③ closest to the target ball was declared the winner. This type of bowling was similar to the modern game of pitching pennies at a line ④ drawn in the dirt. In pitching pennies, the player ⑤ whose penny is nearest the line wins the game.

10

다음 글의 밑줄 친 부분 중, 어법상 틀린 것을 고르시오. | 경찰대학 2015학년도 7번 |

The next time you step into a retail store — ① whether it sells consumer electronics, hardware or high fashion — stop and carefully consider your surroundings. Think about the store's layout and displays. Listen to the background sounds. Smell the smells. Chances are everything in the store from the layout and lighting to the music and even the smells ② has orchestrated to help shape your shopping experience — and to open your wallet. In most cases, you're probably being affected in ways so subtle that you don't even realize ③ what is happening to you. Thus, once inside a store, ④ how you as a shopper move in and around the store is not, really, up to you. The next time you visit a store, see if you can spot the subtle things ⑤ that retailers do to affect your shopping behavior. [3점]

다음 글의 밑줄 친 부분 중, 어법상 틀린 것을 고르시오. | 경찰대학 2015학년도 8번 |

The No. 1 recommendation for great pots is: Think big! Small containers hold too little soil for good root growth and are too much work ① to keep watered. So the larger the container, ② the better. Glazed, fiberglass, and molded-plastic containers hold moisture better than unglazed terra-cotta. Regardless of the type, ③ be sure pots to have drainage holes, and use pot feet or shims to raise them about a half-inch off the ground to allow water to drain away. Fiberglass and plastic pots are less likely to degrade ④ in weather extremes and are easier to move. But heavy containers can give tall plants the foundation needed to prevent toppling in the wind. Lighter pots should ⑤ be secured to prevent tipping. [3점]

12

다음 글의 밑줄 친 부분 중, 어법상 틀린 것을 고르시오. | 경찰대학 2014학년도 10번 |

Insensitivity to pain is dangerous. People with a gene that ① inactivates pain axons suffer repeated injuries and generally fail to learn ② to avoid dangers. One boy with this condition performed street theaterin Pakistan by thrusting a knife through his arm or ③ walking on burning coals. He ④ has died at age 14 by falling off a roof. Nevertheless, although we wouldn't want to eliminate pain, it ⑤ would be good to hold it under control.

13

다음 글의 밑줄 친 부분 중, 어법상 틀린 것을 고르시오.

| 경찰대학 2014학년도 11번 |

Menno Aden is fascinated by the influence of architecture and design on spaces and the people who inhabit ① them. The 41-year-old artist has ② explored both the exteriors of residential developments and interiors of corporate buildings in his home city of Berlin, rearranging images of each into grids and panel mosaics, ③ occasionally transposing them into video works. But the inspiration for his recent project came from a photographic food diary, ④ which he shot his meals by standing on a chair and aiming his camera downward. This view put more emphasis on the space than the food, and he wondered ⑤ if he could capture an overhead view of an entire room. [3점]

14

다음 글의 밑줄 친 부분 중, 어법상 틀린 것을 고르시오.

| 경찰대학 2014학년도 12번 |

One of the ① most contesting issues in using local land-use controls for environmental protection purposes is the "takings" problem. The Fifth Amendment to the U.S. Constitution contains the following language: "No person shall ② be deprived of life, liberty, or property, without due process of law; ③ nor shall private property be taken for a public use, without just compensation." This authorizes the government ④ to "take" private property, but only if it is for a public purpose and only if the owners receive just compensation. Land may be taken physically (e.g., for a public park or highway), and the main question will revolve around ⑤ how much the compensation should be. [3점]

15

다음 글의 밑줄 친 부분 중, 어법상 틀린 것을 고르시오.　　| 경찰대학 2013학년도 11번 |

Julie's main goals for freshmen year were to do well academically and to figure out ① <u>about what</u> kind of engineering she'd major in. But she knew that engineering was tough and that to do well, she'd have to shorten the long list of extracurricular activities she'd participated in for the past ② <u>few years</u>. She'd been a cheerleader and a member of the student government through high school. She'd taken piano lessons and she'd spent the past year as Elkhart's Junior Miss, ③ <u>which</u> had earned her a college scholarship. That's not to say Julie wanted to bury her face in her books for the next four years. She did want to make time ④ <u>to swim</u> and do aerobics for exercise. She knew she'd check out the Purdue social scene, especially weekend fraternity parties. And then there was her boyfriend. "I know I'll go out ⑤ <u>whenever</u> I feel like it," she said. "But homework will be my priority."

16

다음 글의 밑줄 친 부분 중, 어법상 틀린 것을 고르시오.　　| 경찰대학 2013학년도 12번 |

The chickens that saved Western civilization were discovered, according to legend, by the side of a road in Greece in the first decade of the fifth century B.C. The Athenian general Themistocles, on his way to confront the invading Persian forces, stopped ① <u>to watch</u> two cocks fighting. He summoned his troops, saying: "Behold, these do not fight for their household gods, for the monuments of their ancestors, for glory, for liberty or the safety of their children, but only because one will not give way to ② <u>another</u>." The tale does not describe what happened to the loser, nor ③ <u>does it explain</u> why the soldiers found this display of instinctive aggression inspirational rather than pointless and depressing. But history records that the Greeks, thus heartened, went on to repel the invaders, ④ <u>preserving</u> the civilization that today honors those same creatures by breading, frying, and dipping them into one's choice of sauce. The descendants of those roosters might well think — if they ⑤ <u>were</u> capable of such profound thought — that their ancient forebears have a lot to answer for.

다음 글의 밑줄 친 부분 중, 어법상 틀린 것을 고르시오. | 경찰대학 2013학년도 13번 |

Some people today think of work ① <u>as</u> a four-letter word. But when I was an undergraduate during the Depression, work was a very popular word. Those who had it gloried in it, and those who did not ② <u>speak of</u> it with longing. After I completed my university years in Canada I went to Oxford, and there I found a different state of affairs. Work was not mentioned. Sometimes students would leave a party ③ <u>saying</u>, "Well, I have to be getting along now." Everybody knew they were sneaking away to work, but we were all too polite to mention it. Professors were never seen ④ <u>to work</u>. Part of the charm of Oxford was that nobody seemed to work at all. There was an Oxford secret, however, which I soon uncovered: everybody worked like hell, but they thought it bad form ⑤ <u>to admit</u> any such thing. One was supposed to take in one's learning from the air.

18

다음 글의 밑줄 친 부분 중, 어법상 틀린 것을 고르시오. | 경찰대학 2013학년도 14번 |

At least 20 million people have worked in a McDonald's since Ray Kroc opened his first McDonald's hamburger stand 40 years ago. Behind that number ① <u>is</u> several corporate strategies including using armies of part-time workers. In addition, ② <u>hourly pay</u> for McDonald's crew members is typically only a bit higher than the $5.25 minimum wage, and fringe benefits are meager. Employees leave ③ <u>so frequently</u> that this year McDonald's and its franchisees, which employ more than 500,000 workers in the United States and Canada, will have to hire well over that number of new employees to ④ <u>stay fully staffed</u>. But there is an upside to this upheaval. The fast-food chains have been forced to concentrate more than other businesses on training programs with an eye toward ⑤ <u>adapting</u> large numbers of raw recruits.

19

다음 글의 밑줄 친 부분 중, 어법상 **틀린** 것을 고르시오.

One of the most peculiar public health hazards — epidemic fainting at pop-music concerts — is a phenomenon familiar to ① legions of adolescents. Their parents may ② be less aware of the threat, which has barely engaged the attention of modern science despite decades of documentation that many a fan ③ are prone to unconsciousness. ④ Concerned that the mechanism of mass fainting had been neglected in the medical literature, two German physicians recently braved a concert by New Kids on the Block and worked with first-aid staff at a Red Cross infirmary where ⑤ the stricken were treated. According to the doctors' report in the Thursday issue of *The New England Journal of Medicine*, some 400 concertgoers fainted, all of them girls aged 11 to 17.

20

다음 글의 밑줄 친 부분 중, 어법상 **틀린** 것을 고르시오.

Families are the people ① whom it matters if you have a cold, are feuding with your mate or training a new puppy. Family members use magnets ② to fasten the newspaper clipping about your bowling team on the refrigerator door. They save your drawings and homemade pottery. They like to hear stories ③ about when you were young. They'll help you can tomatoes or change the oil in your car. They're the people who will come and visit you in the hospital, will talk to you when you call with a "dark night of the soul" and will ④ loan you money to pay the rent if you lose your job. ⑤ Whether or not they are biologically related to each other, the people who do these things are family.

다음 글의 밑줄 친 부분 중, 어법상 틀린 것을 고르시오.　　| 경찰대학 2012학년도 9번 |

When the mammals ① underline{evolved out of} the reptiles, their brains began to change. First, they developed a new package of instincts, related to the reptilian instincts for sex and procreation, but ② <u>modifying for</u> the special needs of a mammalian lifestyle. Chief among these was the instinct for parental care of the young. Here was ③ <u>a revolutionary advance</u> over the behavior of reptile parents, for whom ④ <u>the newly hatched young</u> provided a tasty snack if they could catch them. But the reptile young were prepared to fight for their lives; they came into the world with all the needed programs of action ⑤ <u>wired into</u> their brain. These hatchlings were miniature adults from the moment of birth. On the other hand, the young mammals arrived in a helpless and vulnerable state, and parental affection was essential for their survival. That is why mammals developed the new instincts for parental care.

22

다음 글의 밑줄 친 부분 중, 어법상 틀린 것을 고르시오.　　| 경찰대학 2012학년도 10번 |

Still no one knows who he was. But scientists are now certain of one thing about the naturally mummified Alpine Iceman, ① <u>whom</u> hikers discovered in September 1991 in the melting ice on the Austrian-Italian border at an elevation of 10,530 feet. In the first genetic analysis of the body, they determined that he was European born and bred, closely ② <u>related to</u> modern northern and alpine Europeans. Scientists said this finding should lay to rest lingering suspicions of a hoax. An international research team, writing in the journal *Science*, said the genetic findings made the possibility of fraud ③ <u>highly unlikely</u>. Among the most recent results of their research ④ <u>is</u> a descriptive inventory of alpine fashions in those remote times. Scientists may not be able to account for the man's presence on the mountain crest, but they know ⑤ <u>that</u> he was wearing, down to his underwear.

23

다음 글의 밑줄 친 부분 중, 어법상 틀린 것을 고르시오.

Grandmother and I lived beside the plaza in a one-room house. It was composed of a traditional fireplace, a makeshift cabinet, and a wooden crate that held our two buckets of all-purpose water. At the far end of the room ① <u>were</u> two rolls of bedding we used as comfortable sitting "couches." ② <u>Consisted</u> of thick quilts, sheepskin, and assorted blankets, these bed rolls were undone each night. A wooden pole, the length of one side of the room, ③ <u>was suspended</u> about 10 inches from the ceiling beams. A dresser, which was traded for some of grandmother's pottery, held the few articles of clothing we owned. Grandmother always had a flour sack filled with candy and store-bought cookies. ④ <u>Tucked securely</u> in my blankets, I listened to one of her stories or accounts of how it was when she was a little girl. These accounts ⑤ <u>seemed so old-fashioned</u> compared to the way we lived.

24

다음 글의 밑줄 친 부분 중, 어법상 틀린 것을 고르시오.

With most men the knowledge that they must ultimately die ① <u>does not weaken</u> the pleasure in being at present alive. To the poet the world ② <u>is appeared</u> still more beautiful as he gazes at flowers that ③ <u>are doomed to</u> wither. The loveliness of May moves him ④ <u>the more deeply</u> because he knows that it is fading even as he looks at it. It is not that the thought of universal mortality gives him pleasure, but that he cherishes the pleasure all the more dearly because he knows it cannot be ⑤ <u>his</u> for long.

25

다음 글의 밑줄 친 부분 중, 어법상 틀린 것을 고르시오. | 경찰대학 2011학년도 7번 |

No matter what road is chosen the travelers who started from different valleys will all meet on the top of the mountain, ① <u>provided</u> they keep on ascending. No one must pride himself on having chosen the best route nor force his neighbor ② <u>to follow</u> him. Everyone takes the path which suits him best, ③ <u>imposed</u> by the structure of the brain, by heredity, by traditions. One can offer support, enlightenment, help. But ④ <u>what succeeds</u> with one may fail with others. Every man must wage his own fight ⑤ <u>without that</u> he cannot progress. There is no short cut to truth.

26

다음 글의 밑줄 친 부분 중, 어법상 틀린 것을 고르시오. | 경찰대학 2011학년도 8번 |

Of course people ① <u>hunger</u> for the strange and wonderful. And they can find it. We can sense what people thousands of miles away ② <u>are</u> thinking by calling them on the phone. And psychic healers ③ <u>relieve people of</u> despair by offering them the false hope of a better life. Authors of innumerable occult books make fortunes by peddling nonsense to ④ <u>the gullible</u>. Even clever people ⑤ <u>are taking in</u> if the rational, practical alternatives are not presented.

27

다음 글의 밑줄 친 부분 중, 어법상 틀린 것을 고르시오.

| 경찰대학 2011학년도 9번 |

Another barrier to peasant migrants to Beijing in China is city workers ① <u>standing at the gate</u>. Although most urban residents now enjoy services provided by migrants, urbanites ② <u>could soon feel</u> the cut of their competitive edge. In tough times city workers would want to reclaim ③ <u>as their own</u> the dirty jobs that urban administrators turn over to newcomers — road pavement, ditch digging, etc. Urban unemployment, grossly under-calculated by the government at just 2.9 percent, could soar once huge ④ <u>state-run enterprises</u> are privatized. Peasants will be their natural competition, and the coming conflict ⑤ <u>hasn't been addressing</u>.

28

다음 글의 밑줄 친 부분 중, 어법상 틀린 것을 고르시오.

| 경찰대학 2011학년도 10번 |

In response to the wave of mergers and the ① <u>growing</u> concentration of industry in the late nineteenth century, Congress passed a bill ② <u>commonly knowing</u> as the Sherman Act. "Every contract, combination in the form of a trust or otherwise, or conspiracy in restraint of trade" ③ <u>was</u> declared illegal. It was likewise illegal to monopolize or ④ <u>attempt to monopolize trade</u>. The surge of legal activity initiated during the presidency of Teddy Roosevelt ⑤ <u>led to</u> the breakup of Standard Oil and America Tobacco Company in 1911.

29

다음 글의 밑줄 친 부분 중, 어법상 <u>틀린</u> 것을 고르시오.

| 경찰대학 2011학년도 11번 |

Trevor and Patricia Janz were walking through a light snowfall in Waterton Lakes Park, Canada, when they experienced a hiker's worst nightmare — a grizzly bear mother with cubs, ① <u>feeding on</u> an animal's body. What happens next ② <u>is captured</u> in the TV program, "Deadly Encounters." The segment shows how humans can protect ③ <u>themselves</u> in the domain of the grizzly. ④ <u>Says</u> Stephen Herrero, a bear behavior expert: "If you surprise a grizzly bear and contact seems inevitable, you've got to protect your face and neck. Lie face down, put your hands behind your neck, and pretend ⑤ <u>being dead</u>."

30

다음 글의 밑줄 친 부분 중, 어법상 <u>틀린</u> 것을 고르시오.

| 경찰대학 2010학년도 7번 |

Although the origins of dances like the waltz and polka in Austrian and Czech folk music ① <u>are</u> clear, it is less easy to see ② <u>that</u> elements the Strausses added — apart, of course, from their genius. The music of Johann I may now seem to us less inspired ③ <u>than</u> that of Johann II or Josef, but it still shows all the distinguishing marks of the later style. Although the only piece of his ④ <u>which</u> is now a household word is the famous *Radetsky March*, his waltzes and gallops and polkas are still enjoyable listening, and it is very hard to discern any influence from contemporary composers such ⑤ <u>as</u> Beethoven or even Schubert.

다음 글의 밑줄 친 부분 중, 어법상 틀린 것을 고르시오.　| 경찰대학 2010학년도 8번 |

The headline is a unique type of text. It has a range of functions that ① <u>specifically</u> dictate its shape, content and structure, and it operates within a range of ② <u>restrictions</u> that limit the freedom of the writer. For example, the space that the headline will occupy is ③ <u>almost always</u> dictated by the layout of the page, and the size of the typeface will similarly be restricted. The headline will rarely, if ever, be written by the reporter who ④ <u>wrote</u> the news story. It should, in theory, encapsulate the story in a minimum number of words, attract the reader to the story and, if it appears on the front page, ⑤ <u>attracting</u> the reader to the paper.

다음 글의 밑줄 친 부분 중, 어법상 틀린 것을 고르시오.　| 경찰대학 2010학년도 9번 |

American shoppers ① <u>have never been</u> so fickle. What are stores, including the new flagship designer boutiques, doing about it? Applying science. Human beings walk the way they drive, ② <u>which is to say</u> that Americans tend to keep to the right when they stroll down shopping mall concourses or city sidewalks. This is why in a well-designed airport travellers ③ <u>drift toward their gate</u> will always find the fast-food restaurants on their left and the gift shops on their right: people will ④ <u>readily cross a lane</u> of pedestrian traffic to satisfy their hunger but ⑤ <u>rarely to make an impulse buy</u> of a T-shirt or a magazine.

다음 글의 밑줄 친 부분 중, 어법상 틀린 것을 고르시오.　　｜경찰대학 2010학년도 10번｜

High blood pressure and high cholesterol ① are more than just numbers. They are risk factors ② that should not be ignored. If your doctor said you have high blood pressure and high cholesterol, you may be at an increased risk for heart attack or stroke. But the good news is, you can take steps to lower your blood pressure and cholesterol. ③ With the help of your doctor and a medicine, along with diet and exercise, you could be on your way ④ to lower your blood pressure and cholesterol. Ready to ⑤ start eating right and exercising more?

34

다음 글의 밑줄 친 부분 중, 어법상 틀린 것을 고르시오.　　｜경찰대학 2010학년도 11번｜

Music has become quite different since Beethoven. While the works of the earlier period contain a certain surprising innovation, there is a predictable element fixed by tradition — an inevitable element ① dictated by formal conventions rather than by lack of originality. However, what Beethoven wanted to express could no longer ② be contained within these conventions. He became the first of music's revolutionaries in ③ what became an age of revolution. Through music, Beethoven sought to illuminate the essence of the human spirit, in a way that ④ had not been attempted before. He soon found the prevailing musical idioms ⑤ inadequately and began to explore new and radical forms of expression.

다음 글의 밑줄 친 부분 중, 어법상 틀린 것을 고르시오.

| 경찰대학 2010학년도 12번 |

Lakes are extremely ① varied and a long list of factors dictates their plants and animals. Among the most ② important is their size. Some lakes are extremely large water bodies ③ approaching the size of smaller seas; at the other extreme are water bodies which we would commonly call small ponds ④ where may be no larger than a few meters in diameter. Another important variable, as with rivers, ⑤ is nutrient status: nutrient-poor lakes contain communities very different from nutrient-rich ones.

01 다음 글의 밑줄 친 부분 중, 어법상 틀린 것을 고르시오.

| 사관학교 2017학년도 12번 |

New experiences trigger change only if they cause us ① to question our beliefs. Remember, whenever we believe something, we no longer question it in any way. The moment we begin to honestly question our beliefs, we no longer feel absolutely certain about ② them. We are beginning to shake the reference legs of our cognitive tables, and as a result start to lose our feeling of absolute certainty. Have you ever doubted your ability to do something? How did you do it? You probably asked ③ yourself some poor questions like "What if it doesn't work out?" But questions can obviously be tremendously empowering if we use them to examine the validity of beliefs we may have just blindly accepted. In fact, many of our beliefs ④ supported by information we've received from others that we failed to question at the time. If we scrutinize them, we may find that ⑤ what we've unconsciously believed for years may be based on a false set of presuppositions.

[3점]

02 다음 글의 밑줄 친 부분 중, 어법상 틀린 것을 고르시오.

| 사관학교 2016학년도 12번 |

In a survey, when the response options are presented visually, it seems reasonable to assume that respondents typically start at the top of the list and ① work their way through the remaining options in order. Primacy effects would, therefore, seem to be the rule: Respondents will tend to prefer options at the beginning of the list over ② those at the end. However, the picture becomes somewhat murkier when the interviewer reads the response options to the respondent. Survey interviewers tend to read questions ③ quickly so that respondents will not generally have time to evaluate the first option before they must turn to the next. It is quite likely that respondents will begin by considering the final option, since that option is the one that will remain in working memory when the interviewer stops ④ to read. Consequently, we should expect recency effects — the tendency to choose options at the end of the list — when the question ⑤ is presented aloud to the respondent.

[3점]

03

다음 글의 밑줄 친 부분 중, 어법상 틀린 것은?

| 수능 2017학년도 홀수형 28번 |

When people face real adversity — disease, unemployment, or the disabilities of age — affection from a pet takes on new meaning. A pet's continuing affection becomes crucially important for ① those enduring hardship because it reassures them that their core essence has not been damaged. Thus pets are important in the treatment of ② depressed or chronically ill patients. In addition, pets are ③ used to great advantage with the institutionalized aged. In such institutions it is difficult for the staff to retain optimism when all the patients are declining in health. Children who visit cannot help but remember ④ what their parents or grandparents once were and be depressed by their incapacities. Animals, however, have no expectations about mental capacity. They do not worship youth. They have no memories about what the aged once ⑤ was and greet them as if they were children. An old man holding a puppy can relive a childhood moment with complete accuracy. His joy and the animal's response are the same. [3점]

04

다음 글의 밑줄 친 부분 중, 어법상 틀린 것은?

| 수능 2016학년도 홀수형 28번 |

The Greeks' focus on the salient object and its attributes led to ① their failure to understand the fundamental nature of causality. Aristotle explained that a stone falling through the air is due to the stone having the property of "gravity." But of course a piece of wood ② tossed into water floats instead of sinking. This phenomenon Aristotle explained as being due to the wood having the property of "levity"! In both cases the focus is ③ exclusively on the object, with no attention paid to the possibility that some force outside the object might be relevant. But the Chinese saw the world as consisting of continuously interacting substances, so their attempts to understand it ④ causing them to be oriented toward the complexities of the entire "field," that is, the context or environment as a whole. The notion ⑤ that events always occur in a field of forces would have been completely intuitive to the Chinese.

*salient: 현저한, 두드러진 **levity: 가벼움 [3점]

Problem Solving Skills

특정 단어가 갖는 어휘상, 문맥상 의미를 파악하는 유형이다. 풍부한 어휘력이 요구되며, 문장에서 주어진 단어가 갖는 의미와 가장 가까운 뜻의 단어를 찾는다.

- 주어진 단어의 뜻을 파악한다.
- 주어진 문장을 정확히 해석한다.
- 선택지 단어의 뜻과 비교하여 정답을 고른다.

Example

밑줄 친 단어의 뜻으로 가장 적절한 것을 고르시오. | 경찰대학 2018학년도 1번 |

2 The students in the movement were deceived into thinking they were in the
1 vanguard of a revolution.

3
① turmoil
② forefront
③ protection
④ opposition
⑤ preparation

Vocabulary

deceive 속이다 vanguard 선봉 turmoil 혼란 forefront 선두

Let's Solve

Point 1 주어진 단어가 가지고 있는 뜻 파악하기

• vanguard
  → the leading position at the front of an army or group of ships moving into battle, or the soldiers who are in this position
  → 사회적인 운동의 선봉, 선두

Point 2 주어진 문장을 정확히 해석하기

• The students in the movement were deceived into thinking they were in the vanguard of a revolution.
  → 그 운동에 참여한 학생들은 그들이 혁명의 선봉에 있다고 생각하도록 기만당했다.

Point 3 선택지 단어의 뜻과 비교하기

① turmoil: a state of confusion, excitement, or anxiety
  → 혼란, 소란
② forefront: a leading position in an important activity that is trying to achieve something or develop new ideas
  → 중심, 가장 중요한 위치, 선두
  → 주어진 문장에서 vanguard는 '선봉'의 의미로 쓰였기 때문에 의미가 가장 비슷하다.
③ protection: an act of keeping someone or something safe from harm, damage, or illness
  → 보호, 보호물
④ opposition: strong disagreement with, or protest against, something such as a plan, law, or system
  → 반대, 항의, 반대 측
⑤ preparation: an act of making plans or arrangements for something that will happen in the future
  → 준비, 대비

01 밑줄 친 단어의 뜻으로 가장 적절한 것을 고르시오. | 경찰대학 2018학년도 2번 |

The government concluded that the manufacturers <u>colluded</u> to sell their products to minors.

① collaborated   ② proposed   ③ pretended
④ intended   ⑤ intervened

02 밑줄 친 단어의 뜻으로 가장 적절한 것을 고르시오. | 경찰대학 2018학년도 3번 |

His <u>penchant</u> for the finer things in life led to the demise of his family fortune.

① obsession   ② aptitude   ③ reproach
④ inclination   ⑤ extravagance

03 밑줄 친 단어의 뜻으로 가장 적절한 것을 고르시오. | 경찰대학 2018학년도 4번 |

Rawls's sternest critics often tried to <u>cabin</u> him as "relevant only for American or at most Anglo-American audiences."

① confine   ② rebuke   ③ introduce
④ safeguard   ⑤ exemplify

04

밑줄 친 단어의 뜻으로 가장 적절한 것을 고르시오. | 경찰대학 2018학년도 5번 |

Questions about the pending lawsuit were met with circumlocutory replies by the pharmaceutical company representative.

① unequivocal   ② succinct   ③ unfounded

④ roundabout   ⑤ conciliatory

05

밑줄 친 단어의 뜻으로 가장 적절한 것을 고르시오. | 경찰대학 2017학년도 1번 |

It was time to devise a new plan of action as the attorneys categorically rejected our offer.

① unequivocally   ② typically   ③ impolitely

④ reluctantly   ⑤ maliciously

06

밑줄 친 단어의 뜻으로 가장 적절한 것을 고르시오. | 경찰대학 2017학년도 2번 |

After emerging victorious in his long-fought bout against cancer, the media tycoon tried to turn over a new leaf by denouncing his opulent way of life.

① immoral   ② proud   ③ luxurious

④ unhealthy   ⑤ incompetent

07

밑줄 친 단어의 뜻으로 가장 적절한 것을 고르시오.

| 경찰대학 2017학년도 3번 |

Sanctions against the country are expected to be among the most <u>contentious</u> issues.

① controversial   ② complex   ③ elusive
④ secretive   ⑤ fruitless

08

밑줄 친 단어의 뜻으로 가장 적절한 것을 고르시오.

| 경찰대학 2017학년도 4번 |

That the days of capitalism were <u>numbered</u>, and that the capitalist era must now give way to socialism: these were assumptions widely held by intellectuals on both sides of the Atlantic.

① limited   ② prolonged   ③ preserved
④ accelerated   ⑤ overlapped

09

밑줄 친 단어의 뜻으로 가장 적절한 것을 고르시오.

| 경찰대학 2017학년도 5번 |

Many politicians viewed that nation's economic hegemony as <u>presumptuous</u>.

① attentive and alert   ② accurate and precise
③ assiduous and diligent   ④ achievable and pragmatic
⑤ arrogant and disrespectful

10

밑줄 친 단어의 뜻으로 가장 적절한 것을 고르시오. | 경찰대학 2016학년도 1번 |

Who would have guessed that the movie star's fame would be ephemeral?

① fleeting   ② residual   ③ perpetual
④ legendary   ⑤ credulous

11

밑줄 친 단어의 뜻으로 가장 적절한 것을 고르시오. | 경찰대학 2016학년도 2번 |

Karen tried to cajole his friend into driving her to the mall, but to no avail.

① coax   ② bully   ③ slander
④ provoke   ⑤ hypnotize

12

밑줄 친 단어의 뜻으로 가장 적절한 것을 고르시오. | 경찰대학 2016학년도 3번 |

She is extremely fastidious about keeping the premises spotless, almost to a fault.

① perilous   ② insidious   ③ insolvent
④ vindictive   ⑤ meticulous

13

밑줄 친 단어의 뜻으로 가장 적절한 것을 고르시오.

| 경찰대학 2016학년도 4번 |

Dreams help people work through the day's emotional <u>quandaries</u>. It is like having a built-in therapist.

① bonds   ② dilemmas   ③ failures

④ ecstasies   ⑤ irritations

14

밑줄 친 단어의 뜻으로 가장 적절한 것을 고르시오.

| 경찰대학 2016학년도 5번 |

He's going to promote me to Clare's level, and he's telling me <u>discreetly</u> so she won't get jealous.

① rashly   ② mildly   ③ enviously

④ cautiously   ⑤ impartially

15

밑줄 친 단어의 뜻으로 가장 적절한 것을 고르시오.

| 경찰대학 2015학년도 1번 |

Silver dollars <u>doled out</u> by my grandfather were kept by my parents, who did not trust us with them.

① distributed   ② incurred   ③ invested

④ withdrawn   ⑤ deposited

16

밑줄 친 단어의 뜻으로 가장 적절한 것을 고르시오.

| 경찰대학 2015학년도 2번 |

Magazine titles play a large part in shaping the reader's expectations. They are always written in large letters <u>conjuring up</u> particular associations in the reader's mind.

① customizing   ② invoking   ③ traversing
④ stripping   ⑤ circumventing

17

밑줄 친 단어의 뜻으로 가장 적절한 것을 고르시오.

| 경찰대학 2015학년도 3번 |

Though the twentieth century saw horrific genocides inspired by Nazi pseudoscience about genetics and race, it also saw horrific genocides inspired by Marxist pseudoscience about the <u>malleability</u> of human nature.   [3점]

① duality   ② fallibility   ③ obscurity
④ plasticity   ⑤ viciousness

18

밑줄 친 단어의 뜻으로 가장 적절한 것을 고르시오.

| 경찰대학 2015학년도 4번 |

The oligarchical power of the aristocracy was <u>coveted</u> by the other class of Roman citizens, the plebeians, who included farmers, laborers, and tradesmen.

① deprived   ② strengthened   ③ granted
④ criticized   ⑤ envied

밑줄 친 단어의 뜻으로 가장 적절한 것을 고르시오. | 경찰대학 2015학년도 5번 |

"Will you take my little brother to New York?" Having lived as a foreigner for a decade, I was accustomed to <u>non sequitur</u> conversations, but that opener left me speechless.

① personal   ② frank   ③ elongated
④ irrelevant   ⑤ practical

20

밑줄 친 단어의 뜻으로 가장 적절한 것을 고르시오. | 경찰대학 2014학년도 1번 |

An experimental method that would be <u>deemed</u> inappropriate for one kind of research may be the method of choice for another kind of research.

① proven   ② coined   ③ considered
④ classified   ⑤ pronounced

21

밑줄 친 단어의 뜻으로 가장 적절한 것을 고르시오. | 경찰대학 2014학년도 2번 |

The World Heritage site has been threatened by the country's civil war. Experts are <u>wielding</u> satellite technology to monitor and protect endangered museums, monuments and other places of historical importance.

① legalizing   ② employing   ③ developing
④ avoiding   ⑤ clarifying

22

밑줄 친 단어의 뜻으로 가장 적절한 것을 고르시오. | 경찰대학 2014학년도 3번 |

Unable to cope with the fact that he was diagnosed with colon cancer, Michael suspected his doctor of being a <u>quack</u> and decided to seek out a second opinion.

① clown　　　　　② demagogue　　　　　③ professional
④ charlatan　　　　⑤ benefactor

23

밑줄 친 단어의 뜻으로 가장 적절한 것을 고르시오. | 경찰대학 2014학년도 4번 |

Aristotle does not <u>hector</u> students with some piety against the desire for material goods. To him, concern for money is a good thing, and one of the good things is that people with money can exercise generosity.

① associate　　　　② incite　　　　　③ criticize
④ appease　　　　　⑤ address

24

밑줄 친 단어의 뜻으로 가장 적절한 것을 고르시오. | 경찰대학 2014학년도 5번 |

The boxing commentator remarked of the heavyweight champion, "His left hook is a real <u>sockdolager</u>. It would take a tank to withstand such impact."

① decisive blow　　　② powerful defense　　　③ sneaky attack
④ elusive punch　　　⑤ fragile delivery

25

밑줄 친 단어의 뜻으로 가장 적절한 것을 고르시오. | 경찰대학 2013학년도 1번 |

Wagner's *The Ring of the Nibelungs* is distinctive in that it is almost entirely operatic; also unusual is the fact that the libretti for his operas were written by the composer himself — a task normally <u>reserved</u> for a poet or literary notable.

① retained　　　② booked　　　③ modified

④ substituted　　⑤ suspended

26

밑줄 친 단어의 뜻으로 가장 적절한 것을 고르시오. | 경찰대학 2013학년도 2번 |

The original garbage crisis occurred when people first settled down to farm and could no longer leave their campsites after their garbage grew too deep. Since then, every society has had problems with discards that are usually <u>odoriferous</u>.

① harmful　　　② futile　　　③ biodegradable

④ invaluable　　⑤ stinky

27

밑줄 친 단어의 뜻으로 가장 적절한 것을 고르시오. | 경찰대학 2013학년도 3번 |

Michael was a very capable salesman. He could sell a refrigerator to an Eskimo. However, Michael's <u>belligerent</u> attitude during team projects had his boss at his wits' end.

① hostile　　　② arrogant　　　③ apathetic

④ gregarious　　⑤ unscrupulous

28

밑줄 친 단어의 뜻으로 가장 적절한 것을 고르시오.

| 경찰대학 2013학년도 4번 |

The prime minister wants to strengthen the <u>rickety</u> alliance with the United States and stress economic growth over redistribution.

① social   ② dominant   ③ clandestine
④ sturdy   ⑤ precarious

29

밑줄 친 단어의 뜻으로 가장 적절한 것을 고르시오.

| 경찰대학 2013학년도 5번 |

The modern version of Shakespeare's "Romeo and Juliet" was met with mixed reviews. One <u>sardonic</u> review of the play called it a "true masterpiece for the uneducated sophist."

① fallible   ② cynical   ③ obsequious
④ charismatic   ⑤ overindulgent

30

밑줄 친 단어의 뜻으로 가장 적절한 것을 고르시오.

| 경찰대학 2013학년도 6번 |

One of your main competitors offers you a <u>lucrative</u> position, more than commensurate with your present duties and at almost double the salary.

① leisurely   ② propitious   ③ charitable
④ classy   ⑤ well-paying

31

밑줄 친 단어의 뜻으로 가장 적절한 것을 고르시오. | 경찰대학 2012학년도 1번 |

For years, concerns about the health effects of cellphones have been largely dismissed because the radio frequency waves emitted from the devices are believed to be <u>benign</u>. Cellphones emit non-ionizing radiation, waves of energy that are too weak to break chemical bonds or to set off the DNA damage known to cause cancers.

① harmless　　　　② vibrating　　　　③ potent
④ transmitting　　　⑤ cancerous

32

밑줄 친 단어의 뜻으로 가장 적절한 것을 고르시오. | 경찰대학 2012학년도 2번 |

The Gods had condemned Sisyphus to ceaselessly rolling a rock to the top of a mountain, whence the stone would fall back of its own weight. They had thought with some reason that there is no more dreadful punishment than <u>futile</u> and hopeless labor.

① repetitive　　　　② fruitless　　　　③ detestable
④ toilsome　　　　⑤ disciplinary

33

밑줄 친 단어의 뜻으로 가장 적절한 것을 고르시오. | 경찰대학 2012학년도 3번 |

Artists past and present understand that manual facility is <u>inextricably</u> bound to observational prowess, and vice versa. In fact, many believe that what the hand cannot draw, the eye cannot see.

① unduly　　　　　② inescapably　　　③ undeservedly
④ incompetently　　⑤ incomprehensively

34

밑줄 친 단어의 뜻으로 가장 적절한 것을 고르시오. | 경찰대학 2012학년도 4번 |

The government is working on a plan for a limited form of <u>mandatory</u> identification. Under a law being prepared, identification would have to be carried in certain situations, such as when applying for a job.

① portable   ② impeccable   ③ makeshift
④ simplified   ⑤ obligatory

35

밑줄 친 단어의 뜻으로 가장 적절한 것을 고르시오. | 경찰대학 2012학년도 5번 |

There are no potholes in the streets of Tucson, Arizona, just "pavement deficiencies." There are no more poor people, just "<u>fiscal</u> underachievers." There was no robbery of an automatic teller machine, just an "unauthorized withdrawal." And the doublespeak goes on. Doublespeak is language that makes the negative appear positive, the unpleasant appear attractive or at least tolerable.

① financial   ② actual   ③ academic
④ physical   ⑤ modest

36

밑줄 친 단어의 뜻으로 가장 적절한 것을 고르시오. | 경찰대학 2012학년도 6번 |

Smells can lift our spirits, calm us, and maybe even help us lose weight. Some odors can <u>repulse</u> us, too, and for good reason: They can tell us that gas is leaking, the milk is sour or the meat is spoiled.

① attract   ② invigorate   ③ repel
④ replenish   ⑤ rebuke

37 밑줄 친 단어의 뜻으로 가장 적절한 것을 고르시오. | 경찰대학 2011학년도 1번 |

The colt was terrified. Separated from the group, he was vulnerable to predators. Anxiously, he walked back and forth, his head close to the ground. It looked like a sign of deference, almost a bow.

① hilarity   ② kindness   ③ submission
④ aggression   ⑤ uncertainty

38 밑줄 친 단어의 뜻으로 가장 적절한 것을 고르시오. | 경찰대학 2011학년도 2번 |

From that day on he specialized in the reptiles. His course included both theory and practice. In the morning there were long lectures on each aspect of the reptiles. He did not distinguish himself in these studies. He had a marvelously versatile gift for forgetting things.

① adaptable   ② upright   ③ vested
④ visible   ⑤ dizzy

39 밑줄 친 단어의 뜻으로 가장 적절한 것을 고르시오. | 경찰대학 2011학년도 3번 |

When the streets are slippery, every nerve and muscle of our bodies is straining to keep our balance; and the fear of falling is the most exhausting of all.

① fatiguing   ② inciting   ③ raging
④ invigorating   ⑤ intriguing

40

밑줄 친 단어의 뜻으로 가장 적절한 것을 고르시오.

| 경찰대학 2011학년도 4번 |

By his own admission, Phillip Johnson plays "a lot of obsolete games." So when Johnson, supervisor of historic house restoration for the Chicago Parks and Recreation Department, walked into the cellar of the city-owned Hurst House, he had no trouble identifying a pattern of lines that someone once carved into a rock there.

① destructive ② elaborate ③ entertaining
④ antiquated ⑤ annoying

41

밑줄 친 단어의 뜻으로 가장 적절한 것을 고르시오.

| 경찰대학 2011학년도 5번 |

The cleavage between the city and the countryside is not a uniquely American idea. The great European social theorists of the nineteenth century described the social changes taking place in terms of a shift from a supportive community based on kinship to a larger, more impersonal society in which ties are based on socioeconomic interests.

① discord ② separation ③ unison
④ resemblance ⑤ integration

42

글의 흐름으로 보아, 밑줄 친 단어의 뜻으로 가장 적절한 것을 고르시오. | 경찰대학 2010학년도 1번 |

Creativity is not simply the doings of genetics but can be substantially influenced by culture. It is not reserved for geniuses only. It is the prerogative of every one of us.

① pursuit ② preference ③ performance
④ perception ⑤ privilege

43

글의 흐름으로 보아, 밑줄 친 단어의 뜻으로 가장 적절한 것을 고르시오. | 경찰대학 2010학년도 2번 |

People respond to seat belts as they would to an improvement in road conditions — by driving faster and less carefully. The result of a seat belt law is a larger number of accidents. The decline in safe driving has a clear adverse impact on pedestrians, who are more likely to find themselves in an accident.

① unfavorable   ② negligible   ③ invariable
④ haphazard   ⑤ visible

44

글의 흐름으로 보아, 밑줄 친 단어의 뜻으로 가장 적절한 것을 고르시오. | 경찰대학 2010학년도 3번 |

All great works of art were created for a purpose, whether religious, social, political or, exceptionally, to express the artist's inner vision. And few artifacts have been created without some regard for aesthetic qualities.

① household items   ② scientific materials
③ religious objects   ④ well-known monuments
⑤ man-made objects

45

글의 흐름으로 보아, 밑줄 친 단어의 뜻으로 가장 적절한 것을 고르시오. | 경찰대학 2010학년도 4번 |

There was a time, not very long ago, in the desperately poor New York City neighborhoods of Brownsville, when the streets would turn into ghost towns at dusk. Children wouldn't ride their bicycles on the streets. The drug trade became so rampant in that part of Brooklyn that most people would take to the safety of their apartment at nightfall.

① prevalent   ② capricious   ③ vicious
④ sparse   ⑤ sporadic

46

글의 흐름으로 보아, 밑줄 친 단어의 뜻으로 가장 적절한 것을 고르시오. | 경찰대학 2010학년도 5번 |

In 1513, Machiavelli had acknowledged in *Il Principe* that citizens might have a right to 'think all things, speak all things, write all things,' but insisted that the prince was always equally entitled to deny them this privilege. A century later, the Scottish prince, James VI, took Machiavelli's position and in a proclamation inveighed against 'freedom of speech.'

① evaluated ② weighed ③ rebuked
④ resolved ⑤ examined

47

글의 흐름으로 보아, 밑줄 친 단어의 뜻으로 가장 적절한 것을 고르시오. | 경찰대학 2010학년도 6번 |

Sales of products decline for many reasons, including technological advances, shifts in consumer tastes, and increased competition. As sales and profits decline, some firms withdraw from the market. Those remaining may prune their product offerings. They may drop smaller market segments and marginal trade channels, or they may cut the promotion budget and reduce their prices further.

① boost ② harvest ③ clip
④ sustain ⑤ detain

01

밑줄 친 단어의 뜻으로 가장 적절한 것을 고르시오. | 사관학교 2017학년도 36번 응용 |

They believe that spirits that live in the wood have to be <u>appeased</u>, of that throwing salt blinds the devil.

① imparted　　　　② pacified　　　　③ deadened
④ overcome　　　　⑤ puzzled

02

밑줄 친 단어의 뜻으로 가장 적절한 것을 고르시오. | 사관학교 2016학년도 21번 응용 |

In the early history of warfare, military leaders were faced with the following <u>predicament</u>.

① quandary　　　　② superstition　　　　③ pundit
④ blunder　　　　⑤ periphery

03 밑줄 친 단어의 뜻으로 가장 적절한 것을 고르시오.

| 수능 2017학년도 홀수형 22번 응용 |

As a system for transmitting specific factual information without any distortion or <u>ambiguity</u>, the sign system of honey-bees would probably win easily over human language every time.

① interpretation   ② obscurity   ③ consequence
④ implementation   ⑤ provision

04 밑줄 친 단어의 뜻으로 가장 적절한 것을 고르시오.

| 수능 2015학년도 홀수형 28번 응용 |

Furthermore, a general lack of knowledge and insufficient care being taken when fish pens were initially constructed meant that pollution from excess feed and fish waste created huge <u>barren</u> underwater deserts.

① primary   ② crucial   ③ desolate
④ imperative   ⑤ legitimate

UNIT 07 어휘 I

사용된 어휘가 문맥에 적합한지 판단하는 유형이다. 정답에 해당하는 어휘의 의미가 문맥상 옳은 의미와 상반되는 경우가 많으므로 제시된 어휘의 반의어를 염두에 두고 접근한다.

• 도입부에서 글의 전개를 추측한다.
• 밑줄 친 낱말이 들어 있는 문장을 정확히 해석한다.
• 맥락상 적절한 어휘인지 검토한다.

Example

밑줄 친 부분 중, 문맥상 낱말의 쓰임이 적절하지 않은 것을 고르시오. | 경찰대학 2018학년도 12번 |

❶ According to one theory, within certain limits the more similar the communicators are, the more effective their communication will be. One limiting condition is that if the similarities between people are so ① pervasive that they have the same attitudes and beliefs about every subject, there is no need for communication. For example, the conversation might be ② lively at a party in which every person was in agreement about every subject from movies to politics. On the other hand, people who are ③ dissimilar in almost every respect lack a common ground, a base from which to share experiences and exchange ideas. According to this theory, the ideal situation is one in which people have many similarities but are dissimilar enough in their attitudes about the subject at hand to interact and perhaps to influence one another's attitudes. Similarity clearly ④ prevails, however. After all, the goal of attitude influence is to change the other person's attitude so that it more closely ⑤ resembles your own.

Vocabulary

pervasive 만연하는 lively 활기 찬 dissimilar 다른 base 바탕 interact 상호작용하다 prevail 압도하다, 우세하다, 승리하다

Let's Solve

Point 1 도입부에서 글의 전개 추측하기

- According to one theory, within certain limits the more similar the communicators are, the more effective their communication will be.

  → 의사소통을 효율적으로 만드는 요인에 관한 내용이 이어질 것이다.

Point 2 밑줄 친 어휘가 들어 있는 문장을 정확히 해석하기

- One limiting condition is that if the similarities between people are so pervasive that they have the same attitudes and beliefs about every subject, there is no need for communication.

  (한 제한적인 상황은 사람들 사이에 유사점이 너무 많아서 그들이 모든 주제에 같은 태도와 신념을 가진다면, 의사소통을 할 필요성이 없어진다는 것이다.)

- For example, the conversation might be lively at a party in which every person was in agreement about every subject from movies to politics.

  (예를 들어, 모든 사람들이 영화부터 정치까지 모든 주제에서 같은 입장을 가진 파티의 대화는 활기찰 것이다.)

- On the other hand, people who are dissimilar in almost every respect lack a common ground, a base from which to share experiences and exchange ideas.

  (반면에, 거의 모든 사항에 대해 다른 사람들은, 경험을 나누고 생각을 교환하는 바탕인 공통점이 없을 것이다.)

- Similarity clearly prevails, however.

  (그러나 유사점이 분명히 우세하다.)

- After all, the goal of attitude influence is to change the other person's attitude so that it more closely resembles your own.

  (결국, 태도 영향의 목표는 다른 사람의 태도를 바꿔 당신 자신의 것과 더 많이 닮도록 하는 것이다.)

Point 3 맥락상 적절한 어휘인지 검토하기

② lively

  → 주어진 지문의 내용은 공통점이 너무 많거나 적으면 의사소통이 잘 이루어지지 못한다는 것이다. 유사점과 차이점이 적절한 수준으로 존재할 때 효과적인 의사소통을 하고 상대방의 의견에 영향을 미치기에 가장 이상적이라는 내용이다. 따라서 모든 사람이 동일한 입장을 가지고 있을 때 대화가 활기를 띤다는 것은 글의 내용과 어긋나므로, '활기 없는, 지루한'의 의미를 갖는 dull이 적합한 단어이다.

01

다음 글의 밑줄 친 부분 중, 문맥상 낱말의 쓰임이 적절하지 않은 것을 고르시오.

| 경찰대학 2018학년도 11번 |

The spiritual dimension is a complex, and controversial area, and is often overlooked within holistic approaches, although it is increasingly being identified as a ① vital element which can have a large influence on the physical, mental and emotional aspects of work. Unfortunately the majority of studies that explore spirituality and resilience treat spirituality as a single entity which is ② easily measured and controlled. Spirituality is in reality a complex, ③ multi-dimensional phenomenon. Hence research which ④ excludes a broad interpretation of spirituality is important in order to expand our understanding. There are some who interpret spirituality using just a religious definition. This ⑤ narrow religious interpretation of spirituality, often seen in America and the UK as a Christian interpretation, is not appropriate for the government agencies that pride themselves on their anti-discriminatory practices.

02

다음 글의 밑줄 친 부분 중, 문맥상 낱말의 쓰임이 적절하지 않은 것을 고르시오.

| 경찰대학 2018학년도 13번 |

The fourth industrial revolution will affect the scale of conflict as well as its character. The distinctions between war and peace and who is a combatant and noncombatant are becoming uncomfortably ① clarified. Similarly, the battlefield is increasingly both local and global. Organizations such as ISIS operate ② principally in defined areas in the Middle East but they also recruit fighters from more than a hundred countries, largely through social media, while related terrorist attacks can occur anywhere on the planet. Modern conflicts are increasingly ③ hybrid in nature, combining traditional battlefield techniques with elements that were previously mostly associated with armed non-state actors. However, with technologies ④ fusing in increasingly unpredictable ways and with state and armed non-state actors learning from each other, the potential magnitude of change is not yet widely ⑤ appreciated.

[3점]

03

다음 글의 밑줄 친 부분 중, 문맥상 낱말의 쓰임이 적절하지 <u>않은</u> 것을 고르시오.

| 경찰대학 2017학년도 11번 |

Sea level rise along any given stretch of coast depends on how far away it is from the globe's two big ice buckets: Greenland and Antarctica. While it's easy to think the closest countries will see the biggest rise as the ice melts, it's not so ① <u>simple</u>. Greenland and Antarctica's massive ice sheets ② <u>exert</u> a strong gravitational pull on the waters around them, but as they melt, the attraction weakens, causing nearby sea levels to fall. In addition, without the burden of weight from the ice, the land uplifts, ③ <u>rising</u> slightly more above the water. The effect diminishes with distance, so it's actually the places farther away from the melting ice that will see the biggest ④ <u>drop</u> in sea level. Ocean currents help push the meltwater around the globe. "It's really an amazing and somewhat ⑤ <u>counterintuitive</u> result, but that's the reality," says Jerry Mitrovica, a geophysicist at Harvard University. [3점]

04

다음 글의 밑줄 친 부분 중, 문맥상 낱말의 쓰임이 적절하지 <u>않은</u> 것을 고르시오.

| 경찰대학 2017학년도 12번 |

Four little heads pop up simultaneously in a pool of blue-black water surrounded by ice as far as the eye can see. They seem to hesitate, reluctant to leave the watery world through which they swim as ① <u>effortlessly</u> as fish. They are Adélie penguins, and the ice ② <u>endangers</u> their existence. The birds leap about excitedly in tight circles, going in and out of the water, perfectly at ease in this ③ <u>frigid</u> sea that surrounds the shores of Antarctica. Their food is tied, literally, to the frozen ocean. Within layers of sea ice, microscopic algae bloom in profusion as sunlight floods in from above. When the sea ice melts with the beginning of summer, the ice algae escape into the water, where they are ④ <u>grazed</u> on by dense swarms of krill — a type of shrimplike crustacean. The krill, ⑤ <u>in turn</u>, are the Adélie penguins' primary food source.

다음 글의 밑줄 친 부분 중, 문맥상 낱말의 쓰임이 적절하지 <u>않은</u> 것을 고르시오.

| 경찰대학 2017학년도 13번 |

The human genome contains an ① <u>enormous</u> amount of information to guide the construction of a complex organism. In a growing number of cases, particular genes can be tied to aspects of cognition, language, and personality. When psychological traits vary, much of the variation comes from ② <u>differences</u> in genes: identical twins are more similar than fraternal twins, and biological siblings are more similar than adoptive siblings, whether ③ <u>raised</u> together or apart. A person's temperament and personality emerge early in life and remain fairly ④ <u>unpredictable</u> throughout the lifespan. And both personality and intelligence show few or no effects of children's particular home environments within their culture: children reared in the same family are similar mainly because of their ⑤ <u>shared</u> genes. Furthermore, neuroscience is showing that the brain's basic architecture develops under genetic control. [3점]

다음 글의 밑줄 친 부분 중, 문맥상 낱말의 쓰임이 적절하지 <u>않은</u> 것을 고르시오.

| 경찰대학 2016학년도 10번 |

In all history, nothing is so surprising or so difficult to account for as the sudden rise of civilization in Greece. Much of what makes civilization had already existed for thousands of years in Egypt and in Mesopotamia, and had ① <u>spread</u> thence to neighbouring countries. But certain elements had been ② <u>lacking</u> until the Greeks supplied them. What they achieved in art and literature is familiar to everybody, but what they did in the purely intellectual realm is even more ③ <u>ordinary</u>. They invented mathematics and science and philosophy; they first wrote history as ④ <u>opposed</u> to mere annals; they speculated freely about the nature of the world and the ends of life, without being ⑤ <u>bound</u> in the fetters of any inherited orthodoxy. [3점]

07

다음 글의 밑줄 친 부분 중, 문맥상 낱말의 쓰임이 적절하지 <u>않은</u> 것을 고르시오.

| 경찰대학 2016학년도 11번 |

For ordinary citizens the electric lights that dispelled the gloom of the city at night offered the most dramatic evidence that times had changed. Gaslight — ① <u>illuminating</u> gas produced from coal — had been in use since the early nineteenth century, but its 12 candlepower lamps lighted the city's public spaces only ② <u>dimly</u>. The first commercial use of electricity was for ③ <u>better</u> city lighting. Charles F. Brush's electric arc lamps, installed in Wanamaker's department store in Philadelphia in 1878, threw a brilliant light and soon ④ <u>established</u> gaslight on city streets and public buildings across the country. ⑤ <u>Electric</u> lighting then entered the American home, thanks to Thomas Edison's invention of a serviceable incandescent bulb in 1879. Edison's motto — "Let there be light!" — truly described the experience of the modern city.

08

다음 글의 밑줄 친 부분 중, 문맥상 낱말의 쓰임이 적절하지 <u>않은</u> 것을 고르시오.

| 경찰대학 2016학년도 12번 |

What else, besides love, gets passed on during a kiss? Dutch researchers tracked how kissing affected the ① <u>oral</u> bacteria of 21 couples. They asked one person in each pair to ② <u>consume</u> a probiotic yogurt drink with specific bacterial strains to track the spread of germs. Then that person was asked to ③ <u>share</u> a ten-second kiss with his or her partner. The average kiss ④ <u>extinguished</u> as many as 80 million bacteria. Although this doesn't sound very hygienic, experts say exposure to someone else's bacteria could actually help ⑤ <u>strengthen</u> your immunity.

다음 글의 밑줄 친 부분 중, 문맥상 낱말의 쓰임이 적절하지 <u>않은</u> 것을 고르시오.

| 경찰대학 2015학년도 10번 |

The backstage area, between the stage wall and the rear of the building, was known as the 'tiring house.' Here costumes and props were ① <u>stored</u> and the players got themselves ready. In the early days, tiring houses had been ② <u>free-standing</u> structures, but now they were built into the framework. Immediately behind the stage was a packed and jumbled room where everyone and everything ③ <u>inessential</u> for the day's play were gathered in readiness. Costumes hung everywhere. Players who had several changes in the play would be dressing or undressing, while 'tiremen' tried to keep the clothes in ④ <u>order</u>. Tables and benches were ⑤ <u>covered</u> with players' gear, false beards and wigs, and make-up.

다음 글의 밑줄 친 부분 중, 문맥상 낱말의 쓰임이 적절하지 <u>않은</u> 것을 고르시오.

| 경찰대학 2015학년도 11번 |

As a rule, law enforcement officials can conduct searches upon consent. To be considered valid, consent searches must satisfy two criteria. First, permission must be freely and voluntarily granted. Second, the individual granting consent must have the authority to do so. Once permission is obtained the police may ① <u>legitimately</u> search, but the search may not extend beyond the limits imposed by the person giving consent. The required voluntary nature of the consent means that permission cannot be granted as a result of ② <u>intimidation</u>. If the police extract consent by actual or threatened physical force or by means of trickery, the permission is ③ <u>invalid</u> and so is the resulting search. The second requirement is that only an ④ <u>authorized</u> person can give permission to search. Normally such permission can be granted only by an adult who owns, occupies, or otherwise ⑤ <u>partially</u> controls the house, automobile, office, or whatever other area the police desire to search. [3점]

11

다음 글의 밑줄 친 부분 중, 문맥상 낱말의 쓰임이 적절하지 <u>않은</u> 것을 고르시오.

| 경찰대학 2015학년도 12번 |

A medical system that deploys social support and caring to help boost patients' quality of life may well enhance their very ability to heal. For example, a patient lying in her hospital bed, awaiting major surgery the next day, can't help but ① <u>worry</u>. In any situation, what one person feels strongly tends to pass to ② <u>others</u>: The more stressed and vulnerable someone feels, the more ③ <u>sensitive</u> they are, and the more likely to catch those feelings. If the worried patient shares a room with another patient who also faces surgery, the two of them may well make each other more ④ <u>anxious</u>. But if she shares a room with a patient who has just come out of surgery successfully — and so feels relatively relieved and calm — the emotional effect on her will be more ⑤ <u>aggravating</u>.

12

다음 글의 밑줄 친 부분 중, 문맥상 낱말의 쓰임이 적절하지 <u>않은</u> 것을 고르시오.

| 경찰대학 2014학년도 7번 |

There is a constant demand for writers who can create good stories, especially for the big screen. However, there is an even greater ① <u>supply</u> of stories and screenplays that don't work and will never make it to the screen. In fact, there are over 100,000 scripts written every year, and only a few hundred actually make it. Even then, most of these movies do not ② <u>succeed</u>. Usually the script is the ③ <u>culprit</u>, and the most common script problem is lack of story. Believe it or not, ④ <u>enormous</u> attention is given to the process of developing good stories and screenplays for the big screen. But these statistics are startling proof of just how ⑤ <u>easy</u> it is to create a good story.

13

다음 글의 밑줄 친 부분 중, 문맥상 낱말의 쓰임이 적절하지 <u>않은</u> 것을 고르시오.

| 경찰대학 2014학년도 8번 |

To different forms of rule ① <u>corresponded</u> different kinds of military organization. In medieval times, independent cities commonly created their own militias and ② <u>obliged</u> citizens to serve. Citizens never included all of the urban population, and often ③ <u>narrowed</u> to elected members of self-renewing councils. In the case of Venice and many other maritime cities, military duties ④ <u>consisted of</u> not only militia but also naval service. In manorial systems, landlords often ⑤ <u>disbanded</u> military units of their own vassals, tenants, and serfs, sometimes carrying on their own private wars, at other times joining an overlord's armies for a season of combat before returning to the country.

*manorial: 장원의, 영지의 [3점]

14

다음 글의 밑줄 친 부분 중, 문맥상 낱말의 쓰임이 적절하지 <u>않은</u> 것을 고르시오.

| 경찰대학 2014학년도 9번 |

Last year, American car buyers named fuel economy the most important consideration when shopping for a car, ① <u>outranking</u> even quality and safety. The change coincides nicely with the ② <u>flood</u> of hybrid and high-efficiency internal-combustion engines on the market. But as efficient as engines may be, they can't compensate for one glaring ③ <u>efficiency</u>: us. Poor driving habits can ④ <u>slash</u> fuel economy by as much as one-third. To ⑤ <u>maximize</u> it, engineers need to not only remake the cars; they need to remake the drivers.

다음 글의 밑줄 친 부분 중, 문맥상 낱말의 쓰임이 적절하지 <u>않은</u> 것을 고르시오.

| 경찰대학 2013학년도 9번 |

The buyers and sellers at the happiness-market seem too often to have lost their sense of the pleasure of difficulty. Heaven knows what they are playing, but it seems a ① <u>dull</u> game. And the Indian holy man, whose idea of happiness is in needing nothing from outside himself, seems boring to us, I suppose, because he seems to be refusing to play anything at all. The Western weakness may be in the ② <u>illusion</u> that happiness can be bought. Perhaps the Eastern weakness is in the idea that there is such a thing as perfect (and therefore static) happiness. Happiness is never more than ③ <u>partial</u>. There are no pure states of mankind. Whatever else happiness may be, it is neither in having nor in being, but in becoming. What the Founding Fathers declared for us as an inherent right, we should do well to remember, was not happiness but the ④ <u>acceptance</u> of happiness. What they might have underlined, could they have foreseen the happiness-market, is the ⑤ <u>cardinal</u> fact that happiness is in the pursuit itself, in the meaningful pursuit of what is life-engaging and life-revealing, which is to say, in the idea of *becoming*.

다음 글의 밑줄 친 부분 중, 문맥상 낱말의 쓰임이 적절하지 <u>않은</u> 것을 고르시오.

| 경찰대학 2013학년도 10번 |

The world does not much like curiosity. The world says that curiosity killed the cat. The world dismisses curiosity by calling it idle, or *mere* idle curiosity — even though curious persons are ① <u>seldom</u> idle. Parents do their best to ② <u>foster</u> curiosity in their children, because it makes life difficult to be faced every day with a string of unanswerable questions about what makes fire hot or why grass grows. They have to ③ <u>halt</u> junior's investigations before they end in explosion and sudden death. Children whose curiosity survives parental ④ <u>discipline</u> and who manage to grow up before they blow up are invited to join the college faculty. Within the university they go on asking their questions and trying to find the answers. In the eyes of a scholar, that is mainly what a university is for. It is a place where the world's hostility to curiosity can be ⑤ <u>defied</u>.

다음 글의 밑줄 친 부분 중, 문맥상 낱말의 쓰임이 적절하지 않은 것을 고르시오.

| 경찰대학 2012학년도 26번 |

Experts disagree about how serious our population and environmental problems are and what we should do about them. Some suggest that ① <u>human ingenuity</u> and technological advances will allow us to clean up pollution to acceptable levels and find substitutes for any scarce resources. They are called technological optimists, who argue that technological innovations can preserve the earth's natural resources. Many leading ② <u>environmental</u> scientists disagree. They appreciate and applaud the significant environmental and social progress that we have made, but they also cite evidence that we are ③ <u>upgrading</u> the earth's life-support systems in many parts of the world at an exponentially accelerating rate. They call for much more action to protect ④ <u>the natural capital</u> that supports our economies and all life. They are called environmental pessimists, who argue that our environmental situations are getting worse and global economy is ⑤ <u>outgrowing</u> the capacity of the earth to support it.

18

다음 글의 밑줄 친 부분 중, 문맥상 낱말의 쓰임이 적절하지 <u>않은</u> 것을 고르시오.

| 경찰대학 2011학년도 26번 |

It is a ① <u>paradox</u> that the greatest gifts of man, the unique faculties of conceptual thought and verbal speech which have raised him to a level high above all other creatures and given him mastery over the globe, are not altogether blessings, or at least are blessings that have to be paid for very ② <u>dearly</u> indeed. All the great dangers threatening humanity with extinction are direct consequences of conceptual thought and verbal speech. They drove man out of the paradise in which he could follow his instincts with ③ <u>impunity</u> and do or not do whatever he pleased. Knowledge springing from conceptual thought robbed man of the ④ <u>insecurity</u> provided by his well-adapted instincts long, long before it was sufficient to provide him with an equally safe adaptation. Man is, as Arnold Gehlen has so truly said, by nature a ⑤ <u>jeopardized</u> creature.

01

다음 글의 밑줄 친 부분 중, 문맥상 낱말의 쓰임이 적절하지 <u>않은</u> 것을 고르시오.

| 사관학교 2017학년도 23번 |

It has been said that the clothes make the man, and nowhere is this truer than in the military. A soldier's uniform ① <u>represents</u> everything from loyalty to title and rank. And as for camouflage, it can mean the difference between life and death — a point brought up by U.S. lawmakers as they prepared to pass a $106 billion emergency war-spending bill that will ② <u>fund</u>, among other things, some 70,000 new uniforms for troops in Afghanistan. Evidently, the country's muddy, mountainous terrain doesn't ③ <u>match</u> the "universal camouflage pattern" designed for dusty desert cities like Baghdad. The emergence of aerial and trench warfare during World War I gave rise to the strategy — and art — of camouflaged battle dress, resulting in a fruitful ④ <u>collaboration</u> among soldiers, artists and naturalists like Abbott Thayer, whose 1909 book *Concealing Coloration in the Animal Kingdom* became required reading for the U.S. Army's newly launched unit of camouflage designers. Now that troops had to avoid bombs and bullets from all directions, the traditional glorious uniform worn in an earlier era of warfare began to seem ⑤ <u>up-to-date</u>, if not downright dangerous.

* camouflage: 위장 ** trench: 참호 [3점]

02

다음 글의 밑줄 친 부분 중, 문맥상 낱말의 쓰임이 적절하지 <u>않은</u> 것을 고르시오.

| 사관학교 2015학년도 15번 |

Not much learning takes place unless you concentrate carefully on what you are learning. Concentration is basically thinking. Concentration can ① <u>enhance</u> your ability to do both mental and physical tasks. This is why many failures in school are due more to poor concentration than to ② <u>low</u> intelligence. Researchers note that one enemy of concentration is indecision: Indecision about when to study and which subject to study first is not only a great time-waster, but also a sure way to ③ <u>eliminate</u> a negative attitude toward studying. Personal problems also interfere with concentration. You will not make good use of your intelligence if you are ④ <u>preoccupied</u> with personal problems. After you have taken some ⑤ <u>constructive</u> action on your problem, you will then be in a better position to learn or perform well.

03 다음 글의 밑줄 친 부분 중, 문맥상 낱말의 쓰임이 적절하지 <u>않은</u> 것은?

| 수능 2013학년도 홀수형 30번 |

Researchers have suggested that maintaining good social relations depends on two ① <u>complementary</u> processes: being sensitive to the needs of others and being motivated to make amends or pay compensation when a violation does occur. In short, maintaining good social relations depends on the ② <u>capacity</u> for guilt. Martin L. Hoffman, who has focused on the guilt that comes from harming others, suggests that the motivational basis for this guilt is empathetic distress. Empathetic distress occurs when people ③ <u>deny</u> that their actions have caused harm or pain to another person. Motivated by feelings of guilt, they are ④ <u>inclined</u> to make amends for their actions. Making amends serves to repair damaged social relations and ⑤ <u>restore</u> group harmony.

04 다음 글의 밑줄 친 부분 중, 문맥상 낱말의 쓰임이 적절하지 <u>않은</u> 것은?

| 수능 2012학년도 홀수형 32번 |

Until the 1920's, there were only three competitive swimming strokes — freestyle, backstroke, and breaststroke — and each had specific rules that described how it was to be performed. The rules of breaststroke ① <u>stated</u> that both arms must be pulled together underwater and then recovered simultaneously back to the start of the pulling position to begin the next stroke. Most people interpreted this arm recovery to mean an ② <u>underwater</u> recovery. In the 1920's, however, someone ③ <u>challenged</u> the rules and reinterpreted this arm recovery to be an out-of-the-water recovery. Since this new breaststroke was about 15% ④ <u>slower</u>, people using the conventional version couldn't effectively compete. Something had to be done to solve the problem. Finally, this new stroke — now known as the 'butterfly' — won ⑤ <u>recognition</u> as the fourth swimming stroke, and became an Olympic event in 1956.

Problem Solving Skills

지문 속에서 한 단어가 지니는 특정한 의미를 그 문맥과 연계하여 파악할 수 있는지 묻는 유형이다. 어휘의 의미를 정확히 알고 문제에 접근한다.

• 도입부에서 글의 전개를 추측한다.
• 네모 안의 표현이 들어 있는 문장을 정확히 해석한다.
• 맥락상 더 적절한 어휘를 고른다.

Example

(A), (B), (C)에 들어갈 말로 가장 적절한 것을 고르시오.　　　| 경찰대학 2017학년도 9번 |

❶ Many of us take broadband Internet for granted, but nearly 1 in 5 Americans lacks access to it, says the Federal Communications Commission (FCC). In rural areas, telecom companies balk at the cost of wiring far-flung homes, while low-income families can find the fees (A) prohibitive / affordable . Closing the broadband gap is about more than being able to stream the latest TV dramas. High-speed Internet is a critical tool of modern life, (B) constraining / enabling kids to learn digitally and adults to work via the cloud. The FCC recently approved a small broadband subsidy, but the real solution may lie in (C) increased / decreased competition for a notoriously consolidated industry.

❷

	(A)	(B)	(C)
①	prohibitive	…… enabling	…… increased
②	prohibitive	…… enabling	…… decreased
③	prohibitive	…… constraining	…… decreased
④	affordable	…… constraining	…… increased
⑤	affordable	…… enabling	…… decreased

❸

Vocabulary

broadband 광대역　take A for granted A를 당연한 것으로 여기다　Federal Communications Commission (FCC) 연방통신위원회　balk at ~에 대해 망설이다　far-flung 멀리 떨어진　prohibitive 엄두도 못 낼 정도로 비싼　notoriously 악명 높게　consolidated 통합된

Let's Solve

Point 1 도입부에서 글의 전개 추측하기

- Many of us take broadband Internet for granted, but nearly 1 in 5 Americans lacks access to it, says the Federal Communications Commission (FCC).
  → 광대역 인터넷 접근성 차이에 대한 내용이 이어질 것이다.

Point 2 네모 안의 표현이 들어 있는 문장 정확히 해석하기

- In rural areas, telecom companies balk at the cost of wiring far-flung homes, while low-income families can find the fees (A) prohibitive / affordable.
  → 시골 지역에서는, 저소득 가정들이 요금이 엄두도 못 낼 정도로 비싼 / 감당할 만한 것을 알게 되는 반면, 통신 회사들은 멀리 떨어진 가정들의 배선 비용을 두고 망설인다.
- High-speed Internet is a critical tool of modern life, (B) constraining / enabling kids to learn digitally and adults to work via the cloud.
  → 고속 인터넷은 현대적 삶의 중요한 도구로, 아이들이 디지털 방식으로 배우고 어른들이 클라우드를 통해 일하는 것을 제한적이게 / 가능하게 한다.
- The FCC recently approved a small broadband subsidy, but the real solution may lie in (C) increased / decreased competition for a notoriously consolidated industry.
  → FCC는 최근 소규모 광대역 보조금을 승인했으나, 실제적인 해결책은 악명 높게도 통합된 산업의 경쟁 증가 / 감소에 있다.

Point 3 맥락상 더 적절한 어휘 고르기

(A) prohibitive / affordable
  → 글 전체에 걸쳐 인터넷 접근성에 지역 간 격차가 존재하는 원인과 해결책을 제시하고 있다. 도시 지역에 비해 시골 지역의 인터넷 접근성이 떨어지는 현상이 문제라는 내용이므로, 시골 지역에 관해 설명하는 해당 문장에는 인터넷 이용을 막는 '엄두도 못 낼 정도로 비싼' 비용이 적합하며, 따라서 prohibitive가 적절하다.

(B) constraining / enabling
  → 고속 인터넷이 현대적 삶에 필수적인 이유, 즉 고속 인터넷의 장점이 나오는 것이 문맥상 자연스러우므로, 클라우드를 통해 일하는 것을 '가능하게' 한다는 뜻의 enabling이 적절하다.

(C) increased / decreased
  → 통합된 산업 내에서는 경쟁이 활발하지 않으므로, 해결책으로는 반대 상황인 경쟁 '증가'가 나오는 것이 논리적이다. 따라서 increased가 적절하다.

01

(A), (B), (C)에 들어갈 말로 가장 적절한 것을 고르시오.

| 경찰대학 2018학년도 9번 |

The realization that the universe consists of atoms and void and nothing else, that the world was not made for us by a providential creator, that we are not the center of the universe, that our emotional lives are no more (A) distinct / indistinct than our physical lives from those of all other creatures, that our souls are as material and as mortal as our bodies — all these things are not the cause for (B) despair / hope. On the contrary, grasping the way things really are is the crucial step toward the possibility of happiness. It is possible for human beings to live happy lives, but not because they think that they are the center of the universe. Unappeasable desire and the fear of death are the principal (C) paths / obstacles to human happiness, but they can be surmounted through the exercise of reason.

	(A)		(B)		(C)
①	distinct	......	despair	......	paths
②	distinct	......	despair	......	obstacles
③	distinct	......	hope	......	obstacles
④	indistinct	......	hope	......	obstacles
⑤	indistinct	......	despair	......	paths

02

(A), (B), (C)에 들어갈 말로 가장 적절한 것을 고르시오.

| 경찰대학 2018학년도 10번 |

Music therapy as an explicit set of practices first developed in the West during the twentieth century — especially during the First World War, when doctors and nurses witnessed the effect that music had on the psychological, physiological, cognitive and emotional states of the wounded. The first major academic study of music's (A) aesthetic / medicinal properties was published in 1948, partly as a response to the continued use of music therapy in military hospitals and in factories during the Second World War. Music therapy is now (B) rarely / widely used for those with mental and/or physical disabilities or illnesses. One of its most significant functions is to relax patients who are preparing for, undergoing or recovering from surgery, notably dental, burns and coronary treatments. It is now well attested that music with slow, steady tempos, legato passages, gentle rhythms, predictable change, and simple sustained melodies is (C) detrimental / conducive to relaxation.

	(A)		(B)		(C)
①	aesthetic	⋯⋯	rarely	⋯⋯	detrimental
②	aesthetic	⋯⋯	widely	⋯⋯	detrimental
③	medicinal	⋯⋯	widely	⋯⋯	detrimental
④	medicinal	⋯⋯	widely	⋯⋯	conducive
⑤	medicinal	⋯⋯	rarely	⋯⋯	conducive

03

(A), (B), (C)에 들어갈 말로 가장 적절한 것을 고르시오.

| 경찰대학 2017학년도 10번 |

As evolutionary scholar Henry Plotkin says, gaining knowledge of the world across countless generations of organisms, evolution conserves knowledge selectively relative to criteria of need, and that collective knowledge is then held within the gene pool of species. Such collective knowledge is doled out to individuals, who come into the world with (A) innate / acquired ideas and predispositions to learn only certain things in specific ways. In other words, whether you're hunting on the savannah or choosing between millions of videos on YouTube, your brain is programmed to (B) adopt / ignore almost everything and home in only on what is most important or interesting. Otherwise, you'd be pointing your spear at every tree and rock or, just as annoyingly, you'd be lost in an infinite trail of video links, hoping in vain to find something worthwhile. With an understanding of the (C) discriminating / integrating nature of our genes, we can begin to construct the basis for stories that grab our attention and stay in our memory.

	(A)		(B)		(C)
①	acquired	······	ignore	······	integrating
②	acquired	······	ignore	······	discriminating
③	innate	······	ignore	······	discriminating
④	innate	······	adopt	······	integrating
⑤	innate	······	adopt	······	discriminating

04

(A), (B), (C)에 들어갈 말로 가장 적절한 것을 고르시오.

| 경찰대학 2016학년도 9번 |

Last summer, a 26-year-old woman in California called 911 to report an emergency. Had she placed her emergency call on a landline, first responders would have been able to (A) pinpoint / overlook her location in a matter of seconds. But because the current 911 system has gone largely unchanged since it was designed in the 1960s, police were forced to use (B) precise / imprecise information provided by her wireless carrier to determine where she might be. When an emergency call is made on a mobile device, telecommunications companies use (C) triangulation / circulation — comparing the signal strength and time the signal takes to reach a number of cell towers — to approximate the phone's position. This technique placed the woman within a one-block radius, and it took over 20 minutes to find her.

(A)	(B)	(C)
① pinpoint ⋯⋯	imprecise ⋯⋯	triangulation
② pinpoint ⋯⋯	imprecise ⋯⋯	circulation
③ overlook ⋯⋯	precise ⋯⋯	circulation
④ overlook ⋯⋯	precise ⋯⋯	triangulation
⑤ overlook ⋯⋯	imprecise ⋯⋯	circulation

05

(A), (B), (C)에 들어갈 말로 가장 적절한 것을 고르시오.

| 경찰대학 2015학년도 9번 |

Marketing's impact on individual consumer welfare has been criticized for its high prices, deceptive practices, and poor service to disadvantaged consumers. Marketing's impact on society has been criticized for creating false wants and too much materialism, too (A) many / few social goods, and cultural pollution. Critics have also criticized marketing's impact on other businesses for harming competitors and reducing competitions through acquisitions, practices that (B) create / lift barriers to entry. Some of these (C) concerns / suggestions are justified; some are not.

	(A)		(B)		(C)
①	many	......	create	......	concerns
②	many	......	lift	......	suggestions
③	few	......	create	......	concerns
④	few	......	lift	......	suggestions
⑤	few	......	lift	......	concerns

06

(A), (B), (C)에 들어갈 말로 가장 적절한 것을 고르시오.

| 경찰대학 2014학년도 6번 |

There has been growing awareness in recent years of the inadequacy of GDP as a measure of true wealth, with its exclusive focus on economic capital formation but with no reference to other forms of capital — the health and biodiversity of the natural environs, the (A) strength / weakness of communities, and the well-being and happiness of people. A society should consciously develop its various forms of capital in a (B) less / more balanced and integrated way. Societies have to substitute other forms of capital for economic wealth, demonstrating how quality of life could be maintained or even enhanced while significantly (C) maximizing / reducing consumption and material throughput.

	(A)		(B)		(C)
①	strength	......	more	......	maximizing
②	strength	......	less	......	reducing
③	strength	......	more	......	reducing
④	weakness	......	less	......	reducing
⑤	weakness	......	less	......	maximizing

(A), (B), (C)에 들어갈 말로 가장 적절한 것을 고르시오.

| 경찰대학 2013학년도 7번 |

Once hunted for their pelts, beavers are back in demand, not for their bodies but for their minds — specifically, for their engineering skills. As changing climate leaves streams short on water in the summer, researchers are (A) | betting / refuting | that the industrious rodents could provide a natural solution. Based on a survey of how dams store water, the Lands Council in Washington State predicts that (B) | prohibiting / reintroducing | beavers to 10,000 miles of suitable habitat in the state could help retain more than 650 trillion gallons of spring runoff, which would slowly be released by the animals' naturally leaky dams. The council began (C) | investigating / terminating | the beaver option after learning that the state was considering artificial dam projects that might cost billions of dollars. It argues that beavers can do the job at a small fraction of the expense.

(A)		(B)		(C)
① betting	......	prohibiting	......	investigating
② betting	......	reintroducing	......	investigating
③ betting	......	reintroducing	......	terminating
④ refuting	......	reintroducing	......	terminating
⑤ refuting	......	prohibiting	......	investigating

(A), (B), (C)에 들어갈 말로 가장 적절한 것을 고르시오.

The need for presidents to travel is (A) obscure / obvious , but it can be asked whether motion is replacing substance. Nixon's cross-country swing was an engineered spectacle that started with his speech in the Oval Office, sped south to Florida, then on to New Orleans, and came to rest by the Pacific. It was supposed to be a triumphal march from coast to coast, but it failed because it was a hollow concept. Ever since John F. Kennedy, there has been the (B) compulsion / abhorrence to fly off some place. There is something about being at 35,000 feet that increases President's sense of omnipotence. Kennedy's spirits lifted when he got on his magic carpet. Even when Nixon is earthbound in California, he often sets out for a spin along the roaring California freeways. The amateur psychologists who travel with Nixon insist that in part he is running from his problems, seeking some (C) vignette / vista where solutions will appear. They may never do.

	(A)		(B)		(C)
①	obscure	……	compulsion	……	vista
②	obscure	……	abhorrence	……	vignette
③	obvious	……	compulsion	……	vista
④	obvious	……	abhorrence	……	vista
⑤	obvious	……	compulsion	……	vignette

09 (A), (B), (C)에 들어갈 말로 가장 적절한 것을 고르시오.

| 경찰대학 2012학년도 23번 |

If ignorance about the nature of pain is widespread, ignorance about the way pain-killing drugs work is even more so. What is not generally understood is that many of the vaunted pain-killing drugs (A) conceal / reveal the pain without correcting the underlying condition. They (B) awaken / deaden the mechanism in the body that alerts the brain to the fact that something may be wrong. The body can pay a high price for (C) suppression / release of pain without regard to its basic cause.

	(A)		(B)		(C)
①	conceal	⋯⋯	awaken	⋯⋯	suppression
②	reveal	⋯⋯	deaden	⋯⋯	release
③	conceal	⋯⋯	awaken	⋯⋯	release
④	reveal	⋯⋯	awaken	⋯⋯	release
⑤	conceal	⋯⋯	deaden	⋯⋯	suppression

How do geniuses come up with ideas? What links the thinking style that produced Mona Lisa with the one that (A) spawned / followed the theory of relativity? What can we learn from the thinking strategies of the Galileos, Edisons, and Mozarts of history? For years, scholars tried to study genius by analyzing statistics. In 1904, Havelock Ellis noted that most geniuses were fathered by men older than 30, had mothers younger than 25, and usually were sickly children. However, other researchers reported that many were celibate (Descartes), fatherless (Dickens), or motherless (Darwin). In the end, the data illuminated (B) something / nothing. Academics also tried to measure the links between intelligence and genius. But they found that run-of-the-mill physicists had IQs much higher than Nobel Prize winner and extraordinary genius Richard Feynman, whose IQ was a merely (C) respectable / respectful 122. Genius is not about mastering 14 languages at the age of seven or being especially smart. Creativity is not the same as intelligence.

*run-of-the-mill : 평범한

	(A)		(B)		(C)
①	spawned	······	something	······	respectful
②	spawned	······	nothing	······	respectable
③	spawned	······	nothing	······	respectful
④	followed	······	something	······	respectable
⑤	followed	······	nothing	······	respectful

11

(A), (B), (C)에 들어갈 말로 가장 적절한 것을 고르시오.

| 경찰대학 2012학년도 25번 |

Scientists are beginning to uncover evidence that meditation has a (A) [negligible / tangible] effect on the brain. Skeptics argue that it is not a practical way to try to deal with the stresses of modern life. But the long years when adherents were unable to point to hard science to support their belief in the technique may finally be coming to an end. When Carol Cattley's husband died, it (B) [tackled / triggered] a relapse of the depression which had not plagued her since she was a teenager. Carol sought medical help and managed to control her depression with a combination of medication and a psychological treatment called Cognitive Behavioral Therapy (CBT) which primarily consists of meditation. One of the (C) [opponents / pioneers] of CBT, Professor Mark Williams from the Department of Psychiatry at the University of Oxford, describes CBT as 80% meditation and 20% cognitive therapy.

	(A)		(B)		(C)
①	negligible	……	tackled	……	pioneers
②	negligible	……	triggered	……	opponents
③	negligible	……	triggered	……	pioneers
④	tangible	……	triggered	……	pioneers
⑤	tangible	……	tackled	……	opponents

(A), (B), (C)에 들어갈 말로 가장 적절한 것을 고르시오.

| 경찰대학 2011학년도 23번 |

Rituals may serve the social function of creating temporary or permanent (A) solicitation / solidarity between people — forming a social community. We see this also in religious practices known as totemism. Totemism was particularly important in the religions of the Native Australians. Totems could be animals, plants, or geographical features. In each tribe, groups of people had particular totems. Members of each totemic group believed themselves to be (B) descendants / dissidents of their totem. They customarily neither killed nor ate it, but this taboo was lifted once a year, when people (C) assented / assembled for ceremonies dedicated to the totem.

	(A)		(B)		(C)
①	solicitation	······	descendants	······	assented
②	solicitation	······	descendants	······	assembled
③	solidarity	······	descendants	······	assembled
④	solidarity	······	dissidents	······	assembled
⑤	solicitation	······	dissidents	······	assented

(A), (B), (C)에 들어갈 말로 가장 적절한 것을 고르시오.

| 경찰대학 2011학년도 24번 |

Contrast the features of renewable energy sources with nonrenewable. Coal and oil are lifeless — thus nonrenewable — quantities. They can be divided and redivided and still the individual parts will contain the same attributes as the whole. A speck of coal is (A) little /very different in composition from a chunk of coal. Nonrenewable resources represent a fixed stock. They can be easily (B) quantified / qualified. They are prone to precise measurement. They can be ordered. Renewable resources, on the other hand, are forever changing and flowing. With the solar energy, the concept of order and decay was an ever-present reminder of the ways the world unfolds. The cycles of birth, life, death, and rebirth were qualitative processes, and renewable resources are (C) hard / easy to subject to precise measurement.

(A)		(B)		(C)
① little	⋯⋯	qualified	⋯⋯	hard
② little	⋯⋯	quantified	⋯⋯	easy
③ little	⋯⋯	quantified	⋯⋯	hard
④ very	⋯⋯	quantified	⋯⋯	easy
⑤ very	⋯⋯	qualified	⋯⋯	easy

(A), (B), (C)에 들어갈 말로 가장 적절한 것을 고르시오.

| 경찰대학 2011학년도 25번 |

In the black community, almost no one is complaining about the resegregation of Leland's schools. In recent months, black activists have been more focused on keeping alive the tradition of the old all-black high school. Last fall, the building's white principal wanted to replace some athletic trophies from the days before (A) integration / segregation in a display case with the work of current students. The black community was outraged. This acute nostalgia reflects a growing sense among some blacks that the cost of giving up schools that they controlled may have been greater than the benefits of integration. Before (B) resegregation / desegregation, black children's schools were woven into the fabric of the community and were a sanctuary from the racial denigration that marks life outside. (C) Resegregation / Integration changed all that, removing blacks from top policy-making positions in the schools and raising racial questions about every faculty promotion and every student disciplinary action.

	(A)		(B)		(C)
①	integration	⋯⋯	desegregation	⋯⋯	Integration
②	integration	⋯⋯	resegregation	⋯⋯	Resegregation
③	segregation	⋯⋯	resegregation	⋯⋯	Resegregation
④	segregation	⋯⋯	desegregation	⋯⋯	Integration
⑤	segregation	⋯⋯	desegregation	⋯⋯	Resegregation

15

(A), (B), (C)에 들어갈 말로 가장 적절한 것을 고르시오.

| 경찰대학 2010학년도 36번 |

Unlike armies, corporations, and other hierarchical organizations, universities are communities in which authority is widely shared instead of being concentrated in the hands of a few leaders. Individual professors are largely (A) distinct / immune from administrative control over their teaching and research by virtue of the (B) doctrine / deficiency of academic freedom. Acting collectively, faculties typically have the power to fix the content of the curriculum, set academic requirements, search for new professors, and (C) shape / shear the standards for admission.

	(A)		(B)		(C)
①	distinct	......	doctrine	......	shape
②	distinct	......	deficiency	......	shape
③	immune	......	deficiency	......	shear
④	immune	......	doctrine	......	shape
⑤	immune	......	doctrine	......	shear

16

(A), (B), (C)에 들어갈 말로 가장 적절한 것을 고르시오.

Like it or not, you are a negotiator. Negotiation is a fact of life. You discuss a raise with your boss. You try to agree with a stranger on a price for his house. Two lawyers try to settle a lawsuit (A) rising / arising from a car accident. A group of oil companies plan a (B) joint / joined venture exploring for offshore oil. A city official meets with union leaders to (C) prevent / protect a transit strike. The United States Secretary of State sits down with his Soviet counterpart to seek an agreement limiting nuclear arms. All these are negotiations.

	(A)	(B)	(C)
①	rising	......	joint	......	prevent
②	rising	......	joined	......	protect
③	arising	......	joined	......	protect
④	arising	......	joint	......	prevent
⑤	arising	......	joined	......	prevent

17

(A), (B), (C)에 들어갈 말로 가장 적절한 것을 고르시오.

Attention, simply defined, is the process of exposing oneself to certain stimuli in the environment. Obviously, there are innumerable such stimuli present in one's immediate environment — so many, in fact, that an individual is incapable of attending to all of them. Thus, attention is a (A) collective / selective process whereby one entirely ignores some stimuli, gives partial attention to others, and devotes full attention to still others. A manager, for example, while involved in an interview with one of his subordinates, may be (B) carefully / casually attending to the subordinate's explanation of his reasons for committing a particular error. Simultaneously, however, other stimuli that may be (C) contingent / impinging upon the manager's attention process could include a noisy, malfunctioning air conditioner, and the telephone ringing in his secretary's office.

	(A)		(B)		(C)
①	collective	······	carefully	······	contingent
②	collective	······	casually	······	impinging
③	collective	······	carefully	······	impinging
④	selective	······	carefully	······	impinging
⑤	selective	······	casually	······	contingent

01

(A), (B), (C)의 각 네모 안에서 어법에 맞는 표현으로 가장 적절한 것을 고르시오.

| 사관학교 2016학년도 22번 |

Stop-motion photography is used to fool the eye into seeing motion. A still photograph is made of an object, such as a clay model of a dinosaur. The object is moved (A) considerably / slightly and another photograph is taken. This delicate process is repeated thousands of times. When the photographs, or frames, are shown at the speed of a motion picture camera, 24 frames per second, the clay model appears to be (B) resting / moving . A major problem with stop-motion filming is that there are no "blurs." If you film a man running down the street, there will be a slight blur on each frame. Although not noticed by the audience, the blur helps make the running motion smooth and realistic. In stop-motion films, a running creature seems to have jerky movements. This problem has been solved with computer animation, which can be used to make frames (C) blurry / jerky to produce realistic movement.

	(A)		(B)		(C)
①	considerably	……	resting	……	blurry
②	considerably	……	moving	……	jerky
③	slightly	……	resting	……	blurry
④	slightly	……	resting	……	jerky
⑤	slightly	……	moving	……	blurry

(A), (B), (C)의 각 네모 안에서 어법에 맞는 표현으로 가장 적절한 것을 고르시오.

| 사관학교 2015학년도 23번 |

Once you have begun to use rewards to control people, you cannot easily go back. When behaviors become (A) irrelevant / instrumental to monetary rewards — in other words, when people behave to get rewards — those behaviors will last only so long as the rewards are forthcoming. In some cases that may be fine, but in most cases the activities we reward are ones that we would like to have (B) persist / cease long after the rewards have stopped. For example, if you offered rewards to your children for studying — a dollar for each "A" on their report cards — you would want the children to remain enthusiastic about studying after your reward system was (C) initiated / terminated. But it is pretty likely that if they study for the rewards, they will stop studying when there are no longer rewards.

	(A)		(B)		(C)
①	irrelevant	......	persist	......	terminated
②	irrelevant	......	cease	......	terminated
③	instrumental	......	cease	......	initiated
④	instrumental	......	persist	......	initiated
⑤	instrumental	......	persist	......	terminated

(A), (B), (C)의 각 네모 안에서 문맥에 맞는 낱말로 가장 적절한 것은?

| 수능 2016학년도 홀수형 29번 |

The Atitlán Giant Grebe was a large, flightless bird that had evolved from the much more widespread and smaller Pied-billed Grebe. By 1965 there were only around 80 birds left on Lake Atitlán. One immediate reason was easy enough to spot: the local human population was cutting down the reed beds at a furious rate. This (A) accommodation / destruction was driven by the needs of a fast growing mat-making industry. But there were other problems. An American airline was intent on developing the lake as a tourist destination for fishermen. However, there was a major problem with this idea: the lake (B) lacked / supported any suitable sporting fish! To compensate for this rather obvious defect, a specially selected species of fish called the Large-mouthed Bass was introduced. The introduced individuals immediately turned their attentions to the crabs and small fish that lived in the lake, thus (C) competing / cooperating with the few remaining grebes for food. There is also little doubt that they sometimes gobbled up the zebra-striped Atitlán Giant Grebe's chicks.

*reed: 갈대 **gobble up: 게걸스럽게 먹다

	(A)		(B)		(C)
①	accommodation	……	lacked	……	competing
②	accommodation	……	supported	……	cooperating
③	destruction	……	lacked	……	competing
④	destruction	……	supported	……	cooperating
⑤	destruction	……	lacked	……	cooperating

(A), (B), (C)의 각 네모 안에서 문맥에 맞는 낱말로 가장 적절한 것은?

| 수능 2013학년도 홀수형 31번 |

Anxiety has a damaging effect on mental performance of all kinds. It is in one sense a useful response gone awry — an overly zealous mental preparation for an anticipated threat. But such mental rehearsal is (A) disastrous / constructive cognitive static when it becomes trapped in a stale routine that captures attention, intruding on all other attempts to focus elsewhere. Anxiety undermines the intellect. In a complex, intellectually demanding and high-pressure task such as that of air traffic controllers, for example, having chronically high anxiety is an almost sure predictor that a person will eventually fail in training or in the field. The anxious are more likely to fail even given (B) inferior / superior scores on intelligence tests, as a study of 1,790 students in training for air traffic control posts discovered. Anxiety also sabotages academic performance of all kinds: 126 different studies of more than 36,000 people found that the more (C) prone / resistant to anxieties a person is, the poorer his or her academic performance is.

*go away: 빗나가다

	(A)		(B)		(C)
①	disastrous	······	inferior	······	prone
②	disastrous	······	superior	······	prone
③	disastrous	······	superior	······	resistant
④	constructive	······	inferior	······	resistant
⑤	constructive	······	superior	······	resistant

PART 03
빈칸 추론하기

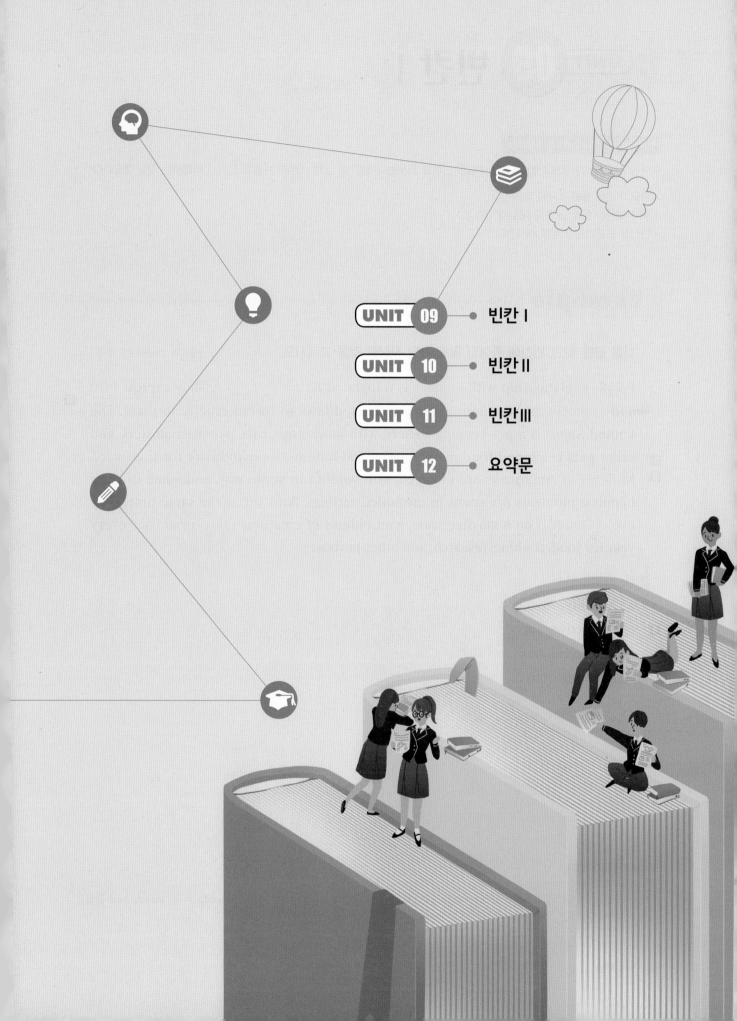

Problem Solving Skills

주어진 지문을 바탕으로 빈칸에 가장 적절한 단어를 고르는 유형이다. 글의 내용과 흐름을 정확히 이해하는 것이 중요하다.

• 주요 어휘를 통해 소재를 파악한다.
• 세부 내용을 통해 글의 요지를 파악한다.
• 빈칸을 포함하는 문장을 해석한다.

Example

다음 글을 읽고, 빈칸에 들어갈 말로 가장 적절한 것을 고르시오. | 경찰대학 2016학년도 18번 |

People's relationship with animals is fraught with _____. They express love and appreciation for them and have enacted laws to forbid cruelty to them. The United States is a pet-keeping society, with more dogs, cats, parrots, hamsters, and other pets combined than people and a $60-billion-a-year industry for their care. Millions of Americans are engaged with wildlife in some way, and some of their happiest moments are spent in unspoiled settings. And yet at the same time, they exploit animals on a massive scale, with billions of creatures killed or abused every year for food, clothing, research, and other purposes.

① gratitude
② hostility
③ protectiveness
④ responsibilities
⑤ contradictions

Vocabulary

fraught with 투성이의 **appreciation** 감사, 감탄 **forbid** 금하다 **enact** 제정하다 **cruelty** 학대 **combined** 결합된
unspoiled 훼손되지 않은 **exploit** 착취하다 **massive** 대량의 **abuse** 남용, 오용

Let's Solve

Point 1 주요 어휘를 통해 소재 파악하기

animals, love, appreciation, care, exploit, kill, abuse

⬇

동물들 + 사랑, 감사, 보살핌 + 착취, 죽임, 학대

⬇

동물에 대한 사람들의 두 가지 태도

Point 2 세부 사항을 통해 글의 요지 파악하기

- They express love and appreciation for them and have enacted laws to forbid cruelty to them
- And yet at the same time, they exploit animals on a massive scale

⬇

인간은 동물을 사랑하는 동시에 착취하는 모순적인 모습을 보인다.

Point 3 빈칸을 포함하는 문장 해석하기

- People's relationship with animals is fraught with _____.
  → 사람들과 동물들의 관계는 _____ 투성이다.

Point 4 정답 풀이하기

① 감사
② 적의
③ 보호
④ 책임
⑤ 모순

→ 지문 전반부에서는 동물을 사랑하고 보살피는 사람들의 행동과 그에 따라 크게 발달한 산업에 대해 설명했고, 마지막 부분에서는 동물을 착취하여 죽이거나 학대하는 경우를 언급하고 있다. 두 가지가 서로 반대되는 현상이기 때문에, 인간과 동물의 관계가 '모순'으로 가득 차 있다는 것을 알 수 있다. 따라서 contradictions가 가장 적절하다.

01

다음 글의 빈칸에 들어갈 말로 가장 적절한 것을 고르시오. | 경찰대학 2018학년도 16번 |

A good rocket launch site has a few important characteristics. An unpopulated patch of land near an ocean is preferable, so no one gets showered with wayward bits of flaming metal. It's also nice if it's on the equator — like all spheres rotating on an axis, the Earth spins fastest in the middle, which provides rocket boosters with extra oomph. In other words, the best sites tend to be in remote, tropical locations. That such places are also often among the world's poorest gives many launches a _____ feel: billions of dollars in futuristic machinery rising up over rainforests and shantytowns.

[3점]

① majestic　　　　② fleeting　　　　③ catastrophic
④ universal　　　　⑤ counterintuitive

02

다음 글의 빈칸에 들어갈 말로 가장 적절한 것을 고르시오. | 경찰대학 2018학년도 21번 |

During the late nineteenth and early twentieth century, the Frenchman Joseph Pujol was famous for his ability to fart _____ by drawing air into his anus. He put on a stage show, calling himself Le Pétomane, which is French for "The Fartiste." Dressed formally, he would open with a rumble of cannon-fire farting. Various routines followed, most spectacularly an imitation of the 1906 San Francisco earthquake. He could rectally project a jet of water a distance of 15 feet (4.5 m) and to close, he sang a rhyme about a farm, punctuated with farts that sounded like different animal noises.

① at will　　　　② silently　　　　③ intermittently
④ to no avail　　　　⑤ inadvertently

03

다음 글의 빈칸 (A), (B)에 들어갈 말로 가장 적절한 것을 고르시오. | 경찰대학 2018학년도 23번 |

In order to promote social engagements among my students, I began encouraging them to bring food and drinks, as well as mats and cushions, to class. With these items, the classroom space is _____(A)_____ in terms of form and function as it gains a "social" aspect. During the reflection exercises, I observed how some students brought not just mats and cushions, but also pillows and stuffed toys as though they were attending a slumber party! When mats and cushions are not in use, students are seated in chairs strategically arranged around the tables, eating and drinking, as they discuss or review each other's drafts. As food and drinks are vital to any sociocultural discourse, they help enhance the social atmosphere, _____(B)_____ communal bonds, and heighten the students' shared identity.

	(A)		(B)
①	altered	······	cement
②	preserved	······	dissolve
③	altered	······	weaken
④	preserved	······	solidify
⑤	modified	······	loosen

04

다음 글의 빈칸에 들어갈 말로 가장 적절한 것을 고르시오. | 경찰대학 2017학년도 18번 |

Judges read statutes and the Constitution for help in devising or refining a rule of conduct that may have a significant impact on the welfare of the community. The community is not always willing to allow its choices to be controlled by what people who lived two centuries ago wrote into the Constitution. The procedure for amending the Constitution is, however, so cumbersome that the judges are under great pressure to use the interpretive process to keep the original document _____.

① obsolete   ② translated   ③ concise

④ flexible   ⑤ judgmental

다음 글의 빈칸 (A), (B)에 들어갈 말로 가장 적절한 것을 고르시오. | 경찰대학 2016학년도 24번 |

The use of tobacco illustrates what happened to what was almost an element of religion in Maya eyes when it became part of Spanish or, for that matter, all Western culture. Tobacco among the Maya had a very important role in religious life; it was an important element in the prevention and cure of disease, and in some parts was deified. Its pleasure-giving qualities seem in Maya eyes to have been quite _____(A)_____ to its other functions. Yet when tobacco was taken over by the Spaniards it was only as a commodity which gave pleasure to the individual; all the Maya ritualistic and community associations were shed. This process was in line with Spanish _____(B)_____ of those cultural elements of the conquered natives which they absorbed. Maize was no longer the beloved and sacred staff of life; it became for the conqueror an item of tribute and commercial transactions. Cacao suffered the same degradation.

[3점]

	(A)		(B)
①	relevant	……	authorization
②	relevant	……	enlightenment
③	identical	……	destruction
④	subordinate	……	inquisition
⑤	subordinate	……	secularization

06

다음 글의 빈칸 (A), (B)에 들어갈 말로 가장 적절한 것을 고르시오. | 경찰대학 2014학년도 23번 |

Earth's upper atmosphere — below freezing, nearly without oxygen, flooded by UV radiation — is no place to live. But last winter, scientists from the Georgia Institute of Technology discovered that billions of bacteria actually ____(A)____ up there. Expecting only a smattering of microorganisms, the researchers flew six miles above Earth's surface in a NASA jet plane. There, they pumped outside air through a filter to collect particles. Back on the ground, they tallied the organisms, and the count was staggering: 20 percent of what they had assumed to be just ____(B)____ or other particles was alive. Earth, it seems, is surrounded by a bubble of bacteria.

	(A)		(B)
①	thrive	……	dust
②	thrive	……	cells
③	thrive	……	germs
④	disintegrate	……	radiation
⑤	disintegrate	……	microorganisms

07

다음 글의 빈칸에 들어갈 말로 가장 적절한 것을 고르시오. | 경찰대학 2013학년도 20번 |

If forgiveness feels so good, why do so many people lug around so much resentment? One reason is that it may compensate for the _____ they experienced when they were hurt. "People may feel more in charge when they're filled with anger," points out Mart Grunte, author of *How to Forgive When You Don't Know How*. "But forgiving instills a much greater sense of power. When you forgive, you reclaim your power to choose. It doesn't matter whether someone deserves forgiveness; you deserve to be free."

① vengefulness ② unforgetfulness ③ powerlessness
④ indebtedness ⑤ guiltlessness

다음 글의 빈칸 (A), (B)에 들어갈 말로 가장 적절한 것을 고르시오. | 경찰대학 2013학년도 26번 |

In the last movie you saw, did you notice the soda the hero was drinking? How about the car the female star was driving? Actors in TV shows and in movies have always drunk sodas and driven cars, but now the name on the soda can and the emblem on the car are more ____(A)____. Advertisers have figured out that they can get exposure for their products by having them featured on TV and in movies. Movie studios have figured out that they can be paid for these so-called "embeds." So what? The next time you order soda X over Y, think about whether the last movie you saw featured X or Y. Have you been ____(B)____ by an advertiser and a movie producer?

	(A)		(B)
①	covert	......	dissuaded
②	covert	......	tricked
③	subliminal	......	manipulated
④	prominent	......	dissuaded
⑤	prominent	......	manipulated

다음 글의 빈칸에 들어갈 말로 가장 적절한 것을 고르시오. | 경찰대학 2012학년도 14번 |

Most men think of themselves as average-looking. Being average does not bother them; average is fine, for men. This is why men never ask anybody how they look. Their primary form of beauty care is to shave themselves, which is essentially the same form of beauty care that they give to their lawns. Women do not look at themselves this way. If I had to express, in three words, what I believe most women think about their appearance, those words would be: "not good enough." No matter how attractive a woman may appear to be to others, when she looks at herself in the mirror, she thinks: woof. Why do women have such _____? There are many complex psychological and societal reasons, by which I mean Barbie. Girls grow up playing with a doll proportioned such that, if it were human, it would be seven feet tall and weigh 81 pounds.

① low self-esteem   ② femininity   ③ high pride
④ reflection   ⑤ appearance

10

다음 글의 빈칸에 들어갈 말로 가장 적절한 것을 고르시오. | 경찰대학 2012학년도 15번 |

If we accept that we cannot prevent science and technology from changing our world, we can at least try to ensure that the changes they make are in the right directions. In a democratic society, this means that the public needs to have a basic understanding of science, so that it can make informed decisions and not leave them in the hands of experts. At the moment, the public has a rather _____ attitude toward science. It has come to expect the steady increase in the standard of living that new developments in science and technology have brought to continue, but it also distrusts science because it has no clear understanding of science.

① ambivalent ② hostile ③ sympathetic
④ amphibious ⑤ amorphous

11

다음 글의 빈칸 (A), (B)에 들어갈 말로 가장 적절한 것을 고르시오. | 경찰대학 2012학년도 19번 |

Because reading demands complex mental manipulations, a reader is required to concentrate far more than a television viewer. An audio expert notes that "with the electronic media it is openness that counts. Openness permits auditory and visual stimuli more direct access to the brain." It may be that a predisposition toward ___(A)___, acquired, perhaps, through one's reading experience, makes one an inadequate television watcher. But it seems far more likely that the reverse situation obtains: that a predisposition toward ___(B)___, acquired through years and years of television viewing, has influenced adversely viewers' ability to concentrate, to read, to write clearly.

	(A)		(B)
①	concentration	·····	involvement
②	concentration	·····	openness
③	manipulation	·····	involvement
④	manipulation	·····	closeness
⑤	stimulation	·····	openness

다음 글의 빈칸 (A), (B)에 들어갈 말로 가장 적절한 것을 고르시오. | 경찰대학 2012학년도 20번 |

Many people, both teens and adults, think that multitasking is the best way to accomplish a lot in a small amount of time. But scientific evidence says this isn't true. "When people try to perform two or more related tasks, either at the same time or quickly switching back and forth between them, they do a worse job on both of them," says David E. Meyer, director of the Brain, Cognition, and Action Laboratory at the University of Michigan. "They make more errors and it takes them much longer than if they worked on the tasks   (A)   ." He says it can take up to 400 percent longer to do a homework assignment if you're trying to do something else at the same time. Why is this? The human brain is simply not wired to process more than one complex task at a time. What your brain does instead is   (B)   tasks. So if you're listening to music and reading a book, your brain will concentrate on the music, and when that's finished, it will focus on taking in the information from the book. "But it takes a lot of mental energy for your brain to keep reorienting itself back to each task," Meyer says. The result is that neither task is done efficiently.

	(A)		(B)
①	simultaneously	······	prioritize
②	sequentially	······	prioritize
③	sequentially	······	perform
④	randomly	······	alienate
⑤	randomly	······	perform

다음 글의 빈칸 (A), (B)에 들어갈 말로 가장 적절한 것을 고르시오. | 경찰대학 2012학년도 21번 |

Television's contribution to family life has been an equivocal one. For while it has, indeed, kept the members of the family from _____(A)_____, it has not served to bring them together. By its domination of the time families spend together, it destroys the special quality that distinguishes one family from another, a quality that depends to a great extent on what a family does, what special rituals, game, recurrent jokes, familiar songs, and shared activities it accumulates. Yet parents have accepted a television-dominated family life so completely that they cannot see how the medium is involved in whatever problems they might be having. Even when families make efforts to control television, too often its very presence _____(B)_____ the positive features of family life.

(A) (B)
① gathering ····· maintains
② gathering ····· counterbalances
③ dispersing ····· enhances
④ dispersing ····· counterbalances
⑤ wavering ····· enhances

14

다음 글의 빈칸에 들어갈 말로 가장 적절한 것을 고르시오. | 경찰대학 2011학년도 14번 |

Chemical wastes have sometimes been dumped into a stream, put into drums and then buried, or simply abandoned in a huge chemical "graveyard." Sometimes they have been spread over deserted country roads by speeding "outlaw trucks" that simply open their valves and let the chemicals slowly spill out. Often this dumping is done by a small firm hired by the large company that has produced the chemical waste. No questions asked; the less the large firm's executives know, the better. But ignorance will no longer be a defense: Congress is now acting to make all parties _____, and to ensure that chemical wastes will be tracked from "the cradle to the grave."

① responsible   ② independent   ③ innocen
④ ready   ⑤ divided

다음 글의 빈칸에 들어갈 말로 가장 적절한 것을 고르시오. | 경찰대학 2011학년도 15번 |

It is said that a first novel is usually autobiographical, in the sense that the writer puts what he knows of life and people into it. But even a twentieth novel is also to some extend a personal document. For the novelist is still writing from his personal experience. The novelist will assert that his characters are purely imaginary, but this only means that they have come out of his own imagination, his own way of thinking about people, his own understanding of them. No novelist remains completely _____.

① hidden ② beautified ③ unrivalled
④ under control ⑤ beyond criticism

다음 글의 빈칸에 들어갈 말로 가장 적절한 것을 고르시오. | 경찰대학 2010학년도 19번 |

Listening to informal everyday conversation, it is possible to discern a number of ways in which people follow the principle of joke — namely, deviating happily from their normal linguistic behaviors, but only within very familiar linguistic territory. Generally, also, only one kind of deviation takes place at a time. If we are playing with sound effects, our grammar and vocabulary tend to stay stable. If we play with vocabulary or grammatical structure, we leave pronunciation _____. Such constraints are important, for without them the language can disintegrate to the point of unintelligibility, and the whole point of the game would be lost.

① intact ② extinct ③ soundless
④ loud ⑤ soft

17

다음 글의 빈칸에 들어갈 말로 가장 적절한 것을 고르시오.

| 경찰대학 2010학년도 20번 |

In the traditional economy, value comes from _____. The conventional icons of wealth — diamonds and gold — are precious because they are rare. And when something rare becomes plentiful — as oil did in the 1980s and 1990s — it loses value. But the logic of the network is exactly the opposite. Power and value now come from abundance. The more copies you make of your software, the more people you add to your network, the more powerful it becomes. This is why e-mail is supposed to be so powerful. It's the ultimate tool for easily creating these kinds of personal networks.

① competition   ② design   ③ advertising

④ demands   ⑤ scarcity

18

다음 글의 빈칸에 들어갈 말로 가장 적절한 것을 고르시오.

| 경찰대학 2010학년도 22번 |

As a twelve-year-old boy in 1942, I was excited about the promise of a professional baseball game on a hot summer night. My father, a hard worker with a heavy six-day-a-week schedule, had rushed through the day so he could take me to the game. As we approached the stadium, the wide doors near the right-field bleachers opened to accommodate the moving of a giant road scraper. Dozens of fans angled toward the opening, some commenting loudly about a free baseball game. Thinking this was our lucky night, I leaned toward the open doors, but my father's firm grip determined otherwise as we continued toward the ticket line. The action on the field and the winner of the game are long forgotten, but not the silent message of _____ from a loving and disciplined father.

① harmony   ② curiosity   ③ passion

④ hope   ⑤ honesty

01 다음 글의 빈칸 (A), (B)에 들어갈 말로 가장 적절한 것을 고르시오. | 사관학교 2018학년도 20번 |

Both internationally and domestically, tourism is seen as an effective means of transferring wealth and investment from richer, developed countries or regions to less developed, poorer areas. This ___(A)___ of wealth occurs, in theory, as a result of both tourist expenditures in destination areas and also of investment by the richer, tourist-generating countries in tourism facilities. In the latter case, developed countries are, in principle, supporting the economic growth and development of less developed countries by investing in tourism. However, it has long been recognized that the net retention of tourist expenditures varies considerably from one destination to another, while overseas investment in tourism facilities more often than not may lead to ___(B)___. This can be seen in profits often largely being diverted away from the less developed countries, potentially leaving them subject to the investor nations and corporations. [3점]

	(A)		(B)
①	concentration	······	exploitation and dependency
②	redistribution	······	exploitation and dependency
③	imbalance	······	prosperity and security
④	redistribution	······	prosperity and security
⑤	imbalance	······	collaboration and development

02

다음 글을 읽고, 빈칸에 들어갈 말로 가장 적절한 것을 고르시오. | 사관학교 2017학년도 15번 |

The producers of manufactured foods have an advantage over farmers because they buy the farm output and have flexibility over what ingredients to use and where to source them. For example, the manufactured food requires a sweetener, but not necessarily sugar derived from the sugarcane plant. It requires oil, yet not necessarily oil from corn. It requires a starch, but that could be derived from a potato or wheat or a number of other grains. The production of potato chips provides a good example of this _____ effect: Producers can fry the chips in whatever oil is cheapest at the moment of production. This illustrates why farmers are often at a disadvantaged position within the agrofood system.

① integration　　　　　　　② substitution
③ conservation　　　　　　 ④ simplification
⑤ overconsumption

다음 글을 읽고, 빈칸에 들어갈 말로 가장 적절한 것을 고르시오. | 수능 2010학년도 홀수형 24번 |

In this modern world, people are not used to living with discomfort. We expect immediate results and satisfaction. We want answers faster than they can be delivered. There is twenty-four-hour repair and round-the-clock shopping. If we are hungry, there is always food available, from microwave dinners to all-night grocery stores and restaurants. People no longer know how to wait, or even what waiting means. It is nice to have what you want when you want it, but the ability to delay satisfaction is important. _____ is clearly an important virtue, yet so many people stand in front of their microwaves thinking "Hurry up!"

① Ambition   ② Patience   ③ Honesty

④ Modesty   ⑤ Diligence

다음 글을 읽고, 빈칸에 들어갈 말로 가장 적절한 것을 고르시오. | 수능 2012학년도 홀수형 25번 |

What you do in the 15 to 30 minutes after eating your evening meal sends powerful signals to your metabolism. You'll set the stage for more vigor throughout the evening hours along with a weight-loss benefit if you stay _____ after your meal. Among many possible activities, walking is one of the easiest ways to get some minutes of exercise after a meal. In fact, research shows that if you walk after a meal, you may burn 15 percent more calories than if you walk the same time, distance, and intensity on an empty stomach.

① active   ② alone   ③ full
④ satisfied   ⑤ silent

Problem Solving Skills

주어진 지문을 바탕으로 빈칸에 가장 적절한 어구를 고르는 유형이다. 글의 내용과 흐름에 더불어 선택지를 정확히 이해하는 것이 중요하다.

- 주요 어휘를 통해 소재를 파악한다.
- 선택지의 내용을 정확히 이해한다.
- 빈칸을 포함하는 문장을 해석한다.

Example

다음 글의 빈칸에 들어갈 말로 가장 적절한 것을 고르시오. | 경찰대학 2017학년도 20번 |

❶ The coyote is a long, slim, sick and sorry-looking skeleton, with a gray wolf-skin stretched over it, a tolerably bushy tail that forever sags down, a furtive and evil eye, and a long, sharp face, with slightly lifted lip and exposed teeth. He has a general slinking expression all over. **❸** The coyote is a living, breathing _____. He is always hungry. He is always poor, out of luck, and friendless. The meanest creatures despise him, and even the fleas would desert him in a blink of an eye.

❷
❹
① epitome of wrath
② analogy of sadism
③ allegory of want
④ symbol of efficiency
⑤ metaphor of dominance

Vocabulary

sorry-looking 초라한   tolerably 웬만큼   bushy 털이 많은   sag 축 처지다   furtive 교활한, 은밀한   slink 살금살금 걷다   out of luck 운이 없는   mean 비열한   despise 경멸하다   flea 벼룩   desert 버리다   in a blink of an eye 눈 깜짝할 사이   epitome 전형   wrath 분노   analogy 유추   sadism 가학증   allegory 우화, 비유, 상징   want 결핍   metaphor 비유, 은유   dominance 지배

Let's Solve

Point 1 주요 어휘를 통해 소재 파악하기

coyote, sorry-looking skeleton, sag, hungry, poor, friendless, despise, desert

↓

코요테 + 초라한 뼈, 축 늘어지다 + 배고픈, 초라한, 친구가 없는, 경멸하다, 버리다

↓

코요테의 초라한 모습

Point 2 선택지의 내용 정확히 이해하기

• epitome of wrath (분노의 전형)
• analogy of sadism (가학성의 유추)
• allegory of want (결핍의 상징)
• symbol of efficiency (효율성의 상징)
• metaphor of dominance (지배의 은유)

Point 3 빈칸을 포함하는 문장 해석하기

• The coyote is a living, breathing _____.
  → 코요테는 살아 있는, 숨 쉬는 _____이다.

Point 4 정답 풀이하기

③ allegory of want
  → 코요테에 대한 글 전반의 묘사에 따르면 코요테는 늘 초라하고 외롭고, 결핍되어 보이는 존재이므로, 분노, 가학성, 효율성, 지배 보다는 결핍, 빈곤 등의 단어가 코요테를 설명하는 데 어울린다. 따라서 '결핍의 상징'이 가장 적절하다.

01 다음 글의 빈칸에 들어갈 말로 가장 적절한 것을 고르시오. | 경찰대학 2018학년도 18번 |

The doublespeak flows in the government, whether people in government are talking to the public or to each other. The Bureau of Land Management issued a press release in 1986 which began, "In a move to add administrative procedures regarding compliance with statutory requirements, the Department of the Interior's Bureau of Land Management (BLM) today published a rulemaking concerning federal coal leasee qualifications." This doublespeak simply means that the BLM intends to crack down on coal leases. An official in the Department of Commerce who had requested an increase in salary was told that "Because of the fluctuational predisposition of your position's productive capacity as juxtaposed to government standards, it would be monetarily injudicious to advocate an increment." In other words, _____.

① the pink slip
② all petitions suspended
③ no pay raise
④ no new openings
⑤ an early retirement

02 다음 글의 빈칸에 들어갈 말로 가장 적절한 것을 고르시오. | 경찰대학 2018학년도 20번 |

Like the iron cage of capitalism in which human needs are sacrificed to the exigencies of production, there is a sense in which science in the modern world has also become _____ : Within the domain of institutionalized science and academic scholarship, creativity and innovation must be accommodated to the specialized criteria of achievement that govern the various professional disciplines.

① a torchlight shining on intellectual avenues
② emancipated from bureaucratic demands
③ a fortress impregnable to any attack
④ vulnerable to moral issues at hand
⑤ the prison house of the mind

03

다음 글의 빈칸에 들어갈 말로 가장 적절한 것을 고르시오. | 경찰대학 2017학년도 19번 |

I go to the Grand Canyon, for instance. I take great pleasure in the views, and I write to you, my good friend, a postcard with the simple message "Wish you were here." What do I mean by this familiar saying? I mean that my pleasure in seeing the Grand Canyon would be greater if I could share it with you. I sense that, as good as it is to be at the Grand Canyon even by myself, it would be that much better if I could share the experience with you. In other words, my postcard is saying that friends share a common good in the special sense that our pleasure in seeing the Grand Canyon together _____ my pleasure and your pleasure in seeing the canyon on separate days.

① can be divided into
② is more than the sum of
③ equals the combined amount of
④ can last in memory longer than
⑤ does not have to take into consideration

04

다음 글의 빈칸에 들어갈 말로 가장 적절한 것을 고르시오. | 경찰대학 2017학년도 21번 |

When I was young I was very impressed by how food producers could fill jars with whole walnuts. Somehow they could crack the shells while leaving the nuts intact. Most of the times I tried it, I ended up with mixed pieces of shell and nut, managing to get the nut out whole only once every ten times or so. Later, however, I learned that although the manufacturers had a better success rate than I did, they often ended up with mixed shell and nut pieces, too. But I also learned that they did something else: they _____. On those occasions when they were successful, they'd take the whole nuts and stick them in a jar labeled "Whole Walnuts." And on the other occasions, they'd separate the nut pieces from the shell and stick them in a jar labeled "Walnut Pieces."

① selected their results ② bred special kinds of nuts
③ used brand new equipment ④ mixed up their nuts for sale
⑤ learned the lesson the hard way

05 다음 글의 빈칸에 들어갈 말로 가장 적절한 것을 고르시오.

We are such social animals that we are completely preoccupied with what others think about us. The social pressure to conform involves being valued by the group because, after all, most success is really defined by what others think. This preoccupation is all too evident in our modern celebrity culture, and especially with the rise of social networking, where normal individuals spend considerable amounts of time and effort _____. Over 1.7 billion people on this planet use social networking on the Internet to share and seek validation from others. When Rachel Berry, a character in a hit musical series about a performing-arts school, said "Nowadays being anonymous is worse than being poor," she was simply echoing our modern obsession with fame and our desire to be liked by many people — even if they are mostly anonymous or casual acquaintances.

① in pursuit of recognition from others
② to extend their domain of friendship
③ despite massive criticism by experts
④ prompting misgivings among the public
⑤ beyond the limits imposed by authorities

다음 글의 빈칸에 들어갈 말로 가장 적절한 것을 고르시오. | 경찰대학 2016학년도 20번 |

Let us unite profound knowledge of the art with the happiest talent for inventing lovely melodies, and then link both with the greatest possible originality, in order to obtain the most faithful picture of Mozart's musical genius. Nowhere in his work does one ever find an idea one had heard before: Even his accompaniments are always novel. One is, as it were, incessantly pulled along from one notion to another, without rest, so that admiration of the latest constantly swallows up admiration for what has gone before, and even by straining all one's forces one is scarcely able to absorb all the beauties that present themselves to the soul. If any fault had to be found with Mozart, it could surely be only this: That such _____ almost tires the soul and the effect of the whole is sometimes obscured thereby. But happy is the artist whose only fault lies in an all too great perfection.

① plethora of faith
② desolation of spirit
③ command of words
④ redundancy of melodies
⑤ abundance of beauty

다음 글의 빈칸에 들어갈 말로 가장 적절한 것을 고르시오. | 경찰대학 2016학년도 21번 |

A picture may be worth a thousand words, but for centuries words ruled the legal domain. Rhetoric, the art of using language, has always been the trademark of lawyers, and trials, especially in Common Law, have been widely understood as battles by words. Alas, all glory is doomed to pass and the second half of the nineteenth century saw a new mode of persuasion rising to dominance, driven by a new class of machine-made testimonies that threatened to turn words into an inferior mode of communicating facts. Ever alert and never involved, machines such as microscopes, telescopes, high-speed cameras and x-ray tubes purported to communicate richer, better, and truer evidence, often inaccessible otherwise to human beings. The emblem for this new type of mechanical objectivity was _____. "Let nature speak for itself," became the watchword, and nature's language seemed to be that of photographs and mechanically generated curves.

[3점]

① visual evidence   ② verbal testimony
③ legal terminology   ④ linguistic eloquence
⑤ subjective expression

다음 글의 빈칸에 들어갈 말로 가장 적절한 것을 고르시오.

| 경찰대학 2016학년도 23번 |

In modern Western society, religion's original explanatory role _____. The origins of the universe as we know it are now attributed to the Big Bang and the subsequent operation of the laws of physics. Modern language diversity is no longer explained by origin myths, such as the Tower of Babel or the snapping of the lianas holding the New Guinea ironwood tree, but is instead considered as adequately explained by observed historical processes of language change. Explanations of sunrises, sunsets, and tides are now left to astronomers, and explanations of winds and rain are left to meteorologists. Bird songs are explained by ethology, and the origin of each plant and animal species, including the human species, is left to evolutionary biologists to interpret.

① provides the basis for scientific theories

② has increasingly become usurped by science

③ has risen to give the best account of nature

④ evokes controversy on the adequacy of science

⑤ is reinforced by creationists and evolutionists alike

다음 글의 빈칸에 들어갈 말로 가장 적절한 것을 고르시오.

A pay increase is a public good in that workers who are not union members, or who choose not to strike in furtherance of the pay claim, are treated equally with union members and those who did strike. This creates opportunities for individuals to become free riders, reaping benefits without incurring the various costs that group membership may entail. This analysis is significant because it implies that there is no guarantee that the existence of a common interest will lead to the formation of an organization to advance or defend that interest. The pluralist assumption that all groups have some kind of political voice therefore _____. It is also argued that group politics may often empower small groups at the expense of large ones. A larger membership encourages free riding because individuals may calculate that the group's effectiveness will be little impaired by their failure to participate.

① is to be developed into a theory
② will not be on the critic's table
③ will face a loose competition
④ becomes highly questionable
⑤ gains more solid grounds

10

Not surprisingly, many contend that America was born with _____. American stories came from Europe. American myths weren't unique. It took Europeans to tell Americans who they were. The American form of government was borrowed from Europe. Until the great capitalists took their stand, Americans had no kings and queens and castles. No amount of wealth and power have erased this sense of voidness, hence millions of Americans travel to Europe each summer to catch and taste a touch of class. (Perversely the obverse is true, for millions of Europeans travel to America each summer to see the last frontier and see what Americans have done with the heritage Europeans gave them.) America is a mirror that Americans and Europeans continually look into, hoping to find 'that which, for whatever reasons, they have been conditioned to see.'

① an inferiority complex
② frontier ethics
③ a perfectionist spirit
④ a pragmatist mind
⑤ a silver spoon

11

다음 글의 빈칸에 들어갈 말로 가장 적절한 것을 고르시오. | 경찰대학 2015학년도 20번 |

With practice in meditation, the whole cognitive system is trained to build models which are less centered on a 'me,' on an imagined self who controls the body's actions and decides what to do. As this illusory self is gently let go, the world appears clearer and less distorted by its needs. Emotions arise and fall away. Ideas form and are let go. To be such a model is to feel free and flowing and able to laugh with the follies of our self-made illusions. It is quite unlike being a closely bound and defended model of self as most of us _____. [3점]

① succeed in doing so
② try to be
③ are allowed to go
④ are most of the time
⑤ depend on each other

12 다음 글의 빈칸에 들어갈 말로 가장 적절한 것을 고르시오. | 경찰대학 2015학년도 21번 |

Art, like most things, is more enjoyable when you know something about it. You can walk for hours through the Louvre admiring paintings, but the experience becomes much more interesting when someone knowledgeable is walking with you. A multimedia document can play the role of guide whether you're at home or in a museum. It can let you hear part of a preeminent scholar's lecture on a work. It can refer you to other works by the same artist or from the same period. You can even zoom in for a closer look. If multimedia reproductions and presentations make art more accessible and approachable, people who see the reproductions will _____. Exposure to the reproductions is likely to increase rather than diminish reverence for the real art and encourage more people to get out to museums and galleries.

① become more creative
② want to see the originals
③ depreciate the delicacy of art
④ elaborate on the multimedia works
⑤ deplete their crave for quality artworks

다음 글의 빈칸에 들어갈 말로 가장 적절한 것을 고르시오.

One of the things that distinguishes television news (and other so-called 'informational' shows) is that unlike drama, the news never attempts to _____. We are always acknowledged by being directly, openly addressed; when we look at television anchors, they look directly back at us, in a kind of staring contest that one might have with one's cat. In this contest, though, it is always we who blink or look away, out of boredom or, more likely, because any television presentation, even the news, is little more than part of an ongoing electronic and informational 'flow' that is only intermittently heeded. We look away, but the anchors never do, for this is the focus of their day, of their existence. We think we watch them, but they watch us, or a virtual us, even harder. [3점]

① fix its gaze on us, the viewers
② divert viewers' attention to trivialities
③ disguise our presence, our looking
④ presuppose our being, our watching
⑤ garner information on viewing figures

다음 글의 빈칸 (A), (B)에 들어갈 말로 가장 적절한 것을 고르시오. | 경찰대학 2015학년도 24번 |

In retrospect, it looks as if Massachusetts made ___(A)___ in 1994 when it let its two most prestigious and costly hospitals — Massachusetts General Hospital and Brigham & Women's Hospital, both affiliated with Harvard — merge into a single system known as Partners HealthCare. Investigations have documented that the merger gave the hospitals enormous market leverage to drive up health care costs in the Boston area by demanding high reimbursements from insurers that were unrelated to the quality or complexity of care delivered. Now, belatedly, Attorney General Martha Coakley is trying to ___(B)___ the hospitals with a negotiated agreement that would at least slow the increases in Partners' prices and limit the number of physician practices it can gobble up, albeit only temporarily. The experience in Massachusetts offers a cautionary tale to other states about the risks of merging big hospitals.

(A)	(B)
① a serious mistake	······ rein in
② a serious mistake	······ shut down
③ a big contribution	······ rein in
④ a big contribution	······ choke up
⑤ remarkable progress	······ shut down

다음 글의 빈칸에 들어갈 말로 가장 적절한 것을 고르시오. | 경찰대학 2014학년도 18번 |

Perhaps the greatest trap ever set for the human race was the coining of the phrase, "Having it all." Bandied about in speeches, headlines, and articles, these three words are intended to be aspirational but instead make all of us feel like we have fallen short. I have never met a person who has stated emphatically, "Yes, I have it all." Because no matter what any of us has, no one has it all. The antiquated rhetoric of "having it all" disregards the basis of every economic relationship: _____. All of us are dealing with the constrained optimization that is life, attempting to maximize our utility based on parameters like career, kids, and relationships, doing our best to allocate the resource of time. Due to the scarcity of this resource, therefore, none of us can "have it all," and those who claim to are most likely lying.

[3점]

① the idea of trade-offs
② the pursuit of happiness
③ the notion of absolute wealth
④ the belief of equal distribution
⑤ the law of supply and demand

다음 글의 빈칸에 들어갈 말로 가장 적절한 것을 고르시오.　　| 경찰대학 2014학년도 19번 |

Discussions of ecological sustainability typically focus on greenhouse gas emissions, bio-diversity, and other measurements of the natural world. They include economic and social trends in production or population. But they rarely feature time use. Yet patterns of human time use are key drivers of ecological outcomes. People combine time, money, and natural resources to carry out their daily lives and activities. Firms combine time, physical capital, and natural capital to create production. To a great extent, time and natural resources are substitutes for each other: doing things faster usually takes a greater toll on Earth. So _____ tend to have heavier ecological footprints and greater per capita energy use.

① misconceptions about time and money
② time-stressed households and societies
③ temporal constraints on resource development
④ time-honored notions of sustainable environments
⑤ cases where recycling resources takes greater time

다음 글의 빈칸에 들어갈 말로 가장 적절한 것을 고르시오.　　| 경찰대학 2014학년도 21번 |

I adore riding fast. I love descending in the drops and turns as if I've escaped the bounds of gravity. Though in pictures I might resemble a bike racer, I am the proud owner of ordinary mitochondria, although that does not stop me from occasionally trying to go as quickly as I can. I discover something significant about myself when I push myself that hard. I equally adore riding slow. When I sit upright and spin, I see the world and feel energized and connected to my community. I feel more complete as a cyclist when I pedal to the farmer's market in jeans or meander through the countryside. I am truly _____.

① on track to be a racer　　② moved by my own body
③ in love with my saddle　　④ convinced of my territory
⑤ at ease with my storytelling

다음 글의 빈칸에 들어갈 말로 가장 적절한 것을 고르시오.

| 경찰대학 2013학년도 21번 |

A train ticket buys a front-row seat to the greatest show on earth: the human condition. Without suffering jet lag or driver fatigue, the passenger is a privileged pilgrim upon whom no demands are made and for whom time is suspended for a while in the rocking of the rail car. He is a witness to life, which passes in vivid pictures outside the window; he glides through the small moments that make a day. Backyards, beautiful trees, city squares — nothing _____. If he chooses, he can step down at any stop along the way to enter what he is observing. There is no adventure quite like that promised by arriving in the middle of the night at a brightly lit station in a foreign country, where a customs officer is smoking a cigarette and a wagon stacked with milk cans rolls by.

① hurts scenic beauty
② adds to driver fatigue
③ reminds him of the past
④ improves quality amenities
⑤ escapes the view

다음 글의 빈칸에 들어갈 말로 가장 적절한 것을 고르시오.

| 경찰대학 2013학년도 22번 |

"At least 80 percent of our statues and sculptures are in bad shape from assaults ranging from acid rain to mechanical damage," said the director of conservation at the Culture Ministry. "Our roads were planned for horse carriages and now we have cars backing into statues." The Culture Ministry has increased the money for restoration in the belief that better-kept statues will reap an economic return from visitors. For Mr. Branda and his fellow restorers, however, the work is _____ than a passion to preserve the soul of the city. Sometimes the passion led them to go to extraordinary lengths. Many nights past midnight Mr. Branda and his colleagues clambered onto the windswept roof of St. Salvator Church at the foot of Charles Bridge to wrap and tie up seven 17th-century stone statues of the disciples. In the dark, a crane then plucked the statues for safekeeping and repair in a workshop.

① more repairs for making money
② less a desire to become famous
③ more research on architecture
④ less cosmetics for tourists
⑤ less a labor of love

다음 글의 빈칸에 들어갈 말로 가장 적절한 것을 고르시오. | 경찰대학 2013학년도 24번 |

One may ask: Why does the great fame of classical authors continue? The answer is that the fame of classical authors is entirely independent of the majority. Do you suppose that if the fame of Shakespeare depended on the man in the street, it would survive a fortnight? The fame of classical authors is originally made, and it is maintained, by a passionate few. Even when a first-class author has enjoyed immense success during his lifetime, the majority have never appreciated him so sincerely as they have appreciated second-rate men. He has always been _____. And in the case of an author who has emerged into glory after his death, the happy sequel has been due to the obstinate perseverance of the few.

① made equal to less-able authors by the elite reader
② indebted to the man in the street for his fame
③ reinforced by the ardour of the passionate few
④ distinguished naturally from second-rate men
⑤ inspired by the immense admiration from the public

다음 글의 빈칸에 들어갈 말로 가장 적절한 것을 고르시오. | 경찰대학 2013학년도 25번 |

If you could take a picture of the soul, it might look something like the black and white photos of certain slaves and soldiers during the Civil War. They are men and women who didn't have time to look at themselves or worry about their appearance, and it shows. Their faces transmit their passions and experiences and never betray their character. One photo shows a large man with a hard stare and a spiky beard that conveys fierceness. In another, a mother's wisdom can be seen in the dark circles under her eyes. A child's skepticism is visible in his small, taut mouth. Somehow, their situations allowed their spirits to develop in their faces, _____.

① mirroring one another's agony and despair
② complemented by their warm souls
③ forever seeking an inner peace
④ unlike in the bodies of modern men
⑤ untainted by luxury and self-examination

다음 글의 빈칸에 들어갈 말로 가장 적절한 것을 고르시오. | 경찰대학 2012학년도 16번 |

My father vehemently opposed my decision to work part-time during the school year at a local grocery store. He wanted me to stop pushing myself and to save work for later life. I agreed with him that quitting my job would have obvious advantages, but I also knew that there were other advantages to working that _____. For example, I enjoy the independence that comes with having my own income, small as it is. His lack of approval has made me angry, but I have listened to his objections, and we have again been able to reach a compromise. I have agreed to quit work at the first sign that I am pushing myself too hard or that my schoolwork is suffering. As a result, both his anger and mine have been effectively dissolved.

① interfered with my independence
② significantly contributed to my schoolwork
③ initially consolidated our relationship
④ eventually opposed my views
⑤ outweighed the disadvantages

다음 글의 빈칸에 들어갈 말로 가장 적절한 것을 고르시오. | 경찰대학 2012학년도 18번 |

To begin with, it was not the hapless victims of the Nazis who named their incomprehensible and totally unmasterable fate the "holocaust." It was the Americans who applied this artificial and highly technical term to the Nazi extermination of the European Jews. But while the event when named as mass murder most foul evokes the most immediate, most powerful revulsion, when it is designated by a rare technical term, we must first in our minds translate it back into emotionally meaningful language. Using technical or specially created terms instead of words from our common vocabulary is one of the best-known and most widely used distancing devices, _____. Talking about the "holocaust" permits us to manage it intellectually where the raw facts, when given their ordinary names, would overwhelm us emotionally — because it was catastrophe beyond comprehension, beyond the limits of our imagination.

① separating the technical from the intellectual terms
② separating the technical from the incomprehensible terms
③ separating the common from the comprehensible terms
④ separating the ordinary from the intellectual experience
⑤ separating the intellectual from the emotional experience

다음 글의 빈칸에 들어갈 말로 가장 적절한 것을 고르시오. | 경찰대학 2011학년도 16번 |

To truly understand a country and its culture, you have to be part of it. That's why, at KAB, we have local banks in more countries than anyone else. All of our offices around the world are staffed by local people. It's their insight that allows us to recognize financial opportunities invisible to outsiders. But these opportunities don't just benefit our local customers. Innovations and ideas are shared throughout the KAB network, so that everyone who banks with us can benefit. Think of it as local knowledge that just happens to _____.

① aim at metropolitan areas   ② enter the next decade
③ stop being universal   ④ cover the world
⑤ return home

다음 글의 빈칸에 들어갈 말로 가장 적절한 것을 고르시오.

| 경찰대학 2011학년도 18번 |

The extension of ethics, so far studied only by philosophers, is actually a process in ecological evolution. Its sequences may be described in ecological as well as in philosophical terms. An ethic, ecologically, is a limitation on freedom of action in the struggle of existence. An ethic, philosophically, is a differentiation of social form from anti-social conduct. These are two definitions of one thing. The thing has its origin in the tendency of interdependent individuals or groups to evolve modes of co-operation. The ecologist calls these symbioses. Politics and economics are advanced symbioses in which the original free–for-all competition has been replaced, in part, by _____.

① a new version of competitive activities
② recent trends in the survival of the fittest
③ co-operative mechanism with an ethical content
④ independence of individual members from the whole groups
⑤ striking similarities between ecological ethic and philosophical one

다음 글의 빈칸에 들어갈 말로 가장 적절한 것을 고르시오.

A close inspection of our countryside would reveal, thrown away over it, thousands of worthless refrigerators, "disposable" containers, broken toasters, mixers, microwave ovens, as well as unregulated food waste. Much of our waste problem is to be accounted for by the intentional unrepairability of the labor-savers and gadgets that we have become addicted to. This amounts to saying that much of the litter that now defaces our country is fairly directly caused by _____.
We have made a social ideal of minimal involvement in the growing and cooking of food. Nevertheless, the more dependent we become on the industries of food and cooking appliances, the more waste we are going to produce. The mess that surrounds us, then, must be understood as a symptom of a greater and graver problem: the centralization of our economy, the gathering of the productive property and power into fewer and fewer hands, and the consequent destruction of the local economies of household, neighborhood, and community.

① the food industry's attempt to recycle its own products
② the excessive consumption that devours natural resources
③ the innumerable local kitchen involved in the food economy
④ the careless behavior of most people who throw away usable products
⑤ the exclusion of most of us from active participation in the food economy

27 다음 글의 빈칸에 들어갈 말로 가장 적절한 것을 고르시오. | 경찰대학 2010학년도 18번 |

Most of us think that athletes would feel happier after winning a silver medal than a bronze in Olympic Games. But research suggests that those who win bronze medals are actually happier than those who win silver medals. The reason for this has to do with the way in which the athletes think about their performance. The silver medalists focus on the notion that if they had performed slightly better, then they would perhaps have won a gold medal. In contrast, the bronze medalists focus on the thought that if they had performed slightly worse, then they wouldn't have won anything at all. Psychologists refer to our ability to imagine what _____, rather than what actually did happen, as 'counter-factual thinking'.

① is happening
② has happened
③ had happened
④ is going to happen
⑤ might have happened

28 다음 글의 빈칸에 들어갈 말로 가장 적절한 것을 고르시오. | 경찰대학 2010학년도 21번 |

The *han'gul* alphabet devised by King Sejong was evidently inspired by the block format of Chinese characters and by the alphabetic principle of Mongol or Tibetan writing. Of course, King Sejong invented the forms of *han'gul* letters and several unique features of his alphabet, including the grouping of letters, the use of related letter shapes, and shapes of consonant letters that depict the position of the articulators. However, we can confidently attribute the *han'gul* to _____ rather than to independent invention in isolation.

① a personal creation
② a scientific system
③ a coincidental happening
④ idea diffusion
⑤ pure originality

29

A girl was asked by her teacher to use the word *cliché* in a sentence. She responded with this statement: "The boy returned home from the test with a *cliché* on his face." When the teacher asked her to explain herself, the girl pointed out that the dictionary defines *cliché* as "_____."

① an ingenious idiom　　　　② a worn-out expression
③ a newly-coined expression　④ a well-defined compound
⑤ a facial expression

30

Twenty years ago, psychology seemed a rather remote and sterile area to individuals interested in the full and creative use of the mind. At that time, the field harbored a trio of uninviting specializations: academic psychology, psychoanalysis, and behaviorism. There was academic psychology, featuring the use of contrived laboratory apparatus to study the perception of visual illusions or the memorization of long lists of nonsense syllables. Such lines of study bore little evident relationship to human beings engaged in thought. _____

_____

There was behaviorism, the approach that emerged from work with rats and pigeons. Behaviorists claimed that we act in the way we do because we are reinforced for doing so and, given their focus on overt activity, these scholars denied inner life — no thoughts, no fantasies, no aspirations.

① reasons why psychoanalysis died out
② description and flaw of psychoanalysis
③ strengths and influences of psychoanalysis
④ how psychoanalysis became popular until nowadays
⑤ comparing academic psychology with psychoanalysis

➔ 빈칸에 올 내용을 선택하는 문제이지만 선택지의 형태를 고려하여 UNIT 10으로 분류하였습니다.

01

다음 글을 읽고, 빈칸에 들어갈 말로 가장 적절한 것을 고르시오. | 사관학교 2017학년도 16번 |

Theodore Berger has achieved successes with _____ by using implanted chips to replace damaged parts of the hippocampus in rats. Berger and his team at the University of Southern California have succeeded in recording and transforming into computer code memories that have been stored for an extended period of time in the hippocampus of these animals. They had the rats perform a memory task. Then, they downloaded and transformed the memory of that task into digital code. Afterwards, they removed the section of the rats' hippocampus that carried these memories and replaced that bit of the brain with a special computer chip, onto which they reloaded the artificially stored memories. They found that the rats' memories could be fully restored using this technique.

*hippocampus: (뇌의) 해마상(狀) 융기

① long-term memory regeneration
② memory capacity increase
③ the selective distortion of memory
④ the deletion of traumatic memories
⑤ memory transfer speed enhancement

다음 글을 읽고, 빈칸에 들어갈 말로 가장 적절한 것을 고르시오. | 사관학교 2016학년도 16번 |

Time adds an important and necessary dimension to our understanding of the world and our place in it — it seems almost impossible to conceive of what our world of experience might be like in the absence of time; after all, events happen in time. This has resulted in physicists treating time, along with space, as a theoretical and an empirical primitive. The view that time constitutes, at some level, part of the physical fabric of the cosmos, and as such is physically real, accords with what I will term the common-place view of time. Most people believe in this view of time, a 'true' time, a time that actually exists in a physical sense; on this account, time _____, as reflected in the physical laws which govern the environment we inhabit. While time may itself be "imperceptible," it is nonetheless real, manifesting tangible consequences. Without time's "passage" there could be no succession and thus no experience of duration. [3점]

① passes with its own driving force
② cannot be perceived physically
③ is not dealt with in the field of physics
④ is objectively embedded in the external world
⑤ is an imaginary construct of human experience

다음 빈칸에 들어갈 말로 가장 적절한 것을 고르시오.

Long before Walt Whitman wrote *Leaves of Grass*, poets had addressed themselves to fame. Horace, Petrarch, Shakespeare, Milton, and Keats all hoped that poetic greatness would grant them a kind of earthly immortality. Whitman held a similar faith that for centuries the world would value his poems. But to this ancient desire to live forever on the page, he added a new sense of fame. Readers would not simply attend to the poet's work; they would be attracted to the greatness of his personality. They would see in his poems a vibrant cultural performance, an individual springing from the book with tremendous charisma and appeal. Out of the political rallies and electoral parades that marked Jacksonian America, Whitman defined poetic fame in relation to the crowd. Other poets might look for their inspiration from the goddess of poetry. Whitman's poet sought _____. In the instability of American democracy, fame would be dependent on celebrity, on the degree to which the people rejoiced in the poet and his work.

* rally: 집회 [3점]

① a refuge from public attention
② poetic purity out of political chaos
③ immortality in literature itself
④ the approval of his contemporaries
⑤ fame with political celebrities

04

다음 빈칸에 들어갈 말로 가장 적절한 것을 고르시오.

| 수능 2013학년도 홀수형 24번 |

Have you ever heard anyone say of a dog, "Well, he's very successful and lives in a beautiful house, but he's not very happy"? One reason most dogs are much happier than most people is that dogs aren't affected by external circumstances the way we are. I notice that even when it's pouring rain outside, my dogs, Blue and Celeste, are still excited to go for a walk. As soon as I open the front door to look outside, they're beside me in a flash, standing expectantly, ready for an adventure. I usually wait for a break in the downpour, and then we all dash out together. The fact that the ground is wet and there are mud puddles dotting the landscape _____. While I'm carefully picking my way around the wet spots, the dogs are joyfully splashing right through them. They aren't afraid to get their paws dirty.

① motivates us to take a shorter walk
② stirs great excitement in me
③ puts the dogs in trouble
④ means nothing to the dogs
⑤ makes me want to wander around

다음 빈칸에 들어갈 말로 가장 적절한 것을 고르시오. | 수능 2015학년도 홀수형 32번 |

My friend was disappointed that scientific progress has not cured the world's ills by abolishing wars and starvation; that gross human inequality is still widespread; that happiness is not universal. My friend made a common mistake — a basic misunderstanding in the nature of knowledge. Knowledge is amoral — not immoral but morality neutral. It can be used for any purpose, but many people assume it will be used to further *their* favorite hopes for society — and this is the fundamental flaw. Knowledge of the world is one thing; its uses create a separate issue. To be disappointed that our progress in understanding has not remedied the social ills of the world is a legitimate view, but _____. To argue that knowledge is not progressing because of the African or Middle Eastern conflicts misses the point. There is nothing inherent in knowledge that dictates any specific social or moral application.

[3점]

① to confuse this with the progress of knowledge is absurd
② to know the nature of knowledge is to practice its moral value
③ to remove social inequality is the inherent purpose of knowledge
④ to accumulate knowledge is to enhance its social application
⑤ to make science progress is to make it cure social ills

다음 빈칸에 들어갈 말로 가장 적절한 것을 고르시오.

| 수능 2016학년도 홀수형 32번 |

Some distinctions between good and bad are hardwired into our biology. Infants enter the world ready to respond to pain as bad and to sweet (up to a point) as good. In many situations, however, the boundary between good and bad is a reference point that changes over time and depends on the immediate circumstances. Imagine that you are out in the country on a cold night, inadequately dressed for the pouring rain, your clothes soaked. A stinging cold wind completes your misery. As you wander around, you find a large rock that provides some shelter from the fury of the elements. The biologist Michel Cabanac would call the experience of that moment intensely pleasurable because it functions, as pleasure normally does, to indicate the direction of _____. The pleasant relief will not last very long, of course, and you will soon be shivering behind the rock again, driven by your renewed suffering to seek better shelter.

*shiver: 떨다 [3점]

① a permanent emotional adjustment to circumstantial demands
② enhancing self-consciousness through physical suffering
③ a biologically significant improvement of circumstances
④ judging desirable and undesirable conditions impartially
⑤ a mentally pre-determined inclination for emotional stability

Problem Solving Skills

주어진 지문을 바탕으로 빈칸에 가장 적절한 어절을 고르는 유형이다. 빈칸이 포함된 문장이 주제문인 경우가 많으므로, 지문의 세부 내용을 통해 정답을 찾는다.

- 빈칸이 포함된 문장을 분석한다.
- 세부 내용을 통해 글의 주제를 파악한다.
- 선택지의 내용을 정확히 이해한다.

Example

다음 글의 빈칸에 들어갈 말로 가장 적절한 것을 고르시오. | 경찰대학 2017학년도 23번 |

2 Social learning in the form of stimulus or local enhancement plays an indispensable role in human development, as it does in the cognitive development of many social species. In some cases, however, human beings learn from one another in a qualitatively different way. Human beings sometimes engage in what we call cultural learning. In cultural learning, learners do not just direct their attention to the location of another individual's activity; rather, _____. It **1** is learning in which the learner is attempting to learn not from another, but through another.

3
① they rely on their own insight to understand others
② they extensively enhance the overall cultural flexibility
③ they attempt to see a situation the way the other sees it
④ they learn to second-guess the hidden agenda of others
⑤ they empower themselves to engage in autonomous learning

Vocabulary

stimulus 자극 indispensable 필수불가결한 cognitive 인지의 insight 통찰 extensively 광범위하게 second-guess 짐작하다 agenda 안건, 의제 empower ~에게 권한을 주다 autonomous 자율적인

Let's Solve

Point 1 빈칸이 포함된 문장 분석하기

• In cultural learning, learners do not just direct their attention to the location of another individual's activity; rather, _____.

→ 문장의 빈칸에는 '타인의 행동의 위치에 대한 주의'의 방식과 대비되는 방법인 문화적 학습에 관한 언급이 들어갈 것이다.

Point 2 세부 내용을 통해 글의 주제 파악하기

• Social learning in the form of stimulus or local enhancement
• however, human beings learn from one another in a qualitatively different way
• to learn not from another, but through another

인간은 타인에게서 배우는 사회적 학습뿐만 아니라
타인을 통해 배우는 문화적 학습으로도 성장한다.

Point 3 선택지의 내용 정확히 이해하기

① 그들은 다른 사람들을 이해하는 데 그들의 통찰력에 의존한다
　→ 통찰력에 대한 언급은 없다.

② 그들은 전반적인 문화적 유연성을 광범위하게 강화한다
　→ 문화적 학습에 대한 이야기이지 문화적 유연성에 대한 내용은 아니다.

③ 그들은 다른 사람들이 보는 방식으로 상황을 보려고 시도한다
　→ 학습자가 다른 사람에게서 배우려고 시도하는 것이 아니라 다른 사람을 통해서 배우려고 하는 것이 바로 문화적 학습이라고 하였으므로 빈칸에 가장 적절한 내용이다.

④ 그들은 다른 사람들의 숨은 의제를 미리 짐작하는 것을 배운다
　→ 숨은 의도를 추리해 내는 것에 대한 언급은 없다.

⑤ 그들은 스스로에게 자율적인 학습에 참여하도록 권한을 부여한다
　→ 학습의 자율성에 대한 언급은 없다.

01

다음 글의 빈칸에 들어갈 말로 가장 적절한 것을 고르시오. | 경찰대학 2018학년도 17번 |

_____. It is not uncommon to find analysts failing to distinguish between facts and inferences or operating on the assumption that an inference was a fact. It is not unusual to hear an analyst state that his conclusions followed "logically" from the evidence, even though generalizations arrived at inductively are not subject to logical proof. That different types of inquiry are subject to different types of "proof" is an alien concept to many researchers. And the common misuse of *infer* and *imply* reflects not only a lack of knowledge of terminology but also an unfamiliarity with underlying concepts of logic as well. [3점]

① Terminological confusion further aggravates flawed logic
② Logical thinking is a precursor to scientific research
③ Examples of the inability to reason well abound
④ Generalizations are subject to rigorous testing
⑤ Inductive logic prevails in academia

02

다음 글의 빈칸에 들어갈 말로 가장 적절한 것을 고르시오. | 경찰대학 2018학년도 19번 |

_____. We've found a hormone that can rejuvenate the muscles of elderly mice. Osteocalcin — a hormone secreted by bone — boosts the ability of muscles to burn fuel and generate energy, researchers at Columbia University discovered. When the team injected the hormone into old mice, the animals were able to run just as far as their younger counterparts, despite being up to a year older — a long time in mouse years. Old mice that did not receive the hormone ran about half as far. Osteocalcin levels decline with age in both mice and humans, and the team now plans to test whether the hormone can improve muscle function in people too. [3점]

① Wind back the clock   ② A stitch in time saves nine
③ Time waits for no man   ④ Give the elderly their due
⑤ Speed up the sands of time

03

다음 글의 빈칸에 들어갈 말로 가장 적절한 것을 고르시오. | 경찰대학 2017학년도 22번 |

In Hobbes's special vocabulary, "natural rights" are what we have already in the state of nature: a right to do anything that protects our vital motions. Hobbes derives the first law of nature from the fear of death in the state of nature. He derives the second law from the first: I should be willing to surrender my natural right to wage war against you, to the extent that you are reciprocally willing to surrender your natural right to wage war against me. _____. Each individually seeks "some Good to himself" in agreeing to surrender the rights of war, and this Good is "nothing else but the security of a man's person."

[3점]

① This mutual disarming is in each person's self-interest
② This shared indifference promotes the peace of the society
③ This reciprocal surrender of rights means fostering animosity
④ This social compromise is conducive to reinforcing the law of nature
⑤ This restraint of waging wars does do good to the weaker of the parties

04

다음 글의 빈칸에 들어갈 말로 가장 적절한 것을 고르시오. | 경찰대학 2016학년도 22번 |

A study in the *Journal of Consumer Psychology* explored the power of repetition by comparing all No. 1 songs on *Billboard*'s Hot 100 list from 1958 to 2012 with tracks that never broke past No. 90. Researchers observed that the simpler and more repetitive a song's lyrics were, the better its chance of reaching the top spot. Such songs also climbed the chart faster than less repetitive ones. This finding supports the theory of processing fluency, which suggests that the easier a message is to digest, _____. Musicians aren't the only ones in on the secret: Similar strategies are used in advertising, through slogans that saturate commercials, and even in comedy; stand-ups often loop to the same punch line throughout a set.

[3점]

① the more effort the brain has to exert
② the more positively people will react to it
③ the higher the likelihood of tuning out the message
④ the less the chances of people singing after the song
⑤ the less likely people will decode the hidden message

다음 글의 빈칸에 들어갈 말로 가장 적절한 것을 고르시오. | 경찰대학 2015학년도 22번 |

_____, he might have lived longer. According to legend, many evil portents preceded his death, among them, according to Plutarch, "the lights in the heavens, the noises heard in the night, and the wild birds which perched in the forum." And, famously, the dictator had been warned by a fortuneteller to "Beware the Ides of March." The morning of his last day, his wife, Calpurnia, told him she'd had terrible dreams during the night; weeping, she begged him not to go to the Senate. Caesar was alarmed, says Plutarch, "for he never before discovered any womanish superstition in Calpurnia." He decided to heed her warning, but changed his mind when one of the conspirators against him, Decimus Brutus, hinted that the Senate planned that day to declare him king of all the Roman provinces outside Italy.

① Had Caesar believed in signs and omens
② Unless Calpurnia had gone to hear the prophecy
③ Had Caesar ignored Calpurnia's womanish superstition
④ As long as Caesar had not listened to the fortunetellers
⑤ Had the Senate declared Caesar king of all the Roman provinces

다음 글의 빈칸에 들어갈 말로 가장 적절한 것을 고르시오.

Plato in his *Republic* criticizes the poets for corrupting the young. Also, he says that an ideal republic controls music even more tightly than it controls poetry and plays. Musical rhythms, Plato remarks, have great capacity to "insinuate themselves into the inmost part of the soul." Sometimes this is for the good, as when music softens the disposition of a citizen made too rough by time in the gymnasium. But at other times, taste in music threatens the moderation we seek in spirit and sets ferocity on fire. _____ if the republic is to train its young citizens well.

*insinuate: (사상 등을) 은근히 심어주다 [3점]

① Aesthetics must defer to politics
② Gymnastics must accompany poetics
③ Moderation must yield to military ferocity
④ Individual taste must prevail over common good
⑤ Citizens must not be indulged in one kind of music

다음 글의 빈칸에 들어갈 말로 가장 적절한 것을 고르시오.

Exactly how a gene increases the probability of a given behavior is a complex issue. Some genes control brain chemicals, but others affect behavior indirectly. Suppose your genes make you unusually attractive. As a result, strangers smile at you and many people want to get to know you. Their reactions to your appearance may change your personality, and if so, the genes altered your behavior by altering your environment. For another example, imagine a child born with genes promoting greater than average height, running speed, and coordination. The child shows early success at basketball, and soon spends more and more time playing basketball. Soon the child spends less time on other pursuits — watching television, playing chess, or collecting stamps. Thus the measured heritability of many behaviors might depend partly on genes that affect leg muscles. This is a hypothetical example, but it illustrates the point: _____. [3점]

① Success depends heavily on genetic formulas
② Genes influence behavior in roundabout ways
③ Personality is a matter of genes and behavior
④ Environmental adaptation is the key to evolution
⑤ Natural selection is stimulated by behavioral cues

다음 글의 빈칸에 들어갈 말로 가장 적절한 것을 고르시오. | 경찰대학 2013학년도 23번 |

Ben Jonson, a well-known playwright and seventeenth-century contemporary of John Donne, wrote that while "the first poet in the world in some things," Donne nevertheless "for not keeping of an accent, deserved hanging." Donne's generation admired the depth of his feeling, but was puzzled by his often irregular rhythm and obscure references. It was not until the twentieth century and modern movements that celebrated emotion and allusion that _____. Writers such as T.S. Eliot and W.B. Yeats admired the psychological intricacies of a poet who could one moment flaunt his earthly dalliances with his mistress and the next, wretched, implore God to "bend your force, to break, blow, burn, and make me new."

① Donne really began to be appreciated
② the forgotten works of Donne were rewritten
③ Jonson admitted that he had misjudged Donne
④ Donne's unclear references became more obscure
⑤ rhythm in poetry became more commonly practiced

다음 글의 빈칸에 들어갈 말로 가장 적절한 것을 고르시오. | 경찰대학 2012학년도 17번 |

The theory of multiple intelligences (MI) challenges traditional ideas about intelligence. It also questions the value of intelligence tests. MI researchers point out that traditional teaching and testing focus only on two of the seven kinds of intelligences that people possess — language and logic skills. So children who don't learn in a style that depends on language and logic are called inadequate. However, according to Thomas Armstrong, author of *Seven Kinds of Smart*, the children are fine but the teaching methods are inadequate. "In traditional education, we try to get students to learn in our way. On the contrary, we need to remake the way we teach so that _____," he explains. "We need to recognize that different children learn in different ways and that all ways of learning are okay. Then we will really be in the business of education," he adds.

① it can fit students
② they can answer questions better
③ we can choose our own teaching methods
④ they can develop language and logic skills
⑤ learning theories can contribute to education

다음 글의 빈칸에 들어갈 말로 가장 적절한 것을 고르시오. | 경찰대학 2011학년도 17번 |

There was a gray-eyed man that I at once hoped would buy me. I knew by the way he handled me that he was used to horses. He offered to buy me, but the sum was too low, and he was refused. A very hard, loud-voiced man came after him, and I was dreadfully afraid he would have me, for he offered a better price. But the gray-eyed man stroked me, saying "Well, I think we should suit each other," and _____. "Done," said the dealer.

① he raised his bid   ② he lowered his voice
③ he cancelled his offer   ④ I roared for mercy
⑤ I suggested another deal

다음 글의 빈칸에 들어갈 말로 가장 적절한 것을 고르시오. | 경찰대학 2011학년도 19번 |

Suburbia today is remarkably diverse. Affluent commuter suburbs have been joined by working-class suburbs, suburbs of condominiums, and industrial-park suburbs. Historically suburbs were considered "sub" because _____. Suburban residents had to commute to the central city in order to earn their livelihood. That no longer holds; suburbs are increasingly becoming major centers of employment. Census figures reveal that as of 1970, in the fifteen largest metropolitan areas, a full of 72 percent of workers who lived in the suburbs also worked in suburban areas. Our image of the suburbs, obviously, has not caught up with reality.

① they consisted of working-class neighbors
② they were not economically self-supporting
③ they did not have sufficient facilities for leisure
④ most people did not want to spend money in them
⑤ their landscape was different from that of the central city

History seeks to link the past with the future in a continuous line along which the historian himself is constantly moving. It is clear that we should not expect to extract from history any absolute judgments, either on the past or on the future. Such judgments it is not in its nature to give. All human judgment, like all human action, is involved in the logical dilemma of determinism and free will. The human being is indissolubly bound, in both his actions and his judgments, by a chain of causation reaching far back into the past; yet _____ at a given point — the present — and so alter the future.

① he is expected to refasten the chain
② he has a qualified power to break the chain
③ it is beyond his natural ability to mould a new chain
④ it is virtually impossible to lift the restrictions of the chain
⑤ he has a moral responsibility to keep away from a stronger chain

다음 글의 빈칸에 들어갈 말로 가장 적절한 것을 고르시오.

A front-page story in a St. Louis newspaper reported an incident in which two men were hospitalized after a fistfight. What had happened was that the driver of an automobile stopped for a red light at a main intersection. A man on the sidewalk called out, "Hey, mister, your left front tire is going flat." The driver got out, looked at the tire, and called to his benefactor, "Thanks for being a Good Samaritan!" Whereupon the pedestrian leapt off the curb and started pounding the driver with his fists, shouting, "You can't call me a dirty name!" The shocked driver struck back, and the result was that both men ended up in the hospitals — all because one of them thought that _____.

① a Samaritan was a dirty name
② the other called him by "mister"
③ the pedestrian lied to him on purpose
④ the driver did not appreciate his kindness
⑤ the driver didn't keep the bus in a clean condition

01

다음 글을 읽고, 빈칸에 들어갈 말로 가장 적절한 것을 고르시오. | 사관학교 2011학년도 18번 |

Primitive peoples' lives are commonly thought to be harsh — their existence dominated by the incessant quest for food. In fact, some primitives do little work. By contemporary standards, we would have to judge them very lazy. If the Kapauka of Papua work one day, they do no labor on the next. Kung Bushmen put in only two and a half days per week and six hours per day. In the Sandwich Islands of Hawaii, native inhabitants only work for four hours per day. The key to understanding why they do not increase their work effort to get more things as we do is that _____. In the race between wanting and having, they have kept their wants low — and in this way, ensure their own kind of satisfaction. They are materially poor by contemporary standards, but in at least one aspect — time — we have to count them as richer.

① they have limited desires
② they live in great material wealth
③ their productivity is relatively low
④ they don't have a concept of time
⑤ they exchange goods with each other

다음 글을 읽고, 빈칸에 들어갈 말로 가장 적절한 것을 고르시오.　| 사관학교 2010학년도 18번 |

In an orchestra, brass players are often told that _____. Brass instruments are made of yards of tubing, coiled up like snakes. If you unrolled all the tubing in a typical French horn, for example, it would be seventeen feet in length. That's as long as three adults of average height standing on each other's shoulders! As you blow into a brass instrument, your air enters the tubing, snakes all the way through its length, deposits some spit on the inside of the instrument, and emerges as a sound at the other end. That's bound to take some time. No wonder the sound comes out a bit late. Good brass players often find that they need to compensate for this time lag to avoid playing behind the other musicians.

[3점]

① their instruments need to be replaced more often
② they should play earlier than the other players
③ their instruments resemble animal shapes
④ they should not avoid the other players
⑤ they have to purchase expensive brass

다음 빈칸에 들어갈 말로 가장 적절한 것을 고르시오. | 수능 2011학년도 홀수형 25번 |

One of the little understood paradoxes in communication is that the more difficult the word, the shorter the explanation. The more meaning you can pack into a single word, the fewer words are needed to get the idea across. Big words are resented by persons who don't understand them and, of course, very often they are used to confuse and impress rather than clarify. But this is not the fault of language; it is the arrogance of the individual who misuses the tools of communication. The best reason for acquiring a large vocabulary is that _____. A genuinely educated person can express himself tersely and trimly. For example, if you don't know, or use, the word 'imbricate,' you have to say to someone, 'having the edges overlapping in a regular arrangement like tiles on a roof, scales on a fish, or sepals on a plant.' More than 20 words to say what can be said in one.

① it keeps you from being long-winded
② you can avoid critical misunderstandings
③ it enables you to hide your true intentions
④ it makes you express yourself more impressively
⑤ you can use an easy word instead of a difficult one

다음 빈칸에 들어갈 말로 가장 적절한 것을 고르시오.

Interestingly, people are more overconfident when they feel like they have control of the outcome — even when this is clearly not the case. For example, it is documented that if people are asked to bet on whether a coin toss is heads or tails, most bet larger amounts if the coin is yet to be tossed. If the coin is tossed and the outcome is concealed, people will offer lower amounts when asked for bets. People act as if _____. In this case, control of the outcome is clearly an illusion. This perception occurs in investing, as well. Even without information, people believe the stocks they own will perform better than stocks they do not own. However, ownership of a stock only gives the illusion of having control of the performance of the stock.

[3점]

① the amount of the bet will influence the outcome

② their involvement will somehow affect the outcome of the toss

③ there is a parallel between a coin toss and stock investments

④ their illusion will not disappear even after the coin is tossed

⑤ they can predict the outcome with credible information

Problem Solving Skills

글 전체의 내용을 하나의 문장으로 압축할 수 있는지 묻는 유형이다. 제시되는 요약문은 글의 주제문에 해당하므로 지문을 읽으며 주제를 파악하는 데 집중한다.

• 요약문을 통해 글의 방향을 예측한다.
• 주요 내용을 통해 글의 요지를 파악한다.

Example

다음 글의 내용을 한 문장으로 나타낼 때, 빈칸 (A)와 (B)에 들어갈 말로 가장 적절한 것은?

| 경찰대학 2018학년도 33번 |

❷ In some cases, researchers simply observe animals in nature as a function of different times of day, different seasons of the year, changes in diet, and so forth. These procedures raise no ethical problems. In other studies, however, animals have been subjected to brain damage, electrode implantation, injections of drugs or hormones, and other procedures that are clearly not for their own benefit. Anyone with a conscience (including scientists) is bothered by this fact. Nevertheless, experimentation with animals has been critical to the medical research that led to methods for the prevention or treatment of polio, diabetes, measles, smallpox, massive burns, heart disease, and other serious conditions. Most Nobel prizes in physiology or medicine have been awarded for research conducted on nonhuman animals. The hope of finding methods to treat or prevent AIDS, Alzheimer's disease, stroke, and many other disorders depends largely on animal research. In many areas of medicine and biological psychology, research would progress slowly or not at all without animals.

⬇

❶ Though some _____(A)_____ studies conducted on animals, unlike simple observational research, raise ethical issues, they are _____(B)_____ in making progress in various medical fields.

	(A)		(B)
❸	① experimental	·····	instrumental
	② statistical	·····	successful
	③ field	·····	critical
	④ developmental	·····	plausible
	⑤ laboratory	·····	negligible

Vocabulary

electrode 전극 implantation 이식 plausible 그럴듯한, 말주변이 좋은 instrumental 중요한 statistical 통계적인
developmental 개발상의 laboratory 실험실 negligible 무시해도 될 정도의

Let's Solve

Point ❶ 요약문을 통해 글의 방향 예측하기

• Though some _____(A)_____ studies conducted on animals, unlike simple observational research, raise ethical issues, they are _____(B)_____ in making progress in various medical fields.

→ 동물대상 연구가 가져오는 윤리적 논쟁과 의학적 발전에 관한 글이다.

Point ❷ 주요 내용을 통해 글의 요지 파악하기

• animals have been subjected to brain damage, ~ that are clearly not for their own benefit

→ 연구 대상 동물들은 그들의 이익을 위한 것이 아닌 절차를 겪음

• Anyone with a conscience is bothered by this fact

→ 윤리적 문제를 일으킬 수 있음

• experimentation with animals has been critical to the medical research ~ and other serious conditions

→ 동물 실험이 다양한 의학적 연구에 기여해 왔음

• In many areas of medicine and biological psychology, research would progress slowly or not at all without animals

→ 의학과 생물심리학 발전에 동물이 필수적임

↓   ↓

동물 실험은 윤리적으로 문제가 있지만 의학 발전에 필수적이다

Point ❸ 정답 풀이하기

• (A): 지문에 나타난 동물을 이용한 연구는 뇌손상, 전극 삽입, 약물 주입, 관찰 등이 있는데 요약문에서 관찰 방식을 제외하고 있으므로 빈칸에는 나머지 연구방식들을 포괄하는 '실험적인'이 가장 적절하다.

• (B): 글 후반부에서 동물 실험의 비윤리성에도 불구하고 동물 없이는 의학, 생물 심리학 발전이 더뎌지거나 불가능할 수 있다고 말하고 있으므로, 빈칸에는 '중요한'이 가장 적절하다.

→ 따라서 (A)에는 experimental이 들어가는 것이 적절하고, (B)에는 instrumental이 들어가는 것이 자연스럽다.

01

다음 글의 내용을 한 문장으로 나타낼 때, 빈칸 (A)와 (B)에 들어갈 말로 가장 적절한 것은?

| 경찰대학 2017학년도 34번 |

Just thinking that a particular brand's products are especially effective may have a kind of placebo effect, researchers have found. In a series of studies, participants received nearly identical tools for skill tests in golf and math. The only difference: Half of the putters bore Nike labels, while half of the earplug sets given to test takers were said to have been made by 3M. Those who thought they were using a Nike putter indeed needed fewer putts, on average, to sink a ball, and participants who thought they had 3M earplugs during the math test answered more questions correctly. It was also found that those with the lowest initial confidence in their abilities seemed to gain the most from the subtle upgrade.

⬇

Studies showed that, on average, the performance of participants on tests was _____(A)_____ when they believed they were using more _____(B)_____ brands.

	(A)		(B)
①	enhanced	⋯⋯	generic
②	enhanced	⋯⋯	athletic
③	enhanced	⋯⋯	prominent
④	diminished	⋯⋯	popular
⑤	diminished	⋯⋯	ordinary

다음 글의 내용을 한 문장으로 나타낼 때, 빈칸 (A)와 (B)에 들어갈 말로 가장 적절한 것은?

| 경찰대학 2016학년도 34번 |

Average life expectancy has risen steadily for decades and except for cancers caused by smoking and exposure to the sun, cancer death rates have dropped or remained relatively stable. Yet surveys have repeatedly shown that people have never been more fretful about their health. "People just seem to see the apocalypse everywhere they turn," said Bruce Ames, who was among the first to point out that natural pesticides are at least 10,000 times more common than those made by man. "There are some important risks, of course. But everyone should just relax a bit and have some fun." At times that seems hard to do. Provocative warnings about too much cholesterol, not enough vitamin A and what can happen to people who do not exercise enough have become part of the tapestry of American life. To some, cancer seems hidden in every meal.

↓

Although Americans have become ____(A)____ than ever, they seem to be experiencing high levels of ____(B)____ about their health.

	(A)		(B)
①	healthier	······	anxiety
②	trendier	······	anxiety
③	healthier	······	hope
④	trendier	······	concern
⑤	slimmer	······	concern

다음 글의 내용을 한 문장으로 나타낼 때, 빈칸 (A)와 (B)에 들어갈 말로 가장 적절한 것은?

| 경찰대학 2015학년도 34번 |

Cinema's status as a spatiotemporal medium owed as much to its historical context as to its technologically granted abilities. Debuting at the end of the nineteenth century, the moving picture stood as the culmination of a series of inventions that emphasized the capacities of technology to collapse conventional boundaries of time and space. The cinema operated as part of a continuum that stretched from the telegraph and the telephone (which had enabled communication to take place between two locations separated by considerable distance), through to the locomotive and automobile (which allowed their passengers to traverse substantial areas with previously unequalled speed, thereby collapsing travel time), and the phonograph and photograph (which had frozen time through the capturing of sound and image, respectively, from reality via a photoelectric process). Cinema was the latest of inventions expanding the traditional sense of how to represent and conceptualize space and time.

⬇

The ___(A)___ of cinema in history represents the culmination of technological achievements that helped ___(B)___ the boundaries of time and space.

	(A)		(B)
①	advent	⋯⋯	condense
②	advent	⋯⋯	surpass
③	waning	⋯⋯	condense
④	waning	⋯⋯	surpass
⑤	revival	⋯⋯	collapse

다음 글의 내용을 한 문장으로 나타낼 때, 빈칸 (A)와 (B)에 들어갈 말로 가장 적절한 것은?

| 경찰대학 2014학년도 34번 |

For hundreds of years in Europe, religious art was almost the only type of art that existed. Churches and other religious buildings were filled with paintings that depicted people and stories from the Bible. Although most people couldn't read, they could still understand biblical stories in the pictures on church walls. By contrast, one of the main characteristics of art in the Middle East was its absence of human and animal images. By Islamic law, artists are not allowed to copy human or animal figures except on small items for daily use such as rugs and bowls. Thus, on palaces, mosques, and other buildings, Islamic artists have created exclusive arabesques — decoration of great beauty with shapes such as circles, squares, and triangles.

⬇

European art differed from Middle Eastern art in that the former contained ____(A)____ images, whereas the latter used ____(B)____ patterns.

	(A)		(B)
①	sacred	······	animal
②	secular	······	non-secular
③	religious	······	circular
④	plain	······	exquisite
⑤	biblical	······	geometric

다음 글의 내용을 한 문장으로 나타낼 때, 빈칸 (A)와 (B)에 들어갈 말로 가장 적절한 것은?

| 경찰대학 2013학년도 38번 |

Perhaps you are one of millions of people who depend on the television to keep you company, or you may have caught yourself actually talking to your computer. But all of your relationships with machines may not be love relationships. You may also hate certain machines — the computer that has a mind of its own, the car that won't start, the toaster that always burns your toast, the vending machine that robs you of your money. Although machines are usually designed to make your life easier, they may also, on occasion, make your life frustrating if not miserable. Machines certainly contribute to much that is bad in our lives: Guns contribute to the high crime rate; automobiles increase air pollution and cause accidents; and machines in general often put people out of work. Yet no one is eager to do without machines. Having become used to them, to the convenience and entertainment and stimulation they provide, people cannot imagine a life in which machines do not play a major role.

⬇

Machines may sometimes be troublesome, frustrating, and even ____(A)____; once accustomed to the advantages they provide, however, you would feel that they are almost ____(B)____ to your daily life.

	(A)		(B)
①	addictive	······	superfluous
②	disappointing	······	inessential
③	harmful	······	superfluous
④	addictive	······	indispensable
⑤	harmful	······	indispensable

다음 글의 내용을 한 문장으로 나타낼 때, 빈칸에 들어갈 말로 가장 적절한 것은?

| 경찰대학 2012학년도 29번 |

If the language of literary work is quite straightforward and simple, this may be helpful but is not in itself the most crucial yardstick in choosing literary works for foreign language learning. Interest, appeal, and relevance are all more important. In order for us to justify the additional time and effort which will undoubtedly be needed for readers to come to grips with a work of literature in a language not their own, there must be some special incentives involved: enjoyment, suspense, and a fresh insight into issues which are felt to be close to the heart of people's concerns. All these are incentives which can lead readers to overcome enthusiastically the linguistic obstacles that might be considered too great in less involving material.

The crucial factor in choosing literary works for foreign language learning is not just the level of language but whether the works _____.

① help the readers learn to overcome linguistic obstacles
② tell the readers something about fundamental human issues
③ justify the readers' time and effort spent reading them
④ provide a fresh insight into foreign language learning
⑤ stimulate the readers' involvement by providing incentives

다음 글의 내용을 한 문장으로 나타낼 때, 빈칸에 들어갈 말로 가장 적절한 것은?

| 경찰대학 2011학년도 27번 |

E-mail deepened my friendship with Ralph. Though his office was next to mine, we rarely had extended conversations because he is shy. Face to face he mumbled so, I could barely tell he was speaking. But when we both got on e-mail, I started receiving long, self-revealing messages; we poured our hearts out each other. A friend discovered that e-mail opened up that kind of communication with her father. He would never talk much on the phone, but they have become close since they both got online. Why, I wondered, would some men find it easier to open up on e-mail? It's a combination of the technology and the obliqueness of the written word, just as many men will reveal feeling in dribs and drabs while riding in the car or doing something, which they could never talk about sitting face to face.

*in dribs and drabs: 조금씩

In e-mail communications, people feel freer to talk because it guarantees _____.

① the freedom of selecting topics
② lengthy and informal encounters
③ a smaller amount of responsibility
④ indirect contacts with the people one writes to
⑤ manifest identities of those who send messages

다음 글의 내용을 한 문장으로 나타낼 때, 빈칸 (A)와 (B)에 들어갈 말로 가장 적절한 것은?

| 경찰대학 2011학년도 29번 |

For more than a thousand years the Japanese have written the *tancho*, a red-crowned crane, into poems and folktales. They have painted it and made sculptures of it. They have revered it as a symbol of long life, happiness, and good luck. From its life habits they have drawn phrases and metaphors to describe their own behaviors. They imitated it and tried to dance as it dances. Most of all, they have made it into an icon and put its image everywhere, so that this extremely rare bird is, ironically, seen throughout Japan — on teacups and trays and fans, on lampposts, on wedding cards, on the backs of thousand-yen notes, and the tail fins of jets.

⬇

Japanese people have long tradition of _____(A)_____ the *tancho*, a red-crowned crane, and their attitude toward it is widely reflected in their _____(B)_____ lives.

	(A)		(B)
①	rearing	······	everyday
②	rearing	······	religious
③	cherishing	······	everyday
④	cherishing	······	traditional
⑤	admiring	······	traditional

다음 글의 내용을 한 문장으로 요약하고자 한다. 빈칸 (A)와 (B)에 들어갈 말로 가장 적절한 것은?

| 경찰대학 2010학년도 43번 |

When we observe flattened "paper cut-out" Egyptian wall painting or the stilted, wooden madonna and child of the mediaeval master Cimabue, we confront artwork that strikes us as being schematic and unrealistic. Then, with the arrival of the Renaissance, we encounter a clear contrast, one exemplified by Giotto's madonna. A march had begun towards increasing realism, a march that continued from the fifteenth to the nineteenth century. By the time the English artist John Constable painted "Wivenhoe Park" in the early nineteenth century, audiences had begun to encounter landscapes and scenes that rivaled photographs in their degree of depicted realism.

⬇

A tour through the ___(A)___ of art reveals a great progression toward ___(B)___ in the past three millenia.

	(A)		(B)
①	materials	⋯⋯	excellence
②	museums	⋯⋯	accuracy
③	history	⋯⋯	realism
④	books	⋯⋯	copying
⑤	techniques	⋯⋯	imitation

10

다음 글의 결론을 한 문장으로 나타낼 때, 빈칸 (A)와 (B)에 들어갈 말로 짝지은 것으로 가장 적절한 것은?

| 경찰대학 2008학년도 39번 |

An understanding of basic psychology can help a person in many ways–but there are limits to what psychology can do for you. It is one thing to understand the origins of offensive or antisocial behavior and another thing to excuse it. Knowing that your short temper is a result, in part, of your unhappy childhood doesn't give you a green light to yell at your family. Nor does scientific neutrality mean that a society must be legally or morally neutral. A better understanding of the origin of child beating may help us to reduce child abuse and treat offenders, but we can still hold child beaters accountable for their behavior.

⬇

Although knowledge of ____(A)____ may help us understand certain behaviors, it does not relieve us of ____(B)____ of our actions.

	(A)		(B)
①	psychology	⋯⋯	morality
②	psychology	⋯⋯	responsibility
③	humanity	⋯⋯	morality
④	humanity	⋯⋯	offensiveness
⑤	psychology	⋯⋯	offensiveness

01

다음 글의 내용을 한 문장으로 요약하고자 한다. 빈칸 (A)와 (B)에 들어갈 말로 가장 적절한 것은?

| 사관학교 2018학년도 37번 |

In a psychological study, researchers gave questionnaires to two groups of students and asked them to respond by email. All the questions had to do with some mundane task, such as opening a bank account. But the two groups were given different instructions for answering the questions. The students in the first group were to write about what the activity implied about some intangible information such as personal traits — what kind of person has a bank account, for example. The second group wrote simply about the specific steps in the process — speaking to a bank teller, filling out forms, making an initial deposit, and so forth. There proved to be a significant difference between the response times of the two groups. The students in the first group tended to delay — in fact, some never completed the task at all. By contrast, the students in the second group, who were focused on the how, when, and where of the task, completed the task sooner than the first group.

*mundane: 일상적인

⬇

In the study, the first group of students, who were given a task requiring thinking in more _____(A)_____ terms, turned out to _____(B)_____ their answers to a greater extent than the other group of students.

	(A)		(B)
①	abstract	······	postpone
②	abstract	······	emphasize
③	quantitative	······	postpone
④	practical	······	exaggerate
⑤	practical	······	emphasize

다음 글의 내용을 한 문장으로 요약하고자 한다. 빈칸 (A)와 (B)에 들어갈 말로 가장 적절한 것은?

| 사관학교 2016학년도 37번 |

Many teenagers want to be like everyone in the school lunchroom. "We are not as unique as we would like to think," said Erica van de Waal, who conducted a study on monkey behavior. "We can find many of the roots of our behaviors in animals." Her study team gave 109 vervet monkeys, living in groups in the wild, food tinted pink or blue. One color for each group was tainted with aloe to give it a bad flavor, but only for the first few meals. Even after the flavor returned to normal the monkeys would not eat the color that they thought was bad. Then some blue-eating monkeys went to the pink-eating tribes and some pink-eating monkeys went to the blue-eating tribes. That is when the researchers saw peer pressure in action. The blue-food eaters that moved to an area full of pink-food eaters switched even though they had avoided pink food before. Pink eaters also changed when they moved to a blue-food area. They ate what everyone else ate.

⬇

The vervet monkeys' act of _____ (A) _____ is thought to be a result of _____ (B) _____ in a new group.

	(A)		(B)
①	switching food	⋯⋯	social conformity
②	switching food	⋯⋯	food abundance
③	refusing to eat	⋯⋯	power struggle
④	refusing to eat	⋯⋯	food abundance
⑤	avoiding contact	⋯⋯	social conformity

다음 글의 내용을 한 문장으로 요약하고자 한다. 빈칸 (A)와 (B)에 들어갈 말로 가장 적절한 것은?

| 수능 2017학년도 홀수형 40번 |

The impacts of tourism on the environment are evident to scientists, but not all residents attribute environmental damage to tourism. Residents commonly have positive views on the economic and some sociocultural influences of tourism on quality of life, but their reactions to environmental impacts are mixed. Some residents feel tourism provides more parks and recreation areas, improves the quality of the roads and public facilities, and does not contribute to ecological decline. Many do not blame tourism for traffic problems, overcrowded outdoor recreation, or the disturbance of peace and tranquility of parks. Alternatively, some residents express concern that tourists overcrowd the local fishing, hunting, and other recreation areas or may cause traffic and pedestrian congestion. Some studies suggest that variations in residents' feelings about tourism's relationship to environmental damage are related to the type of tourism, the extent to which residents feel the natural environment needs to be protected, and the distance residents live from the tourist attractions.

*tranquility: 고요함 **congestion: 혼잡

↓

Residents do not ___(A)___ tourism's environmental influences identically since they take ___(B)___ postures based on factors such as the type of tourism, opinions on the degree of protection, and their distance from an attraction.

	(A)		(B)
①	weigh	······	dissimilar
②	weigh	······	common
③	weigh	······	balanced
④	control	······	favorable
⑤	control	······	conflicting

04

다음 글의 내용을 한 문장으로 요약하고자 한다. 빈칸 (A)와 (B)에 들어갈 말로 가장 적절한 것은?

| 수능 2016학년도 홀수형 40번 |

Performance must be judged in terms of what is under the control of the individuals being evaluated rather than those influences on performance that are beyond their control. There can be broad, influential factors, sometimes of an economic nature, that hold down the performance of everyone being judged. One example is in sales. If there is a general downturn in the economy and products or services are not being purchased with the same frequency as in the previous year, sales could be down, for example, by an average of 15%. This 15% (actually −15%) figure would then represent "average" performance. Perhaps the best salesperson in the year had only a 3% drop in sales over the previous year. Thus, "good" performance in this situation is a smaller loss compared to some average or norm group.

⬇

In performance evaluation, we should consider ___(A)___ factors affecting the individual's performance rather than ___(B)___ figures only.

	(A)		(B)
①	contextual	······	put aside
②	contextual	······	rely on
③	controllable	······	put aside
④	positive	······	ignore
⑤	positive	······	rely on

PART 04
논리 추론하기

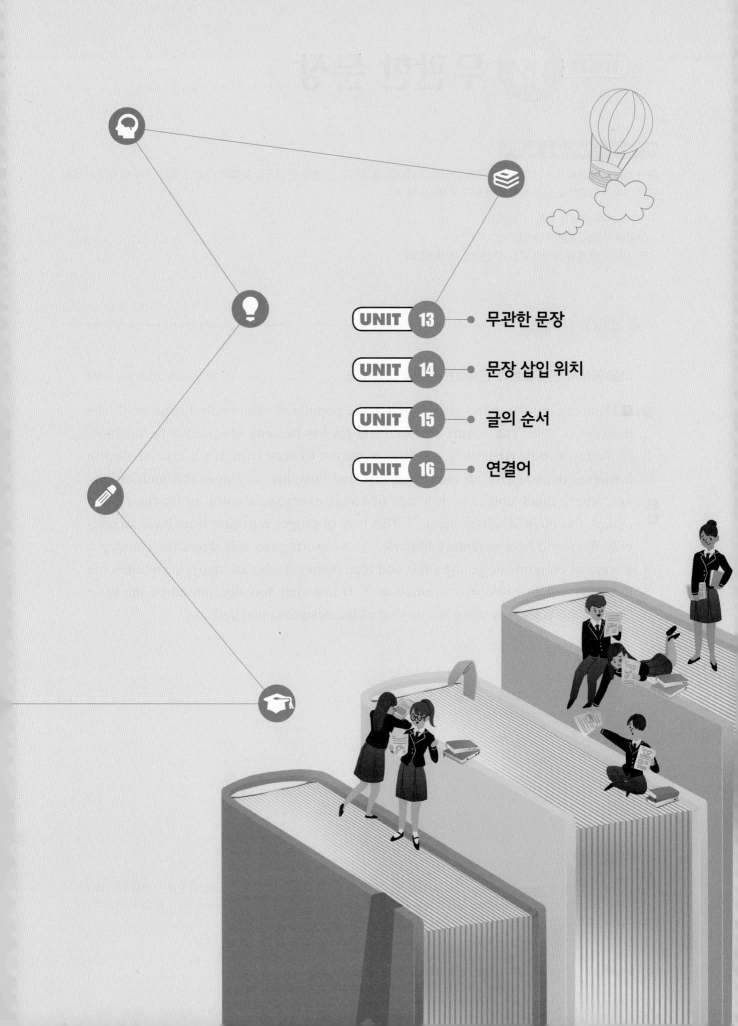

Problem Solving Skills

글의 흐름과 무관하거나 반대되는 내용의 문장을 찾아내는 유형이다. 무관한 문장에도 주제와 관련된 핵심 단어 및 어구가 포함되는 경우가 많으므로 모든 문장을 꼼꼼히 해석하도록 한다.

- 도입부에서 글의 소재를 파악한다.
- 선택지 문장을 꼼꼼히 해석한다.
- 글 전체의 흐름과 선택지 문장 간 연관성을 분석한다.

Example

다음 글에서 전체 흐름과 관계<u>없는</u> 문장을 고르시오.　　　　　　　| 경찰대학 2016학년도 32번 |

1 From the artfully styled grain bowls to the popular slow-simmered bone broth, the message is clear: The beauty-and-wellness set has become obsessed with nutrition. ① Today, eating virtuously isn't just a means to stay trim; it's a crucial step in fortifying the body for an increasingly fit, and busy, life. ② But in this multitasking age, where lunch comes with a side of email, everyone's got a lot on their plate except, too often, a square meal. ③ This lack of proper nutrition from local foods is only worsened by a sedentary lifestyle. ④ Answering the call across the country is a wave of enterprising young chefs and tech pioneers who are marrying wholesome meals with door-to-door convenience. ⑤ If last year was dominated by the juice cleanse, this is shaping up to be the year of the designer meal delivery.

Vocabulary

grain bowl 그레인 볼　bone broth 사골탕　virtuously 정숙하게　trim 말쑥한, 군살 없는　crucial 중대한, 결정적인　fortify 강화하다　nutrition 영양　sedentary 주로 앉아서 하는　pioneer 개척자, 선구자　convenience 편의　shape up 되어가다　designer (명사 앞에서) 유명 디자이너의, 고급의

Let's Solve

Point ➊ 도입부에서 글의 소재 파악하기

• From the artfully styled grain bowls to the popular slow-simmered bone broth, the message is clear: The beauty-and-wellness set has become obsessed with nutrition.

→ 건강을 강조하는 흐름

Point ➋ 선택지 문장을 꼼꼼히 해석하기

• Today, eating virtuously isn't just a means to stay trim; it's a crucial step in fortifying the body for an increasingly fit, and busy, life.

(오늘날, 정갈하게 먹는 것은 단지 군살 없는 몸을 유지하는 수단이 아니다. 그것은 점점 더 빡빡하고 바쁜 삶에 맞게 몸을 튼튼히 하는 중요한 단계이다.)

• But in this multitasking age, where lunch comes with a side of email, everyone's got a lot on their plate except, too often, a square meal.

(그러나, 점심에 곁들여 메일이 오는, 이 멀티태스킹의 시대에, 모든 사람은 너무 자주, 그들의 접시에 실속 있는 식사를 뺀 많은 것들을 올린다.)

• This lack of proper nutrition from local foods is only worsened by a sedentary lifestyle.

(이러한 지역 식품에서 얻는 적절한 영양의 결여는 바로 좌식 생활 습관 때문에 악화된다.)

• Answering the call across the country is a wave of enterprising young chefs and tech pioneers who are marrying wholesome meals with door-to-door convenience.

(전국적인 요구에 대한 대답은 집집마다 찾아가는 편리함과 건강에 좋은 식사를 결합시켜 사업을 시작하는 젊은 요리사와 기술적 선구자들의 물결이다.)

• If last year was dominated by the juice cleanse, this is shaping up to be the year of the designer meal delivery.

(지난해가 해독주스로 성황이었다면, 지금은 고급 음식 배달의 해가 되어가고 있다.)

Point ➌ 글 전체의 흐름과 선택지 문장의 연관성 분석하기

지문에서는 사람들이 평상시에 먹는 음식의 성향이 바뀌고 있음을 설명하고 있다. 오늘날 사람들은 바쁜 와중에 건강을 챙길 수 있는 음식에 관심을 가지고 있으며, 이러한 관심을 충족시키기 위해 생긴 새로운 사업이 음식을 포장해 배달해주는 일이라는 내용이다. ①, ②, ④, ⑤는 이러한 내용과 자연스럽게 연결된다.

→ 반면에, ③은 앉아서 일하는 생활 방식의 단점에 대한 문장으로 문맥상 적절하지 않다.

01

다음 글에서 전체 흐름과 관계 없는 문장을 고르시오.

| 경찰대학 2018학년도 31번 |

As a rule, physicians should not be considered altruistic when acting in their patients' best interests because they do not have the choices in acting that we ordinarily associate with altruism. Doctors have professional duties to patients that they cannot discharge as a matter of choice. To be sure, becoming a doctor and thereby entering into a professional relationship with patients is an optional act. ① Once a doctor enters into this relationship, however, he or she cannot choose obligations. ② A doctor can choose not to treat a particular patient in a particular situation if doing so would compromise personal and professional integrity. ③ Thus there arises a potential conflict for a physician who sees patients as individuals needing therapeutic treatments. ④ But the doctor must ensure that the patient's care is transferred to another physician. ⑤ Once one becomes a physician, one promises to promote the best medical interests of one's patients. This is not optional, but obligatory.

[3점]

02

다음 글에서 전체 흐름과 관계 없는 문장을 고르시오.

| 경찰대학 2018학년도 32번 |

Unlike other climate issues, the science of sea level rise is fairly simple. ① Ocean levels are increasing mostly because of what heat does to water, in all its various states. ② To combat the rise in ocean levels, it is of utmost importance to understand the molecular structure of water. ③ As global temperature rises, most of the extra heat in the atmosphere — about 90 percent — sinks into the ocean. ④ As the water warms, it expands like mercury in a thermometer. ⑤ This thermal expansion accounts for one-third of sea level rise. The other two-thirds comes from melting mountain glaciers and ice sheets in Greenland and Antarctica.

다음 글에서 전체 흐름과 관계 <u>없는</u> 문장을 고르시오.

| 경찰대학 2017학년도 31번 |

Pasta's ethnic roots have been long debated. ① Many theories have been put forward, some notably far-fetched. ② An enduring myth, based on the writings of the 13th-century explorer Marco Polo, that pasta was brought to Italy from China, rose from a misinterpretation of a famous passage in Polo's *Travels*. ③ In it, Polo mentions a tree from which something like pasta was made. ④ It was probably the sago palm, which produces a starchy food that resembles, but is not pasta. ⑤ This tree, native to Asia, provided undeniable evidence that Pasta originated in China.

다음 글에서 전체 흐름과 관계 <u>없는</u> 문장을 고르시오.

| 경찰대학 2017학년도 32번 |

Another difference in the concept of justice lies in various societies' ideas of what laws are. In the West, people consider "laws" quite different from "customs." There is also a great contrast between "sins" (breaking religious laws) and "crimes" (breaking laws of the government). ① In many non-Western cultures, however, there is little separation of customs, laws, and religious beliefs; in other cultures, these three may be quite separate from one another, but still very much different from those in the West. ② For these reasons, an action may be considered a crime in one country but be socially acceptable in others. ③ For instance, although a thief is viewed as a criminal in much of the world, in a small village where there is considerable communal living and sharing of objects, the word thief may have little meaning. ④ In small villages, everyone, in a sense, becomes a judge; in such societies, social disapproval of people's activities can serve both as powerful punishment for and as strong deterrent to crime. ⑤ Someone who has taken something without asking is simply considered an impolite person.

[3점]

다음 글에서 전체 흐름과 관계 <u>없는</u> 문장을 고르시오.

| 경찰대학 2016학년도 31번 |

On the face of it, industrialized agriculture promised to be a most welcome solution to the timeless problem of world hunger. ① But some so-called solutions, as writer and farmer Wendell Berry observed, led to ramifying sets of new problems. ② And during the past several decades, it has become increasingly clear that industrial agriculture has indeed created a host of new problems impacting the health of people and the planet. ③ So corporations and governments, recognizing the opportunity presented by the new technologies, fostered the rapid spread of industrialized agriculture. ④ The use of fertilizers and pesticides, for example, has led to higher rates of cancer and the contamination of soil, streams, and groundwater. ⑤ Monoculture farming has led to the loss of biodiversity, undermining the productivity and stability of ecosystems.

다음 글에서 전체 흐름과 관계 <u>없는</u> 문장을 고르시오.

| 경찰대학 2015학년도 31번 |

To conclusively set new safety standards for CT radiation, researchers are beginning to directly investigate the number of cancers among people who have received CT scans. ① About a dozen such studies from different countries will be published in the next few years. ② In the meantime, some researchers have started testing whether good images can be produced with radiation doses lower than those generated in typical CT scans. ③ Radiologists at Mass General Hospital have an unusual way of conducting such investigations. ④ A single CT scan subjects the human body to between 150 and 1,100 times the radiation of a conventional X-ray. ⑤ In that way, they scan bodies many times without worrying about making people sick and perform an autopsy to check whether the scan has correctly identified a medical problem. Rather than recruiting living, breathing human volunteers for their studies, they work with cadavers.

07

다음 글에서 전체 흐름과 관계 없는 문장을 고르시오.

Foreign language learners may perform different speech acts than native speakers in the same contexts, or, alternatively, they may elect not to perform any speech act at all. The best examples of this come from authentic conversations and role-plays where speakers have some flexibility in determining what they will say or do. In academic advising sessions, native speakers and learners favor different speech acts. ① Native speakers produce more suggestions than learners per advising session, whereas learners produce more rejections per advising session than native speakers do. ② In addition, the absence of the speech act of advice was salient for academic advisers. ③ The two speech acts of suggestion and rejection seem to serve the same function, that of control. ④ Native speakers exert control over their course schedules by making suggestions; in contrast, the learners do so through rejections, by blocking the suggestions of the advisers. ⑤ Although both groups of students participate in determining what courses they ultimately take, the resulting feeling of harmony in the interview is perceived by the advisers to be noticeably different.

08

다음 글에서 전체 흐름과 관계 없는 문장을 고르시오.

Thanks to advances in cell cultivation, researchers are closer than ever to growing real, edible meat in labs. Beyond the ethics of raising some 9 billion animals to be killed for food each year in the U.S., factory farms produce vast amounts of waste. ① Scientists are working to come up with efficient ways to recycle this waste. ② The 2 trillion pounds of animal waste pollutes the air and water. ③ Besides the pollution problem, the global demand for meat is expected to grow 60% by 2050, and the amount of farmland and grain needed to feed those chickens, pigs, and cows may be unsustainable. ④ But producing in vitro meat — muscle tissue that is cultured from animal cells and grown in a laboratory — has none of those hang-ups. ⑤ In fact, it's mouthwateringly efficient compared with existing methods of meat production, using 45% less energy and 99% less land.

*hang-up: 고민, 곤란 [3점]

다음 글에서 전체 흐름과 관계 <u>없는</u> 문장을 고르시오.

An infant's lack of sparkling dialogue may obscure the fact that we are all born with an ability to communicate. ① A capacity for language exists in our tiny, screaming bodies in the delivery room, along with our eyes, ears, arms, legs, and vital organs. ② The capacity must be stimulated — we need to hear people talk in order to form words — but we are born eager to speak. ③ The newborn baby is patiently waiting for answers to questions: "What will I call the objects that surround me? How will I form positive and negative sentences? How can I express feelings about objects and people?" ④ Only when the baby is able to clearly articulate such questions, do the parents initiate communication. ⑤ The child's brain instinctively searches for answers to these questions and then, like a sponge, soaks them up.

다음 글에서 전체 흐름과 관계 <u>없는</u> 문장을 고르시오.

Some of the men working nearby would watch me and laugh. ① <u>Two or three of the older men took the trouble to teach me the right way to shovel.</u> "You're doing it wrong," one man scolded. ② <u>Beginning around seven each morning, I would feel my body resist the first thrust of the shovel.</u> "Don't make your back do so much work," he instructed. ③ <u>I stood impatiently listening, vaguely watching, then noticed his work-thickened fingers clutching the shovel.</u> I was annoyed and wanted to tell him that I enjoyed shoveling the wrong way. I was about to, but, as it turned out, I didn't say a thing. ④ <u>Rather it was at that moment I realized that I was fooling myself if I expected a few weeks of labor to gain me admission to the world of laborer.</u> I would not learn in three months what my parents had meant by "real work." For me the sensations of exertion and fatigue could be savored. ⑤ <u>For my parents, working at comparable jobs when they were my age, such sensations were to be feared.</u> Fatigue took a different toll on their bodies and minds.

다음 글에서 전체 흐름과 관계 <u>없는</u> 문장을 고르시오.

| 경찰대학 2013학년도 36번 |

"What is your blood type?" is an unusual question from the Western point of view. From the Korean and Japanese perspective, such a question is quite normal. ① People of these cultures believe that specific personality traits are related to blood type. ② These days, however, more and more Westerners are buying into the idea of a connection between these two seemingly distinct features. ③ This belief is very similar to Western notions of astrology and signs of the zodiac. ④ Most Westerners are surprised by such a question because they are unaware of the concept of a relationship between blood type and personality. ⑤ In fact, many Westerners do not even know their own blood type.

다음 글에서 전체 흐름과 관계 <u>없는</u> 문장을 고르시오.

| 경찰대학 2012학년도 36번 |

On May 18, at 8:32 in the morning, Mount St. Helens blew its top, literally. Suddenly, it was 1,300 feet shorter than before. At the same moment, an earthquake with an intensity of 5 on the Richter scale was recorded. ① It triggered an avalanche of snow and ice, mixed with hot rock. ② A wave of scorching volcanic gas and rock fragments shot horizontally from the volcano's flank, at 200 miles per hour. ③ There is no doubt that the activity of Mount St. Helens has influenced our climate. ④ As the sliding ice and snow melted, it touched off devastating torrents of mud and debris, which destroyed all life in their path. ⑤ Pulverized rock climbed as a dust cloud into the atmosphere. Finally, lava, accompanied by burning clouds of ash and gas welled out of the volcano's new crater and cracks in its flanks.

다음 글에서 전체 흐름과 관계 <u>없는</u> 문장을 고르시오.

| 경찰대학 2012학년도 37번 |

Since skeletal remains of Giganotosaurus do not include skin, scientists must theorize as to their coloring. ① They tried to make educated guesses about the dinosaurs' skin colors. ② Since a Giganotosaurus hunted smaller prey, it is likely that the appearance of its skin allowed it to blend into its surroundings for camouflage. ③ The Giganotosaurus lived in the grassy wetlands of what is now Argentina, an environment similar to the African savanna. ④ It had big teeth which were much larger than those of other dinosaurs eating grass. ⑤ Therefore, this dinosaur probably had skin that closely matched the colors of the vegetation around it.

다음 글에서 전체 흐름과 관계 <u>없는</u> 문장을 고르시오.

| 경찰대학 2011학년도 37번 |

If the moon can stir oceans, why not the blood of humans? We are, after all, more than 60 per cent water ourselves. Perhaps tides within our blood cause an ebb and flow in our emotions and self-control. ① Shakespeare sensed some truth in this, charging that the moon "makes men mad." ② And, in fact, that was the claim of the man who served as a model for Mr. Hyde in Robert Louis Stevenson's *Strange Case of Dr Jekyll and Mr Hyde* — he blamed his crimes on moon-induced lunacy. ③ Some observations also support the notion, suggesting that violent crime increases under a full moon: as the moon waxes, ice hockey players were said to spend more time in the penalty box, while casualty departments gear up for busier times. ④ And the moon's regular appearance through our skies — 29 days, 12 hours and 44 minutes from one new moon to the next — is a comforting constant. ⑤ Still, there's no denying the restlessness some of us feel beneath the moon — the sudden desire to climb mountains, cower in the shadows or just rear up and howl.

15 다음 글에서 전체 흐름과 관계 <u>없는</u> 문장을 고르시오. | 경찰대학 2011학년도 38번 |

All intentional actions which we perform enjoy a certain latitude. ① Our intention applies as a rule only to the *what* and not so much to the *how*. ② Whether I want to lift the receiver of the telephone or put the key into the lock, I always gratefully rely on my eyes, which guide the hand to its target and save me the effort of groping, because any false movement is immediately corrected by visual control. ③ In the language of engineers this kind of interaction is known as feedback. ④ Engineers' words are always concise and precise in order to communicate ideas without any confusion. ⑤ On the whole we may say that the intention determines the *what* and the feedback the *how*. It is the character of this interaction which enables humans to deal with the environment effectivity.

16 다음 밑줄 친 부분 중에서 글의 흐름상 어색한 부분은? | 경찰대학 2010학년도 39번 |

Uncertainty avoidance is the degree to which a culture feels threatened by ambiguity. Cultures with "weak" uncertainty avoidance are more accepting of uncertainty, live from day to day, have lower stress levels, accept dissent, are unthreatened by social deviations, are more risk prone, are youth oriented, believe time is free, and are not fascinated by many rules. "Strong" uncertainty avoidance cultures ① <u>perceive uncertainty to be continuous threat</u>, ② <u>experience greater stress</u>, ③ <u>promote consensus over dissent</u>, ④ <u>consider deviance to be desirable</u>, ⑤ <u>are security conscious</u>, are distrustful of the young, believe time is money, and like many rules.

→ 무관한 '구'를 선택하는 문제이지만 출제 의도를 고려하여 UNIT 13으로 분류하였습니다.

01 다음 글에서 전체 흐름과 관계 없는 문장을 고르시오.

When the first Olympic victor was recorded in 776 B.C., Rome was a mere farm community surrounded by warring tribes. ① By 500 B.C., as the athletic program at Olympia settled into a fixed, predictable pattern, the Romans were rising up against the rule of the Etruscans, their hostile neighbors to the north. ② Within two centuries Roman military might, administrative officials, language, and culture dominated all of Italy. ③ Then began their imperial conquest of Sicily, Carthage, and Greece. ④ Furthermore, Greek sports and games were too individualistic, too geared to the participants rather than to spectator appeal. ⑤ By the end of the first century B.C., the Roman empire covered the entire rim of the Mediterranean, extending to the northern reaches of Britain, to the Danube in Europe, and east to the Caspian Sea.

02 다음 글에서 전체 흐름과 관계 없는 문장을 고르시오.

One study evaluated the efficacy of a daily multivitamin to prevent cognitive decline among 5,947 elderly males. ① After 12 years of follow-up, there were no differences between the multivitamin and placebo groups in overall cognitive performance or verbal memory. ② The researchers concluded that the use of a multivitamin supplement in a well-nourished elderly population did not prevent cognitive decline. ③ This conclusion was further supported by a review of some other studies that evaluated supplementation with multivitamins, B vitamins, vitamins E, C and omega-3 fatty acids, in persons with mild cognitive impairment or mild to moderate dementia. ④ While all vitamins are required for optimal health and brain function, there are a few that stand out above the rest as being essential for a healthy brain. ⑤ None of the supplements improved cognitive function, indicating that multivitamin intake has no effect on the treatment of dementia.

* dementia: 치매

전체 흐름과 관계 없는 문장은? | 수능 2012학년도 홀수형 22번 |

During the 1997 Kyoto negotiations, Brazil made a suggestion that has since become known as the Brazilian Proposal. ① Its idea was that countries should now share the burden of emissions cuts according to how historically responsible they were for the problem. ② In other words, we should calculate what concentration of greenhouse gases each country has put into the atmosphere over time and use those figures to allocate emissions cuts. ③ That would mean, for instance, that countries such as Germany and the United Kingdom, which have been emitting for longer than most countries, would bear a larger share than their current emissions implied. ④ Greenhouse gases have been known to absorb heat and hold this heat in the atmosphere, instead of reflecting it back into space. ⑤ It would also mean that big emitters that had developed their industries more recently, such as Australia, would bear less of a share.

전체 흐름과 관계 없는 문장은? | 수능 2017학년도 홀수형 35번 |

Most often, you will find or meet people who introduce themselves in terms of their work or by what they spend time on. These people introduce themselves as a salesman or an executive. ① There is nothing criminal in doing this, but psychologically, we become what we believe. ② Identifying what we can do in the workplace serves to enhance the quality of our professional career. ③ People who follow this practice tend to lose their individuality and begin to live with the notion that they are recognized by the job they do. ④ However, jobs may not be permanent, and you may lose your job for countless reasons, some of which you may not even be responsible for. ⑤ In such a case, these people suffer from an inevitable social and mental trauma, leading to emotional stress and a feeling that all of a sudden they have been disassociated from what once was their identity.

Problem Solving Skills

글의 흐름상 주어진 문장이 들어가기에 자연스러운 위치를 찾는 유형이다. 글의 흐름을 파악하는 것을 기본으로, 주어진 문장의 내용이나 연결어 등 흐름과 관련된 단서에 유의한다.

• 주어진 문장의 단서를 분석한다.
• 도입부에서 글의 소재를 파악한다.
• 주어진 문장에 적합한 위치를 찾는다.

Example

글의 흐름으로 보아 주어진 문장이 들어가기에 가장 적절한 곳은? | 경찰대학 2018학년도 34번 |

❶ It preserves, and sometimes further simplifies, the relevant information.

❷ Generally speaking, a model is a simplified representation of reality created to serve a purpose. (①) It is simplified based on some assumptions about what is and is not important for the specific purpose, or sometimes based on constraints on information or tractability. (②) For example, a map is a model of the physical world. (③) It abstracts away a tremendous amount of information that the mapmaker **❸** deemed irrelevant for its purpose. (④) For example, a road map keeps and highlights the roads, their basic topology, their relationships to places one would want to travel, and other relevant information. (⑤) Various professions have well-known model types: an architectural blueprint, an engineering prototype, and so on. Each of these abstracts away details that are not relevant to their main purpose and keeps those that are.

Vocabulary

constraint 제약 **tractability** 순종 **tremendous** 굉장한 **deem** 여기다 **irrelevant** 무관한 **topology** 위상 기하학
blueprint 청사진 **prototype** 원형

Let's Solve

Point 1 주어진 문장의 단서 분석하기

• It preserves, and sometimes further simplifies, the relevant information.
- 단서: It이 가리키는 개념의 역할을 설명하고 있다.
  → 주어진 문장의 앞에는 It이 가리키는 개념이 언급되고, 뒤에는 문장에서 언급한 It의 보존과 심화된 단순화의 예시가 이어질 것이다.

Point 2 도입부에서 글의 소재 파악하기

• Generally speaking, a model is a simplified representation of reality created to serve a purpose.
  → '모형'의 의의

Point 3 주어진 문장에 적합한 위치 찾기

a. a model is a simplified representation of reality created to serve a purpose.
  → '모형'의 기본적인 의미

(①)

b. It is simplified based on some assumptions ~, or sometimes based on constraints~.
  → a에 대한 추가 설명

(②)

c. For example, a map ~.
  → a의 예시: 지도

(③)

d. It abstracts away a tremendous amount of information that the mapmaker deemed irrelevant for its purpose.
  → c의 설명

(④)

e. For example, a road map ~ and other relevant information.
  → 목적에 따라 지도가 "관련 정보"를 강조하는 사례

(⑤)

f. Various professions have well-known model types ~ and so on.
  → 분야에 따라 다양한 모형이 있음.

  → 주어진 문장의 It이 '지도'를 가리킴을 알 수 있다. 또한 주어진 문장에 언급된 '보존', '심화된 단순화', '관련 정보'라는 어구들이 문장 e 에서 'keep', 'highlight', 'relevant information' 등으로 반복되면서 도로 지도의 사례를 설명하고 있는 것으로 볼 때, 주어진 문장이 들 어갈 곳으로는 ④가 가장 적절하다.

01 글의 흐름으로 보아, 주어진 문장이 들어가기에 가장 적절한 곳은? | 경찰대학 2017학년도 33번 |

Humans also automatically adjust their behavior to blend with the people around them.

When you interact with other people, you are quite likely to find yourself mimicking them in certain ways. (①) You may, for example, unconsciously match your friends' speech patterns and accents. (②) Social psychologists labeled this type of mimicry the chameleon effect. (③) Chameleons automatically change their color to blend in with their environment. (④) It is speculated that this form of mimicry functions as a type of "social glue." (⑤) By producing identical motor gestures, people make themselves more similar to the other individuals around them.

[3점]

02 글의 흐름으로 보아, 주어진 문장이 들어가기에 가장 적절한 곳은? | 경찰대학 2016학년도 33번 |

At one point, he clapped me on the back and said: "Son, make sure you talk with everyone here tonight and see that each one feels better about himself when he leaves than he did when he walked in the door."

One of my daughters was married recently, and I spent the evening celebrating with 200 people of all ages. (①) They ranged from my 3-year-old granddaughters to my 85-year-old uncle, who fought in World War II and ran successful law and accounting practices for 5 decades. (②) The advice made me consider what it means to be mentally sharp. (③) Although our ability to learn and remember gradually declines throughout adulthood, there's mounting evidence that our skill at making sense of important information and experiences increases. (④) This is what's known as wisdom, and it's something that scientists are just beginning to study. (⑤) Its classic elements include sound judgment, psychological insight, long and diverse life experience, emotional control, empathetic understanding, and, of course, knowledge.

글의 흐름으로 보아, 주어진 문장이 들어가기에 가장 적절한 곳은? | 경찰대학 2015학년도 33번 |

Other promising leads come from a major source virtually untapped by both traditional and modern medicine systems — the ocean.

All frogs and toads secrete defensive fluids, many of which possess antibiotic properties. (①) That's why Chinese folk healers have treated wounds such as sores and dog bites with toad secretions, sometimes obtained by surrounding the toads with mirrors to scare them. (②) While such methods may sound strange, a large percentage of medicines used in Western countries come from nature or from chemical formulas found in nature. (③) Steroids, penicillin, digitalis, morphine, and aspirin are only a few examples. (④) One of the most exciting discoveries in medicine is Taxol, which fights breast and ovarian cancer and is derived from the bark of the yew tree. (⑤) Candidates include an anticancer drug from the Antarctic seabed and a painkiller from the venom of a tropical cone snail.

글의 흐름으로 보아, 주어진 문장이 들어가기에 가장 적절한 곳은? | 경찰대학 2014학년도 33번 |

Who's going to take care of all of those people?

For a country that has managed to outspend every other developed nation in the world on health care, the U.S. is oddly short on doctors. (①) We have about 30 primary-care physicians per 100,000 people. (②) That is far fewer than any other industrialized country. (③) You may have seen the headlines about U.S. physician shortages and how they're posed to get even worse, with baby boomers entering retirement. (④) This is only worsened by the millions of previously uninsured people about to enter the health care system. (⑤) The most viable solution is a growing population of nurses and other clinicians who have obtained advanced and academic training and are licensed to do many of the same things as physicians.

글의 흐름으로 보아, 주어진 문장이 들어가기에 가장 적절한 곳은?　| 경찰대학 2013학년도 37번 |

If, instead, an enlightened course is pursued, allowing workers to benefit from increases in productivity with shorter workweeks and adequate income, more leisure time will exist than in any other period of modern history.

In the future, a growing number of people around the world will be spending less time on the job and have more time on their hands. (①) Whether their "free" time will be coerced, involuntary, and the result of forced part-time work, layoffs, and unemployment, or leisure made possible by productivity gains, shorter workweeks, and better income remains to be worked out in the political arena. (②) If massive unemployment of a kind unknown in history were to occur as a result of the sweeping replacement of machines for human labor, then the chances of developing a compassionate and caring society are unlikely. (③) The more likely course would be widespread social upheaval, violence on an unprecedented scale, and open warfare, with the poor lashing out at each other as well as at the rich elites who control the global economy. (④) That free time could be used to renew the bonds of community and rejuvenate the democratic legacy. (⑤) A new generation might transcend the narrow limits of nationalism and begin to think and act as common members of the human race, with shared commitments to each other, the community, and the larger biosphere.

글의 흐름으로 보아, 주어진 문장이 들어가기에 가장 적절한 곳은? | 경찰대학 2010학년도 42번 |

So must be the "point of view."

The sequence of events in a narrative is called the "plot." (①) Unlike random events in real life, the plot of a narrative must be controlled and directed by the narrator. (②) Point of view is the vantage from which a narrative is told. (③) It is not a difficult concept to master if you think of the difference between watching a football game in the stadium and watching it on television. (④) The camera controls your point of view on the screen. You see only what the camera focuses on. (⑤) In the stands, however, you are free to scan the entire field, to watch the quarterback or the line, to concentrate on the cheerleaders. Your point of view is determined by your eyes alone.

01 글의 흐름으로 보아, 주어진 문장이 들어가기에 가장 적절한 곳을 고르시오.

| 사관학교 2018학년도 27번 |

In a stable, fully occupied habitat, there may not be enough nest sites or food available in a given year for new breeders to strike out on their own.

Flamingos, penguins, ostriches, giraffes, dolphins, crocodiles, and many other species leave their young in the care of other adults for a while. This gives parents the freedom to track down the most nutritious foods for their growing family. (①) Just who are these surrogate parents that care for the young? (②) The sitters may be parents taking random turns, or they may be nonbreeding individuals that are related to the parents. (③) Though it may look like altruism, the sitters are merely promoting their own genes tied up in the young nieces, nephews, or siblings that they are caring for. (④) If their aim is to further their genes, you may ask, why not just have their own brood? (⑤) Rather than be forced into a marginal nesting site, they might hold off for a year, learning tricks in the meantime that will make them better parents.

*surrogate: 대리의 [3점]

글의 흐름으로 보아, 주어진 문장이 들어가기에 가장 적절한 곳을 고르시오.

| 사관학교 2017학년도 27번 |

Yet nations tend to restrict the import of certain goods for a variety of reasons.

There are a growing number of companies, large and small, that are doing business with firms in other countries. Some companies sell to firms in foreign countries; others buy goods around the world to import into their countries. (①) Whether they buy or sell products across national borders, these businesses are all contributing to the volume of international trade that is fueling the global economy. (②) Theoretically, international trade is every bit as logical and worthwhile as interstate trade between, say, California and Washington. (③) For example, in the early 2000s, the United States restricted the import of Mexican fresh tomatoes because they were undercutting the price levels of domestic fresh tomatoes. (④) Despite such restrictions, international trade has increased almost steadily since World War II. (⑤) Many of the industrialized nations have signed trade agreements intended to eliminate problems in international business and to help less-developed nations participate in world trade.

글의 흐름으로 보아, 주어진 문장이 들어가기에 가장 적절한 곳을 고르시오.

| 수능 2016학년도 홀수형 37번 |

Surprised by the vision of an unfamiliar silhouette pushing into the house, these dogs were using their eyes instead of their noses.

Remember when you were little and you imagined that adults had infinite power? Surely someone who could drive the car, open the juice container, and reach the sink could make it stop raining. (①) I think that's the same expectation that we have with respect to our dogs and their ability to smell. (②) Because they are so good at using their noses, we assume that they can smell anything, anytime. (③) But dogs use other senses, too, and the brains of both humans and dogs tend to intensify one sense at a time. (④) Many owners have been snapped at by their dogs when they returned home with a new hairdo or a new coat. (⑤) Their noses may be remarkable, but they're not always switched on.

글의 흐름으로 보아, 주어진 문장이 들어가기에 가장 적절한 곳을 고르시오.

| 수능 2016학년도 홀수형 38번 |

Even so, it is not the money *per se* that is valuable, but the fact that it can potentially yield more positive experiences.

Money — beyond the bare minimum necessary for food and shelter — is nothing more than a means to an end. Yet so often we confuse means with ends, and sacrifice happiness (end) for money (means). It is easy to do this when material wealth is elevated to the position of the ultimate end, as it so often is in our society. (①) This is not to say that the accumulation and production of material wealth is in itself wrong. (②) Material prosperity can help individuals, as well as society, attain higher levels of happiness. (③) Financial security can liberate us from work we do not find meaningful and from having to worry about the next paycheck. (④) Moreover, the desire to make money can challenge and inspire us. (⑤) Material wealth in and of itself does not necessarily generate meaning or lead to emotional wealth.

per se: 그 자체로 [3점]

Problem Solving Skills

주어진 문장의 방향성을 전제로 나머지 짧은 문단들을 자연스럽게 배열하는 유형이다. 문장 또는 문단 말단의 화제가 다음 문장 또는 문단의 서두에 등장하는 방식으로 글이 전개되는 경우가 많으므로 이러한 사슬구조를 찾으며 지문을 읽는다.

• 주어진 문장으로 글의 전개를 추측한다.
• 앞뒤의 단서를 찾으며 문단을 읽는다.
• 논리적인 글의 순서를 추론한다.

Example

주어진 글 다음에 이어질 글의 순서로 가장 적절한 것은?

| 경찰대학 2017학년도 35번 |

❶ From all the meals you've shared with family and friends, you are probably aware that people have very different taste preferences.

❷
(A) The group of individuals who have considerably more than an average number of taste buds are called supertasters. The variations in the density of taste buds on different people's tongues appear to be genetic. Women are much more likely than men to be supertasters.

(B) In fact, the foods mothers eat change the flavor of amniotic fluid, so some food preferences may be shaped in utero. However, people also show remarkable differences in the numbers of taste buds they possess.

(C) Some people love spicy food, for example, whereas others shudder at the thought of a hot pepper. Some preferences are explained by differences in the flavors people experience quite early in life.

*in utero: 자궁 내에

❸
① (A) – (C) – (B)
② (B) – (A) – (C)
③ (B) – (C) – (A)
④ (C) – (A) – (B)
⑤ (C) – (B) – (A)

Vocabulary

preference 선호도　considerably 상당히　taste bud 미뢰　variation 차이　density 밀집도　genetic 유전적인　flavor 풍미, 맛　amniotic fluid 양수　shudder 몸서리치다

Let's Solve

Point 1 주어진 문장으로 글의 전개 추측하기

• From all the meals you've shared with family and friends, you are probably aware that people have very different taste preferences.

→ 사람들마다 서로 다른 음식 취향에 관련한 내용이 이어질 것이다.

Point 2 앞뒤의 단서를 찾으며 문단 읽기

From all the meals you've shared with family and friends, you are probably aware that people have very <u>different taste preferences</u>.

→ 뒷부분: 사람들은 다양한 음식 취향을 가지고 있다.

(A) The group of individuals who have considerably <u>more than an average number of taste buds</u> are called supertasters. The variations in the density of taste buds on different people's tongues <u>appear to be genetic</u>. Women are much more likely than men to be supertasters.

→ 앞부분: 평균치 이상의 미뢰를 가진 사람들

→ 뒷부분: 미뢰 수는 유전적으로 결정되는 것 같다.

(B) In fact, the foods mothers eat change the flavor of amniotic fluid, so some <u>food preferences may be shaped in utero</u>. However, people also show remarkable differences <u>in the numbers of taste buds they possess</u>.

→ 앞부분: 어떤 음식 취향은 태아일 때 형성됨

→ 뒷부분: 미뢰 수의 차이도 영향을 줌

(C) <u>Some people</u> love spicy food, for example, <u>whereas others</u> shudder at the thought of a hot pepper. Some preferences are explained by <u>differences in the flavors people experience quite early in life</u>.

→ 앞부분: 같은 매운맛에 대해 서로 다른 선호도를 가질 수 있음

→ 뒷부분: 취향의 차이는 어렸을 때 경험한 맛에 의해 생길 수 있음

Point 3 논리적인 글의 순서 추론하기

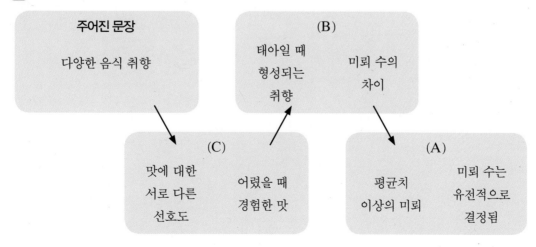

01 주어진 글 다음에 이어질 글의 순서로 가장 적절한 것은?

| 경찰대학 2018학년도 35번 |

Common law is otherwise known as case law, which is the law developed by the judges in their judgments (or rulings) on particular cases. The judges are guided by the theory and rules of precedent, which means they are bound by previous rulings that set "precedents."

(A) Equally, judges must sometimes interpret laws that Parliament has passed. One such example involved the Abortion Act 1967. A secretary declined to type a referral letter for a termination, claiming that the right to conscientiously object to participation in an abortion protected her refusal.

(B) This essentially means that they must take into account similar cases decided in the past, particularly those decided in the highest courts. This area of judge-made law is important because there will be situations where Parliament has not enacted a law and it falls to the judges to plug the gap.

(C) The judges looked at the word "participation" and decided that the secretary was not covered, as she was not sufficiently involved in the procedure. [3점]

① (A) – (C) – (B)　　　② (B) – (A) – (C)　　　③ (B) – (C) – (A)
④ (C) – (A) – (B)　　　⑤ (C) – (B) – (A)

주어진 글 다음에 이어질 글의 순서로 가장 적절한 것은?

| 경찰대학 2018학년도 36번 |

As robotics starts to spread, the degree to which countries can succeed in the robot era will depend in part on culture — on how readily people accept robots into their lives.

(A) As a result, Japanese culture tends to be more accepting of robot companions as actual companions than is Western culture, which views robots as soulless machines.

(B) The ancient Shinto religion, practiced by 80 percent of Japanese, includes a belief in animism, which holds that both objects and human beings have spirits.

(C) Western and Eastern cultures are highly differentiated in how they view robots. Not only does Japan have an economic need and the technological know-how for robots, but it also has a cultural predisposition.

① (A) – (C) – (B)　　　② (B) – (A) – (C)　　　③ (B) – (C) – (A)
④ (C) – (A) – (B)　　　⑤ (C) – (B) – (A)

주어진 글 다음에 이어질 글의 순서로 가장 적절한 것은?

Many people don't want to be travelers. They would rather be tourists, flitting over the surface of other people's lives while never really leaving their own.

(A) To be a real traveler, however, you must be willing to give yourself over to the moment and take yourself out of the center of your universe. You must believe totally in the lives of the people and the places where you find yourself.

(B) Become part of the fabric of their everyday lives. You will realize that the possibilities of life in this world are endless, and that beneath our differences of language and culture we all share the same dream of loving and being loved, of having a life with more joy than sorrow.

(C) They try to bring their world with them wherever they go, or try to recreate the world they left. They do not want to risk the security of their own understanding and see how small and limited their experiences really are.

① (A) – (C) – (B)   ② (B) – (A) – (C)   ③ (B) – (C) – (A)
④ (C) – (A) – (B)   ⑤ (C) – (B) – (A)

주어진 글 다음에 이어질 글의 순서로 가장 적절한 것은?

Imagine that you are feeling a bit down because you have just moved to a new neighborhood and are finding it difficult to meet people.

(A) After a few weeks you find that you are indeed surrounded by a close circle of friends. In fact, it is quite possible that the fortuneteller did not actually see into the future but instead actually helped to create it.

(B) Just for fun, you decide to go along to the local fortuneteller to find out what the future holds for you. The fortuneteller gazes into her crystal ball, smiles and says that the future looks bright. She says that within a few months you will be surrounded by many close and loyal friends.

(C) You are reassured by her comments and walk away feeling much happier than when you arrived. Because you now feel happy and confident about the future, you smile more, go out more and chat to more people.

① (A) – (B) – (C)   ② (A) – (C) – (B)   ③ (B) – (A) – (C)
④ (B) – (C) – (A)   ⑤ (C) – (A) – (B)

주어진 글 다음에 이어질 글의 순서로 가장 적절한 것은?

| 경찰대학 2014학년도 35번 |

Judging by the moon, I knew it was almost four weeks since I had been trapped by the snowstorm. I had stopped counting days on January 6, because on that day my prospects had suddenly taken a turn for the worse.

(A) Blustering clouds engulfed my mountainside in snow, quickly undoing all the good works of the sun. Still, I had made some progress during the sunny spell.

(B) The sensation of cool water trickling down my throat felt so good that I almost became addicted to it. I anticipated the small pleasure for hours beforehand.

(C) I discovered that if I compacted snow into balls of ice and set them in the sun, water would drip off the bottom for drinking. This was much easier than melting snow or ice in my mouth. Melting snowballs became a part of my daily ritual.

[3점]

① (A) – (B) – (C) ② (A) – (C) – (B) ③ (B) – (A) – (C)
④ (B) – (C) – (A) ⑤ (C) – (A) – (B)

주어진 글 다음에 이어질 글의 순서로 가장 적절한 것은?

| 경찰대학 2013학년도 39번 |

Logic promotes truth; yet we can go far in logic without knowing or caring much whether a particular statement is true or false, in the ordinary acceptation of those words. By *true* in ordinary speech we mean true to fact, and by *false* we mean the opposite. Now a statement, true to fact, may in its context infringe a rule of logic; and a statement, false in fact, may in its context conform to the rules of logic.

(A) The logician, as such, is not directly concerned with fact, but is much more concerned with the observance of the rules of logic, and therefore he uses a pair of technical terms, *valid* and *invalid*, to express, respectively, what conforms to the rules of logic and what does not conform thereto.

(B) A valid passport may make mistakes in fact, but if duly signed and not out of date, it may do its work and get you through the barrier. On the other hand, it may give the color of the eyes and all the other facts correctly, but if it is out of date, it will not do its work; it is invalid.

(C) By the aid of these terms he can set out the rules of reasoning without committing himself as to whether a particular statement is true to fact, or not. *Valid* comes from the Latin, *validus*, or strong.

① (A) – (B) – (C)　　② (A) – (C) – (B)　　③ (B) – (A) – (C)

④ (B) – (C) – (A)　　⑤ (C) – (A) – (B)

주어진 글 다음에 이어질 글의 순서로 가장 적절한 것은?

| 경찰대학 2012학년도 41번 |

The sense of sight has been served and illuminated by the visual arts for as long, almost, as we have been human. For a little over a hundred years, it has also been served by the camera.

(A) Since relatively few of its operators are notably well endowed in any of these respects, save perhaps in technical skill, the results are, generally, disheartening. It is now probably well on the conservative side to estimate that during the past ten to fifteen years, the camera has corrupted thousands of pairs of eyes.

(B) Well used, the camera is unique in its power to develop and to delight our ability to see. Ill or indifferently used, it is unique in its power to defile and destroy that ability. It is clear enough by now to most people that "the camera never lies" is a foolish saying.

(C) Yet it is doubtful whether most people realize how extraordinarily slippery a liar the camera is. The camera is just a machine, which records with impressive and as a rule very cruel faithfulness what is in the eye, mind, spirit, and skill of its operator.

① (A) – (B) – (C)   ② (B) – (A) – (C)   ③ (B) – (C) – (A)
④ (C) – (A) – (B)   ⑤ (C) – (B) – (A)

주어진 글 다음에 이어질 글의 순서로 가장 적절한 것은?

Spend a day among elephants, and you will come away mystified. Sudden, silent, synchronous activities — a herd taking a flight for no apparent or audible reason, a mass of scattered animals simultaneously raising ears and freezing in the tracks — such events demand explanation, but none is forthcoming.

(A) It turned out that the elephants, like the organ pipe, were the source of the throbbing. Elephants communicate with one another by means of calls too low pitched for human beings to hear.

(B) Some unknown capacity beyond memory and the five senses seems to inform elephants, silently and from a distance, of the whereabouts and activities of other elephants.

(C) Only later did a thought occur to me: As a young choir girl in New York, I used to stand next largest deepest organ pipe in the church. When the organ blasted out the bass line in a Bach chorale, the whole chapel would throb, just as the elephant room did at the zoo.

(D) I stumbled on a possible clue to these mysteries during a visit to a zoo in Portland, Oregon. While observing three Asian elephant mothers and their new calves, I repeatedly noticed a palpable throbbing in the air like distant thunder, yet all around me was silent.

① (A) – (C) – (B) – (D)   ② (B) – (A) – (D) – (C)
③ (B) – (D) – (C) – (A)   ④ (C) – (B) – (A) – (D)
⑤ (C) – (D) – (B) – (A)

다음 주어진 두 글 사이에 이어질 글의 순서로 가장 적절한 것은? | 경찰대학 2010학년도 33번 |

Lucky people are more likely than unlucky people to create, notice and act upon chance opportunities.

(A) More people start to chat to them because of their social magnetism. They are good at keeping in touch with people, too.

(B) Lucky people are also more relaxed than unlucky people, and this makes them more able to notice unexpected chance opportunities in many different aspects of their lives.

(C) They do this in various ways. They initiate conversations with more people because they are extroverts.

Finally, lucky people also introduce more variety and new experiences into their lives, and this also helps them to experience and maximize chance opportunities.

① (A) – (B) – (C)　　　② (B) – (A) – (C)　　　③ (C) – (A) – (B)

④ (A) – (C) – (B)　　　⑤ (C) – (B) – (A)

주어진 글 다음에 이어질 글의 순서로 가장 적절한 것은? | 경찰대학 2010학년도 34번 |

Gutenberg seems to have made two original technical contributions to the work of the books. He invented a new ink base.

(A) As his ink was better for vellum than paper, this improvement was not so critical, given paper was anyway replacing vellum.

(B) As many sorts were needed for every page of text and wore out quickly with repeated use, the mould was a critical development.

(C) It enabled individual letters — which are called "sorts" — to be made which could be assembled into texts, printed and taken down to be reused. The mould was also reusable, producing up to four sorts a minute, and could be easily disassembled.

(D) On the other hand, his refinement of the type-casting process was an essential advance. Gutenberg seems to have developed a little hand-held mould, a type-founder's tool, into which the liquid metal could be poured.

* vellum: 가죽으로 만든 피지

① (A) – (B) – (C) – (D)　　　② (A) – (B) – (D) – (C)

③ (A) – (D) – (C) – (B)　　　④ (B) – (A) – (C) – (D)

⑤ (B) – (C) – (A) – (D)

01 **주어진 글 다음에 이어질 글의 순서로 가장 적절한 것을 고르시오.** | 사관학교 2018학년도 35번 |

One of the most valuable outcomes from coaching people is that you also develop yourself in the process of coaching. It is the genuine passion and intention to grow others that spurs us on to transform ourselves.

(A) This cycle of learning returns over and over again throughout the entire coaching relationship. As we coach more people, we inculcate knowledge, skills, and competencies in coaching that will help us in many aspects of our professional and personal lives.

(B) During the coaching session, we gain hands-on experience and practice coaching skills and techniques. After coaching, we reflect on what happened during the dialogue and what went well, what didn't, and how we can do better next time.

(C) To develop others, we have to first develop ourselves. And to continuously change others, we can't help but continuously transform ourselves. Before we coach, we learn, we prepare, and we reflect on how we can be an effective coach.

*inculcate: 되풀이하여 가르치다 [3점]

① (A) – (C) – (B) ② (B) – (A) – (C) ③ (B) – (C) – (A)
④ (C) – (A) – (B) ⑤ (C) – (B) – (A)

주어진 글 다음에 이어질 글의 순서로 가장 적절한 것을 고르시오. | 사관학교 2017학년도 35번 |

There are certain rules that, to break them, would give us such intense pain that we don't even consider the possibility. We will rarely, if ever, break them. I call these rules threshold rules.

(A) Conversely, we have some rules that we don't want to break. I call these personal standards. If we do break them, we don't feel good about it, but depending upon the reasons, we're willing to break them in the short term. The difference between these two rules is often phrased with the words must and should.

(B) We have certain things that we *must* do, certain things that we *must not* do, certain things that we *must never* do, and certain things that we *must always* do. The "must" and the "must never" rules are threshold rules; the "should" and "should never" rules are personal standard rules. All of them give a structure to our lives.

(C) For example, if I asked you, "What's something you would never do?," you'd give me a threshold rule. You'd tell me a rule that you would never violate. Why? Because you link too much pain to it. [3점]

① (A) – (C) – (B)   ② (B) – (A) – (C)   ③ (B) – (C) – (A)
④ (C) – (A) – (B)   ⑤ (C) – (B) – (A)

주어진 글 다음에 이어질 글의 순서로 가장 적절한 것을 고르시오. | 수능 2017학년도 홀수형 37번 |

Evolution works to maximize the number of descendants that an animal leaves behind. Where the risk of death from fishing increases as an animal grows, evolution favors those that grow slowly, mature younger and smaller, and reproduce earlier.

(A) Surely these adaptations are good news for species hard-pressed by excessive fishing? Not exactly. Young fish produce many fewer eggs than large-bodied animals, and many industrial fisheries are now so intensive that few animals survive more than a couple of years beyond the age of maturity.

(B) This is exactly what we now see in the wild. Cod in Canada' Gulf of St. Lawrence begin to reproduce at around four today; forty years ago they had to wait until six or seven to reach maturity. Sole in the North Sea mature at half the body weight they did in 1950.

(C) Together this means there are fewer eggs and larvae to secure future generations. In some cases the amount of young produced today is a hundred or even a thousand times less than in the past, putting the survival of species, and the fisheries dependent on them, at grave risk. [3점]

① (A) – (C) – (B)   ② (B) – (A) – (C)   ③ (B) – (C) – (A)
④ (C) – (A) – (B)   ⑤ (C) – (B) – (A)

주어진 글 다음에 이어질 글의 순서로 가장 적절한 것을 고르시오. | 수능 2016학년도 홀수형 35번 |

Some people make few intentional changes in life. Sure, over time they may get fatter, gather lines, and go gray.

(A) They train for marathons, quit smoking, switch fields, write plays, take up the guitar, or learn to tango even if they never danced before in their lives. What is the difference between these two groups of people?

(B) But they wear their hair the same way, buy the same brand of shoes, eat the same breakfast, and stick to routines for no reason other than the ease of a comfortable, predictable life. Yet as both research and real life show, many others do make important changes.

(C) It's their perspective. People who change do not question whether change is possible or look for reasons they cannot change. They simply decide on a change they want and do what is necessary to accomplish it. Changing, which always stems from a firm decision, becomes job number one.

① (A) – (C) – (B)　　　② (B) – (A) – (C)　　　③ (B) – (C) – (A)
④ (C) – (A) – (B)　　　⑤ (C) – (B) – (A)

글의 흐름을 바탕으로 빈칸에 적절한 연결어를 고르는 유형이다. 다양한 연결어가 어떤 기능을 하는지 알아두고 빈칸 전후의 논리적 구조에 부합하는 기능의 연결어를 고른다.

- 도입부에서 글의 주제를 파악한다.
- 빈칸 앞뒤의 내용을 확인한다.
- 빈칸에 들어갈 연결어의 역할을 파악한다.

Example

빈칸 (A)와 (B)에 들어갈 말로 가장 적절한 것을 고르시오.

| 경찰대학 2018학년도 22번 |

❶ For most of your past life experiences, you would probably agree that you need to reconstruct the memories. For example, if someone asked you how you celebrated your birthday three years ago, you'd likely count backwards and try to reconstruct the context. _____(A)_____, there are some circumstances in which people believe that their memories remain completely faithful to the original events. These types of **❷** memories — which are called flashbulb memories — arise when people experience **❸** emotionally charged events: People's memories are so vivid that they seem almost to be photographs of the original incident. The first research on flashbulb memories focused on people's recollections of public events. _____(B)_____, the researchers asked participants if they had specific memories of how they first learned about the assassination of President John F. Kennedy. All but one of the 80 participants reported vivid recollections.

	(A)		(B)
①	As a result	……	Consequently
②	As a result	……	For example
❹ ③	Moreover	……	However
④	Moreover	……	Consequently
⑤	However	……	For example

Vocabulary

reconstruct 재구성하다　flashbulb 플래시 전구　assassination 암살　recollection 회상

Let's Solve

Point 1 도입부에서 글의 주제 파악하기

• For most of your past life experiences, you would probably agree that you need to reconstruct the memories.

→ 기억을 되살리는 일에 관련된 내용이 이어질 것이다.

Point 2 빈칸 앞뒤의 내용 확인하기

if someone asked you how you celebrated your birthday three years ago, you'd likely count backwards and try to reconstruct the context.

→ 오래된 기억을 떠올릴 때 일반적으로 시간을 되돌려 상황을 재구성하려 함

(A)
➡

there are some circumstances in which people believe that their memories remain completely faithful to the original events.

→ 실제 상황이 완벽하게 남아 있는 기억들이 있음

The first research on flashbulb memories focused on people's recollections of public events.

→ 초창기 플래시 전구 기억 연구는 대중적 사건에 대한 회상에 초점을 맞춤

(B)
➡

asked participants if they had specific memories of how they first learned about the assassination of President John F. Kennedy.

→ John F. Kennedy 대통령 암살에 대해 기억을 떠올려 보라고 요구함

Point 3 빈칸에 들어갈 연결어의 역할 파악하기

• (A): 빈칸 앞의 문장은 기억을 재구성하는 방식에 관한 내용이고 빈칸 뒤의 문장은 완벽한 형태로 기억이 남아 있는 경우에 대한 내용이므로, (A)에는 역접의 연결어가 적절하다.

• (B): 빈칸 앞의 문장은 초창기 연구가 대중적 사건에 초점을 두었다는 특성에 관한 내용이고 빈칸 뒤의 문장은 대통령 암살 사건을 대상으로 연구를 진행한 사례이므로, (B)에는 예시의 연결어가 적절하다.

Point 4 정답 풀이하기

① 결과적으로 …… 따라서
② 결과적으로 …… 예를 들어
③ 게다가 …… 그러나
④ 게다가 …… 따라서
⑤ 그러나 …… 예를 들어   → 역접 – 예시로 구성된 ⑤가 답이다.

01 빈칸 (A)와 (B)에 들어갈 말로 가장 적절한 것은?

| 경찰대학 2017학년도 24번 |

One basic criterion for comparing countries is their levels of economic development. The most common tool that economists use to measure economic development is gross domestic product (GDP). GDP provides a basic benchmark for the average per capita income in a country.   (A)   , GDP statistics can be quite misleading. For one thing, people may earn far more in some countries than they do in others, but those raw figures do not take into account the relative costs of living in those countries.   (B)   , as exchange rates between national currencies rise or fall, countries can look richer or poorer than they are.

	(A)		(B)
①	In contrast	······	However
②	In contrast	······	For example
③	Moreover	······	Therefore
④	However	······	Moreover
⑤	However	······	In contrast

빈칸 (A)와 (B)에 들어갈 말로 가장 적절한 것을 고르시오.

| 경찰대학 2013학년도 27번 |

Chain reactions are occurring all the time on Earth. Chain reactions occur in chemical plants when a single excited molecule prompts its neighbors into a cascade of combination to create plastics. _____(A)_____, they are commonplace in nuclear reactors, where a speeding subatomic particle slams into a heavy atom and splits it apart, releasing more particles that repeat and amplify the process in bursts of energy. Now, experts say, a dangerous new kind of chain reaction is getting under way in space, where it threatens to limit mankind's endeavors beyond the planet. _____(B)_____, it could put billions of dollars worth of advanced communications and weather satellites at risk of destruction. The problem is that some orbits near Earth have become junkyards of dead and active satellites, spent rocket stages and billions of bits of whirling debris.

	(A)		(B)
①	In consequence	······	However
②	In addition	······	However
③	By contrast	······	For instance
④	In addition	······	For instance
⑤	By contrast	······	Unfortunately

빈칸 (A)와 (B)에 들어갈 말로 가장 적절한 것을 고르시오.

The nineteenth-century American philosopher Henry David Thoreau was famous for saying, "Simplify, simplify." Unfortunately, the trend these days seems to be "complicate, complicate" instead. Many people are working longer hours, spending more money, and getting in more debt than ever before. They are also relaxing less and spending less time with family and friends. _____(A)_____, there is also a trend toward voluntary simplicity. People in the voluntary simplicity movement take various steps to make their lives both simpler and more enjoyable. Some people work fewer hours each week. Others plant a vegetable garden; this gives them fresh air, exercise, and time with their families — not to mention organic produce. Still others try to buy less; they stop buying unnecessary items. _____(B)_____, the priority for people in the voluntary movement is to follow Thoreau's suggestion: simplify.

	(A)		(B)
①	Furthermore	……	Besides
②	Furthermore	……	In short
③	Therefore	……	Besides
④	However	……	Similarly
⑤	However	……	In short

빈칸 (A)와 (B)에 들어갈 말로 가장 적절한 것끼리 짝지은 것은? | 경찰대학 2011학년도 22번 |

Black women whose ancestors were brought to the United State beginning in 1619 have lived through conditions of cruelties so horrible that the women had to reinvent themselves. They had to find safety and sanctity inside themselves or they would not have been able to tolerate those tortuous lives. They had to learn to be self-forgiving quickly, for often their exterior exploits were at odds with their interior beliefs. ___(A)___ . they had to survive as wholly and healthily as possible in an infectious and sick climate. Lives lived in such environment are either obliterated or forged into impenetrable alloys. ___(B)___ , early on and consciously, black women as reality became possibilities only to themselves. To others they were mostly seen and described in the abstract, concrete in their labor but surreal in their humanness.

	(A)		(B)
①	Similarly	⋯⋯	However
②	Still	⋯⋯	Moreover
③	Still	⋯⋯	Thus
④	Further	⋯⋯	Moreover
⑤	Further	⋯⋯	However

다음 글을 읽고 빈칸에 들어갈 가장 적절한 표현을 고르시오. | 경찰대학 2010학년도 15번 |

We use the term "motivate" to designate any way that we are "moved" to act or want something. Early attempts to explain motivation assumed that a measurable physical "need" or "drive" existed for reinforcers such as food, social support and recognition. But such theories could not explain certain activities and behaviors: Why would someone spend two years sailing around the world alone? Why would someone risk his or her life to jump out of an airplane at 10,000 feet? In these instances, no process in the body can be measured to confirm that a need or drive is really operating. _____ the idea of a need does not explain the motivating cause for many behaviors, it is a useful term when describing how a behavior persists among people or within individuals.

① Because   ② If   ③ Although

④ Considering   ⑤ When

빈칸 (A)와 (B)에 들어갈 말로 가장 적절한 것끼리 짝지은 것은? | 경찰대학 2010학년도 16번 |

Piaget's contributions need no defense. Like nearly all social scientists, I have learned much from him. Nor have his contributions been merely academic. ___(A)___, much of the recent interests in child-centered learning and in "open instruction" has been directly inspired by Piaget's views of mental development and the nature of thought. ___(B)___, it would be misleading to suggest that Piaget was oblivious to the limitations. It was with explicit intent that he elected to fix his powerful intellect upon scientific thought and thus to neglect realms of imagination, emotion, and "lived" experience.

	(A)		(B)
①	However	······	Indeed
②	However	······	Incidentally
③	Therefore	······	Likewise
④	That is	······	Otherwise
⑤	For example	······	Besides

빈칸 (A)와 (B)에 들어갈 말로 가장 적절한 것끼리 짝지은 것은? | 경찰대학 2010학년도 17번 |

Social scientists distinguish between what are known as treatment effects and selection effects. The Marine Corps, _____(A)_____, is largely a treatment effect institution. It doesn't have an enormous admissions office grading applicants along four separate dimensions of toughness and intelligence. It's confident that the experience of undergoing Marine Corps basic training will turn you into a formidable soldier. A modelling agency, _____(B)_____, is a selection-effect institution. You don't become beautiful by signing up with an agency. You get signed up by an agency because you're beautiful.

	(A)		(B)
①	therefore	……	in addition
②	for instance	……	by contrast
③	that is	……	on the other hand
④	however	……	therefore
⑤	in fact	……	likewise

01

다음 글의 빈칸 (A)와 (B)에 들어갈 말로 가장 적절한 것을 고르시오. | 사관학교 2018학년도 21번 |

A kind of personal knowledge that we have stored in our memory is the knowledge of our likes and dislikes. This is a highly personal kind of knowledge, dependent on individual taste. If we ask you,   (A)   , what your favorite kind of soup is, you might tell us that it's Borscht or Chicken Noodle or Egg Drop. You know because you have eaten many kinds of soup before, and you remember which one you liked the best. Based on that memory, you probably ask for it over and over again at home or in restaurants.   (B)   , you can easily tell us who your best friend is, who your favorite singer is, and which soccer team you like best, as well as what your favorite color or book or television program is. All of these things you remember because you have had extensive direct experience with them in the past, and you can easily compare and contrast the various experiences to determine which one gave you the most pleasure.

	(A)		(B)
①	for example	······	Similarly
②	for example	······	Therefore
③	on the contrary	······	Similarly
④	on the contrary	······	Otherwise
⑤	in other words	······	Therefore

다음 글의 빈칸 (A)와 (B)에 들어갈 말로 가장 적절한 것을 고르시오. | 사관학교 2015학년도 21번 |

A transition to an alternate energy cannot be motivated by a scarcity of fossil fuels. For decades, energy producers have continually identified new fossil fuel reserves and developed technologies to economically recover oil and gas from deposits previously deemed too difficult to access.   (A)   , Japan recently announced that they were able to extract methane from undersea hydrate deposits, which appear to contain more than twice as much carbon as in all of Earth's fossil fuel combined. This means that humanity has burned just a small portion of our fossil fuels to date. Even though we have used such a small fraction of our fossil fuels, the planet has already experienced serious warming problems. If we continue to rely heavily on fossil fuels for our energy supply, climate-change related damage will become very severe long before there is any real pressure on our fossil fuel supply.   (B)   , movement for an alternate energy must be driven by a concerted effort to keep the climate livable and healthy.

	(A)		(B)
①	For example	⋯⋯	Therefore
②	On the other hand	⋯⋯	Nevertheless
③	For example	⋯⋯	On the contrary
④	On the other hand	⋯⋯	Therefore
⑤	In the same way	⋯⋯	Nevertheless

다음 글의 빈칸 (A), (B)에 들어갈 말로 가장 적절한 것은? | 수능 2015학년도 홀수형 34번 |

New media can be defined by four characteristics simultaneously: they are media at the turn of the 20th and 21st centuries which are both integrated and interactive and use digital code and hypertext as technical means. It follows that their most common alternative names are multimedia, interactive media and digital media. By using this definition, it is easy to identify media as old or new. _____(A)_____ , traditional television is integrated as it contains images, sound and text, but it is not interactive or based on digital code. The plain old telephone was interactive, but not integrated as it only transmitted speech and sounds and it did not work with digital code. In contrast, the new medium of interactive television adds interactivity and digital code. _____(B)_____ , the new generations of mobile or fixed telephony are fully digitalized and integrated as they add text, pictures or video and they are connected to the Internet.

	(A)		(B)
①	For example	······	Additionally
②	Nevertheless	······	In other words
③	Therefore	······	Additionally
④	For example	······	In other words
⑤	Nevertheless	······	Consequently

다음 글의 빈칸 (A), (B)에 들어갈 말로 가장 적절한 것은? | 수능 2014학년도 B형 홀수형 37번 |

Oil and gas resources are not likely to be impacted by climate change because they result from a process that takes millions of years and are geologically trapped. _____(A)_____. climate change may not only force the shutting down of oil-and gas-producing areas, but increase the possibility of exploration in areas of the Arctic through the reduction in ice cover. Thus, while climate change may not impact these resources, oil and gas reserves and known or potential resources could be affected by new climate conditions, since climate change may affect access to these resources. In Siberia, _____(B)_____, the actual exploration challenge is the time required to access, produce, and deliver oil under extreme environmental conditions, where temperatures in January range from -20°C to -35°C. Warming may ease extreme environmental conditions, expanding the production frontier.

	(A)		(B)
①	On the other hand	······	however
②	On the other hand	······	for instance
③	As a result	······	for instance
④	As a result	······	however
⑤	In other words	······	therefore

PART 05
정보 파악하기

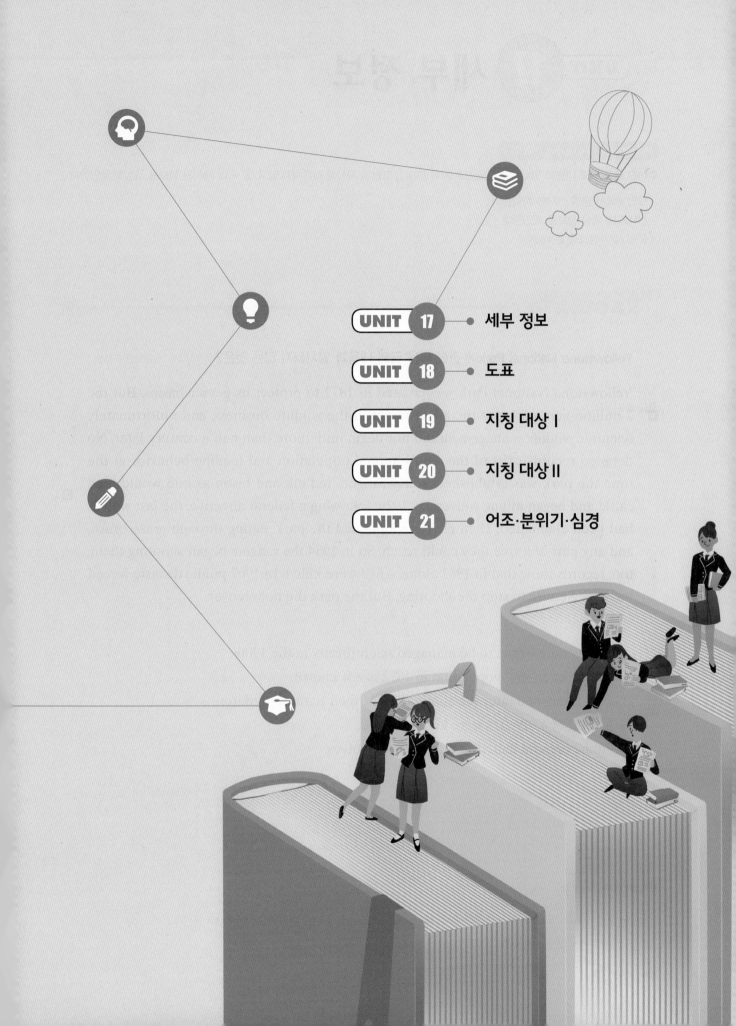

주어진 글을 읽고 내용과 일치하는 것을 고르는 유형이다. 자신의 지식에 의존하지 말고, 글 속에 제시된 정보를 세심히 확인한다.

• 도입부에서 글의 소재를 파악한다.
• 선택지의 핵심 정보를 확인한다.
• 글의 세부 정보를 분석한다.

Example

Yellowstone National Park에 관한 다음 글의 내용과 일치하지 <u>않는</u> 것은? | 경찰대학 2018학년도 15번 |

1 Yellowstone National Park was created in 1872 to protect its geyser basins. But the 2-million-acre park put the government in the wildlife business, and unfortunately scientific wildlife management did not begin until more than half a century later. No detailed records exist of the area's animal population and feeding behavior at the time the park was established. Early rangers fed elk and bison as one would feed cattle and began killing wolves. By 1926, following a federal directive, the last wolves had been eliminated. Then elk overpopulated the park, eating through grass, brush, and any part of a tree they could reach. So in 1934 the rangers began shooting them, too; records show that in 1962 alone, 4,619 were killed. In 1967 public distaste forced the Park Service to stop the shooting. But the park did not recover. **3**

2
4
① The wildlife began to be managed scientifically in the 1900s.
② The exact animal population in 1872 is not known.
③ Elks flourished after the elimination of their natural predator.
④ A total of 4,619 elks were killed in 1962.
⑤ Public opinion halted the shooting of wolves.

Vocabulary

basin 분지 bison 들소 directive 지시, 명령 eliminate 제거하다 distaste 불쾌함 predator 포식자

Let's Solve

Point 1 도입부에서 글의 소재 파악하기

• Yellowstone National Park was created in 1872 to protect its geyser basins. But ~ scientific wildlife management did not begin until more than half a century later.

→ Yellowstone National Park의 야생 동물 관리

Point 2 선택지의 핵심 정보 확인하기

① The wildlife began to be managed <u>scientifically in the 1900s</u>.
② The exact <u>animal population in 1872</u> is not known.
③ Elks flourished after <u>the elimination of their natural predator.</u>
④ A total of <u>4,619 elks were killed</u> in 1962.
⑤ <u>Public opinion</u> halted the shooting of <u>wolves</u>.

Point 3 글의 세부 정보 분석하기

• 1872년: Yellowstone National Park was created → <u>No detailed records</u> exist of the area's animal population and feeding behavior → fed elk and bison and began killing wolves
• 1926년: the last wolves had been eliminated → <u>elk overpopulated</u>
• 1934년: the rangers began shooting them
• 1962년: <u>4,619 were killed</u>
• 1967년: public distaste forced the Park Service to <u>stop the shooting</u> → the park did not recover

Point 4 정답 풀이하기

① 1900년대에 야생 동물이 과학적으로 관리되었다.
  → 도입부에서 1872년에 개장한 공원의 과학적인 관리는 반세기 이후, 즉 50년 이후까지도 시작되지 않았다고 하였으므로 과학적 관리가 시작된 것은 1900년대라고 볼 수 있다.

② 1872년의 정확한 동물 개체수는 알 수 없다.
  → 1872년 공원의 개장 당시의 동물에 대한 정확한 정보가 없다.

③ 엘크는 그들의 자연적 천적의 제거 이후에 잘 자랐다.
  → 늑대가 제거된 뒤 엘크가 번성했다.

④ 총 4,619 마리의 엘크는 1962년에 도살당했다.
  → 1962년 한 해만 4,619마리의 엘크를 죽였다.

⑤ 여론은 늑대 사냥을 중지시켰다.
  → 대중의 불쾌감으로 중지된 것은 엘크 사냥으로, 늑대가 이미 사라진 1967년의 일이다.

01 ger에 관한 다음 글의 내용과 일치하는 것은?

| 경찰대학 2018학년도 14번 |

The large, white felt tent, known as a *ger* and seen all over Mongolia, is probably the most identifiable symbol of the country. (The word "yurt" is a Turkic word introduced to the west by the Russians. If you don't want to offend the nationalistic sensibilities of the Mongolians, use the word "ger.") Most Mongolians still live in gers, even in the suburbs of Ulaan Baatar. And it's not hard to understand why: wood and bricks are scarce and expensive, especially out on the steppes, and animal hides are cheap and readily available. Nomadic people obviously have to be flexible and mobile and gers can be moved easily — depending on the size, a ger can be assembled in one to three hours. If the opportunity arises, an invitation to visit or stay in a ger is one that should not be missed.

① Most Mongolians prefer to call it a "yurt."
② You can only find it in urban areas of Ulaan Baatar.
③ It is made of wood and bricks.
④ It can be built in three hours or less.
⑤ It is not recommended for the modern traveler.

Walter Reed에 관한 다음 글의 내용과 일치하는 것은?

Walter Reed, medical doctor, was a U.S. Army physician who in 1901 found that yellow fever is transmitted by a particular mosquito species. He was born in Virginia and completed the M.D. degree in 1869 at the University of Virginia. Reed obtained his second M.D. in 1870 at New York University's Bellevue Hospital Medical College. Reed joined the U.S. Army as a medical doctor. Then, he got married in 1876. The couple had a son and a daughter, and they adopted a Native American girl later. He also served as the curator of the Army Medical Museum, which later became the National Museum of Health and Medicine. He was stationed to Cuba to study yellow fever, which killed thousands of soldiers. With the help of other doctors, Reed confirmed that the disease is transmitted by mosquitoes. This finding saved countless lives. To commemorate his achievements, many U.S. hospitals were named after Reed.

① yellow fever의 백신을 개발했다.
② medical doctor 학위를 두 번 취득했다.
③ 두 아이의 아버지가 된 후에 중국 아이를 입양했다.
④ 버지니아 의대 박물관 curator를 역임했다.
⑤ 쿠바에 자신의 이름을 딴 병원을 설립했다.

Lewis와 Clark의 탐사에 관한 다음 글의 내용과 일치하는 것은? | 경찰대학 2017학년도 15번 |

In 1803, the U.S. government purchased the entire area of Louisiana from France. The territory stretched from the Mississippi River to the middle of the Rocky Mountains, but no one was really sure where the Mississippi River started or where exactly the Rocky Mountains were located. President Thomas Jefferson commissioned an expedition in this area. It comprised a selected group of U.S. Army volunteers under the command of Captain Meriwether Lewis and Second Lieutenant William Clark. Their perilous journey lasted from May 1804 to September 1806. Their primary objective was to explore and to map the newly acquired territory, and to find a practical route across the western half of the continent. Lewis and Clark departed with forty-three men and supplies for two years. They became acquainted with a sixteen-year-old Native American woman named Sacajawea, which means Bird Woman. With her help, Lewis and Clark obtained horses from the Indians and passed the Indian territory without much trouble.

① 미국은 영국으로부터 Louisiana 지역을 매입했다.
② 탐사는 이미 알려진 Mississippi 강의 시작점에서 출발했다.
③ 탐사 대원들은 육군의 추천을 통해 선발됐다.
④ 모든 탐사를 마치기까지 4년 이상의 기간이 걸렸다.
⑤ 탐사 중에 원주민 여성의 도움을 받았다.

halibut에 관한 다음 글의 내용과 일치하지 <u>않는</u> 것은?

Halibut is a common name principally applied to the two flatfish from the family of right-eye flounders in the North Atlantic and the North Pacific. Halibut is dark brown on the top side with an off-white underbelly and has very small scales invisible to the naked eye embedded in its skin. At birth, it has an eye on each side of the head. After six months, one eye migrates to the other side. Halibut is often boiled, deep-fried or grilled while fresh. Smoking is more difficult with halibut meat than it is with salmon, due to its ultra-low fat content. Currently, the Atlantic population is so depleted through overfishing that it may be declared an endangered species.

① 북대서양과 북태평양에 서식하는 넙치과 생선이다.

② 육안으로 볼 수 없는 비늘을 가지고 있다.

③ 부화 후 6개월까지는 눈이 머리 양쪽에 있다.

④ 지방 함유량이 낮기 때문에, 연어보다 훈제하기가 어렵다.

⑤ 태평양 지역에서 멸종위기 종으로 공표되었다.

alien species에 관한 다음 글의 내용과 일치하지 <u>않는</u> 것은?

Ecologists generally define an alien species as one that people, inadvertently or deliberately, carried to its new location. "Only a small percentage of alien species cause problems in their new habitats," says a professor of ecology and evolutionary biology. Yet appearances can deceive, ecologists caution, and many of these exotics may be considered acceptable only because no one has documented their harmful effects. What is more, non-native species can appear innocuous for decades, then turn invasive. Faced with such uncertainty, many ecologists argue for strong steps to be taken. Their approach is to remove exotics from natural ecosystems. But a number of experts question the scientific wisdom of trying to roll back ecosystems to a time when they were more natural. Even many ecologists who would like to rid ecosystems of all exotics admit that this goal is impractical. Further, Professor Rosenzweig at the University of Arizona challenges the prevailing view that invasive alien species reduce biodiversity. The exotics increase the number of species in the environment. Even if alien species cause extinctions, the extinction phase will eventually end, and new species may then begin to evolve, he explains.

① 새 환경에서 거의 문제를 일으키지 않는다고 생각하는 것은 잘못된 관측일 수 있다.

② 새 환경에서 수 십 년간 무해했으나, 그 이후 환경을 해치는 경우도 있다.

③ alien species가 제거된 생태계를 선호하는 생태학자들이 있다.

④ Rosenzweig 교수는 alien species가 생태 다양성을 저해한다는 견해를 반박한다.

⑤ 다른 species의 멸종을 초래하기 시작하면 그 현상은 멈추지 않는다.

Temple Grandin에 관한 다음 글의 내용과 일치하는 것은?

What do neurologists, cattle and fast-food restaurants have in common? They all owe a great deal to one woman, a renowned animal scientist born with autism, Temple Grandin. Though she did not utter a word until her fourth birthday, she splashed onto the stage of public awareness in 1995, thanks to the famed neurologist Oliver Sacks. But as with many psychological disorders, autism is a spectrum, and Temple is on one edge. Living on this edge has allowed her to be an extraordinary source of inspiration for autistic children. She is also a source of hope for another mammal: the cow. Using her unique window into the minds of animals, she has developed housing for cattle that improves their quality of life by reducing stress. And though the fast-food industry continues to use cattle in its patties, it has come to appreciate the ethics and compassion of a Grandin burger.

① 자폐증을 갖고 태어난 동물 과학자다.
② 1995년 한 사회 비평가에 의해서 알려지게 되었다.
③ 모든 어린이들에게 영감의 원천이었다.
④ 소의 스트레스를 줄이는 사료를 개발했다.
⑤ Grandin 버거의 비윤리성을 비난했다.

filefish에 관한 다음 글의 내용과 일치하는 것은?

Now you see it, now you don't. The slender filefish has a neat way to avoid its predators. It has evolved the ability to become almost invisible. Justine Allen of Brown University was amazed by how fast the fish camouflaged themselves when she saw them in the Caribbean. It took them just two seconds to match the colors of the sea fans, or gorgonians, they swam past. How does it work? To see an object for what it is, you need to be able to perceive its edges, which mark it out as being separate from the background. Allen found that the filefish changes its coloration to create "false edges." For example, it can make a dark, longitudinal stripe appear on its body that looks like a real edge. The eye sees this false edge, and so can miss the true outline of the fish.

① 천적을 피하는 기술이 없다.
② 눈에 안 띄게 하는 능력을 상실했다.
③ 2초 만에 몸의 색을 바꿀 수 있다.
④ 몸의 크기를 늘려서 가짜 윤곽을 만든다.
⑤ 몸에 가로 줄무늬를 만든다.

A source of confusion and misunderstanding that leads to disappointment is the often complex and ambiguous language in insurance contracts. Much of the billions of dollars of damage wrought by Hurricane Katrina on the Gulf Coast of Mississippi occurred when Katrina's huge storm surge damaged or destroyed thousands of homes and businesses. Homeowners, infuriated when they realized that their policies covered wind—not water—damage, teamed with their state governments to sue insurance carriers. They argued that, even if their insurance did not cover water damage, it still should pay because Katrina's screaming winds drove a wall of water that damaged their property. The homeowners lost the suit, but the insurance industry lost much credibility and people became more concerned that their coverage was much less than it appeared to be on paper.

① 보험 계약서 상의 언어로 인해 오해가 일어나기도 한다.
② Hurricane Katrina로 수십억 달러의 피해가 발생했다.
③ 주택 소유자들은 보험회사를 상대로 소송했다.
④ 주택 소유자들은 물로 인한 피해도 보상하라고 요구했다.
⑤ 주택 소유자들은 보험회사를 상대로 한 소송에서 승소했다.

Candace Hill에 관한 다음 글의 내용과 일치하지 <u>않는</u> 것은?

Eleven seconds is the benchmark that separates the women from the girls in the 100 meters. Last Saturday, at the Brooks PR Invitational in Seattle, 16-year-old Candace Hill joined the elite group with a scorching win in 10.98 seconds, becoming the first U.S. high school girl to break the 11-second barrier, smashing the American junior and world youth records. Candace, who finished her second year at Rockdale County High in Georgia last month, is a five-time national champion, and already held Georgia state records in the 100- and 200-meter dash. Her record-setting race would have earned third place at this year's NCAA championships and tied for 10th best in the world this season.

① Seattle에서 개최된 대회에 참가했다.
② 11초 벽을 깬 최초의 미국 여고생이다.
③ 지난달에 고등학교 2학년을 마쳤다.
④ Georgia주 200미터 경주 기록 보유자이다.
⑤ 올해 NCAA 대회에서 3등을 차지했다.

Garth Brooks에 관한 다음 글의 내용과 일치하는 것은?

Garth Brooks has had a nice, long retirement. Now, it appears to be over. During a news conference Thursday in Nashville, Brooks, 52, is expected to announce details of his comeback, most likely including plans for a world tour. The country superstar, who ranks behind only The Beatles and Elvis Presley in U.S. album sales, walked away from the music business in 2001 to raise his three daughters. Since then, he has only sporadically performed and released music. With Brooks' youngest daughter, Allie, entering college in the fall, the stage is set for his return. He's a master at building anticipation: Last week, his website teased an announcement about the day he'd make his real announcement. It's entirely possible he'll reveal only a portion of his big plan at the event. Or a tour could be only part of what he announces. What else might Brooks be ready to talk about?

[3점]

① 2001년 은퇴에 대한 이유가 밝혀지지 않았다.
② 은퇴 이후에는 음악 활동을 하지 않았다.
③ 미국 내 앨범 판매량에서 2위를 차지한다.
④ 자신의 행보에 대한 궁금증을 잘 유발시킨다.
⑤ 세계 순회공연의 세부계획을 발표하였다.

Youth Ambassadors campaign에 관한 다음 글의 내용과 일치하는 것은?

| 경찰대학 2015학년도 15번 |

Starting this summer the Hong Kong government plans to have 200,000 youths search Internet discussion sites for illegal copies of copyrighted songs and movies, and report them to the authorities. The campaign has delighted the entertainment industry, but prompted misgivings among some civil liberties advocates. The so-called Youth Ambassadors campaign will start on Wednesday with 1,600 youths pledging their participation at a stadium in front of leading Hong Kong film and singing stars and several Hong Kong government ministers. The Youth Ambassadors represent a new reliance on youths to keep order on the Internet. All members of the Boy Scouts, Girl Guides, and nine other uniformed youth groups, ranging in age from 9 to 25, will be expected to participate.

① 홍콩 젊은이들이 노래와 영화에 대해 토론하는 장이다.
② 연예계뿐만 아니라 모든 계층의 환영을 받았다.
③ 참가 선서는 체육계 인사들 앞에서 할 예정이다.
④ 비슷한 캠페인이 예전에도 시도된 적이 있다.
⑤ 열 개 이상의 단체가 참여할 예정이다.

Utah offers the advanced skier the opportunity to ski up to five world-class resorts in a single day with the Interconnect Adventure Tour. The tours, operated by Ski Utah under a special-use permit granted by the U.S. National Forest Service, are conducted by experienced backcountry guides trained in avalanche safety and control. Skiers registering for the tour must be in good physical condition with ski experience in various snow conditions. Each participant's ability is tested prior to the tour's departure. Tours operating on Sunday, Monday, Wednesday and Friday begin at Park City and take in Park City, Brighton, Solitude, Alta and Snowbird; it takes eight hours to complete, with a rest stop for lunch. Tours operating on Tuesday, Thursday and Saturday begin at Snowbird and include Snowbird, Alta, Brighton and Solitude.

① 하루 동안 여러 개의 리조트에서 스키를 즐길 기회를 제공한다.
② 참가자는 눈사태 발생에 대비한 안전 교육을 받아야 한다.
③ 다양한 조건의 눈에서 스키를 탄 경험이 있어야 등록할 수 있다.
④ 출발 전에 모든 참가자의 스키 실력을 테스트한다.
⑤ 토요일에 진행되는 투어는 Park City를 이용할 수 없다.

Gersenson에 관한 다음 글의 내용과 일치하지 <u>않는</u> 것은?

Even as he was disassembling cardboard boxes in a garage that served as the warehouse for his just-launched organic produce home-delivery venture, David Gersenson's gut told him Door to Door Organics was destined for big things. "While I was breaking down the boxes, I knew this thing was going to take off," he recalls of that moment in 1997 when he foresaw the future of his company. Started for about $700 in Upper Bucks County, Pa., the business was based on an idea he hatched in his early 20s after eating organic produce on a trip to India. While Gersenson's vision proved prophetic, he could hardly have predicted the outcome of the strategic decisions he made along the way to turn Door to Door Organics into the bustling multistate company it is today. The online grocer of natural and organic produce employs more than 200 people in five metro markets around the country, posted $26 million in revenue in 2013 and is projected to grow to more than $40 million this year.

① 사업을 시작한 초창기에는 차고를 창고로 활용하였다.
② 사업에 대한 구상은 20대 때 인도 여행을 준비하면서 착안하였다.
③ 그의 회사는 유기농 식품을 온라인으로 주문받아 집으로 배달해 준다.
④ 회사 성장 과정에서 내린 결정들이 가져올 결과를 거의 예측할 수 없었다.
⑤ 올해 회사의 수익은 2013년 대비 50% 이상 성장할 것으로 추정된다.

14

Kevin Han에 관한 다음 글의 내용과 일치하는 것은?

| 경찰대학 2014학년도 14번 |

Twenty-seven-year-old lawyer Kevin Han is frugal. Breakfast is 5 yuan (82 cents) for a cup of soybean milk and a hard-boiled egg. He has a 20-yuan lunch of white rice with small portions of meat and vegetables in the cafeteria at his workplace in Beijing. He spends the same for dinner. Han gets deals buying clothes online, lives in a cheap rental apartment, and takes the subway to work (4 yuan round-trip). Scrimping is a must if he's to buy his own place. He makes 13,000 yuan per month and saves about half. "My parents are not rich. So I have to save everything by myself."

① 저축하기 위해 아침을 거른다.
② 점심보다 비싼 저녁식사를 한다.
③ 온라인 의류 사업을 한다.
④ 매달 약 6,500 yuan을 저축한다.
⑤ 부유한 부모 밑에서 자랐다.

15

Ed Sheeran에 관한 다음 글의 내용과 일치하는 것은?

| 경찰대학 2014학년도 15번 |

"I'm going to go home and watch TV," says Ed Sheeran after serenading a sold-out crowd at his Radio City Music Hall show. The 22-year-old Grammy-nominated singer-songwriter isn't concerned with being anything other than who he really is: the folk-pop rapper your parents might actually listen to. And so far, this refreshing approach seems to be getting him places. Don't believe us? Ask his 6.5-plus million Twitter followers and the thousands of screaming girls who show up at countless concerts simply to see him. Some think Ed is an overnight music sensation, but the Halifax, England native grew up in an artistic home where his love of music was nurtured at a young age.

① 관중들에게 노래하기 전에 TV를 시청할 거라고 말했다.
② Grammy상 후보가 되는 것 말고는 관심이 없다.
③ 6천 5백 만 명 이상의 Twitter follower가 있다.
④ 아무도 그가 하루 밤 사이에 성공했다고 믿지 않는다.
⑤ England 출신으로 예술적 가정 분위기에서 자랐다.

Pete Bodharamik에 관한 다음 글의 내용과 일치하지 <u>않는</u> 것은? | 경찰대학 2014학년도 16번 |

Five years ago Pete Bodharamik was a 35-year-old with a big challenge. He had just taken over Jasmine International, the telecom holding company his father had started back in 1982. It was going through rough times, emerging from years in bankruptcy court after his father had diversified on borrowed money in the 1990s. And expectations weren't high that Pete was the one to turn things around. But Pete had spent his time delving into content for new forms of media and pursuing his love of pop culture and entertainment. He invested heavily in expanding Jasmine's limited broadband network in the provinces far from Bangkok, where there was little competition. He fed those big pipes with movies, television shows, music videos, games and other rich content, sometimes produced by the media company he had started.

① 부친이 시작한 회사를 인수했다.
② 부친은 돈을 빌려 사업을 다양화했다.
③ 대중문화에 대한 애정을 버리지 않았다.
④ Bangkok 시내 지역에 투자를 집중했다.
⑤ 자기가 시작한 회사가 콘텐츠를 생산하기도 했다.

Sousa에 관한 다음 글의 내용과 일치하지 <u>않는</u> 것은?

John Philip Sousa started his music education by playing the violin at the age of six. At the age of thirteen, his father, a trombonist in the Marine Band, enlisted Sousa in the U.S. Marine Corps as an apprentice. Several years after serving his apprenticeship, Sousa joined a theatrical orchestra where he learned to conduct. The marching brass bass, or sousaphone, was created in 1893 by J. W. Pepper, a Philadelphia instrument maker, with several of Sousa's suggestions in its design. He organized the Sousa Band the year he left the Marine Band. The band played both in America and around the world, including at the World Exposition in Paris. Sousa passed away from a heart attack at the age of 77 in Pennsylvania. He had conducted a rehearsal of "The Stars and Stripes Forever" the previous day with the Ringgold Band. He was posthumously enshrined in the Hall of Fame for Great Americans in 1976.

① 어릴 때 바이올린을 연주하였으며, 아버지는 미 해병대 밴드의 트롬본 연주자였다.
② 미 해병대 실습생 생활을 마치고, 극장 오케스트라 단원이 되었고, 거기서 지휘를 배웠다.
③ 필라델피아 악기제작자 J. W. Pepper의 제안으로 sousaphone을 만들었다.
④ 그의 Sousa Band는 파리 세계 엑스포에서도 연주하였다.
⑤ 심장 마비로 갑자기 죽은 후, 명예의 전당의 일원이 되었다.

Hollywood sign에 관한 다음 글의 내용과 일치하는 것은?

The Hollywood sign in the hills that line the northern border of Los Angeles is a famous landmark recognized the world over. The white-painted, 50-foot-high sheet metal letters can be seen from great distances across the Los Angeles basin. The sign was not constructed, as one might suppose, by the movie business as a means of celebrating the importance of Hollywood to this industry; instead, it was first constructed in 1923 as a means of advertising homes for sale in a 500-acre housing subdivision in a part of Los Angeles called "Hollywoodland." The sign that was constructed at the time, of course, said "Hollywoodland." Over the years, people began referring to the area by the shortened version "Hollywood," and after the sign and its site were donated to Los Angeles in 1945, the last four letters were removed. The sign suffered from years of disrepair, and in 1973 it was completely replaced, at a cost of $27,000 per letter. Various celebrities including Alice Cooper were instrumental in helping to raise needed funds.

① Los Angeles 북쪽 경계인 평야지대에 있다.
② Hollywood의 영화 산업을 홍보하기 위해 제작되었다.
③ 1945년에 부지와 함께 Hollywoodland에 기부되었다.
④ 1973년에 총 $27,000의 비용을 들여 교체되었다.
⑤ 유명 인사들이 교체 비용을 모금하는 데에 기여했다.

다음 글의 내용과 일치하지 <u>않는</u> 것을 고르시오.

India is part of the Asian subcontinent and is home to over 1 billion people. Only China has a larger population. A little over half of India's land is suited to agriculture, but about 65 percent of Indians are farmers or farm laborers. They raise rice, wheat, cotton, cattle, sheep and water buffalo. To increase output, the government instituted irrigation and land reclamation projects. Newer types of crops and fertilizers have also been tried. India is one of the nations benefiting from the Green Revolution. Unfortunately, India's initial high hopes for the Green Revolution have proven to be illusory because of the high costs for the seeds and fertilizer and the environmental issues arising from the massive use of pesticides.

① India의 인구는 10억이 넘는다.

② India에서 농업에 적합한 토지는 전 국토의 절반을 조금 넘는다.

③ India의 농부들은 물소를 숭배한다.

④ India 정부는 관개 사업과 토지 개간 사업을 실시했다.

⑤ Green Revolution에 대한 India의 기대치가 처음에는 높았다.

Thoreau noted that "many a traveler came out of his way to see me," including his friends, schoolchildren, aimless tourists, and the down and out from local almshouses who were far more interesting than some of his more affluent drop-ins. Thoreau had no tolerance for babble but was responsive to children who brought him flowers, weeds, and dead animals. On the whole, they entertained themselves, unlike some of his adult "unreckoned guests." Some of the more shameless, Thoreau suspected, came when he was out walking in the woods and rooted through his drawers and cabinets. Most of the guests came from nearby Concord and Lincoln, or from Boston. "Girls and boys and young women generally seemed glad to be here in the woods," Thoreau wrote. "They looked in the pond and at the flowers, and improved their time. Men of business, even farmers, thought only of solitude and employment, and of the great distance at which I dwelt from something or other; and though they said they loved a ramble in the woods occasionally, it was evident that they did not."

① Thoreau의 방문객 중에는 부유층뿐만 아니라 빈민층도 있었다.
② Thoreau는 죽은 동물을 가져오는 어린이들에게 화를 내기도 했다.
③ Thoreau는 일부 방문객들이 그의 서랍을 뒤진다고 의심했다.
④ Thoreau를 찾는 대부분의 방문객은 Concord, Lincoln, Boston에서 왔다.
⑤ Thoreau는 사업가나 농부가 숲속 산책을 즐기지 않는다고 생각했다.

21 다음 글의 내용과 일치하는 것을 고르시오.

The Whistling Swan is an all-white bird of amazing grace and beauty, except its bill and feet which are black. Its name does not refer to the call of the bird which is a low, melodic sound, but refers to the sound the bird's powerful wings make in flight. The migration of this swan is an incredible 3,725 miles round trip. While these animals flock together during migration, they are solitary nesters, choosing a site near a pond or slow-moving river. An excellent nesting site may be used year after year by the same birds. The female usually lays four to five eggs and incubates them for about a month with some help from the male. After the eggs hatch, both parents tend to the young swans and lead them to food source. Although the young can fly at two to three months of age, they usually stay with the parents through the first winter.

① Whistling Swan의 부리는 하얀색이다.
② Whistling Swan의 이름은 울음소리에서 유래되었다.
③ Whistling Swan은 둥지를 숲에 짓는다.
④ Whistling Swan의 수컷은 새끼를 돌보지 않는다.
⑤ Whistling Swan은 부화 후 2-3달이 지나면 날 수 있다.

다음 글의 내용과 일치하는 것을 고르시오.

It is not enough to say, "We must not wage war." It is necessary to love peace and sacrifice for it. We must concentrate not merely on the eradication of war but on the affirmation of peace. A fascinating story about Ulysses and the Sirens is preserved for us in Greek literature. The Sirens had the ability to sing so sweetly that sailors could not resist steering toward their island. Many ships were lured upon the rocks, and men forgot home, duty and honor as they flung themselves into the sea to be embraced by arms that drew them down to death. Ulysses, determined not to succumb to the Sirens, first decided to tie himself tightly to the mast of his boat and his crew stuffed their ears with wax. But finally he and his crew learned a better way to save themselves: They took on board the beautiful singer Orpheus, whose melodies were sweeter than the music of the Sirens. When Orpheus sang, who would bother to listen to the Sirens? So we must see that peace represents a sweeter music, a cosmic melody that is far superior to the discords of war. Somehow we must transform the dynamics of the world power struggle from the nuclear arms race, which no one can win, to a creative contest to harness man's genius for the purpose of making peace and prosperity a reality for all the nations of the world.

① 평화를 위해 노력하는 것보다 전쟁을 억제하는 것이 더 중요하다.
② 사이렌의 유혹에서 벗어나기 위해 선원들은 돛대에 몸을 묶었다.
③ 선원들은 사이렌의 노래보다 달콤한 오르페우스의 노래에 귀를 기울였다.
④ 오르페우스의 노래는 전쟁의 승리를 상징한다.
⑤ 핵무기 경쟁을 피하기 위해 인간의 천재성을 발휘해야 한다.

다음 글의 내용과 일치하지 <u>않는</u> 것을 고르시오.

The Pleiades, also known as Messier 45, are among those objects which are known since the earliest times. According to Kenneth Glyn Jones, the earliest known references to this cluster are mentionings by Homer in his *Iliad* (about 750 B.C.) and his *Odyssey* (about 720 B.C.). The stars in the Pleiades are thought to have formed together around 100 million years ago, making them 1/50 the age of our sun. Even though they lie some 425 light years away, at least 6 member stars are visible to the naked eye, while under clear dark skies this number jumps up to more than a dozen. Modern observing methods have revealed that at least about 500 mostly faint stars belong to the Pleiades star cluster, spread over a 2 degree (four times the diameter of the Moon) field. Their density is pretty low, compared to other open clusters. This is one reason why the life expectation of the Pleiades cluster is also pretty low.

① Homer는 그의 저서에서 Pleiades에 대해 언급하였다.
② Pleiades는 태양보다 훨씬 오래 전에 생성되었다.
③ Pleiades는 약 425광년 떨어져 있다.
④ Pleiades에는 적어도 약 500개의 별들이 무리를 이루고 있다.
⑤ Pleiades에 속하는 일부의 별은 육안으로 관찰할 수 있다.

After I realized the extent to which men work from a base of unacknowledged privilege, I understood that much of their oppressiveness was unconscious. Then I remembered the frequent charges from women of color that white women whom they encounter are oppressive. I began to understand why we are justly seen as oppressive, even when we don't see ourselves that way. I began to count the ways in which I enjoy unearned skin privilege and have been conditioned into oblivion about its existence. My schooling gave me no training in seeing myself as an oppressor, as an unfairly advantaged person, or as a participant in a damaged culture. I was taught to see myself as an individual whose moral state depended on her individual moral will. My schooling followed the pattern my colleague Elisabeth Minnich has pointed out: whites are taught to think of their lives as morally neutral, normative, and average, and also ideal, so that when we work to benefit others, this is seen as work which will allow "them" to be more like "us".

① 화자는 남성들이 대개 무의식적으로 억압자의 역할을 한다고 믿는다.
② 유색인 여성들은 종종 백인여성들이 억압적이라고 비난한다.
③ 학생시절 화자는 백인여성들이 억압적이라고 생각하지 않았다.
④ 화자는 개인의 윤리가 집단 윤리에 근거한다고 배웠다.
⑤ 화자는 백인들의 삶이 도덕적으로 중립적이고 이상적이라고 학교에서 배웠다.

25

다음 글에서 추론할 수 있는 내용으로 적절하지 <u>않은</u> 것은?

| 경찰대학 2012학년도 38번 |

Taking turns attempts to build consensus while recognizing political or social differences, and it encourages everyone to play. The taking-turns approach gives those with the most support more turns, but it also legitimates the outcome from each individual's perspective, including those whose views are shared only by a minority. I do not believe that democracy should encourage rule by the powerful — even a powerful majority. Instead, the idea of democracy promises a fair discussion among self-defined equals about how to achieve our common aspirations. To redeem that promise, we need to put the idea of taking turns at the center of our conception of representation. Particularly as we move into the twenty-first century as a more highly diversified citizenry, it is essential that we consider the ways in which voting and representational systems succeed or fail at encouraging the system in which majority rules but is not tyrannical.

① The idea of monolithic majority should not be encouraged.
② The majority that rules, but is not overbearing is desirable.
③ The majority should not be shifting, but fixed for effectiveness.
④ The minority will show active participation under the taking turns system.
⑤ Despotism comes not just from kings or lords, but from the majority of people as well.

26 다음 글의 내용과 일치하는 것을 고르시오.

Unlike its avian peers, the ostrich spawns a variety of luxury products. Start with the meat, which aficionados liken in taste to beef tenderloin. At about $20 per lb., there's a wealth of cuts to be had from the average 400-lb. bird. Ostrich meat is healthful as well: half the calories of beef, one-seventh the fat and considerably less cholesterol, and it even bests chicken and turkey in those categories. "Our customers thought we were kidding at first. Ostrich?" says a restaurant manager. "But then they became fascinated by it." One out of four diners orders the lean meat in the restaurant. Even if ostriches don't become high class cuisine, investors are hoping the big birds achieve greater fame than a spot on *Sesame Street*. Ostrich eyelashes are used as paintbrush bristles, feathers for dusting and hats and coats, and the thick, tough hide is prized for everything from cowboy boots to sofas.

*aficionado: 애호가

① 타조 고기는 육질이 떨어져 상품화 가능성이 낮은 편이다.
② 타조 고기는 칼로리 함유량이 쇠고기의 절반이다.
③ 타조 고기는 닭이나 칠면조 고기에 비해 콜레스테롤 함유량은 낮지만 칼로리 함유량은 높다.
④ 타조 요리는 초창기에는 식당에서 인기가 많았으나 점차 열기가 식어갔다.
⑤ 타조 깃털은 카우보이 부츠와 소파에 사용된다.

다음 글의 내용과 일치하는 것을 고르시오.

| 경찰대학 2011학년도 32번 |

Long ago on the little island of Nauru, far away in the western Pacific, a happy people lived and had everything they needed there: coconut trees for food and drink, abundant bird life and an ocean full of fish. And the natives of Nauru were living on one of the richest piles of phosphate rock on the globe. Then it happened one hundred years ago that a piece of fossilized wood, carried off from Nauru to Australia as a souvenir, caught the eye of a chemist He examined it and found it was quite valuable. For most of the 20th century, millions of tons of the phosphate were shipped to Australia and New Zealand, where they fertilized fields and farms. Following the island's independence in 1968, the phosphate mines were nationalized, and the citizens of the smallest republic in the world joined the ranks of the wealthiest. Today, however, these once self-sufficient people are caught up in a grim fairy tale. The phosphate is almost gone, and most of the money, too. The heart is dug out of four-fifths of the island.

*phosphate: 인산염. 인산 광물

① 나우루 사람들은 조상 대대로 인산염을 생계 수단으로 삼았다.
② 오스트레일리아 화학자가 검사한 인산염은 별로 가치가 없었다.
③ 오스트레일리아와 뉴질랜드로 선적된 인산염은 비료로 사용되었다.
④ 인산염이 국유화한 직후부터 나우루 사람들은 가난해졌다.
⑤ 나우루 섬에서 인산염을 채굴한 면적은 절반 정도 이다.

다음 글의 내용과 일치하지 <u>않는</u> 것을 고르시오.

The first humans to give up the hunter–gatherer way of life settled down on the eastern Mediterranean coast to grow wheat and barley, then tamed sheep and goats for meat and milk, most archaeologists believe. But excavations at a 10,000-year-old village in Turkey paint a different picture. Residents of round stone houses hunted wild sheep and goats and ate nuts and legumes but also raised pigs, perhaps 500 years before the earliest known domesticated sheep and goats. The dig led by Michael Rosenberg of the University of Delaware, reveals a community that lasted several hundred years. Evidence that villagers raised pigs includes teeth that are generally smaller than those of wild pigs. Most of the pig bones came from males; females were likely spared for breeding. Methods learned in raising pigs were later applied to wild sheep and goats, Rosenberg believes.

① 대부분의 고고학자들은 Rosenberg의 발굴 결과와 다른 의견을 가지고 있다.
② Rosenberg가 발굴한 돌집에 거주했던 사람들은 양과 염소를 사냥했었다.
③ Rosenberg가 발굴한 마을은 수백 년 동안 지속되었던 것으로 밝혀졌다.
④ 돼지를 길렀다는 증거는 발견된 뼈가 야생 돼지 뼈보다 크다는 점이다.
⑤ Rosenberg는 돼지를 기르는 방법이 양과 염소에 적용되었다고 믿는다.

다음 글에서 추론할 수 있는 내용으로 적절하지 <u>않은</u> 것은?

In coming years, NASA and other space agencies will intensify the search for life in the solar system. But the search is complicated by a fundamental mystery: What is life, anyway? NASA has been using a simple working definition: "Life is a self-sustained chemical system capable of undergoing Darwinian evolution." Other scientists have circulated their own definition, such as, "Life is a chemical system able to replicate itself through autocatalysis and to make mistakes that gradually increase the efficiency of the autocatalysis." Life tends to elude capture by any single definition. Maybe life, for example, doesn't have to evolve. Imagine creatures that have no information-bearing molecules like DNA. They might reproduce but not replicate. The parent would be no more biologically related to the child than to a complete stranger.

*autocatalysis: 자가 촉매작용

① Definition of life complicate the search for life in the solar system.
② The concept of Darwinian evolution is reflected in NASA's definition of life.
③ Many scientists have their own definition of life different from that of NASA.
④ It is very difficult for a single definition to capture the nature of life.
⑤ If an organism replicates, its child is not biologically related to its parent.

다음 글에서 추론할 수 있는 것으로 가장 적절한 것은?　　| 경찰대학 2011학년도 39번 |

You are sharpest in your 20's; around 30, memory begins to decline, particularly your ability to perform mathematical computations. But your I.Q. for other takes climbs. Your vocabulary at age 45, for example, is three times as great as when you graduated from college. At 60, your brain possesses almost four times as much information as it did at age 21. Though the peak in most fields comes early — most Nobel prize winners did their top research in their late 20's and 30's, and most of the great music was written by men between 33 and 39 — some people continue to produce quality work throughout their lives. At 71, Tolstoi completed *Resurrection;* Voltaire wrote his marvelous satire *Candide* at 64. Will Durant began to write five volumes of the monumental *History of a Civilization* when he was 69.

① Memory loss does not affect the well-conditioned body.
② Aged women tend to be better at figures than aged men.
③ Life has certain achievement patterns, but it has some exceptions.
④ People can have only one prime period in their lives, so don't miss it.
⑤ There are times in which the balance between loss and gain is broken.

다음 글의 내용과 일치하지 <u>않는</u> 것은?

A momentary flash of lightning and the sound of a tree branch snapping represent stimulation of exceedingly brief duration, but they may nonetheless provide important information that can require some response. Such stimuli are initially — and briefly — stored in sensory memory, the first repository of the information that the world presents to us. Actually, the term "sensory memory" encompasses several types of sensory memories, each related to a different source of sensory information. There is iconic memory, which reflects information from our visual system; echoic memory, which stores information coming from the ears; and corresponding memories for each of the other senses. Regardless of the individual subtypes, sensory memory in general is able to store information for only a very short time, and if material does not pass to another form of memory, that information is lost for good.

① Even a brief stimulation provides information that can require some response.

② Some subtypes of sensory memories store information for a long period.

③ There are more than two types of sensory memories.

④ The information we are exposed to is first stored in sensory memory.

⑤ Iconic and echoic memories store visual and auditory information, respectively.

01 Andy Warhol에 관한 다음 글의 내용과 일치하지 <u>않는</u> 것은? | 사관학교 2017학년도 32번 |

In 1967, Andy Warhol was asked to lecture at various colleges. He hated to talk, particularly about his own art; "The less something has to say," he felt, "the more perfect it is." But the money was good, so Warhol always found it hard to say no. His solution was simple: he asked an actor, Allen Midgette, to impersonate him. Midgette was dark-haired, tan, part Cherokee Indian. He did not resemble Warhol in the least. But Warhol and friends covered his face with powder, sprayed his brown hair silver, gave him dark glasses, and dressed him in Warhol's clothes. Since Midgette knew nothing about art, his answers to students' questions tended to be as short and enigmatic as Warhol's own. The impersonation worked. Warhol may have been an icon, but no one really knew him, and since he often wore dark glasses, even his face was unfamiliar in any detail.

*enigmatic: 수수께끼 같은

① 자신의 예술에 대해 이야기하는 것을 싫어했다.
② 돈 때문에 강연 요청을 거절하기 힘들었다.
③ 자신을 전혀 닮지 않은 배우를 자신처럼 분장시켰다.
④ 예술에 조예가 깊은 사람을 골라 대신 강연하게 했다.
⑤ 짙은 색의 안경을 자주 썼기에 얼굴이 상세하게 알려지지 않았다.

러시아 문학에 관한 다음 글의 내용과 일치하지 않는 것은? | 사관학교 2016학년도 32번 |

During the century that it has existed in adequate English translation, the Russian canon of novels and plays has acquired a reputation and a certain "tone." It is serious (that is, tragic or absurd, but rarely lighthearted and never trivial), somewhat preacherly, often politically oppositionist, and frequently cast in a mystifying genre with abrupt or bizarre beginnings and ends. The novels especially are too long, too full of metaphysical ideas, too manifestly eager that readers not just read the story for fun or pleasure but learn a moral lesson. These books are deep into good and evil even while they parody those pretensions. If there is comedy, there is a twist near the end that turns your blood to ice. Russian literary characters don't seek the usual money, career, success in society for its own sake, trophy wife or husband, house in the suburbs, but instead crave some other unattainable thing.

*canon: 진짜 작품(목록)

① 소설과 희곡은 명성을 얻었다.
② 소설과 희곡은 다소 설교적인 색채를 띤다.
③ 소설은 도덕적 교훈을 배제하고 즐거움을 추구한다.
④ 희극의 끝부분에서는 뜻밖의 전개가 일어난다.
⑤ 문학작품의 등장인물은 얻기 어려운 것을 갈망한다.

Great Salt Lake에 관한 다음 글의 내용과 일치하지 <u>않는</u> 것은? | 수능 2013학년도 홀수형 34번 |

The Great Salt Lake is the largest salt lake in the Western Hemisphere. The lake is fed by the Bear, Weber, and Jordan rivers and has no outlet. At the close of the Ice Age the entire region was submerged beneath a lake of meltwater, and overflow from the lake flowed into the Pacific Ocean through the Snake and Columbia rivers. The great climatic change the lake underwent and continued evaporation, exceeding the inflow of fresh water, reduced the lake to one-twentieth of its former size. The majority of salt in the Great Salt Lake is a remnant of dissolved salts that are present in all fresh water. As the water evaporated, the traces of dissolved salts were gradually concentrated in the shrinking lake.

① 서반구에서 가장 큰 소금호수이다.

② Bear 강, Weber 강, Jordan 강에서 물이 유입된다.

③ 전 지역이 물에 잠긴 적이 있다.

④ 심한 기후 변화와 계속된 증발로 크기가 줄었다.

⑤ 대부분의 소금은 바닷물이 증발하여 남은 것이다.

Fourier에 관한 다음 글의 내용과 일치하지 <u>않는</u> 것은?

Jean Baptiste Joseph Fourier was a French mathematician and physicist. When he was eight years old, his father died, and less than a year after this tragedy, his mother passed away, leaving him an orphan. A charitable lady helped him attend a local military school. He wanted to become an officer but was not allowed to because he was the son of a tailor. In 1795, he became a teacher at the École Normale in Paris. During the post-Revolution frenzy, he spoke out against the use of the guillotine, for which he almost lost his life. When Napoleon invaded Egypt in 1798, Fourier and other scholars accompanied the expedition. Having returned to France, Fourier began his research on heat conduction. His mathematical theory of heat conduction earned him lasting fame. During his stay in Egypt he contracted a strange illness that confined him to well-heated rooms for the rest of his life. On May 16, 1830, Fourier died in Paris.

*guillotine: 단두대

① 프랑스의 수학자이자 물리학자였다.
② 재단사의 아들이라는 이유로 장교가 되지 못했다.
③ 단두대 사용에 반대하다가 목숨을 잃을 뻔했다.
④ 열전도에 관한 수학 이론으로 명성을 얻었다.
⑤ 이집트에서 프랑스로 돌아온 후 이상한 병에 걸렸다.

Problem Solving Skills

도표 속의 정보를 영어로 설명했을 때 이해할 수 있는지 묻는 유형이다. 도표의 수치, 제목, 단위 등과 관련된 영어식 표현법을 이해하고 도표의 내용을 지문의 설명과 꼼꼼히 비교한다.

• 도표 제목과 첫 문장으로 소재를 파악한다.
• 선택지와 비교하여 일치 여부를 확인한다.

Example

다음 도표의 내용과 일치하지 않는 것은? | 경찰대학 2012학년도 30번 |

1

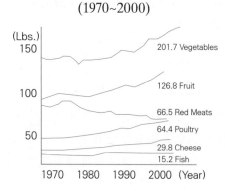

Annual Food Consumption by the Average American
(1970~2000)

The graph above shows the changes in the amount of the consumption of different foods during the period ranging from 1970 to 2000. ① The consumption of vegetables and fruits increased more than 20 percent during the 30 year span. ② The difference between red meats and poultry consumption was minimized in the year 2000. ③ The consumption of cheese had increased continuously while that of fish had stayed almost still throughout these three decades. ④ No food showed any decrease in the consumption rate during the same period. ⑤ The total amount of fruits and vegetables consumed by the average American in the year 2000 exceeded that of all other foods in the same year.

2

Vocabulary

poultry 가금류 span 한 뼘, 일정한 거리, 기간 exceed 초월하다, 능가하다

Let's Solve

Point 1 도표 제목과 첫 문장으로 소재 파악하기

> Annual Food Consumption by the Average American

> The graph above shows the changes in the amount of the consumption of different foods during the period ranging from 1970 to 2000.

⬇

> 1970년부터 2000년까지 미국인의 식품별 연간 소비량 변화 추이

Point 2 선택지와 비교하여 일치 여부 확인하기

① 30년의 기간 동안 채소와 과일의 소비는 20퍼센트 이상 증가했다.
　➜ 채소 소비량은 1970년 150파운드에서 2000년 201.7파운드로, 과일 소비량은 1970년 100파운드에서 2000년 126.8파운드로 증가해, 둘 모두 소비량이 20퍼센트 이상 증가했다.

② 붉은 육류와 가금육 소비량의 차이는 2000년에 가장 작았다.
　➜ 붉은 육류 소비량은 2000년에 가장 적고 가금육 소비량은 2000년에 가장 많으므로 두 식품의 소비량 차이는 2000년에 가장 작다.

③ 치즈 소비량은, 생선 소비량이 최근 30년 간 거의 고정적으로 유지되었던 것에 반해, 지속적으로 증가했다.
　➜ 생선 소비량 곡선에는 큰 변동이 없는 반면에 치즈 소비량 곡선은 꾸준히 상승하고 있다.

④ 같은 기간 동안 소비율 하락을 보인 음식은 없다.
　➜ 다른 식품들이 모두 전반적인 소비량 증가를 보이는 반면에 붉은 육류 소비량은 지속적으로 감소하고 있으므로, 붉은 육류 소비율이 하락하고 있음을 알 수 있다.

⑤ 2000년에 평균적 미국인이 소비한 과일과 채소의 양은 같은 해 다른 모든 식품의 소비량을 초과했다.
　➜ 2000년 과일과 채소 소비량 곡선이 모두 다른 식품의 소비량 곡선보다 위에 위치해 있다.

01 다음 도표의 내용과 일치하지 <u>않는</u> 것은?

| 경찰대학 2011학년도 30번 |

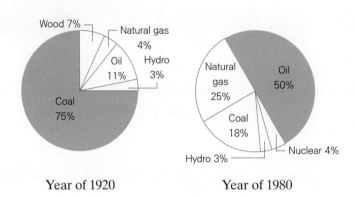

Year of 1920   Year of 1980

It is worth studying how energy sources changed during the twentieth century for finding a solution to possible energy shortage in the near future. The above graphs show how energy sources changed in America between 1920 and 1980. ① Coal was the king in the picture of energy supply, and exactly consisted of three quarters of the total energy supply in 1920. ② However, it constituted only 18 percent of the supply in 1980 and dropped to the third place from the first. ③ The percentage of oil use had been more than quadrupled between 1920 and 1980 and it became the greatest energy source in 1980. ④ Natural gas stepped up from the fifth to the second in 1980 and consisted exactly of a quarter of the total energy supply. ⑤ In 1980, wood was dropped out of the picture, while hydropower maintained the same percentage and nuclear power was newly included.

다음 도표의 내용과 일치하지 <u>않는</u> 것은?

Religious Preferences in the United States

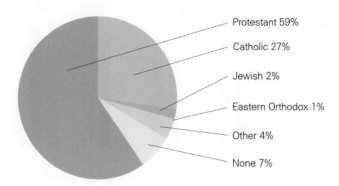

Protestant 59%
Catholic 27%
Jewish 2%
Eastern Orthodox 1%
Other 4%
None 7%

The great diversity of ethnic backgrounds of the United States has produced religious pluralism. ① Ninety-three percent of all Americans say that they have religious beliefs. ② Only 11 percent say they have no religious preferences or beliefs. ③ About 87 percent of Americans are Christians, 2 percent are Jewish, and the other 4 percent belong to other religious faiths such as Moslem, Buddhism, or Hindu. ④ Among the 87 percent who are Christians are Protestant, Catholic, and Eastern Orthodox religious groups. ⑤ Although the Protestants are 59 percent, they constitute the largest religious group in the United States.

01 다음 도표의 내용과 일치하지 <u>않는</u> 문장은?

| 사관학교 2017학년도 33번 |

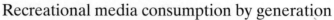

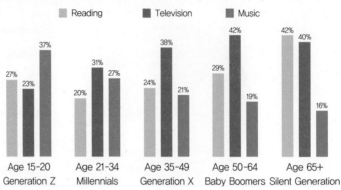

The graph above shows the generational participation percentages for three popular recreational media activities. ① Of the three leisure pursuits, music is the most popular spare-time activity among Generation Z, while reading is the most popular among the silent generation. ② The percentage of millennials who spend their spare time reading is visibly smaller than that of their counterparts from other generations. ③ Television is the most popular spare-time activity for all generations, except for Generation Z, less than a quarter of whom chose television as their favorite recreational activity. ④ Among Generation X, baby boomers, and the silent generation, music is less popular than reading. ⑤ The two generations that read more than the youngest are baby boomers and the silent generation.

02 다음 도표의 내용과 일치하지 <u>않는</u> 문장은?

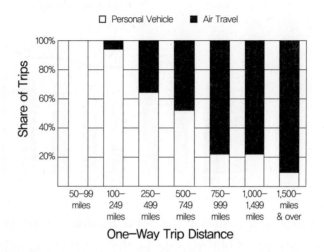

The graph above shows the share of the personal vehicle and air travel in long-distance business trips by miles traveled one-way. (This graph does not reflect other modes of transportation.) ① The decision to take a personal vehicle or fly to a destination changes with the distance of the trip; and the longer the distance, the greater the percentage of business trips traveled by air. ② For business trips of 100-249 miles, the personal vehicle is the dominant means of transportation, with only a few percent for the other type of transportation. ③ If a destination is between 250-499 miles away, over 60 percent of business trips are taken with a personal vehicle. ④ On the other hand, if the destination is 500-749 miles away, more than two-thirds of business trips are taken by air. ⑤ Between business trips of 750-999 miles and 1,000-1,499 miles, there is no apparent difference in the percentage of travelers who prefer to fly.

Number of Researchers in Korea

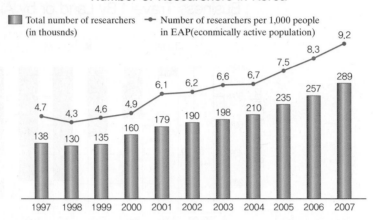

The above graph shows the total number of researchers and the number of researchers per 1,000 people in the EAP (economically active population) of Korea from 1997 to 2007. ① Compared to the previous year, both numbers recorded each year showed an increase except for the numbers recorded in 1998. ② The highest annual growth in the number of researchers per 1,000 people in the EAP was recorded between 2000 and 2001. ③ From 2004 to 2007 Korea had more than 200,000 researchers each year, recording the largest number in 2007. ④ The number of researchers per 1,000 people in the EAP in 2007 was twice as large as that in 1999. ⑤ The annual increase in the total number of researchers was the largest between 1998 and 1999.

04

다음 도표의 내용과 일치하지 <u>않는</u> 문장은?

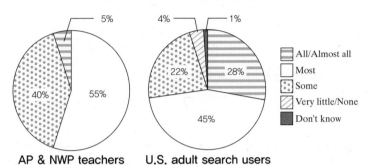

Accuracy or Trustworthiness of the Information Found Using Search Engines

- AP: Advanced Placement courses
- NWP: National Writing Project

The two pie charts above show how much of the information found using search engines is considered to be accurate or trustworthy by two groups of respondents (AP & NWP teachers and U.S. adult search users) in 2012. ① As for AP & NWP teachers, five percent say that "All / Almost all" of the information found using search engines is accurate or trustworthy, while 28 percent of U.S. adult search users say the same. ② The largest percentage of both AP & NWP teachers and U.S. adult search users answer that "Most"of the information is accurate or trustworthy. ③ In addition, 40 percent of AP & NWP teachers say that "Some"of the information is accurate or trustworthy, and more than 30 percent of U.S. adult search users respond the same. ④ U.S. adult search users saying that "Very little / None" of the information found using search engines is accurate or trustworthy account for less than five percent. ⑤ The percentage of U.S. adult search users who answer "Don't know"is only one percent.

Problem Solving Skills

문장과 내용에 대한 정확한 이해를 통해 대명사나 명사구가 가리키는 대상을 추론해 내는 유형이다. 주어진 문장들의 정보를 종합하여 지칭하는 대상을 추론한다.

- 글의 소재를 파악한다.
- 등장인물과 상황을 확인한다.
- 글의 흐름을 따라가며 인물 간 상호작용을 정확히 파악한다.

Example

밑줄 친 it이 가리키는 대상이 다른 것은? | 경찰대학 2014학년도 13번 |

❶ It started off like just any other winter day on the farm. But in the afternoon, all hell broke loose. The snow that had accumulated on the roof of the pig pen proved to be too much for it. The roof caved in and a heavy wooden beam trapped one of the baby pigs. The beam pinned ① it down and it couldn't move. When I arrived at the scene, ② it was squealing in pain. I tried to lift the beam off of ③ it but faced an unexpected obstacle. The mother pig was protecting the baby pig. It would not let anyone get near its offspring. Little did ④ it understand that I was just trying to help. Only when another farm hand restrained the mother with a rope was I able to reach the baby and set ⑤ it free.

Vocabulary

all hell break loose 큰 소란(혼란)이 일어나다   pen 동물의 우리, 축사   cave 휘다, 내려앉다   squeal 비명을 지르다, 울다 offspring 자식, 새끼   restrain 구속하다, 억누르다

Let's Solve

Point **1** 글의 소재 파악하기

• It started off like just any other winter day on the farm.
  ➜ 어느 겨울날 농장에서 생긴 일

Point **2** 등장인물과 상황 파악하기

• 등장인물: one of the baby pigs, I, the mother pig
• 상황: The roof caved in and a heavy wooden beam trapped one of the baby pigs.
  ➜ 농장 지붕이 휘어지면서 나무 지지대가 쓰러져 새끼 돼지 한 마리를 덮쳤다.

Point **3** 글의 흐름을 따라가며 인물 간 상호작용 정확히 파악하기

one of the baby pigs	I	the mother pig
• The beam pinned it down and it couldn't move. ➜ 나무 지지대가 그것을 가둬 그것은 움직일 수 없었다. • it was squealing in pain. ➜ 그것은 고통에 울부짖고 있었다.	• I tried to lift the beam off of it ➜ 나는 지지대를 그것에서 들어내려고 했다. • Only when~was I able to reach the baby and set it free. ➜ 어미를 붙잡고서야 그것을 풀어줄 수 있었다.	• The mother pig was protecting the baby pig. ➜ 어미 돼지가 새끼 돼지를 보호하고 있었다. • Little did it understand that I was just trying to help. ➜ 그것은 내가 도우려 한다는 것을 이해하지 못했다.

Point **4** 정답 풀이하기

  ➜ ①, ②, ③, ⑤는 '아기 돼지'를, ④는 '어미 돼지'를 가리킨다.

01 밑줄 친 ①~⑤ 중에서 의미하는 바가 나머지와 <u>다른</u> 것은?

| 경찰대학 2016학년도 13번 |

It's really not that hard to build a flying car — the first working model got up in 1947. The real challenge turns out to be building ① <u>a flying car</u> that makes sense. Elon Musk, CEO of both Tesla and SpaceX, keeps getting asked why he can't mate his two companies and give birth to ② <u>a rocket car</u>. He answered in a series of recent tweets, including: "③ <u>Airborne auto</u> pros: travel in 3D fast. Cons: risk of car falling on head much greater than ④ <u>one moving in two vectors</u>." And Peter Thiel, the famous investor, goes around saying, "We wanted ⑤ <u>real sky cars</u>; instead we got junk."

02 밑줄 친 부분이 가리키는 대상이 나머지 넷과 <u>다른</u> 것은?

| 경찰대학 2015학년도 13번 |

There used to be ① <u>a tradition at Eton</u>, known as 'capping' — when boys would salute the beaks in the street by pointing a finger at their heads, as an abbreviated doffing of the hat (like a naval or military salute); this would be reciprocated by the beaks. Recently, despite government drives for the promotion of what ② <u>it</u> is pleased to call 'respect,' ③ <u>this tradition</u> has died out: I suppose it takes too much time and effort and shows too much deference — so, like many similar customs, ④ <u>it</u> is doomed in modern Britain. In fairness, soon after having written the above, I was cheered to note that many of the golfers on TV are still following ⑤ <u>the old custom</u> to salute the crowd.

*beak: (영국 학생 속어) 교사, 교장

03 밑줄 친 It[it]이 가리키는 대상이 다른 것은?　　　| 경찰대학 2013학년도 15번 |

Many of us have an item of endearment that we cannot dare part with. Perhaps ① it is an old tattered T-shirt with an autograph from your favorite movie star. ② It could also be a lucky pen that is out of ink, but has been your trusty sidekick through countless exams. For others, ③ it may be a tarnished silver ring that has long lost its shine. Although the ring no longer serves its purpose as an item of adornment, ④ it can conjure up a memory of a loved one, such as a grandmother who passed away. Whatever the item, the real reason for keeping it is not for its face value, but because ⑤ it represents part of our past, a memory we hold dear to our hearts.

01 밑줄 친 부분이 가리키는 대상이 나머지 넷과 다른 것은? | 사관학교 2017학년도 7번 |

J. R. Kline liked to tell stories of other mathematicians. This one about Norbert Wiener was a favorite: One summer, the Klines and the Wieners had adjacent cottages on a lake in New Hampshire. Wiener was in the habit of swimming from ① his dock to a small island in the middle of the lake. On these swims, Kline would keep Wiener company by paddling a rowboat alongside, and they would carry on a conversation while Wiener was steadfastly progressing towards ② his goal. Wiener always tried to keep control of the conversation, even as ③ he was puffing and gasping towards the small land mass. On one such day, near the end of the swim, ④ he bleated out, "Kline, who are the five greatest living mathematicians?" Quietly, Kline replied, "That is an interesting question. Let's see." ⑤ He quickly ticked off four names (none of them "Wiener"). "Yes, yes, go on," spluttered Wiener. With delicate humor, Kline avoided mentioning the name of the fifth one.

02 밑줄 친 부분이 가리키는 대상이 나머지 넷과 다른 것은? | 사관학교 2016학년도 7번 |

Misty May-Treanor and Kerri Walsh are great athletes, and they are great people. In the semifinals of the beach volleyball event at the 2008 Olympics in Beijing, ① they defeated a very good Brazilian team. Afterward, they shook hands with the members of the Brazilian team and said "thank you." ② They then shook hands with many, many volunteers who do such things as retrieve balls and rake the sand. In awe, journalist Mike Celizic wrote, "They literally chased down some of the volunteers from behind as they were leaving the court, not wanting ③ them to get away without knowing how much their efforts were appreciated." ④ They also waved to the fans and promised to come back after the mandatory drug testing. They did come back, posing for photographs and signing autographs for many, many fans. And yes, the fans really appreciated shaking hands with ⑤ them.

밑줄 친 They[they]가 가리키는 대상이 나머지 넷과 다른 것은? | 수능 2008학년도 홀수형 19번 |

The first true piece of sports equipment that man invented was the ball. In ancient Egypt, pitching stones was children's favorite game, but a badly thrown rock could hurt a child. Egyptians were therefore looking for something less dangerous to throw. And ① they developed what were probably the first balls. ② They were first made of grass or leaves held together by strings, and later of pieces of animal skin sewn together and stuffed with feathers or hay. Even though the Egyptians were warlike, ③ they found time for peaceful games. Before long ④ they devised a number of ball games. Perhaps ⑤ they played ball more for instruction than for fun. Ball playing was thought of mainly as a way to teach young men the speed and skill they would need for war.

밑줄 친 부분이 가리키는 대상이 나머지 넷과 다른 것은? | 수능 2015학년도 홀수형 29번 |

Nancy was struggling to see the positive when ① her teen daughter was experiencing a negative perspective on her life and abilities. In her desire to parent intentionally, ② she went into her daughter's room and noted one positive accomplishment she had observed. "I know you've been having a hard time lately, and you aren't feeling really good or positive about your life. But you did a great job cleaning up your room today, and ③ I know that must have been a big effort for you." The next day, to Nancy's surprise, the teen girl seemed somewhat cheerful. In passing, ④ she said, "Mom, thanks for saying the positive thing about me yesterday. I was feeling so down and couldn't think of anything good about myself. After ⑤ you said that positive thing, it helped me see one good quality in myself, and I've been holding onto those words."

Problem Solving Skills

지문에 밑줄로 표시된 지시어의 의미를 고르는 유형이다. 지문 내용 전체가 지시어의 특성에 관한 설명이므로, 지문을 꼼꼼히 파악하고 모든 내용에 적합한 선택지를 고른다.

· 주요 내용을 정리하며 지문을 읽는다.
· 지문의 내용에 모두 부합하는 선택지를 고른다.

Example

밑줄 친 this가 의미하는 것으로 가장 적절한 것은?

| 경찰대학 2012학년도 13번 |

❶ People often show <u>this</u> — even when doing so means contradicting their own perceptions of the world. A major reason for <u>this</u> is to gain the approval or avoid the disapproval of other people. We often want others to accept us, like us, and treat us well. In growing up, people often learn that one way to get along with a group is to go along with group standards. In deciding how to dress for the senior prom, we may try to wear the right clothes so that we will fit in, give a good impression, and avoid disapproval. We may not really like wearing formal clothes, but do it anyway because it's socially appropriate for the occasion. When we're with our weight-conscious friends, we may eat salads and health foods even though we don't especially like them; when we're alone, we're more likely to follow our personal preferences by eating hamburgers and fries. In such situations, <u>this</u> leads to an outward change in public behavior, but not necessarily to a change in the individual's private opinions.

❷ ① authority
② conformity
③ obstinacy
④ independence
⑤ dominance

Vocabulary

contradict 부정하다, 모순되다 perception 지각, 인식 the senior prom 졸업생 무도회 disapproval 반감 appropriate 적절한 occasion 경우, 행사 conscious 의식하는 outward 외면적인

Let's Solve

Point **1** 주요 내용 정리하며 지문 읽기

- contradicting their own perceptions of the world
  - ➡ 자신의 세계관과 모순된다고 하더라도 그렇게 행동하는 경우가 있다.
- to gain the approval or avoid the disapproval of other people
  - ➡ 남에게서 인정을 받기 위해서 또는 거절당하지 않기 위해서
- to go along with group standards
  - ➡ 집단의 준거와 충돌하지 않게 행동한다.
- socially appropriate for the occasion
  - ➡ 때에 따라 사회적으로 적절한 행동을 한다.
- <u>this</u> leads to an outward change in public behavior, but not necessarily to a change in the individual's private opinions
  - ➡ <u>이것</u> 때문에 공적인 행동에 외형적인 변화가 생기지만 개인의 사적인 의견도 변화하는 것은 아니다.

<u>이것</u>: 개인이 남과 어울리기 위해 집단의 준거에 따르고 상황에 맞춰 사회적 행동을 하는 동기이지만 개인의 의견을 변화시키는 힘은 없다.

Point **2** 지문의 내용에 모두 부합하는 선택지 고르기

① 권한
  - ➡ 지문의 내용과 관계없다.
② 순응
  - ➡ 개인의 선호를 억제하고 타인과 집단, 사회의 기준에 따른다는 내용과 행동의 변화는 외면적일 뿐 내면 변화와는 별개라는 내용 모두에 부합하는 단어이므로 this의 의미로 가장 적합하다.
③ 고집
  - ➡ 지문의 내용과 반대된다.
④ 독립
  - ➡ 개인의 의견은 유지된다는 부분과 일부 연관되지만, 타인과의 관계를 중시하는 행동을 강조하고 있는 글의 나머지 부분과는 맞지 않다.
⑤ 지배
  - ➡ 지문의 내용과 반대된다.

01 밑줄 친 This[this]가 의미하는 것으로 가장 적절한 것은?

| 경찰대학 2013학년도 16번 |

This not only affects expectations for success or failure; it also influences motivation through goal setting. If we have a high sense of this in a given area such as foreign language learning, we will set higher goals, be less afraid of failure, and persist longer when we encounter difficulties. If our sense of this is low, however, we may avoid a task altogether or give up easily when problems arise. This also seems to be related to attributions. People with a strong sense of this for a given task attribute their failures to lack of effort. But people with a low sense of this tend to attribute their failures to lack of ability. You can see that motivation would be destroyed when failures were attributed to lack of ability.

① self-efficacy   ② proportion   ③ empathy

④ self-consciousness   ⑤ interest

02 밑줄 친 it이 의미하는 것으로 가장 적절한 것은?

| 경찰대학 2012학년도 12번 |

Closely related to the societal customs of touching are those of spatial relationships. Anthropologists tell us that each of us walks around inside "bubbles of personal space." The size of the bubble represents our personal territory, territorial imperatives, or "personal buffer zones." We neither like nor tolerate it when someone invades our bubbles. We become distinctly uncomfortable. But as we travel to different places around the world, we learn that some cultural bubbles are larger or smaller than others.

① feeling uncomfortable

② walking inside the bubble

③ the size of the bubble

④ someone's invasion of our bubbles

⑤ our personal territory

03

밑줄 친 "demon"이 의미하는 것으로 가장 적절한 것은?

In late October, I began rehearsal for a play. The rehearsal schedule was not rigorous at first, and did not rule my life. But it was there and the demon assured me I had nothing to worry about. I was persuaded because the January deadline was still a long way off. It was not long into rehearsal when the other, smaller deadlines began to creep up and rear their ugly heads, and paper after paper after test struck me unmercifully. It was almost Christmas and the responsibilities of shopping allied themselves with my academic obligations and thrashed me mercilessly while the demon chuckled, knowing that the real deadline would be painful to meet. I began the ordeal that would increase my misery daily until when the real deadline was met. I cursed the demon, loudly at first. However, I think I learned from this experience that all I need to do is seize the deadline in the distance and never shall the demon haunt me again.

① competitiveness   ② obsession   ③ procrastination

④ agitation   ⑤ fastidiousness

04

밑줄 친 "these"가 가리키는 것으로 가장 적절한 것은?

One of the questions which interested the ancient Greeks was "what is the ultimate structure of matter?" Let us imagine ourselves doing what they pictured, taking a piece of matter and cutting it into smaller pieces, and then each piece into smaller pieces still. Could one go on for ever, or would one in the end arrive at bits which could not be divided any more and were the final bricks of which all matter is built? The final bits which could not be cut are called these. Scientists are very prone to give graphic illustrations of very small size of these, such as the well-known one that if a drop of water were magnified to the world, these in it would be about as large as cricket balls.

① cells   ② units   ③ atoms

④ bacteria   ⑤ essences

05

밑줄 친 "It"이 가리키는 것으로 가장 적절한 것은? | 경찰대학 2011학년도 13번 |

It is a major part of administration and is concerned with helping staff use their knowledge and skill in getting the job done efficiently and well. It has been defined by Dr. Towle as "an administrative process which has as one of its purposes to contribute to staff development." Towle further explains that staff members responsible for the work of other staff have the obligation of giving leadership that results in the development of worker competence. It focuses upon helping others acquire knowledge and apply it to practice. It is a teaching-learning situation, educational as well as administrative.

① selection   ② supervision   ③ promotion
④ distribution   ⑤ introduction

06

밑줄 친 "a morality play"가 의미하는 것으로 가장 적절한 것은? | 경찰대학 2011학년도 28번 |

In the bullfighting, the bull is often honored and the man falls into despair. The bull is never left to die, but killed in the open, in hairsbreadth contact with a man on foot who has nothing to defend himself with except his courage and only a piece of red cloth. Yet the bullfighting tells us something. It tells us much about the love of contradiction in a race of intense individualists. It aims at an ideal of bravery and style, and falls into dullness and squalor. It is in miniature one image of life as Latin people tend to see it: a challenge to high romance always defeated by the rich and fatuous disorder of life itself. It is a morality play, that isolates, and sets against each other, the qualities which this courteous, passionate, and chivalrous people value most: which I take to be — courage, manners, pride of self cautioned by its opposite reminder that nothing is more helpful to humanity than the immediate prospect of a violent death.

① 자만과 수치를 분간하는 척도
② 윤리적 삶의 추구와 예절의 실천
③ 영웅적 삶의 품격과 이미지의 재현
④ 개인주의적 가치관에 내재된 득실의 재인식
⑤ 삶의 높은 가치 추구와 그것의 붕괴 사이의 긴장

다음 글에서 밑줄 친 "this"가 가리키는 것은?

In Germany in January 1921, a daily newspaper cost 0.30 marks. Less than 2 years later, in November 1922, the same newspaper cost 70,000,000 marks. All other prices in the economy rose by similar amounts. This episode is one of history's most spectacular examples of this. Although the United States has never experienced this even close to that in Germany in the 1920s, this has at times been an economic problem. During the 1970s, for instance, the overall level of prices more than doubled, and President Gerald Ford called this "public enemy number one."

① inflation　　② tax　　③ unemployment
④ deficit　　⑤ depression

01 다음 글에서 밑줄 친 This가 뜻하는 의미로 가장 적절한 것은? | 수능 2004학년도 홀수형 18번 |

I have been living in this foreign country for five years. Near my house is a tiny dry-cleaning shop run by two chatty old ladies. They are probably in their 60s, which isn't all that old, but their service is slow enough to say, "It takes forever." Sometimes they try my patience. Once I had to go back five times to pick up a couple of items. "My, you are in a hurry," they cheerfully said. "How slow of us! We are terrible!" Despite the slow service, their shop is constantly packed with customers and their counter piled high with clothes. This I do not understand at all.

[2점]

① 세탁물 처리가 느려도 영업이 잘 되는 것
② 작업 중 끊임없이 잡담을 나누는 것
③ 세탁소 주인들이 불친절한 것
④ 세탁물을 찾으러 여러 번 가야 하는 것
⑤ 세탁소 내부를 깨끗이 정리하지 않는 것

다음 글에서 밑줄 친 this의 의미로 가장 적절한 것은?

| 수능 2005학년도 홀수형 19번 |

For a long time, <u>this</u> irritated me a great deal. I once got a chance to interview one of my favorite comedians, Mike Myers. After our session was over, he teased me saying, "Wow, you look like you're 11." At the time, I was 26. It was sort of embarrassing, because someone I had been attracted to told me that I looked like I was in elementary school. Six years later, I no longer have that problem. I recently renewed my driver's license and was pleased to discover that the picture smiling back at me looked just like a 32-year-old woman. It has taken a long time, but I finally look my age.

① 인터뷰에 실패한 것
② 사진을 찍는 것
③ 운전 면허를 갱신하는 것
④ 유명 인사를 만나는 것
⑤ 나이보다 어려 보이는 것

Problem Solving Skills

지문의 내용을 바탕으로 필자의 태도나 등장인물의 심경, 장면의 분위기를 판단하는 유형이다. 지문의 논리적 구성보다는 배경 상황이나 행동 등의 의미를 생각하며 문제를 해결한다.

• 글의 도입부에서 상황에 대해 파악한다.
• 태도나 심경, 분위기와 관련된 표현을 찾아가며 지문을 읽는다.
• 분위기를 잘 설명하는 선택지를 고른다.

Example

다음 글에 나타난 David의 심경으로 가장 적절한 것은?　　　｜ 경찰대학 2017학년도 30번 ｜

① When the elevator began its descent, a broad smile began to form on David's face. The spinning and nausea were gone. The pressure on his chest vanished. He was doing it. He was leaving the job and saying farewell to a nightmare. He found the spine to walk away that gloomy morning. He was standing in the empty elevator, watching with a wide grin as the floor numbers went down in bright red digital numbers. The elevator rocked gently as it fell through the center of the building. **②** When it stopped, David got off and darted to the descending escalators. Somebody called out, "Hey, David, where are you going?" David smiled and waved in the general direction of the voice, as if everything was under control. He went outside, and the air that had seemed so wet and dreary earlier now held the promise of a new beginning.

③
① sad and agitated
② relieved and hopeful
③ bored and indifferent
④ nervous and confused
⑤ empty and abandoned

Vocabulary

descent 하강　spinning 현기증　nausea 메스꺼움　rock (앞뒤 · 좌우로) 흔들다, 흔들리다　dreary 황량한　agitated 흥분한

Let's Solve

- When the elevator began its descent, a broad smile began to form on David's face. ~ He was leaving the job and saying farewell to a nightmare.

→ 지문의 주인공은 힘들었던 직장을 그만두고 즐거워하고 있다.

Point **2** 심경과 분위기에 관련된 표현 찾기

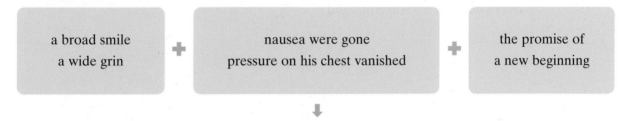

| a broad smile / a wide grin | + | nausea were gone / pressure on his chest vanished | + | the promise of / a new beginning |

즐거워서 웃음이 나고, 멀미나 압박감이 사라졌으며 새로운 시작을 맞이하여 설레고 있다.

Point **3** 분위기를 잘 설명하는 선택지 고르기

① 슬프고 흥분한

② 편안하고 희망찬

→ 글의 시작부터 마음이 편안해지고 있음과 웃는 모습이 계속 묘사되어 주인공이 마음의 편안함을 느끼고 있음을 알 수 있다. 또한 마지막 부분에서 축축하고 황량했던 공기가 지금은 새로운 시작의 약속을 머금고 있다고 하고 있으므로 새 시작에 대한 희망을 품고 있음을 알 수 있다. 따라서 David의 심경으로 가장 적절한 것은 '편안하고 희망찬'이다.

③ 지루하고 무관심한

④ 초조하고 혼란스러운

⑤ 공허하고 자포자기한

01 다음 글에 나타난 "I"의 심경으로 가장 적절한 것은?

경찰대학 2018학년도 30번

Taking a deep breath, I began sprinting again, counting my strokes, telling myself that I wouldn't look up again until I'd swum one thousand strokes. Slowly I gained a foot, then a few hundred yards. Now I realized why the English Channel was the Mount Everest of swimming: though everyone's goal is to get to the top, the summit is where the air grows thinner, where everything becomes challenging. *Don't look up for five hundred strokes. Go as fast as you can go. Push it. Pull your arms with everything you have. Kick. Yes. Kick those legs. Pull deeper. Faster. Come on. Pull.*

① frustrated but resilient
② determined and persistent
③ daunted and disappointed
④ surprised but exhilarated
⑤ overwhelmed and discouraged

02 다음 글에 나타난 Dave의 심경으로 가장 적절한 것은?

경찰대학 2016학년도 30번

Dave was never quite sure how it happened. He only knew that he awoke as he was being hurled from his bed and, mingled with the startled awakening, there was a terrific explosion. For a moment or more he lay absent-mindedly on the deck of his room, struggling to regain his senses. Then slowly he realized the steady throb of the engines, to which he had grown so accustomed in the week since boarding the ship, had abruptly ceased. What happened? He got up and, feeling his way to the light switch, gave it a turn with a trembling hand. Nothing happened, and he tried it again. The lights did not come on.

① distracted and angry
② confused and nervous
③ overjoyed and proud
④ indifferent and bored
⑤ irritated and stimulated

03 다음 글에 나타난 "I"의 심정으로 가장 적절한 것은?

| 경찰대학 2015학년도 30번 |

During the day the air was hot and dry, and filled with fine particles of dust. At night, when it was cooler, gnats and mosquitoes made me appreciate all the more their absence in the forest. My hut, ten times the size of my home in the hunting camp, seemed close and stuffy, and as I lay in bed I could hear the huge spiders, some several inches across, crawling about in the leaves of the roof. Occasionally one dropped onto the bed with a dull thud and lay there for a while before stalking away. At first I carried out an active campaign to get rid of them, but it was useless — and a mosquito net would have been unbearably hot. The familiar night sounds of the forest were replaced by the cries of drunks coming home from a dance at the nearby hotel.

① gloomy and detached   ② depressed but curious

③ daunted but anticipating   ④ exhilarated and energized

⑤ reminiscent and displeased

04 다음 글의 상황에 나타난 분위기로 가장 적절한 것은?

| 경찰대학 2014학년도 30번 |

It was just another dog day of summer. The sun was shining down brightly but Jake was in the comfort of the shade in his backyard. He had a glass of iced tea in his right hand and a good read in his left. Jake was without a single care in the world. Today, he was just going to sit around and vegetate until dusk. His playful puppy was playing with a ball. She looked at Jake as if to invite him to a game of fetch. But he would not oblige her today. Only an earthquake of 10 points on the Richter scale could drive him from his snug nest.

① bored   ② relaxed   ③ nervous

④ surprised   ⑤ playful

다음 글의 분위기로 가장 적절한 것은?

| 경찰대학 2013학년도 34번 |

The sun was just far enough in the west to send inviting shadows. In the center of a small field, and in the shade of a haystack which was there, a girl lay sleeping. She had slept long and soundly when she was awoken by a gentle breeze. She opened her eyes and stared a moment up in the sky of blue and white. She yawned and stretched her long brown legs and arms, lazily. Then she arose, never minding the bits of straw that clung to her black hair, to her red sweater, and to the blue cotton skirt that did not reach her ankles. The girl absentmindedly watched a cloud that floated lazily overhead, trying to decide what kind of animal it most looked like.

① calm and relaxing   ② lively and exciting
③ funny and amusing   ④ sad and frightening
⑤ urgent and desperate

06

이민자들에 대한 필자의 태도로 가장 적절한 것은?

| 경찰대학 2012학년도 35번 |

Ten years ago, Jefferson Boulevard in south Dallas was a dying inner-city business district filled with vacant storefronts. Today, there are almost 800 businesses there and on neighboring streets, and about three-quarters of them are owned by Hispanics, many of them first- and second-generation immigrants. "They were hungry enough to start their own businesses," says Leonel Ramos, president of the Jefferson Area Association. And sociologist Kasarda adds, "There is a whole multiplier effect throughout the community." Immigrants provide a hardworking labor force to fill the low-paid jobs that make a modern service economy run. In many cities, industries such as hotels, restaurants, and child care would be hardpressed without immigrant labor.

① appreciating   ② cynical   ③ indifferent
④ arrogant   ⑤ shunning

다음 글의 마지막 부분에 나타난 "I"의 심정으로 가장 적절한 것은? | 경찰대학 2010학년도 14번 |

This was in 1943, right in the middle of the war years, and there wasn't a new bike to be found anywhere. At that time, I just had to have a bike. I can remember pleading with my dad for one — any kind, as long as it had two wheels. He was very patient with me and explained that it just wouldn't be possible that year. Deep down I understood, but a little begging never hurt, so I persisted. Christmas Eve finally arrived and I looked everywhere; there wasn't a bike in the house. But as I came downstairs the next morning, my eyes almost popped out of my head. There, right next to the Christmas tree, stood the biggest, most beautiful red and silver bicycle I had ever seen. I don't think my feet even touched the bottom stairs as I dashed to inspect that miraculous sight.

① embarrassed ② envious ③ delighted
④ puzzled ⑤ disappointed

인도와 중국의 온실가스 배출에 대한 다음 글의 마지막 부분에 나타난 필자의 태도로 가장 적절한 것은? | 경찰대학 2010학년도 44번 |

If everyone lived like the average Chinese or Indian, you wouldn't be reading about global warming. On a per capita basis, China and India emit far less greenhouse gas than energy-efficient Japan, environmentally scrupulous Sweden, and especially the gas-guzzling U.S. For example, the average American is responsible for 20 times as much CO_2 emission annually as the average Indian. There's only one problem: 2.4 billion people live in China and India, a great many of whom aspire to an American-style energy-intensive life. And thanks to the fast growth of the two countries' economies, they will soon get there — with potentially disastrous results for the world's climate.

① approving ② indifferent ③ contented
④ worried ⑤ skeptical

01 다음 글의 상황에 나타난 분위기로 가장 적절한 것은?

| 수능 2010학년도 홀수형 29번 |

After dinner he built a fire, going out into the weather for wood he had piled against the garage. The air was bright and cold against his face, and the snow in the driveway was already halfway to his knees. He gathered logs, shaking off their soft white caps and carrying them inside. He sat for a time in front of the fireplace, cross-legged, adding logs, and gazing at the warm fire. Outside, snow continued to fall quietly in the cones of light cast by the streetlights. By the time he rose and looked out the window, his car had become a soft white hill on the edge of the street.

① calm and peaceful
② lively and festive
③ funny and amusing
④ exciting and thrilling
⑤ promising and hopeful

02 다음 글에 드러난 'I'의 심경으로 가장 적절한 것은?

| 수능 2016학년도 홀수형 19번 |

I'm leaving early tomorrow morning, finally! I've always wanted to explore the Amazon, the unknown and mysterious world. At this hour, the great Emerald Amazon Explorer should be at the port waiting for me to get on board. Freshwater dolphins will escort me on the playful river, and 500 species of birds, half a dozen species of monkeys, and numerous colorful butterflies will welcome me into their kingdom. I wish I could camp in the wild and enjoy the company of mosquitos, snakes, and spiders. I'd love to make the world's largest rainforest home. My heart swells as much as my chubby bags; yet, I'd better get some sleep since a long, tough journey is ahead of me.

① excited
② exhausted
③ frustrated
④ indifferent
⑤ relieved

PART 06
다문항 지문 독해하기

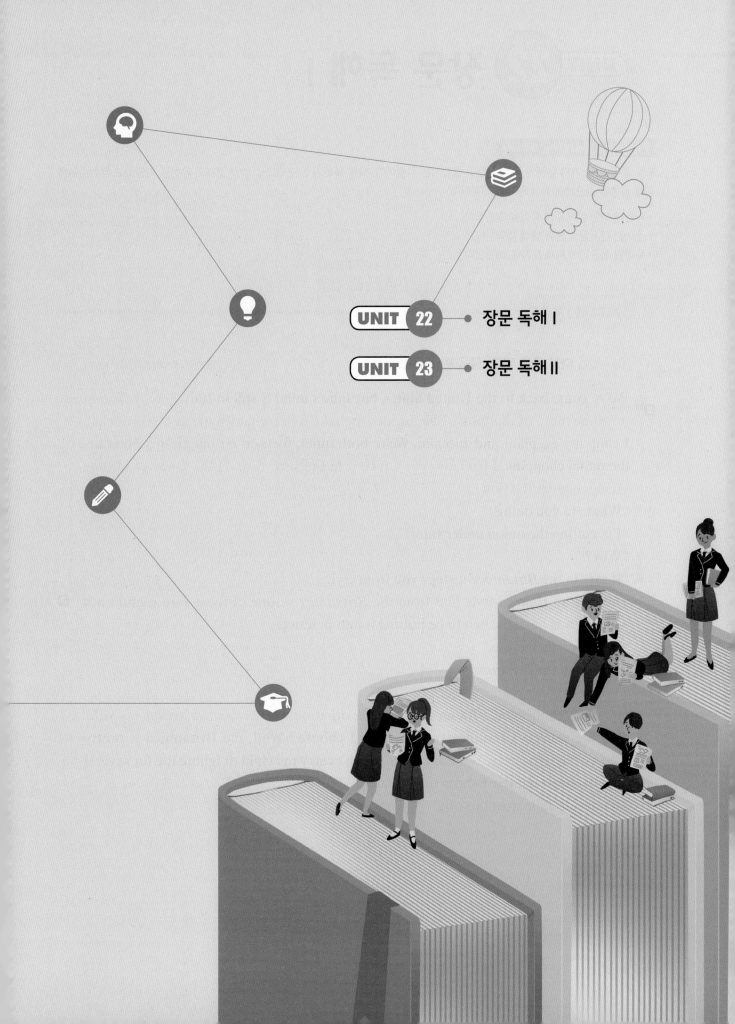

Problem Solving Skills

지문 하나에 두 가지 유형의 문제가 묶여 출제되는 유형이다. 빠른 독해가 요구되므로 엮인 문제의 유형을 확인하고 우선순위를 정해 유형별 접근법에 따라 문제를 해결한다.

• 지문에 엮인 문제들의 유형을 확인한다.
• 주어진 단서들로 글에 대해 파악한다.
• 유형별 접근법에 따라 문제를 해결한다.

Example

[01~02] 다음 글을 읽고, 물음에 답하시오. | 경찰대학 2018학년도 37~38번 |

2 We've come back to the United States, but Julie's mind is still in Italy. She's yearning for some more of that pizza. She decides to make it herself, with me as her sous chef. I chop my eggplant and zucchini. We're both quiet, focused on our chores. Next up, the onion chopping. I peel my onion, take it to the sink, turn on the faucet, and start slicing it under the flow.

"What are you doing?"

"I'm cutting the onion underwater."

"Why?"

"It says in the *Britannica* it stops you from crying."

3 This was an Heloise-style hint from the *Britannica* — one of those rare useful ones — and I was quite excited to be putting it into practice.

"Nope, too dangerous."

"But it's in the *Britannica*."

"Nope, I'm the executive chef. You're the sous chef."

Here I'm confronted with an unfortunate situation: the *Britannica* versus my wife. Two big sources of authority. Which do I choose? Well, the Britannica is pretty trustworthy. However, as far as I know, it can't carry my child or ignore me for several days or throw out the T-shirts that it hates.

So I decide Julie wins this one. _____.

Vocabulary

eggplant 가지   zucchini 주키니   sous chef 부주방장   confront 맞서다   aftermath 여파

01 윗글의 제목으로 가장 적절한 것은?

① Peel Onions Underwater to Avoid Tears
② Battle of Genders Ending in a Draw
③ Aftermath of an Italian Cooking Tip
④ Real Boss in My Home
⑤ Sous Chefs in the *Britannica*

02 윗글의 빈칸에 들어가기에 가장 적절한 것은?

① Which attests to how strong working women are
② I might have to call the *Britannica* for corrections
③ The onion will be cut without water and I will cry
④ I will ignore her for the next few days
⑤ But I'll be the executive chef tomorrow

Let's Solve

Point **1** 지문에 엮인 문제들의 유형 확인하기

• 01 제목(UNIT 03)
• 02 빈칸 III(UNIT 11)
  → 빈칸을 먼저 채운 뒤 제목을 찾는다.

Point **2** 주어진 단서들로 글에 대해 파악하기

• She's yearning for some more of that pizza. She decides to make it herself, with me as her sous chef.
  → Julie가 주방장, '나'가 부주방장이 되어 피자를 만들고 있다.

Point 3 유형별 접근법에 따라 문제 해결하기

02 빈칸에 들어가기에 가장 적절한 것 – 빈칸III 유형

• 빈칸이 포함된 문장 분석하기

So I decide Julie wins this one. _____.

→ 문장의 빈칸에는 Julie의 주장을 받아들인 결과가 이어져야 한다.

• 세부 내용을 통해 글의 주제 파악하기

> **'나'의 행동**
>
> I peel my onion, take it to the sink, turn on the faucet, and start slicing it under the flow.
> (Britannica의 팁에 따라 물 속에서 양파를 자르려고 함)

> **Julie의 말**
>
> "Nope, I'm the executive chef. You're the sous chef."
> (물 속에서 양파를 자르지 못하게 함)

> the Britannica versus my wife.
> (Britannica의 팁에 따를지 아내의 말에 따를지 선택하게 된 '나')

• 선택지의 내용 정확히 이해하기

① Which attests to how strong working women are
　　→ 일하는 여성이 얼마나 강한지를 입증하는 것

② I might have to call the Britannica for corrections
　　→ 수정을 요청하기 위해 Britannica에 전화를 해야 할지도 모른다.

③ The onion will be cut without water and I will cry
　　→ 양파는 물 없이 썰리고 나는 울 것이다.

④ I will ignore her for the next few days
　　→ 다음 며칠 간 나는 그녀를 무시할 것이다.

⑤ But I'll be the executive chef tomorrow
　　→ 하지만 내일은 내가 총주방장이 될 것이다.

• 정답 풀이하기

③ The onion will be cut without water and I will cry
　　→ Julie의 주장을 받아들인 '나'의 행동이 빈칸에 와야 하므로, 위험하기 때문에 물속에서 양파를 깎지 말라는 Julie의 말에 따라 ③ '양파는 물 없이 썰리고 나는 울 것이다'가 빈칸에 가장 적절하다.

01 글의 제목으로 가장 적절한 것 – 제목 유형

• 도입부에서 글의 소재 파악하기
  → Julie와 '나'의 이탈리아식 피자 만들기

• 글의 요지 파악하기
  → Britannica의 양파 깎는 팁 대신 아내의 말에 따르기를 선택한 '나'

• 소재와 관련된 글의 흐름 파악하기

> Julie가 이탈리아 피자를 먹고 싶어 해서 집에서 만들게 됨

⬇

> 양파를 썰게 된 '나'는 Britannica에서 본 팁에 따라 물속에서 양파를 자르려 함

⬇

> Julie가 위험하다며 물속에서 양파를 자르지 말라고 함

⬇

> 내 생활에 직접적으로 영향을 줄 수 있는 아내의 말에 따르기로 한 '나'

• 정답 풀이하기
  → '나'가 백과사전의 정보를 신뢰하고 있지만 실제로 '나'의 생활에 영향을 줄 수 있는 것은 아내이기 때문에 아내의 의견을 따르겠다고 하고
  있으므로, 글의 제목으로는 ④ Real Boss in My Home이 가장 적절하다.

다음 글을 읽고, 물음에 답하시오. | 경찰대학 2018학년도 39~40번 |

We have long known that ravens are no birdbrains. They have been spotted caching food for later, gathering string to pull up hanging food and even trying to deceive one another. A study published today in *Science* adds an especially impressive twist: Ravens can _____ that they never encounter in nature.

The new study was led by cognitive zoologists in Sweden, who replicated a series of experiments previously used to (a) <u>testing</u> apes' planning abilities, this time using ravens. The ravens were first taught to use a stone to knock a food pellet out of a puzzle box. The next day, without the box present, the birds were (b) <u>offered</u> a choice between the stone tool and "distracter" objects — toys too light or bulky to use as tools. The box (c) <u>would</u> then be brought back 15 minutes after the selection. Despite the delay, the ravens chose the correct tool nearly 80 percent of the time, and successfully used the tools they selected 86 percent of the time. The birds performed almost (d) <u>as well</u> when they had to give an experimenter a bottle cap in exchange for a piece of food. The birds almost always selected the bottle cap over distracters, even though they would have (e) <u>to wait</u> 15 minutes to barter with it. The preference for soon-to-be-useful items persisted when the ravens had to pass up a smaller treat in favor of either the tool or the bartering token — and even when they could use each item only after a 17-hour delay.

01 윗글의 밑줄 친 부분 중 어법상 <u>틀린</u> 것은?

① (a)　　　② (b)　　　③ (c)　　　④ (d)　　　⑤ (e)

02 윗글의 빈칸에 들어가기에 가장 적절한 것은?　　　[3점]

① preserve tools for emergencies
② work in groups for situations
③ predict events yet to happen
④ trick potential competitors
⑤ plan for future needs

I had decided to go and I would go, and I had to be there by my mother's birthday. This was extremely important. I believed that if there was any chance to bring my mother back home it would happen on her birthday. If I had said this aloud to my father or to my grandparents, they would have said that I might as well try to catch a fish in the air, so I did not say it aloud. But I believed it. (①) My father says I lean on broken reeds and will get a face full of swamp mud one day.

When at last Gram and Gramps Hiddle and I set out that first day of the trip, I prayed for the first thirty minutes solid. I prayed that we would not be in an accident (I was terrified of cars and buses) and that we would get there by my mother's birthday — seven days away — and that we would bring her home. Over and over, I prayed the same thing. I prayed to trees. This was easier than praying directly to God. There was nearly always a tree nearby. As we pulled onto the Ohio Turnpike, which is the flattest, straightest piece of road in God's whole creation, Gram interrupted my prayers. "Salamanca — " (②)

I should explain right off that my real name is Salamanca Tree Hiddle. Salamanca, my parents thought, was the name of the Indian tribe to which my great-great-grandmother belonged. (③) My parents were mistaken. The name of the tribe was Seneca, but since my parents did not discover their error until after I was born and they were, by then, used to my name, it remained Salamanca. (④) My middle name, Tree, comes from your basic tree, a thing of such beauty to my mother that she made it part of my name. She wanted to be more specific and use Sugar Maple Tree, her very favorite, but Salamanca Sugar Maple Tree Hiddle was a bit much even for her. (⑤) My mother used to call me Salamanca, but after she left, only my grandparents Hiddle called me Salamanca (when they were not calling me chickabiddy). To most other people, I was Sal, and to a few boys who thought they were especially amusing, I was Salamander.

03

윗글의 'I'에 관한 내용과 일치하지 <u>않는</u> 것은?

① The purpose of her trip was to bring her mother home.

② Her grandparents accompanied her on the trip.

③ She found it easier to pray to trees than to God.

④ Her parents had a misunderstanding when they named her.

⑤ Most people called her Salamanca or Salamander.

04

다음 문장이 들어가기에 가장 적절한 곳은?

Sometimes I am as ornery and stubborn as an old donkey.

So effective was the mass conversion to the new engineering values that even when the depression hit in 1929, Americans continued to defend the technological vision. (①   ) They chose instead to vent their anger and fear against greedy businessmen who, in their mind, had undermined and thwarted the lofty aims and goals of the nation's new heroes—the engineers. (②   ) Quite a few Americans agreed with the earlier criticism of economist and social theorist Thorstein Veblen. He contended in 1921 that only by entrusting the nation's economy to the professional engineers — whose noble standards stood above pecuniary and parochial concerns — could the economy be saved and the country transformed into a new Eden. (③   ) Internal bickering among its leaders led to a splintering of the movement into warring factions. (④   ) Then too, Hitler's meteoric rise to power and the Third Reich's fanatical obsession with technological efficiency gave many social thinkers second thoughts about the Technocrats' call for a technological dictatorship in the United States. (⑤   ) The technological world view suffered an even more critical setback in 1945 when U.S. airplanes dropped atomic bombs on Japanese cities: the entire world was abruptly forced to look at the dark side of the techno-utopian vision. The postwar generation was the first to live with the constant reminder of modern technology's awesome power to destroy as well as create the future.

05   윗글의 흐름으로 보아, 주어진 문장이 들어가기에 가장 적절한 곳은?

But the success of technocracy was to be short-lived.

06   윗글의 주제로 가장 적절한 것을 고르시오.

① the technocratic vision and its downfall
② the brief honeymoon for democracy and technology
③ the inevitable arrival of the technological world view
④ the belligerent approach of Technocrats for a better society
⑤ the imbalance between the bright and dark sides of technocracy

Even before there is a nation or other organized community to take over from the victims of aggression and their families the responsibility for catching and punishing aggressors, customs evolve that alleviate some of the problems of revenge practices. Among these is the principle of retribution, that is, exact retaliation for a wrong — an eye for an eye. Rather than being bloodthirsty, which is the modern connotation of the word, retribution reduces the likelihood of overreactions (your life for my eye) that are likely to engender feuds. Another _____ (A) _____ principle is "composition" (blood money), whereby the victim or the victim's family is required, or at least encouraged, to accept payment in compensation for an injury, discharging the injurer's liability. A transfer of money or goods is less costly to society as a whole than an act of violence, which besides inflicting a net social loss rather than merely transferring wealth from one person to another may provoke further violence. Another _____ (B) _____ institution is bilateral kinship. Icelanders reckoned kinship through both the father and the mother (many societies reckon it only through the father and some only through the mother). This not only increased the credibility of revenge as a deterrent to aggression by strengthening the family; it made it more likely that a disputant would have kin on both sides of the dispute. The *Iliad* hints at the further possibility that pity and empathy might limit the savagery of revenge.

07 윗글의 빈칸 (A)와 (B)에 공통으로 들어갈 말로 가장 적절한 것은?   [3점]

① modifying   ② penalizing   ③ conflicting

④ moderating   ⑤ captivating

08 윗글의 내용과 일치하는 것은?

① 국가가 가해자를 처벌할 책임을 맡기 전 보복은 주로 폭력으로 이루어졌다.

② '눈에는 눈' 원칙은 피해자의 과잉대응 가능성을 줄였다.

③ 피해자에 대한 물질적인 보상은 공동체가 담당했다.

④ 부모는 가족 구성원의 폭력에 대한 책임을 질 필요가 없었다.

⑤ 연민이나 공감은 보복의 가능성을 줄이는 데 도움이 되지 않았다.

Since 2008 Zsófia Virányi and her colleagues at the Wolf Science Center in Austria have been raising dogs and wolves to figure out what makes a dog a dog — and a wolf a wolf. "You can leave a piece of meat on a table and tell one of our dogs, 'No!' and he will not take it," Virányi says. "But the wolves ignore you. They'll look you in the eye and grab the meat." And when this happens, she wonders yet again how the wolf ever became (A) the domesticated dog. "You can't have an animal — a large carnivore — living with you and behaving like that," she says. "You want an animal that's like a dog: one that accepts 'No!'"

Dogs' understanding of the absolute no may be connected to the structure of (B) their packs, which are not egalitarian like those of the wolves but dictatorial, the center's researchers have discovered. Wolves can eat together, Virányi notes. Even if a dominant wolf flashes its teeth and growls at a subordinate, (C) the lower-ranked member does not move away. The same is not true in dog packs, however. "Subordinate dogs will rarely eat at the same time as the dominant one," she observes. "They don't even try." Their studies also suggest that rather than expecting to cooperate on tasks with humans, dogs simply want to be told what to do.

How the independent-minded, egalitarian wolf changed into (D) the obedient, waiting-for-orders pet and what role ancient humans played in achieving this feat baffle Virányi. She is not alone in her bafflement. Although researchers have successfully determined the time, location and ancestry of nearly every other domesticated species, from sheep to cattle to chickens to guinea pigs, they continue to debate these questions for (E) our best friend, *Canis familiaris*.

09　윗글의 밑줄 친 부분 중 그 의미하는 바가 나머지와 다른 하나는?

① (A)　　　② (B)　　　③ (C)　　　④ (D)　　　⑤ (E)

10　윗글의 내용과 일치하지 않는 것은?

① Virányi는 개와 늑대를 키우며 그들의 본질에 대해 연구한다.
② 늑대는 고기를 먹지 말라는 사람의 명령을 무시하고 먹는다.
③ 무리 중 강한 늑대가 약한 늑대에게 으르렁대면 약한 늑대는 먹이로부터 물러난다.
④ 무리 중 약한 개와 강한 개가 먹이를 동시에 먹는 일은 없다.
⑤ 양, 소, 닭이 가축화된 시간이나 장소는 알려져 있다.

Why do people try to make their expectations _____ their best possible guess of the future, using all available information? The simplest explanation is that it is costly for people not to do so. Joe Commuter has a strong incentive to make his expectation of the time it takes him to drive to work as accurate as possible. If he underpredicts his driving time, he will often be late to work and risk being fired. If he overpredicts, he will, on average, get to work too early and will have given up sleep or leisure time unnecessarily. Accurate expectations are desirable, and the incentives are strong for people to try to make them equal to optimal forecasts by using all available information.

The same principle applies to businesses. Suppose that an appliance manufacturer knows that interest-rate movements are important to the sales of appliances. If the company makes poor forecasts of interest rates, it will earn less profit, because it might produce either too many appliances or too few. The incentives are strong for the company to acquire all available information to help it forecast interest rates and use the information to make the best possible guess of future interest-rate movements. The incentives for equating expectations with optimal forecasts are especially strong in financial markets. In these markets, people with better forecasts of the future get rich.

11 윗글의 제목으로 가장 적절한 것은?

① Set Your Goals As High As Possible
② Reap the Rewards of Optimal Predictions
③ Maximize Profit by Manipulating Interest Rates
④ The Gap Between Theory and Practice in Business
⑤ How Does Commuting Distance Affect Productivity?

12 윗글의 빈칸에 들어갈 말로 가장 적절한 것은?   [3점]

① match   ② exceed   ③ negate

④ transform   ⑤ underestimate

Professor Balak at the Indian Institute of Technology (IIT) in Delhi heads a team behind the Smartcane™, a new device using ultrasound to guide the visually impaired through the busy streets of India by building upon the widely used white cane. "A white cane is an excellent device, providing a lot of information to users," he says. (A) "But it is poor at detecting obstacles that are above waist height and do not have a touch-point on the ground, such as a tree branch sticking out into your path." (B) The smart technology version instead sends out ultrasound waves via a device attached to a standard white cane; it detects them on their return, and uses vibrations to inform users of any obstacles in their way. (C) The real benefit comes from the ultrasound scanning a 45 degree span above the knee, providing information a regular cane simply can't provide. (D) As people move the cane from left to right when they walk, vibrations detected on one side mean they should move towards the other. (E) Differing patterns and intensities of vibration tell users the distance of the object obstructing their path, as far as three meters away.

13 다음 문장이 들어가기에 가장 적절한 곳은?

The team at Smartcane™ took on this challenge by copying the skills of animals such as bats, which emit sonar calls into their surroundings and use the echoes bouncing back from nearby objects to divert around them.

① (A) ② (B) ③ (C) ④ (D) ⑤ (E)

14 Smartcane™에 관한 윗글의 내용과 일치하지 <u>않는</u> 것은?

① IIT의 한 교수가 이끄는 팀에 의해 개발되었다.
② 기존에 사용되던 제품을 토대로 만들었다.
③ 이용자의 무릎 위 45도 범위를 감지한다.
④ 이용자는 진동이 탐지된 방향과 반대로 이동한다.
⑤ 진동의 패턴으로 장애물의 높이를 식별한다.

Once, a long time ago, I was a young lieutenant in the 82nd Airborne Division, trying to orient myself on a field problem at Fort Bragg, North Carolina. As I stood studying a map, my platoon sergeant, a veteran of many junior officers, approached. "You figure out where we are, lieutenant?" he asked. "Well, the map says there should be a hill over there, but I don't see it," I replied. "Sir," he said, "if the map doesn't agree with the ground, then the map is wrong." Even at the time, I knew I had just heard a profound truth.

Over the many years I have spent listening to people's stories, especially all the ways in which things can go awry. I have learned that our passage through life consists of an effort to get the maps in our heads to conform to the ground on which we walk. Ideally, this process takes place as we grow. Our parents teach us, primarily by example, what they have learned. Unfortunately, we are seldom wholly _____ to these lessons. And often, our parents' lives suggest to us that they have little useful to convey, so that much of what we know comes to us through the frequently painful process of trial and error.

15 윗글의 주제로 가장 적절한 것은?

① reasons for teaching students how to read maps
② difficulties of transferring leadership to subordinates
③ value of maps drawn on our mind
④ importance of personal experience in life
⑤ ways to expose children to direct experiences

16 윗글의 빈칸에 들어갈 말로 가장 적절한 것은?　　　　　[3점]

① receptive
② inappropriate
③ restricted
④ addicted
⑤ conducive

Near-Earth Objects (NEOs) is a contemporary term for massive objects that periodically cross Earth's orbit, and in doing so come close to our planet. They include asteroids, meteoroids, and comets. (A) Almost all asteroids are confined to the asteroid belt, situated between Mars and Jupiter. It is estimated that more than a thousand asteroids are at least a mile wide. (B) Perhaps a dozen are three or more miles wide. There is no lower limit to asteroid size because they grade down to tiny rocks and particles of dust, but no asteroid is big enough to hold an atmosphere. What produced the asteroids? Isaac Asimov posed the once popular science fiction idea that asteroids are remnants of a small planet whose inhabitants discovered nuclear energy and blew their world to tiny pieces of fragments. (C) But not even a nuclear explosion would be great enough to form the asteroid belt. The prevailing scientific view is that asteroids are material that failed to combine into a planet. (D) One of the recent appearances of the massive NEO was its 1908 crash in Siberia. (E) Earth is spotted with dozens of visible craters that testify to similar impacts. It is widely believed that the impact of a giant NEO caused a mass extinction of life that included the dinosaurs, 65 million years ago.

17   다음 문장이 들어가기에 가장 적절한 곳은?

It flattened trees for many miles around and killed a herd of reindeer.

① (A)   ② (B)   ③ (C)   ④ (D)   ⑤ (E)

18   asteroids에 관한 윗글의 내용과 일치하는 것은?

① 대기권을 형성할 수 있을 만큼 큰 것도 있다.
② 핵폭발로 인해 발생했다는 생각이 한때 유행했다.
③ 행성으로 만들어지기 쉬운 물질로 이루어져 있다.
④ 일반적으로 지구에 떨어지면 높은 언덕을 만든다.
⑤ 1908년에 처음 발생한 것으로 알려져 있다.

Two historical facts highlight a fundamental problem that needs to be addressed in the area of computer security. First, all complex software systems have eventually revealed flaws or bugs that subsequently needed to be fixed. Second, it is extraordinarily difficult to build a computer hardware/software system that is not vulnerable to a variety of security attacks. An illustration of this difficulty is the Windows NT operating system (OS), introduced by Microsoft in the early 1990s. Windows NT was promised to have a high degree of security. Sadly, Windows NT did not deliver on this promise. This OS and its successor Windows versions have been _____.

Problems to do with providing strong computer security involved both design and implementation. It is difficult, in designing any hardware or software module, to be assured that the design does in fact provide the level of security that was intended. This difficulty results in many unanticipated security vulnerabilities. Even if the design is in some sense correct, it is difficult, if not impossible, to implement the design without errors or bugs, providing yet another host of vulnerabilities.

19 윗글의 주제로 가장 적절한 것은?

① finding solutions to design and implementation problems
② building secure computer programming companies
③ difficulty of building secure computer systems
④ responsibilities of bug-free software developers
⑤ requirements for installing a new hardware system

20 윗글의 빈칸에 들어가기에 가장 적절한 것은?

① recently stabilized after numerous trial and error
② constantly updated to outperform their predecessors
③ unduly promoted and sold to over ten million consumers
④ erroneously recognized by software developers as the strongest
⑤ chronically plagued with a wide range of security vulnerabilities

This much is known. Neuron No. 28, say, fires an electrical signal, and in the synapse where one of 28's connectors touches a receiver of neuron No. 29, a chemical change triggers an electrical signal in 29. That signal gets passed on to neuron No. 30, and on and on. If the connection between 28 and 29 is made often enough, the bond between the two neurons grows stronger. This crucial marriage seems to be the stuff that memory is made of. Unlike cells elsewhere in the body, neurons don't divide. By the time someone reaches 65 or 70, neuron No. 28 and some of its neighbors may be dead, or so feeble they no longer transmit electrical charges efficiently.

Still, there are billions more neurons remaining. And even though the brain cannot grow new ones, the neurons can probably sprout new synapses and thereby form new connections with one another. A researcher supplied certain lab rats with new toys daily and changed the chutes and tunnels in their cages. When he cut open their brains, he counted many more synapses than in rats that got no toys and no new decor. It's a good guess that the human brain, too, grows more synapses when stimulated and challenged. So the brain — even while shrinking — may be able to blaze ever more trails for laying down memory. If neuron No. 28's path is no longer easily passable, _____ . The trick is to force the brain to make them.

*synapse: 신경세포의 자극 전달부

21 윗글의 주제로 가장 적절한 것은?

① the vital role of neurons in creating new memory
② the mechanism of neurons for overcoming weakening memory
③ the similarity in memory function between human and rat brains
④ the function of brain cells in triggering and transmitting electrical signals
⑤ the brain cell's demand of stimulation and challenge for its reproduction

22 윗글의 빈칸에 들어가기에 가장 적절한 것은?

① the number of alternate routes may be virtually limitless
② the memory functions in one's brain stop temporarily
③ the neuron can probably make its channel even stronger
④ the brain still tries to bring it back to life by lengthening it
⑤ the brain creates new neurons to deliver electrical signals

In the past few decades, the term *The Other* has become an increasingly common one in discussions about difference, diversity, prejudice, and racism. It is even sometimes used as an odd-sounding verb: You can be "othered" — That is, you can be categorized as "other" than something, which usually means less than that something. Most often, people belonging to minority groups or non-mainstream cultures are "othered" in this way, but the idea can apply to any person or group treated in a way that reflects prejudice or bias. All of us have probably been in circumstances in which we have been *The Other*, but it's clear that some groups have long been categorized as *Other* in systematic ways that are damaging and disturbing. It's worth thinking about what this idea of *The Other* says about how we respond to each other's identities. In discussions of injustices based on such things as race, gender, ethnicity, religion, and culture, this term has acquired a particular kind of meaning. It suggests something more than prejudice. To have prejudice is to dislike or have negative feelings about someone or something; conversely, we can have a prejudice in favor of something — for example, a sports fan can be prejudiced toward a favorite team. But to consider someone as an *Other* is to place that person in a category that is separate from ourselves and, importantly, somehow _____ ourselves. It is to consider that person's identity undesirable in some way.

23 윗글의 빈칸에 들어갈 말로 가장 적절한 것은?

① specific to ② different from ③ tantamount to
④ inferior to ⑤ more than

24 윗글의 내용과 일치하지 <u>않는</u> 것은?

① 타자(Other)라는 용어는 명사뿐 아니라 동사로도 활용될 수 있다.
② 소수집단이나 비주류집단이 종종 타자화의 대상이 된다.
③ 어떤 집단은 체계적인 방식으로 오랜 기간 타자로 분류되었다.
④ 편견을 갖는다는 말은 무엇을 선호하는 경우에도 쓰인다.
⑤ 타자화는 긍정적 또는 부정적 의미로 사용될 수 있다.

Whatever (A) <u>they</u> may be in theory, in the workplace, biological incapacity and natural preference are the counters used to defend against accusations of discrimination. Larry Summers, President of Harvard University, argues that competition makes discrimination irrational; that wouldn't hold, though, if an entire field is pervaded with discrimination, if there's a consensus that women don't belong there and if female candidates are judged more harshly by all potential employers. It also doesn't work if the threat of competition isn't so credible; it will be a long time before Ivies* feel the heat from Northwestern, which has improved its profile by hiring the first-rate women (B) <u>they</u> foolishly let go. The history of women and minorities in the workplace shows that vigorous enforcement of antidiscrimination law is what drives progress. Moreover, the competition argument can be turned against Summers; after all, given its prestige and wealth, Harvard could compete for women with any university on the planet. So why doesn't it?

* Ivies: 미국 동부의 유명 사립대학들

25 다음 중 필자의 의견으로 적절하지 <u>않은</u> 것은?

① Summers는 여성의 기회 균등을 경쟁이라는 논리로 부정한다.
② Harvard 대학은 여성에게 동등한 기회를 부여하는 데 앞장서지 않고 있다.
③ 생물학적 능력의 결핍, 자연적 선호가 모두 여성을 차별하는 수단으로 이용된다.
④ Ivies와 Northwestern 대학은 여성에 대해 차별적이다.
⑤ 반차별 정책을 강력하게 적용해야 여성과 소수자의 권리가 신장된다.

26 위 (A)와 (B)의 <u>they</u>가 각각 가리키는 것은?

(A)	(B)
① biological incapacity and natural preference	Ivies and Northwestern
② biological incapacity and natural preference	Ivies
③ counters	Ivies and Northwestern
④ accusations	Ivies
⑤ accusations	Ivies and Northwestern

(A)

In their recent report, "One Nation, Many Peoples: A Declaration of Cultural Interdependence," a committee of scholars and teachers recommends that public schools provide a multicultural education. What that means, according to the report, is recognizing that America was shaped and continues to be shaped by people of diverse ethnic backgrounds and its history is an ongoing process of discovery and interpretation of the past, and that there is more than one way of viewing the world.

(B)

Several dissenting committee members publicly worry that America will splinter into ethnic fragments if this multicultural curriculum is adopted. They argue that the committee's report puts the focus on ethnicity at the expense of national unity.

(C)

In particular, according to the report, the curriculum should help children "to assess critically the reasons for the inconsistencies between the ideals of the U.S. and social realities. It should provide information and intellectual tools that can permit them to contribute to bringing reality closer to the ideals." In other words, show children what really happened, and give them the skills to help improve their country. What could be more patriotic?

(D)

Downplaying ethnicity, however, will not bolster national unity. The history of America is the story of how and why people from all over the world came to the United States, and how in struggling to make a better life for themselves, they changed each other, they changed the country, and they all came to call themselves Americans.

(E)

Thus, the westward migration of white Americans is not just a heroic settling of an untamed wild, but also the conquest of indigenous peoples. Immigrants were not just white, but Asian as well. Blacks were not merely passive slaves freed by northern whites, but active fighters for their own liberation.

27 주어진 글 (A)에 이어질 내용을 순서에 맞게 배열한 것으로 가장 적절한 것은?

① (E) – (C) – (B) – (D)　　　　② (C) – (D) – (E) – (B)

③ (E) – (C) – (D) – (B)　　　　④ (C) – (E) – (B) – (D)

⑤ (B) – (D) – (E) – (C)

28 윗글의 내용과 일치하는 것은?

① 위원회의 모든 구성원들이 다문화 교육 과정의 도입에 동의했다.

② 미국은 이상과 실제가 일치하는 국가이다.

③ 민족성을 부각시키지 않을 때 비로소 미국의 국가적 통합이 가능하다.

④ 백인의 영웅적인 서부 이주와 정착의 이면에는 원주민에 대한 정복이 있었다.

⑤ 흑인 노예는 남부 백인에 의해 해방되었을 뿐 아니라 스스로 해방을 위해 싸웠다.

The majority of persons, if asked what the uses of dust, would reply that did not know it had any, but they were sure it was a great nuisance. It is true that dust, in our towns and in our houses, is often not only a nuisance, but a serious source of disease, sometimes resulting in total blindness. Dust, however, is only matter in the wrong place, and whatever injurious or disagreeable effects it produces are largely due to our own dealing with nature. If we adopt purely mechanical means of conveyance, we can almost wholly abolish disease-bearing dust from our streets; while another kind of dust, that is caused by the imperfect burning of coal, may be got rid of with equal facility if we consider pure air and sunlight to be of more importance to the population as a whole than are the prejudices or the interests of those who produce the smoke. But though we can minimize the dangers and the inconveniences arising from dust, we cannot wholly abolish it; and _____, since it has now been discovered that it is to the presence of dust we owe much of the beauty, and perhaps even the very habitability, of the earth we live upon. Were it not for dust, we could not admire the blue sky or the gorgeous tints seen at sunset and sunrise not only in the atmosphere but also on the clouds near the horizon.

윗글의 빈칸에 들어갈 말로 가장 적절한 것은?

① we are very busy searching for the ways to do so
② we will be easily forgetful of having done so
③ it is one of our greatest missions to do so
④ it is indeed fortunate we cannot do so
⑤ no one knows how to avoid doing so

30

위 글의 내용과 일치하는 것은?

① 먼지가 쓸모 있다는 점이 널리 알려져 있다.
② 먼지는 질병과 실명의 원인이 될 수 있다.
③ 석탄의 불완전 연소에 의한 먼지는 제거될 수 없다.
④ 질병을 옮기는 먼지는 제거될 수 없다.
⑤ 먼지 때문에 지구의 아름다움을 음미할 수 없다.

I was eight years old and a tomboy. I had a cowboy hat, cowboy boots, checkered shirt and pants, all red. My playmates were my brothers, two and four years older than I. My parents decided to buy my brothers guns. These were not "real" guns. They shot "BBs," copper pellets that my brother said would kill birds. Because I was a girl, I did not get a gun. Instantly I was relegated to the position of Indian. Now there appeared a great distance between us. They shot at everything with their new guns. I tried to keep up with my bow and arrows. Then I felt an incredible blow in my right eye. I looked out just in time to see my brother lower his gun. I remember the accident now: I confront for the first time, consciously, the meaning of the doctor's words years ago: "Eyes are sympathetic. If one is blind, the other will likely become blind too." I realize I have dashed about the world madly, looking at this, looking at that, storing up images against the fading of the light. Then, the gratitude that I have still maintained my sight for over twenty-five years sends me literally to my knees. Word after word comes — which is perhaps how one prays.

*pellet: 작은 총알

31   윗글의 내용과 일치하지 <u>않는</u> 것은?

① 여덟 살 때 나는 카우보이 복장을 한 말괄량이 소녀였다.
② 오빠들이 BB총알을 사용하는 총을 갖게 된 후에 나는 인디언 역할을 했다.
③ 내가 눈에 상처를 입은 것을 보고나서 오빠들은 가해자를 찾아 나섰다.
④ 한 쪽 눈을 실명한 이후 나는 많은 것들을 보고 기억에 저장하려 했다.
⑤ 한쪽 눈의 시력을 상실하면 다른 쪽 눈도 실명할 수 있다고 의사가 말했다.

32   윗글의 나타난 필자의 현재 심경으로 가장 적절한 것은?

① apologetic   ② regretful   ③ reserved
④ appreciative   ⑤ absent-minded

After a man died several months ago at the Virginian Retirement Community, his family went to collect his worldly goods. His home was crammed, floor to ceiling, with possessions they never knew (a) he had: kitchen gadgets, costume jewelry, bed linens, and cleaners, all by the dozens. (b) He had bought it all from the home shopping networks that came through his television into his living room 24 hours a day, seven days a week. He ordered a package almost every day. Some of what came (c) he gave away. Most of it simply piled up, unused. What had brought him to line his walls with the fruits of home shopping? Companionship. Home shopping hosts didn't just sell to him — they spoke to him. An employee at the retirement community recalls that (d) he saw him spending a lot of time by himself. He spoke of being lonely. But when he bought, (e) he said he could keep operators chatting to him for half an hour. He had found a way to fill his days and sleepless nights. He was not alone in his discovery. As the hours cycle past on home shopping channels, the disembodied voices of buyers float above the sparkling descriptions of jewelry. Most are female. Many of the voices are beginning to crack with age.

33

윗글의 밑줄 친 'He was not alone in his discovery'의 의미로 가장 적절한 것은?

① There were many people in the retirement community.
② He was lonely in the Virginian Retirement Community.
③ He kept all the items he bought from home shopping.
④ Many people sought companionship from home shopping channels.
⑤ He did not feel lonely by finding things at home shopping channels.

34

윗글의 밑줄 친 (a)~(e) 중에서 가리키는 바가 나머지 넷과 다른 하나는?

①(a)   ②(b)   ③(c)   ④(d)   ⑤(e)

It's hard to listen to a politician or pundit these days without hearing that America is losing jobs to poorer nations — manufacturing jobs to China, back-office work to India, just about every job to Latin America. This lament distracts our attention from the larger challenge of preparing more Americans for better jobs.

It's true that U.S. manufacturing employment has been dropping for many years, but that's not primarily due to foreigners taking these jobs. Factory jobs are vanishing all over the world. I recently toured a U.S. factory containing two employees and 400 computerized robots. The two live people sat in front of computer screens and instructed the robots. In a few years this factory won't have a single employee on site, except for an occasional visiting technician who repairs and upgrades the robots, like the gas man changing your meter.

Manufacturing is following the same trend as agriculture. As productivity rises, employment falls because fewer people are needed. In 1910, a third of Americans worked on farms. Now, fewer than 3 percent do. Since 1995, even as manufacturing employment has dropped around the world, global output has risen more than 30 percent. Want to blame something? Blame _____ which created the electronic gadgets and software that can now do almost any routine task. This goes well beyond the factory floor.

35 윗글의 주제로 가장 적절한 것은?

① why manufacturing jobs disappear
② why free trade destroys domestic jobs
③ how to beat global competitions
④ how to deal with the loss of manufacturing jobs
⑤ how to save manufacturing jobs

36 윗글의 빈칸에 들어갈 말로 가장 적절한 것은?

① poor nations   ② international trade   ③ low employment rate
④ new knowledge   ⑤ trade deficits

A corporate president recently made a visit to a nearby Indian reservation as part of his firm's public relations program. "We realize that we have not hired any Indians in the five years our company has been located in this area," he told the assembled tribesmen, "but we are looking into the matter very seriously." "Hora, hora," said some of the Indians. "We would like to eventually hire 5 percent of our total work force from this reservation," he said. "Hora, hora," shouted more of the Indians. _____ their enthusiasm, the president closed his short address by telling them that he hoped his firm would be able to take some hiring action within the next couple of years. "Hora, hora, hora," cried the total group. With a feeling of satisfaction the president left the hall and was taken on a tour of the reservation. Stopping in a field to admire some of the horses grazing there, the president asked if he could walk up closer to the animals. "Certainly," said his Indian driver, "but be careful not to step in the hora."

37 윗글의 내용으로 추론할 수 있는 것은?

① The president thought the Indians deserved to be hired.
② The firm had a stated policy never to hire Indians.
③ The Indians did not believe the president's speech.
④ The Indians offered the company to build its factory in their area.
⑤ The president thought hiring the Indians would be bad for his company.

38 윗글의 빈칸에 들어갈 말로 가장 적절한 것은?

① In spite of   ② Not noticing   ③ To calm down
④ Encouraged by   ⑤ Feeling gloomy about

[01~02]   다음 글을 읽고, 물음에 답하시오.

| 사관학교 2018학년도 42~43번 |

During World War II, the composer Dmitry Shostakovich and several of his colleagues were called into a meeting with the Russian ruler Joseph Stalin, who had commissioned them to write a new national anthem. Shostakovich heard meetings with Stalin were (A) ⎡fascinating / terrifying⎤; one misstep could lead you into a very dark alley. He would stare you down until you felt your throat tighten. And, as meetings with Stalin often did, this one took a bad turn: The ruler began to criticize one of the composers for his poor arrangement of his anthem. Scared silly, the man admitted he had used an arranger who had done a bad job. Here he was digging several graves: Clearly the poor arranger could be called to task. The composer was responsible for the (B) ⎡hire / dismissal⎤, and he, too, could pay for the mistake. And what of the other composers, including Shostakovich? Stalin could be relentless once he smelled fear.

Shostakovich had heard enough: It was foolish, he said, to blame the arranger, who was mostly following orders. He then subtly redirected the conversation to a different subject — whether a composer should do his own orchestrations. What did Stalin think on the matter? Always eager to prove his expertise, he swallowed the bait. The dangerous moment passed.

Shostakovich maintained his presence of mind in several ways. First, instead of letting Stalin intimidate him, he forced himself to see the man as he was: short, fat, ugly, unimaginative. So the dictator's famous piercing gaze was just a trick, a sign of his own (C) ⎡creativity / creativity⎤. Second, Shostakovich faced up to Stalin, talking to him normally and straightforwardly. By his actions and tone of voice, the composer showed that he was not intimidated.

01

(A), (B), (C)의 각 네모 안에서 문맥에 맞는 표현으로 가장 적절한 것은? [3점]

(A)		(B)		(C)
① fascinating	……	hire	……	creativity
② fascinating	……	dismissal	……	insecurity
③ terrifying	……	hire	……	insecurity
④ terrifying	……	dismissal	……	insecurity
⑤ terrifying	……	hire	……	creativity

02

윗글의 내용으로 적절하지 <u>않은</u> 것은?

① Shostakovich와 그의 동료들은 Stalin으로부터 국가를 작곡하라는 의뢰를 받았다.

② Stalin은 국가를 잘 편곡하지 못한 작곡자 중 한 명을 비난했다.

③ Shostakovich는 지시를 따른 편곡자를 나무라는 것은 어리석은 일이라고 말했다.

④ Stalin은 자신이 전문적 지식을 지녔음을 입증하는 것을 원하지 않았다.

⑤ Shostakovich는 Stalin을 두려워하지 않는다는 것을 보여줬다.

(A)

When Don was 25, he went backpacking around South East Asia. For three of those weeks, he traveled around Indonesia, including a stop in a lovely town called Bukittinggi. At his guesthouse, he met a nice fellow from Sweden, Stephen, who recommended that (a) he explore a nearby lake atop a long inactive volcano.

(B)

In starting (b) his trek around the lake, Don knew that the last bus down the mountain left at 5:00p.m., so he had to be sure to be back at the bus stop by then. As it was 1:00p.m., he figured he had loads of time to make it all the way around the lake and back in time to catch the last bus down the mountain. It was an amazing hike. However, at about 4:00p.m. he realized that (c) he was nowhere near half-way around the lake.

(C)

He decided to race back the way he came. As he neared the bus stop, he saw the last bus driving away without (d) him. Breathless, he had no choice but to start walking down the mountain and hope that some kind person would pick him up. He walked for hours before any vehicles even came by. Fortunately, eventually, a wonderful Indonesian gentleman stopped to help. He was very sympathetic to the situation and offered Don a ride all the way back to his guesthouse. Don was more grateful than words could express.

(D)

Following (e) his advice, Don found a bus that would take him up there. It turned out to be not so close, but rather a four-hour ride up steep, windy, and rather dangerous roads. It was worth it, though, because the view was unbelievable at the top. There was an absolutely majestic lake at the top of the mountain where the mouth of the volcano once was. It was surrounded by a lovely walking path, which according to Stephen, would take about two hours to walk around.

03 주어진 글 (A)에 이어질 내용을 순서에 맞게 배열한 것으로 가장 적절한 것은?

① (B) – (D) – (C)

② (C) – (B) – (D)

③ (C) – (D) – (B)

④ (D) – (B) – (C)

⑤ (D) – (C) – (B)

04 밑줄 친 (a)~(e) 중에서 가리키는 대상이 나머지 넷과 <u>다른</u> 것은?

① (a)

② (b)

③ (c)

④ (d)

⑤ (e)

We might describe science that has no known practical value as basic science or basic research. Our exploration of worlds such as Jupiter would be called basic science, and it is easy to argue that basic science is not worth the effort and expense because it has no known practical use. Of course, the problem is that we have no way of knowing what knowledge will be of use until we acquire that knowledge. In the middle of the 19th century, Queen Victoria is supposed to have asked physicist Michael Faraday what good his experiments with electricity and magnetism were. He answered, "Madam, what good is a baby?" Of course, Faraday's experiments were the beginning of the electronic age. Many of the practical uses of scientific knowledge that fill our world — transistors, vaccines, plastics — began as basic research. Basic scientific research provides the raw materials that technology and engineering use to solve problems.

Basic scientific research has yet one more important use that is so valuable it seems an insult to refer to it as merely functional. Science is the study of nature, and as we learn more about how nature works, we learn more about what our existence in this universe means for us. The seemingly _____ knowledge we gain from space probes to other worlds tells us about our planet and our own role in the scheme of nature. Science tells us where we are and what we are, and that knowledge is beyond value.

*space probe: 우주탐사기(機)

05 윗글의 제목으로 가장 적절한 것은?

① What Does Basic Science Bring to Us?
② The Crisis of Researchers in Basic Science
③ Common Goals of Science and Technology
④ Technology: The Ultimate Aim of Basic Science
⑤ Michael Faraday, Frontiersman of the Electronic Age!

06 윗글의 빈칸에 들어갈 말로 가장 적절한 것은?   [3점]

① applicable   ② impractical   ③ inaccurate
④ priceless   ⑤ resourceful

There is a difference between getting what you want and getting what you think you want. Technology gives us more and more of what we think we want. These days, looking at sociable robots and digitized friends, one might assume that what we want is to be always in touch and never alone, no matter who or what we are in touch with. One might assume that what we want is plenty of weak ties, the informal networks that underpin online acquaintanceship. But if we pay attention to the real consequences of what we think we want, we may discover what we really want. We may want some stillness and solitude. As an American writer once put it, we may want to live less 'thickly' and wait for more infrequent but meaningful _____.
As we put in our many hours of typing — with all fingers or just thumbs — we may discover that we miss the human voice. We may decide that it is fine to play chess with a robot, but that robots are unfit for any conversation about family or friends. A robot might have needs, but to understand desire, one needs language and flesh. We may decide that for these conversations, we must have a person who knows, firsthand, what it means to be born, to have parents and a family, to wish for love and perhaps children, and to anticipate death. And, of course, we must not let the virtual take us away from the real world that doesn't go away with a power outage.

07   윗글의 제목으로 가장 적절한 것은?

① Plug In and Log On: Farewell to Loneliness
② Ethical Issues in the Online Community
③ Humans and Robots: Friends or Foes?
④ Connected yet Detached in Virtuality
⑤ Explore the Net, Go Beyond Reality

08   윗글의 빈칸에 들어갈 말로 가장 적절한 것은?

① adventurous endeavors
② technological outbursts
③ face-to-face encounters
④ dialogs with social robots
⑤ supernatural interventions

Problem Solving Skills

장문 독해 I과 유사하나 엮인 문항이 3문항으로 한 문항 더 많으며 지문의 길이도 좀 더 길다. 장문 독해 I와 같은 방식으로 접근하되 시간 관리에 유의한다.

• 지문에 엮인 문제들의 유형을 확인한다.
• 주어진 단서들로 글에 대해 파악한다.
• 유형별 접근법에 따라 문제를 해결한다.

Example

[01~03] **다음 글을 읽고 물음에 답하시오.** | 경찰대학 2017학년도 43~45번 |

I have always had an interest in the art of magic. By the time I was ten, I could make handkerchiefs vanish and shuffle a deck of cards thoroughly without altering their order. In my early teens I joined one of the world's best-known magic societies in London. By my early twenties I had been invited to the U.S. to perform several times at prestigious shows.

My love for the world of fascinating tricks and illusion had started with a chance encounter. When I was eight I was asked to complete a school project on the history of chess. Being a diligent young student, I decided to pay a visit to my local library to find books on the topic. I was directed to the wrong shelf and came across some books on magic. I was curious, and started to read all about the secrets that magicians use to achieve the impossible. I have no idea what might have happened if I had been directed to the correct shelf and found the chess books.

Many people have reported how chance meetings and unplanned encounters with strangers frequently led to a significant shift in career directions. Each one of us could tell stories of how crucial, unplanned events have had a major career impact and how untold thousands of minor unplanned events have had at least a small impact. Influential unplanned events _____; they are everyday occurrences. Serendipity is not serendipitous. Serendipity is ubiquitous.

Take Joseph Pulitzer as an example. He was born in Hungary. As a young man Pulitzer suffered from both poor health and extremely bad eyesight. When he was seventeen, he came to America for a better life. However, he could not find a job there. Pulitzer spent a great deal of time playing chess in his local library. On one such visit he happened to meet an editor of a local newspaper. This unexpected meeting resulted in Pulitzer being offered a job as a junior reporter. He was quite successful in his newspaper career, and became an editor, and eventually owner of two of the best-known newspapers of his day.

01 윗글의 제목으로 가장 적절한 것은?

① Diligence Always Pays Off
② Chances Are It's a Great Chance
③ Joseph Pulitzer: Untold Anecdotes
④ Prestige and Your Career Choices
⑤ Magical Moments Long Remembered

02 윗글의 빈칸에 들어가기에 가장 적절한 것은?

① are preconceived
② are not welcome
③ are not uncommon
④ can predict the future
⑤ can lose their influence

03 윗글에서 Joseph Pulitzer에 관한 내용과 일치하지 않는 것은?

① Hungary에서 출생했다.
② 시력이 나빠서 고생했다.
③ 열일곱 살 때 미국에 갔다.
④ 프로 chess 기사가 됐다.
⑤ 두 개의 신문사를 소유했다.

Vocabulary

vanish 사라지다 shuffle 섞다 thoroughly 완전히 alter 바꾸다 prestigious 저명한 direct 향하다 serendipity 우연한 사건 serendipitous 우연한 ubiquitous 어디에나 있는 pay off 수지가 맞다 anecdote 일화 prestige 명성 preconceive 예상하다

Let's Solve

Point ❶ 지문에 엮인 문제들의 유형 확인하기

- 01 제목(UNIT 03)
- 02 II(UNIT 10)
- 03 세부 정보(UNIT 17)
  - → 빈칸을 먼저 채우고 제목과 세부 정보 문제를 해결한다.

Point ❷ 주어진 단서들로 글에 대해 파악하기

- My love for the world of fascinating tricks and illusion had started with a chance encounter.
- Serendipity is not serendipitous. Serendipity is ubiquitous.

삶을 바꾸는 예기치 않은 사건은 흔히 일어난다.

Point ❸ 유형별 접근법에 따라 문제 해결하기

02 빈칸에 가장 적절한 것 – 빈칸 II 유형

- 빈칸을 포함하는 문장 해석하기

  Influential unplanned events _____; they are everyday occurrences.
  - → 영향력 있는 예기치 못한 사건들은 _____. 그것들은 매일 일어난다.

- 정답 풀이하기
  - → 우연한 사건들은 매일 일어난다고 하였으므로, 빈칸에는 ③ '드물지 않다'가 가장 적절하다.

01 제목으로 가장 적절한 것 – 제목 유형

- 글의 흐름 파악하기

어렸을 때 우연히 마술에 흥미를 갖게 되어 마술사의 길을 걷게 된 글쓴이의 사례	➡ 삶의 방향을 바꿔놓는 예기치 못한 사건은 흔히 일어남	➡ Joseph Pulitzer의 사례

- 정답 풀이하기
  - → 글쓴이가 우연한 기회에 마술을 하게 된 이야기와 풀리처가 우연한 기회에 신문기자가 되어 신문사를 소유하게 되는 과정을 통해 인생을 바꾼 우연한 사건들을 보여주는 글이므로, 이 글의 제목으로는 ② '우연한 일들이 좋은 기회이다'가 가장 적절하다.

03 Joseph Pulitzer에 관한 내용과 일치하지 <u>않는</u> 것 − 세부 정보 유형

- **글의 소재 파악하기 마지막 문단**
  - 마지막 문단 도입부: Take Joseph Pulitzer as an example. He was born in Hungary.
    → Joseph Pulitzer의 삶

- **선택지의 핵심 정보 확인하기**
  ① <u>Hungary</u>에서 출생했다.
  ② <u>시력이 나빠서</u> 고생했다.
  ③ <u>열일곱 살 때</u> 미국에 갔다.
  ④ <u>프로 chess 기사</u>가 됐다.
  ⑤ <u>두 개의 신문사</u>를 소유했다.

- **글의 세부 정보 분석하기**
  - 어릴 때: Hungary에서 태어나 나쁜 건강과 시력으로 고생했다.
  - 17살 때: 미국에 왔지만 직업을 찾지 못했다.
  - 지역 도서관: 체스로 시간을 보냈고 그곳에서 우연히 지역신문 편집자를 만났다.
  - 기자 생활: 견습 기자가 된 뒤 성공적인 경력을 쌓았다.
  - 이후: 당대 가장 유명한 신문사 두 곳을 소유했다.

- **정답 풀이하기**
  Pulitzer spent a great deal of time playing chess in his local library. On one such visit he happened to meet an editor of a local newspaper. This unexpected meeting resulted in Pulitzer being offered a job as a junior reporter.
  → ④ 심심풀이로 체스를 하러 다니다 우연히 지역신문 편집자를 만나 견습 기자가 되었다.

[01~03]   다음 글을 읽고, 물음에 답하시오. | 경찰대학 2018학년도 43~45번 |

On disembarking at Amsterdam's Schipol Airport, I am struck, only a few steps inside the terminal, by the appearance of a sign hanging from the ceiling, which shows the way to the arrivals hall, the exit and the transfer desks. It is a bright-yellow sign, one meter high and two meters across, simple in design, a plastic fascia in an illuminated aluminum box suspended on steel struts from a ceiling webbed with cables and air-conditioning ducts. Despite its simplicity, even its mundanity, the sign delights me, a delight for which the adjective *exotic*, though unusual, seems apt. The exoticism is located in particular areas: in the double a of *Aankomst*, in the neighborliness of the *u* and the *i* in *Uitgang*, in the use of English subtitles, in the word for "desk," *balies*, and in the choice of practical, modernist fonts, Frutiger or Univers.

If the sign provokes in me genuine pleasure, it is in part because it offers the first conclusive evidence of my having arrived elsewhere. It is a symbol of being abroad. Although it may not seem distinctive to the casual eye, such a sign would never exist in precisely this form in my own country. There it would be less yellow, the typeface would be softer and more nostalgic, there would — out of greater indifference to the _____ of foreigners — be no subtitles, and the language would contain no double *a*s, a repetition in which I sense, confusedly, the presence of another history and mind-set.

That a sign could be different in different places is evidence of a simple but pleasing idea: countries are diverse, and practices variable across borders. Yet difference alone would not be enough to elicit pleasure, or not for long. The difference has to seem like an improvement on what my own country is capable of. If I call the Schipol sign exotic, it is because it succeeds in suggesting, vaguely but intensely, that the country that made it and that lies beyond the *uitgang* may in critical ways prove more congenial than my own to my temperament and concerns. The sign is a promise of happiness.

01 윗글의 제목으로 가장 적절한 것은?

① At Once Exotic and Nostalgic
② Too Esoteric a Sign Kills Curiosity
③ Sweet Bewilderment: Am I Elsewhere?
④ Various Languages on the Same Platter
⑤ Across the Border: The Pioneering Traveler

02 윗글의 빈칸에 들어가기에 가장 적절한 것은?

① talent   ② excitement
③ confusion   ④ intimacy
⑤ number

03 Schipol Airport의 표지판에 관한 윗글의 내용과 일치하지 <u>않는</u> 것은? [3점]

① Its length is twice its height.
② It is written in two languages.
③ Its simplicity is the main reason for its exoticism.
④ It gives proof of arriving in another country.
⑤ The writer could not find a sign like it back home.

(A)

Many states have laws requiring individuals to wear a helmet while riding a motorcycle. These laws are frequently challenged, on the grounds that their sole purpose is to protect cyclists from injuring themselves.

(B)

In college I had a motorcycle-riding friend who steadfastly refused to wear a helmet. He had been ridiculed so often by the rest of us for his foolishness that (a) he developed a rather eloquent defense that went something like this: "Look, I'm tired of this bourgeois life; I'm out for a little adventure, that's why I ride a bike in the first place. I want it to be dangerous; the thrill is the risk. And the more I risk, the bigger the thrill."

(C)

It would seem from the episode that the helmet-free motorcyclist is engaged in other-regarding conduct after all. It is not that the public cares much about what happens to the motorcyclist; we care about the costs to the rest of us that flow from daredevil behavior. Not everyone's lifestyle is equal in terms of the burden or tax (b) he places on public resources. My reckless pal seems a particularly extreme example of an egoist asking the public to support his choice, not just leave (c) him alone.

(D)

Was my friend's decision to ride without a helmet a decision that affected only himself? Stones or other objects might fly up from the road, causing (d) him to swerve into others. Even were he to injure only himself, that injury might involve head trauma that could have been avoided by wearing a helmet. My friend would then expect not to be left alone but to be ministered to by ambulance drivers, medics, and EMTs. Valuable time and money would be expended to subsidize his thrill seeking. The medics might not get to another victim in time because they were busy working to stuff brain tissue back inside (e) his cracked skull. Hospital space and resources would also be taxed, doctors called upon, and medical and auto insurance rates pushed upward for all of us.

04

윗글의 (A)에 이어질 내용을 순서에 맞게 배열한 것으로 가장 적절한 것은?

① (B) – (C) – (D)　　　② (B) – (D) – (C)　　　③ (C) – (B) – (D)

④ (C) – (D) – (B)　　　⑤ (D) – (C) – (B)

05

윗글의 주제로 가장 적절한 것은?

① the psyche of a helmetless biker
② a recipe for an accident-free society
③ lifestyles of risk and non-risk takers
④ personal freedom at the expense of others
⑤ a controversial regulation for traffic violators

06

밑줄 친 (a)~(e) 중에서 지칭하는 대상이 나머지와 다른 것은?

① (a)　　　② (b)　　　③ (c)　　　④ (d)　　　⑤ (e)

Motivation gains refer to circumstances that increase the effort expended by group members in a collective task. Motivational gains in which the less capable member works harder is known as the Köhler effect. In some investigations, athletes curled a bar attached to a pulley system until exhaustion. They did this first individually and then in groups of two. Motivation gains happened when the athlete pairs had moderately different abilities.   (A)   , motivation gains did not emerge when athletes had equal or very unequal abilities. It was the weaker member of the group who was responsible for the motivation gain. The psychological mechanisms underlying the Köhler effect are social comparison (particularly when someone thinks that their teammate is more capable) and the feeling that one's effort is indispensible to the group. Group members are willing to exert effort on a collective task when they expect their efforts to be instrumental in obtaining outcomes that they value personally. Moreover, in particular, the weakest member of a team is more likely to work harder when everyone is given feedback about people's performance in a timely fashion.

A more common observation in groups is motivation losses, also known as social loafing. A French agricultural engineer named Max Ringelmann was interested in the relative efficiency of farm labor supplied by horses, oxen, machines, and men. In particular, he was curious about their relative abilities to pull a load horizontally, such as in a tug-of-war. In one of his experiments, groups of 14 men pulled a load, and the amount of force they generated was measured. The force that each man could pull independently was also measured. There was a steady decline in the average pull-per-member as the size of the rope-pulling team increased. One person pulling on a rope alone exerted an average of 63 kilograms of force.   (B)   , in groups of three, the per-person force dropped to 53 kilograms, and in groups of eight, it plummeted to only 31 kilograms — less than half of the effort exerted by people working alone. This revealed a fundamental principle of teamwork: People in groups often do not work as hard as they do when alone.

07 윗글의 제목으로 가장 적절할 것은?

① Mechanisms of a Tug of War
② Motivational Effects in Teamwork
③ How to Measure Work Efficiency
④ Boosting Motivation in Individual Tasks
⑤ Psychology Behind the Ringelmann Effect

08 윗글의 내용과 일치하지 <u>않는</u> 것은? [3점]

① The Köhler effect occurs when the less capable person works harder in a group.
② Motivation gains are likely to happen when working with people of the same ability.
③ The weakest member tends to work harder when timely feedback is provided.
④ Max Ringelmann studied the efficiency of labor between different groups.
⑤ Max Ringelmann found that people tend to expend less effort when working collectively.

09 윗글의 빈칸 (A)와 (B)에 들어갈 말로 가장 적절한 것은?

	(A)		(B)
①	Likewise	⋯⋯	However
②	Instead	⋯⋯	Meanwhile
③	Conversely	⋯⋯	However
④	Conversely	⋯⋯	As a result
⑤	Likewise	⋯⋯	Meanwhile

Sheldon Cohen, a psychologist at Carnegie Mellon University, has intentionally given colds to hundreds of people. Under carefully controlled conditions, he systematically exposes volunteers to a rhinovirus that causes the common cold. About a third of people exposed to the virus develop the full panoply of symptoms, while the rest walk away with nary a sniffle.

On the first day, Cohen's experimental volunteers are quarantined for twenty-four hours before they are exposed, to be sure they have not picked up a cold elsewhere. For the next five days the volunteers are housed in a special unit with other volunteers, all of whom are kept at least three feet from one another, lest they reinfect someone. During those five days their nasal secretions are tested for technical indicators of colds (like the total weight of their mucus) as well as the presence of the specific rhinovirus, and their blood samples are tested for antibodies. We know that low levels of vitamin C, smoking and sleeping poorly all increase the likelihood of infection. The question is, can a stressful relationship be added to that list? Cohen's answer: definitely. Cohen assigns precise numerical values to the factors that make one person come down with a cold while another stays healthy. Those with an ongoing personal conflict were 2.5 times as likely as the others to get a cold, putting rocky relationships in the same causal range as vitamin C deficiency and poor sleep. Conflicts that lasted a month or longer boosted susceptibility, but an occasional argument presented no health hazard. While perpetual arguments are bad for our health, isolating ourselves is worse. Compared to those with a rich web of social connections, those with the fewest close relationships were 4.2 times more likely to come down with the cold.

The more we socialize, the less susceptible to colds we become. This idea seems counterintuitive: Don't we *increase* the likelihood of being exposed to a cold virus the more people we interact with? Sure. But vibrant social connections boost our good moods and limit our negative ones, suppressing cortisol and enhancing immune function under stress. Relationships themselves seem to _____ the risk of exposure to the very cold virus they pose.

10

윗글의 제목으로 가장 적절할 것은?

① The Nature of Antibiotic Metabolism in the Human Body
② Rhinovirus Exposure: A Methodology of Utmost Precision
③ The More Social Interactions, the More Severe the Cold
④ Uncommon Findings from the Common Cold Experiment
⑤ New Health Hazards Discovered in Cyberspace

11

윗글의 빈칸에 들어가기에 가장 적절한 것은?   [3점]

① be modified by   ② push them to
③ be weakened by   ④ protect us from
⑤ gradually increase

12

Cohen의 실험과 일치하는 것은?

① 첫날 피험자를 감기 바이러스에 노출시킨다.
② 총 5일 동안 진행된다.
③ 피험자 간 신체적 접촉을 허용한다.
④ 코 분비물을 검사한다.
⑤ 혈액 샘플 검사는 생략한다.

Hunter-gatherers reached Australia about 50,000 years ago. Armed with fire and primitive tools they were able to have a significant impact on the environments they colonized. The fossil record shows a sudden extinction of many large mammals in Australia, which appears to coincide with human colonization, but the evidence for cause and effect is (A) equivocal. There is some debate as to whether the extinctions were caused by human activity or by a period of rapid climate change to which many species were (B) able to adapt. During the late Pleistocene, humans arrived in Australia and more than 85% of large (body mass exceeding 44kg) marsupials and birds were extinct. Was this just coincidence? Dr. David Miller examined evidence for the cause of extinction of the mihirung (a large flightless bird) related to the emu. The time of extinction corresponds to a period of only moderate climate change and he concludes that human impact on this bird's habitat is the most likely (C) cause. However, Dr. Susan Bowman argues that there is no convincing evidence that human predation was the direct cause of the extinction of such a large amount of the Australian megafauna unless the aboriginal population was considerably (D) denser than today. A more likely scenario is that the impact of the use of fire by early aboriginal populations changed the landscape so radically that many species were unable to survive. Aboriginal landscape burning played a crucial role in the (E) formation of typical Australian grassland plant communities before the arrival of Europeans. This has created habitats suitable for some species that are adapted to grazing, but hostile to many browsing animals reliant on scrubby vegetation: browsing is a characteristic of many of the extinct species.

13 윗글의 제목으로 가장 적절한 것은?

① What the Burning Brought to the Landscape
② Magnitude of Human Activity on Climate Change
③ Footprints of Humans' Arrival in Australia
④ How Australians Colonized the Environment
⑤ The Effects of Disappearance of Habitats for Animals

14 밑줄 친 단어 중에서, 글의 흐름에 적절하지 <u>않은</u> 것은?

① (A)　　　② (B)　　　③ (C)　　　④ (D)　　　⑤ (E)

15 윗글의 내용과 일치하지 <u>않는</u> 것은?　　　　　　[3점]

① A sudden disappearance of a number of large mammals in Australia can be substantiated by fossils.
② Dr. Miller believes that people's arrival in Australia and the extinction of many birds during the late Pleistocene is not coincidental.
③ Dr. Bowman says human predation cannot be blamed for the extinction of large Australian animals on a massive scale.
④ The mihirung got extinct in a period of moderate climate change.
⑤ Grassland plant communities created habitats for both grazing and browsing species.

(가)

When you slap some meat inside two slices of bread, you have a sandwich, at least according to the U.S. Department of Agriculture, which enforces the safety and labeling of meat and poultry. "We're talking about a traditional closed-face sandwich," says Mark Wheeler, who works in food safety at the USDA. "A sandwich is a meat or poultry filling between two slices of bread, a bun or a biscuit." That excludes items like burritos, wraps or hot dogs.

(나)

The debate got so heated that in 2006, a contract dispute over whether Qdoba Mexican Grill's burritos qualify as sandwiches went to trial. Expert witnesses including chefs and food critics testified, much deliberation took place, and in the end, Superior Court Judge Jeffrey Locke ruled burritos are not sandwiches. That settled it in Massachusetts. But for every solid definition in every place, you can find ____(A)____. An ice cream sandwich isn't really a sandwich, according to the feds. But we call it that. A taco is not a sandwich in New York. But a burrito somehow is. But New York hasn't explained why — at least not yet.

(다)

What do all these say? Sliced bread brought us sandwiches. But they keep changing. Food trends flash in and out. And keeping up with all the innovation is a losing game for ____(B)____. Whether it's sandwiches or smartphones, the government tries to classify these things to protect the public. But innovation moves faster than the standards can change — a tension Veltman sees again and again. "The people that write these memos are in the business of trying to classify the unclassifiable. Human behavior is kind of infinitely varied. You can never come up with a scheme for it that actually fits everything," Veltman says.

(라)

But the USDA isn't the only place that must define a sandwich. It matters to jurisdictions across the country, mainly for inspection and tax purposes. Noah Veltman, a computer developer, has a weird hobby, which is reading obscure government memos. He says, "My new home state of New York has a special tax category for sandwiches. So they publish this memo that explains that a sandwich includes club sandwiches, BLTs, hot dogs and burritos. And then you wonder, are burritos really a sandwich?" New York says yes, the USDA says no, and it makes a difference when it's inspection time.

16 주어진 글 (가)에 이어질 내용을 순서에 맞게 배열한 것으로 가장 적절한 것은?

① (나) – (다) – (라)　　　② (다) – (나) – (라)
③ (다) – (라) – (나)　　　④ (라) – (나) – (다)
⑤ (라) – (다) – (나)

17 윗글의 제목으로 가장 적절한 것은?

① Superior Courts Sandwiched between Two Forces
② When Is the Right Time to Call Burritos Sandwiches?
③ Tension between New York vs. USDA: A Story Behind
④ Defining Sandwiches: A Lesson on Regulations and Innovation
⑤ Local Food Always Wins: The Case of Burritos and Sandwiches

18 윗글의 빈칸 (A)와 (B)에 들어갈 말로 가장 적절한 것은?

	(A)	(B)
①	an edge case	······ regulators
②	an edge case	······ chefs and food critics
③	a lucid case	······ software developers
④	a lucid case	······ chefs and food critics
⑤	a lucid case	······ regulators

Like many stories, certain details of who or what the Bell Witch was vary from version to version. The prevailing account is that it was (A) the ghost of a woman named Kate Batts, a mean old neighbor of John Bell. Batts believed Bell cheated her in a land purchase and on her deathbed she swore that she would haunt John Bell and his family. This version appears in a Tennessee guidebook published in 1933:

"Sure enough, the Bells were tormented for years by the malicious spirit of Old Kate Batts. John Bell and his daughter Betsy were the principal targets. Toward the other members of the family the witch was either indifferent or, as in the case of Mrs. Bell, friendly. No one ever saw (B) her, but every visitor to the Bell home heard her all too well. The spirit of Old Kate led John and Betsy Bell on a merry chase. She threw furniture and dishes at them. She pulled their noses, yanked their hair, poked needles into them. She yelled all night to keep them from sleeping, and snatched food from their mouths at mealtimes."

News of the Bell Witch spread quickly. When word of the haunting reached Nashville, one of its most famous citizens, General Andrew Jackson, decided to gather a group of friends to investigate it. The future president of the U.S. wanted to either expose it as a hoax or send (C) the spirit away. Jackson and his men were traveling when suddenly the wagon stopped. The men pushed and pushed, but the wagon could not be moved. Then came the sound of a voice from the bushes saying, "All right general, let the wagon move on. I will see you tonight." The astonished men could not find the source of the voice. The horses then unexpectedly started walking on their own and the wagon moved along again. Jackson indeed encountered (D) the witch that night and left early the next morning, claiming he would rather fight the British than the Bell Witch.

A few explanations of the Bell Witch phenomena have been offered over the years. One is that the haunting was a hoax created by Richard Powell, the schoolteacher of Betsy Bell and Joshua Gardner, the boy with whom Betsy was in love. It seems Powell was deeply in love with Betsy and would do anything to destroy (E) her relationship with Gardner. Through a variety of tricks, it is believed that Powell created all of the ghostly effects to scare Gardner away. In fact, Gardner eventually did break up with Betsy and left the area. It has never been satisfactorily explained, however, how Powell achieved all the effects. But Powell did come out the winner. In the end, he married Betsy Bell.

19 윗글의 제목으로 가장 적절한 것은?

① Story Behind the Bell Witch
② Watch Out for a Witch's Tricks
③ Don't Fall in Love with a Witch
④ General Jackson's Unsuccessful Witch Hunt
⑤ Invention of Witchcraft in the American South

20 밑줄 친 부분 중 가리키는 대상이 <u>다른</u> 것은?

① (A)   ② (B)   ③ (C)   ④ (D)   ⑤ (E)

21 윗글의 내용과 일치하지 <u>않는</u> 것은?

① Bell Witch는 Mrs. Bell에게는 우호적이었다.
② Bell Witch는 가구를 던지고 머리카락을 잡아당기기도 했다.
③ Andrew Jackson 장군은 후에 대통령이 되었다.
④ Andrew Jackson은 영국과 싸우기 위해 남부에서의 전투를 중지하였다.
⑤ Powell은 Betsy와 결혼하는 데 성공했다.

(가)

I first heard about Veranda Beach on my grandparents' porch the summer I was 13. It was a lazy night that left the hills a smoky blue and the air heavy with the smell of rain. The last shadows were melting into dusk as conversation turned to the summer ahead.

(나)

Well, summer passed, and with age came wisdom. I realized the front porch was no enemy to adventure. It was a window on the world and a lesson in how that world works. What's more, the love affair continues to this day — with new lessons adding to the old. On my family's porch, I learned about life and love, hopes and dreams, and promises and trust. One day it was the front door to Tara, as my sister and I assumed awful Southern accents and scouted the horizon for Rhett Butler. The next day it was a castle fortress or a ship at sea. For the adults, lighthearted bantering and games of checkers were _____(A)_____ ; talk about taxes and checkbooks was not. The veranda was a place to enjoy the little things. Life was slower there.

(다)

Now, more than a few verandas later, I have become a connoisseur of the porch. This summer I am spending time perched on a porch rail, trading stories with my children. As I watch a new generation write their names in the sweat of a lemonade pitcher, I hope they, too, are learning the lessons of Veranda Beach. Be strong against the wind. Be colorful and imaginative — grow in unexpected ways. Watch for the shooting stars. Above all, know that sometimes it's better to have a place to be yourself than to have a place to go.

(라)

"Any plans?" my grandfather asked. Tipping his chair back, my father answered, "Just Veranda Beach." They all chuckled. My heart pounded. Veranda Beach? Where was it? When would we go? "Why, you're there already," my father teased. There was a gentle chorus of laughter as they told me the awful truth. Veranda Beach was the front porch. We were going nowhere. My adolescent spirits _____(B)_____ . What did they see in that boring porch? Didn't they know the grass was surely greener in some distant place?

*connoisseur: 감식가, 전문가

22 주어진 글 (가)에 이어질 내용을 순서에 맞게 배열한 것으로 가장 적절한 것은?

① (나) – (다) – (라)   ② (나) – (라) – (다)
③ (다) – (나) – (라)   ④ (다) – (라) – (나)
⑤ (라) – (나) – (다)

23 윗글의 제목으로 가장 적절한 것은?

① The Gentle Chorus in the Front Porch
② The Greener Grass in My Front Yard
③ Veranda Beach: The Place to Be Yourself
④ The Memory Never Gone with the Wind
⑤ Life's Lesson: Getting Older, but Wiser

24 윗글의 빈칸 (A)와 (B)에 들어갈 말로 가장 적절한 것은?   [3점]

	(A)		(B)
①	encouraged	⋯⋯	plunged
②	discredited	⋯⋯	plunged
③	explored	⋯⋯	arose
④	favored	⋯⋯	arose
⑤	altered	⋯⋯	drooped

(A)

When ordinary young adults realize how little they learned in school, they usually assume there was something wrong with the school they attended or with the way they spent their time there. But the fact is that the best possible graduate of the best possible school needs to continue learning in the days to come.

(B)

However, never just read, for reading without discussion with others who have read the same book is not nearly as profitable. And as reading without discussion can fail to yield the full measure of understanding that should be sought, so discussion without the substance that good and great books afford is likely to degenerate into little more than an exchange of

_____.

(C)

How should they go about doing this? In a book published last year, I tried to answer the question, "How should persons proceed who wish to conduct for themselves the continuation of learning after all schooling has been finished?" The brief and simple answer to this crucial question is: Read and discuss.

(D)

Those who take this prescription seriously would, of course, be better off if their schooling had given them the intellectual discipline and skill they need to carry it out. But even the individual who is fortunate enough to leave school or college after extensive reading followed by insightful discussions, would still have a long road to travel before he or she became an educated person.

25 윗글의 (A)에 이어질 내용을 순서에 맞게 배열한 것으로 가장 적절한 것은?

① (B) – (D) – (C)　　　② (C) – (B) – (D)　　　③ (C) – (D) – (B)
④ (D) – (B) – (C)　　　⑤ (D) – (C) – (B)

26 윗글의 주제로 가장 적절한 것은?

① the importance of reading and discussion in continuing learning
② the contribution of schooling to lifelong education
③ problems of schooling for young adults
④ the necessity for extensive reading for young adults
⑤ factors affecting reading and discussion throughout schooling

27 윗글의 빈칸에 들어갈 말로 가장 적절한 것은?

① critical questions
② profound schooling
③ superficial opinions
④ insightful understanding
⑤ intellectual discipline

(A)

It happened one day that a fisherman putting out to sea in a boat was just about to cast a net, when right in front of him he saw a man on the point of drowning. Being a stout-hearted and at the same time an agile man, he jumped up and, seizing a boathook, thrust it toward the man's face. It caught him right in the eye and pierced it. The fisherman hauled the man into the boat and made for shore without casting any of his nets. He had the man carried to his house and given the best possible attention and treatment, until he had got over his ordeal.

(B)

The other promptly spoke up and said, "Gentlemen, I cannot deny that I knocked his eye out, but if what I did was wrong, I'd like to explain how it all happened. This man was in mortal danger in the sea, in fact he was on the point of drowning. I went to his aid. I won't deny I struck him with my boathook, but I did it for his own good. I saved his life on that occasion. I don't know what more I can say. For God's sake, give me justice!"

(C)

The court was quite at a loss when it came to deciding the rights of the case, but a fool who was present at the time said to them, "Why this hesitation? Let the first speaker be thrown back into the sea on the spot where the other man hit him in the face, and if he can get out again, the defendant shall compensate him for the loss of his eye. That I think, is a fair judgment." Then they all cried out as one man, "You're absolutely right! That's exactly what we'll do!" Judgment was then pronounced to that effect. When the man heard that he was to be thrown back into the sea, just where he had endured all that cold water before, he wouldn't have gone back there for all the world. He released the goodman from any liability, and his earlier attitude came in for much criticism.

(D)

For a long time, that man thought about the loss of his eye, considering it a great misfortune. "That wretched fellow put my eye out, but I didn't do him any harm. I'll go and lodge a complaint against him — why, I'll make things really hot for him." Accordingly he went and complained to the magistrate, who fixed a day for the hearing. They both waited till the day came round, and then went to the court. The one who had lost an eye spoke first, as was appropriate. "Gentlemen," he said, "I'm bringing a complaint against this worthy, who, only the other day, savagely struck me with a boathook and knocked my eye out. Now, I'm handicapped. Give me justice, that's all I ask. I've nothing more to say."

28

윗글의 (A)에 이어질 내용을 순서에 맞게 배열한 것으로 가장 적절한 것은?

① (B) – (D) – (C)   ② (C) – (B) – (D)   ③ (C) – (D) – (B)
④ (D) – (B) – (C)   ⑤ (D) – (C) – (B)

29

윗글이 시사하는 바로 가장 적절한 것은?

① It's All Water under the Bridge.
② Don't Bite the Hand That Feeds You.
③ Beauty is in the Eye of the Beholder.
④ You Can't Judge a Book by Its Cover.
⑤ The Grass is Always Greener on the Other Side.

30

밑줄 친 as one man이 의미하는 것으로 가장 적절한 것은?

① uniquely   ② humanely   ③ unanimously
④ as he believed   ⑤ one after another

I am not by nature a country person. But once, long ago, the country was forced upon me. It was 1942, and we were evacuated to a farmhouse about 15 miles out of Cardiff, my home town. We'd watch the bombers comb the country sky on their way to Cardiff docks. We stuck it out in that farmhouse for almost six months and during that time I underwent a radical change. It all started one morning when I was leaving for school. My mother was standing at the window, watching a lone cow ambling across a distant field. "I wonder where that cow is going," she said, "and when it will get there." My mother was a woman with a practical head on her shoulders, and I thought for a frightening moment that the countryside had finally sent her round the bend.

That morning I did miss the train for school, because I dawdled on my way to the station. My mother's wonderings had unnerved me. I caught a later train. But all day I couldn't concentrate, and after school, on my way back from the station, I found myself studying the hedgerow flowers and finding pleasure in their discovery. When I got home to the farm, I said, "I saw some pretty flowers in the hedges today. I wish I knew their names."

Thereafter we took walks every day, my mother and I. At first we said little to each other, as was our wont in the city. Because city subjects — homework neglected, drawers untidied, piano unpractised — were beyond discussion, best covered with 　　(A)　　. As the days passed, we identified each hedgerow flower. We also watched birds and savoured their newly discovered names. Moreover, at night when the bombers had quit the skies, we looked at the stars and whispered, Orion, the Plough and the Bear.

When we returned to Cardiff, we slipped back into our urban 　　(B)　　, into the sham priorities of exams and tidy drawers. But often we would smile at each other as we recalled that rural magic, that sane wand that tapped everything into its right and proper place. And even now, so many years later, and urban-riddled, I can still watch a dog wandering in a crowded street, and wonder where it is going.

*round the bend: 정신이 나간

31 윗글의 'I'에 관한 내용과 일치하는 것은?

① 전쟁 때문에 Cardiff에서 15마일 떨어진 농장을 비우고 떠났다.
② 어머니는 원래 감성적인 성격의 소유자였다.
③ hedgerow flowers를 본 이후 어머니와 함께 산책을 매일 했다.
④ 시골생활 중에 꽃, 새, 별들의 이름을 새로 지어주었다.
⑤ 도시로 돌아와서는 시골생활을 회상할 겨를이 없었다.

32 윗글의 제목으로 가장 적절한 것은?

① Disenchanted from the Rural Beauty
② A Dangerous Pastime Amidst the War
③ Rural Magic: Opening Our Eyes to a New World
④ An Unexpected Exodus from Rural Imprisonment
⑤ Surviving the War: The Unwithering Hedgerow Flower

33 윗글의 빈칸 (A), (B)에 공통으로 들어갈 말로 가장 적절한 것은?

① eloquence   ② rush   ③ melody
④ riddle   ⑤ silence

(A)

Researchers who have spent thousands of hours observing the behavior of bottlenose dolphins off the coast of Australia have discovered that the males form ＿＿＿＿＿＿ with one another that are far more sophisticated than any seen in animals apart from human beings.

(B)

Should the female be so unimpressed as to attempt to flee, the males will chase after her, bite her, slap her with their fins or slam into her with their bodies. The scientists call this effort to control females "herding," but they acknowledge that the word does not convey the aggressiveness of the act.

(C)

And after they have succeeded in spiriting a female away, the males remain in their tight-knit group to assure that the female stays in line, performing a series of feats that are spectacular and threatening. Two or three males will surround the female, leaping, bellyflopping, and somersaulting, all in perfect synchrony with one another.

(D)

They have found that one team of male dolphins will recruit the help of another team of males to gang up against a third group. According to scientists, this sort of battleplan requires considerable mental calculus to work out. But the purpose of these complex ＿＿＿＿＿＿ is not exactly sportive. Males collude with their peers as a way of stealing fertile females from competing dolphin bands.

34 주어진 글 (A)에 이어질 내용을 순서에 맞게 배열한 것으로 가장 적절한 것은?

① (B) – (D) – (C)　　　② (C) – (B) – (D)　　　③ (C) – (D) – (B)

④ (D) – (B) – (C)　　　⑤ (D) – (C) – (B)

35 윗글의 제목으로 가장 적절한 것은?

① Symbiosis Between Male and Female Dolphins
② Dolphins Display Cunning in Courtship
③ Gender Differences of Dolphins
④ Male Dolphins Threaten Their Female Counterparts
⑤ Spectacular Behaviors of Endangered Species

36 윗글의 빈칸에 공통으로 들어갈 말로 가장 적절한 것은?

① altruistic coalitions
② attractive skills
③ age groups
④ interfering relations
⑤ social alliances

(A)

Government programs such as Comprehensive Employment and Training Act (CETA), which provide jobs for the unemployed might be made more ambitious. The government might act as the employer of _____. That is, the government might stand ready to provide jobs to all those who want work but are unable to find it in the private sector.

(B)

On the other side, opponents object that such a program would be expensive. Just how expensive was indicated during 1977-1978, when the new Carter administration more than doubled the size of Public Service Employment Programs to 725,000 jobs, at a cost of $8.4 billion. That works out to more than $11,500 per job. The average worker got considerably less than that—about $7,200. Part went into administration and supporting services.

(C)

Proposals to make the government _____ are controversial. (Because of opposition, those provisions were dropped from later versions of the Humphrey-Hawkins bill. And President Reagan suggested that CETA be eliminated by the end of 1983.) On the positive side, government projects might give the unemployed something useful to do. For example, the unemployed might do maintenance jobs in the cities and carry out public works projects similar to those of Roosevelt's recovery program in the 1930s.

(D)

Although the government has no such commitment to provide jobs for those who are rejected by private companies, a closely related proposal was included in the original 1976 draft of the Humphrey-Hawkins bill. That bill would have committed the government to offer whatever jobs were needed to get the unemployment rate down to a target of 3 percent per year.

37 주어진 글 (A)에 이어질 내용을 순서에 맞게 배열한 것으로 가장 적절한 것은?

① (B) – (D) – (C)　　　② (C) – (B) – (D)　　　③ (C) – (D) – (B)

④ (D) – (B) – (C)　　　⑤ (D) – (C) – (B)

38 윗글의 빈칸에 공통으로 들어갈 말로 가장 적절한 것은?

① public loan
② last resort
③ optimal condition
④ short supply
⑤ security check

39 윗글의 제목으로 가장 적절한 것은?

① Today's Tough job Market Situations
② Necessary Conditions for Full Employment
③ Controversial Government Policies for the Unemployed
④ Official Guidelines for Government Employment
⑤ History of Employment-related Legislation

[01~03] 다음 글을 읽고, 물음에 답하시오.

| 수능 2014학년도 B형 홀수형 43~45번 |

(A)

How much space do you need to be happy? Part of the American story is that bigger is better, and with cheap credit and tax breaks for home buyers, it's tempting to stretch one's finances to build or buy a larger house. My grandpa Otto chose a different path. (a) He didn't want to find himself working longer and longer hours just to pay for more space and the stuff to fill it. He grew up in a farming community and within a very large family, so living simply was integral to his life philosophy.

(B)

Yet my grandpa loved his little home and was content with what he had. Even though the house was small, it didn't feel cramped. As my dad said, "Everyone was happy and content. The size of the house didn't matter." My grandpa taught me that living a simple life isn't about self-deprivation. Instead, it's about giving yourself the time, freedom, and money to pursue your dreams. In many ways, I've modeled my life after that of my grandpa. I learned from (b) him that simplicity isn't about austerity. It's a revolution in personal growth.

(C)

In the 1950s, when my dad was a little boy, my grandpa built a 600-square-foot cottage. (c) He put the twenty-by thirty-foot structure on a small plot of land in Pleasant Hill. Dad remarked, "Reusing and recycling was a necessity. In essence, (d) he was recycling before it became 'cool.'" Grandpa got most of the materials for his little house from the Oakland docks, where he was working. It took four years to build the small cottage, and when they moved in, the roof wasn't even on!

(D)

My dad recalled looking up at the stars in the roofless house as a twelve-year-old kid before falling asleep. Dad didn't mind living in an unfinished house. (e) He described Pleasant Hill as "open and private. It felt like all the homes were on ten acres." Over the years, my dad and grandpa noticed dramatic changes in their community. Each year more farmland was devoured to build strip malls and neighborhoods with larger homes. As real estate prices rose, many of their neighbors sold their homes and lots. Soon my grandpa had the only small house on the block, surrounded by a sea of homes four times the size of his dwelling.

01 주어진 글 (A)에 이어질 내용을 순서에 맞게 배열한 것으로 가장 적절한 것은?

① (B)−(D)−(C)

② (C)−(B)−(D)

③ (C)−(D)−(B)

④ (D)−(B)−(C)

⑤ (D)−(C)−(B)

02 밑줄 친 (a)~(e) 중에서 가리키는 대상이 나머지 넷과 다른 것은?

① (a)　　② (b)　　③ (c)　　④ (d)　　⑤ (e)

03 윗글의 grandpa에 관한 내용과 일치하지 않는 것은?

① 농촌 사회의 대가족 속에서 성장했다.

② 여러 가지 면에서 필자의 삶의 모델이 되었다.

③ 1950년대에 600제곱 피트의 집을 지었다.

④ 집을 짓는 데 필요한 대부분의 자재를 부두에서 구했다.

⑤ 지역 사회의 급격한 변화를 알아차리지 못했다.

(A)

The midday sun was glorious. The high school grounds were filled with well-dressed people, posing in fancy dresses and suits for cheerful photographers. Congratulations, hugs, and laughter were contagious. Hannah looked at all the familiar faces that had been part of (a) her life for the last few years. Soon her mother would be joining them. She recalled the first day of school when she had stood in that same place, in the middle of many anxious freshmen, some of whom had become her closest friends.

(B)

"Hannah, you look so serious. What are you thinking about?" "Oh, Mom, just, you know." Her mother smiled. "You'll miss this place, won't you?" Hannah nodded. "Quick," her mother said, "stand over there ... and smile, Hannah. You have such a pretty smile." (b) She hurried out her cell phone, zoomed in on her daughter, and realized suddenly that she was looking at a young lady. "You're all grown-up," she whispered. Hannah took more photos with her teachers in the school garden. She wished all the memories would remain in her mind forever.

(C)

Hannah struggled with the many class hours, the endless assignments, and the exams. However, there were exciting events like sports days and school festivals. How could (c) she ever forget her second year! She had sung and danced with her friends in the festival, part of a sensational performance. After that, she had become more confident and active. Her thoughts wandering, Hannah vaguely heard her mother's voice. "Here you are!" Her mother hurried over, and gave (d) her a bundle of lilies and roses and a big hug.

(D)

That day was unusually foggy as if something mysterious were ahead. Hannah was nervous and trembling. The principal was energetically addressing them, talking of the challenges and thrills of high school life, but she could not concentrate. Later, a tall, strict-looking man introduced himself as (e) her homeroom teacher. The classroom was old, but neat and inviting. Hannah was seated in the fifth row, hallway side, even though she had wanted a window seat. High school life soon proved as challenging as the principal had predicted.

04

주어진 글 (A)에 이어질 내용을 순서에 맞게 배열한 것으로 가장 적절한 것은?

① (B)—(D)—(C)　　　　　② (C)—(B)—(D)

③ (C)—(D)—(B)　　　　　④ (D)—(B)—(C)

⑤ (D)—(C)—(B)

05

밑줄 친 (a)~(e) 중에서 가리키는 대상이 나머지 넷과 <u>다른</u> 것은?

① (a)　　　② (b)　　　③ (c)　　　④ (d)　　　⑤ (e)

06

윗글의 Hannah에 관한 내용과 일치하지 <u>않는</u> 것은?

① 다른 신입생들과 함께 운동장에 서 있었다.

② 학교 정원에서 선생님들과 사진을 찍었다.

③ 축제에서 노래를 부르고 춤을 추었다.

④ 교장 선생님의 말씀에 집중할 수가 없었다.

⑤ 교실에서 다섯 번째 줄 창가 자리에 앉았다.

정답 및 해설

UNIT 01 주제

Example

답 ①

혐오감의 감정적인 반응은 종종 특정한 채소를 먹는 것에 대한 어린이들의 고집 센 거부와 연관된다. 그러한 혐오감은 자식에게 영양가 있는 음식을 제공하려고 결심한 부모에게는 말도 안 되는 것처럼 보일 수 있지만, 위생 행동에 관심 있는 과학자들은 합리적인 설명을 한다. 이러한 이론은 사람들이 낯설거나 해로울 수도 있는 대상에 대해 보호 기제로써 혐오감을 발달시켜왔다고 주장한다. 최근 연구는 혐오감이 위험한 물질을 섭취하는 것을 저지할 뿐 아니라 사람들이 잠재적으로 전염성 있는 상태에 들어가지 않도록 만류한다는 것을 보여준다. 예를 들면, 연구의 피험자들은 혼잡한 기동차가 빈 차보다 더욱 역겹고, 기생충이 장수말벌보다 더 혐오스럽다고 발표했다.

① 사람을 보호하는 혐오의 역할
② 적절한 영양 섭취의 이점
③ 위험과 전염의 차이
④ 유해 물질을 피하는 일의 중요성
⑤ 좋은 위생 행동 실천의 필요성

주 제) 사람을 보호하는 혐오의 역할

Practice

01 ③	02 ③	03 ②	04 ⑤	05 ③
06 ⑤	07 ③	08 ③	09 ①	10 ④
11 ④	12 ②	13 ⑤	14 ②	15 ①
16 ⑤				

01 ③ 천주교는 유일한 신이 내린 천직은 사제직이라고 믿었지만, 개신교는 사람들이 그 어떤 세속적 기술과 상업에도 소명 받을 수 있다고 생각했다. 그들이 신을 섬기고 있다는 믿음은 그들이 종교적 열정으로 일을 하도록 독려하여, 더 많은 상품을 생산하고 더 많은 돈을 벌도록 이끌었다. Weber는 개신교의 믿음이 불가피하게 자본주의 경제의 사회로 이어졌다고 믿었는데, 그것이 신자들에게 이윤 추구를 탐욕이나 야망 같이 도덕적으로 의심스러운 동기보다는 헌신의 증거로 바라볼 기회를 주었기 때문이다. 운명예정설의 개념 역시 신자들이 사회적 불평등과 가난을 고민

하지 않아도 된다는 것을 의미했는데, 물질적 부는 영적 부의 상징이었기 때문이다.

① 사회적 평등을 일구는 종교의 역할
② 개신교적 믿음이 부상한 이유
③ 경제적 이상에 관한 개신교의 영향
④ 경제적 활동에서 도덕성의 중요성
⑤ 개신교와 천주교의 차이점

주 제) 개신교가 경제적 이상에 끼친 영향

정답 해설) 글의 초반부에서 가톨릭교와 개신교의 차이를 설명하기 때문에 ⑤가 답이라고 생각할 수 있지만 중반부와 후반부에서는 가톨릭교에 대한 언급이 없고 경제와 개신교의 연결고리에 대해 중점적으로 이야기하고 있다. 따라서 이 글의 주제로는 ③이 가장 적절하다.

어 휘) vocation 천직 priesthood 사제직 Protestant 개신교도 secular 세속적인 fervor 열정 devotion 헌신 predestination 운명, 숙명, 운명예정설

02 ③ 호기심, 자만심 또는 아직 알려지지 않은 원동력에서 나오는 것이든지 간에 시대를 통틀어 사람들은 자기 자신의 반영을 보고 싶어해 왔다. 기원전 2500년에 이미 이집트인들은 주로 청동 또는 때때로 은이나 금의 매우 잘 닦여진 금속을 거울로 가지고 있었다. 최초의 상업적 유리 거울은 1564년에 베니스에서 만들어졌다. 그것들은 납작하게 눌려 수은과 주석 합금으로 덮인 분유리로 만들어졌다. 베니스인들은 수 세기동안 유럽에 거울을 공급하기에 이르렀다. 1840년에 이르러서야 Justus Liebig이라는 독일인 화학자가 우리가 오늘날 사용하고 있는 은도금의 방법을 고안해냈다. 이 기술로 인해, 은·암모니아 혼합물은 인버트 슈거, 로셸염, 포름알데히드와 같은 환원체의 화학적 작용을 받게 되고 생성된 금속성 은은 판유리의 부드러운 뒷면에 고르게 퍼진다.

① 거울 발명 뒤의 경제적인 동기
② 독일 화학자의 굉장한 업적
③ 상업 유리 거울 기술의 발전
④ 상업 유리 거울 속에 숨겨진 인간의 욕망
⑤ 유럽 고대 거울 기술의 공통점

주 제) 상업 유리 거울 기술의 발전

정답 해설) 고대 이집트에서는 잘 닦인 금속을 거울로 썼고, 그 후 베니스에서 수은과 주석의 합금으로 유리 거울을 만들었으며, 1840년에 이르러 은도금 방법으로 오늘날 사용하는 거울을 만들었다는 내용의 글이다. 시대별로 거울이 어떻게 발전해 왔

는지 보여주고 있기 때문에 ③이 주제로 가장 적절하다.

(어 휘) vanity 허영심　blown glass 분유리(불어서 만든 유리) amalgam 혼합물　commonality 공통점

---

03 ②　과학자로서의 성공은 단순히 우리 머릿속에 가지고 있는 아이디어나 우리가 손에 쥐고 있는 데이터의 질의 작용일 뿐 아니라, 우리가 그것을 묘사하기 위한 언어의 질의 작용이기도 하다. 우리 모두는 "출간하지 않으면 죽는다"는 것이 진짜이고, 우리의 직업적인 삶을 지배한다는 것을 이해한다. 그러나 "출간하지 않으면 죽는다"는 것은 생존에 관한 것이지 성공에 관한 것은 아니다. 당신은 논문을 출간함으로써 과학자로서 성공하지 않는다. 당신은 그것들이 인용되게 하면서 과학자로서 성공한다. 당신의 연구를 중요하게 만드는 것이 중요하다. 성공은 얼마나 많은 페이지를 인쇄하는 것이 아니라 그것들의 영향력에 의해서 결정된다. 동료들이 당신의 연구를 이해하고 그것을 그들의 동기부여를 위해 사용할 때 당신은 성공한다.

① '더 많이 쓸수록 더 좋다'는 지속적인 믿음
② 과학 논문에서 다른 이들에게 영향을 미치는 것의 중요성
③ 탐구되지 않은 영역의 연구를 추구하는 것의 필요성
④ 논문 승인에 필요한 동료들의 우호적인 검토
⑤ 출판에서 직업윤리와 엄격한 품질 통제

(주 제) 과학 논문에서 인용의 중요성

(정답 해설) 과학자로서의 성공은 논문을 얼마나 많이 쓰는가가 아니라 논문이 다른 과학자들에 의해 얼마나 많이 인용되는가에 달려 있다는 내용의 글이므로 ②가 주제로 가장 적절하다.

(어 휘) perish 죽다

---

04 ⑤　우리가 지금 그들의 문화를 나누지는 못하지만, 바흐와 베토벤의 동시대 사람들에게 흥미로웠던 음악은 지금도 흥미롭다. 비록 불행히도 비틀즈는 해산됐지만, 여전히 초기 비틀즈의 노래들은 듣기 좋다. 이와 유사하게, 수백 년 전에 작곡된 벤다의 노래들은 여전히 날 즐겁게 해준다. 우리들 중 많은 사람들은 일본의 Koto 음악, 인도의 시타르 음악, Chopi 실로폰 음악 등의 노래들을 통해 전율을 느낀다. 나는 우리가 연주자들이 느끼는 정확히 그대로를 느낀다고 말할 순 없지만, 우리 자신의 경험은 여러 문화 사이의 소통의 가능성을 암시한다. 표면 구조상에 드러나지 않더라도, 나는 이것을 위한 설명을 음악의 심오한 구조의 단계에 인간의 정신에 흔한 요소들이 있다는 사실에서 찾을 수 있다고 확신한다.

① 문화를 풍요롭게 만들 음악의 가능성
② 문화로부터의 점차적인 음악의 다양화
③ 사람에게 정신적인 풍요를 주는 음악의 능력
④ 음악의 상호 문화 간 전달의 장점
⑤ 시간과 문화를 초월한 음악의 보편성

(주 제) 시간과 문화를 초월한 음악의 보편성

(정답 해설) 수백 년 전에 만들어진 음악들이 지금의 우리들을 즐겁게 해준다는 내용의 글이다. 사람들은 과거 베토벤부터 비틀즈까지 시대를 한정하지 않고 좋은 음악들을 여전히 즐겨 듣는다고 말하고 있다. 따라서 글의 제목으로 ⑤ '시간과 문화를 초월한 음악의 보편성'이 적절하다.

(어 휘) contemporary 동시대의　unfortunately 불행히도 compose 작곡하다　cross-cultural 여러 문화가 섞인　convince 확신하다, 납득시키다　explanation 설명, 해설　psyche 정신

---

05 ③　우리는 종종 아름다운 성공과 동기부여가 되는 사람들의 이야기를 보곤 한다. 우리 중 몇몇은 그들의 사진을 벽에 붙여놓거나, 그들의 유명한 인용구를 고정시켜 놓기도 한다. 하지만 우리가 과거에도 할 수 없었고 앞으로도 해낼 수 없는 일들을 이룬 그 사람들이 우리들에게 어떠한 동기부여가 될까? 우리 중 대다수에게 롤 모델의 선택은 비교를 불러오고, 만약 우리의 능력과 결과가 기대에 미치지 못한다면 롤 모델은 더 이상 동기부여가 아닌 열등감과 패배감을 일으키는 존재가 된다. 당신이 이룰 수 있거나 이루고 싶은 목표를 이룬 사람을 롤 모델로 골라라. 대단한 성공을 이루었지만 우리와 별로 연관이 없는 유명한 운동선수, 지도자 그리고 역사적 인물을 롤 모델로 삼는 것보다 당신과 같이 일하는 동료나 가족을 동기부여의 대상으로 삼을 때 더 큰 가치를 만들어 낸다.

① 현실적인 롤 모델의 성공 이야기
② 롤 모델을 모방하는 일을 좌절시키는 근원
③ 접근 가능한 롤 모델을 고르는 것의 중요성
④ 동기부여가 되는 사람을 주변에 두는 것의 중요성
⑤ 높은 직위에 있는 사람을 따라하는 것의 긍정적인 효과

(주 제) 접근 가능한 롤 모델 선택의 중요성

(정답 해설) 주어진 글은 대다수의 사람들이 롤 모델을 고를 때 자신과는 비교가 불가능하고 전혀 경험적 연관이 없는 사람들을 선택한다고 말한다. 하지만 이러한 선택은 오히려 자신감을 잃게 하고 패배감을 일으키기 때문에 현실적인 롤 모델을 고르는 일이 더 긍정적인 효과를 낳을 수 있다고 말하고 있다. 따라서 글의 주제로는 ③ '접근 가능한 롤 모델을 고르는 것의 중요

성'이 적절하다.

어 휘 inspire 격려시키다, 영감을 주다 quote 인용구 frustration 불만, 좌절감 defeat 좌절시키다 accomplish 이루다, 성취하다 tremendous 굉장한

---

06 ⑤ 관찰 연구 결과들은 엄마가 자녀 주변에서 하는 것들에 관해서는 정보를 제공해 줄 수 있지만, 그들의 감정, 그들과 관련된 생각이나 신념, 그리고 자녀들과 자녀들을 돌보는 것에 대해서는 거의 알려주지 못한다. 엄마들은 자녀들과 양육에 대해서는 다양한 관점을 고수하게 되고, 그것들이 언제나 정형화된 심리학과 일치하게 되는 것은 아니며, 그것들은 그들이 그들의 자녀들과 상호작용하는 방식에 영향을 주게 될 것이다. 어떤 엄마들은 자녀들에 대해 세심하게 잘 살피는 것이 쉽게 되지 않는다고 생각한다. 그 것은 아마도 그들이 자녀들과 쉽게 관계를 맺지 못하기 때문이거나, 그들이 우울한 상태 또는 외로운 상태이기 때문일 수도 있고, 또는 그들이 세심함이 자녀들과의 관계에 있어서 중요한 부분이라고 생각하지 않기 때문일 수도 있다. 어떤 엄마들에게는 그들의 감정과 행동이 심리학적인 이론으로 규정된 그것들과 불일치하는 현상이 일어날 수도 있다. 그리고 엄마들의 요구사항과 자녀들의 요구사항 사이에서 갈등이 생기게 될 것이다.

① 아이 양육에서 엄마들의 부주의에 대한 이유
② 엄마들의 육아 철학 확립의 필요성
③ 엄마들과 아이들이 원하는 것의 차이
④ 엄마들과 아이들의 갈등의 심리학적 기반
⑤ 엄마들과 심리학자들의 양육 개념에 대한 불일치

주 제 엄마들과 심리학자들의 양육 개념 불일치
정답 해설 글의 초반부에서 엄마들이 취하는 양육과 자녀에 대한 관점이 심리학과 일치되는 것은 아니라고 말하였고, 후반부에서는 엄마들의 감정이나 행동이 심리학에서 규정한 부분과 차이가 있을 수도 있다고 언급하고 있다. 따라서 글의 주제로는 ⑤가 가장 적절하다.

어 휘 as to ~에 관해서는 observational 관찰상의, 실측하는 parenting 육아, 양육 a range of 다양한 sensitive to ~에 대해 세심하게 알아채는, (감정 등을) 잘 살피는 sensitivity (남의 기분을 쉽게 알아채는) 세심함, 감수성 prescribe 처방을 내리다 discrepancy 불일치

---

07 ③ Alexander the Great(알렉산더 대왕)은 기원전 332년에 이집트의 그리스 · 로마 시대를 열었

다. 서아시아를 정복한 후에 그 마케도니아의 장군은 수백 년 간 이어진 불안한 정세와 외부인들의 점령으로 인해 정치적으로 매우 지쳤던 이집트 사람들에 의해 환영을 받았다. 이미 풍부한 이집트 문화와 그리스(이후 로마)의 영향을 복합시킨 문화는 지중해 지역을 돌며 사회적인 그리고 종교적인 변화의 기틀을 마련했다. 이 새로운 역동의 시기에 이집트 사람들의 의복이나 조각의 양식은 그리스와 로마까지 퍼져나간 반면, 이집트의 신들과 신격화된 통치자들은 그리스와 로마 신화에 나오는 신들과 융합되었다. 이집트의 모신인 Isis는 결국에는 Caesars가 통치하는 땅에 세워진 신전을 갖게 되는 한편 많은 그리스 · 로마의 신들과 영웅들은 이집트 전역에 걸쳐 있는 신전에서 숭배를 받곤 했었다.

① 그리스 · 로마 시대 이집트의 사회 개혁 노력
② 알렉산더 대왕에 의해서 생긴 이집트의 정치적 불안
③ 이집트와 그리스 · 로마 사이의 문화 교류
④ 그리스 · 로마 세계에 이집트식 생활의 침투
⑤ 이집트 농부들의 일상생활에 끼친 그리스와 로마의 영향

주 제 이집트와 그리스 · 로마 사이의 문화 교류
정답 해설 그리스 로마의 영향을 받은 이집트 문화가 다시 유럽에 영향을 끼치는 과정에서 생겨난 문화 교류에 대한 내용을 설명하고 있다. 따라서 ③이 주제로 가장 적절하다.

어 휘 Greco-Roman 그리스의 영향을 받은 로마 스타일의 weary 몹시 지친, 실증난 unrest 불안 spin around 반대 방향으로 빠르게 방향을 바꾸다 the Mediterranean 지중해 vibrancy 활력, 활기, 맥박, 떨림 demigod 신격화된 통치자, 반인 반신 mingle with ~과 섞다, 혼합하다 counterpart (동등한 지위를 갖는) 상대

---

08 ③ '낙관주의가 당신의 생명을 살릴 수 있다. 또는 적어도 암의 진행을 늦출 수 있다.'라는 믿음은 1979년 Lancet의료 저널에서 유방암 환자들의 회복에 대한 연구가 발표된 이후부터 주목되기 시작했다. 그 때 이후로 "극복하려는 의지"가 있는 환자가 무기력함을 느끼는 환자들에 비해 훨씬 더 잘 지낸다는 것은 일반적인 상식이 되어왔다. 하지만 최근에 있었던 대규모의 메타 분석을 통해 낙관주의가 암에 걸린 환자들의 생명을 실제로 연장시켜줬는가 하는 문제에 대해서는 설득력 있는 증거가 부족하다는 사실을 발견하게 되었다. 결정적인 정보가 부족함에도 불구하고 긍정적인 생각에 대한 그 믿음은 너무나도 광범위하게 퍼져서 실제로는 해로운 기능을 하게 될지도 모른다. 암에 걸린 환자들은 실제로는 마음이 괴로울 때도 밝은 것처럼 행동하고자 할지도 모른다. 그리고 위로나 치료를 찾는 것 대신 그들의 절망감을 숨기려고 할지도 모른다. 또한 병이 진행이 될 경우 그들 스스로 자신을 비난하게 될지도 모른다.

① 암 치료에서의 절망감의 위험
② 회복하는 환자들을 위한 낙관주의의 필요성
③ 암 환자들이 긍정적이어야 한다는 생각의 몰락
④ 환자와 의사의 건전한 관계의 중요성
⑤ 새로운 암 예방 조치의 발견

주 제 암 환자들이 긍정적이어야 한다는 생각의 몰락

정답 해설 이 글은 정확한 근거 없이 맹신하는 낙관주의가 암 환자에게 줄 수 있는 역효과에 대해서 설명하고 있다. 그러므로 ③이 주제로 알맞다.

어 휘 optimism 낙천주의, 낙관론 stave off (안 좋은 일을) 늦추다, 피하다 traction 끌림, 관심(인기) fare better 더욱 잘 지내다(fare well의 비교급) meta analysis 메타 분석(학술적 분석의 한 방법) inclined to ~로 향하게 되다, ~하고자 하다 upbeat 긍정적인, 낙관적인 distraught 괴로운, 마음이 심란한 solace 위안, 위로가 되는 것(사람) preventative 예방을 위한, 예방하는

---

09 ① 사모스의 에게 해의 섬에 살던 Aristarchus는 처음으로, Copernicus가 2,000년이 지난 뒤에 다시 주장하기 전까지 천문학자들에 의해 인정받지 못했던 개념인, 지구와 다른 행성들이 태양의 주위를 돌고 있다는 주장을 했다. Copernicus 이후에는 덴마크의 천문학자인 Tycho Brahe 가 후벤의 발틱 섬에 있는 그의 관측소에서 화성의 움직임을 관찰했다. 그 결과로 Johannes Kepler는 화성과 지구, 그리고 다른 행성들이 태양 근처를 타원형으로 돌고 있다는 사실을 증명해낼 수 있었다. 그 이후, Isaac Newton 이 만유인력의 법칙과, 운동의 법칙을 고안했고, 이를 통해 전체 태양계에 대한 정밀한 묘사를 해내는 것이 가능해졌다. 이것은 이후 수 세기에 걸쳐서 여러 위대한 과학자들과 수학자들의 마음을 사로잡았다.

---

① 태양계를 이해하기 위한 인간들의 노력
② 고대 과학자들에 의한 태양계의 왜곡
③ 고대의 태양계에 대한 미신
④ 뉴턴의 학설 전의 물리적 법칙과 규칙의 역사
⑤ 행성 움직임에 대한 몇몇 새로운 사실들

주 제 태양계를 이해하기 위한 인간의 노력

정답 해설 태양계의 운동 법칙이 오랜 세월 수많은 학자들의 노력에 의해 밝혀졌음을 설명하고 있는 글이다. 따라서 ①이 글의 주제로 적절하다.

어 휘 ellipse 타원, 타원형 universal law of gravitation 만유인력의 법칙 laws of motion (뉴턴의) 운동의 법칙 distortion 일그러짐, 왜곡 pre-Newtonian 뉴턴 이전의

---

10 ④ 자유를 옹호하는 몇몇 사람들이 너무 중요하지 않게 생각하는 고려할 사항이 있다. 어른들의 간섭 없는 상태의 아이들의 집단에서는 대부분의 어른들의 폭정보다 훨씬 더 잔인할 가능성이 높은, 더 힘이 강한 아이의 폭정이 있다. 만약 두세 살 정도의 아이들 두 명이 함께 놀도록 남겨졌을 때, 몇 번의 싸움을 거친 뒤 아이들은 어느 쪽이 항상 승리자가 되는지 알게 되고 다른 한쪽은 그의 노예가 되고 말 것이다. 아이들의 수가 더 많은 곳에서는 한 명 또는 두 명의 아이가 완벽한 지배력을 갖게 되고, 다른 아이들은 어른들이 약하고 싸우기 싫어하는 아이들을 보호하기 위해 간섭했을 때에 비해 훨씬 적은 자유만을 누릴 수 있다. 대부분의 아이들에게 다른 사람들을 위한 숙고는 자발적으로 발생하지 않는다. 그러나 반드시 배워야만 하는 것이고, 권위에 의해 직접 체험해 보지 않고서는 거의 배울 수 없는 것이다. 이것은 아마도 어른들이 한발 물러서는 것에 대한 가장 중요한 주장이 될 것이다.

---

① 육아에서의 자유의 중요성
② 여러 학습 맥락에서 아이들의 행동 이해하기
③ 아이들 사회에서 노예와 정복자의 관계
④ 육아에 있어서 어른의 개입의 필요성
⑤ 아이의 리더십에 영향을 주는 여러 가지 요인들

주 제 육아에서 간섭의 필요성

정답 해설 아이들 집단의 놀이에서 지배 구조가 발생하는 부작용을 막기 위해 어른의 개입이 필요하다는 내용의 글이다. 따라서 ④가 글의 주제로 가장 적절하다.

어 휘 attach 붙이다, 부여하다 tyranny 포학, 학대, 전제정치 brutal 야만적인, 잔인한 mastery 지배력, 통제권 pugnacious 싸우기 좋아하는 abdication (권리 등을) 포기함, 양도함

---

11 ④ 질병을 유발하는 간접 흡연의 역할에 대한 연구가 몇 년간 진행되었다. 그 중 서부 지역의 한 중소 도시가 뜻밖에 이 연구 자료에 추가되었다. 공공장소와 일터에서의 흡연이 금지되었고, 6개월 후 그 조치는 해제되었다. 공공장소에서 흡연이 금지되었던 그 기간 중에는 병원에 심장 질환으로 입원한 환자는 24명이었다. 금지 기간이 아닌 보통 때에는 6개월간 평균 40명의 입원 환자가 있었다. 연구자들은 입원 환자의 감소가 간접 흡연의 부정적인 영향에 대한 증거라고 생각한다. 간접 흡연은 심박 수를 올려놓고, 혈관의 팽창하는 능력을 감소시키므로 심장 질환의 원인이 된다.

---

① 직장에서의 흡연의 영향들

② 중형의 도시에서 심장 발작의 원인
③ 스트레스 없는 근무 환경의 중요성
④ 간접 흡연과 심장 발작의 관계
⑤ 공공장소와 직장에서 흡연을 금지할 필요성

[주 제] 간접흡연과 심장 발작의 관계
[정답 해설] 간접흡연이 심장 질환에 끼치는 영향을 설명하는 글이다. 따라서 ④가 주제로 가장 적절하다.

[어 휘] unexpectedly 예상 외로, 예상치 않게 admission 입장, 등장, 입학, 입원

12 ② 1950년대에 엄청나게 쏟아져 나온 청소년 비행에 대한 우려는 영화 산업에 위험하지만 수익성 있는 가능성을 제시했다. 대부분의 영화 관객이 줄어들었던 시기에 자극 받은 부모들, 청소년 상담 센터, 교사들, 청소년들, 그리고 경찰관들은 비행 영화의 거대한 잠재적 관객층을 형성하고 있었다. 하지만 이것은 이용하기에 위험한 소재였는데, 청소년들에게 건전한 모범을 제시해야 한다는 영화 산업에 대한 공공의 압력이 끈질기게 남아있었기 때문이었다. 게다가 대중문화가 청소년 비행을 조장한다는 비난이 당시 사회적으로 주요 쟁점이었다. 만약 영화 산업이 청소년 비행에 접근하려면 반드시 신중하고 조심스럽게 진행해야 했다. 비행을 미화해서는 안 되며, 모든 이야기는 영화 코드에 맞게 도덕적 체계 안에서 설정되어야 할 것이기 때문이다. 하지만 성공하기 위해, 영화는 비행이 하나의 변형이라고 보는 성장하는 청년 문화에 점점 더 큰 흥미를 가진 젊은 사람들로부터 공감을 자아내야 했다.

---

① 50년대의 촬영 환경
② 50년대의 청소년 범죄 영화가 마주한 과제
③ 50년대의 청소년 범죄 영화의 도덕적 원칙
④ 50년대의 청소년 범죄 영화의 성공과 종말
⑤ 50년대의 수익성 있는 사업으로서의 청소년 범죄 영화

[주 제] 50년대 청소년 범죄 영화가 마주한 과제
[정답 해설] 50년대 영화계에서 청소년 비행에 대한 영화의 위험성과 그런 영화의 성공 전략에 대해 이야기하고 있다. 그러므로 이 글의 주제로는 ②가 가장 적절하다.

[어 휘] juvenile delinquency 청소년 비행 arouse 깨우다, 자극하다, 촉진하다 perilous 위험한 exploit 개발하다, 사용하다 unremitting 끊임없는, 끈질긴 accusation 비난, 규탄, 죄 cautiously 주의 깊게, 신중하게 firmament 하늘, 창공, 천계 evoke 떠올려 주다, 환기시키다 variant 다른, 여러 가지의 intrigue 흥미를 갖게 하다, 호기심이 생기게 하다

13 ⑤ 어떤 사람들은 '지금까지는 참 좋았다'라고 말할 것이다. "우리는 포유류인 영장류이다. 그러나 우리는 언어가 있고 동물들은 그렇지 않다." 몇몇 정의에 의하면 아마도 동물들은 언어를 가지고 있지 않다. 그러나 그들은 광범위하게 의사소통을 하고, 우리는 호출 시스템을 통해서 이제야 이해하기 시작하고 있다. 언어를 먼저 생각하고 그 다음에 사회를 두는 것은 잘못일 것이다. 언어와 문화는 우리였고 (현재) 우리인 동물들, 즉 우리의 사회생물학적, 자연적 존재로부터 나온다. 언어는 우리의 필요와 신경과 함께 발달해 온 심신 체계이다. 상상력과 신체처럼, 언어는 예상 밖으로 떠오른다. 이것은 우리의 합리적인 지적 능력을 벗어나는 복잡한 것이다. 언어학자들이 선뜻 고백하듯이, 자연 언어의 과학적 설명의 모든 시도는 완전함에 미치지 못해왔다. 그렇지만 어린 아이들은 모국어를 쉽게 배우며 사실상 6살이면 습득을 마친다.

[주 제] 생물학적 자연 상태와 연관된 인간 언어의 이해
[정답 해설] 이 글의 핵심 내용은 '언어와 문화는 우리였고 (현재) 우리인 동물들, 즉 우리의 사회 생물학적, 자연적 존재로부터 나온다.'라는 것이므로 주제로는 ⑤가 가장 적절하다.

[어 휘] primates 영장류 unbidden 명령 받지 않은, 예상 밖의 complexity 복잡성 elude 벗어나다 rational intellectual capacities 합리적인 지적 능력 attempt 시도 readily 쉽게 virtually 실질적으로, 거의

14 ② 우리는 당신이 먹는 것과 먹지 않는 것이 당신의 건강에 영향을 미칠 수 있다는 것을 알고 있다. 하지만 (이상한 나라의 앨리스에서) 흰토끼가 Alice에 충고한 것처럼 "머리에 양식을 주는 것"이 가능할까? 뇌에 좋은 음식이 존재하는 것일까? 나는 있다고 확신한다. 생선과 같은 몇 가지 음식들이 녹황색 야채와 같은 다른 음식들보다 좋다는 증거가 있다. 하지만 그 음식들 중 당신에게 해로운 것은 없으며, 절대로 당신을 멍청하게 만들지 않을 것이다. 생선이 두뇌에 좋은 이유는 생선에 함유되어 있는 오메가3 지방산이라 불리는 물질 때문이다. 오직 연어, 정어리, 고등어, 대구와 같은 지방이 많은 생선만이 이 특별한 지방의 원천이다. 오메가3 중 하나인 DHA는 뇌의 세포막의 주성분이고, 이것의 부족은 뇌의 구조를 약화시키고 질병에 취약한 상태로 만들 수도 있다.

---

① 어떻게 뇌를 활동적으로 유지하나
② 뇌를 위한 좋은 식단인 생선
③ 오메가3를 함유한 채소들
④ 뼈에 좋은 음식인 오메가3

⑤ 오메가3의 일일 섭취량

주 제) 뇌에 좋은 식단인 생선
정답 해설) 다른 음식들보다 오메가3를 포함한 생선이 두뇌에 좋다는 내용이다. 그러므로, 주제로는 ② '뇌를 위한 좋은 식단인 생선'이 알맞다.

어 휘) sardine 정어리, 꽉꽉 채우다 mackerel 고등어 cod 대구 deficiency 결핍, 부족 membrane (인체 피부 조직의) 막, 점막 constituent 요소, 성분, 구성하는

15 ① 많은 환자들이 의사에게 자신들의 증상을 설명하기를 꺼려한다는 사실이 당신을 놀라게 할지 모른다. 하지만 이러한 상황은 평범한 일이다. 많은 사람들은 의사들의 기술이 뛰어나기 때문에, 숙련된 수리공이 자동차의 문제를 진단해 낼 수 있는 것처럼, 검사를 통해서 환자들의 문제를 쉽게 알아낼 수 있을 것이라고 생각한다. 게다가 상대적으로 높은 의사들의 사회적 지위와 권력이 환자들 스스로의 문제가 사소하고 하찮다고 느끼게 하거나, 그들이 좋지 않게 보일 정보를 자발적으로 알려주는 것을 꺼리게 하여 환자들에게 겁을 줄 수도 있다. 반면에 의사들은 환자들이 적절한 정보를 제공하도록 독려하는데 어려움을 겪을지도 모른다. 많은 경우 의사들은 전문적인 성격의 질문으로 면담을 주도해가는 반면에 환자들이 병에 대한 개인적인 느낌이나 병이 생활에 주는 영향을 이야기하고자 한다.

① 의사와 환자 사이의 의사소통의 어려움
② 환자의 협조를 이끌어내는 의사의 능력
③ 환자에게 미치는 의사의 영향력
④ 환자의 문제를 진찰하는 효과적 방법
⑤ 환자를 면담하는데 쓰이는 기술적 질문

주 제) 의사와 환자 간 의사소통의 어려움
정답 해설) 병원에서 병에 대해 상담할 때, 의사와 환자 간의 입장 차이에서 오는 의사소통의 어려움에 대해 설명하고 있다. 의사의 지위가 환자를 부담스럽게 하거나 환자의 불안감을 해소시키지 못하는 이유가 의사와 환자의 초점이 다르기 때문이므로 글의 주제로는 ①이 가장 적절하다.

어 휘) diagnose 진단하다 trivial 하찮은, 사소한 dominate 지배하다, 다스리다 intimidate 위협하다, 협박하다 reluctant 꺼리는, 내키지 않는

16 ⑤ 영국 정부는 2차 대전 기간 동안 모든 영화 제작을 통제했고 전투 부대에 대해 긍정적으로 다루는 영화를 제작하도록 요구했다. 이러한 영화들은 '영국인다움'이라는 이야기를 이용하였는데, 영국의 모든 사람들이 영국적인 가치를 공유한다는 것을 내포하는 '영국적 캐릭터'의 개념을 구축하였다. '군대' 영화 속의 등장인물들은 공정하고 용감할 뿐만 아니라 유머 감각과 같은 다정한 성격도 지니고 있다. '영국'과 '영국인다움'은 서로 다른 계층, 문화, 지역, 나라의 영국인들로 하여금 군대가 '영국의' 가치를 위해 싸우고 있다고 믿도록 하는 강력한 주제 전달 방법이었다.

① 영국 영화의 우월성
② 군대 영화의 캐릭터
③ 영화 제작의 어려움
④ 군인 교육을 위한 영화들
⑤ 통합을 위한 영화 제작

주 제) 영국의 국민 통합을 위한 영화 제작
정답 해설) 영국 정부가 영화 제작을 통제하면서 이야기에 반영한 '영국'과 '영국인다움'은 서로 다른 계층, 문화, 지역, 나라의 영국인들로 하여금 군대가 '영국의' 가치를 위해 싸우고 있다고 믿게 하는 강력한 주제 전달 방법이었다는 내용의 글이므로 주제로는 ⑤ '통합을 위한 영화 제작'이 가장 적절하다.

어 휘) discourse 강연, 연설, 설교 homely 가정적인, 검소한, 꾸밈없는

More Practice

01 ③   02 ②   03 ⑤   04 ③

01 ③ "무엇이 스포츠를 정의하는가?"라는 겉으로 보기에 단순한 질문은, 몇 년 간 프로 선수들과 이론뿐인 운동선수들을 막론하고 그 사이에서 똑같이 논쟁과 대화의 주제였다. 야구와 미식축구, 축구와 같은 활기차고 매우 경쟁적인 운동은 진정한 "스포츠"라는 데 의심의 여지가 없지만, 다트나 체스, 셔플보드와 같은 다른 활동의 주제가 제기될 때, 우리는 논쟁의 한가운데 있는 우리 자신을 발견하게 된다. 만일 당구가 스포츠가 아니라고 한다면, 그것은 정확히 무엇인가? 그것이 스포츠라는 것에 이의를 제기하는 사람들은 그것이 단순한 여가 활동이라고 답변할 것이다. 그들은 진정한 스포츠는 첫째로 무엇보다도 일정한 형태의 신체적인 힘의 발휘를 요한다고 계속해서 주장할 것이다. 더 중요한 것은, 만약 선수가 열심히 땀을 흘리지 않는다면, 그나 그녀가 하는 것은 스포츠가 아니다. 그 밖에, 더욱 중요한 기준은, 훌륭하게 손과 눈의 동작을 일치시키는 능력과 항상 존재하는 부상을 입을 가능성을 필요로 한다. 당구는 단지

그러한 세부사항들 중 한 가지(손과 눈의 동작을 일치시키는 능력)에 들어맞을 뿐이어서 회의론자들에 따르면, 그것은 진정한 스포츠가 아니다.

① 스포츠에 구현된 여가활동
② 매우 경쟁적인 활동의 인기
③ 스포츠를 정의하는 기준에 대한 논쟁
④ 스포츠가 인간의 정신 건강에 미치는 영향
⑤ 당구를 스포츠로 정의하는 특성

주제 스포츠를 정의하는 기준에 대한 논쟁

정답 해설 본문의 시작 부분에서 스포츠를 정의하는 기준에 대하여 질문을 던지고 있으며, 여러 사례를 통해 그에 대한 답변이 간단하지 않다는 것을 보여주고 있다. 따라서 이 글의 주제로는 ③이 가장 적절하다.

어휘 seemingly 겉으로는 armchair 탁상공론의 vigorous 원기 왕성한 exertion 발휘, (힘의) 행사

---

02 ② 아마도 우리가 자신에 대한 평가를 생각하는 방법의 가장 중요한 차원은 자신감의 수준일 것이다. 우리가 대외적으로 보여준 우리의 모습은 우리가 어떻게 행동했는지, 특히 다른 사람들과 어떻게 지내는지에 영향을 끼친다. 어느 정도까지는 자기 평가의 확고한 기준은 다른 사람들과 비교하는 것에 달려있다. 예를 들어 우리의 판단들을 판단하는 특별한 능력들은 상대적일 수밖에 없다. 테니스 선수, 음악가, 요리사가 얼마나 잘하는지에 대한 질문은 다른 사람들의 업적에 의해 만들어진 척도를 참고할 때에만 의미가 있다. 우리가 다른 관계있는 사람과 스스로를 비교해 기회를 찾는다는 많은 증거가 있다. 관계자라 함은 유의미한 비교를 위한 전체적인 척도의 측면에서 우리에게 충분히 가까운 경향이 있는 사람들을 의미한다. 예를 들어 지역 테니스 클럽은 국제 챔피언보다 우리의 테니스 기술에 대한 더 유의미한 비교들을 제공해 준다.

① 지나치게 집중된 경쟁의 폐해
② 자체 평가에서의 비교의 역할
③ 높은 자부심을 가지는 것의 중요성
④ 경쟁력 있는 정신의 개발
⑤ 자기 가치의 척도로서 스포츠

주제 자기 평가에 있어서 관련인의 역할

정답 해설 다른 사람들과 비교함으로써 자기 자신을 평가할 수 있다는 내용의 글로 해당되는 다양한 사례를 들고 있다. 따라서 글의 주제로 가장 적절한 것은 ②이다.

어휘 dimension 차원 evaluation 평가 comparison 비교 ample 풍부한, 충분한 sufficiently 충분히 relevant 관계자

---

03 ⑤ 역사의 바다에는 한 쌍의 사이렌이 숨어 있는데, 그것들은 과거를 이해하고 제대로 인식하려고 하는 사람들을 유혹해 오해와 오역의 암초 위에 올려놓는다. 이 한 쌍의 위험은 시대 중심주의와 민족 중심주의이다. 시대 중심주의는 당신의 시대가 모든 가능한 시대 중에 최고라는 믿음이다. 모든 다른 시대는 따라서 열등하다. 민족 중심주의는 당신의 문화가 모든 가능한 문화 중에 최고라는 믿음이다. 모든 다른 문화는 따라서 열등하다. 시대 중심주의와 민족 중심주의는 결합하여 개인과 문화가 다른 모든 개인과 문화를 그들의 당대 문화의 '우월한' 기준에 의해 판단하게 한다. 이것은 과거나 외국의 문화를 다룸에 있어 총체적인 관점의 결핍과 이에 따른 그것들에 대한 오해와 잘못된 평가를 초래한다. 시대 중심주의와 민족 중심주의는 현대인들을 유혹해 과거의 인간에 대한 정당하지 않은 비판에 빠지게 한다.

① 역사를 기록하는 방식에 있어서 명확한 차이점들
② 다양한 문화에서 발견되는 보편적인 특징들
③ 그들 자신의 문화를 옹호하려는 역사가들의 노력들
④ 비교 문화 관점의 장단점
⑤ 과거에 대한 편향된 해석을 야기하는 믿음들

주제 시대 및 민족 중심주의적 사고의 위험성

정답 해설 시대 중심주의와 민족 중심주의라는 두 가지 잘못된 믿음이 과거를 잘못 이해하는 결과를 초래한다는 내용의 글이므로, 글의 주제로는 ⑤가 가장 적절하다.

어휘 temporocentrism 시대 중심주의 ethnocentrism 민족 중심주의 unjustified 정당하지 않은 tempt 유혹하다 appreciate 제대로 인식하다 reef 암초 misinterpretation 오역 inferior 열등한 current 현재의 lead to ~을 초래하다, perspective 관점 resultant 그에 따른, 결과적인 misappreciation 제대로 평가하지 못함

---

04 ③ 가장 정상적이고 유능한 아이라 하더라도 살면서 극복할 수 없는 문제처럼 보이는 것을 만난다. 하지만 그것들을 끝까지 해결함으로써 아이는 한 단계씩 해나가는 과정을 통해 그것들에 대처할 수 있게 될지도 모른다. 그는 그 기원이 자신의 무의식 깊이 숨겨져 있을 수도 있는 내부의 과정에 반응하고 있기 때문에, 흔히 자기조차 이해하기 힘든 상징적인 방식으로 그렇게 한다. 이것은 그 순간에

는 우리가 거의 이해할 수 없는 놀이가 될 수 있는데, 우리가 그것이 기여하는 목적을 모르기 때문이다. 당면한 위험이 없을 때는, 대개 간섭하지 말고 아이의 놀이를 인정해 주는 것이 가장 좋다. 선의라 하더라도, 그 아이가 애쓸 때 도와주려는 노력은 그가 자신에게 가장 도움이 될 해결책을 모색해 마침내 찾아내는 것을 방해할 수 있다.

① 정신 건강에 대한 폭력적인 게임의 위험성
② 어렸을 때 야외에서 노는 것의 유익한 영향
③ 최소의 간섭이 수반되는 문제 해결로서의 아이들의 놀이
④ 형제간의 다툼에 있어서 개입의 필요성
⑤ 아이들의 신체적 발달에 있어서 부모의 역할

주제 아이의 문제 해결력 향상에 관련된 놀이의 역할
정답 해설 아이는 놀이를 통하여 어려운 문제들에 대처하는 방법을 배우게 되므로, 당면한 위험이 없으면 아이의 놀이에 간섭하지 말라는 내용의 글이다. 따라서 주제로는 ③이 가장 적절하다.

어휘 competent 유능한, 능력 있는 insurmountable 극복할 수 없는, 넘을 수 없는 play out 끝까지 (연주, 소모)하다/풀다 cope with ~에 대처[대응]하다 symbolic 상징적인 unconscious 무의식; 의식이 없는 serve 기여하다, 도움이 되다 immediate 당면한, 직접적인 interfere 간섭하다, 방해하다 minimal 최소의, 아주 적은 intervention 간섭, 사이에 끼어듦 intervene 개입하다, 끼어들다 dispute 논쟁 sibling 형제자매

UNIT 02 주장 · 요지

Example
답 ⑤

당신은 건강한 습관에서 장수의 이점을 얻기 위해 채식주의자가 되거나, 운동 숭배 집단에 충성을 서약하거나, 하루 종일 명상가가 될 필요는 없다. 최근 과학은 사실상 그 반대를 보여준다. 건강한 삶을 연장하는 것은 우리 중 많은 이들이 특별히 어렵지 않은 작은 변화들을 통해 달성 가능한 것이며, 당신을 비참하게 만들지 않을 것이다. 예를 들어 연구자들은 체육관에서의 시간은 오랜 기간 앉아 있는 것의 부정적인 효과를 없애지 못하지만, 꼼지락거리는 것만큼 간단한 것은 그럴 수 있다는 것을 알게 되었다. 그들은 또한 당신이 먹는 양을 줄이는 것이 몹시 고통스러울 필요가 없다는 점을 발견하게 되었고, 이는 당신이 더 오래 살 가능성을 높여줄 것이다.

① 건강한 생활 방식을 실천하기보다 말하기가 쉽다.
② 식단의 주요 변화가 장수를 도울 것이다.
③ 운동은 앉아서 생활하는 사람들에게 중요하다.
④ 신체적이고 정신적인 건강은 열심히 운동해서 얻을 수 있다.
⑤ 장수하는 것은 생각보다 어렵지 않다.

주제 오래 살기 위한 쉬운 방법들

Practice

01 ⑤	02 ③	03 ④	04 ①	05 ②
06 ④	07 ⑤	08 ⑤	09 ①	10 ③

01 ⑤ 당신은 행복을 살 수 없다. 당신은 가까운 마트에 가서 한 파운드의 버터를 사듯이 한 파운드의 행복을 살 수는 없다. 그러나 행복은 내면에서 오기 때문에 우리는 당신의 행동으로 행복의 척도를 보장할 수 있다. 당신은 불행한 이웃을 도움으로써 만족감을 얻을 수 있다. 당신은 불행한 운명 때문에 우리가 함께 나누지 않는 한 행복한 크리스마스를 보낼 수 없을 사람들을 도울 수 있다. 이 평화와 선의의 계절에 도움을 필요로 하는 사람들이 우리의 눈을 통해 행복을 보도록 강요하지 말자. 오히려, 그들 자신의 눈을 통해 행복을 보고 찾을 수 있도록 도움을 주자. 지역 사회의 불행한 사람들을 낙담시키지 말자.

① 선의의 행동으로 당신의 진정한 행복의 수준을 측정하라.
② 당신의 지역 사회에서 행복 바이러스를 잡아라.

③ 당신의 이웃에게 당신의 행복의 방법을 강요하지 마라.
④ 정신적인 건강을 위해 자기만족을 연습하라.
⑤ 당신 주위의 도움이 필요한 사람을 도움으로써 행복을 찾아라.

주 제) 불행한 이웃을 도우면서 찾는 내면의 행복
정답 해설) 행복은 내면에서 오는 것이기 때문에 주위에 불행한 이웃을 도움으로써 만족감을 얻고 또한 그들도 행복해지도록 도와주자는 내용의 글이다. 따라서 ⑤가 글의 요지로 가장 적절하다.

어 휘) contentment 만족 fellowman 동포

02 ③ 최근에 나는 브리티시컬럼비아 연안에 서식하는 멸종위기의 회색 곰에 대해 읽은 적이 있다. 글쓴이는 새끼 곰이 먹이를 찾고 섭취하는 어미 곰의 기술에 대해 얼마나 예리한 관찰자인지 강조했다. 새끼 곰이 어미 곰의 모범을 통해 배우는 것은 생존의 문제였다. 이러한 지식 없이 새끼 곰은 살아남을 수 없다. 똑같은 원리는 우리에게도 적용된다. 우리들은 무한경쟁 시대를 살아가면서 어떻게 아이들은 어쨌든 그렇지 않을 거라고 생각할 수 있을까? 우리가 함부로 자원과 에너지를 낭비하면서, 아이들이 미래에 절제를 배우고 물건들과의 관계의 의미를 알 수 있을까? 만약 내가 자주 사소한 것을 속인다면 — 예를 들어 점원에게 더 받은 잔돈을 돌려주지 않는다거나, 주인 잃은 돈을 돌려줄 노력을 하지 않은 채 내가 챙긴다면 — 나는 이러한 행동을 아이들에게 가르치게 되는 것이다.

① 부모들은 야생동물에 대한 책을 읽는 데 더 많은 시간을 쓴다.
② 주의 깊은 소비는 좋은 부모가 되기 위한 중심에 있다.
③ 좋은 부모 역할은 좋은 예시와 함께 시작하고 끝난다.
④ 아이들에게 좋은 품행을 가르치는 것은 돈을 버는 것보다 더 가치 있다.
⑤ 아이들의 행동은 무의식적으로 그들의 부모를 모방한다.

주 제) 자녀에게 부모가 모범이 될 필요성
정답 해설) 지문에서 아이들을 교육하기 위해서는 부모가 모범을 보여야 한다는 점을 브리티시컬럼비아 연안의 회색 곰을 예시로 들면서 설명하고 있다. 부모가 자녀들에게 어떠한 모습을 보여주느냐에 따라서 아이들이 보고 배우며 성장하기 때문에, 자녀들 앞에서 좋은 행동을 보여주어야 한다고 언급하고 있다. 그렇기 때문에, ③ '좋은 부모의 처음과 끝은 좋은 예시와 함께 한다.'가 지문의 요지로 적절하다.

어 휘) endangered 멸종위기에 처한 grizzly bear 회색

곰 emphasize 강조하다 cub 새끼 곰 principle 원리, 원칙 mindlessly 부주의한, 조심성 없는 acquire 손에 넣다, 획득하다 moderation 완화, 절제 cheat on 속이다

03 ④ lapse란, 당신이 바꾸려고 노력 중인 오래된 행동을 다시 하는 하나의 사건이다. 그 실수를 극복하는 방법은 고속도로에서의 교통 정체나 도로 공사 등이 당신을 지체시킬 경우처럼 가끔 그것들을 예상해 보는 것이다. 지난 번에 다녀왔던 장거리 자동차 여행을 출발할 때를 생각해 보라. 아마도 당신은 도중에 당신을 지체시켰던 무언가를 맞닥뜨렸을 것이다. 하지만 당신은 포기하고 차를 돌려 집으로 돌아오지 않았다. 비록 그 사건을 통해 당신이 예상했었던 것보다 조금 더 긴 시간이 소모되었지만, 당신은 여전히 당신이 의도한 목적지에 다다랐다. 이것은 개인적 변화에서도 똑같다. 당신이 접시에 더 많은 과일과 야채를 담으면서 균형을 맞추고 있는 상황이라고 생각해 보자. 하지만 문득 패스트푸드 햄버거를 먹고 싶은 충동을 이기지 못하고 굴복하게 된다. 이러한 경우 당신은 lapse를 하게 된 것이다.

① 당신은 당신이 어디로 향하고 싶은지 자신에게 상기시켜 주어야 한다.
② 당신이 옛 버릇을 다시 시작하고자 하는 욕구가 생긴다면, 그 욕구에 저항하려 노력해라.
③ 당신의 변화를 위한 계획이 뜻하지 않은 지연을 만나면 지름길로 가라.
④ 변화로 향하는 길 도중에 때때로 만나는 일탈은 비정상적인 것이 아니다.
⑤ 당신과 동일한 행동을 변화시키려고 노력하는 사람들로부터 지지를 구해라.

주 제) 바꾸려고 노력 중인 행동이 반복되는 현상
정답 해설) 잘못에 대해 알면서도 문득 깜빡하고 저지르는 실수인 lapse를 극복하려면 그것들을 때때로 예상해 보라는 내용의 글이다. 그 사례로 장거리 여행이 지체된 경우, 충동적으로 패스트푸드를 먹게 된 경우를 언급하고 있다. 따라서 글쓴이의 주장으로는 ④ '변화로 향하는 길 도중에 만나는 일탈은 비정상적인 것이 아니다'가 가장 적절하다.

어 휘) lapse (깜빡 하고) 저지르는 실수 traffic tie up 교통 정체 embark on ~에 착수하다, 나서다 chances are ~할 가능성이 높다. 아마 ~일 것이다 give in to ~에 굴복하다

04 ① 교환을 기초로 하는 상업 사회하에서, 모든 사람들은 "어느 정도 상인이 된다." 시장에서 개인이

이윤을 추구하는 것은 노동의 분업과 그에 따른 타인에 대한 의존성에 의해 개인의 행동을 다른 사람들의 기대치에 맞추도록 하는 결과로 이끈다. 따라서 시장은 그 자체가 하나의 훈육 기관이라고 할 수 있다. "노동자들에게 실시되는 실질적이고 효율적인 훈육은 회사에 대한 것이 아니다."라고 애덤 스미스는 기록했다. "(그것은) 바로 고객에 대한 훈육이다. 거짓으로 속이지 못하도록 규제하고, 태만한 행동을 바로잡는 것은 바로 실직에 대한 두려움이다." 다른 사람들과의 경제적인 거래에서 성공하기 위해서 각 개인은 스미스가 "예절"이라고 불렀던 자제력을 적절한 수준까지 개발시키게 된다. 시장이 장려하는 특성에는 신중함과, 장기 이익을 위해 단기간의 만족감을 유보할 줄 아는 능력이 포함된다.

[주 제] 시장 경제 활동이 제공하는 자기 훈육

[정답 해설] 시장에서 성공적인 경제활동이 이루어지려면 신중함, 장기 이익을 위해 단기간의 만족감을 유보할 줄 아는 능력과 같은 덕목에 대한 훈육이 뒷받침되어야 한다는 논지의 글이다. 따라서 글의 요지로는 ①이 가장 적절하다.

[어 휘] in some measure 약간, 어느 정도 division of labor 분업 fraud 사기, 사기꾼 negligence 태만, 과실 propriety 예절, 행동의 적절함 prudence 신중함 gratification 만족감

05 ② 열병에서부터 홍역과 간질에 이르기까지 다양한 질병에 효과가 있다고 주장되는 코뿔소의 뿔은 중국 의학에서 수천 년 동안 중요하게 여겨져 온 약재였다. 그들의 뿔에 대한 수요 때문에, 1910년 남아프리카의 흰코뿔소는 개체 수가 100마리 이하로 떨어지기도 했다. 오늘날에는 1977년에 공포된 코뿔소의 신체 부위에 대한 판매금지령에도 불구하고 아프리카의 코뿔소들은 또다시 멸종위기에 직면해 있다. 금지령이 코뿔소들을 불법적인 밀렵으로부터 보호할 수 없었으므로, 반어적으로 코뿔소 뿔에 대해서 엄격한 기준을 적용한 거래는 그 동물을 지켜낼 수 있을 것이다. 코뿔소의 뿔은 그들을 상처 입히지 않으면서도 잘라내거나 일부 깎아낼 수 있고, 그것들은 다시 자라난다. 만약 하나로 집중된 조직에 의해 엄격하게 관리가 된다면, 암시장에서 몰수된 뿔들과 자연사한 코뿔소로부터 수집한 뿔과 더불어, 현재의 수요는 합법적인 뿔의 절단을 통해 충분히 충족될 것이다.

① 코뿔소 뿔은 전통적인 약물의 대체물로 여겨져야 한다.
② 코뿔소 뿔의 거래를 합법화하고 규제하는 것이 코뿔소를 살릴 수 있다.
③ 정부는 불법 밀렵에 대한 형벌을 엄격하게 집행해야 한다.
④ 암시장에서 압수한 코뿔소 뿔은 더 좋은 곳에 쓰여야 한다.

⑤ 코뿔소의 뿔을 자르는 건 비인도적인 것으로, 폐지되어야한다.

[주 제] 코뿔소 뿔 거래 합법화의 필요성

[정답 해설] 전적인 금지보다는 엄격한 통제 하에서 거래를 허용해 주는 것이 코뿔소의 보호에 더 효과적일 것이라는 논지의 글이다. 따라서 글쓴이의 주장으로는 ②가 가장 적절하다.

[어 휘] purport 주장하다 ailment 질병 measles 홍역 epilepsy 간질 rhinoceros 코뿔소 seek after ~을 찾다, 구하다 poaching (밀렵 등을 위한) 불법 침입 confiscate 몰수하다, 압수하다 along with ~에 덧붙여, ~와 마찬가지로

06 ④ 만약 쓰레기의 위기가 존재한다면 그것은 바로 우리가 쓰레기를 환경적인 위협으로 생각할 뿐, 관리 가능하지만 명백히 복잡한 도시의 문제 그 자체로 보고 있지 않다는 것이다. 비록 많은 오래된 도시의 쓰레기 매립지는 수용 한계 용량에 근접했지만, 실제로는 안전한 쓰레기 매립지를 위한 공간은 나라 안에 얼마든지 있고, 또 앞으로도 언제나 존재할 것이다. 우리는 지금까지 쓰레기를 관리 차원의 문제로 보지 않고, 도덕적 위기로 보는 편을 택해왔다. 그 결과로 오늘날 재활용은 손익에 대한 평가로부터 자유롭고 결코 비난할 수 없는 미덕이 되어 버렸다. 하지만 실제로 자치단체들이 재활용을 하는 데 소비하는 돈은 학교와 도서관, 병원, 그리고 경찰에서 소비되지 못하는 돈이다. 현실 세계에서 많은 도시들과 마을에서 착수한 대규모 쓰레기 재활용 프로그램과 같은 것들은 부족한 정부 예산을 가장 합리적으로 사용하는 방법이 아닐지도 모른다.

[주 제] 쓰레기 재활용 비용의 재고 필요성

[정답 해설] 쓰레기 재활용의 비효율성에 대한 글이다. 특히 마지막 문장에서는 쓰레기 재활용이 정부의 부족한 예산을 효율적으로 사용하는 방법이 아니라고 명백히 밝히고 있다. 따라서 글쓴이의 주장으로 ④가 가장 적절하다.

[어 휘] admittedly 명백하게, 분명하게 landfill 쓰레기 매립지 irreproachable 흠잡을 데 없는, 비난할 수 없는 municipality 지방 자치단체 embark upon 착수하다 scarce 부족한, 적은

07 ⑤ 학자들은 정확히 왜 인간에 의한 무한한 진보의 개념이 지배적인지에 대해서 궁금하게 여겨 왔다. 해답은 에너지 기반을 확보하는 기술의 개발에서 찾을 수 있다. 거대하고 겉으로는 한계가 없어 보이는 — 정확하게 30년의 가치가 있는 태양 에너지는 — 처음부터 거기에 존재해 있었다. 그러나 우리는 점차 태양을 대체하는 데

필요한 모든 에너지를 갖게 되었고, 자연의 진행과정을 기다릴 필요가 전혀 없었다. 그 후 시간의 개념이 변경되었다. 그것은 우리가 얼마나 빨리 석탄층과 석유 매장지에 깊이 위치한 저장된 에너지를 활용할 수 있는지의 기능과 동등해졌다. 우리는 우리가 마음만 먹으면 태양을 두 배나 멀리 있게도 만들 수 있다. 왜냐하면 현재 우리는 땅에서 받아 마음대로 조작할 수 있는 "저장되어 있는 태양"을 다루고 있기 때문이다. 이러한 에너지 자원을 가지고, 사람들은 그들이 더 이상 자연에 의존하지 않음과 그들 스스로의 결정에 의해 세상을 재정렬할 수 있음을 점점 더 확신하게 되었다.

(주 제) 에너지 확보 기술 개발로 인해 자연의 지배로부터 벗어난 인간

(정답 해설) 이 글의 마지막에 나오는 '이러한 에너지 자원을 가지고, 세상을 재정렬할 수 있음을 점점 더 확신하게 되었다.'로 미루어 볼 때, 글의 요지로는 ⑤가 가장 적절하다.

(어 휘) notion 개념 progress 발전 secure 확보하다 gigantic 거인의, 거대한 seemingly 겉보기에, 외관상 equivalent 동등한, 평등한 reorder 다시 질서를 잡다 harness 동력원으로 이용하다, 사용하다 reservoir 저장고, 저장 탱크 deal with 다루다 manipulate 조작하다 at will 마음대로 convince 확신시키다 dependent 의존하는

08 ⑤ 시민들은 몇 년이 걸릴지도 모르는, 공공 신탁 개념을 연방 정부와 주정부 소유의 토지와 야생동물에 관한 법률에 주입하는 운동을 시작해야 한다. 책임 기관은 피신탁인이며, 법은 이를 강조 조항으로 규정해야 한다. 공공 신탁정책에서 중요한 문제는 법원이 그것을 강제할 것인가에 대한 문제가 아니라, 그 신탁이 연방 및 주정부 정책의 작용하는 일부가 될 수 있는가이다. 우리는 이 기관들을 압박하여 관리정책의 문제로서 신탁 관리 업무와 높은 의무감을 인정하도록 해야 한다. 연방 토지 기관의 관리들은 설득력과 자부심을 갖고 이렇게 말해야 할 것이다. "예, 우리는 국가의 경이로움의 피신탁인입니다." 이런 종류의 선언은 더 높은 기준을 설정하고 원칙에 입각한 행동에 대한 분위기를 만들어 줄 것이다.

(주 제) 정부 소유 토지 및 야생 동물 관리 기관의 의무감 자각 필요성

(정답 해설) 이 글의 핵심 내용은 야생동물 보호를 위하여 공공 신탁 개념을 정부 차원에서 시작해야 한다는 것이다. 그러므로 글쓴이의 주장으로 ⑤가 가장 적절하다.

(어 휘) inject 주입하다, 주사하다 trust 신탁, 맡김 notion 개념 federal 동맹의, 연합의, 연방의 statute 법령, 법규 matter 중

요하다, 문제, 사정 doctrine 주의, 정책, 원리 court 법원 enforce 시행하다 acknowledge 동의(시인)하다, 인정하다 trusteeship 신탁 관리 업무, 신탁 통치

09 ① 자원을 절약하기 위해 재활용을 해야 할까? 아니다, 실제로는 그렇지 않다. 재활용이 수익성이 없는 이유는 대부분의 재활용품들이 나무 농장에서 나오는 재생지거나 또는 모래로 만들어지는 싸고 풍부한 유리이기 때문이다. 알루미늄은 재활용하면 이득이 되며, 이미 법에 의한 명령 전에 개인 사업자들은 그것을 재활용하고 있었다. 재활용은 그 비용이 정해지고 쓰레기의 양에 미치는 영향이 예상보다 적다는 것이 밝혀져 빛을 잃기 시작했다. 할당제와 벌금이 쓰레기를 분리수거하도록 강제할 수는 있지만 이것으로는 우리가 재활용하는 쓰레기가 쓰이는 산업 시장이 형성될 수는 없다. 재활용은 지역 단위나 상품 단위로는 매우 효율적으로 작용할 수 있지만 정부 차원에서는 그렇지 못하다.

① 정부 수준의 재활용은 효과적으로 실행되지 않을 것이다.
② 재활용은 정부 차원에서 이루어져야 한다.
③ 우리는 쓰레기를 분리수거해야 한다.
④ 우리는 쓰레기를 길에 버리지 말아야 한다.
⑤ 재활용은 수익성 있는 정부의 프로젝트이다.

(주 제) 정부 차원 재활용의 비효율성

(정답 해설) 재활용이 실질적으로는 특별한 효과가 없음을 설명하고 있는 글이다. 기대치보다 효과가 적으며 정부 차원에서 실시하기에는 적절하지 못하다. 따라서 ①이 글쓴이의 주장으로 가장 적절하다 할 수 있다.

(어 휘) unprofitable 이익이 없는 silica 규토(모래의 종류) commodity 일용품, 물자, 생활필수품 mandate 명령, 권한의 위임, 명령하다, 위임하다

10 ③ 동아시아의 경제적 변화는 20세기 후반 전 세계에서 가장 놀랄 만한 발전 중의 하나이다. 1990년대까지 이러한 경제적 발전은 동아시아를 국가 간 평화와 균형을 보장할 지속적으로 확장되는 상업망으로 보는 많은 관찰자들 사이에서 기대를 불러 일으켰다. 그러나 이러한 낙관론은 상업적인 교류가 반드시 평화를 유지시킬 것이라는 매우 불확실한 가정에 기초하고 있다. 실제 상황은 그렇지 못하다. 경제 성장은 국가 간의 힘의 균형을 변화시키고 국가 내부와 국가들 사이의 정치적 불안정을 초래한다. 경제적 교류는 사람들을 접촉하게 하지만 그들의 의견을 하나로 일

치시키는 것은 아니다.

---

① 국제 정치가 경제 침체를 야기한다.
② 동아시아는 계속해서 경제 성장을 누려왔다.
③ 경제적 교류가 필연적으로 평화를 가져오지는 않는다.
④ 동아시아의 민주주의는 많이 발전했다.
⑤ 경제 발전은 국제 협력을 보장한다.

[주 제] 평화를 보장하지 못하는 동아시아 경제 발전
[정답 해설] 동아시아의 눈부신 경제적 성장이 평화가 아니라, 국가 간의 긴장을 초래하고 있다는 내용의 글이다. 그러므로 ③ '경제적 교류가 필연적으로 평화를 가져오지는 않는다.'가 글의 요지로 가장 알맞다.

[어 휘] insure 보증하다, 보장하다 optimism 낙천주의, 낙관주의 assumption 가정, 가설 interchange 교환하다, 교체하다 invariably 변함없이, 항상 instability 불안정, 불안정한 상태 dubious 불확실한, 의심스러운, 수상한

More Practice

| 01 ④ | 02 ② | 03 ⑤ | 04 ⑤ |

01 ④ 일상생활에서 사람들은 소비의 여러 가지의 측면에 반복적으로 노출된다. 광고, 기차 여행, 식료품 쇼핑, 텔레비전 시청, 음악 청취, 인터넷 서핑, 의류 쇼핑, 그리고 책 읽는 것은 모두 다 사람들이 소비하는 것들의 예시들이다. 인간이 참여하는 거의 모든 행동들은 직간접적으로 소비와 관련되어 있다. 심지어 크리스마스와 같은 전통적인 휴일도 요즘에는 주로 소비에 관한 것이다. 원래는 종교적 휴일이었던 것이 선물을 전달하는 산타클로스라는 가장 전형적인 예를 동반한 소비 측면에 대부분 압도됐다. 기본적으로 소비는 인간 일상생활의 일부라는 사실을 피할 방법이 없다. 그러므로 소비가 개인과 집단에 어떤 영향을 미치는가에 대한 연구 없이는, 우리가 인간을 이해한다고 진정으로 말할 수는 없다.

[주 제] 인간의 소비 연구의 필요성
[정답 해설] 글은 인간의 삶에서 소비를 떼어놓고 생각할 수 없으며 이러한 소비를 이해하는 것이 인간을 진정으로 이해하는 것이라고 말하고 있다. 따라서 이 글의 후반부에서 말하는 소비의 영향에 대한 연구를 언급하는 ④번이 이 글의 요지로 가장 적절하다.

[어 휘] consumption 소비 overtake 압도하다

02 ② 공간 인식은 고정된 영역이나 근거지를 둔 모든 움직이는 종에게 필수적인 구상 요건이다. 그리고 그것이 인간의 사고와 사유에 중심적인 역할을 한다는 데는 의심의 여지가 없다. 정말로, 그러한 중심에 대한 증거는 우리 주변 모든 곳, 많은 다른 영역에 대해 공간적인 은유가 쓰이는 우리의 언어와 우리 기억에서 장소의 특별한 역할에 있다. 공간이 우리의 본성에 장착된 근본적인 직관이라는 관념은 최소한 칸트까지 거슬러 올라가고, 공간에 대한 우리의 인식이 인식론적인 일반법칙에 의해 지배된다는 관념은 현재의 많은 인지 과학에 정보를 제공한다. 그러나 어떠한 측면에서 인간의 공간 인식은 당황스럽게 한다. 첫째, 그것은 평범하다. 우리는 벌이나 비둘기, 박쥐나 고래와 비교해 볼 때 길을 찾는 데 능숙한 종이 아니다. 둘째, 인간의 공간 인식은 분명히 변화한다. 사냥꾼, 항해사와 택시 운전자들은 평범한 도시 거주자들과 다른 부류이다. 이는 효율적인 공간 사고의 많은 측면이 문화적 요소에 달려 있고, 이는 결국 이 영역에서 인지적 보편성의 한계가 있다는 점을 보여준다.

[주 제] 인간의 공간적 사고의 한계
[정답 해설] 인간에게 있어서 공간 인식의 필요성을 언급한 후에 인간이 공간을 인식할 때의 특징을 설명한 글이다. 즉 인간의 공간 인식은 평범하며 개인에 따라 차이가 있으므로 보편적이라고 하기에는 한계가 있다는 내용이다. 따라서 주어진 글의 요지로는 ②가 가장 적절하다.

[어 휘] spatial 공간적인 cognition 인식 metaphor 비유, 은유 unspectacular 평범한 universal 보편성

03 ⑤ 인간의 진보를 지키고 유지하며, 인간의 필요를 충족하고, 인간의 야망을 실현하기 위한 많은 현재의 노력들은, 부유하고 가난한 나라 모두에서 명백히 지속 불가능하다. 그들은 이미 초과 인출된 환경 자원의 계좌에서, 그 계좌들이 먼 미래에도 파산 당하지 않고 사용 가능할 수 있기에는 지나치게 많이, 지나치게 빨리 가져다 쓰고 있다. 그들은 우리 세대에서는 대차대조표에서 이득을 보일 수도 있지만, 우리의 자손들은 손실을 물려받게 될 것이다. 우리는 상황의 의지도 예정도 없이 미래 세대로부터 환경 자본을 빌려온다. 그들은 우리의 낭비적인 방식의 책임을 우리에게 물을 테지만, 그들은 절대로 우리의 빚을 받아갈 수 없다. 우리는 우리가 그것을 피할 수 있기 때문에 우리가 하는 대로 행동한다. 미래 세대는 투표하지 못하므로, 그들은 정치적, 재정적인 힘이 없고, 우리의 결정에 문제를 제기할 수 없다.

정답 해설 과도하게 인출된 계좌에 비유하여 현재 세대가 미래 세대를 전혀 고려하지 않고 환경 자원을 낭비하는 행태를 설명하고 있으므로, 글의 요지로는 ⑤가 가장 적절하다.

어 휘 unsustainable 지속불가능한 overdrawn 초과 인출된 affordable 감당할 수 있는 bankrupt 파산시키다 balance sheet 대차대조표 inherit 물려받다 collect on ~을 수령하다 get away 벗어나다, 피하다

---

04 ⑤ 승자와 패자 간의 한 가지 차이점은 그들이 패배를 다루는 방식이다. 최고의 회사와 가장 뛰어난 전문가에게도 긴 성공의 실적이 헛디딤, 미끄러짐 그리고 작은 전환으로 중단된다. 게임에서 이기는 팀이라도 실수를 하고 일부분 뒤쳐질 수 있다. 빠르게 회복하는 능력이 중요한 이유이다. 난관은 어디에나 있다. 깜짝 놀랄 일은 화산재처럼 하늘에서 떨어질 수 있고 모든 것을 바꿀 듯 보인다. 한 저명한 학자가 "모든 것이 중간에는 실패처럼 보일 수 있다"고 말한 까닭이다. 즉, 높은 성취의 핵심요소는 최악의 상태를 딛고 일어서는 것이다.

주 제 성공의 핵심인 회복력

정답 해설 유능한 사람에게도 크고 작은 실패가 찾아오므로, 최종적인 성공에 가장 중요한 요소는 실패에서 빨리 회복하는 능력이라는 내용으로, 글의 요지로는 ⑤가 가장 적절하다.

어 휘 accomplished 기량이 뛰어난 track record 실적 punctuate 중단시키다 slip 헛디딤, 미끄러짐 slide 미끄러짐, 저하 turnaround (진로, 방침의) 전환 lag behind 뒤지다, ~보다 뒤떨어지다 ubiquitous 어디에나 있는, 아주 흔한 prominent 유명한 bounce back from ~에서 회복하다, 딛고 일어서다 low point 최악의 상태

UNIT 03 제목

Example

답 ⑤

최초의 Robin Hood 이야기는 1450년에 인쇄되었고, 대중문화에서 우리가 알게 된 늠름한 영웅을 그리지는 않는다. 그는 소작농이었고, 때로 거칠고 잔인했다. 전설은 부자에게서 훔친 돈을 갖고 있다가 가끔씩 가난한 사람을 도왔던 강도에 더 기반하는 편이다. 그는 숲 속에 이상적인 사회를 세우고 싶어 하지 않았다. 그와 그의 사람들은 주로 사회적인 부정의를 교정하고 잘 살기를 추구했다. Robin Hood는 17세기 무렵 매우 인기가 생겨서 사람들이 장소와 배에 그의 이름을 따올 정도였다. 19세기에 이르러 많은 이야기와 노래에서 Robin Hood 전설의 주요한 변화가 발생했다. 그의 소작농이라는 출신은 사라졌고, 그는 점점 가난한 사람의 권리를 수호하는 Sherwood 숲의 영웅적인 무법자가 되었다.

---

① 강도로서의 Robin Hood
② 중세 자작농의 시초
③ 초창기 Robin Hood의 고난
④ Sherwood Forest의 이상적 사회
⑤ Robin Hood 캐릭터의 변화

주 제 시대에 따른 Robin Hood 전설의 변화

Practice

01 ④	02 ①	03 ③	04 ③	05 ②
06 ①	07 ①	08 ④	09 ②	10 ③
11 ④	12 ③	13 ⑤	14 ③	15 ①
16 ②	17 ⑤	18 ①	19 ②	20 ④

---

01 ④ 광산과 갑옷 기술의 중심지는 독일의 Augsburg이며 이것은 우연의 일치가 아니었다. Augsburg는 유럽의 주요 철광석 매장층과 가까이 있으며 봉건 국가의 갑옷 입은 기사 집단을 만들 금속에 대한 수요는 곧 급성장하는 광업과 그와 함께 번성한 병장기 제조업을 창출했다. 유럽의 봉건 국가들 도처에 있는 고객들의 성가심에, 고객들이 다른 대안이 없다는 것을 아는 독일은 아주 높은 가격을 책정했다. 독일 갑옷은 세계에서 최고였고 어떤 고객이 만약 가격을 마음에 들어 하지 않는다면 그는 다음 전투에 막대와 돌을 가지고 출전하면 되었다. 이런 지나치게 높은 가격을 담보로 독일의 무기 제조업자들은 엄청난 연구와 개발 노력이 가능했다. 예를 들어, 머리 전체를 덮고 움직이는 차

양이 있는 강철 헬멧 같은 더 강한 갑옷으로 이어졌다.

① 무기와 갑옷에 대한 작별
② 갑옷 사업의 과거와 미래
③ 돌 대 철 : 뻔한 선택
④ 독일, 갑옷 기술의 중심
⑤ 고급과 싼 가격 : 양면의 칼

[주 제] 갑옷 기술의 중심지 독일

[정답 해설] 독일이 갑옷 기술의 중심지가 된 배경, 높은 가격을 책정하게 된 이유, 연구 개발이 가능했던 배경에 대해 설명하고 있다. 따라서 글의 제목으로는 ④가 가장 적절하다.

[어 휘] armor 갑옷 coincidence 우연의 일치 feudal 봉건적인 annoyance 성가심 alternative 대안 sally forth 힘차게 떠나다 underwrite 동의하다 lavish 아낌없는, 지나친 visor 차양

02 ① 흥정하기 싫은가? 당신은 혼자가 아니다. 전국 조사에 따르면 쇼핑객의 오직 48퍼센트만이 지난 3년 동안 일상용품과 서비스의 더 나은 거래를 위해 흥정을 하려고 했는데, 이것은 2007년의 61퍼센트에서 감소한 것이다. 그러나 만약 당신이 겁쟁이라면, 당신이 진다. 흥정을 했던 이들 중에 89퍼센트는 적어도 한 번은 보상을 받았다. 건강과 관련된 가격에 문의를 했던 사람들처럼 성공적인 가구 흥정가는 평균적으로 300달러를 아꼈다. 휴대폰 요금제에 이의를 제기했던 사람들은 80달러를 절약했다. 확실하게, 흥정을 하지 않는 사람은 돈을 버리는 것이다.

① 물어봐서 나쁠 것은 없다
② 흥정을 잘 하기 위한 기본
③ 쉬운 가구 흥정
④ 둘러보는 것: 보상을 얻어내다
⑤ 흥정은 정말로 가격을 부풀리는가?

[주 제] 흥정의 이점

[정답 해설] 주어진 글은 흥정을 통해 이익을 얻은 사례들을 언급하고 있다. 또한, 흥정에 있어서 겁쟁이라면 당신이 진다고 언급한 것으로 보아 흥정을 독려하는 글임을 알 수 있다. 따라서 ①이 제목으로 가장 적절하다.

[어 휘] haggle 흥정을 하다 inflate 부풀리다

03 ③ 당신이 초과 체중을 짊어지고 다닐 때, 의료 보험부터 시작하여 추가적 비용이 증가한다. 2013년

뉴크대 연구에 따르면, 연구자들은 의료보험 지출을 비만지수(BMI)에 따라 추적했다. 1인당 연간 평균은 저체중인 비만지수 19일 때, 2,541 달러였다. 과체중으로 여겨지는 BMI 지수 25일 때, 그것은 2,893 달러였다. 비만으로 여겨지는 BMI 지수 33에서 비용이 3,439 달러로 가장 높았다. "질병 위험은 '정상 체중'의 낮은 지점에서부터 증가하기 시작한다"고 수석 연구원 Truls Ostbye가 말한다. 초과 체중인 사람들은 병원에서 끝나지 않는다. 2010 맥킨지 보고서는 비만 미국인들은 옷에 총 300억 달러의 추가 비용을 쓴다고 추정했다. 40살 비만 남성은 생명보험에 두 배의 비용을 지불해야 한다고 또한 추정된다.

① 의료 서비스의 증가하는 비용
② 체중을 줄이면 질병 위험도 줄어든다
③ 초과 체중에 대해 지불해야 하는 대가
④ 비만인들이 옷에 돈을 더 많이 쓰는가?
⑤ BMI: 체중의 부정확한 지표

[주 제] 초과 체중이 야기하는 비용

[정답 해설] 체중 증가에 따라 의류 구입 비용, 생명보험료 등이 증가한다는 내용이므로 ③이 제목으로 가장 적절하다.

[어 휘] track 추적하다 deem ~으로 생각하다 obese 비만인 top 가장 높다 add-on 추가 aggregate 합계, 총액 indicator 지표

04 ③ 자동차의 사다리에 올라가는 것은 어려운 일이었고 그 꼭대기에 서 있는 것은 더욱 더 힘든 일이었다. 매년, 노후화되었다고 인식된 방식을 채택하면서 Chevrolet은 완전히 새롭게 설계되고 대개 더 큰 모델을 출시했다. 어제 유행의 정상에 있던 차는 내일 작고 당혹스럽고 진부한 것으로 보일 것이다. 당신이 상상하는 바와 같이 이 모든 것은 미국 사회의 바닥에서부터 정상에 이르기까지 상당한 근심을 유발한다. 그러다 1959년에 난데없이 나타난 듯한, 꾸미지 않은 Volkswagen Beetle과 "Think Small."이라는 제목을 가진 신문의 전면광고가 나타나기 시작했다. 그 광고는 자동차가 간소하고 효율적이라는 것 이외에는 더 이상 이야기하지 않았다. 그 광고는 심지어 Beetle을 쓰레기를 말하는 당시의 속어인 "싸구려 자동차"라고 불렀다. 사람들은, 그것들이 공식적으로 마케터들이 몇 년 동안 그것들에 주입한 이름 없는 근심을 공개적으로 표현하도록 하면서 광고가 충격적으로 정직하고 유쾌하다는 것을 알게 되었다. 내가 사다리 꼭대기에 올라갈 수 있을 것인가? 누가 신경 쓸 것인가?

① 어려운 경제 시절: 간소한 것을 생각하라

② 자동차의 지위의 정상
③ 새로운 광고: 당신의 사다리에서 내려오시오
④ 자동차가 당신의 사회적 지위를 나타내는가?
⑤ 국제 자동차 전쟁: 사이즈가 중요하다

주 제 간소함과 효율성을 표방한 Volkswagen Beetle

정답 해설 기존의 자동차에 대한 관념에서 벗어나 간소함과 효율성을 표방한 1959년 Volkswagen의 Beetle과 그 광고를 언급하고 있다. 자동차의 사다리에 올라가는 것을 추구했던 것이 기존의 관념이라면 사다리 꼭대기에 올라갈 수도 없을 뿐만 아니라 그것을 아무도 신경 쓰지 않을 것이라는 내용이 변화된 관념이다. 따라서 ③이 글의 제목으로 가장 적절하다.

어 휘 ladder 지위 obsolescence 노후화 roll out 출시하다 out of nowhere 난데없이 unadorned 꾸미지 않은 flivver 싸구려 자동차 slang 비속어

---

05 ② 한 실험에서 백 명의 남성과 여성은 누군가와 만날 때마다 그들의 혈압을 측정하는 장비를 착용했다. 실험자들이 가족이나 친한 친구들을 만났을 때, 그들의 혈압은 떨어졌다. 이러한 상호작용은 즐겁고 (마음을) 진정시켰다. 그들이 관계가 좋지 않은 사람들을 만났을 때는 혈압이 올라갔다. 그러나 과잉보호하는 부모, 변덕스러운 연애 상대, 혹은 경쟁자라고 생각하는 친구 등 그들이 애증 관계라고 느끼는 사람과 있을 때 가장 큰 급등이 왔다. 변덕스러운 상사의 모습이 전형적인 예로 어렴풋이 보이지만 이러한 동력은 우리의 모든 관계에서 작용한다.

① 고혈압: 조용한 암살자
② 쉽지 않은 관계: 당신의 몸은 거짓말을 하지 않는다.
③ 당신의 바이오리듬에 휘둘리지 마라.
④ 건강 감지 도구가 당신의 건강을 지킬 수 있을까?
⑤ 당신은 어떻게 불편한 관계를 다루나?

주 제 인간관계에 따른 혈압의 변화

정답 해설 사람들이 편한 사람들을 만날 때는 차분해져서 혈압이 내려가고, 불편한 사람들을 만났을 때는 흥분해서 혈압이 올라가는 것을 언급하는 글이다. 몸은 만나는 사람의 유형에 따라 반응한다는 것을 알 수 있다. 따라서 ② '쉽지 않은 관계: 당신의 몸은 거짓말을 하지 않는다.'가 제목으로 적절하다.

어 휘 interact 상호 작용하다, 서로 영향을 주다 pleasant 기분 좋은, 유쾌한 soothing 진정되는 troublesome 골치 아픈 ambivalent 애증의 volatile 휘발성의, 변덕스러운 loom 어렴풋이 보이다 archetype 전형, 원형

---

06 ① 당신은 대륙 간 거대 기업(CCE)의 절차를 지켜야 하고, 공급자를 선정하는 것에 대한 내부적 통제 시스템을 충실히 따라야만 한다. 공급자를 선정하는 것은 절대로 선물 수령이나, 융숭한 대접, 또는 보답에 기초한 것이어선 안 된다. 공급자에 대한 선정이 상품이나 서비스의 제공자(우리가 보통 입찰이라고 부르는)에 대한 정형화되고 구조화된 초청일 때는, 우리의 내부적 통제를 뒷받침할 수 있는 문서를 유지하는 것이 가장 중요한 일이다. 공공사업 분야에서 그러한 입찰 과정은 공공 자금을 사용하는 것에 대한 경쟁 과정이 투명하고 공정하며 부정부패로부터 자유롭다는 것을 확실하게 보장하기 위해, 법에 의해 구체적으로 요구되고 결정될지도 모른다. 입찰 과정은 관련된 계약에 대해 어떤 경쟁도 입찰에 대한 대응으로 실행되어야 한다는 것과, 어떤 당사자도 입찰 과정이 자격을 갖춘 모든 입찰자들에게 공개되고 봉함입찰이 조사를 위해 공개되며 가격과 질을 기반으로 선택되는 계약을 위한 개별적, 우선적, 밀실 협상의 불공평한 이익을 얻지 않는다는 조건을 기반으로 다른 당사자들이 제안하도록 하는 초청을 포함한다.

① 공급자 선택 과정에서 CCE의 규제
② 왜 공급자 선택이 CCE에서 중요한가?
③ 회사 고용인의 사기를 올리는 방법
④ 입찰 경쟁 과정에 대한 법적 문제
⑤ 입찰자 선택 과정에서 필요한 문서

주 제 공급자 선정에서 CCE의 규제 사항

정답 해설 공급자 선정을 위한 입찰 규제들을 설명하고 있는 글이므로 ①이 제목으로 가장 적절하다.

어 휘 adhere to 충실히 따르다, 들러붙다 tender 입찰 corruption 부정부패 relevant 관련이 있는 in response to ~에 응하여, ~에 답하여 on the understanding that ~이라는 조건하에 in the open 공공연하게, 개방되게 scrutiny 정밀 조사, 철저한 검토

---

07 ① 빛이 지구의 표면에 부딪치면 서로 다른 색들은 다른 방식으로 반응한다. 그들 중 일부는 다른 색들과는 달리, 기체의 분자에 흡수된다. (빨간색이나 오렌지색과 같이) 상대적으로 파장의 길이가 긴 대부분의 색들은 대기를 바로 통과하며 영향을 받지 않는 반면에, (보라색이나 파란색과 같이) 상대적으로 파장의 길이가 짧은 색들은 기체 분자에 흡수된다. 왜냐하면 이러한 색들의 파장(즉, 각 파동의 정점 사이의 거리)의 길이는 산소 원자의 직경과 크기가 비슷하기 때문이다. 이 때 기체 분자는 이러한 색들을 방출하고 하늘에 분산시키며, 이를 통해 하늘을 파랗게 보이게 한다.

① 파장에 의해서 결정되는 색깔의 운명
② 과학의 이면 가스 분자의 과학
③ 빛의 본질: 더 길수록 더 밝다
④ 가스 분자 vs 파장: 누가 이기는가?
⑤ 우리의 육안이 어떻게 색깔을 인지하는가?

[주제] 파장에 따른 색깔별 반응

[정답 해설] 파장의 길이에 따라 빛이 다른 방식으로 반응을 하게 되고, 이에 따라 우리가 볼 수 있는 색이 결정된다는 것을 파란색을 예로 들어서 설명하고 있다. 따라서 제목으로 ①이 가장 적절하다.

[어휘] react 반응하다 molecule 분자 radiate 내뿜다, 방출하다 scatter 분산시키다

---

08 ④ 억만장자들이 그들의 부를 이룩한 이후에 자선 사업으로 관심을 돌릴 때, 그들은 종종 가난한 학생들을 위해 장학재단을 설립하거나, 건강 복지를 향상시키기 위한 일을 하거나, 예술에 공헌하곤 한다. Chang Yung-Fa의 사명은 바로 사회적인 가치들을 "다시 구축하는 것"이다. 5년 전 그는 '도덕'이라는 삽화가 포함되어있는 잡지를 발간했고, 그리고 매달 그것은 타이완과 전 세계의 사람들의 도덕성을 고양시키기 위해 노력하고 있다. 그가 돈을 벌던 거저 주든, 도덕성은 85세의 Chang이 하는 많은 일들의 토대가 되어준다. 그는 세계에서 4번째로 큰 화물 운송 회사와 호텔, EVA 항공, 그리고 섬의 주 공항으로 가는 유일한 장거리 버스 회사를 포함하고 있는 그의 Evergreen 그룹이 큰 성공을 이룬 것은 도덕성이라는 회사의 문화를 바탕으로 뜻이 잘 통하는 직원 관계 덕분이라고 믿는다.

① 타이완의 박해받는 자선가
② 더 높은 도덕성, 더 많은 행복
③ 타이완 기업에 도덕성 심어주기
④ 도덕성 전파에 눈을 돌린 사업가
⑤ 사업과 도덕성: 물과 기름과 같은 존재

[주제] 사업가 Chang의 도덕성 전파 노력

[정답 해설] Chang이라는 사업가가 하는 많은 일들의 토대가 도덕성이라는 내용의 글이다. 따라서 글의 제목으로는 ④가 가장 적절하다.

[어휘] philanthropy 자선 행위, 자선 사업 nothing less than 다름 아닌, 바로 그 underpin 지지하다, 토대가 되다 airway 항공회사, 항공로 congenial 뜻이 잘 맞는, 마음이 맞는 philanthropist 자선가, 박애주의자

---

09 ② 달에 관한 프로그램을 다시 시작하는 것에 대해서 가장 흥분하는 과학자들은 아마도 달에 대한 전문가들이 아니라 대상을 광범위하게 연구하는 천문학자들일 것이다. 그러한 과학자들은 달의 반대편에 직경 30미터의 거대한 망원경을 설치하는 새로운 임무를 좋아할 것이다. 망원경의 최적의 작동을 위한 두 가지 조건은 극한의 추위가 있을 것, 그리고 진동이 거의 없어야 하는 것이다. 달의 어두운 쪽에 있는 분화구의 안에서는 온도가 섭씨 영하 200도까지도 내려갈 수 있다. 지진 활동이 없기 때문에 달은 매우 안정적인 장소이다. 영구적인 어둠 역시 망원경이 계속해서 사용될 수 있음을 의미한다. 지지자들은 이러한 조건에 의해 달을 기반으로 한 망원경으로 대체하면 Hubble 망원경이 10년에 걸쳐서 이룰 수 있는 것들을 불과 17일 만에 이룰 수 있다고 주장한다.

① 달 프로그램: 극히 드문 일
② 달 우주 관측소에 대한 사례
③ 달 탐험 인류의 작은 발자취
④ 새로운 허블 망원경: 가치가 있는 것인가?
⑤ 달 전문가 vs. 보통의 천문학자

[주제] 달에 망원경이 설치될 경우의 효용

[정답 해설] 달을 통해 우주를 관찰하는 프로그램에 대해서 설명하고 있는 글이다. 따라서 ②의 '달 우주 관측소에 대한 사례'가 가장 적절한 제목이다.

[어휘] reignite 다시 불을 붙이다 astronomer 천문학자 far side 저쪽, 멀리, 반대쪽 install 설치하다 optimum 최적의, 가장 알맞은 frigid 추운, 혹한의 crater 분화구 seismic 진동의, 지진의 proponent 제안자, 발의자, 지지자 once in a blue moon 극히 드물게

---

10 ③ 지구에 도달하는 태양광의 총량은 1950년대 초기에서 1990년대 초기 사이에 10퍼센트 가까이 감소했다. 과학자들은 그것이 태양의 문제가 아니라는 사실을 밝혀냈다. 그 어떤 기구도 태양광이 어두워졌다는 것을 기록하지는 못했다. 그 문제는 태양과 지구 사이에 있는 것으로 보인다. 환경오염이 사이에서 방해를 했다. 오염 물질 속의 소립자가 태양광을 다시 우주 밖으로 반사시켰다. 또한 환경오염은 대기의 농도를 더욱 진하게 만들었다. 이 짙은 농도는 더 두툼하고 어두운 구름을 형성한다. 과학자들은 그들의 이론을 증명하기 위해 오염이 아주 없거나 적은 지역을 예로 든다. 그러한 장소에서 실시한 태양광의 측정 결과는 여전히 밝다는 것을 보여준다.

① 해에게 휴가를 줍시다
② 햇빛: 많을 수록 더 좋다
③ 환경 오염: 인공적인 차양 장막
④ 어떻게 해가 어두워지는 걸 멈출 수 있을까?
⑤ 모든 구름 속에서 한 줄기 빛을 찾아라

주 제) 환경오염 때문에 어두워진 태양광

정답 해설) 햇빛의 양이 감소하는 것은 자연적인 이유 때문이
아니라, 환경오염에 기인한다는 내용의 글이다. 따라서 가장 적
당한 제목은 ③의 '환경오염: 인공적인 차양 장막'이다.

어 휘) dim 희미한, 어두운, 어둡게 하다 get in the way 방해
하다 particulate 미립자 condensation 응결, 응축 verify 증명
하다

11 ④ Walter Benjamin은 이야깃거리를 가지고 방랑
에서 돌아온 여행가뿐만 아니라 고향에 근간을
두고 전통을 지키는 사람들도 스토리텔링과 동일시한다. 중
세시대에는 지역에 거주하는 장인 수공업자와 이동해 다니
는 기술자들이 같은 작업장에 모이게 되는 수공업의 구조로
인하여, 두 종류의 스토리텔링은 서로 밀접한 연관성을 갖게
되었다. 하지만 '역사 속의 세속적인 생산 노동력'에 의한 작
업을 통해, 이야기를 전하는 것은 직접 말하는 담화의 영역
에서 점차 배제되어갔다. 스토리텔링과 대척점에 있으며 스
토리텔링을 완전하게 대체하고 있는 그것은, 당연히 인쇄 기
술의 발명 그리고 책이라는 개념과 뗄 수 없는 관계에 있는,
바로 소설이다. 소설가는 필연적으로 고립되어 있으며 눈에
보이지 않는, 숨어있는 신과 같은 존재로 독자들과의 직접적
인 대화에는 끼어들 수 없으며, 따라서 훌륭한 충고가 되는
좋은 이야기도 직접 전해줄 수 없다.

① 두 시대, 하나의 이야기
② 스토리텔링: 생기 있는 말 vs 죽은 글자
③ 현대 이야기의 고독한 영웅
④ 스토리텔링의 쇠퇴, 소설의 번영
⑤ 장인과 날품팔이: 동전의 양면

주 제) 스토리텔링을 대체한 소설

정답 해설) 스토리텔링이 쇠퇴하고 소설이 출연하게 된 배경
에 대해서 설명하는 글이다. 전반부에는 스토리텔링에 대한
Walter Benjamin의 견해가 나오고 후반부에는 소설의 특징과
발생 배경에 대한 설명이 나온다. 내용을 모두 포함할 수 있는
적절한 제목은 ④이다.

어 휘) storytelling 이야기(구비 문학) whereby 그것에 의하
여, 그렇게 하여 craftsman 장인 journeyman 날품팔이(숙련 노동
자) secular 현세의, 세속적인 colloquy 대화, 대담

12 ③ 현대 심리학은 "대학 2학년 학생들의 행동에 관
한 과학"이라고 불려왔다. 1960년대에서 1970년
대에, 여러 심리학자들은 그 분야의 4개의 학술지를 직접 분
석했고, 58퍼센트에서 96퍼센트에 달하는 논문이 대학생들
에 대한 연구를 기반으로 작성되었다는 사실을 알게 되었
다. 더욱 최근에 나는 1991년에 그 학술지 중 2종류에 실린
논문들을 분석해 보았고, 77퍼센트는 대학생들에 대해 수행
된 연구를 보고했다는 사실을 알게 되었다. Michigan 대학
의 심리학자이자 연구 대상이 되었던 학술지의 편집자이기
도 한 Melvin Manis는 편리함은 다른 분야에서 연구 대상
을 선택할 때도 영향을 준다고 해명했다. 그는 말했다. "코끼
리에 대해 이루어지는 유전학 연구는 거의 없어요. 대부분은
초파리에 대해 이루어집니다. 그것은 초파리의 생애 주기가
더 짧은 것뿐만 아니라 훨씬 더 저렴하기 때문입니다." 물론
코끼리와 초파리가 비교할 만한 유전자 구조를 가지고 있다
면 이는 옳은 말이다. 하지만 대학생들이 대학생이 아닌 동
년배들처럼 생각하고 행동하고 느끼는가? 또는 같은 문제에
대해서 더 나이 많은 성인이 그러하는 것처럼 할 수 있을까?
이 두 가지 질문에 대한 정답은 "아니다."이다.

① 대학생들: 지금과 그때
② 유전의 연구: 작은 것이 더 낫다?
③ 심리학 연구에서의 표본 선정 오류
④ 심리학과의 대학생들: 너무 많다?
⑤ 대학생들과 나이가 더 많은 어른들의 생각 패턴

주 제) 심리학 표본의 높은 대학생 비중

정답 해설) '심리학 분야의 여러 연구는 표본의 보편성이 부족
하다'는 내용의 글이다. 이를 가장 잘 표현한 제목은 ③이라 할
수 있다.

어 휘) sophomore 대학 2학년생 article 기사, 상품, 연구 논
문 dictate ~하게 하다, 받아쓰게 하다

13 ⑤ 인도에서는 10월 말에 새해 축하행사에서 음식
이 아니라 맛의 균형에 초점을 둔다고 Classic
Indian Cooking의 저자 Julie Sahni는 말한다. 쌀가루 반
죽과, 코코넛, 우유 그리고 일종의 야자나무 수액으로 만
들어진 전통 빵인 Appam은 사탕인 barifi와 함께 제공된
다. 두 가지 모두 행운이 있는 삶에 대한 기원의 상징이다.
그러나 Sahni는 새해의 향연에는 달콤한 맛, 시큼한 맛, 매
운 맛을 포함해야 하기 때문에(숙취에 좋은 것으로 알려진)
mulligatawny 수프와 달고 매운 녹색 망고 처트니처럼 다
른 음식들도 제공되는 것이 특징이다. Sahni는 "이 생각은

삶이 쾌락과 고통의 많은 요소를 가지고 올 것이고, 당신이 기분 좋게 모든 것을 받아 들여야 한다는 희망과 함께 당신의 입에 많은 맛을 주는 무언가를 제공하기 위함이다."라고 말했다.

---

① 전통적인 인도 음식의 레시피
② 인도에서의 신년 의식
③ 건강에 대한 음식의 관계
④ 인도에서의 즐거움과 괴로움의 요소
⑤ 인도에서의 행운과 지혜를 위한 식품

주 제 인도 새해 축하 행사에서 행운과 지혜를 상징하는 음식들

정답 해설 인도의 신년 행사 때 여러 가지 맛이 나는 음식을 먹어야 하는 이유를 설명하고 있다. 이 음식의 여러 맛들은 기쁨과 슬픔이 혼재한 삶에 행운이 깃들길 바라며 지혜를 알려준다는 교훈적인 글이다. 따라서 글의 제목으로 ⑤가 가장 적절하다.

어 휘 celebration 기념행사, 기념 fudge 물렁물렁한 캔디 mulligatawny 카레가 든 스프 chutney 인도의 달콤하고 매운 양념 hangover 숙취 savory 맛 좋은, 향기로운

14 ③ Mr. Halle은 사람들이 자신의 주머니를 털어서, 생물체 중 더욱 불쾌한 말썽을 피우는 동물들을 구하도록 하는 것이 어려웠다고 인정했다. "우리가 논거를 찾는데 어려움을 겪고 있는 수많은 종들이 있다."고 그가 말했다. "또한 환경 운동가들에게 불명예가 되는 것들 중 하나는, 어떤 특정한 종을 지나치게 고집하는 것이다. 예를 들면, California Condor를 보호하기 위하여 사용된 수백만 달러는 내가 더 잘 쓰일 수도 있었다고 생각한다. 그럼에도 불구하고 Mr. Halle은 유전적인 다양성이 중요하고 사람들은 어떤 종은 멸종 위기에 처해서 사라지도록 방치하기 전에 넓은 결과에 대해 신중하게 생각한다고 말했다. 모든 것은, 아무리 역겹더라도 뭔가 다른 종의 점심이다. Jonathan Swift는 "벼룩은 자신에게 더 작은 벼룩이 먹잇감인데 그것들을 그들을 물 더 작은 것들이 있으며 이들은 여전히 물리면서 무한히 진행된다."고 말했다. 따라서 존재의 대 사슬이라 불렸던 것으로부터 어떤 식물이나 동물을 잃는 것이라도 수많은 종류의 예기치 못한 결과를 가져올 수 있다.

---

① 멸종 위기 종의 다양한 종류
② 캘리포니아 콘도르를 유지하는 방법
③ 생물 다양성의 유지
④ 환경 운동가의 접근 방식의 문제
⑤ 불편한 동물을 지키는 방법

주 제 생물 다양성 유지의 중요성

정답 해설 어떤 종은 보호하고, 어떤 종은 멸종 위기에 처해 사라지도록 방치하기 전에 한 종이 다른 종의 먹이가 될 수 있으며 존재의 대 사슬에서 한 종이 없어지는 것이 예기치 못한 결과를 가져올 수 있음을 생각해야 한다고 말하고 있다. 따라서 이 글의 제목으로 가장 적절한 것은 ③ '생물 다양성의 유지'이다.

어 휘 dig into one's pocket 자기 돈을 내다 disgusting 역겨운, 혐오스러운 varmint 해충, 해로운 것 flea 벼룩 hath have의 고어 ad infinitum (라틴어에서) 무한히, 끝없이 unforeseen 예상치 못한 do A credit A를 자랑스럽게 하다

15 ① 학생들이 내용을 완벽하게 해석하고, 심지어 유창하게 읽을 수 있게 되어도 그들은 진정으로 그 자료를 이해하지 못한다. 그들이 행간의 의미를 이해하지 못하고 의미를 추론하지 못하며 혹은 다른 것들 사이에서 작가의 성향을 파악하지 못한다면 말이다. 독서는 단순히 음소 인지와 알파벳 인식에 통달하는 것보다 훨씬 복잡하다. 독서란 믿을 수 없을 만큼 복잡한 심리 언어학적 활동으로 문자의 발음뿐만 아니라 모든 측면에서의 이해를 포함하고 다양한 목적과 문학 감상, 그리고 무엇보다도 중요하게, 평생 동안의 진실한 응용에 적용하는 일이다. 또한 독서는 기술을 요구한다. 내가 즐거움을 위해 이것을 읽는 것인가, 아니면 시험을 준비하기 위해 읽는 것인가? 마지막으로 만약 학생이 관심이 없거나 참여 동기를 부여받지 못한 경우 또는 그 경험을 즐겁게 여기지 않을 때, 이러한 완전한 지식들도 거의 이용되지 않을 것이다. 독서는 어려운 작업이고 많은 집중력과 에너지를 필요로 한다. 그것이 아이들에게 재미있게 보이지 않으면 관심을 유지하기 어렵다.

---

① 단순한 해독이 아닌 복잡한 활동으로서의 독서
② 암호화와 해독 사이의 미묘한 균형을 유지하는 것
③ 행간을 읽다가 함정에 빠짐
④ 독서 기술을 가르치기 위한 경험적 접근
⑤ 학습 경험의 즐거움과 어려움

주 제 복합적 활동인 독서

정답 해설 독서는 단순한 읽기가 아니라 다양한 목적에 따른 읽기 기술, 여러 측면에서의 이해와 삶에 대한 적용을 포함하는 매우 복잡한 활동이라는 내용의 글이다. 따라서 글의 제목으로는 ①이 가장 적절하다.

어 휘 decode 해석하다 fluent 유창한 comprehend 이해하다 infer 추론하다 detect 파악하다 bias 편견 complex 복잡한 phonemic awareness 음소론적 이해 recognition 인지, 인식 incredibly 놀라울 정도로 psycholinguistic 심리언어학적인 involve 관련하다 facet 면, 양상 adjust 조절하다 motivate 자극

을 주다 concentration 집중 sustain 유지하다

16 ② 캐나다에 있는 작은 광산 마을인 'Flin Flon'에서는 추위 때문에 정원이 오래가지 못한다. 하지만 현재 광산 마을의 주민들은 1년 내내 신선한 과일과 장미를 즐긴다. 그 풍부함은 지표면에서 1,770피트 아래에 있는 구리와 아연 광산의 텅 빈 공간이었던 곳에서 자란다. 이 실험은 지하 정원의 품질, 생산량과 비용을 시험하기 위해 Prairie Plant Systems 사의 Wayne Fraser와 Brent Zettle에 의해 고안되었다. Zettle은 "그 공간은 지면으로부터 완벽하게 고립되어 있어서 그 공간의 환경은 저렴하고 정확하게 제어될 수 있다."라고 말한다. 그 광산에는 높은 강도의 조명과 물방울 관개시설 및 컴퓨터가 설치되어 있다. "목본 식물이 놀라운 속도로 우거지게 성장한다." 라고 Zettle은 강조한다. 심은 지 석 달 후, 80그루의 장미 나무가 평균적인 700송이 대신에 1,100송이를 생산했다. 이 결과물들은 지역 시장에서 판매되고 있다. 광부들은 큰 자부심을 갖고 있다.

① 광산의 어두운 측면
② 광산의 깊은 곳에서 핀 장미
③ 한기 속에서의 따뜻한 마음
④ 야생화에 대한 광부의 사랑
⑤ 광부를 위한 번영하는 현지 시장

주 제 지하 광산 정원의 성공

정답 해설 방치되었던 광산의 지하에 장미를 심어 생산 판매하여 수익성이 좋다는 내용의 글이다. 따라서 제목으로는 ②가 가장 적절하다.

어 휘 prosperous 번창한 chill 추위, 한기 mining town 탄광촌 resident 주민 drip 액체가 똑똑 떨어지다 woody plant 목본 식물 chamber 방, 실내 공간 bounty 축하금, 너그러움, 풍부함 subterranean 지하의, 땅속의 zinc 아연 phenomenal 놀라운, 경이로운 irrigation 관개, 관개시설

17 ⑤ 추천서는 업무 수행 능력에 대한 가장 정확하지 못한 예측요소 중 하나일 뿐이다. 어떤 사람들은 심지어 기준과 역의 관계를 가진 추천을 하기도 한다. 즉, 지원자가 고용되도록 추천 받았다면 회사는 최선을 다해 그 지원자를 거절하는 것이다! 추천서의 가장 큰 문제 중 하나는 그것의 제한된 범위이다. 당신이 예상하듯 당연히 대부분의 추천장은 긍정적이다. 대개 추천장을 써줄 사람은 지원자가 선택한다. 그래서 자신을 훌륭하게 보여줄 사람을 선택하는 것은 놀라운 일이 아니다. 이러한 제약 때문에 추천서의

역량 예측 부족은 전혀 예상 밖의 일이 아니다.

① 개인 채용의 변호 전략
② 추천서 잘 쓰는 방법
③ 좋은 추천서의 특징
④ 추천서의 의도적인 속임수
⑤ 추천서의 제약

주 제 역량 예측에서 추천서의 한계

정답 해설 추천서가 실제 지원자의 업무 수행 능력을 보장해 줄 수 없다는 내용을 설명하고 있다. 추천서는 지원자에 대해 좋은 이야기만 늘어놓기 때문이다. 따라서 ⑤가 이 글의 제목으로 타당하다.

어 휘 criterion 판단 기준, 표준 predictive 예언하는, 예언적인

18 ① Charlotte Church는 십대처럼 보이지만 그녀는 보통의 십대와는 거리가 멀다. 그녀는 놀라운 목소리를 가지고 있다. 그녀의 팬들은 그녀의 콘서트 입장권을 구하기 위해 몇 시간 동안 줄을 서서 기다린다. 그녀의 가수 경력은 TV 쇼에 출연했던 11살 때부터 시작됐다. 레코드 회사 사장은 그녀의 노래하는 목소리에 매우 감명 받아 바로 그 자리에서 계약을 했다. 그녀의 첫 앨범은 1위로 떠올랐다. 그녀는 여전히 갈 수 있을 때 학교를 간다. 하지만 그녀는 종종 한 번에 몇 주씩 걸리는 투어를 떠난다. 그래도 그녀는 개인 교사를 동반하기 때문에 학업에 뒤처지지 않는다. 그녀는 매일 아침 3시간씩 개인 교사와 공부를 한다. 하지만 그녀는 어떻게 이런 특별한 생활을 감당할 수 있을까? 그녀는 친구들이 전과 다름없다고 주장한다. 그것은 사실일지도 모르지만 사람들이 그녀를 막아 세우고 사인을 요청하기 때문에 더 이상 친구들과 시내에 갈 수 없다. 대부분의 유명 스타들처럼 그녀도 이러한 제약들을 참고 사는 법을 배워야 한다.

① 유명세에 대한 대가
② 위험에 처한 10대 스타
③ 10대 소녀와 그녀의 공적인 생활
④ 여기서 그녀는 얼마나 멀리 갈 수 있을까?
⑤ 슈퍼스타의 숨은 매력

주 제 유명 십대 스타의 고충

정답 해설 이 글은 십대 유명 가수가 겪는 어려움을 묘사한 글이다. 그녀의 유명세 때문에 학업에 뒤처지지 않기 위해 투어마다 개인교사를 동반하고, 친구들과 시내에 평범하게 놀러가지 못한다. 이로 보아 ① '유명세에 대한 대가'가 글의 제목으로 알맞다.

19 ②
아이를 양육하는 동안에 거의 모든 부모들은 아이의 발달에 관한 어떤 '사실'들에 대해 우연히 발견해 왔다고 믿는다. 그들의 발견은 그 분야의 전문가들이 실시한 수많은 연구에 의해 확실히 뒷받침될 수 있었다. 아이들의 초기 신체적 발달은 거의 표준적인 모습을 제공한 체계적 관찰의 영역이다. 만약 아이의 성장이 그 기준을 따르지 않는다 해도, 개인차가 나타날 수 있기 마련이므로 문제가 있음을 의미하지는 않는다. 그러나 어떤 연령대의 집단 내에서 아이들은 특정 능력을 공통적으로 보이거나 유사한 방식으로 행동을 많이 한다. 자신의 아이와 동갑인 다른 아이와의 극단적인 차이는 발달 장애를 의미하는 것일 수도 있다. 그래서 성장 기준은 부모가 언제 전문가의 도움과 조언을 구해야 하는지 알게 한다.

① 아이들 사이에서 극단적인 차이가 생기는 이유가 무엇인가?
② 초기 발달 기준의 유용성
③ 갓난아기에 대해 전문가의 조언을 구할 때
④ 아이들이 언어를 배우는 방식에 대한 어머니들의 우려
⑤ 어머니들은 자신의 아이들에 대한 도움을 누구에게 청해야 할까?

주 제 초기 신체 발달 표준의 유용성
정답 해설 아이들의 초기 성장에서 '성장 기준'이 갖는 유용함에 대해 설명하는 글이다. 이 기준에 따라 아이의 발달이 빠른지 늦은지 판단하여 전문가와 상담할 수 있을 것이라는 내용이다. 따라서 ②가 적절하다.
어 휘 possibly 어쩌면, 아마도 not necessarily 항상 ~하는 것은 아닌 emerge 출현하다, 나타나다 conform 따르다, 순응하다 stumble 넘어지다, 비틀거리다

20 ④
정부 기관의 컴퓨터 디스크 분실을 포함하여 일련의 세간의 이목을 끈 사건은 경찰력으로 하여금 그들이 기밀 정보를 전달하는 방식을 다시 생각해 보게 했다. 런던 경찰은 시스템을 더 복잡하게 만들지 않고 더 안전하게 만드는 창의적인 소프트웨어로 그 문제를 이미 해결했다. DeviceStick은 관계자들에게 특별히 고안된 USB에만 정보를 내려 받도록 허용하는데, 그 USB는 정확한 지문과 암호가 있어야 이용할 수 있다. 그 시스템은 또한 경찰력이 컴퓨터 시스템에 누가, 언제 접근했는지를 추적

할 수 있도록 한다. 런던 경찰의 정보 관리 책임자인 Gary Brailsford-Hart는 장치를 분실하는 경우에도 "어느 누구라도 그 정보에 접근하는 것은 사실상 불가능하다."라고 말했다.

① 경찰력에 의해 개발된 기술
② 정보 이용을 위해 고안된 기술
③ 범죄에 대한 투쟁을 위해 사용된 기술
④ 기밀 정보를 보호하기 위한 기술
⑤ 컴퓨터 디스크 분실을 예방하기 위한 기술

주 제 기밀 정보 보호를 위한 런던 경찰의 기술
정답 해설 기밀 정보를 보호 문제를 해결한 사례로 런던 경찰의 특수한 USB를 들고 있다. 정확한 지문과 암호가 있어야 이 USB에 정보를 내려받을 수 있고, USB를 분실하는 경우에도 타인이 정보에 접근하는 것이 불가능하다고 설명하고 있다. 따라서 ④ '기밀 정보를 보호하기 위한 기술'이 글의 제목으로 가장 적절하다.
어 휘 high-profile 세간의 이목을 끄는 confidential 기밀의 secure 안전한 complicated 복잡한 access 이용하다 fingerprint 지문 virtually 사실상, 실질적으로

More Practice

01 ①　　02 ④　　03 ①　　04 ①

01 ①
사람들은 무의식적으로 자신의 비언어적인 행동의 불일치를 통해 그들이 거짓말을 하고 있다는 신호를 보낸다. 거짓말을 하는 누군가를 붙잡은 적이 있다면, 대화의 말미에서 한 진술은 대화의 초반부의 진술과 모순되거나 아마도 그나 그녀가 말한 단어와 몸짓이 모순되는 것처럼 보였을 것이다. 그 사람은 차분하고 초연한 듯 행동했을지 모르지만 동시에 자신의 발을 계속해서 두드리고, 단추나 보석을 만지작거리고, 더 높은 톤으로 말할 것이다. 법정에서의 증언에 대한 사람들의 인식 실험은 틀에 박힌 거짓된 행동이 꼭 의심을 불러일으키는 것은 아님을 보여주지만, 일관성 없는 비언어적인 행동은 수행되는 특정 행동에 관계없이 종종 기만적이라고 해석된다. 연구에 따르면 사람의 전형적인 비언어적 행동에 대한 친숙함은 속임수를 쉽게 발견할 수 있게 한다. 특히 사람들은 상대방의 진실된 행동에 대한 이전의 경험이 있을 때 상대방이 진실을 말하고 있는지 거짓말하는지 더 잘 알 수 있다.

① 기만을 나타내는 행동의 패턴

② 기만으로 이끄는 심리적 요인
③ 비언어적 메시지의 공통된 특성
④ 기만적이지 않은 강한 관계의 형성
⑤ 사람들의 진실과 기만의 부정확한 평가

주 제 거짓과 비언어적인 행동
정답 해설 거짓말을 할 때의 언어적인 신호에 대한 언급과 함께 비언어적인 행동 양상도 보여주는 글이다. 따라서 이 글의 제목으로 가장 적절한 것은 ①번이 된다.
어 휘 inconsistency 불일치 contradict 반박하다, 모순되다 testimony 증언 deception 기만

02 ④ 우리는 매일 이를 닦는 것에 익숙하다. 우리는 그것이 치아와 잇몸을 보호하고 우리가 편하게 미소를 짓도록 하는 건강에 유익한 의식이라고 알고 있다. 그것의 이점은 사회적일 뿐만 아니라 개인적이기도 한 것이다. 하지만 18세기 Annapolis — 새로운 계층의 사람들이 일자리를 찾으려고 애썼던 곳 — 의 유적지를 다루는 고고학자들은 어떻게, 그리고 왜 우리 모두 이렇게 양치질을 하고, 치실을 사용하며 법석을 떠는지에 대한 새로운 관점을 제시했다. Mark Leone과 그의 도시 고고학자 팀은 Annapolis의 도로 아래에서 수많은 칫솔을 발견했다. 18세기 칫솔은 개인 위생에 대한 새로운 강조와 스스로 관리하는 개인의 개념을 시사한다. 그것은 중요하다. 근로자들이 제시간에 도착해서 일을 하게 하려면 그들 사이에 규율이 생겨나야 한다. 따라서 산업 사회는 칫솔, 그리고 빗이나 시계와 같은 많은 다른 것들을 강조하여 사람들이 스스로를 정돈하는 일을 돕기에 이른다. 칫솔은 우리를 산업혁명 체제 안으로 손쉽게 편입되도록 하는 도구적 기능을 한 것으로 드러났다.

① Annapolis: 고고학의 웅장한 명소
② 영어에서 '칫솔'이라는 단어의 출현
③ 칫솔이 치아 관리 산업에 미친 영향
④ 산업 노동력을 발전시키는 데 기여한 칫솔의 역할
⑤ 산업혁명이 가져온 경제 변화

주 제 산업혁명 시기에 칫솔이 가졌던 기능
정답 해설 이 글은 칫솔질이 치아와 잇몸을 보호하는 건강 차원의 행위라는 기존의 해석과는 다른 관점을 소개하고 있다. 18세기 산업혁명 시기의 노동자들이 질서와 자기 관리의 필요에 부응하여 자연스럽게 산업 사회의 노동력으로 편입되도록 도구적인 기능을 하였다는 것이 이 글의 요지이다. 따라서 이 글의 제목으로는 ④가 가장 적절하다.
어 휘 be accustomed to ~에 익숙하다 ritual 의식 gum

잇몸 archaeologist 고고학자 flossing 치실 사용하기 hygiene 위생 self-maintained 자기 관리되는 comb 빗 orderly 질서 있는, 정연한

03 ① 음 높이의 명칭은 특정한 진동수와 관련이 있다. 현재 체계는 A440이라고 불리는데, 우리가 A라고 부르는, 피아노 건반의 가운데에 있는 음이 440 Hz의 진동수를 가지도록 고정되어 있기 때문이다. 이것은 전적으로 자의적이다. 가령 439나 424처럼 어떤 진동수에도 'A'를 고정할 수 있었고, 모차르트가 살았던 시대에는 오늘날과는 다른 기준이 사용되었다. 어떤 이들은 정확한 진동수가 악곡의 전반적인 소리와 악기의 소리에 영향을 끼친다고 주장한다. 70년대에 인기 있었던 밴드 Led Zeppelin은 종종, 그들의 음악에 독특한 소리를 주고, 아마도 자신들의 음악을 그들의 많은 곡에 영감을 준 유럽의 민속 동요와 연결하기 위해 현대의 A440 표준에서 벗어나도록 그들의 악기를 조율했다. 많은 순수주의자들은 시대 악기로 바로크 음악을 들어야 한다고 주장하는데, 그 악기가 다른 소리를 지니고 있기 때문이고 그 악기들이 원래의 조율 기준, 즉 순수주의자들이 중요하다고 여기는 것으로 음악을 연주하도록 설계되어 있기 때문이다.

① 'A'가 늘 440Hz에 맞춰져야 하는가?
② 자의적인 음 조율: 음악에서의 새로운 경향
③ 진동수 값을 바르게 측정하는 방법
④ 음악가들은 어떻게 음 높이 차이를 찾아내는가?
⑤ 불안정한 음 높이: 음악의 공통된 맥락

주 제 음의 진동수 기준의 자의성
정답 해설 현대에 음높이 표준으로 사용되는 A가 440Hz의 진동수에 고정되어 있는데 이것은 전적으로 자의적이라서 얼마든지 다른 진동수로 A를 고정할 수 있다고 말하고 있으므로, 글의 제목으로는 ①이 가장 적절하다.
어 휘 pitch 음 높이 frequency value 진동수, 주파수 note 음 arbitrary 자의적인 precise 정밀한 overall 전반적인 tune 음을 맞추다 uncommon 흔하지 않은 inspire 영감을 주다 composition 작품, 작곡 purist 순수주의자 period instrument 시대 악기 deem 여기다

04 ① 우리가 놀라서 누군가에게 그 사람의 실제 나이에 비해 "젊어 보인다"라고 말할 때, 우리는 우리가 모두 서로 다른 속도로 생물학적으로 노화한다는 것을 관찰하고 있다. 과학자들은 이 겉으로 보이는 차이가 실제

한다는 좋은 증거를 가지고 있다. 나이의 변화는 몸의 다른 부분에서 다른 시간에 시작되고 연간 변화 속도는 사람에 따라서 뿐만 아니라 다양한 세포, 조직, 기관 사이에서도 달라지는 것으로 보인다. 시간의 경과와 달리 생물학적 노화는 간편한 측정이 어렵다. 우리가 갖고자 하는 것은, 예컨대, 우리가 실제 나이가 80세인 어떤 사람이 생물학적으로는 60세라고 말할 수 있게 하는, 시간의 경과와 관계없이 다른 모든 생물학적 노화를 반영하는 한두 가지의 측정 가능한 생물학적 변화이다. 이런 종류의 측정기준은 어째서 어떤 80세의 사람이 생물학적으로 80세 또는 90세에 이르는 다른 80세의 사람들 보다 그렇게 더 많은 젊음의 특성을 가지는지를 설명하는 데 도움을 줄 것이다.

① 생물학적 노화를 비추는 거울을 찾아
② 현대의 느린 노화의 까닭
③ 실제 나이를 추측하는 몇 가지 요령
④ 밝혀진 생물학적 노화의 비밀
⑤ 젊음의 샘 찾기

주 제 생물학적 노화 측정 기준의 필요성

정답 해설 생물학적 노화가 그 다양성으로 인해 측정하기 어려우며 실제 나이와 생물학적 나이의 차이를 설명하기 위해 생물학적 노화를 반영하는 측정기준이 필요하다는 내용이므로, 글의 제목으로는 ①이 가장 적절하다.

어 휘 chronological age 생활 연령, 실제 나이 biologically 생물학적으로 rate 속도, 비율 apparent 외관상의 분명한 annual 매년의, 연례의 tissue 조직 organ 기관, 장기 mirror 반영하다 without reference to ~에 관계없이 quality 특성, 품질

UNIT 04 목적

Example
답 ②

당신의 강아지나 고양이가 행복한 잠에 빠져 몸을 말고 있는 것을 보는 것보다 더한 기쁨이 무엇이겠는가? 두 동물 모두 하루의 거의 절반을 어떤 형태로든 잠을 자는 데 쓴다. 그러나 그 모두가 편안한 것은 아니다. 근육이나 관절의 문제가 있는 나이 든 동물들이나 매우 활달한 강아지들은 자주 서성거리거나 움직일 것이다. 만약 당신의 애완동물이 이 경우들 중 하나에 해당한다면 치료 침대가 도움이 될 수도 있다. 이 전문화된 제품은 일반 침대나 즉석에서 고른 잠자리와는 다르게 지탱함과 편안함을 제공한다. 나이와 건강에 관계없이, 좋은 침대는 근육과 골격의 건강을 증진시키고 추가적인 활기와 치유의 이점을 제공한다.

① 가축 학대를 예방하기 위해
② 전문화된 애완동물 가구를 홍보하기 위해
③ 좋은 수면의 이점을 설명하기 위해
④ 애완동물 주인들에게 가구의 위험성을 알리기 위해
⑤ 애완동물의 나쁜 습관에 대해 주인들에게 경고하기 위해

주 제 애완동물 치료용 침대 홍보

Practice

01 ④   02 ⑤   03 ⑤

01 ④ 예술사에서 정확한 시대의 경계를 세우는 것은 어렵다. 하지만 입체파의 경우, 그 흐름이 1906년 말 Picasso가 생각해 낸 뒤, 이어지는 해에 그대로 방치돼 있었던 '아비뇽의 여자들'로 예고되었다고 말할 수 있다. 그것은 오늘날 충격적이고 참신한 화법이다. 60년 전, 그것은 아주 터무니없어 보였음에 틀림없다. 그것은 Picasso의 가장 우호적인 지지자들조차 명백히 실망하고 당황하게 만들었다. 지적이고 개방적인 젊은 화가 Braque는 그것을 처음 보고 진심으로 경악했다. 하지만 몇 달 후 그의 위대한 '목욕하는 여인들'은 '아비뇽의 여자들'이 그의 예술적 진화의 경로 전체를 바꿔 놓았다는 것을 증명한다.

주 제 입체파의 시작을 알린 Picasso의 작품

정답 해설 입체파는 예술사에서 예외적으로 사조의 등장 시점을 확정할 수 있다는 점을 지적하고 사조의 시작을 알린 Picasso의 작품이 입체파 등장에 어떻게 작용했는지 설명하는 글이므로, 이 글의 목적으로는 ④ '미술사에서의 입체파의 등장

소개'가 가장 적절하다.

어 휘 Cubism 입체파 usher in ~의 예고가 되다, ~의 도래를 알리다 conceive 상상하다 disturbing 충격적인, 불안한 daring 대담한, 참신한 painting 그림, 화법 nothing short of 아주 ~한, ~와 다름없는 dismay 실망시키다 baffle 당황시키다

02 ⑤ 이 현대적 카우보이 이야기는 1949년을 배경으로 한다. 이것은 텍사스를 떠나 멕시코 북부로 말 등에 올라 거침없이 달리는 세 젊은 남자를 따라간다. 그들의 모험은 20세기 미국에서 그들을 꺼내 완전히 다른 세계에 데려다 놓는데, 그곳에서는 말, 자연과 더불어 사는 것이 아직 가능하다. 고전 영화에서처럼, 그곳에는 악인과 호인이 있지만, 그것은 단순한 John Wayne 영화의 재기록은 아니다. 등장인물들은 설득력 있고, 자연에 대한 묘사는 아주 뛰어나다. 문체는 야심차고, 액션으로 가득한 줄거리에 바탕을 둔 능란한 저술이 우리의 주의를 끝까지 잡아둔다. 우리는 이것만큼 만족스러운 2권을 기대한다.

① 스토리텔링 연습에 초대하기 위해
② 대학의 문학 수업을 소개하기 위해
③ 유명한 서부 영화에 대한 정보를 주기 위해
④ 새 영화를 광고하기 위해
⑤ 새 책의 비평을 제공하기 위해

주 제 현대적 카우보이 소설에 대한 서평
정답 해설 volume이라는 단어로 대상이 책이라는 것을 알 수 있고, 이야기의 차별성과 장점에 대해 평가하고 있으므로, 이 글의 목적으로는 ⑤ '새 책의 비평을 제공하기 위해'가 가장 적절하다

어 휘 convincing 설득력 있는 rewrite 다시 쓰다, 고쳐 쓰다 natural world 자연계 brilliant 눈부신, 뛰어난 masterful 능수능란한, 거장의 review 비평, 논평 volume 권(卷), 용적, 음량

03 ⑤ 나는 이 풍요로운 대륙에 접근한 우리의 초기 정착민들의 야만성과 경솔함에 놀랐다. 그들은 이곳이 마치 적국인 것처럼 왔고, 이곳은 물론 그랬다. 그들은 숲을 태우고 강수량을 변화시켰다. 그들은 평원의 버팔로를 휩쓸어갔고, 강줄기를 폭파했으며, 초원에 불을 놓고, 미답의 장엄한 산림을 난폭한 낫질로 모조리 베어냈다. 아마도 그들은 이곳이 무한하고 절대 고갈될 수 없으며, 인간은 끝없이 새로운 미지로 떠날 수 있는 곳이라고 느꼈을 것이다. 분명 반대의 사례도 많이 있지만 초기의 사람들은 대부분 그들이 이곳을 증오하고, 이곳을 일시적으로 가졌다가 언제

든 떠나게 될 것처럼 이 땅을 약탈했다.

① 초기 미국 정착자의 동기를 설명하기 위해
② 초기 개척자들의 거주지가 어떻게 만들어졌는지 기술하기 위해
③ 초기 정착민들이 자연 자원을 착취한 방식을 변호하기 위해
④ 초기 정착민들의 인디언에 대한 잔인한 대우를 비판하기 위해
⑤ 초기 정착민들이 그들 주변의 자연을 파괴한 이유와 방식을 기술하기 위해

주 제 초기 미 대륙 개척자들의 야만적 행동
정답 해설 초기 정착민들이 적국에 오듯이 대륙에 도착했고 실제로 그 대륙을 적국처럼 대했다고 말하며 초기 정착민들의 자연에 대한 폭력적인 행위를 비판적 어조로 서술하고 있으므로, 이 글의 목적으로는 ⑤ '초기 정착민들이 그들 주변의 자연을 파괴한 이유와 방식을 기술하기 위해'가 가장 적절하다.

어 휘 wonder 궁금해 하다, 놀라다 savagery 야만성 thoughtlessness 경솔함, 인정 없음 rainfall 강우, 강수량 run through ~을 다 써버리다, 낭비하다 reckless 무모한, 난폭한 scythe 큰 낫, 낫으로 베다 to a large extent 대단히, 주로 pillage 약탈하다 drive off 떠나다

More Practice

01 ②   02 ①   03 ③   04 ②

01 ② 이것처럼 큰 회사에서 일하는 것은 이상하게도 고립시키는 것일 수 있다. 만약 우리가 몇몇 운 좋은 동료처럼 밖에서 일한다면, 우리는 새로운 사람들을 만나고 돌아다니면서 활동적이 될 것이다. 하지만, 우리와 같은 사무직 종사자들은 차를 지하 주차장에 주차하고, 엘리베이터를 타고 하루 종일 일을 하는 구석 자리로 향하게 된다. 구내식당은 사람들이 모이는 장소가 되지만, 사람들은 같은 사무실과 같은 층의 사람들과 함께 앉는 경향이 있다. 나는 체력 단련장이 회사 내의 모든 다양한 부서와 사무실, 모든 다양한 연령대와 배경을 가진 직원들을 맺어줄 비공식적인 장소를 제공할 것이라고 생각한다. 만약 이 생각이 받아들여진다면 적당한 장소는 아마 현재 창고로 사용 중인 지하의 뒤쪽 방이나 거의 사용되지 않는 10층의 라운지가 될 것이라고 생각한다. 나는 이러한 투자가 우리의 건강뿐만 아니라 회사의 단합을 이루는 데 도움을 준다면 틀림없이 그럴 가치가 있을 거라고 믿는다.

회사 내 체력 단련장 신설 건의

대규모 회사에서 고립된 직장생활을 하는 사무직 노동자를 위해 운동 시설(gym)을 마련하여 다양한 부서와 연령과 배경의 직원들을 맺어 주는 비공식적 장소로 활용하자고 제안하고 있으므로, 글의 목적으로는 ②가 가장 적절하다.

oddly 이상하게 isolating 고립시키는 colleague 동료 work away 계속 일하다 cafeteria 회사 내 식당 bring together 결합하다, 맺어주다 personnel 직원 department 부서 suitable 적합한 basement 지하실 currently 현재 storage 저장 unity 단합

02 ① 제가 지난 회의에서 언급했듯이, 저는 당신이 Pacific Rim 시장을 포함한 우리의 사업을 확장하는 제안에 대해 한 달 가량의 타당성 조사를 수행해 주기를 바랍니다. 만약 결과가 긍정적인 경우 당신의 보고서는 이번 확장을 위한 재정 자원 확보를 위해 이사회에 제출될 것입니다. 현재 예산에 따라 일을 수행하고 있기 때문에 당신의 여행 경비는 빠듯할 것입니다. 그러나 당신이 신중한 선택을 할 것임을 알고 있습니다. 저는 이 문제에 대한 Neumann 보고서 한 부를 포함했습니다. 이것은 약간 구식이긴 하지만, 아마도 여전히 유용한 모델일 것입니다. 저는 주간 보고서를 기대하고 있으며 물론 늦어도 7월 14일까지 제출하기로 되어 있는 당신의 마지막 보고서도 기대하고 있습니다.

① 연구 조사 계획을 위임하기 위해
② 사적인 충고를 요청하기 위해
③ 특별한 회의를 알리기 위해
④ 공식 초대장을 만들기 위해
⑤ 재정적인 기부에 감사해 하기 위해

사업 확장을 위한 타당성 조사 의뢰

글의 서두에 필자는 상대방에게 사업을 확장하려는 계획에 관해 1개월 가량 타당성 조사를 수행하라고 요청하고 있으므로 ①이 알맞다.

feasibility 실행 가능성 feasibility study 타당성 조사 extend 늘이다, 확장하다 operation 사업 board of directors 이사회 secure 확보하다 financing 재정 allowance 수당, 용돈

03 ③ 당신의 한국어 글쓰기를 증진하고 싶습니까? 쓰기는 당신이 한국의 대학생활에 적응하도록 도와줄 기초적인 도구입니다. 하랑 글쓰기 센터는 우리 대학의 모든 외국인 학생들에게 열려 있는 무료 개인교습 프로그램을 제공합니다. 우리는 당신이 이것의 혜택을 보기를 권합니다. 이 프로그램은 외국인 학생 사이에서 인기가 항상 매우 좋았습니다. 등록은 11월 28일부터 3일 동안만 열립니다. 일단 등록하시면, 우리가 당신에게 완벽한 개인 교사를 연결하고 당신이 일정을 조정할 수 있도록 연락할 것입니다. 우리는 당신이 우리의 경험 많은 개인 교사들에 만족할 것이라 확신합니다. 당신의 한국어 글쓰기를 증진할 이 엄청난 기회를 놓치지 마세요. 더 많은 정보를 원하신다면, 부담없이 HRWC 담당자 윤지영에게, jyoon@hrwc.org로 이메일을 보내주세요.

외국인 학생의 한국어 글쓰기 교습 프로그램 등록 안내

하랑 글쓰기 센터의 한국어 글쓰기 교습의 장점을 설명하면서 외국인 학생에게 프로그램 등록을 권하고 안내하고 있으므로, 이 글의 목적으로는 ③이 가장 적절하다.

registration 등록 arrange 정하다 feel free to 거리낌 없이 ~하다

04 ② Johnson 코치님께.
저는 Bradley Markle의 엄마인 Christina Markle이라고 합니다. Bradley와 저는 당신이 당신의 여름 체조 캠프를 올해 다시 여신다는 소식을 듣고 기뻤습니다. 그래서 망설임 없이 등록하고 7월 13일부터 17일까지인 2주 차 프로그램의 환불 불가 보증금을 지불했습니다. 그런데 오늘 저는 우리 가족이 7월 13일에 여행에서 돌아온다는 것을 기억해 냈고, Bradley가 프로그램의 맨 첫날에 도착하지 못할 것 같습니다. 그날을 건너뛰게 하기보다, 혹시 그가 셋째 주 프로그램으로 변경할 수 있는지 확인하고 싶습니다. 가능하다면 저희에게 알려주세요. 감사합니다.
Christina Markle 드림.

Bradley의 체조 캠프 일정 조정 문의

Bradley가 체조 캠프의 둘째 주 프로그램에 등록했는데, 가족 여행 일정 때문에 첫날 출석이 어려워 셋째 주 프로그램으로 변경할 수 있을지 문의하고 있으므로, 이 글의 목적으로는 ②가 가장 적절하다.

gymnastics 체조 sign up 등록하다 non-refundable 환불이 안 되는 deposit 보증금

UNIT 05 어법

Example
답②

백악관 입법부 직원이 즉시 나를 마중 나왔고 나는 골드 룸으로 안내받았는데, 그곳에는 이미 새로 당선된 대부분의 하원과 상원 의원들이 모여 있었다. 16시 정각, 활기차고 건강해 보이는 부시대통령이 호명되어, 그가 예정대로 움직이고 있으며, 우회를 최소화하고 싶어함을 보여주는 그 경쾌하고 단호한 걸음으로 단상에 올랐다. 10분 남짓 그는 농담을 하고 나라가 협력해야 한다는 것을 요구하며 방에 있는 사람들과 이야기를 한 뒤 우리를 백악관 반대편으로 초대하여 다과를 즐기고 그와 영부인과 함께 사진을 찍자고 하였다.

주 제 | 백악관에 초대 받은 경험

Practice

01 ⑤	02 ⑤	03 ④	04 ②	05 ②
06 ④	07 ④	08 ⑤	09 ②	10 ②
11 ③	12 ④	13 ④	14 ①	15 ①
16 ②	17 ②	18 ①	19 ③	20 ①
21 ②	22 ⑤	23 ②	24 ②	25 ⑤
26 ⑤	27 ⑤	28 ②	29 ②	30 ②
31 ⑤	32 ③	33 ④	34 ⑤	35 ④

01 ⑤ San Francisco Giants의 투수인 Ryan Vogelsong과 그의 아내 Nicole은 그들의 아파트 옥상에서 미국의 독립기념일 불꽃놀이를 보았는데, 그곳에서는 Bay Bridge, Alcatraz Island와 Coit Tower 같은 랜드마크의 장관을 볼 수 있다. 또한 그곳은 그가 부평초 같은 직종에서 적어도 지금까지는 믿을 수 없이 좋은 자리인 올스타팀의 내셔널리그에 선발되었을 때 샴페인 축배를 들었던 곳이기도 하다. San Francisco Chronicle은 최근에 그를 최우수 투수 상(사이 영 상)의 후보로 지명했다. 월드 시리즈 챔피언십에서 8-1의 기록과 2.23의 방어율을 가진 34세의 Vogelsong에게는 꿈만 같은 시즌이었다. 올해의 그의 업적이 야구에서 그가 이전에 보여줬던 것들을 무색하게 만들기는 하지만, 샌프란시스코, 피츠버그, 일본과 베네수엘라를

10개의 마이너 리그에 더해 거쳐 온 긴 여정의 고난 없이는 그것들이 가능하지 않았을 것이다.

주 제 | 긴 여정과 고난을 이겨낸 투수 Vogelsong의 영광
정답 해설 | ⑤가 포함된 문장은 without이 포함된 가정법 과거 완료 형태가 되어 '과거의 고난 없이는 최근의 업적을 세울 수 없었다'라고 해석되는 것이 문맥상 자연스럽다. 따라서 be는 have been으로 수정되어야 한다.

어 휘 | improbable 가능성이 없는 itinerant 떠돌아다니는 overshadow 무색하게 만들다 toil 고역 odyssey 긴 여정, 오랜 방랑

02 ⑤ 자연 상태에서 (발생하는) 비교의 부재는 루소에게 정말 중요하다. 지속적인 관계에서 분리되어 사는 생물은 사람들을 평가하는 마음을 발달시킬 수 없다고 주장함으로써 루소는 두 가지 위대한 결론을 도출한다. 첫째, 자연적인 불평등, 예를 들어 더 좋은 체력, 노래하기에 더 좋은 목소리, 더 높은 지능 같은 것은 우리가 우연히 갖게 된 자질이 타인의 눈으로 보기에 존경, 찬사, 부, 가치에 해당하는 것을 우리에게 가져다 줄 때에만 중요한 것이 된다. 두 번째 결론은 자연인이, 그리고 자연인만이 정직하다는 것이다. 사회에서는 우리는 항상 다른 사람들이 우리를 어떻게 생각하는지를 걱정한다. 우리는 우리에게 영광과 타인으로부터의 존경을 가져다 줄 일을 하는 데 동기부여가 된다. 이로써 나 자신에 대한 나의 감각은 다른 사람들이 나에 대해 갖는 인상으로부터 얻게 된다는 결론에 이르게 된다.

주 제 | 타인의 영향을 받는 스스로에 대한 감각
정답 해설 | 마지막 문장은 다른 사람들이 나에 대해 갖는 인상으로부터 나 자신에 대한 감각을 얻게 된다는 내용이어야 문맥상 자연스럽다. 'Other people have the impressions of me'에서 the impressions가 선행사가 되어 other people 앞으로 나오게 된 형태이므로 ⑤의 have me는 have of me로 수정되어야 적절하다.

어 휘 | sustain 살아가게 하다 derive A from B B에서 A를 얻다

03 ④ 에너지의 일상적인 흐름에서 중대한 차단은 분명히 육지 식물과 해양 유기체들의 성장이 그것들을 재활용하는 분해자들의 능력을 초과하였던 몇 백만 년 전에 발생했다. 에너지가 풍부한 유기물질의 축적하는 층은 위에서 누르는 지상의 압력에 의해 점차 석탄과 석유로 변하고 있었다. 그것들의 분자 구조에 저장된 에너지는 우리가

지금 태움으로써 배출할 수 있다. 그리고 우리의 현대 문명은 지구로부터 채굴되는 그러한 화석 연료에서 나오는 어마어마한 양의 에너지에 의존하고 있다. 화석 연료를 태우면서 우리는 마침내 저장된 에너지의 대부분을 열기로 환경에 내보내고 있다. 우리는 또한 상대적으로 매우 짧은 시간에 몇백만 년 동안 천천히 제거되었던 많은 양의 이산화탄소를 대기에 되돌려 보내고 있다.

주 제) 화석 연료 사용에 따른 에너지 과다 배출
정답 해설) fossil fuel은 채굴되는 대상이므로 ④ recovering이 아닌 recovered로 수정되어야 한다.
어 휘) decomposer 분해자 molecular 분자 release 배출하다 immense 거대한

04 ② 지구는 인간의 생명에 매우 중요한 자원을 많이 가지고 있다. 어떤 것들은 손쉽게 재생이 가능하고, 어떤 것들은 막대한 비용을 들여야만 재생이 가능하며, 어떤 것들은 아예 재생이 불가능하다. 지구는 그것들을 구성하는 성분의 역사뿐만 아니라 그것들이 어떻게 형성되었는지에 의해 그 속성이 결정되는 온갖 종류의 광물들로 구성되어 있다. 그들의 존재도 희소한 것에서부터 거의 무한대에 이른다. 그러나 그것들을 환경에서 채취해내는 것의 어려움은 그들의 풍부함만큼이나 중요한 문제이다. 매우 다양한 종류의 광물은 철, 알루미늄, 마그네슘, 구리와 같은 산업 물질에 필수적인 자원이다. 최고의 자원 중 많은 것들은 고갈되고 있어서 그 광물들을 얻기 점점 더 어렵게 하고 비용이 많이 들게 한다.

주 제) 자원 고갈에 따른 문제점
정답 해설) be composed of ~는 '~로 구성되다'라는 의미이다. 여기서 of는 생략될 수 없다. 따라서 ②의 which 앞에 of가 와야 한다.
어 휘) readily 손쉽게 renewable 재생 가능한 comprise 구성하다 extract 채취하다 abundance 풍부, (물리) 존재도 deplete 고갈시키다

05 ② 유럽 대륙에서 칸트는 자유주의의 공리주의적인 방어를 거부했지만, 선한 삶에 대한 자신의 개념을 자유롭게 선택하는 사람에게만 오는 자율성의 양립 가능한 경우를 제시했다. 동시대의 훔볼트의 저작에 영감을 받았다고 〈자유론〉의 권두 삽화에서 언급한 것처럼 밀은 독일의 다른 자유주의자들에게서 영감을 받았다. 그러나 독일과 앵글로-미국의 자유주의적 수렴의 이 순간은 곧 지나갔다. 헤

겔, 그 다음 마르크스와 함께, 독일의 지적인 사상은 자유주의적 사회를 특징짓기 위해 수용된 개인주의 윤리에서의 결함을 중점적으로 탐구했다. 칸트로부터 헤겔, 마르크스에 이르는 사상의 전달은 너무나 극적이어서 플라톤에서 아리스토텔레스, 아우구스티누스에 이르는 사상의 초기의 흐름에 필적한다.

주 제) 자유주의 사상의 변화
정답 해설) 분사구문으로서 ②는 being noted가 아니라 noting으로 수정되어야 한다.
어 휘) continent 대륙 utilitarian 공리주의의 liberalism 자유주의 autonomy 자율성, 자치 frontispiece 권두 삽화 contemporary 동시대의

06 ④ 나는 한 때 파푸아뉴기니의 연안 마을에 살았었다. 어린이들은 그들의 부모님들과 같이 살지 않았지만, 그들은 집에서 집으로 그들이 원하는 한 옮겨 다니며 살았다. 10살짜리 어린이들이 아기를 안고 다니거나 요리용 불을 돌보는 모습을 볼 수 있었다. 14살쯤 되면 그들은 신뢰와 자존심을 갖고 어른들의 일을 하였다. 이 마을에 있으면서 가장 새롭고 흥미로웠던 일은 12명 혹은 그 이상의 아이들이 우리 집 베란다에서 자는 일이었다. 나는 늦은 밤에 열대 지방성 설사가 왔을 때, 나는 카펫처럼 널브러진 작은 갈색 몸들 사이로 나올 길을 찾아 헤매야 했다. 이 때 문득 들었던 생각은 어차피 여기 마을 전체가 부모로서 해야 할 일과 그에 대한 기쁨을 공유하고 있기 때문에 여기는 부모가 되기에는 쉬운 장소일 거라는 것이다. 사실 여기에 살고 있는 어떠한 어른도 부모였다.

주 제) 모든 어른이 부모 역할을 하는 마을
정답 해설) ④ 지문의 경우 what 이후에 주어, 동사 그리고 목적어로 이루어진 완벽한 문장이 나오기 때문에 what은 that으로 수정되어야 한다.
어 휘) tend 돌보다, 보살피다 confidence 신뢰, 자신감 tropical diarrhea 열대성 설사 pleasure 기쁨

07 ④ 나는 부유한 집안에서 태어났지만 십대에 급격히 가난해져서, 자라면서 성공을 얻는 비밀보다 성공을 잃는 일에 대한 위험을 더 많이 알게 되었다. 비록 나의 부모님들은 중년의 나이에 들어서 잃었던 모든 걸 원상복귀시켰지만, 그들은 결코 부유한 사고 방식을 다시 갖지 못했다. 그리고 나는 그들의 성공보다 그들의 실패에 대한 두려움을 더 크게 받아들이게 되었다. 그런 두려움은 내가 금전

적으로 더 성공할 수 있도록 하는 동력이 되었고, 어떤 면에서는, 어떻게 하면 성취를 이룰 것인가에 대해 사람들을 가르치면서 생계를 유지하도록 나를 이끌었다. 나는 수천 명의 사업가와 운동선수들이 가치 있는 성공의 원리를 통해 자신들의 성공을 이룰 수 있도록 도와주는 동기부여 강사로 성장했다.

주제 가난에서 얻은 교훈으로 이룬 성공

정답 해설 ④에서 be 동사가 수식하는 주어는 fears라는 복수 형태의 명사이기 때문에 was가 아닌 were을 사용해야 한다.

어휘 peril 위험, 모험 attain 이르다, 도달하다 be stripped of 빼앗기다 prosperous 번영한, 번창한, 부유한 principle 원칙, 원리

---

08 ⑤ 보석과 관련된 신화나 전설들은 수없이 많다. 소유자에게 어떤 이들은 저주받은 보석에 대해 말하고, 다른 사람들은 특별한 치유력이 있거나 보호해주거나 소유자에게 행운을 가져다주는 보석이 있다고 이야기한다. 사람들에게 가장 잘 알려진 다이아몬드들의 전설은 몇 세기 동안 입에서 입으로 전해져 내려왔고, 현재는 없어진 몇몇은 음모와 살인에 대한 이야기로 둘러싸여있다. 몇몇의 탄광들의 경우 저주를 받았다고 여겨지는데, 아마도 탄광의 주인이 자신의 탄광을 반갑지 않은 탐광자들로부터 지키기 위해 퍼뜨린 루머일 수 있다. 예를 들어 탄광의 원석들은 전부 군주의 소유가 되었던 미얀마의 경우, 국가의 재산이 손실되는 것을 막기 위해 누군가가 탄광에서 원석을 가져가게 되면 그 당사자는 저주에 걸릴 것이라는 믿음이 의도적으로 키워졌을 것이다.

주제 보석에 관한 신화나 전설

정답 해설 ⑤의 경우 믿음을 의도적으로 키웠다는 문장이 되는데, 여기서 믿음은 스스로 커진 것이 아니라 사람들에 의해 커진 것이기 때문에 자동사가 아닌 타동사가 수동태로 사용되어야 한다. 그렇기 때문에 이 문장은 may have been deliberately cultivated이 되어야 한다.

어휘 myths 신화, 전설 intrigue 흥미를 불러일으키다, 음모 curse 저주하다 prospector 탐광자, 투기자 monarch 군주, 제왕 deliberately 일부러 cultivate 재배하다, 양식하다 curb 억제, 제어 asset 자산, 재산

---

09 ② 볼링은 식민지에서 매우 인기가 높았다. 최초에 그것은 Ninepins라고 불렸다. Ninepins는 사실

식민지 주민들에 의해 진행되던 몇몇 볼링 게임 중 하나였다. 또 다른 종류의 볼링은 플레이어가 좀 더 큰 공을 굴려서 잔디밭 위에 놓여 있는 상대적으로 작은 공에 최대한 가깝게 멈추는 것을 시도하는 게임이었다. 대상이 되는 공에 가장 가깝게 근접한 플레이어가 승리자가 되었다. 이러한 형태의 볼링은 오늘날 흙바닥 위에 그어진 선에 동전을 던지는 게임과 흡사하다. 동전 던지기에서는 동전이 선에 가장 가까운 플레이어가 게임에서 승리하게 된다.

주제 식민지에서 볼링의 인기와 경기 방법

정답 해설 ② attempted의 주체는 바로 앞의 players이다. 따라서 주체가 능동적으로 행위를 하는 것이므로, rolling과 마찬가지로 현재분사 형태인 attempting으로 표기하는 것이 적절하다. 목적 보어는 (동사 involved의 목적어가 players이므로) 행위의 주체가 능동일 경우에는 현재분사로, 수동일 경우에는 과거분사로 수식해 준다.

어휘 pitching pennies 동전 던지기

---

10 ② 다음에 당신이 소매점에 방문할 때에는, 그곳에서 가전제품을 팔든, 철물이나 자재 혹은 최신 유행 제품을 팔든, 멈춰 서서 주변에 대해 주의 깊게 생각해 보라. 상점의 배치와 진열에 대해 생각해 보라. 배경으로 들려오는 소리를 들어 보라. 냄새를 맡아 보라. 아마도 전체적인 배치와 조명에서부터 음악과 심지어는 냄새까지도 당신의 쇼핑 경험을 결정하는 데 도움을 주고, 당신의 지갑을 열기 위해 조직되어 있을 것이다. 대부분의 경우, 당신은 아마도 매우 미묘한 방법으로 자극을 받기에 당신은 심지어 당신에게 어떤 일이 일어나고 있는지도 알아차리지 못한다. 그렇기 때문에 일단 상점 안으로 들어가게 되면, 당신이 쇼핑객으로서 주변을 돌아보는 방식은 실제로는 당신에게 달려있지 않다. 다음에 상점에 방문하게 되면, 판매자들이 당신의 구매 활동에 영향을 끼치도록 해놓은 미묘한 것들을 알아챌 수 있는지 한 번 확인해 보라

주제 구매를 촉진하기 위해 설정된 환경

정답 해설 'Chances are (that) ~'은 '아마도 ~ 일 것이다, ~ 일 확률이 높다'라고 해석되며 that 다음에는 주어와 동사로 구성된 절이 온다. that 이후의 주어는 'everything ~ smells'인데 이때 주어는 조직되는 대상이므로 ②의 has orchestrated는 has been orchestrated로 수정되어야 한다.

어휘 retail store 소매점 consumer electronics 가전제품 hardware 철물 high fashion 최신 유행 (주로 옷) layout 배치 orchestrate (세밀하게, 은밀하게) 조직하다 chances are (that) 아마도 ~일 것이다 in and around ~의 주변에 spot 감지하다, 알아채다

11 ③ 좋은 화분에 대한 첫 번째 추천은 다음과 같다. 큰 것을 고려해라! 작은 용기들은 뿌리들이 잘 성장하기에는 너무 적은 양의 흙밖에 담을 수 없고, 물기를 유지하기 위해서 너무 많은 노력이 필요하다. 그러므로 용기는 크면 클수록 더 좋다. 유약 처리 되거나, 유리 섬유, 그리고 사출 성형 플라스틱 재질로 된 용기들이 유약 처리가 되지 않은 질그릇에 비해 더욱 수분을 잘 유지한다. 모양에 상관없이 물이 빠져나갈 구멍이 있는지 확인하고, 물이 빠져나갈 수 있도록 지면에서부터 1/2인치 정도 되는 높이로 화분을 올려두는 데는 화분 받침이나 쐐기 등을 이용하라. 유리 섬유나 플라스틱 재질의 화분은 극단적인 기후에서도 망가질 가능성이 적고, 옮기기도 쉽다. 하지만 무거운 재질의 용기는 키가 큰 식물들이 바람에 넘어지는 것을 방지할 수 있도록 토대를 제공한다. 상대적으로 가벼운 화분들은 기울어지는 현상이 일어나지 않도록 확실히 해 두어야 한다.

(주 제) 좋은 화분의 조건

(정답 해설) ③에서 '화분이 물이 빠져나갈 구멍을 가지고 있는지 확인하라'는 내용이 문맥상 자연스러우므로 be sure to pots to have는 be sure that pots have로 수정되어야 한다.

(어 휘) glaze (도자기에) 유약을 바르다 fiberglass 유리 섬유 molded-plastic 사출 성형된 플라스틱 terra-cotta 질그릇, 유약을 바르지 않은 토기 shim 쐐기, (틈을 메꾸는) 작은 조각 topple 넘어지다, 넘어뜨리다 tip 기울어지다

12 ④ 고통에 대해 무감각한 것은 위험한 것이다. 고통을 느끼는 (신경 세포의) 축색 돌기를 비활성화하는 유전자를 갖고 있는 사람은 반복되는 부상에서 고통을 당하고, 일반적으로는 위험을 피하는 방법을 배우지 못한다. 이러한 증세를 갖고 있는 한 소년은 파키스탄의 노상 공연장에서 나이프를 그의 팔에 찔러 넣거나 불타는 석탄 위를 걷는 등의 공연을 했다. 그는 14살 때 지붕에서 떨어져서 사망했다. 비록 우리가 고통을 아예 없애는 것은 바라지 않을지라도, 그럼에도 불구하고, 고통을 통제할 수 있는 것은 좋은 일일 것이다.

(주 제) 고통의 필요성

(정답 해설) 시기가 분명한 과거의 내용을 표현할 때에는 완료 시제를 사용할 수 없다. ④에는 at age 14라는 정확한 시기가 명시되었기 때문에 과거 시제를 사용해야 한다. 따라서 has died를 died로 고치는 것이 적절하다.

(어 휘) insensitivity 무감각, 둔감 axon (신경 세포의) 축색 돌기 thrust 밀다, 찌르다

13 ④ Menno Aden은 건축물과 공간에 대한 디자인이 미치는 영향력과 그곳에 거주하고 있는 사람들에 대해 매료되어 있었다. 그 41세의 예술가는 그의 고향인 베를린에서 각각의 이미지를 격자 모양과 사각 모자이크 이미지로 재배치하거나 때때로는 그것들을 영상물로 바꾸어가며 주거 단지의 외부와 회사 건물의 내부에 대해서 탐구해 왔다. 하지만 그의 최근 프로젝트의 영감은 그가 의자 위에 서서 카메라를 아래로 향하고 그의 식사를 찍은 음식에 대한 사진 일기에서 받았다. 이러한 관점은 음식보다도 공간에 대해 더욱 많은 강조를 두고 있었다. 그리고 그는 그가 방 전체를 볼 수 있는 높은 곳에서의 조망이 가능한지에 대해 궁금해했다.

(주 제) Menno Aden의 공간 탐구

(정답 해설) ④의 which 다음에 주어, 동사, 목적어를 갖춘 완전한 문장이 왔으므로 목적격 관계대명사나 주격 관계대명사인 which는 이 자리에 적절하지 않다.

(어 휘) residential developments 주거 단지, 택지 개발 grid 격자, 격자무늬 panel 패널, 네모꼴의 물건 mosaic 모자이크 transpose 바꾸어 놓다, 옮기다 overhead 머리 위에, 높이

14 ① 환경보호를 목적으로 지역 토지의 이용 통제를 하는 것에 있어서 가장 논쟁이 되는 화두 중 하나는 바로 "취득"의 문제이다. 미국 헌법의 5차 개정판에는 다음과 같은 내용이 포함되어 있다. "그 누구도 적법한 법적 절차 없이는 삶, 자유, 재산을 빼앗겨서는 안 된다. 또한 개인의 재산은 적절한 보상 없이는 공공의 목적을 위해 빼앗겨서는 안 된다." 이 조항은 국가에게 국민의 사적 재산을 취득할 수 있는 권한을 부여했지만, 그것은 오직 공공의 목적을 위할 때여야 하고 주인이 합당한 보상을 받았을 때에만 가능하다. 토지는 물리적으로 취득하는 것이 가능하고 (예를 들면 공공 공원과 고속도로를 위해) 가장 중요한 문제는 보상이 얼마나 이루어져야만 하는지에 대한 것을 핵심으로 한다.

(주 제) 환경 보호를 위한 토지 취득 문제

(정답 해설) ① 다음에 오는 issue는 논쟁의 대상이므로 contesting은 contested로 수정되는 것이 적절하다.

(어 휘) contest 논쟁하다, 겨루다, 다투다 land-use control 국토계획안, 토지이용 통제 be deprived of ~을 빼앗기다, 약탈당하다 compensation 보상 revolve around ~을 중심으로 돌다, 핵심으로 하다

15 ①　Julie의 대학 신입생으로서의 목표는 학사 과정을 잘 마치고 어떤 종류의 공학을 전공할지 생각해 내는 것이었다. 하지만 그녀는 공학이 힘들고, 그것을 잘 하기 위해서는 그녀가 지난 몇 년 동안 참여해왔던 수많은 특별활동을 줄여야만 할 것이라는 사실을 알고 있었다. 그녀는 고등학교 시절 치어리더와 학교 자치 기구의 일원으로 활동해왔다. 그리고 그녀는 피아노 수업을 받아 왔고, 지난 몇 년 동안은 엘크하트의 그녀가 대학생활을 위한 장학금을 받아온 청소년 미인 대회 수상자로서 활동해왔다. Julie가 앞으로 4년간을 오직 공부에만 몰두하고 싶어 하는 것은 아니었다. 그녀는 에어로빅과 수영을 할 시간을 내고 싶어했다. 그리고 그녀는 그녀가 Purdue 대학의 사교장, 특히 주말 친목 파티 등은 꼭 확인할 거란 사실을 알고 있었다. 그리고 그녀는 남자친구가 있었다. "나는 내가 놀고 싶을 때 언제든지 나갈 거라는 걸 알고 있어요." 그녀는 말했다. "하지만 과제는 나에게 가장 먼저 해야 할 일이 될 거에요."

주 제　Julie의 대학 생활 목표
정답 해설　① 앞의 figure out 다음에는 명사나 명사 상당 어구가 와야 하므로 about what은 what으로 수정되어야 한다.
어 휘　Junior Miss 청소년 미인 대회 우승자

16 ②　전설에 따르면 서구 문명을 구원한 닭들이 기원 전 5세기의 10년대경에 그리스의 어떤 길가에서 발견되었다. 아테네의 장군인 Themistocles는 페르시아 군대의 침략에 맞서기 위해 행군하던 중 두 마리의 수탉이 싸우는 것을 보기 위해 잠시 멈췄다. 그는 그의 군사들을 불러 다음과 같이 말했다. "보아라! 이 닭들은 그들의 신을 위해 싸우지 않는다. 그리고 조상들의 유적이나, 영예나, 자유 혹은 저들의 자식들의 안전을 위해 싸우지도 않는다. 오직 한 마리가 또 다른 한 마리에게 굴복하지 않는다는 이유 때문에 싸우는 것이다." 그 이야기는 싸움의 패자에게 어떤 일이 일어났는지는 묘사하지 않고 있다. 또한 어째서 병사들이 이렇게 본능적인 공격 행위를 보여주는 것을, 지루하거나 우울한 것이 아닌 영감을 주는 것으로 생각했는지는 설명해 주고 있지 않다. 하지만 역사는 그렇게 용기를 얻은 그리스인들이 침략자들을 격퇴하기 위해 진군하였고, 오늘날 그 때의 닭들과 똑같은 생명체를 빵가루를 입히고 튀기거나, 누군가가 선택한 소스에 담그는 것으로써 존경을 표하는 그 문명을 보존한다고 기록한다. 그 닭들의 후손들은, 만약 그들이 그렇게 심오한 생각을 할 수만 있다면 아마도 그들의 고대 조상들이 대답해야 할 일이 많을 것이라고 생각할지도 모른다.

주 제　닭요리의 유래
정답 해설　②에서 문맥상 '한 마리가 또 다른 한 마리에게 굴복하지 않는다는 이유 때문에 싸우는 것이다'라고 해석되어야 자연스럽다. 따라서 ②는 둘 중 하나를 뜻하는 the other로 수정되어야 한다.
어 휘　Athenian 아테네인　summon 소환하다, 호출하다　behold 보다　give way to 굴복하다, 복종하다　tale 이야기　instinctive 본능적인　inspirational 영감을 주는　pointless 무딘, 요점이 없는, 지루한　repel 격퇴하다, 쫓아버리다　dip 담그다, 적시다　rooster 수탉　profound 심오한, 깊이 있는　forebear 선조, 조상

17 ②　오늘날 어떤 사람들은 '노동'을 굉장히 혐오스러운 단어로 생각한다. 하지만 내가 불경기에 대학생이었을 때에는 노동은 아주 인기 있는 단어였다. 그것을 영광스럽게 생각하는 사람이든, 아닌 사람이든 모두 노동에 대해 갈망하며 이야기했다. 내가 캐나다에서 대학 생활을 마치고 난 뒤 나는 옥스퍼드로 갔고, 거기에서 나는 또 다른 상황을 발견했다. '노동'이 언급되지 않았다. 때때로 학생들은 "나는 이제 가봐야 되는데"라고 말하며 파티를 떠나곤 했다. 모두가 그들이 일을 하기 위해 살짝 빠져나가고 있다는 사실을 알고 있었다. 하지만 우리는 모두 너무 점잖아서 그것을 말하지 않았다. 교수들이 일하는 모습 또한 보이지 않았다. 옥스퍼드 지역의 매력 중의 하나는 어느 누구도 일하는 것처럼 보이지 않는다는 것이었다. 하지만 그곳에는 내가 얼마 지나지 않아 알게 된 옥스퍼드 지역의 비밀이 있었다. 모든 사람들은 매우 열심히 일했지만, 그들은 그러한 일을 인정하는 것은 나쁜 것으로 생각한다는 것이다. 사람들은 분위기를 통해 학습하게 되어 있었다.

주 제　노동에 대한 인식 변화
정답 해설　②가 포함된 문장의 주어 'Those who ~ did not'은 과거 필자가 대학생이었던 불경기 때의 사람들이다. 따라서 문장의 동사는 과거 시제로 쓰여야 하므로 ②의 speak of는 spoke of로 수정되어야 한다.
어 휘　four-letter word 네 글자 단어, 욕설, 안 좋은 말　glory 기뻐하다, 자랑스럽게 여기다, 영광　longing 동경, 갈망, 간절히 원하는　sneak away 살금살금 걷다, 몰래 떠나다

18 ①　Ray Korc가 40년 전 처음으로 맥도날드 햄버거 노점을 개업한 이후로 최소한 2천만 명이 맥도날드 사에서 근무해 왔다. 이러한 수치 뒤에는 많은 시간제 근무자들을 활용하는 것 등을 비롯한 경영 전략들이 숨어 있

다. 게다가 일반적으로 맥도날드 직원의 시간당 임금은 최저 임금인 5.25달러보다 약간 더 높을 뿐이었다. 그리고 추가 수당은 거의 없었다. 오늘날 직원들이 너무 자주 그만두기 때문에 미국과 캐나다에서 50만 명 이상의 직원을 고용하고 있는 맥도날드 사와 그 가맹점들은 공백이 생기지 않도록 하기 위해 그 숫자 이상의 새로운 직원들을 고용해야 할 것이다. 그러나 이러한 격변에는 좋은 점도 있다. 패스트푸드 체인점들은 수많은 신입사원들을 신속히 적응시키기 위해 다른 업무 이상으로 교육 프로그램에 집중할 수밖에 없었다.

주 제) McDonald's 고용 수치의 이면

정답 해설) ①이 포함된 문장은 '부사 + 동사 + 주어' 순으로 도치되었으며 이 때 주어는 'Several corporate ~ workers'로 복수형이다. 따라서 is는 are로 수정되어야 한다.

어 휘) strategy 전략 typically 일반적으로 staff 직원, 직원을 고용하다 raw 미숙한 with an eye toward ~ing ~하기 위하여

---

19 ③ 대중의 건강을 해치는 것 중 하나인, 대중음악 콘서트에서 전염병과 같이 기절하는 현상은 청소년 집단에게 익숙한 현상이다. 많은 팬들이 의식을 잃는 경향이 있다는 수십 년 간의 보고서에도 불구하고 현대 의학의 주목을 거의 받지 못한 이 위험성에 대해 그들의 부모들은 잘 알고 있지 못할 수 있다. 집단 혼절의 메커니즘이 의학에서 간과되어 왔던 것을 걱정하며, 두 명의 독일 의사가 최근 New Kids on the Block의 콘서트에 용감하게 참여하여 구급요원들과 함께 쓰러진 사람들이 치료를 받는 적십자 요양소에서 일했다. 그 의사들이 New England Journal of Medicine의 목요일 발행물에서 밝힌 내용에 따르면, 약 400여 명의 콘서트 관람객들이 기절했고, 그 소녀들의 나이는 11세에서 17세였다고 한다.

주 제) 대중음악 콘서트에서 소녀들이 기절하는 현상

정답 해설) 'many a + 단수 명사'는 '여러, 수많은~'이라는 의미이며 단수로 취급한다. 따라서 ③ are prone to는 is prone to로 수정되어야 한다.

어 휘) peculiar 특별한, 특유한 hazard 위험 epidemic 유행병, 전염병 legions of 수많은 be prone to ~하는 경향이 있다 infirmary 병원, 진료소

---

20 ① 가족은 네가 감기에 걸리거나, 네가 친구들과 사이가 좋지 않거나, 새 강아지를 훈련시키는 등의

일을 중요하게 여기는 사람들이다. 가족은 너의 볼링 팀에 대한 신문기사를 냉장고 문에 자석을 이용하여 붙여둔다. 그들은 너의 그림들이나 손으로 만든 도자기 등을 모은다. 그들은 너의 어렸을 때의 이야기를 듣는 것을 좋아한다. 그들은 네가 토마토 통조림을 따거나 자동차의 오일을 교체하는 일에 도움을 줄 것이다. 그들은 병원에 있는 너를 병문안 올 것이고, 네가 "아주 힘들고 어려운 상황 속에서" 불러도 너에게 대답해 줄 것이고, 네가 직업을 잃으면 집세를 낼 수 있도록 돈을 빌려줄 것이다. 생물학적으로 서로 연관이 있든 없든, 이러한 것들을 행하는 사람들이 가족이다.

주 제) 가족의 의미

정답 해설) ①에서 동사 matter는 자동사이므로 다음에 목적어가 이어지지 않는다. ①이 포함된 문장 'Families are ~ puppy.'는 'Families are the people'과 'It matters to them if you~'가 합쳐진 문장이다. 따라서 whom은 to whom으로 수정되어야 한다.

어 휘) feud 불화를 빚다 homemade 손으로 만든 pottery 도기, 도자기 dark night of the soul 영혼의 어두운 밤, 인생에 가장 어려운 시기

---

21 ② 포유류가 파충류에서 진화했을 때 그들의 뇌는 변하기 시작했다. 우선 그들은 성과 번식을 위한 파충류적인 본능들과 관련이 있으나 포유류적인 생활 방식의 특별한 필요성을 위해 수정된 새로운 일련의 본능들을 발전시켰다. 이것들 중 가장 대표적인 것은 새끼들을 양육하는 본능이다. 여기에 파충류 부모의 행동의 혁명적인 진화가 있었는데, 갓 부화된 새끼는 만약 그들(파충류 부모)이 그들(갓 부화된 새끼)을 잡을 수만 있다면 파충류 부모들에게 맛있는 간식을 제공하였다. 하지만 어린 파충류 새끼들은 그들의 생존을 위해 싸울 준비가 되어 있었고, 그들은 필요한 모든 행동양식이 뇌에 각인된 채 세상에 태어났다. 이 새끼들은 태어난 순간부터 아주 작은 어른과 같다. 반면에 포유류 새끼들은 무력하고 연약한 상태로 태어났으며, 부모의 관심은 그들의 생존에 필수적이었다. 그것이 바로 포유류가 부모의 양육이라는 새로운 본능을 발전시킨 이유이다.

주 제) 파충류와 포유류의 본능 차이

정답 해설) ② 부분은 앞의 'related ~ procreation'과 같이 a new package of instinct를 수식한다. 이때 a new package of instinct는 수정되는 대상이므로 modifying for는 modified for로 수정되어야 한다.

어 휘) procreation 자식 낳기, 번식 modify 수정하다, 변경하다 hatchling 갓 부화한 새[동물] vulnerable 취약한, 연약한

22 ⑤ 아직까지 그가 누구였는지 아는 사람은 아무도 없다. 그러나 과학자들은 오늘날 자연적으로 미라가 된, 1991년 9월, 해발 10,530피트에서 오스트리아와 이탈리아의 국경지역의 녹아내리는 얼음 속에서 등산객이 발견한 알프스의 빙하 인간에 관하여 한 가지 사실만은 확신한다. 그 시신에 대한 첫 번째 유전자 분석에서 그들은 그가 유럽에서 태어나고 키워졌으며 현대의 북유럽과 알프스 지방의 유럽인들과 밀접한 관련이 있음을 밝혔다. 과학자들은 이 발견이 계속되는 설인에 대한 조작의 혐의를 끝내야만 한다고 말했다. 어떤 국제적인 연구팀은 과학 잡지인 Science에서 그 유전학적인 발견이 사기의 가능성을 아주 있을 법하지 않은 것으로 만들어 주었다고 말했다. 그들의 최근 연구 중에는 격리된 그 시기의 알프스 지역의 패션에 대해 묘사한 목록이 있다. 과학자들은 산꼭대기에 있는 그 사람의 존재에 대해서는 설명할 수 없지만, 그들은 그가 무엇을 입었는지에 대해, 속옷에 이르기까지 알고 있다.

(주 제) 알프스 빙하 인간에 대한 연구
(정답 해설) ⑤에서 문맥상 '그가 무엇을 입고 있었는지'로 해석되어야 자연스러우므로 that은 what으로 수정되어야 한다.
(어 휘) mummify 미라로 만들다 Alpine 알프스 산맥의 hiker 도보 여행자, 하이커 elevation 고도, 해발 genetic 유전의, 유전학의 lingering 오래 끄는 suspicion 의혹, 의심 hoax 거짓말, 감쪽같이 속이다 lay to rest 끝마치다, 종결하다 crest 산꼭대기

23 ② 할머니와 나는 광장 옆에 있는 원룸에 살았다. 그 원룸은 전통적인 벽난로와 임시 캐비닛 그리고 여러 용도로 사용하는 물 양동이 두 통이 담긴 나무 상자로 이루어져 있었다. 방의 한쪽 끝에는 우리가 편안하게 앉는 '긴 의자'로 사용했던 두 채의 침구가 있었다. 두꺼운 솜과 양가죽, 담요로 구성되어, 이 침구는 밤마다 펼쳐졌다. 방의 한쪽 측면의 길이인 나무로 만들어진 기둥이 천장 빔으로부터 10인치 정도 연장되어 있었다. 할머니의 도자기 몇 개와 교환한 옷장은 우리가 갖고 있는 몇 안 되는 옷들이 걸려 있었다. 할머니는 항상 사탕과 상점에서 파는 쿠키들로 가득 채워진 밀가루 자루를 가지고 있었다. 담요를 단단히 덮은 채 나는 할머니의 이야기나 그녀가 어린 소녀였을 때 어땠는지에 대한 설명을 들었다. 이런 이야기들은 우리가 당시 살던 방법과 비교했을 때 매우 구식인 것처럼 느껴졌다.

(주 제) 할머니와 함께 살던 방
(정답 해설) ②가 포함된 문장에서 'Consisted of ~ blankets'는 분사 구문으로 주어는 these bed rolls, 즉 침구이다. consist of는 '구성되다'라는 뜻이고 문맥상 'Consisted of ~ blankets'는

'두꺼운 솜과 양가죽, 담요로 구성되어'라고 해석되어야 하므로 Consisted of는 Consisting of로 수정되어야 한다.
(어 휘) fireplace 난로, 벽난로 makeshift 임시변통의 수단 crate 나무틀, 상자 bedding 침구류 sheepskin 양가죽 assorted 여러 가지, 갖은

24 ② 대부분의 사람들에게 그들이 결국에는 반드시 죽는다는 사실이 지금 살아서 존재한다는 즐거움을 약화시키진 않는다. 시인에게는 시들 운명에 처한 꽃을 바라볼 때 세상이 훨씬 더 아름답게 여겨진다. 5월의 사랑스러움은 그가 바라보고 있는 순간에도 사라져가고 있다는 것을 알기 때문에 그를 더욱 더 감동시킨다. 모든 것이 필멸할 운명이라는 생각이 그에게 기쁨을 주는 것은 아니지만, 그는 그 즐거움이 오래도록 자신의 것이 될 수 없다는 것을 알기 때문에 그 기쁨을 훨씬 더 진심으로 소중히 여기는 것이다.

(주 제) 죽음에 대한 시인의 관점
(정답 해설) ②에서 appear는 '~라고 여겨지다, ~ 인 것 같다'라는 뜻의 자동사이다. ②가 포함된 문장은 시들 운명에 처한 꽃을 바라볼 때 시인에게 세상이 훨씬 더 아름답게 여겨진다고 해석되는 것이 문맥상 자연스러우므로 is appeared는 appears로 수정되어야 한다.
(어 휘) mortality 죽어야 할 운명 dearly 애정 있게, 비싼 값으로

25 ⑤ 어떤 길이 선택됐는가와 상관없이 서로 다른 계곡에서 출발한 여행자들도 올라가기를 계속한다면 결국에는 모두 산 정상에서 만나게 될 것이다. 누구도 자신이 가장 좋은 길을 선택했다고 자랑스러워해서는 안 되며 다른 사람들에게 자신을 따라오라고 강요해서도 안 된다. 모든 사람들은 자신의 두뇌 구조와, 유전, 그리고 전통에 의해 영향을 받아 가장 적합한 길을 택한다. 누구나 지원해 줄 수 있고, 가르쳐 줄 수 있으며, 도움을 줄 수 있다. 하지만 누군가에게 성공적이었던 것은 다른 사람에게는 실패일 수 있다. 모든 사람들은 그들 자신만의 싸움을 해 나가야만 하고, 그것 없이는 발전할 수 없다. 진리를 (혹은 진실을) 향한 길에는 어떤 지름길도 존재하지 않는다.

(주 제) 저마다 다른 자신의 길
(정답 해설) ⑤의 that은 선행사 his own fight를 가리키는 관계대명사이다. 관계대명사 that은 전치사 다음에 사용되지 않는다.
(어 휘) wage 싸움 등을 수행하다, 임금, 급료 valley 골짜기, 계곡 heredity 유전, 세습

26 ⑤

사람들은 당연히 기묘하고 불가사의한 것을 갈망한다. 그리고 그들은 그것을 발견할 수 있다. 우리는 수천 마일 떨어진 사람들이 생각하고 있는 것을 그들에게 전화를 걸어 느낄 수 있다. 그리고 심리 치료사들은 더 나은 삶의 거짓된 희망을 주어 절망에 빠진 사람들을 안도하게 한다. 셀 수 없이 많은 오컬트 책을 저술한 작가는 속기 쉬운 사람들에게 허튼 소리를 퍼뜨려서 돈을 번다. 심지어 현명한 사람들조차도 이성적이고 현실적인 대안이 보이지 않을 때 그러한 것들에 속는다.

주제 기묘함에 대한 사람들의 갈망을 이용한 행태

정답 해설 ⑤에서 문맥상 '심지어 현명한 사람들조차도 ~ 때 속는다'가 자연스러우므로 are taking in은 are taken in으로 수정되어야 한다.

어휘 despair 절망, 자포자기 peddle 행상하다, 퍼뜨리다 psychic 마음의, 정신적인 occult 신비한, 불가사의한 gullible 속기 쉬운, 순진한

27 ⑤

중국의 베이징으로의 농민 이주를 막는 장벽 중 하나는 바로 문 앞에 서있는 도시 노동자들이다. 대부분의 도시 거주자들이 현재 이주민들로부터 제공되는 서비스에 만족함에도 불구하고 도시 거주자들은 곧 경쟁의 한 단면을 느낄 수 있었을 것이다. 어려운 시기에 도시 노동자들은 도시 관리자들이 이주민들에게 떠넘겼던 하수구 파기, 도로 포장과 같은 더러운 직업들을 되찾고 싶을 것이다. 정부에 의해 심하게 적게 추산된 고작 2.9퍼센트의 도시의 실업률은 일단 국영 회사들이 사유화 되면 치솟을 수 있었다. 농부들은 자연스럽게 그들의 경쟁자가 될 것이며 닥쳐올 갈등은 (아직) 다뤄지지 않았다.

주제 중국의 도시 노동자들

정답 해설 ⑤의 주어인 the coming conflict는 다뤄지는 대상이므로 hasn't been addressing은 hasn't been addressed로 수정되어야 한다.

어휘 ditch 도랑, 하수도 urbanite 도시 사람 pavement 도로 포장, 포장된 도로 peasant 농부, 시골 사람 migrant 이주자, 이주 노동자 reclaim 되찾다, 교화시키다

28 ②

19세기 후반 합병의 물결과 증가하는 산업 집중화에 대한 대응으로 의회는 Sherman Act라고 익히 알려진 법률을 통과시켰다. "트러스트 혹은 다른 형태의 계약, 조합이나 무역을 제한하는 음모"는 불법이라고 선언되었다. 독점을 하는 것이나 독점 무역을 하려고 시도하는 것 또한 마찬가지로 불법이었다. Teddy Roosevelt 대통령 시절에 그 법의 파장은 1911년 Standard Oil과 American Tobacco Company의 파산으로 이어졌다.

주제 Sherman Act의 효과

정답 해설 ② 앞의 bill은 알려지는 대상이므로 commonly knowing은 commonly known으로 수정되어야 한다.

어휘 merger 합병, 통합 likewise 마찬가지로, 똑같이 monopolize 독점하다 conspiracy 음모, 계략 surge 큰 파도가 일다, 큰 파도

29 ⑤

Trevor와 Patricia Janz은 Canada의 Waterton 호수 공원에서 가볍게 내리는 눈을 맞으며 걷고 있었을 때 그들은 도보 여행자들의 가장 큰 악몽인 동물의 사체를 먹고 있는 거대 회색 어미 곰과 새끼를 마주치는 경험을 하게 된다. 그 다음에 일어난 일들은 "치명적인 조우"라는 TV 프로그램에서 다뤄졌다. 그 일부분은 인간이 회색 곰의 영역에서 자신을 어떻게 보호할 수 있는지를 보여준다. 곰 행동 전문가인 Stephen Herrero는 말한다. "만약 당신이 회색 곰을 놀라게 했고 그들과의 접촉이 불가피할 것 같으면 당신은 당신의 얼굴과 목을 보호해야 할 것입니다. 얼굴을 아래로 한 채 엎드리고, 당신의 손을 목 뒤에 댄 다음, 죽은 척 하십시오."

주제 곰과 마주칠 경우 취할 행동

정답 해설 'pretend to + 동사'는 '~하는 것을 가장하다'라는 뜻이다. 문맥상 ⑤는 '죽은 척 하다'라는 의미이므로 being dead가 아니라 to be dead로 수정되어야 한다.

어휘 capture 포획하다, 사로잡다 inevitable 피할 수 없는 grizzly 회색의, 회색인, 회색 불곰. domain 영토, 범위, 세력권 cub 동물의 새끼, 애송이

30 ②

오스트리아와 체코의 전통 음악인 왈츠와 폴카 같은 무도곡의 기원은 분명하지만, Strauss 부자의 천재성과는 상관없이 무슨 요소들을 그들이 첨가했는지 파악하는 것은 쉽지 않다. 현대에 Johann Strauss 1세의 작품들은 Johann Strauss 2세나 Josef의 작품에 비해 영감이 부족한 듯 보이지만, 여전히 후기 스타일의 독보적인 특징들을 잘 보여준다. 그의 작품 중 현대까지 잘 알려진 곡으로는 유명한 '라데츠키 행진곡'이 유일하지만, 그의 왈츠, 갤럽, 폴카 곡들은 즐겁게 감상할 만하며, Beethoven이나 심지어 Schubert와 같은 동시대의 작곡가들로부터의 영향을 알아

보기는 매우 어렵다.

31 ⑤ 헤드라인은 독특한 스타일의 문장이다. 그것은 특별한 형태와 내용 그리고 모양을 결정하는 다양한 범위의 기능을 지니고, 작가의 자유를 한정하는 제약된 범위 내에서 기능한다. 예를 들어 헤드라인이 차지할 공간은 거의 항상 페이지 할당 계획에 의해 결정되어 있고, 마찬가지로 글씨 크기도 제한적이다. 뉴스 기사를 작성한 기자가 헤드라인을 쓰는 일은, 혹시 있다고 할지라도 거의 드문 일이다. 이론적으로 그것은 기사 내용을 최소의 단어들로 압축해야 하고, 독자들의 주의를 기사로 이끌어야 한다. 그리고 그것이 1면에 실릴 경우 독자들이 신문에 관심을 갖도록 해야만 한다.

주 제 헤드라인의 특징
정답 해설 문맥상 ⑤ attracting은 주어를 문장 맨 처음에 나오는 It으로 하고 should에 이어지는 동사이므로 attract로 수정되어야 한다.
어 휘 dictate 구술하다, 받아쓰다, 명령하다 layout 설계, 배치, 계획 typeface 인쇄된 글자

32 ③ 지금까지 미국 소비자들이 이토록 변덕스러웠던 적은 없었다. 디자이너의 플래그십 부티크를 비롯한 상점들은 이에 어떻게 대처할까? 바로 과학을 적용하는 것이다. 사람은 그들이 차를 운전하는 방향으로 걷는 습성이 있다. 즉, 미국인들은 쇼핑몰의 중앙 홀이나 도시의 인도를 걸을 때 우측통행을 하는 경향이 있음을 의미한다. 이것이 잘 설계된 공항에서 출구로 이동하는 여행자들이 항상 패스트푸드 식당은 왼쪽에서, 선물 가게는 오른쪽에서 발견하게 되는 이유이다. 사람들은 허기를 채우기 위해 보행자들로 붐비는 통로를 기꺼이 가로질러 가지만, 잡지나 티셔츠를 충동적으로 사기 위해 그러는 경우는 거의 드물기 때문이다.

주 제 소비자 구매 촉진을 위한 설계
정답 해설 ③은 앞의 travellers를 수식하고 drift의 주체도 travellers이므로 drift toward their gate는 drifting toward

their gate로 수정되어야 한다.
어 휘 drift 표류하다, 이동하다 fickle 변하기 쉬운, 변덕스런 flagship 함대의 기함, 주력 상품 boutique 고급 양품점 stroll 산책하다, 어슬렁거리다 concourse 중앙 홀 readily 기꺼이, 즉시, 쉽게

33 ④ 높은 혈압과 높은 콜레스테롤 수치는 단순한 숫자 이상이다. 그것들은 무시되어서는 안 될 위험 요소이다. 만일 의사가 당신에게 혈압과 콜레스테롤 수치가 높다고 말한다면 당신은 심장 발작이나 뇌졸중의 더 높아진 위험에 처해 있는 것일지도 모른다. 하지만 희소식은 당신이 혈압과 콜레스테롤을 낮추기 위한 조치를 취할 수 있다는 것이다. 의사와 약물의 도움과 식단 조절과 운동을 같이 해나간다면, 당신은 혈압과 콜레스테롤을 낮출 수 있을 것이다. 제대로 먹고 더 많이 운동할 준비가 되었는가?

주 제 고혈압과 고콜레스테롤의 위험성
정답 해설 ④에서 on your way to는 '당신이 ~로 향하는 길'이라는 뜻으로 to 다음에는 명사나 명사구가 올 수 있다. 따라서 to lower your blood pressure는 to lowering your blood pressure로 수정되어야 한다.
어 휘 blood pressure 혈압 cholesterol 콜레스테롤 stroke 타격, 뇌졸중

34 ⑤ 음악은 베토벤 이후로 상당히 변화하였다. 이전 시기의 작품들은 놀라운 혁신을 담고 있음과 동시에, 독창성 부족이라기보다는 전통에 의해 자리잡아 불가피한 성분이 된, 예측 가능한 필수 요소가 존재했다. 그러나 베토벤이 표현하고자 했던 것들은 더 이상 이러한 관습 속에 포함될 수 없었다. 그는 혁신의 시대였던 그 시기의 최초의 음악적 혁명가가 되었다. 베토벤은 음악을 통해서 이전에 없던 새로운 방식으로 인간 정신의 정수를 밝히고자 했다. 그는 이내 당시 널리 퍼져있는 음악적 표현 방식이 부적합하다는 것을 발견하고 새롭고 급진적인 표현 방식을 탐험하기 시작했다.

주 제 베토벤이 음악에 끼친 변화
정답 해설 ⑤가 포함된 문장은 'find + 목적어 + 목적보어'의 형태이다. 따라서 문맥상 자연스러운 '널리 퍼져 있는 음악적 표현이 부적합하다는 것을 발견했다'라는 내용을 완성하려면 inadequately는 inadequate로 수정되어야 한다.
어 휘 predictable 예상 가능한, 예견 가능한 formal 형식적인, 격식에 맞는 convention 집회, 관습 prevail 우세하다, 이기다, 널리 퍼지다 idiom 숙어, 관용어구, 표현 방식 radical 급진적인, 과격한

35 ④ 호수는 매우 다양하며 많은 요인들이 (그곳에서 서식하는) 식물들과 동물들에게 영향을 준다. 그 중 가장 중요한 것은 바로 크기이다. 어떤 호수들은 작은 편인 바다에 견줄 수 있을 정도로 엄청나게 넓은 수역들이고, 반대의 극단에는 직경이 몇 미터 정도에 지나지 않는, 우리가 흔히 연못이라고 부를 법한 수역들이 있다. 또 다른 중요한 변수는, 강과 마찬가지로, 영양 상태이다. 영양 상태가 나쁜 호수에는 영양 상태가 좋은 호수와는 매우 다른 (생물의) 군집이 있다.

[주 제] 호수의 특성이 생물에 미치는 영향

[정답 해설] ④ 앞의 ponds는 ④ 뒤의 내용의 의미상 주어이므로 where는 that이나 which로 수정되어야 한다.

[어 휘] pond 연못, 샘물 diameter 직경, 지름, 배율(렌즈)

More Practice

01 ④   02 ④   03 ⑤   04 ④

01 ④ 새로운 경험들은, 그들이 우리로 하여금 우리의 신념에 의문을 던지게만 한다면, 변화를 촉발한다. 우리가 무언가를 믿을 때마다, 우리는 더 이상 어떤 식으로든 그것에 의문을 던지지 않는다는 점을 기억해라. 우리가 우리의 신념들에 정직하게 질문을 던지기 시작하는 순간, 우리는 더 이상 그것들에 대해 절대적으로 확신을 느낄 수 없다. 우리는 우리 인식의 탁자의 준거의 다리를 흔들기 시작하고 있으며, 결과적으로 우리의 절대적인 확신감을 잃어가기 시작한다. 무언가를 하는 당신의 능력에 대하여 의심해본 적이 있는가? 당신은 어떻게 그것을 했는가? 당신은 아마도 당신 자신에게 "그것이 잘 풀리지 않으면 어쩌지?"와 같은 몇 가지 초라한 질문을 했을 것이다. 그러나 질문은, 우리가 그것들을 우리가 맹목적으로 수용한 신념의 타당성을 검증하는 데 사용한다면 분명히 엄청나게 힘을 실어줄 수 있다. 사실, 우리 신념의 많은 부분들은 그 당시에 우리가 질문하는 데 실패한 다른 사람들로부터 얻은 정보에 의해 뒷받침된다. 만일 우리가 그것들을 자세히 조사한다면 우리는 우리가 몇 년 간 무의식적으로 받아들여 왔던 것들이 일련의 거짓된 가정에 근거하고 있을지도 모른다는 점을 알게 될 수도 있다.

[주 제] 신념의 타당성에 대한 질문의 힘

[정답 해설] ④가 포함된 문장에서 '우리 신념의 많은 부분'들은 정보에 의해 뒷받침되는 대상이므로 supported는 are supported로 수정되어야 한다.

[어 휘] trigger 유발하다 reference 참조, 준거 cognitive 인

식의 work out 잘 풀리다 tremendously 엄청나게 empower ~에게 힘을 주다 validity 타당성 blindly 맹목적으로 scrutinize 세심하게 조사하다 presupposition 가정

02 ④ 설문조사에서, 응답 선택지가 시각적으로 제시되었을 때, 응답자들이 보통 목록의 위부터 시작하여 남아있는 선택지들을 차근차근 처리해 나간다고 가정하는 것은 타당해 보인다. 그러므로 초두 효과는 법칙처럼 보인다. 응답자들은 끝에 있는 선택지보다 처음에 있는 선택지를 선호하는 경향이 있을 것이다. 그러나 이 상황은 인터뷰 진행자가 응답 선택지를 응답자들에게 읽어줄 때 다소 흐릿해진다. 설문조사 응답자들이 다음으로 넘어가기 전에 첫 번째 선택지를 평가할 시간을 갖지 못할 정도로 인터뷰 진행자들은 질문들을 빨리 읽는 경향이 있다. 인터뷰 진행자가 읽기를 멈추었을 때, 응답자가 마지막 선택지 고려부터 시작할 가능성이 높은데 왜냐하면 그 선택지는 작업 기억에 남아있을 것이기 때문이다. 결과적으로 질문이 응답자에게 소리로 제시될 때 우리는 최신 효과, 즉 목록의 끝에 있는 선택지들을 선택하는 경향을 기대할 것이다.

[주 제] 설문조사의 답변 경향 기대

[정답 해설] ④의 stops to read는 '읽기 위해 멈추다'라고 해석되므로 문맥상 부자연스럽다. '읽기를 멈춘 것'이라는 뜻이 적절하므로 to read는 reading으로 수정되어야 한다.

[어 휘] option 보기, 선택 respondent 답변자 primacy 최고, 으뜸 murky 흐릿한 recency 새로움, 최신

03 ⑤ 사람들이 질병, 실직, 혹은 연령으로 인한 장애 등 진짜 역경 직면할 때, 애완동물이 주는 애정은 새로운 의미를 띤다. 애완동물의 지속적인 애정은 고난을 견디고 있는 사람들에게 그들의 핵심적인 본질이 손상되지 않았다고 안심시켜 주기 때문에 매우 중요해진다. 그러므로 애완동물은 우울증이 있거나 만성적인 질병이 있는 환자들의 치료에 중요하다. 게다가, 애완동물은 시설에 수용된 노인들에게 매우 유익하게 이용된다. 그런 시설에서 직원들은 모든 환자가 건강이 나빠지는 와중에 낙관주의를 유지하기가 힘들다. 방문하는 자녀들은 부모님이나 조부모님이 예전에 어떠했는지를 기억하고 그들의 무능함에 의기소침해할 수밖에 없다. 그러나 동물은 정신적인 능력에 대한 기대를 하지 않는다. 그들은 젊음을 숭배하지 않는다. 그들은 노인들이 예전에 어떠했는지에 대한 기억이 전혀 없어서 그들이(노인들이) 마치 어린이들인 것처럼 그들을 반긴다. 강아지를 안고 있는 노인은 완전히 정확하게 어린 시절을 다시 체험할

수 있다. 그의 기쁨과 그 동물의 반응은 동일하다.

주제 노인 시설에서 애완동물의 긍정적 역할

정답 해설 ⑤ 주어인 the aged는 'the+형용사'의 형태로, '나이 든 사람들'이라는 복수의 의미를 띠므로 동사 was를 were로 고쳐야 한다.

어휘 to advantage 유익하게, 유리하게 institutionalize 시설에 수용하다 retain 유지하다 adversity 역경 disability 장애 affection 애정 chronically 만성적으로 optimism 낙관주의 worship 숭배하다 relive 다시 체험하다 accuracy 정확성

04 ④ 그리스인의 두드러진 물체와 그것의 속성에 에 대한 집중은 인과 관계의 근본적인 성질을 이해하지 못하는 결과를 낳았다. 아리스토텔레스는 돌이 공중에서 떨어지는 것은 돌이 '중력'이라는 성질을 가지고 있기 때문이라고 설명했다. 하지만 물론 물에 던져진 나무 조각은 가라앉는 대신 뜬다. 이 현상을 아리스토텔레스는 나무가 '가벼움'이라는 성질을 가지고 있기 때문이라고 설명했다! 두 경우 모두 그 물체 밖에 있는 어떤 힘이 관련 있을지도 모른다는 가능성에 주의를 기울이지 않고, 초점은 오로지 그 물체에 있다. 그러나 중국인은 세계를 계속적으로 상호 작용하는 물질로 구성된 것으로 보았고, 그래서 그것을 이해하고자 하는 그들의 시도는 그들로 하여금 전체적인 '장(場)', 즉 전체로서의 맥락이나 환경의 복잡성에 중점을 두도록 했다. 사건은 언제나 여러 힘의 장에서 발생한다는 개념은 중국인에게 전적으로 직관적이었을 것이다.

주제 그리스 철학과 중국 철학의 세계관 차이

정답 해설 ④ so 이하 절의 주어가 their attempts to understand it이므로, causing을 동사 caused로 고쳐야 한다.

어휘 attribute 속성, 자질 causality 인과 관계 property 성질, 속성 gravity 중력 toss (가볍게) 던지다 phenomenon 현상 exclusively 오로지, 배타적으로 relevant 관련 있는 substance 물질 oriented toward ~에 중점을 둔, complexity 복잡성 context 맥락, 전후 사정

UNIT **06** 동의어

Example
답 ②

그 운동에 참여한 학생들은 그들이 혁명의 <u>선봉</u>에 있다고 생각하도록 기만당했다.

① 혼란	② 선두
③ 보호	④ 반대
⑤ 준비	

Practice

01 ①	02 ④	03 ①	04 ④	05 ①
06 ③	07 ①	08 ①	09 ⑤	10 ①
11 ①	12 ⑤	13 ②	14 ④	15 ①
16 ②	17 ④	18 ⑤	19 ④	20 ③
21 ②	22 ④	23 ③	24 ①	25 ①
26 ⑤	27 ①	28 ①	29 ②	30 ⑤
31 ①	32 ①	33 ②	34 ⑤	35 ①
36 ③	37 ③	38 ①	39 ①	40 ④
41 ②	42 ⑤	43 ①	44 ⑤	45 ①
46 ③	47 ③			

01 ① 정부는 제조업자들이 미성년자들에게 그들의 제품을 판매하기 위해 <u>공모했다</u>는 결론을 내렸다.

① 협력하다	② 제안하다
③ 가장하다	④ 의도하다
⑤ 개입하다	

정답 해설 collude는 '공모하다'라는 뜻으로 사용되었으므로 colluded는 ① collaborated와 바꿔 쓸 수 있다.

어휘 collude 공모하다 collaborate 협력하다 intervene 개입하다

02 ④ 사치에 대한 그의 <u>선호</u>는 그의 가족의 재산을 소멸시켰다.

① 집착	② 소질
③ 비난	④ 애호
⑤ 낭비	

정답 해설 penchant는 '선호'라는 뜻으로 사용되었으므로 ④ inclination과 바꿔 쓸 수 있다.

어휘 penchant 선호, 경향 demise 종말 obsession 집착 aptitude 소질 inclination 경향, 애호 reproach 비난 extravagance 낭비

03 ① Rawls의 가장 엄격한 비평가들은 그를 종종 "미국인들 또는 기껏해야 영국계 미국인 청중들하고만 관련이 있다"고 한정지으려 했다.

① 가두다　　　　　② 꾸짖다
③ 소개하다　　　　④ 보호하다
⑤ 예증하다

정답 해설 cabin은 '가두다, 감금하다'라는 뜻으로 사용되었고 문맥상 '한정짓다'라고 해석될 수 있으므로 ① confine과 바꿔 쓸 수 있다.

어휘 cabin 가두다, 감금하다 confine 국한시키다, 가두다 rebuke 꾸짖다 exemplify 예증하다

04 ④ 미결된 소송에 대한 질문은 제약회사 대표의 완곡한 답변에 맞닥뜨렸다.

① 명백한　　　　　② 간결한
③ 근거 없는　　　　④ 우회적인
⑤ 회유하는

정답 해설 circumlocutory는 '완곡한, 빙 둘러서 말하는'이라는 뜻으로 사용되었으므로 ④ roundabout과 바꿔 쓸 수 있다.

어휘 pending 미결의 circumlocutory 완곡한 unequivocal 명백한 succinct 간결한 unfounded 근거 없는 roundabout 우회적인, 에두르는 conciliatory 회유하는

05 ① 그 변호사들이 우리의 제안을 분명하게 거절했기 때문에 새로운 행동 계획을 고안해야 할 때이다.

① 분명하게　　　　② 전형적으로
③ 무례하게　　　　④ 마지못해
⑤ 심술궂게

정답 해설 categorically는 '분명하게'라는 뜻으로 사용되었으

므로 ① unequivocally와 바꿔 쓸 수 있다.

어휘 devise 고안하다 attorney 변호사

06 ③ 오랜 시간 암 투병을 이겨낸 후에 그 미디어 거물은 그의 부유한 삶의 방식을 비난하면서 새사람이 되기 위해 노력했다.

① 부도덕한　　　　② 자부하는
③ 호화로운　　　　④ 병든
⑤ 무능한

정답 해설 opulent는 '부유한'이라는 뜻으로 사용되었으므로 ③ luxurious와 바꿔 쓸 수 있다.

어휘 victorious 이긴 long-fought 오랜 시간 싸워 온 bout 한판 승부 tycoon 거물 turn over a new leaf 새사람이 되다 denounce 비난하다

07 ① 그 국가에 대한 제재는 가장 논쟁적인 이슈들 중 하나가 될 것으로 예상된다.

① 논쟁적인　　　　② 복잡한
③ 파악하기 어려운　④ 숨기는
⑤ 무익한

정답 해설 contentious는 '논쟁적인'이라는 뜻으로 사용되었으므로 ① controversial과 바꿔 쓸 수 있다.

어휘 sanction 제재 among the most 최고로

08 ① 자본주의 시대가 얼마 안 남았다는 것, 자본주의 시대는 사회주의에 길을 내주어야 한다는 것. 이것들은 대서양 양측의 지성인들 사이에 널리 퍼진 가정이다.

① 제한된　　　　　② 장기의
③ 보전된　　　　　④ 가속화된
⑤ 겹쳐진

정답 해설 numbered가 '국한된, 얼마 남지 않은'이라는 뜻으로 사용되었으므로 ① limited와 바꿔 쓸 수 있다.

어휘 capitalism 자본주의 give way to ~에 길을 내주다

09 ⑤ 많은 정치인들은 그 국가의 경제적 패권을 <u>주제넘은</u> 것으로 여겼다.

① 주의 깊고 기민한
② 정확하고 정밀한
③ 근면하고 성실한
④ 달성할 수 있고 실용적인
⑤ 거만하고 무례한

정답 해설 presumptuous가 '주제넘은'이라는 뜻으로 사용되었으므로 ⑤ arrogant and disrespectful과 바꿔 쓸 수 있다.

어휘 hegemony 헤게모니, 패권

10 ① 누가 그 영화배우의 인기가 <u>덧없다고</u> 추측이나 했을까?

① 덧없는   ② 나머지의
③ 영구의   ④ 전설의
⑤ 쉽사리 믿는

정답 해설 ephemeral이 '덧없는, 단명한'이라는 뜻으로 사용되었으므로 ① fleeting과 바꿔 쓸 수 있다.

어휘 fame 인기

11 ① Karen은 그의 친구를 <u>부추겨</u> 그녀를 자동차에 태워 쇼핑몰로 데려가도록 애썼지만 소용이 없었다.

① 설득하다, 꾀다
② 괴롭히다
③ 비방하다
④ (감정 따위를) 일으키다, 성나게 하다
⑤ 최면술을 걸다, 매혹시키다

정답 해설 cajole이 '부추기다, 구워삶다'라는 뜻으로 사용되었으므로 ① coax와 바꿔 쓸 수 있다.

어휘 to no avail 보람없이, 헛되이

12 ⑤ 그녀는 자신의 전제들이 결점이 없도록 하는 데 있어서 과도할 정도로 <u>까다롭다</u>.

① 위험한, 모험적인   ② 교활한
③ 파산한   ④ 원한을 품은
⑤ 지나치게 세심한, 매우 신중한

정답 해설 fastidious는 '까다로운, 가림이 심한'이라는 뜻으로 사용되었으므로 ⑤ meticulous와 바꿔 쓸 수 있다.

어휘 premise 전제 spotless 결점이 없는

13 ② 꿈은 사람들이 그날의 감정적인 <u>곤경들을</u> 헤쳐 나갈 수 있도록 도와준다. 꿈은 마치 타고난 치료사를 갖고 있는 것과 같다.

① 유대감, 인연   ② 궁지, 딜레마
③ 실패   ④ 무아경, 황홀
⑤ 흥분, 초조

정답 해설 quandaries는 '궁지, 곤경'이라는 뜻으로 사용된 복수형 명사이므로 ② dilemmas와 바꿔 쓸 수 있다.

어휘 therapist 치료사

14 ④ 그는 나를 클레어와 같은 직급으로 승진시켜 줄 것이고, 그녀가 질투하지 않도록 <u>조심스럽게</u> 얘기해 주고 있다.

① 경솔하게   ② 부드럽게
③ 질투심을 가지고   ④ 신중하게
⑤ 편견 없이

정답 해설 discreetly는 '신중하게, 조심스럽게'라는 뜻으로 사용되었으므로 ④ cautiously와 바꿔 쓸 수 있다.

어휘 promote 승진시키다 jealous 질투하는

15 ① 할아버지에 의해 <u>나누어진</u> 1달러짜리 은화들은 부모님에 의해 보관되었고 부모님은 우리에게 그 것들을 맡기지 않았다.

① 분배된   ② 초래된
③ 투자된, 부여된   ④ 인출된
⑤ 예금된

정답 해설 dole A out B는 'A에게 B를 (조금씩) 나누어주다' 라는 뜻이므로 doled out은 ① distributed와 바꿔 쓸 수 있다.

어 휘 silver dollar 1달러 은화 dole ~ out ~을 (조금씩)나눠 주다 trust A with B A에게 B를 맡기다 incur (좋지 못한 상황)을 초래하다, 비용을 발생하게 하다 withdraw (돈을) 인출하다.

---

16 ② 잡지의 제목은 독자들의 예상에 결정적인 역할을 한다. 그것들은 항상 독자들에게 특별한 연상을 불러일으키는 큰 글씨로 쓰인다.

① 맞추는   ② 연상시키는
③ 횡단하는   ④ 벗기는
⑤ 피해가는

정답 해설 conjure A up은 'A를 상기시키다, A가 떠오르게 하다'라는 뜻이므로 conjuring up은 ② invoking과 바꿔 쓸 수 있다.

어 휘 a large part 대부분, 상당 부분 conjure up ~을 떠올리게 하다, 상기시키다 association 연상, 연상 작용 customize 취향에 맞게 만들다, 특별 제작하다 invoke ~을 떠올리게 하다, 연상시키다 traverse 가로지르다, 횡단하다 strip (옷, 껍질 등을) 벗기다, 벗다 circumvent 우회하다, 피하다, 돌아가다

---

17 ④ 비록 20세기는 유전과 인종에 대한 나치의 사이비 과학에 의한 끔찍한 대량 학살을 목격했지만, 마르크스주의자들의 사이비 과학에 의해 인간 본성의 순응성에 대한 대량 학살이 일어나는 것 역시 지켜보게 되었다.

① 이중성   ② 틀리기 쉬운 것
③ 잊힘, 모호함   ④ 가소성
⑤ 악함

정답 해설 malleability는 '유연성, 순응성'이라는 뜻으로 사용되었으므로 ④ plasticity와 바꿔 쓸 수 있다. '가소성'이란 원하는 대로 모양을 만들 수 있다는 뜻이므로 '순응성'과 의미가 상통한다.

어 휘 Nazi 나치 genocide 대량 학살 pseudoscience 사이비 과학 Marxist 마르크스주의자 malleability (사상 등에) 영향을 받기 쉬움, 순응성 duality 이중성, 이원성 fallibility 불완전성, 오류를 범하기 쉬움 obscurity 불분명성, 애매함, 모호함 plasticity 적응성, 유연성, 가소성 viciousness 사악함, 잔인함

---

18 ⑤ 귀족들의 소수 독재 정치적 권력은 로마의 시민들 중 다른 계층, 즉 농부와 노동자, 상인들을 포함한 평민들로부터 갈망되었다.

① 가난한   ② 강화된
③ 주어진   ④ 비판받는
⑤ 부러움을 받는

정답 해설 covet은 '탐내다, 갈망하다'라는 뜻으로 사용되었으므로 coveted는 ⑤ envied와 바꿔 쓸 수 있다.

어 휘 oligarchical 소수 독재의, 과두 정치의 aristocracy 귀족 정치, 귀족 계층 covet (남의 것을) 탐내다 plebeian 평민, 서민 grant 승인하다, 인정하다

---

19 ④ "내 남동생을 뉴욕까지 바래다주겠니?" 10년간을 이방인으로 살아왔기 때문에, 나는 얼토당토않은 대화에는 익숙해져 있었지만 그 첫마디는 내가 할 말을 잃게 만들었다.

① 개인적인   ② 솔직한
③ 가늘고 긴   ④ 관계없는
⑤ 실용적인

정답 해설 non sequitur는 논리적으로 인과 관계가 없는 불합리한 추론라는 뜻으로 사용되었으므로 ④ irrelevant와 바꿔 쓸 수 있다.

어 휘 non sequitur 불합리한 추론(결론), 논리적인 모순 irrelevant 부적절한, 무관한 elongated (비정상적으로) 길쭉한, 가늘고 긴 opener (병, 캔) 따개, 시작하는 것, 처음의 것

---

20 ③ 한 종류의 연구에서 부적절한 것으로 여겨지는 실험 방법은 다른 종류의 연구에서 선택되는 방법이 될 수도 있다.

① 증명된   ② 만들어진
③ 여겨지는   ④ 분류된
⑤ 뚜렷한

정답 해설 deemed는 '~로 여겨지는'이라는 뜻으로 사용되었으므로 ③ considered와 바꿔 쓸 수 있다.

어 휘 deemed ~으로 여겨지는, ~으로 간주되는 coined (새로운 낱말이) 만들어진, (화폐 등이) 주조된 pronounced 뚜렷한, 현저한

21 ②

국가들의 내전에 의해 세계 문화 유적지가 위협받고 있다. 전문가들은 위험에 처한 박물관들과 기념물, 그리고 역사적으로 중요한 다른 장소들을 보호하고 감시하기 위해 위성 기술을 <u>사용하고</u> 있다.

① 합법화하는 ② 사용하는
③ 개발하는 ④ 회피하는
⑤ 명확하게 하는

정답 해설 wield는 '사용하다, 휘두르다'라는 뜻으로 사용되었으므로 wielding은 ② employing과 바꿔 쓸 수 있다.

어 휘 wield (도구나 칼 등을) 사용하다, 휘두르다 legalize 합법화하다 avoid 꺼리다, 회피하다 clarify 명확하게 하다

22 ④

그가 대장암에 걸렸다는 진단을 받은 사실을 받아들일 수가 없어서 Michael은 그의 주치의가 <u>돌팔이 의사</u>가 아닌지 의심했고 다른 의사의 진단을 찾아보기로 결심했다.

① 어릿광대 ② 선동자
③ 전문가 ④ 사기꾼, 돌팔이 의사
⑤ 자선가

정답 해설 quack은 '돌팔이 의사'라는 뜻으로 사용되었으므로 ④ charlatan과 바꿔 쓸 수 있다.

어 휘 cope with 감당하다, 대응하다 diagnose 진단하다 colon cancer 대장암 quack 돌팔이 의사 clown 광대 demagogue 정치가, 선동가 charlatan 사기꾼, 돌팔이 의사 benefactor 자선가

23 ③

Aristotle은 물질적인 욕망에 대해서 다소 경애심을 가진 학생들에게 <u>호통치지</u> 않는다. 그에게 있어서 돈에 대한 관심은 좋은 일이고, 그 좋은 일들 중 한 가지는 바로 돈을 가진 사람들이 관대함을 실천할 수 있다는 사실이다.

① 연상하다, 어울리다 ② 선동하다
③ 비판하다 ④ 달래다
⑤ 언급하다

정답 해설 hector는 '호통을 치다'라는 뜻으로 사용되었으므로 ③ criticize와 바꿔 쓸 수 있다.

어 휘 piety 신앙심, 경애심 hector 호통을 치다, 못살게 굴다 incite 선동하다, 부추기다 appease 달래다, 진정시키다

24 ①

권투 해설자는 헤비급 챔피언에 대해 언급했다. "그의 왼쪽 훅은 정말 <u>결정적 타격</u>입니다. 그런 충격을 견딜 수 있는 것은 탱크 정도나 되어야 할 것입니다."

① 결정적 타격 ② 강력한 방어
③ 교활한 공격 ④ 교묘한 펀치
⑤ 허술한 전달

정답 해설 sockdolager는 '결정적 타격'이라는 뜻으로 사용되었으므로 ① decisive blow와 바꿔 쓸 수 있다.

어 휘 commentator 해설자, 방송원 remark 주목하다, ~에 대해 말하다 sockdolager 결정적 타격, 최후의 일격 sneaky 은밀한, 남몰래 하는 elusive 파악하기 어려운, 포착하기 어려운 fragile 부서지기 쉬운 delivery (탄환 등의)발사, 배달(물)

25 ①

Wagner의 '니벨룽겐의 반지'는 그 작품이 거의 전체적으로 오페라풍이라는 점에서 특별함을 갖는다. 그리고 오페라의 대본을 쓰는 것은 보통 시인이나 저명한 문학인을 위해 <u>남겨진</u> 업무였음에 반해, 그의 오페라에서는 작곡가인 그 자신이 스스로 가사를 썼다는 사실 또한 흔치 않다.

① 유지되다 ② 예약되다
③ 수정되다 ④ 교체되다
⑤ 연기되다

정답 해설 reserve는 '남겨두다, 보유하다'라는 뜻으로 사용되었으므로 reserved는 ① retained와 바꿔 쓸 수 있다.

어 휘 operatic 가극의 libretti(libretto) 가사, 대본(오페라의) literary 문학적인 notable 주목할 만한, 저명한, 유명한 사람 reserve 비축해두다, 남겨두다 retain 보유하다, 유지하다

26 ⑤

최초의 쓰레기 위기는 사람들이 농장에 정착하고, 쓰레기가 너무 많아진 후 주거지를 떠날 수 없게 되었을 때 발생하였다. 그때부터 모든 사회는 대개 냄새가 고약한 폐기물들에 대한 문제가 있었다.

① 해로운 ② 무익한

③ 생분해성의   ④ 매우 귀중한
⑤ 악취가 나는

[정답 해설] odoriferous는 '냄새가 고약한, 구린'이라는 뜻으로 사용되었으므로 ⑤ stinky와 바꿔 쓸 수 있다.

[어 휘] campsite 거주지, 정착지 discard 폐기하다, 버리다, 폐기물, 처분 odoriferous 냄새가 고약한, 구린 futile 쓸데없는, 무익한, 하찮은

27 ① Michael은 굉장히 유능한 판매사원이었다. 그는 에스키모에게도 냉장고를 팔 수 있었다. 하지만 팀 프로젝트 수행 중 그의 적대적인 태도는 그의 상사가 어찌할 바를 모르게 했다.

① 적의 있는   ② 거만한
③ 냉담한   ④ 사교적인
⑤ 부도덕한

[정답 해설] belligerent는 '적대적인'이라는 뜻으로 사용되었으므로 ① hostile과 바꿔 쓸 수 있다.

[어 휘] belligerent 적대적인, 호전적인 at one's wits' end 어찌할 바를 모르는, 당황하는 hostile 적대적인, 비우호적인 arrogant 거만한, 건방진 apathetic 냉담한, 무관심한 gregarious 사교적인, 떼 지어 다니는 unscrupulous 부도덕한, 파렴치한, 못된

28 ⑤ 수상은 미국과의 곧 무너질 것 같은 동맹을 강화하길 원하고 재분배에 앞서 경제적 성장을 강조하기를 바란다.

① 사회적인   ② 지배적인
③ 은밀한   ④ 튼튼한
⑤ 위태로운

[정답 해설] rickety는 '곧 무너질 것 같은'이라는 뜻으로 사용되었으므로 ⑤ precarious와 바꿔 쓸 수 있다.

[어 휘] rickety 곧 무너질 것 같은 redistribution 재분배 dominant 지배적인, 유리한 clandestine 비밀의, 은밀한 sturdy 억센, 완강한, 착실한 precarious 불확실한, 믿을 수 없는

29 ② 현대판으로 구성된 셰익스피어의 '로미오와 줄리엣'은 복합적인 평가를 받았다. 그 연극의 한 냉소

적인 비평은 그 작품을 '교육 받지 못한 궤변가를 위한 걸작'이라고 불렀다.

① 실수할 수 있는   ② 냉소적인
③ 아첨하는   ④ 카리스마적인
⑤ 지나치게 방임하는

[정답 해설] sardonic은 '냉소적인, 빈정대는'이라는 뜻으로 사용되었으므로 ② cynical과 바꿔 쓸 수 있다.

[어 휘] sardonic 냉소적인, 빈정대는 sophist 고대 그리스의 철학자, 궤변가 fallible 틀리기 쉬운, 속기 쉬운 obsequious 아첨하는, 비굴한 charismatic 카리스마 있는 overindulgent 지나치게 방임하는, 멋대로 굴게 하는

30 ⑤ 당신의 주된 경쟁자 중 한 명은 당신에게 현재의 임무에 적합한 것 이상이면서도, 봉급도 거의 2배에 가까운, 수익성이 좋은 지위를 제공할 것이다.

① 느긋한   ② (일하기) 좋은, 징조가 좋은
③ 자비로운   ④ 고급의
⑤ 보수가 좋은

[정답 해설] lucrative는 '수익성이 좋은'이라는 뜻으로 사용되었으므로 ⑤ well-paying과 바꿔 쓸 수 있다.

[어 휘] lucrative 수익성이 좋은 commensurate ~에 상응하는, 대응하는, ~에 비례하는 leisurely (일하기) 좋은, 징조가 좋은 propitious 좋은 charitable 자비로운, 관대한, 자선의 classy 고급의, 세련된

31 ① 오랫동안 휴대전화가 건강에 미치는 영향에 대해서 광범위하게 간과되어 왔다. 왜냐하면 휴대전화에서 방출되는 주파수의 파동은 무해한 것으로 믿어져 왔기 때문이다. 휴대전화는 비전이성 방사선을 방출하는데, 이는 굉장히 미약해서 화학적인 연결 상태를 해체하거나 암을 유발하는 것으로 알려진 유전자 손상을 일으키지는 못한다.

① 무해한   ② 진동하는
③ 강력한   ④ 전송하는
⑤ 암에 걸린, 불치의

[정답 해설] benign은 '상냥한, 양호한'이라는 뜻인데 휴대전화의 파동이 인체에 큰 영향을 주지 못한다는 글의 내용을 미루어 볼 때 ① harmless와 바꿔 쓸 수 있다.

frequency 자주 일어남, 빈번함 dismiss 떠나게 하다, 해산하다 benign 상냥한, 온화한 non-ionizing radiation (원자력) 비전이성 방사선 vibrating 떠는, 진동하는 potent 세력이 있는, 효력이 있는 transmitting 운송, 발송 cancerous 암의, 암에 걸린, 불치의

---

32 ② 신들은 시시포스에게 끊임없이 산 정상으로 바위를 굴리게 하는 벌을 내렸는데, 그 돌은 그 무게 때문에 다시 굴러 내려왔다. 신들은 <u>헛되고</u> 희망이 없는 노동보다 더 끔찍한 벌은 없다고 생각했다.

① 반복적인   ② 성과 없는
③ 혐오스러운   ④ 고생스러운
⑤ 징계의

정답 해설 futile은 '헛된, 소용없는'이라는 뜻으로 사용되었으므로 ② fruitless와 바꿔 쓸 수 있다.

어 휘 ceaselessly 끊임없이 futile 쓸데없는, 무익한

---

33 ② 예술가들은 과거나 지금이나 관찰의 기량에는 손재주가 <u>불가피하게</u> 엮여있다고 생각하고, 그 반대의 경우도 마찬가지라고 생각한다. 실제로 많은 사람들이 손으로 그릴 수 없는 것은 눈으로 볼 수 없다고 믿는다.

① 과도하게   ② 필연적으로
③ 과분하게   ④ 무능하게
⑤ 좁은 범위로

정답 해설 inextricably는 '불가피하게'라는 뜻으로 사용되었으므로 ② inescapably와 바꿔 쓸 수 있다.

어 휘 inextricably 탈출할 수 없게, 불가분하게 bound to 반드시 ~하게 되어 있다 prowess 훌륭한 솜씨, 기량 observational 관찰하는, 관측의 vice versa 반대로

---

34 ⑤ 정부는 <u>의무적인</u> 신원 확인의 제한적인 형태에 대해 논의를 하고 있는 중이다. 준비되고 있는 법률 하에서, 신원 확인은 구직과 같이 특정한 상황에서는 반드시 수행되어야만 한다.

① 휴대용의   ② 결점 없는

③ 임시변통의   ④ 간소화한
⑤ 의무적인

정답 해설 mandatory는 '의무적인, 필수의'라는 뜻으로 사용되었으므로 ⑤ obligatory와 바꿔 쓸 수 있다.

어 휘 mandatory 명령의, 강압적인 identification 신원 확인, 신분 확인서

---

35 ① Arizona 주, Tucson 지역에는 도로에 움푹 패인 곳이 없고 다만 '포장도로의 부족현상'이 있을 뿐이다. 가난한 사람들도 더 이상은 없고 '<u>재정적으로</u> 적게 획득하는 사람들'이 있을 뿐이다. 자동인출기 강도 역시 없으나 '허가받지 않은 인출'이 있다. 이런 애매모호한 말들은 계속된다. 애매모호한 말들은 부정적인 것들을 긍정적으로, 기분 나쁜 것을 매력적으로 또는 최소한 인내할 만한 것으로 보이게 한다.

① 재정상의   ② 실제의
③ 학업의   ④ 신체의
⑤ 보통의

정답 해설 fiscal은 '재정상의'라는 뜻으로 사용되었으므로 ① financial과 바꿔 쓸 수 있다.

어 휘 pothole 도로에 생긴 깊은 구멍, deficiency 결핍, 결함 doublespeak 사실을 호도하기 위한 말, (고의적으로 쓰는) 모호한 말

---

36 ③ 냄새는 우리의 정신을 고취시키고, 진정시킬 수 있으며 심지어는 우리가 살을 빼는 데 도움을 줄 수 있다. 일부 냄새들은 좋은 측면에서 우리에게 <u>혐오감을 줄</u> 수 있는데, 우리에게 가스가 새고 있다는 것과 우유가 상했다는 것, 고기가 부패했다는 것을 알려 줄 수 있다.

① 마음을 끌다   ② 활성화하다
③ 혐오감을 주다   ④ 보충하다
⑤ 비난하다

정답 해설 repulse는 '혐오감을 주다'라는 뜻으로 사용되었으므로 ③ repel과 바꿔 쓸 수 있다.

어 휘 odor 냄새, 악취 repulse 구역질나게 하다, 혐오감을 주다 spoil 상하다, 망치다 rebuke 비난하다, 꾸짖다

37 ③ 그 망아지는 겁에 질려있었다. 무리에서 따로 떨어져 있었기 때문에 포식자들에게 공격받기 쉬웠다. 그 망아지는 초조하게 앞뒤로 움직이고 있었으며 그의 머리는 땅에 박을 듯이 하고 있었다. 그것은 거의 경례하는 것처럼, 마치 복종의 표시처럼 보였다.

① 아주 우스움
② 친절
③ 복종
④ 공격
⑤ 불확실

정답 해설 deference는 '복종, 존경'이라는 뜻으로 사용되었으므로 ③ submission과 바꿔 쓸 수 있다.

어 휘 colt 망아지, 애송이 back and forth 앞뒤로 bow 머리를 숙이다, 절하다

38 ① 그날 이후로 그는 파충류를 전공했다. 그가 수료한 과정은 이론과 실습을 모두 포함하고 있었다. 아침에 파충류들의 각각의 모습에 대한 긴 강의가 있었다. 그는 그 수업에서 특별히 두각을 나타내지는 못했다. 그는 무엇인가 잊어버리는 데 놀라우리만치 융통성 있는 재주를 가지고 있었다.

① 융통성 있는
② 똑바로
③ 부여된
④ 보이는
⑤ 난잡한

정답 해설 versatile은 '유용한, 융통성 있는, 다재다능한'이라는 뜻으로 사용되었으므로 ① adaptable과 바꿔 쓸 수 있다.

어 휘 reptile 파충류 marvelously 신비하게도 versatile 재주가 많은, 다재다능한, 융통성이 있는

39 ① 도로가 미끄러우면, 우리 몸의 모든 신경과 근육은 균형을 잡기 위해 긴장하고, 넘어질지도 모른다는 공포심은 모든 것들 중 가장 심신을 지치게 하는 것이다.

① 심신을 지치게 하는
② 자극적인
③ 격노한
④ 격려하는
⑤ 궁금하게 하는

정답 해설 exhausting은 '심신을 지치게 하는, 소모적인'이라는 뜻으로 사용되었으므로 ① fatiguing과 바꿔 쓸 수 있다.

어 휘 slippery 미끄러운, 매끄러운 straining 팽팽한, 긴장한

40 ④ 그가 시인한 바에 따르면 필립 존슨은 "많은 한물간 일들"을 하게 되었다. 그래서 시카고 공원과 재건축부의 역사 유적지 복원의 감독관인 존슨이 시 소유의 Hurst house 지하실에 들어섰을 때 그는 어렵지 않게 누군가 그곳의 바위에 새겨놓은 선들을 식별해 냈다.

① 파괴적인
② 정성들인
③ 재미있는
④ 낡은
⑤ 귀찮은

정답 해설 obsolete는 '낡은, 한물간'이라는 뜻으로 사용되었으므로 ④ antiquated와 바꿔 쓸 수 있다.

어 휘 historic 역사적인, 역사적으로 중요한 restoration 회복, 복구 carve 새기다, 조각하다

41 ② 도시와 지방 간의 분열이 단지 미국인들만의 독특한 생각은 아니다. 19세기의 가장 훌륭한 유럽의 사회 이론가들은 그때 발생하고 있던 사회적인 변화가 혈연관계에 기초한 협력 공동체에서 사회 경제적인 관심사에 기초한 더 거대하고 냉정한 사회로 변화하는 것이라고 설명했다.

① 불일치
② 분리
③ 조화
④ 닮음
⑤ 완성

정답 해설 cleavage는 '분열'이라는 뜻으로 사용되었으므로 ② separation과 바꿔 쓸 수 있다.

어 휘 cleavage 갈라진 틈, 분열 theorist 이론가 impersonal 비인간적인, 개인적이지 않은

42 ⑤ 창의성이란 단지 유전에 의한 결과물만은 아니며 문화에 의해 상당히 영향을 받을 수 있다. 그것은 천재들만의 전유물은 아니다. 그것은 우리들 모두가 누릴 수 있는 특권이다.

① 추구, 추적
② 선호, 우선권
③ 실행, 수행
④ 지각, 인식
⑤ 특권, 특전

정답 해설 prerogative는 '특권'이라는 뜻으로 사용되었으므로 ⑤ privilege와 바꿔 쓸 수 있다.

어휘 substantially 실질적으로, 상당히 prerogative 특권, 특전

43 ① 사람들은 도로 사정의 개선에 반응하는 것처럼 더 빠르고 부주의하게 운전함으로써 안전띠에 반응한다. 안전띠 법률 시행의 결과는 증가한 사고 건수이다. 안전 운전 소홀은 보행자들에게 명백한 해로운 영향을 끼치게 되었고, 그들은 훨씬 더 사고 위험이 높아졌다.

① 불리한   ② 사소한
③ 불변의, 일정한   ④ 무계획적인, 우연의
⑤ 보이는

정답 해설 adverse는 '불리한, 부정적인'이라는 뜻으로 사용되었으므로 ① unfavorable과 바꿔 쓸 수 있다.

어휘 improvement 향상 decline 감소

44 ⑤ 모든 위대한 예술 작품들은 종교적이든, 사회적이든 정치적이든 혹은 이례적으로 예술가의 내면의 상상을 표현하기 위한 것이든 상관없이 어떤 목적에 따라 창조되었다. 미적인 수준을 감안하지 않고 창조된 인공물은 거의 없다.

① 생활용품   ② 과학 물질
③ 종교적인 물건   ④ 잘 알려진 기념물
⑤ 인공물, 인간이 만든 물체

정답 해설 artifact는 '인공물'이라는 뜻으로 사용되었으므로 artifacts는 ⑤ man-made objects와 바꿔 쓸 수 있다.

어휘 exceptionally 예외적으로 aesthetic 미술의, 미적인

45 ① 멀지 않은 과거에 뉴욕의 매우 빈곤한 마을인 Brownsville은 해만 떨어지면 거리가 유령 마을처럼 변했던 때가 있었다. 아이들은 거리에서 자전거를 타려 하지 않았다. Brooklyn의 그 지역에서는 마약 거래가 만연하여 대부분의 사람들은 해질녘에 그들의 안전한 아파트로 가곤 했다.

① 일반적인, 널리 퍼져있는   ② 변덕스러운
③ 사악한, 부도덕한   ④ 희박한
⑤ 산발적인

정답 해설 rampant는 '만연한'이라는 뜻으로 사용되었으므로 ① prevalent와 바꿔 쓸 수 있다.

어휘 dusk 어둑어둑함, 땅거미 vicious 과격한, 사나운, 거친 nightfall 해질녘, 황혼

46 ③ 1513년 마키아벨리는 '군주론'에서 시민들이 '무엇이든 생각하고, 말하고, 저술할 권리'를 지녔다고 인정했다. 그러나 그는 군주에게 그들의 그러한 권리를 얼마든지 부정할 수 있는 권리가 동등하게 주어진다고 주장했다. 백년 뒤 스코틀랜드의 군주 제임스 6세는 마키아벨리의 이러한 주장을 인용하여 한 선언서에서 '표현의 자유'를 통렬히 비난했다.

① 평가했다   ② 무게를 달았다
③ 비난했다   ④ ~을 결심했다
⑤ ~을 조사했다

정답 해설 inveigh against는 '~을 통렬히 비난하다'라는 뜻으로 사용되었으므로 inveighed against는 ③ rebuked와 바꿔 쓸 수 있다.

어휘 acknowledge 인정하다 privilege 특권, 특전 proclamation 선언, 포고, 공포 inveigh 통렬히 비난하다, 호되게 비난하다

47 ③ 상품의 판매량은 기술의 진보, 소비자의 취향 변화와 경쟁 심화 등의 여러 가지 이유로 감소한다. 판매량과 이익이 감소하게 되면, 일부 회사들은 시장에서 철수한다. 남아 있는 회사들은 제품 공급량을 축소할 수도 있다. 그들은 소규모 시장이나 주요하지 않은 판매처를 배제할 수도 있고 또는 홍보 예산을 삭감하거나 가격을 더 내릴 수도 있다.

① 강화하다   ② 추수하다
③ 자르다   ④ 유지하다
⑤ 붙들어두다

정답 해설 prune은 '축소하다, 불필요한 부분을 잘라내다'라는 뜻으로 사용되었으므로 ③ clip과 바꿔 쓸 수 있다.

어 휘 prune 불필요한 부분을 잘라내다, 축소하다 segment 단편, 조각, 부분 marginal 가장자리의, 여분의

어 휘 factual 사실에 기반을 둔 distortion 왜곡 ambiguity 모호함

More Practice

| 01 ② | 02 ① | 03 ② | 04 ③ |

01 ② 그들은 숲 속에 사는 영들이 <u>달래져야</u> 한다거나, 소금을 뿌리는 일이 악마를 눈멀게 한다고 믿었다.

① 전해져야 ② 달래져야, 진정되어야
③ 약해져야 ④ 극복되어야, 정복되어야
⑤ 당황해야

정답 해설 appease는 '달래다, 진정시키다'라는 뜻이므로, 밑줄 친 부분은 ② pacified와 바꿔 쓸 수 있다.

어 휘 appease 달래다, 충족시키다

02 ① 전쟁의 역사 초기에, 군대의 수장은 다음과 같은 <u>곤경</u>에 맞닥뜨렸다.

① 곤경 ② 미신
③ 권위자, 전문가 ④ 큰 실수
⑤ 주변, 겉면

정답 해설 predicament는 '곤경, 궁지'라는 뜻으로 사용되었으므로, ① quandary와 바꿔 쓸 수 있다.

어 휘 warfare 전쟁, 전투 be faced with ~에 직면하다 predicament 곤경, 궁지, 상황

03 ② 특정한 사실적 정보를 어떠한 왜곡이나 <u>모호함</u>이 없이 전달하는 체계로서, 꿀벌의 신호 체계는 아마 인간의 언어를 항상 쉽게 이길 것이다.

① 해석 ② 불분명함
③ 결과 ④ 이행
⑤ 공급

정답 해설 ambiguity는 '애매함, 모호함'이라는 뜻으로 사용되었으므로, ② obscurity와 바꿔 쓸 수 있다.

04 ③ 게다가, 수산 양식용 가두리가 처음 지어질 때의 일반적인 지식 부족과 불충분하게 실행된 관리는 과다한 사료 공급과 어류 폐기물로 발생한 오염이 거대한 <u>불모의</u> 해저 사막을 만들어냈다는 것을 의미했다.

① 기본적인 ② 중대한
③ 황량한 ④ 긴요한
⑤ 정당한

정답 해설 barren은 '불모의, 황폐한'이라는 뜻으로 사용되었으므로, ③ desolate와 바꿔 쓸 수 있다.

어 휘 insufficient 불충분한 pen 울타리 initially 초기의 excess 과잉의 barren 불모의, 황폐한

Example

답 ②

한 이론에 따르면, 특정한 제한 내에서는 의사소통하는 사람들이 더 비슷할수록, 그들의 의사소통이 더 효율적이어진다. 한 제한적인 상황은 사람들 사이에 유사점이 너무 많아서 그들이 모든 주제에 같은 태도와 신념을 가진다면, 의사소통을 할 필요성이 없어진다는 것이다. 예를 들어, 모든 사람들이 영화부터 정치까지 모든 주제에서 같은 입장을 가진 파티의 대화는 ② 활기찰(→ 지루할) 것이다. 반면에, 거의 모든 사항에 대해 다른 사람들은, 경험을 나누고 생각을 교환하는 바탕인 공통점이 없을 것이다. 이 이론에 따르면, 이 상적인 상황은, 사람들이 많은 공통점을 가지고 있지만 상호작용하고 어쩌면 상대방의 태도에 영향을 줄 당장의 주제에 대해 그들의 태도가 충분히 다른 경우이다. 그러나 유사점이 분명히 우세하다. 결국, 태도 영향의 목표는 다른 사람의 태도를 바꿔 당신 자신의 것과 더 많이 닮도록 하는 것이다.

주제 참여자 특성에 따른 의사소통의 효율성

Practice

01 ④	02 ①	03 ④	04 ②	05 ④
06 ③	07 ④	08 ④	09 ③	10 ⑤
11 ⑤	12 ⑤	13 ⑤	14 ③	15 ④
16 ②	17 ③	18 ④		

01 ④ 영적 차원은 복잡하고 논쟁적인 분야이며 그것이 일의 신체적, 정신적, 그리고 감정적인 측면에 커다란 영향을 줄 수 있는 중요한 요소임이 점점 더 밝혀지고 있음에도 종종 전체론적 접근법 안에서 간과되곤 한다. 안타깝게도 영성과 탄력성을 탐구하는 연구의 대다수는 영성을 쉽게 측정되고 제어될 수 있는 단일실체로 본다. 현실의 영성은 복잡하고 다차원적인 현상이다. 이런 이유로 영성에 대한 넓은 범위의 해석을 ④ 배제한(→포함한) 연구는 우리의 이해를 확장시키기 위해서 중요하다. 종교적인 정의만을 사용하여 영성을 해석하는 사람들이 있다. 미국과 영국에서 종종 보이는 기독교적 해석으로서 미국과 영국에서 자주 보이는 영성에 대한 이 편협한 종교적 해석은 그들의 차별 반대 관행을 자랑스럽게 여기는 정부 기관에는 부적절하다.

주제 광범위한 영성 연구의 필요성
정답 해설 주어진 글은 영성은 복잡하고 다차원적인 현상이라고 언급한다. 우리의 이해를 확장시키려면 영성에 대한 넓은 범

위의 해석을 포함하는 것이 문맥상 자연스럽다. 따라서 '배제하다'라는 뜻의 ④ excludes는 '포함하다'라는 뜻의 includes로 수정되는 것이 적절하다.

어휘 overlook 간과하다 holistic 전체론적인 spirituality 영성 resilience 탄력성 entity 독립체 phenomenon 현상 interpretation 해석 definition 정의 anti-discriminatory 차별 반대

02 ① 4차 산업 혁명은 그것의 특성뿐만 아니라 갈등의 규모에도 영향을 미칠 것이다. 전쟁과 평화, 그리고 전투자와 민간인의 구별은 불편하게 ① 명확해지고(→모호해지고) 있다. 마찬가지로, 전쟁터는 점점 더 지역적인 동시에 세계적이 되어 간다. ISIS와 같은 단체는 주로 중동의 특정 지역에서 활동하지만 지구 어디서든 연관된 테러리스트 공격이 일어날 수 있는 한, 그들은 100개국 이상에서 주로 소셜미디어를 통해 전사를 모집하기도 한다. 현재의 갈등은 전통적인 전쟁터의 기술과 전에는 주로 무장한 비국가 활동 세력과 연계되었던 요소의 결합으로 특성상 점점 더 혼합되고 있다. 그러나 예측 불가능한 방식으로 융합하는 기술과 서로를 학습하는 국가 및 비국가 무장 활동 세력으로 말미암아 잠재적 변화의 크기는 아직 널리 알려져 있지 않다.

주제 4차 산업 혁명이 세계 갈등에 끼칠 영향
정답 해설 주어진 글은 전투자, 전쟁 지역, 전쟁 기술의 경계가 모호해지는 상황을 설명하고 있으므로 '명확한'이라는 뜻의 ① clarified는 '모호한'이라는 뜻의 ambiguous로 수정되어야 한다.

어휘 combatant 전투원 principally 주로 hybrid 혼합의 armed 무장한 non-state actor 비국가 활동 세력 magnitude 중요도, 크기

03 ④ 어느 해안선이든 해수면 상승은 지구의 두 큰 얼음 양동이인 그린란드와 남극으로부터 그것이 얼마나 멀리 떨어져 있는가에 달려 있다. 얼음이 녹으면서 가장 가까운 나라들이 가장 큰 상승을 보일 것이라고 생각하기 쉽지만 그리 간단하지 않다. 그린란드와 남극의 거대한 얼음장은 그들 주변의 물 위에서 강력한 중력의 인력을 발휘하는데, 그들이 녹으면서 인력이 약화되어 근처 해수면을 하강하게 만든다. 게다가 얼음의 무게에 대한 부담 없이 육지는, 바다보다 살짝 올라가면서 부상한다. 그 효과는 거리와 함께 감소하므로, 실제로 해수면의 가장 큰 ④ 하강(→상승)을 보게 되는 곳은 녹는 얼음에서 멀리 떨어진 곳이다. 대양의 해류는 지구의 녹은 해수를 밀어내는 것을 도와준다.

"그것은 놀랍기도 하고 반직관적이지만, 그것은 현실이다."라고 하버드 대학의 지구물리학자인 Jerry Mitrovica가 말했다.

해수면 상승 현상

본문의 내용은 그린란드와 남극의 얼음장의 인력 효과가 얼음이 녹는 곳으로부터 거리가 멀어질수록 감소한다고 말하고 있으므로, 얼음이 녹는 곳으로부터 가장 멀리 떨어진 곳에서 해수면이 상승한다고 보는 것이 자연스럽다. 따라서 ④는 글의 흐름에 적절하지 않다.

gravitational 중력의 attraction 인력, 끌어당김 counterintuitive 반직관적인 geophysicist 지구물리학자

04 ② 네 개의 작은 머리가 끝이 안 보이는 얼음에 둘러싸인 검푸른 바닷물 웅덩이에서 동시에 튀어 나온다. 그들은 물고기처럼 쉽게 헤엄쳐 온 바다 세계에서 떠나기를 꺼리며 망설이는 것처럼 보인다. 그들은 Adélie 펭귄이고, 얼음은 그들의 존재를 ② 멸종 위기에 빠뜨린다(→ 살게 해준다). 그 새들은 남극 해변을 둘러싼 이 차가운 바다에서 완전히 편하게 물에 들어갔다 나오면서 작은 원에서 흥분해서 뛰어오른다. 그들의 음식은 말 그대로 얼어 있는 바다에 묶여 있다. 바다 얼음의 층 안에는 위에서 햇볕을 받아서 미세한 조류가 다량으로 피어난다. 여름이 시작하면서 얼음이 녹을 때 얼음 조류는 물속으로 나오게 되는데, 물속에서 그들은 빽빽한 무리의 크릴 — 새우와 유사한 갑각류의 일종 — 에 의해 뜯어 먹힌다. 크릴은 결국 Adélie 펭귄의 주요 먹이가 된다.

Adélie 펭귄의 생태

Adélie 펭귄은 얼음에서 먹이를 구하며 살아가므로 ②는 글의 흐름상 적절하지 않다.

simultaneously 동시에 microscopic 매우 작은 algae 말, 조류 profusion 다량

05 ④ 인간 게놈은 복잡한 유기체의 구성을 안내하는 수많은 양의 정보를 포함한다. 많은 수의 경우들에서, 특정 유전자는 인식, 언어와 성격의 측면에 연결될 수 있다. 심리학적 특성이 다를 때, 변화의 많은 부분은 유전자의 차이에서 비롯된다. 일란성 쌍둥이는 이란성 쌍둥이보다 더 닮았고, 생물학적인 형제자매는 함께 혹은 따로 길러졌든지 간에 입양된 형제자매보다 더 비슷하다. 한 개인의 성향과 성격은 인생의 초기에 나타나고, 수명이 다할 때까지 ④ 예측불가능한(→ 예측가능한) 상태로 남아 있다. 그리

고 성격과 지능 둘 다 어린이들이 속한 문화의 특정 가정환경의 영향은 거의 보여주지 않는다. 같은 가정에서 길러진 아이들은 주로 그들의 공유된 유전자로 인해 비슷하다. 더욱이 뇌과학은 뇌의 기본적인 구조가 유전적인 통제 아래 발달한다는 것을 보여주고 있다.

유전자가 개인의 성격에 미치는 영향

유전자로 인해서 개인의 성향과 성격이 인생 초기에 나타나고 이를 통해 예측 가능한 상태로 남아 있다고 보는 것이 문맥상 자연스럽다. 따라서 ④는 글의 흐름상 적절하지 않다.

enormous 수많은 identical twins 일란성 쌍둥이 fraternal twins 이란성 쌍둥이 adoptive 입양의 temperament 기질

06 ③ 모든 역사에서, 갑작스런 그리스 문명의 발흥만큼 놀랄 일도, 설명하기 어려운 일도 없다. 문명을 만드는 요소들은 이미 이집트와 메소포타미아에서 수천 년 동안 존재했고, 거기에서 주변국들로 전파되었다. 하지만 그리스가 그들에게 제공하기까지는 특정한 요소들이 부족했다. 그들이 미술과 문학에서 이뤄낸 것들은 다들 비슷했지만, 그들이 순수하게 지적인 영역에서 이뤄낸 것들은 더욱 ③ 평범했다(→ 특별했다). 그들은 수학과 과학 그리고 철학을 발명했고, 그들은 처음으로 역사를 1년 주기 기록에 반(反)해서 작성했고, 그들은 세상의 이치와 사후 세계에 대해서 그동안의 정설의 족쇄에 묶이지 않고 좀 더 자유롭게 사색했다.

그리스 문명의 독특성

그리스가 더욱 더 지적으로 뛰어난 문화를 다른 나라에 전파했기 때문에, 문맥의 흐름상 ③ '평범했다'는 어울리지 않는다.

civilization 문명 thence 거기에서, 그 뒤에 neighbour 이웃 lack 부족하다 achieve 달성하다 realm 범위, 영역 ordinary 평범하다 philosophy 철학 opposed to 반대하다 annal 1년간의 기록 fetter 족쇄 orthodoxy 정설(正說)

07 ④ 밤에 도시의 어둠을 떨쳐버린 전등은 평범한 시민들에게 시대가 변했다는 가장 극적인 증거를 제공했다. 석탄에서 만들어진 가스로 밝히던 가스등은 19세기 초기부터 사용되어 왔지만, 12개의 촛불 세기에 불과한 불빛은 도시의 공간을 어스레하게 만들 뿐이었다. 전기의 최초로 사업적인 사용은 도시를 더 밝게 하기 위함이었다. 1878년 필라델피아의 Wanamaker 백화점에 처음 설

치된 Charles F. Brush의 아크등은 더욱 밝은 빛을 내뿜었고, 곧 국가의 도시의 거리와 공공건물에 가스등이 ④ 설치되었다(→ 필요없어졌다). 전기 등은 그 후 1879년 Thomas Edison의 실용적인 백열등의 발명 덕분에 미국 가정집에 도입되었다. Edison의 좌우명 "빛이 있게 하라!"는 현재 도시의 삶을 사실적으로 묘사한다.

[주 제] 전등이 가져온 변화
[정답 해설] 지문에서 더 밝은 아크등의 개발로 이전까지 설치되어 있던 어두운 가스등은 필요가 없어졌기 때문에 ④ '설치되었다'는 문맥상 어울리지 않는다.

[어 휘] dispel 떨쳐버리다 gloom 어둠 dramatic 극적인 gaslight 가스등 illuminate 밝게 비추다 dimly (빛이) 어둑한, 어스레한 commercial 상업 arc lamp 아크등 incandescent bulb 백열등

08 ④ 사랑 말고, 키스를 하는 동안 또 옮겨지는 게 뭐가 있을까? 네덜란드의 연구원들은 키스가 어떻게 21쌍의 커플들의 구강 세균에 영향을 끼치는지 추적해보았다. 그들은 커플당 한 명에게 세균증식을 추적하기 위한 특정 세균주가 들어있는 생균제 요거트를 마시게 했다. 그러고 나서 그 당사자는 10초간 그 혹은 그녀의 파트너와 키스를 나누도록 부탁했다. 평균적으로 그들이 키스를 나눈 동안 약 8000만 마리의 박테리아를 ④ 없앴다(→ 공유했다). 비록 이것이 매우 위생적으로 들리진 않지만, 전문가들은 다른 누군가의 박테리아에 노출되는 것은 사실 당신의 면역성을 강화하는 데 더 도움을 줄 수 있다고 말한다.

[주 제] 박테리아를 옮기는 키스
[정답 해설] '사랑 말고 키스하는 동안 또 옮겨지는 게 뭐가 있을까?'에서 이 글은 키스를 통해 이동하는 어떤 대상에 대한 글임을 알 수 있다. 마지막 문장의 '매우 위생적으로 들리지는 않는다'와 '다른 누군가의 박테리아에 노출되는 것은 당신의 면역성을 강화하는 데 도움을 준다'로 미루어 볼 때 이전 문장의 박테리아는 키스하는 동안 서로 공유된다는 내용이 문맥상 적절하다. 따라서 ④의 '제거했다, 없앴다'라는 뜻의 extinguished는 문맥상 적절하지 않다.

[어 휘] Dutch 네덜란드의 track 추적하다 probiotic 바이오 유 제품의, 생균제의 bacterial strain 세균주 hygienic 위생적인 exposure 노출

09 ③ 무대 뒤의 공간, 무대의 벽과 건물의 뒤쪽 사이에 있는 그곳은 '분장실'로 알려져 있었다. 여기에 의

상과 각종 소품들이 보관되어 있었고, 연기자들은 그곳에서 자신을 준비된 상태로 만들었다. 초창기에 분장실은 건물과는 별도로 세워진 간이 구조물이었지만, 오늘날에는 골조 구조로 지어진다. 무대 바로 뒤는 그날의 연극에 ③ 불필요한 (→ 필수적인) 모든 물건들과 사람들이 준비된 상태로 모여 있는, 빽빽하고 뒤죽박죽으로 뒤섞인 공간이 되었다. 의상은 어디에나 걸려있었다. 연극에서 의상을 자주 바꿔야 하는 연기자들은 옷을 입거나 벗고 있었고, 그 틈에 '분장실 조수'들은 그 옷들을 질서 정연하게 정리하려고 노력했다. 탁자와 의자는 연기자들의 소품 그리고 가짜 턱수염이나 가발, 화장품 등으로 뒤덮였다.

[주 제] 연극 무대 뒤 광경
[정답 해설] 문맥상 '그날의 연극 공연을 위해 필요한 모든 것들이 준비된 상태로 모여 있어야 한다.'라는 내용이 오는 것이 자연스럽다. 따라서 '불필요하다.'라는 의미의 inessential 보다는 '필요한, 필수적인'이라는 의미를 갖는 essential과 같은 어휘가 적절하다.

[어 휘] tiring house 분장실(의상실) prop (연극을 위한) 소도구, 소품 free-standing 지지대 없이 별도로 서있는 framework 골조, 뼈대 jumble (뒤죽박죽으로, 마구) 뒤섞다 pack (사람이나 짐으로) 가득 채우다 tiremen 분장실(의상실) 직원, 조수 beard (턱)수염 wig 가발

10 ⑤ 일반적으로 법 집행 기관은 동의를 얻어 수색을 할 수 있다. 그것이 유효한 것으로 인정받으려면, 동의하에 이루어지는 수색은 반드시 다음 두 가지 기준을 충족시켜야 한다. 첫 번째, 허가는 반드시 자유롭게 그리고 자발적으로 승인되어야 한다. 두 번째, 동의를 인정하는 사람은 반드시 그럴 수 있는 권한을 갖고 있어야 한다. 일단 허가가 떨어지면 경찰은 적법하게 수색을 하겠지만, 수색은 동의를 한 사람이 설정한 한계 이상으로 확장되어 이루어지지는 않을 것이다. 동의의 필수적인 자발적 성질은 동의를 수락하는 과정이 협박의 결과로 이루어질 수는 없다는 것을 의미한다. 만약 경찰이 실제적인 혹은 위협적인 물리적 폭력, 또는 속임수를 통하여 동의를 끌어낸다면, 그 수락은 효력을 잃게 되고 수색의 결과도 그렇게 된다. 두 번째 필수 요건은 오직 권한이 있는 사람만이 수색에 대해 허가를 해줄 수 있다는 것을 의미한다. 일반적으로 그러한 수락은 집, 자동차, 사무실, 또는 경찰이 수색하고자 하는 어떤 공간을 소유하고 있거나 점유하고 있는 또는 ⑤ 부분적으로(→ 전체적으로) 통제하에 두고 있는 성인에 의해서만 주어질 수 있다.

[주 제] 동의를 얻은 수색의 필수 조건
[정답 해설] 법적으로 권한이 있는 사람만이 수색에 대해 동의를

해줄 수 있다고 하였으므로 부분적으로 통제하고 있는 사람이 수색에 동의할 수 있다고 보기 어렵다. 문맥상 wholly와 같은 뉘앙스의 단어를 사용하는 것이 적절하다.

as a rule 대체로, 일반적으로 **criteria** 기준(criterion 의 복수형) **consent search** 동의를 받고 이루어지는 수색 **intimidation** 협박, 위협 **trickery** 속임수, 사기

11 ⑤ 환자들의 삶의 질을 개선시키도록 도와주는 사회적 지원과 보살핌을 효율적으로 활용하는 의료 시스템은 그들의 치유 능력을 상당히 발전시켜줄 것이다. 예를 들면, 병원의 침상에 누워있는, 그리고 다음날에 있을 큰 수술을 기다리고 있는 환자는 걱정하지 않을 수 없을 것이다. 어떤 상황에서건, 한 사람이 강하게 느끼는 것은 다른 사람들에게도 전달되기 마련이다. 누군가 더 많은 스트레스를 받고, 나약하다고 느끼면 느낄수록 그들은 더욱 더 민감한 상태가 되고, 그러한 감정을 계속해서 느끼게 될 가능성이 높다. 만약 걱정하는 환자들이 역시 수술을 앞두고 있는 다른 환자들과 같은 병실을 쓰고 있다면, 그들은 서로 상대방을 더 불안하게 만들지도 모른다. 하지만 만약 그녀가 이제 막 수술을 성공적으로 마치고 나와서 상대적으로 안도하고 평온한 환자와 같은 병실을 공유하게 된다면, 그녀에게 미칠 정신적인 영향은 더 ⑤ 상황을 악화시키는(→ 상황을 완화하는) 것이 될 것이다.

주 제 환자 간 감정의 상호 전달
정답 해설 감정은 전이될 수 있는 것이라고 하였으므로 수술을 잘 받고 나온 환자와 같은 병실을 사용하게 될 경우 훨씬 더 긍정적인 효과를 기대할 수 있을 것이다. 따라서 '상황을 더 나쁘게 만드는, 질병을 악화시키는'과 같은 의미를 갖고 있는 aggravating은 적절하지 못하다.

어 휘 **boost** 신장시키다, 발전시키다 **deploy** 배치하다, 북돋다 **can't help but** ~하지 않을 수 없다 **vulnerable** 나약한, 취약한 **aggravate** (상황이나 질병 등을) 악화시키다

12 ⑤ 좋은 이야기들, 특히 영화를 위한 좋은 이야기를 창작해 줄 작가들에 대한 수요는 지속적으로 존재해 왔다. 하지만 사용되지 않거나, 앞으로도 절대 영화로 만들어지지 않을 이야기와 시나리오의 공급은 훨씬 더 많다. 사실, 매해 100,000개 이상의 대본이 쓰여지고, 이 중 몇 백 개의 작품만이 실제 영화로 제작된다. 그럼에도 불구하고 이 영화들의 대부분은 흥행하지 못한다. 대개는 대본이 (문제의) 원인인 경우이다. 그리고 대부분의 대본들이

갖고 있는 문제점은 바로 이야기가 부족하다는 것이다. 믿거나 말거나, 영화를 위한 좋은 이야기와 시나리오를 만들어내는 과정에는 엄청나게 많은 관심이 든다. 하지만 이러한 통계상의 수치는 좋은 이야기를 만들어내는 것이 얼마나 ⑤ 쉬운지(→ 어려운지)에 대해 알려주는 놀라운 증거일 뿐이다.

주 제 좋은 이야기 창작의 어려움
정답 해설 전반적으로 좋은 이야기와 시나리오를 만들어 내는 것이 굉장히 중요하고 어려운 일이라고 말하고 있으므로 ⑤의 easy는 difficult로 수정되어야 한다.

어 휘 **screenplay** 영화 대본, 시나리오 **culprit** 범인, 범죄자, (문제의) 원인 **startling** 놀라운, 깜짝 놀라게 하는

13 ⑤ 다른 형태의 통치에는 다른 형태의 군사 조직이 대응된다. 중세시대에 자주 도시들은 보통 그들만의 군대를 조직했고, 시민들에게 병역의 의무를 부과했다. 시민의 개념은 모든 도시의 인구를 포함하는 것은 아니었고, 종종 자기 혁신 조직의 선출된 구성원들만으로 범위를 좁히기도 하였다. 베니스와 다른 여러 해양 도시의 경우에는, 병역 의무는 민병대뿐만 아니라 해군에 대한 복무로 이루어져 있었다. 장원제도 하에서 지주는 종종 그들의 신하, 소작인, 농노로 구성된 자신만의 군대를 ⑤ 해체했고(→ 형성했고) 때때로 그들의 사적인 전투를 수행하거나, 전쟁기간 중에는 복귀하기 전까지 왕의 부대에 합류하기도 하였다.

주 제 통치 형태에 따른 군사 조직 차이
정답 해설 지문의 마지막 부분에서 지주들이 군대를 어떻게 활용했는지 언급하고 있으므로 '해체했다'라는 뜻의 ⑤ disbanded는 '형성했다'라는 뜻의 단어로 수정되어야 한다.

어 휘 **correspond** 대응하다, 해당하다, 부합하다 **oblige** 의무를 지우다, 부과하다 **narrow** 폭이 좁은, 좁히다, 줄이다 **maritime** 바다의, 해양의 **militia** 의용군, 시민군 **naval service** 해군 복무 **manorial** 장원의, 영지의 **disband** (군대 등이) 해산하다, 해체하다. **vassal** 신하, 가신 **tenant** 소작인 **serf** 농노 **overlord** 지배자, 왕

14 ③ 지난해 미국의 자동차 구매자들은 자동차를 살 때 품질과 안전 이상으로 연비를 가장 중요한 고려 대상으로 꼽았다. 이러한 변화는 자동차 시장에서의 하이브리드와 고효율 내부연소 엔진에 대한 관심의 쇄도와 정확하게 일치한다. 하지만 엔진은 효율적으로 되어갈지 몰라도 단 하나의 명백한 ③ 효율성(→ 비효율성)은 어떻게 보완할

방법이 없다. 그것은 바로 우리 자신이다. 나쁜 운전 습관은 연비를 1/3 만큼이나 감소시킬 수 있다. 연비를 극대화하기 위해서, 기술자들은 자동차를 새로 만드는 것뿐만 아니라, 운전자들 또한 개선시킬 필요가 있다.

주 제 연비를 극대화하기 위한 운전 습관 개선 필요성

정답 해설 운전자의 나쁜 운전 습관이 연비 감소의 원인이라는 언급으로 미루어 볼 때 우리 자신이 바로 명백한 비효율성이라는 내용이 문맥상 자연스럽다. 따라서 ③의 효율성을 뜻하는 efficiency는 비효율성을 뜻하는 inefficiency로 수정되어야 한다.

어 휘 fuel economy 연비, 연료소비율 outrank ~의 위를 차지하다 nicely 좋게, 잘, 정확히 coincide 일치하다, 동시에 일어나다 combustion 연소 glaring 반짝이는, 명백한, 틀림없는 slash 상처를 입히다, 삭감하다

15 ④ 행복의 시장에서 물건을 사고 파는 사람들은 어려움에서 오는 기쁨을 너무 자주 잊어버리는 것같다. 하늘은 그들이 하는 일들을 다 알고 있다. 하지만 그것은 미련한 것처럼 보인다. 그리고 그 자신 외에는 아무것도 필요로 하지 않는 것에 행복이 있다고 생각하는 인도의 성인은, 내가 생각하건데 우리에게 지루해 보인다. 왜냐하면 그는 그 어떤 것도 하기를 거부하고 있는 것처럼 보이기 때문이다. 서양인들의 부족한 점은 행복도 돈으로 구매할 수 있다고 믿는 환상에 있을지도 모른다. 아마도 동양인들의 약점은 완벽하고, 따라서 절대 변하지 않는 행복과 같은 것이 존재한다는 생각일 것이다. 하지만 행복이란 것은 불완전한 것에 불과하다. 사람에게 있어 완벽하게 순수한 상태란 존재하지 않는다. 어떤 행복이라 할지라도, 행복은 소유나 존재하는 것이 아니라 되어 가는 것에 있다. 헌법 제정자들이 우리를 위해 고유의 권리로 선언했던 것, 우리가 반드시 기억해야만 하는 그것은 행복이 아니라 행복에 대한 ④ 인정(→추구)이었다. 아마도 행복의 시장에 대해 미리 예상할 수 있었을 그들이 강조했던 것은 '행복은 그것을 추구하는 것 자체에 있고, 삶에 열중하고, 삶을 드러내 보일 수 있는 의미 있는 추구, 즉 되어 가는 과정이라는 믿음 속에 있다.'는 중요한 사실 일지도 모른다.

주 제 행복의 속성

정답 해설 글의 주제는 '진정한 행복은 그것을 추구하는 과정 중에 있다'이므로 우리가 반드시 기억해야만 하는 것은 행복의 추구라고 하는 것이 문맥상 자연스럽다. 따라서 ④의 acceptance는 pursuit로 수정되는 것이 적절하다.

어 휘 weakness 약점, 약함 static 정적인, 고요한, 움직임이 없는 partial 부분적인, 불완전한 Founding Father 미국 헌법 제정자들 inherent 선천적인, 타고나는 cardinal 주요한, 중요한, 기본적인

16 ② 세상은 호기심을 그리 좋아하지 않는다. 사람들은 '호기심이 고양이를 죽였다.'라고 말한다. 심지어는 호기심이 많은 사람은 좀처럼 게으르지 않음에도 불구하고, 세상은 호기심을 나태한 것이라고 하거나, 단순히 한가한 호기심이라고 불러서 묵살하려 한다. 부모들 역시 아이들의 호기심을 ② 길러주기(→ 억누르기) 위해 최선을 다한다. 왜냐하면 무엇이 불을 뜨겁게 하는지나 왜 잔디가 자라는지에 관한 대답할 수 없는 연속된 질문들과 마주하게 되는 것은 삶을 피곤하게 만들기 때문이다. 부모들은 아이들이 폭발로 목숨을 잃거나 급사를 당하기 전에 그들의 탐구활동을 멈추게 해야만 한다. 부모의 훈육으로부터 생존한 호기심을 소유하거나, 폭발 사고가 나기 전까지 가까스로 살아남은 아이들은 대학으로부터 함께 하기를 요청 받는다. 대학 안에서 그들은 질문하고 정답을 찾기 위해 노력하는 것을 계속해 나간다. 학자의 눈으로 보았을 때 그것이야말로 대학의 주된 목적이다. 대학은 호기심에 대한 세계의 적대감이 도전받을 수 있는 장소이다.

주 제 호기심을 존중하는 장소인 대학

정답 해설 문맥상 부모들은 자녀의 호기심을 반기지 않기 때문에 ② foster는 흐름에 어긋난다. 억누르거나 제거하다는 의미를 가진 단어가 오는 것이 적절할 것이다.

어 휘 curiosity 호기심 foster 기르다, 양육하다 halt 멈추어 서다 faculty 학부, 교수단 hostility 적의, 적개심 defy 도전하다, 반항하다

17 ③ 전문가들은 우리의 인구와 환경 문제가 얼마나 심각한지와 우리는 그것들에 대해 무엇을 해야 하는지에 대해 의견이 분분하다. 몇몇 사람들은 인간의 창의성과 기술 진보가, 우리가 오염들을 용인되는 수준까지 정화하도록 할 것이고, 어떤 부족한 자원이든 그 대체물을 발견하게 해줄 것이라고 말한다. 그들은 기술 혁신이 지구의 천연 자원을 보존할 수 있다고 주장하는 기술 낙관론자들이다. 많은 선구적인 환경 과학자들은 이에 반대한다. 그들은 우리가 만든 중요한 환경 및 사회 발전에 감사하고 박수를 보내지만 우리가 기하급수적인 가속 속도로 세계의 많은 지역에서 지구의 생명 유지 시스템을 ③ 개선시키고(→ 손상시키고) 있다는 증거를 인용한다. 그들은 우리의 경제와 모든 삶을 지탱하는 자연 자본을 보호할 수 있도록 훨씬 더 많은 실천을 요구한다. 그들을 환경론적 비관론자라고 하는데 그들은 우리의 환경 상황이 악화되고 있고, 세계 경제가 그것을 지원하기 위해 지구의 수용력을 초과하고 있다고 주장한다.

주 제 인간이 환경에 끼칠 영향에 대한 상반된 주장

정답 해설 인구 증가가 환경 상황을 악화시키고 있다고 주장하는 과학자들의 언급과 관련하여 우리가 지구의 생명 유지 시스템을 '손상시킨다'는 내용이 문맥상 자연스럽다. 따라서 ③의 upgrading은 downgrading으로 수정되는 것이 적절하다.

어 휘 ingenuity 창의성, 발명 exponential 기하급수적인 natural capital 자연자본 call for ~을 요구하다

18 ④ 사람에게 가장 큰 선물 즉, 인간을 다른 모든 생물보다 우위에 올려놓았고, 전 세계를 지배하게 해 준 개념적 사고와 언어적 표현의 고유 능력들은 전적으로 축복은 아니며, 또한 적어도 비싼 값을 치러야만 하는 축복이라는 것은 역설이다. 인류를 멸종으로 위협하는 모든 큰 위험은 개념적인 생각과 언어적 표현의 직접적인 결과이다. 그것들은 인간이 본능을 따라도 처벌받지 않고, 무슨 일이건 그의 마음대로 해도 되었던 낙원으로부터 사람들을 끌어냈다. 오래 전에는 사람들에게 동등하게 안전한 적응을 제공하기에 충분했지만, 개념적 사고에서부터 발전된 지식들은 사람에게서 적절히 순응한 본능으로부터 오랫동안 제공되었던 ④ 불안(→ 안전)을 강탈해갔다. Arnold Gehlen이 진정으로 말한 바와 같이 인간은 본질적으로 위태로운 동물이다.

주 제 개념적 사고가 인간에게 가져온 위태로움

정답 해설 개념적 사고와 언어적 표현이 인간이 본능을 따를 때의 이점들을 빼앗았다는 내용의 글이다. 따라서 개념적 사고에서 발전된 지식들이 강탈해 간 것은 오랫동안 제공되었던 '불안'이 아니라 '안전'으로 수정되는 것이 더 자연스럽다. 따라서 ④의 insecurity는 security로 수정되는 것이 적절하다.

어 휘 paradox 독설 unique 유일한 faculty 재능, 기능 blessing 축복, 신의 은총 springing 도약, 큰 발전 insecurity 불안 sufficient 충분한 jeopardize 위태롭게 하다, 위험에 빠뜨리다

More Practice

01 ⑤   02 ③   03 ③   04 ④

01 ⑤ 옷이 사람을 만든다는 말이 있는데, 이 말이 군대만큼 사실인 곳은 없다. 군복은 충성심에서부터 직위와 지위까지 모든 것을 나타낸다. 그리고 위장에 있어서 그것은 생사의 차이, 즉 미국의 입법자들이 다른 무엇보다 아프가니스탄의 군대에 70,000벌의 새로운 군복에 비용을 대는 1060억 달러의 긴급 전쟁 비용 법안을 통과시키

기 위해 준비할 때 그들에 의해 제기된 논점을 의미할 수 있다. 분명히, 그 나라의 진흙투성이의, 산이 많은 지형은 바그다드와 같은 먼지 날리는 사막 도시를 위해 디자인된 "보편적인 위장 방식"에는 맞지 않을 것이다. 제1차 세계대전 동안 항공기와 참호 전투의 출현은, 군인들과 예술가들, 미국 군대의 새로 출범한 위장 디자이너들의 필독 도서가 된 'Concealing Coloration in the Animal Kingdom'이라는 1909년 책의 저자 Abbott Thayer와 같은 자연주의자들의 풍성한 협업의 결과를 낳으며, 위장 전투복의 전략과 예술이 생겨나게 했다. 군대는, 모든 방향에서 폭탄과 총알을 피해야만 했기 때문에 이전 전쟁 시대에 착용되던 전통적인 영광의 군복은, 완전히 위험하지 않다면, ⑤ 최신식(→ 구식)으로 보이기 시작했다.

주 제 시대 흐름에 따른 군복의 변화

정답 해설 ⑤의 앞부분은 상황과 환경에 따라 적합한 군복의 형태가 다르다는 내용이다. 따라서 이전 전쟁 시대에 착용되던 전통적인 군복은 '최신식'이 아니라 '구식'으로 보이기 시작했다는 내용이 문맥상 적절하다.

어 휘 terrain 지형, 지역 give rise to ~이 생기게 하다 collaboration 협업 launch 출범하다 now that ~이기 때문에 downright 완전한

02 ③ 만약 당신이 학습하고 있는 것에 세심하게 집중하지 않는다면 학습은 그다지 많이 일어나고 있는 것이 아니다. 집중이란 기본적으로 사고하는 것이다. 집중은 정신적 과제든 육체적 과제든 그것을 하는 당신의 능력을 향상시킬 수 있다. 따라서 학교 공부에서 실패를 많이 하는 이유는 낮은 지능보다는 형편없는 집중력 때문이다. 연구자들은 집중의 한 가지 적은 망설임이라고 언급한다. 언제 공부하고 어느 과목부터 공부할 것인지를 결정하지 못하고 망설이는 것은 굉장한 시간 낭비일 뿐만 아니라 공부에 대한 부정적인 태도를 ③ 제거하는(→ 조장하는) 확실한 방법이다. 개인적인 문제 또한 집중에 지장을 준다. 만약 당신이 개인적인 문제에 사로잡혀 있다면 당신은 지능을 충분히 사용하지 못할 것이다. 당신의 문제에 어느 정도 건설적인 조치를 취하고 나면 당신은 학습이든 수행이든 잘할 수 있는 더 나은 상태에 있을 것이다.

주 제 학습에서 집중력의 중요성

정답 해설 망설임은 집중력의 적이라 했으므로, 언제 공부하고 어느 과목을 공부할 것인지를 결정하지 못하고 망설이는 것은 시간낭비일 뿐만 아니라 공부에 대한 부정적인 태도를 조장하는 방법이라고 써야 문맥상 자연스럽다. 이때

③ eliminate는 encourage로 수정할 수 있다.

어휘 **enhance** 높이다, 끌어올리다 **indecision** 망설임, 우유부단 **eliminate** 제거하다, 없애다 **interfere with** 방해하다 **make use of** ~을 이용하다 **preoccupied with** ~에 사로잡힌, 몰두한 **constructive** 건설적인

03 ③ 연구자들은 좋은 사회적 관계를 유지하는 것이 두 가지 상호보완적인 과정, 즉 타인의 요구에 민감한 것과 위반 행위가 정말로 일어나면 보상이나 배상이 가능하도록 자극을 받는 것에 달려있다는 점을 언급해왔다. 요컨대, 좋은 사회적 관계를 유지하는 것은 죄책감의 수용 능력에 달려 있다. Martin L. Hoffman은, 타인에게 해를 입히면 생기는 죄책감에 초점을 맞춰왔는데, 그는 이러한 죄책감의 동기 유발 기반은 공감적 고통이라고 말한다. 공감적 고통은 자신들의 행동이 다른 사람에게 손해나 고통을 일으켰음을 ③ 부인할(→ 깨달을) 때 생긴다. 죄책감으로 인해 자극을 받을 때, 사람들은 자신의 행동에 대해 보상을 하려는 경향이 있다. 보상하는 것은 손상된 사회적 관계를 회복하고 집단의 화합을 재건하는 역할을 한다.

주제 공감적 고통의 발생과 역할

정답 해설 공감적 고통은 죄책감에서 나오고 죄책감은 타인에게 해를 입혔을 때 생긴다고 했으므로, 공감적 고통은 타인에게 해를 입혔다는 것을 알게 되었을 때 생기는 것이 자연스럽다. 따라서 ③의 deny를 realize로 바꾸는 것이 적절하다.

어휘 **complementary** 상호보완적인 **sensitive** 민감한, 예민한 **make amends** 보상해 주다 **compensation** 배상, 변상 **capacity** 수용 능력 **guilt** 죄책감, 죄의식 **empathetic** 공감할 수 있는, 감정 이입의 **distress** 고통, 비탄, 고민

04 ④ 1920년대까지 경쟁하는 수영 영법에는 자유형, 배영, 그리고 평영 이 세 가지 밖에 없었고, 각 영법에는 그것이 어떻게 행해져야 하는가를 묘사하는 구체적인 규칙들이 있었다. 평영의 규칙은 두 팔이 물 밑에서 함께 당겨져야 하고, 그런 다음 다음번 팔 젓기를 시작하기 위한 당기기 자세의 시작점으로 동시에 돌아와야 한다고 설명했다. 대부분의 사람들은 이런 팔의 복귀를 물 밑 복귀를 뜻하는 것으로 이해했다. 그러나 1920년대 누군가가 그 규칙에 문제를 제기하여 이런 팔의 복귀를 물 밖 복귀를 뜻하는 것으로 재해석했다. 이런 새로운 평영이 약 15퍼센트나 ④ 더 느렸기(→더 빨랐기) 때문에, 전통적인 평영을 이용하는 사람들은 효과적으로 경쟁을 할 수 없었다. 그 문제를 해결하기 위해서 무언가가 행해져야만 했다. 마침내, 현재 "접영"으로 알려진 이 새 영법은 네 번째 수영 영법으로 인정을 받게 되었고, 1956년에 올림픽 종목이 되었다.

주제 접영이 등장한 과정

정답 해설 전통적 평영 영법으로 수영하는 사람들이 효과적으로 경쟁할 수 없었던 이유는 새로운 평영이 더 빨랐기 때문이라고 하는 것이 자연스러우므로, ④의 slower를 faster로 바꾸는 것이 적절하다.

어휘 **competitive** 경쟁을 벌이는, 경쟁의 **stroke** (수영의) 영법, 팔 젓기 **freestyle** 자유형 **backstroke** 배영 **breaststroke** 평영 **conventional** 전통적인 **butterfly** 접영

UNIT 08 어휘 II

Example
답 ①

연방통신위원회(FCC)에 의하면, 우리 중 많은 사람이 광대역 인터넷을 당연한 것으로 받아들이지만, 미국인 5명 중 1명에 가까운 사람이 이것에 접근할 수 없다. 시골 지역에서는, 저소득 가정들이 요금이 (A) 엄두도 못 내게 비싼 것을 알게 되는 반면, 통신회사들은 멀리 떨어진 가정들의 배선 비용을 두고 망설인다. 광대역 격차를 좁히는 일은 최신 TV 드라마를 재생할 수 있게 되는 것보다 더 큰일이다. 고속 인터넷은 현대적 삶의 중요한 도구로, 아이들이 디지털 방식으로 배우고 어른들이 클라우드를 통해 일하는 것을 (B) 가능하게 한다. FCC는 최근 소규모 광대역 보조금을 승인했으나, 실제적인 해결책은 악명 높게도 통합된 산업의 경쟁 (C) 증가에 있다.

	(A)	(B)	(C)
①	엄두도 못 내게 비싼	가능하게 하는	증가
②	엄두도 못 내게 비싼	가능하게 하는	감소
③	엄두도 못 내게 비싼	제한적이게 하는	감소
④	감당할 만한	제한적이게 하는	증가
⑤	감당할 만한	가능하게 하는	감소

주 제 광대역 인터넷의 높은 비용과 접근성 차이

Practice

01 ②	02 ④	03 ③	04 ①	05 ③
06 ③	07 ②	08 ③	09 ⑤	10 ②
11 ④	12 ③	13 ③	14 ①	15 ④
16 ④	17 ④			

01 ② 우주는 원자와 빈 공간으로만 구성되어 있다는 것, 세계는 신적인 창조자가 우리를 위해 만든 것이 아니라는 것, 우리가 우주의 중심이 아니라는 것, 우리의 육체적 삶에 비해 우리의 감정적 삶이 다른 생물들의 그것과 (A) 뚜렷이 다른 것이 아니라는 것, 우리의 영혼은 우리의 신체만큼이나 물질적이고 필멸한다는 것에 대한 인식이 모두 (B) 절망의 원인은 아니다. 반대로, 일의 실정을 파악하는 것은 행복의 가능성을 향한 중요한 단계이다. 인간은 행복한 삶을 살 수도 있지만 그들이 우주의 중심이라고 생각하기 때문은 아니다. 채울 수 없는 욕망과 죽음에 대한 두려움은 인간의 행복의 주된 (C) 장애물이지만 이성의 단련

을 통해 그것은 극복될 수 있다.

	(A)	(B)	(C)
①	뚜렷이 다른	절망	길
②	뚜렷이 다른	절망	장애물
③	뚜렷이 다른	희망	장애물
④	희미한	희망	장애물
⑤	희미한	절망	길

주 제 이성적 현실 인식에 기인한 행복

정답 해설 (A) 인간과 다른 생물의 감정적 삶의 차이가 크지 않다는 의미가 문맥상 자연스럽다. 따라서 distinct가 적절하다. (B) 실정을 파악하는 것이 행복을 추구하는 데 도움이 된다는 언급으로 미루어 볼 때 주어진 상황을 인식하는 것이 절망의 원인이 아니라는 내용이 문맥상 자연스럽다. 따라서 despair가 적절하다. (C) '인간의 행복의 주된 길'보다는 '인간의 행복의 주된 장애물'이 이성의 단련을 통해 극복될 수 있는 대상으로 더 자연스럽다. 따라서 obstacles가 적절하다.

어 휘 void 빈 공간 providential 신의, 천우신조의 distinct from ~와 뚜렷이 다른 indistinct 희미한 surmount 극복하다

02 ④ 확정된 일련의 관행으로서 음악 치료는, 20세기, 특히 의사와 간호사들이 부상자들의 심리적, 신체적, 인지적, 정서적 상태에 음악이 주는 효과를 목격했던 제 1차 세계대전 기간 서양에서 처음 개발되었다. 음악의 (A) 치유적인 특성에 대한 최초의 주요한 학문적인 연구는 1948년에 발표되었는데, 어느 정도는 2차 세계 대전 동안에 군인 병원과 공장에서의 음악 치료의 지속적인 사용에 대한 반응이었다. 음악 치료는 이제 정신적 또는 신체적 장애나 병을 가지고 있는 사람들에게 (B) 널리 사용된다. 그것의 가장 중요한 기능 중에 하나는 특히 치과, 화상, 그리고 관상동맥 치료의 수술을 준비하거나, 겪고 있거나, 수술 후에 회복 중인 사람들을 안정시키는 것이다. 느리고 일정한 템포, 부드러운 흐름, 조용한 리듬, 예상 가능한 변화, 그리고 단순하게 지속되는 멜로디를 가진 음악이 긴장 완화에 (C) 도움이 된다는 것이 충분히 입증되었다.

	(A)	(B)	(C)
①	심미적인	드물게	해로운
②	심미적인	널리	해로운
③	치유력이 있는	널리	해로운
④	치유력이 있는	널리	도움이 되는
⑤	치유력이 있는	드물게	도움이 되는

주제 음악 치료의 역사와 효용

정답 해설 (A) 이 글은 음악 치료, 즉 음악이 가지고 있는 치유적인 면에 대한 글이기 때문에 medicinal이 적절하다. (B) 음악 치료가 1차 세계 대전 때 개발되어 부상자 대상으로 쓰이다가 2차 세계 대전 때 군인 병원, 공장에서 사용된 후 이제는 정신적, 신체적인 질병을 가진 환자들을 위해 널리 사용된다는 내용이 문맥상 자연스럽다. 따라서 widely가 적절하다. (C) 앞서 나온 문장은 음악 치료가 환자들을 안정시킨다는 내용이다. 따라서 주어진 문장에서 제시된 음악들이 긴장 완화에 도움이 된다는 내용이 문맥상 자연스럽다. 따라서 conducive가 적절하다.

어휘 explicit 분명한, 충분히 해명된 aesthetic 심미적인 medicinal 치유력이 있는 coronary 관상동맥의 attest 증명하다 detrimental 해로운 conducive (~에) 도움이 되는

03 ③ 진화론 학자인 Henry Plotkin이 말한 바와 같이, 무한한 유기체 세대를 넘나드는 세계의 지식을 얻으면서 진화는 필요라는 기준과 관련하여 선별적으로 지식을 보존하고, 그러한 집합적인 지식은 종의 유전적 풀 안에서 유지된다. 그러한 집합 지식은 개인들에게 분배되고, 이들은 (A) 선천적인 생각과 오로지 구체적인 것들을 특한 방식으로 배우는 경향을 가지고 세상에 태어난다. 달리 말하면, 당신이 사바나에서 사냥을 하든 유튜브에서 수백만 개의 동영상 중 선택을 하든, 당신의 뇌는 거의 모든 것을 (B) 무시하고 가장 중요하거나 재미있는 것으로 곧장 나아가도록 설계되어 있다. 그렇지 않으면 당신은 모든 나무와 돌에 창을 던지거나 흔들 것이고, 성가시게도 당신은 가치 있는 무언가를 찾을 것이라는 헛된 희망을 안고 무한한 비디오 링크의 줄에서 길을 잃을 것이다. 우리 유전자의 (C) 구별하는 본성에 대한 이해를 통해, 우리는 우리의 주의력을 이해하고 우리 기억 속에 머무르는 이야기에 대한 기초를 구성하는 것을 시작할 수 있다.

	(A)		(B)		(C)
①	후천적인	……	무시하다	……	통합하는
②	후천적인	……	무시하다	……	구별하는
③	선천적인	……	무시하다	……	구별하는
④	선천적인	……	채택하다	……	통합하는
⑤	선천적인	……	채택하다	……	구별하는

주제 지식을 선별하는 인간 본성

정답 해설 (A) 세상에 태어날 때 지니고 있는 생각은 선천적이라는 내용이 문맥상 자연스럽다. 따라서 innate가 적절하다. (B) 뇌는 가장 중요하거나 재미있는 것으로 나아가려면 그렇지 않은 것들을 무시하도록 프로그램되었다는 내용이 문맥상 자연스럽다. 따라서 ignore가 적절하다. (C) 본문의 내용은 정보를 선별하는 우리의 능력을 언급하고 있다. 따라서 '우리 유전자의 구별하는 본성에 대한 이해'라는 내용이 문맥상 자연스럽다. 따라서 discriminating이 적절하다.

어휘 evolutionary 진화론적인 selectively 선별적으로 collective 집합의 dole 분배하다 innate 타고난, 선천적인 acquired 후천적인 predisposition 경향, 성질 home in 목표를 향해 나아가다 annoyingly 성가시게

04 ① 작년 여름, 캘리포니아의 26세 여성은 응급상황을 신고하기 위해 911에 전화를 걸었다. 그녀가 유선전화를 사용했다면, 처음 전화를 받은 응답자는 그녀의 위치를 몇 초 이내에 (A) 정확히 찾을 수 있었을 것이다. 하지만 지금의 911 시스템은 1960년대에 설계된 이후로 크게 변한 적이 없기 때문에, 경찰은 그녀의 통신사에서 제공하는 (B) 자세하지 않은 정보를 통해 그녀의 위치를 파악하도록 강요받았다. 휴대전화로 일단 응급전화를 걸게 되면, 통신회사에서는 (C) 삼각측량을 통해 신호의 강도와 신호가 여러 기지국에 도달하는 시간을 비교해서 휴대전화 위치의 근사치를 낸다. 이 방법을 통해 최소 20분 이상을 소요하여 전화를 건 여성의 위치를 한 시가지의 반지름 정도로 정확하게 찾아낼 수 있다.

	(A)	(B)	(C)
①	정확히 찾아내다	… 자세하지 않은	… 삼각측량
②	정확히 찾아내다	… 자세하지 않은	… 순환
③	대충 훑어보다	자세한	… 순환
④	대충 훑어보다	자세한	… 삼각측량
⑤	대충 훑어보다	자세한	… 순환

주제 휴대전화 신호를 이용한 위치 측정

정답 해설 (A) 유선전화를 사용했다면 전화를 받은 응답자는 그녀의 위치를 정확히 찾을 수 있었을 것이라는 내용이 문맥상 자연스럽다. 따라서 pinpoint가 적절하다. (B) 911 시스템이 1960년대에 설계된 이후 크게 변한 적이 없으므로 경찰이 받은 그녀의 위치에 대한 정보는 자세하지 않다는 것이 문맥상 자연스럽다. 따라서 imprecise가 적절하다. (C) 신호의 강도와 신호가 기지국에 도달하는 시간을 비교하여 휴대전화 위치의 근사치를 내는 방법으로는 삼각측량이 적절하다. 따라서 triangulation이 들어가야 한다.

어휘 emergency 비상, 응급사태 landline 유선전화기 pinpoint 정확히 찾아내다 overlook 대충 훑어보다 precise 정확한 imprecise 부정확한 triangulation 삼각 측량 circulation 순환 approximate 근접하다 radius 반지름

05 ③ 마케팅이 개별 소비자들의 복지에 끼치는 영향은 그것들의 높은 비용, 기만하는 행위, 그리고 손해를 본 소비자들에 대한 부실한 서비스를 이유로 비판받아 왔다. 그리고 마케팅이 사회에 끼치는 영향은, 그것이 그릇된 소유욕을 낳고 지나치게 과도한 물질만능주의를 조장하며 사회적 재화는 너무 (A) 적게 생산하는 반면, 문화적 공해를 불러일으킨다는 점에서 비판받아 왔다. 비평가들은 또한 경쟁사들에게 손해를 끼치고 진입 장벽을 (B) 만드는 관습인 인수를 통해서 경쟁을 감소시키는 것에 대하여 다른 사업에 대한 마케팅의 영향을 비판해 왔다. 이러한 (C) 염려들 중에 일부는 정당화되지만, 일부는 그렇지 못하다.

	(A)		(B)		(C)
①	많게	……	만드는	……	염려들
②	많게	……	없애는	……	제안들
③	적게	……	만드는	……	염려들
④	적게	……	없애는	……	제안들
⑤	적게	……	없애는	……	염려들

주제 마케팅에 대한 비판

정답 해설 (A) social goods는 사회적 재화로, 사회 전체에 이로운 공공재인 성격을 갖는 것을 가리키는 말이다. 마케팅이 사회에 가져오는 해악에 대해 설명하고 있는 글이므로, '사회적 재화는 너무 적게 생산하고 있다.'라는 내용이 문맥상 자연스럽다. (B) 마케팅이 주는 악영향 중에 다른 기업, 즉 경쟁사에 끼치는 영향에 대해 비판하고 있는 내용이므로, 인수 합병을 통해 타 기업이 해당 사업 분야로 진입을 하지 못하게 막는다는 의미가 문맥상 적절하다. (C) 위에서 전체적으로 마케팅의 악영향에 대해 이야기하였으므로 그 자체가 어떤 제안(suggestions)이 된다고 보기는 어렵다. 오히려 해악에 대한 염려, 걱정(concerns)라고 표현하는 것이 자연스럽다.

어휘 deceptive 기만하는, 현혹시키는 materialism 물질만능주의 acquisition 구매, 습득, 취득

06 ③ 최근 수년 간 GDP가 경제적인 자본의 형태에만 초점이 맞춰져 있고 자연 환경의 건강과 생물학적 다양성, 지역 사회의 (A) 강점, 사람들의 행복과 복지 등과 같은 다른 형태의 자본들과의 연관성은 참고하지 않기에, 진정한 부의 척도로서의 GDP의 부적절함에 대한 인식이 증가해왔다. 사회는 그것의 다양한 형태의 자본을 훨씬 (B) 더 균형 잡히고 완전한 방법으로, 의식적으로 발전시켜야만 한다. 사회는 경제적인 부를 다른 형태의 자본으로 대체해야만 하는데, 삶의 질이 어떻게 유지될 수 있었고 심지어 사회가 소비와 물질적 생산을 대폭 (C) 줄이는 동안 삶의 질이

어떻게 향상될 수 있었는지를 보여 주어야 한다.

	(A)		(B)		(C)
①	강점	……	더	……	최대화하는
②	강점	……	덜	……	줄이는
③	강점	……	더	……	줄이는
④	약점	……	덜	……	줄이는
⑤	약점	……	덜	……	최대화하는

주제 다양한 사회적 자본을 보여줄 척도의 필요성

정답 해설 (A) 경제적 자본 이외의 자본 중 한 가지 사례이므로 '지역 사회의 강점'이 문맥상 자연스럽다. 따라서 strength가 적절하다. (B) 사회가 자본을 더 균형 잡히고 완전한 방법으로 발전시켜야 한다는 내용이 문맥상 자연스럽다. 따라서 more가 적절하다. (C) 앞에서 언급한 자연환경의 건강, 사람들의 행복과 복지 등과 관련지어 생각했을 때 '사회는 소비와 물질적인 생산을 대폭 줄일 때 삶의 질이 어떻게 향상될 수 있었는지를 보여 주어야 한다.'는 내용이 문맥상 자연스럽다. 따라서 reducing이 적절하다.

어휘 awareness 인식, 인지 inadequacy 부적절함 exclusive 배타적인 reference 참고, 참조 biodiversity 생물의 다양성 environs 주변지역, 외곽, 근교 integrate 통합하다, 완성하다 substitute A for B B를 A로 대체하다 enhance 향상하다, 발전하다 throughput 처리량, 일의 양

07 ② 한때 털가죽 때문에 사냥 당했던 비버는, 그들의 몸이 아닌 그들의 정신, 특히 그들의 만드는 기술 때문에 다시 수요가 생겼다. 기후의 변화가 여름에 강가의 물이 부족하게 만들기 때문에, 연구자들은 근면한 설치류들이 자연적인 해결책을 제시할 수 있다고 (A) 단언한다. 댐이 물을 어떻게 저장하는지에 대한 설문조사에 기초하여, 워싱턴 주의 국토부는 주에 있는 10,000마일의 적합한 서식지에 비버들을 (B) 다시 들여오는 것은 자연적으로 새는 동물들의 댐에서 천천히 방출되어 흐르는 650조 갤런의 물을 저장하는 데 도움을 줄 수 있다고 예측한다. 국토부는 몇십억 달러의 비용이 드는 인위적 댐 프로젝트를 고려하고 있다는 걸 안 후에 비버 옵션을 (C) 조사하기 시작했다. 그것은 비버가 일을 그 비용의 적은 부분으로 할 수 있다고 주장한다.

	(A)		(B)		(C)
①	단언한다	……	금지하는	……	조사하기
②	단언한다	……	다시 들여오는	……	조사하기
③	단언한다	……	다시 들여오는	……	제거하기
④	반박한다	……	다시 들여오는	……	제거하기

⑤ 반박한다 …… 금지하는 …… 조사하기

주제 자연적 물 저장 수단인 비버

정답 해설 (A) 물 부족 현상을 해결하는 데 비버가 도움을 줄 수 있다는 문맥에 비추어 볼 때 연구자들은 근면한 설치류들이 자연적인 해결책을 제시할 수 있다고 단언한다는 내용이 자연스럽다. 따라서 betting이 적절하다. (B) 물 저장에 도움이 되려면 비버들을 다시 들여와야 한다는 내용이 자연스럽다. 따라서 reintroducing이 적절하다. (C) 몇십억을 들여야 하는 인위적 댐 프로젝트에 대한 대안으로 비용이 적게 드는 비버 옵션을 조사했다는 내용이 문맥상 자연스럽다. 따라서 investigating이 적절하다.

어휘 in demand 필요에 의해, 수요에 의해 pelt 털가죽 refute 반박하다, 논박하다 rodent 설치류 trillion 1조의 runoff 흘러나가는 것, 흐르는 빗물 fraction 파편, 작은 양, 일부분 reintroduce 다시 도입하다, 다시 소개하다 terminate 없애다, 끝내다

주제 실패로 끝난 Nixon 대통령의 여행

정답 해설 (A) 대통령이 여행을 할 필요성이 명백한 가운데 그 여행에 대해 의문을 던지는 것이 문맥상 자연스러우므로 obvious가 적절하다. (B) 대통령이 35,000피트 상공에서 권력감이 상승했다는 뒷부분 내용으로 미루어 볼 때 어딘가로 날아가고자 하는 충동이 있어 왔다는 내용이 자연스럽다. 따라서 compulsion이 적절하다. (C) 파도치는 캘리포니아 고속도로를 달리면서 볼 수 있는 것으로는 '멋진 경치'가 자연스럽다. 따라서 vista가 적절하다.

어휘 obscure 애매모호한, 어두컴컴한, 희미한 substance 본질, 실질, 실체 Oval Office 백악관 집무실 triumphal 승리의, 개선하는 hollow 속이 빈, 텅 빈, 공허한 compulsion 강한 충동, 강요, 강제 abhorrence 혐오, 싫어하는 것 omnipotence 전능함, 무한한 힘 set out 떠나다, 출발하다 for a spin 드라이브하다 vignette 삽화, 초상화 vista 멋진 경치

---

08 ③ 대통령이 여행을 하는 것의 필요성은 (A) 명백하지만 그것은 과연 그 움직임이 본질을 대체하고 있는지에 대한 질문은 할 수 있다. Nixon 대통령의 국토횡단은 그의 백악관 집무실 연설에서 시작하여, 플로리다를 향해 남쪽으로 속도를 낸 뒤, 뉴올리언스를 거쳐 태평양 연안을 따라 나머지 지역으로 가는 연출된 볼거리였다. Nixon의 이 여행은 전국에 걸친 승리의 행진이 될 예정이었지만 특별한 의미가 없었기 때문에 실패하고 말았다. John F. Kennedy 대통령 이후로 어딘가로 날아가고자 하는 (B) 충동이 있어 왔다. 대통령의 막강한 권력감을 증대시켜주는 35000피트 상공에 있다는 것에는 뭔가 특별한 것이 있다. Kennedy 대통령의 기분은 그가 그의 마법의 양탄자 위에 올라탔을 때 더욱 고취되었다. 심지어 비행을 할 수 없었을 때에도 Nixon 대통령은 캘리포니아에서 종종 파도가 치는 캘리포니아 고속도로를 드라이브하기 위해 떠나곤 했다. Nixon 대통령과 함께 여행을 했던 아마추어 심리학자는 'Nixon이 어느 정도는 그가 처한 문제들로부터 도피하고 해결책들이 나타날만한 (C) 멋진 경치를 찾아 헤맨 것이었다.'라고 주장했다. 하지만 해결책들은 전혀 나타나지 않았을 것이다.

	(A)		(B)		(C)
①	모호한	……	충동	……	멋진 경치
②	모호한	……	혐오	……	삽화
③	명백한	……	충동	……	멋진 경치
④	명백한	……	혐오	……	멋진 경치
⑤	명백한	……	충동	……	삽화

---

09 ⑤ 통증의 기본 성질에 대한 무지가 일반화되었다면 진통제가 작용하는 방식에 대한 무지는 그보다 더 심하다. 일반적으로 알려지지 않은 것은 성능이 극구 칭찬받는 수많은 진통제들이(통증을 일으키는) 기본 상태를 바로잡는 것 없이 그저 통증만을 (A) 은폐한다는 것이다. 그 약들은 우리의 몸이 뭔가 잘못될 수 있다는 사실을 전달하는 신체의 뇌 경고 메커니즘을 (B) 무감각하게 한다. 우리 몸은 그 기본 원인에 관계없이 통증의 (C) 억제에 대해 높은 가격을 지불할 수 있다.

	(A)		(B)		(C)
①	은폐하다	……	일깨우다	……	억제
②	드러내다	……	무감각하게 하다	……	발산
③	은폐하다	……	일깨우다	……	발산
④	드러내다	……	일깨우다	……	발산
⑤	은폐하다	……	무감각하게 하다	……	억제

주제 진통제 작용의 실체

정답 해설 (A) 진통제의 기본 성질은 통증을 감추는 것이므로 문맥상 conceal이 적절하다. (B) 진통제는 통증을 은폐하기 때문에 신체의 뇌 경고 메커니즘을 무감각하게 한다는 것이 문맥상 자연스럽다. 따라서 deaden이 적절하다. (C) 우리가 값을 지불하는 진통제는 통증을 억제한다는 내용이 문맥상 자연스러우므로 suppression이 적절하다.

어휘 widespread 광범위한, 널리 퍼진 vaunted 과시된, (과도하게) 칭찬받는 conceal 숨기다, 봉인하다 deaden 누그러뜨리다, 무감각하게 하다, 죽게 만들다 suppression 억제, 진압 without regard to ~을 고려하지 않고

10 ② 천재는 어떻게 사고를 하는 걸까? 무엇이 Mona Lisa를 만들어낸 사고방식과 상대성 이론을 (A) 낳은 사고방식을 연결하는가? 우리는 역사 속 인물 Galileo와 Edison, Mozart 등의 사고 전략으로부터 무엇을 배울 수 있을까? 오랜 시간동안 학자들은 통계적 분석으로 천재성을 연구하는 데 주력했다. 1904년에 Havelock Ellis은 대부분의 천재들은 아버지가 30세 이상이었고, 어머니가 25세 이하였으며 대개 허약한 유년기를 보냈다고 말했다. 그러나 다른 연구자들은 많은 수가 독신이었으며 (Descartes), 아버지가 없거나(Dickens), 또는 어머니가 없다고(Darwin) 보고했다. 결국 그 자료는 (B) 아무것도 밝혀내지 못했다. 학자들은 또한 지능과 천재성 사이의 관계를 측정하려고 했다. 하지만 그들은 평범한 물리학자가 노벨상 수상자이며 IQ는 (C) 꽤 괜찮은 122였던 특별한 천재 Richard Feynman보다 훨씬 더 높은 IQ를 가졌었다는 것을 발견했다. 천재성은 14개의 언어를 7살에 완벽히 구사하거나, 아주 특별하게 똑똑한 것이 아니다. 창의성은 지능과 동일한 것이 아니다.

	(A)		(B)		(C)
①	낳다	……	뭔가	……	공손한
②	낳다	……	아무것도	……	꽤 괜찮은
③	낳다	……	아무것도	……	공손한
④	따르다	……	뭔가	……	꽤 괜찮은
⑤	따르다	……	아무것도	……	공손한

[주 제] 천재성에 대한 연구
[정답 해설] (A) 모나리자를 창안하여 그린 사람과 상대성 이론을 발견한 사람과 대등한 관계이므로 '낳다'라는 의미의 spawned이 적절하다. (B) 두 가지 연구 결과가 명확하게 밝힌 것이 없기에 nothing이 적절하다. (C) 122 정도 되는 아이큐도 나쁘지 않다는 의미가 와야 하므로 respectable이 적절하다.

[어 휘] run-of-the-mill 평범한 spawn 알, 알을 낳다 the theory of relativity 상대성 이론 illuminate 조명하다, 밝게 비추다 celibate 독신주의자 extraordinary 놀라운, 보기 드문 respectable 존경할만한, 훌륭한 respectful 공손한, 예의 바른

11 ④ 과학자들은 명상이 뇌에 (A) 실질적인 영향을 끼친다는 증거를 밝혀내기 시작했다. 회의론자는 명상이 현대 생활의 스트레스에 대처하려고 하는 실용적인 방법이 아니라고 주장한다. 그러나 지지자들이 그들의 테크닉에 대한 그들의 신념을 지지하기 위해 자연 과학을 제시할 수 없었던 오랜 세월이 마침내 끝나게 될 것이다. Carol Cattley의 남편이 사망했을 때, 그것은 십대 이후로 그녀를 괴롭히지 않았던 우울증을 (B) 촉발시켰다. Carol은 의학적인 도움을 구했고 기본적으로 명상으로 구성된 인지행동치료(CBT)라고 불리는 심리학적 치료와 약물의 조합으로 우울증을 극복하였다. CBT의 (C) 개척자들 중 하나인 Oxford 대학의 정신학과 교수인 Mark Williams는 CBT를 인지 치료 20%와, 명상 80%로 구성되어 있다고 설명했다.

	(A)		(B)		(C)
①	무시할 정도의	……	맞붙다	……	개척자들
②	무시할 정도의	……	촉발시키다	……	반대자들
③	무시할 정도의	……	촉발시키다	……	개척자들
④	실질적인	……	촉발시키다	……	개척자들
⑤	실질적인	……	맞붙다	……	반대자들

[주 제] 명상의 효과에 대한 과학자들의 증거
[정답 해설] (A) 문맥상 명상이 뇌에 실질적인 효과를 미친다는 의미의 단어 tangible이 적절하다. (B) 남편이 죽고 우울증이 다시 시작되어 치료를 목적으로 의학적 도움을 요청하는 내용이 이어지므로 triggered가 적절하다. (C) Mark Williams는 CBT 분야의 개척자 중의 한 사람이라는 내용이 문맥상 자연스러우므로 pioneers가 적절하다.

[어 휘] negligible 무시해도 좋은, 사소한 tangible 만져서 알 수 있는, 유형의 skeptic 회의론자 adherent ~을 신봉하는, 신봉자 tackle 맞붙다, 달려들다 plague 역병, 전염병 psychiatry 정신의학

12 ③ 제례 의식은 지역 사회를 이루는 사람들 사이에 임시 또는 영구적인 (A) 결속을 형성하는 사회적 기능을 수행할 수 있다. 우리는 이것을 토템 숭배로 알려진 종교적 관행에서 찾아볼 수 있다. 토템 숭배는 호주 원주민들의 종교에서 특히 중요한 것이다. 토템은 동물, 식물, 혹은 지리적 특징이 될 수 있다. 각각의 부족이나 지파에서 사람들은 그들만의 특별한 토템을 갖는다. 각 토템 그룹의 구성원은 자신들이 그 토템의 (B) 후손이라고 믿는다. 그들은 습관적으로 그 토템을 죽이거나 먹지 않았다. 하지만 이 금기는 일 년에 한 번 사람들이 토템에 전념하여 의식을 하기 위해 (C) 모였을 때만 해제된다.

	(A)		(B)		(C)
①	간청	……	후손	……	동의하다
②	간청	……	후손	……	모이다
③	결속	……	후손	……	모이다
④	결속	……	반체제 인사	……	모이다
⑤	간청	……	반체제 인사	……	동의하다

[주 제] 토템 숭배의 기능

정답 해설 (A) '각각의 부족이나 지파에서 사람들은 그들만의 특별한 토템을 갖는다'는 내용으로 미루어 볼 때 제례 의식이 지역 사람들을 결속하는 역할을 한다는 것이 문맥상 자연스럽다. 따라서 solidarity가 적절하다. (B) 토템은 부족이나 지파에게 있어서 특별한 존재이고 사람들은 자신들의 토템을 함부로 죽이지 않았다는 내용으로 미루어 볼 때 후손을 뜻하는 descendants가 적절하다. (C) 의식을 위해 사람들이 모이는 것이 문맥상 자연스러우므로 assembled가 적절하다.

어휘 ritual 제례 function 기능 temporary 일시적인 permanent 항구적인 solidarity 결속, 단결, 일치 lift 해제하다 assent 찬성하다 assemble 모이다

---

13 ③ 재생 불가능한 에너지원과 신재생 에너지원의 기능을 대조해 보자. 석탄과 석유는 생명이 없는, 따라서 재생 불가능한 수량적인 것이다. 그것들은 반복해서 분할되고 재분할될 수 있으며, 여전히 각각의 부분은 전체와 같은 속성을 포함하고 있다. 석탄 알갱이는 석탄 덩어리와 조성이 (A) 거의 차이가 없다. 재생 불가능한 에너지 자원은 고정된 주식으로 묘사된다. 그것들은 쉽게 (B) 정량화할 수 있다. 그것들은 측정이 정확하게 되는 경향이 있다. 그것들은 주문될 수 있다. 다른 한편으로는, 재생 자원은 영원히 변화하며 흐른다. 태양 에너지에 대해서, 질서와 쇠퇴의 개념은 세계가 전개되는 방법을 항상 우리에게 알려주고 기억하게 해주는 요소이다. 탄생, 삶, 죽음, 그리고 재생의 순환 과정은 질적인 과정이고 재생 가능 자원들은 정확한 측정 대상이 되기 (C) 어렵다.

	(A)		(B)		(C)
①	거의	……	자격이 주어진	……	어려운
②	거의	……	정량화할	……	쉬운
③	거의	……	정량화할	……	어려운
④	매우	……	정량화할	……	쉬운
⑤	매우	……	자격이 주어진	……	쉬운

주제 재생 불가능 에너지원과 신재생 에너지원의 차이

정답 해설 (A) 각각의 부분은 전체와 같은 속성을 포함하고 있다는 내용으로 미루어 볼 때 석탄 알갱이는 석탄 덩어리와 조성이 거의 차이가 없다는 내용이 문맥상 자연스럽다. 따라서 little이 적절하다. (B) 그것들은 측정이 정확하게 되는 경향이 있다는 내용으로 미루어 볼 때 그것들은 쉽게 정량화할 수 있다는 내용이 문맥상 자연스럽다. 따라서 quantified가 적절하다. (C) 측정이 정확하게 이루어지는 재생 불가능한 에너지원과 대비되는 재생 가능 에너지원의 특징을 언급하고 있으므로 재생 가능 에너지는 정확한 측정 대상이 되기 어렵다는 내용이 문맥

상 자연스럽다. 따라서 hard가 적절하다.

어휘 contrast 대조하다 feature 특징 renewable 재사용할 수 있는 lifeless 생명 없는 precise 정밀한, 정확한 measurement 측량, 측정, 치수 chunk 두꺼운 조각, 덩어리 speck 작은 반점, 소량, 작은 점을 찍다 qualitative 질적인, 성질상의 decay 쇠퇴하다 unfold 전개되다 be subject to ~의 대상이다, 예속되다 precise 정밀한

---

14 ① 흑인 사회에서 Leland 학교의 인종 분리 재시행에 대해 불평을 하는 사람은 거의 없다. 최근 몇 개월, 흑인 활동가들은 기존의 올 블랙 고등학교의 전통을 유지시키는 데 더욱 집중하고 있다. 지난 가을, 그 학교의 백인 교장은 진열장에 있는 (A) 인종 통합되기 전 체육 관련 트로피를 최근의 학생들의 것으로 교체하고 싶어 했다. 흑인 사회는 분노했다. 이 급성 향수병은 흑인들 사이에서 그들이 통제했던 학교의 포기 비용이 학교 통합의 이점보다 훨씬 더 크다는 생각이 증가하고 있음을 반영한다. (B) 인종 분리 폐지 전에, 흑인 아이들의 학교는 공동체의 조직으로 구성되었으며, 외부 생활을 의미하는 인종적 명예 훼손으로부터의 성역이었다. 통합은 이 모든 것을 바꾸어 놓았다. (C) 인종 통합은 학교의 최종 정책 결정 위치에서 흑인을 제거하고 모든 교직원들의 승진 및 모든 학생 징계 조치에 인종적 문제를 증폭시켰다.

	(A)	(B)	(C)
①	인종 통합 …	인종 분리 폐지 …	인종 통합
②	인종 통합 …	인종 분리 재시행 …	인종 분리 재시행
③	인종 분리 …	인종 분리 재시행 …	인종 분리 재시행
④	인종 분리 …	인종 분리 폐지 …	인종 통합
⑤	인종 분리 …	인종 분리 폐지 …	인종 분리 재시행

주제 Leland 학교의 인종 통합이 야기한 갈등

정답 해설 (A) 흑인 사회는 인종 통합 이전에 대한 향수를 가지고 있으므로 백인 교장이 인종 통합 이전의 트로피를 인종 통합 이후의 트로피로 교체하는 것에 대해 분노했다는 것이 문맥상 자연스럽다. 따라서 integration이 적절하다. (B) 학교가 흑인 아이들로만 구성되었던 것은 인종 분리 폐지 이전의 상황이다. 따라서 desegregation이 적절하다. (C) 앞부분에서 언급된 인종 통합이 바꾸어 놓은 상황에 대한 예시이다. 따라서 Integration이 적절하다.

어휘 complain 항의하다, 불평하다 resegregation 인종 재분리 replace 대체하다 sanctuary 신성한 장소, 보호소 weave-wove-woven 직물 등을 짜다, 엮다 denigration 명예 훼손, 더럽힘 desegregation 인종 분리 폐지 mark 나타내다, 표시하다 faculty promotion 교직원 승진 disciplinary 훈련 상의, 규율 상의

④ 발생한 …… 합동의 …… 막다
⑤ 발생한 …… 연결된 …… 막다

주 제 삶 속 협상의 사례

정답 해설 (A) 소송이 자동차 사고 때문에 발생했다는 내용이 문맥상 자연스러우므로 arising이 적절하다. (B) 정유 회사들이 합동해서 석유 탐사를 계획한다는 내용이 문맥상 자연스러우므로 joint가 적절하다. (C) 공무원들이 교통 파업을 막기 위해 노동조합의 대표와 만난다는 것이 문맥상 자연스러우므로 prevent가 적절하다.

어 휘 negotiator 협상가 joint 이음매, 접합 부분, 공동의, 합동의 offshore 연안의, 근해의 lawsuit 소송, 고소 counterpart 상대방, 상대

15 ④ 군대나 회사 그리고 여타 계급에 따른 조직과는 달리, 대학은 권위가 소수 지도급들에게 집중되기보다는 폭넓게 공유되는 공동체이다. 각각의 교수들은 학문적 자유의 (B) 원칙에 의해 행정적 통제로부터 그들의 강의와 연구들에 대해 대체로 (A) 영향을 받지 않는다. 집단적으로 행동하면서 교수진들은 교과 과정 내용을 수정하고, 학술 연구에 필요한 지원을 요구하고, 신임 교수에 대한 물색과 입학 기준을 (C) 형성하는 등의 권한을 갖는다.

	(A)		(B)		(C)
①	구별되는	……	원칙	……	형성하는
②	구별되는	……	결핍	……	형성하는
③	영향을 받지 않는	……	결핍	……	깎아내는
④	영향을 받지 않는	……	원칙	……	형성하는
⑤	영향을 받지 않는	……	원칙	……	깎아내는

주 제 대학 내부 권한의 양상

정답 해설 (A) 대학의 권위가 집중되지 않고 폭넓게 공유된다고 언급했으므로 각각의 교수들은 행정적 통제로부터 영향을 받지 않는다는 것이 문맥상 자연스럽다. 따라서 immune이 적절하다. (B) 교수들이 행정적 통제로부터 영향을 받지 않기 위한 근거로는 학문적 자유의 원칙이 문맥상 자연스럽다. 따라서 doctrine이 적절하다. (C) 행정적 통제를 받지 않는 상태에서 교수진들의 권한에 관한 내용을 언급하고 있으므로 신임 교수에 대한 물색과 입학 기준을 형성한다는 내용이 문맥상 자연스럽다. 따라서 shape이 적절하다.

어 휘 immune 면역의, 면역을 가진 authority 권위, 권한 administrative 행정의, 관리하는, 경영상의 hierarchic 계급을 가진, 권력의, 정치의 doctrine ~주의, 신조, 교리

17 ④ 간단히 정의하자면 '주의'란 누군가를 환경의 특정 자극에 노출시키는 과정이다. 확실히 지금 한 사람이 당면한 환경 속에서도 무수히 많은 자극이 존재하는데, 이는 너무나도 많아서 사실상 한 개인이 모든 자극에 주의를 기울이는 것은 불가능하다. 따라서 주의란 (그에 따라) 한 사람이 어떤 자극을 전적으로 무시하고, 어떤 자극에 부분적으로 주의를 기울이고, 나머지에 모든 주의를 다하는 (A) 선택적인 과정이다. 부하 직원과 면담을 하고 있는 지배인을 예로 들면 그는 특정한 실수를 했던 이유에 대해 (B) 신중하게 주의를 기울일 것이다. 하지만 이와 동시에 고장난 에어컨의 소음이라든가 비서실에서 울리는 전화벨 소리와 같은 다른 자극들이 지배인의 주의 집중 과정에 (C) 영향을 줄 수도 있다.

	(A)		(B)		(C)
①	집합적인	……	신중하게	……	혹 있을
②	집합적인	……	우연히	……	영향을 줄
③	집합적인	……	신중하게	……	영향을 줄
④	선택적인	……	신중하게	……	영향을 줄
⑤	선택적인	……	우연히	……	혹 있을

주 제 주의의 정의

정답 해설 (A) 부분적으로 주의를 기울일 자극과 주의를 집중할 자극을 선택하는 과정이라는 내용이 문맥상 자연스럽다. 따라서 selective가 적절하다. (B) 앞의 내용으로 미루어 볼 때 부하 직원이 실수를 했던 이유에 대해 주의를 기울이기로 선택했다고 볼 수 있으므로 신중하게 주의를 기울인다는 내용이 문맥상 자연스럽다. 따라서 carefully가 적절하다. (C) 에어컨 소음이나 전화벨 소리는 부분적으로 주의를 기울이게 되는 자극이므로 지배인이 부하 직원과의 면담에 주의를 집중하는 과정에 영향을 줄 수 있다는 것이 문맥상 자연스럽다. 따라서

16 ④ 좋든 싫든 간에 당신은 협상가이다. 협상은 어쩔 수 없는 현실이다. 당신은 월급과 승진에 대해 상사와 의견을 나눈다. 당신은 집값에 대해 낯선 사람과 의견을 맞추려고 노력한다. 두 명의 변호사는 자동차 사고로 (A) 발생한 소송을 처리하려고 노력한다. 정유 회사 집단은 앞바다의 석유를 탐사하는 (B) 합동의 모험을 계획한다. 시 공무원은 교통 파업을 (C) 막기 위해 노동조합의 대표와 만난다. 미 국무장관은 핵무기 제한에 대해 합의하기 위해서 구소련의 대표와 한 자리에 앉는다. 이 모든 것들이 협상이다.

	(A)		(B)		(C)
①	떠오른	……	합동의	……	막다
②	떠오른	……	연결된	……	보호하다
③	발생한	……	연결된	……	보호하다

impinging이 적절하다.

어휘 innumerable 셀 수 없이 많은 subordinate 부하, 직원, 종속시키다 simultaneously 동시에, 일제히 impinge 영향을 미치다, 침해하다 malfunction 제 기능을 못하다

More Practice

| 01 ⑤ | 02 ⑤ | 03 ③ | 04 ② |

01 ⑤ 정지 장면 사진술은 움직임을 보는 눈을 속이는 것을 이용한다. 정지한 사진은 진흙 모형 공룡과 같은 대상에 의해 만들어진다. 대상이 (A) 약간 움직이면 또 다른 사진이 찍힌다. 이런 섬세한 과정은 수천 번 반복된다. 사진, 또는 프레임들이 영화 카메라의 초당 24프레임의 속도에 노출되면 진흙 모형은 (B) 움직이는 것처럼 보인다. 정지 장면 촬영의 가장 주된 문제는 "흐릿함(잔상)"이 없다는 것이다. 만약 어떤 사람이 거리를 달려가는 것을 찍는다면 각 프레임마다 약간의 흐릿함이 생길 것이다. 관중이 알아차리지 못해도 흐릿함은 달리는 동작을 부드럽고 현실적으로 만들어준다. 정지 장면 영화에서 달리는 피사체는 덜컥거리는 것처럼 보인다. 이 문제는 현실적 움직임을 만들기 위해 프레임들을 (C) 흐릿하게 하는 컴퓨터 애니메이션으로 해결되었다.

	(A)		(B)		(C)
①	상당히	……	쉬고 있는	……	흐릿한
②	상당히	……	움직이는	……	덜컥거리는
③	약간	……	쉬고 있는	……	흐릿한
④	약간	……	쉬고 있는	……	덜컥거리는
⑤	약간	……	움직이는	……	흐릿한

주제 운동하는 피사체 촬영물의 문제점
정답 해설 (A) 정지 장면 사진술은 '섬세한' 과정이므로 빈칸에는 '약간'을 의미하는 slightly가 적절하다. (B) 영화 카메라는 초당 24 프레임의 정지된 사진들을 보여주므로 진흙 모형은 움직이는 것처럼 보이는 것이 문맥상 자연스럽다. 따라서 moving이 가장 적절하다. (C) 흐릿함은 달리는 동작을 부드럽고 현실적으로 만들어 준다는 앞부분의 내용으로 미루어 볼 때 정지 장면 영화에서 덜컥거리는 것처럼 보이는 문제를 해결하기 위한 방안으로는 프레임들을 흐릿하게 하는 것이 문맥상 자연스럽다. 따라서 빈칸에는 blurry가 가장 적절하다.

어휘 delicate 섬세한 jerky 덜컥거리는 blur 흐려짐

02 ⑤ 일단 사람들을 통제하기 위하여 보상을 이용하기 시작했다면, 당신은 쉽게 돌아갈 수 없다. 행동이 금전적인 보상의 (A) 수단이 될 때, 다시 말해 사람들이 보상을 얻기 위해 행동할 때 그러한 행동들은 보상이 이루어지고 있는 동안만 지속될 것이다. 어떤 경우에는 아무래도 상관없을 수 있겠지만, 대부분의 경우 우리가 보상하는 행위는 보상이 중단된 후에도 오랫동안 (B) 지속되기를 바라는 것들이다. 예를 들어, 만약 당신이 공부하는 것에 대해 아이들에게 보상 — 성적표에 기재된 'A' 점수에 대해 1달러씩 — 을 제시한다면 당신은 보상 제도가 (C) 종료된 후에도 아이들이 계속해서 열심히 공부하기를 원할 것이다. 하지만 만약 보상을 받으려고 공부한다면 더 이상 보상이 없을 때 그들은 공부를 하지 않을 가능성이 높아진다.

	(A)		(B)		(C)
①	무관한	……	지속하다	……	종료된
②	무관한	……	중단하다	……	종료된
③	수단이 될	……	중단하다	……	시작된
④	수단이 될	……	지속하다	……	시작된
⑤	수단이 될	……	지속하다	……	종료된

주제 보상이 주어지는 행동의 지속 가능성
정답 해설 (A) '다시 말해 사람들이 보상을 얻기 위해 행동할 때'와 같은 뜻인 '행동이 금전적인 보상의 수단이 될 때'가 문맥상 자연스럽다. 따라서 빈칸에는 instrumental이 적절하다. (B) 아이들이 공부를 계속 하기를 원한다는 예시로 미루어 볼 때 빈칸에는 '지속되다'라는 뜻의 persist가 적절하다. (C) 보상이 중단된 후에도 보상하는 행위가 오랫동안 지속되기를 바라는 것이므로 빈칸에는 '종료되다'라는 뜻의 terminated가 적절하다.

어휘 reward 보상 monetary 금전의 forthcoming 곧 있을 report card 성적표

03 ③ Atitlán Giant Grebe는 훨씬 더 널리 퍼져 있던 더 작은 Pied-billed Grebe(얼룩부리논병아리)에서 진화한 날지 못하는 큰 새였다. 1965년 무렵에는 Atitlán 호수에 약 80마리만이 남아 있었다. 한 가지 직접적인 원인은 매우 찾기 쉬웠는데, 현지의 인간들이 맹렬한 속도로 갈대밭을 베어 넘어뜨리는 것이었다. 이런 (A) 파괴는 빠르게 성장하는 매트 제조 산업의 필요에 의해 추진되었다. 그러나 다른 문제들이 있었다. 한 미국 항공사가 그 호수를 낚시꾼들의 관광지로 개발하는 데 전념하고 있었다. 하지만 이 생각에 큰 문제가 있었는데, 그 호수에는 적절한 스포츠용 물고기가 (B) 없었다! 이런 다소 분명한 결함을 보충하

기 위해 큰 입 배스라 불리는 특별히 선택된 물고기 종이 도입되었다. 그 도입된 개체는 즉각 그 호수에 사는 게와 작은 물고기에게 관심을 돌렸고, 이리하여 몇 마리 안 남은 논병아리와 먹이를 놓고 (C) 경쟁하였다. 또한, 가끔 그들이 얼룩말 줄무늬가 있는 Atitlàn Giant Grebe 새끼들을 게걸스럽게 먹어치웠다는 데 의심의 여지가 거의 없다.

	(A)		(B)		(C)
①	수용	……	없었다	……	경쟁하는
②	수용	……	지원했다	……	협력하는
③	파괴	……	없었다	……	경쟁하는
④	파괴	……	지원했다	……	협력하는
⑤	파괴	……	없었다	……	협력하는

주제 인간이 Atitlàn Giant Grebe의 생태에 끼친 악영향

정답 해설

(A) 인간이 갈대밭을 훼손한 행위를 가리키는 단어가 와야 하므로 destruction이 가장 적절하다. (B) 관광지로서 호수가 가지고 있는 결함을 보충하기 위해 큰 입 배스를 도입한 것으로 볼 때 그 호수에는 스포츠용 물고기가 없었을 것이므로, lacked가 가장 적절하다. (C) 새로 도입된 큰 입 배스가 호수의 게와 물고기를 먹기 시작했다는 것으로 보아 먹이를 두고 Atitlàn Giant Grebe와 경쟁하게 되었다는 것이 자연스러우므로, competing이 가장 적절하다.

어휘 flightless 날지 못하는 evolve 진화하다 spot 알아내다, 발견하다 reed bed 갈대밭 furious 맹렬한, 몹시 화가 난 be intent on ~에 전념하다 tourist destination 관광지 compensate for ~을 보충[보상]하다 obvious 분명한 defect 결함 chick 새끼 새, 병아리

04 ②
걱정은 모든 종류의 정신적인 활동에 해로운 영향을 준다. 그것은 어떤 면에서 실패로 돌아간 유용한 반응 — 예상된 위협에 대한 지나치게 열성적인 정신적 준비이다. 그러나 그러한 정신적 예행연습이 주의력을 빼앗아 다른 곳에 집중하려는 온갖 시도를 방해하는 진부한 일상에 사로잡힐 때, 그것은 (A) 파멸적인 인지적 정지상태가 된다. 걱정은 지적능력을 약화시킨다. 예를 들어 항공교통관제사와 같이 복잡하고 지적으로 힘들고 압박이 심한 업무에서는 만성적으로 많은 걱정을 하는 것은 그 사람이 결국 훈련이나 실전에서 실패할 것이라는 거의 확실한 예언이다. 항공 교통관제사 훈련을 받는 1,790명의 학생들에 대한 연구에서 밝혀진 바와 같이, 걱정이 많은 사람들은 지능검사에서 더 (B) 우수한 성적을 받았을 때조차도 통과하지 못할 가능성이 높다. 걱정은 또한 모든 종류의 학업을 방해한다. 36,000명 넘는 사람을 대상으로 한 126가지의 다른 연구는 걱정에 (C) 빠지기 쉬운 사람일수록 학업 성취도가 더 부진

하다는 것을 발견했다.

	(A)		(B)		(C)
①	파멸적인	……	열등한	……	빠지기 쉬운
②	파멸적인	……	우수한	……	빠지기 쉬운
③	파멸적인	……	우수한	……	잘 견디는
④	건설적인	……	열등한	……	잘 견디는
⑤	건설적인	……	우수한	……	잘 견디는

주제 걱정의 다양한 악영향

정답 해설 (A) 걱정이 지적능력을 약화시킨다고 했으므로, disastrous가 적절하다. (B) 걱정이 많은 사람들이 더 우수한 성적을 받았을 때조차도 통과하지 못할 가능성이 높다고 하는 것이 문맥상 자연스러우므로, superior가 적절하다. (C) 걱정이 학업에 악영향을 준다는 내용이므로 걱정을 잘 하는 사람일수록 학업 성취도가 낮은 것이 자연스럽다. 따라서 prone이 적절하다.

어휘 zealous 열광적인 cognitive 인식의 static 공전상태, 정지상태 stale 진부한, 상해는 intrude on ~에 끼어들다, 방해하다 demanding 지나친 요구를 하는 air traffic controller 항공교통관제사 chronically 만성적으로 sabotage 고의로 방해하다

UNIT 09 빈칸 I

Example
답 ⑤

사람들과 동물들의 관계는 <u>모순투성</u>이다. 사람들은 동물들에 대해 사랑과 감사함을 표현하고 동물들에 대한 잔인한 행동을 막기 위한 법들을 제정했다. 미국은 사람들보다 더 많은 강아지들, 고양이들, 앵무새들, 햄스터들, 그리고 다른 애완동물과 함께 살아가는 사회가 되었으며 이 동물들의 관리를 위해 연간 600억 정도의 산업이 형성되어 있다. 수백만의 미국인들은 다양한 방법으로 야생 동물과 관계되어 있고, 그들 중의 몇몇은 때 묻지 않은 곳에서 보내는 걸 가장 행복한 순간이라고 여긴다. 하지만 그와 동시에 사람들은 수십억의 동물들을 음식, 의류, 연구 그리고 다른 목적들을 위하여 죽이거나 남용하면서 대량의 동물들을 착취한다.

① 감사 ② 적의
③ 보호 ④ 책임
⑤ 모순

주 제 사람과 동물의 모순된 관계

Practice

01 ⑤	02 ①	03 ①	04 ④	05 ⑤
06 ①	07 ③	08 ⑤	09 ①	10 ①
11 ②	12 ②	13 ④	14 ①	15 ①
16 ①	17 ⑤	18 ⑤		

01 ⑤ 좋은 로켓 발사 장소는 몇 가지 중요한 특징을 가지고 있다. 제어가 어려운 불타는 금속 조각의 세례를 받는 사람이 없도록, 바다 근처의 비거주지역이 더 좋다. 또한 만약 그 장소가 적도라면 좋을 것이다. 축을 기준으로 도는 모든 구와 마찬가지로, 지구도 가운데에서 가장 빨리 돌고 이것은 로켓 추진체에 추가적인 힘을 실어준다. 다시 말해서, 최고의 장소는 열대의 외진 장소인 경향이 있다. 이러한 장소가 또한 종종 세상에서 가장 가난한 나라에 있다는 것은 많은 발사에 직관에 어긋나는 느낌을 준다. 수십억 달러짜리 초현대적 기계는 열대 우림과 판자촌 위를 날아간다.

① 장엄한 ② 일시적인

③ 큰 재앙의 ④ 보편적인
⑤ 직관에 어긋나는

주 제 로켓 발사 장소의 조건
정답 해설 여러 가지 측면에서 로켓 발사를 위한 최적의 장소는 세계에서 가장 가난한 나라가 위치한 곳이 된다는 내용의 글이다. 그렇게 가난한 나라들 위로 엄청난 돈을 들인 초현대적 기계가 날아간다는 것은 직관에 어긋나는 느낌을 준다는 것이 자연스럽다. 따라서 빈칸에는 ⑤ counterintuitive가 가장 적절하다.

어 휘 unpopulated 사람이 살지 않는 wayward 다루기 힘든 equator 적도 axis 축 oomph 힘 majestic 장엄한 fleeting 순식간의 catastrophic 큰 재앙의 counterintuitive 직관에 어긋나는 shantytown 판자촌

02 ① 19세기 말과 20세기 초에, Joseph Pujol이라는 프랑스인은 자신의 항문으로 공기를 빨아들여 마음대로 방귀를 뀔 수 있는 능력으로 유명했다. 그는 자신을 Le Petomane, 프랑스어로 '방귀 전문가'라고 지칭하며 무대 공연을 열었다. 잘 차려입은 그는 우르렁거리는 대포 발사의 방귀로 시작했다. 다양한 흉내가 이어졌고, 1906년 샌프란시스코 대지진을 흉내낸 것이 가장 볼 만 했다. 그는 직장으로 15피트의 거리에서 물줄기를 쏠 수 있었고, 쇼를 끝내기 위해서 여러 동물의 소리를 간간이 끼워 넣어 농장에 대한 노래를 부르는 것으로 대미를 장식했다.

① 마음대로 ② 조용하게
③ 간헐적으로 ④ 헛되이
⑤ 우연히

주 제 Joseph Pujol의 방귀 뀌는 능력
정답 해설 방귀 전문가에 대한 글로 그가 할 수 있었던 다양한 재주들에 대해 구체적으로 이야기하고 있다. 이러한 재주를 부릴 수 있었던 것은 그가 그의 의지대로 방귀를 뀔 수 있었기 때문이므로 빈칸에는 ①이 가장 적절하다.

어 휘 fart 방귀를 뀌다 at will 마음대로 anus 항문 rumble 우르렁거리는 소리 spectacularly 볼만하게 rectally 직장으로 punctuate with 간간이 끼워 넣다 intermittently 간헐적으로 to no avail 헛되이 inadvertently 우연히

03 ① 학생들 사이의 사회적 연대감을 독려하기 위해서 나는 그들에게 매트와 쿠션 그리고 음식과 음료수

틀 수업시간에 가져올 것을 권했다. 이 물건들 덕분에, 교실은 '사회적' 측면이 더해져 형태와 기능 면에서 (A) 바뀌었다. 성찰 활동 시간에, 나는 몇 명의 학생들이 마치 파자마 파티를 하는 듯이 매트와 쿠션뿐만 아니라 베개와 인형까지 어떻게 가져오는지 보았다! 매트와 쿠션을 쓰지 않을 때 학생들은 서로의 글에 대해 논의하거나 수정하면서 탁자 주위에 전략적으로 놓인 의자에 앉아 먹거나 마셨다. 음식과 음료수가 어떠한 사회 문화적인 담화에 필수적이듯이 그것들은 사회적 분위기를 강화하고 공동의 연대감을 (B) 결속시키며 학생들의 공통된 정체성을 고조시키는 데 도움을 준다.

	(A)		(B)
①	바꾸다	……	결속시키다
②	보존하다	……	녹이다
③	바꾸다	……	약화시키다
④	보존하다	……	고체화하다
⑤	보존하다	……	느슨하게 하다

주 제 │ 학생들의 사회적 연대감을 향상시킨 소품

정답 해설 │ (A) 학생들이 가져온 물건들 때문에 교실에서 사회적 분위기가 강화되었다는 전체 내용으로 보아 교실의 환경이 '바뀌었다'라는 뜻의 alter가 적절하다. (B) 사회적 분위기를 강화하고 학생들의 공통된 정체성을 고조시킨다는 앞뒤 내용과 문맥상 연결되려면 공동의 연대감을 결속시킨다는 내용이 적합하다. 따라서 빈칸에는 cement가 적절하다.

어 휘 │ slumber party 파자마 파티 sociocultural 사회 문화적인 discourse 담화 alter 달라지다 cement 결속시키다 communal 공동의 dissolve 녹다

04 ④ 판사들은 공동체의 복지에 중대한 영향을 미칠지도 모르는 행동에 대한 규율을 고안하거나 개선하는 데 도움을 얻기 위해 법령과 헌법을 읽는다. 공동체는 항상 기꺼이 그 선택이 2세기 전에 살았던 사람들이 헌법에 썼던 것에 의해 통제되도록 하지는 않는다. 그러나 헌법을 개정하는 과정은 너무 성가시므로, 판사들은 본래 내용을 유연하게 유지하는 해석 과정을 이용해야 하는 압박에 놓이게 된다.

① 시대에 뒤떨어진   ② 번역된
③ 간결한   ④ 유연한
⑤ 재판의

주 제 │ 유연한 법률 해석의 필요성

정답 해설 │ 헌법 개정은 부담스러운 일이지만 시대의 변화에 맞

추어 법을 해석해야 하므로 빈칸에는 본래 내용을 유연하게 해석한다는 내용이 들어가는 것이 자연스럽다. 따라서 빈칸에는 ④ flexible이 적절하다.

어 휘 │ statute 법령 the Constitution 헌법 refine 가다듬다 amend 개정하다 cumbersome 다루기 힘든, 성가신 obsolete 시대에 뒤떨어진 concise 간결한

05 ⑤ 담배의 사용은 그것이 스페인의 일부, 혹은 그 점에 대해서는 전부 다 서양문화가 되었을 때 마야의 견해로는 거의 종교적 요소였던 담배에 무슨 일이 있었는지를 설명해준다. 담배는 마야문명에서 종교적인 삶에 아주 중요한 역할을 했다. 담배는 병을 치유하고 막는 데 중요한 요소였고, 어떤 부분에서는 신성시되었다. 마야 사람들에게 기분을 좋게 만드는 담배의 특성은 담배의 많은 기능들에 비해 (A) 부차적으로 보였다. 하지만 담배를 스페인 사람들에게 빼앗겼을 때 그것은 그들 개인의 기호품으로 전락되었다. 마야인들의 모든 의식적이고 공동체적인 연관은 사라졌다. 이러한 과정은 그들이 흡수한, 정복당한 원주민들의 문화적 요소의 스페인식 (B) 세속화와 함께 이루어졌다. 옥수수는 더 이상 사랑받는 신성한 삶의 양식이 되지 못했다. 이것은 정복자에게 공물과 상업적 거래의 물품이 되었다. 카카오도 똑같은 수모 때문에 고통을 받았다.

	(A)		(B)
①	연관 있는	……	권한
②	연관 있는	……	계몽
③	동일한	……	파괴
④	부차적인	……	탐색
⑤	부차적인	……	세속화

주 제 │ 마야에서 담배 위상의 추락

정답 해설 │ (A) 담배는 마야 문명에서 종교나 치료의 목적 때문에 신성시되었으나 스페인의 마야 정복 이후에는 기호품으로 전락했다는 내용의 글이다. 따라서 스페인 정복 전에 담배의 기분을 좋게 만드는 기능은 담배의 많은 기능들, 즉 종교적인 기능이나 치료의 기능에 비해 부차적인 것이었다는 내용이 문맥상 자연스럽다. 따라서 빈칸에는 subordinate가 적절하다. (B) 담배가 '공물'과 '상업적 거래의 물품'이 되었다는 내용으로 볼 때 세속화와 함께 담배가 기호품으로 전락하고 마야인들의 모든 의식적이고 공동체적인 연관은 사라졌다고 언급하는 것이 자연스럽다. 따라서 빈칸에는 secularization이 적절하다.

어 휘 │ tobacco 담배 illustrate 설명하다 prevention 예방 commodity 일용품 ritualistic 의식의 conquer 정복하다 sacred 신성한 transaction 거래, 교류 degradation 격하, 강직

06 ① 지구의 상층부의 대기는 영하의 온도에, 산소도 희박하고 자외선으로 넘쳐나는, 생명이 살 수 없는 공간이다. 하지만 지난 겨울 Georgia Institute of Technology(기술 연구소)의 과학자들은 수십억의 박테리아가 그곳에서 실제로 (A) 번성하고 있다는 것을 발견해냈다. 아주 적은 수의 미생물밖에 없을 것으로 예상하고, 연구자들은 NASA의 제트기를 타고 지구 표면 6마일 높이로 비행했다. 그곳에서 그들은 작은 조각들을 모으기 위해 필터를 통해 외부의 공기를 빨아들었다. 지상으로 돌아와서, 그들은 미생물들의 수를 계산했고 그 수는 굉장히 놀라울 만한 것이었다. 그들이 (B) 먼지나 다른 물질들이라고 가정했었던 것들 중 20%가 생명이 있는 것들이었다. 지구는 아마도, 박테리아의 기포 속에 둘러 싸여 있는 것 같다.

	(A)		(B)
①	번성하다	……	먼지
②	번성하다	……	세포
③	번성하다	……	균
④	붕괴하다	……	방사선
⑤	붕괴하다	……	미생물

［주 제］ 지구 상층부 대기 속 작은 생명체

［정답 해설］ (A) 지구 상층부에서 빨아들인 공기에 포함된 미생물의 수가 놀라울 만한 것이라는 내용으로 미루어 보았을 때 '번성하다'라는 뜻의 thrive가 적절하다. (B) 생명이 없다고 여겨졌던 것들이 생명이 있다고 밝혀졌다는 내용이 문맥상 자연스럽다. 또한 미생물은 매우 작으므로 빈칸에는 먼지를 뜻하는 dust가 적절하다.

［어 휘］ UV radiation 자외선 복사 smattering 적은 수, 조금 microorganism 미생물, 박테리아 pump (공기나 물 등을) 주입하다, 퍼내다 tally 계산하다, 기록하다 staggering 놀라운, 엄청난, 경이로운 thrive 번성하다 disintegrate 분해시키다, 붕괴시키다

07 ③ 만약에 용서가 정말로 기분 좋다면 왜 그렇게 많은 사람들은 엄청난 분노를 질질 끌고 다니는 것일까? 한 가지 이유는, 그렇게 하는 것이 그들이 상처를 받았을 때 경험했던 무력감에 대해 보상해 줄지도 모르기 때문이다. "사람들은 그들이 분노로 가득 차 있을 때 더 책임감을 느낄지도 몰라요." '당신이 방법을 모를 때 어떻게 용서하는가'의 저자인 Mart Grunte이 지적했다. "하지만 용서하는 것은 점차적으로 엄청난 힘을 갖게 해줍니다. 당신이 용서를 하게 되면 당신은 선택할 수 있는 힘을 다시 찾게 됩니다. 대상이 용서받을 자격이 있는지 없는지는 중요하지 않습니다. 하지만 당신은 자유로워질 자격이 있습니다."

① 복수심   ② 잊지 못함
③ 무력감   ④ 빚, 은혜 입음
⑤ 결백함

［주 제］ 용서의 이유

［정답 해설］ 보기 중 상처를 받았을 때 경험할 수 있는 감정으로 가장 적절한 것은 무력감이므로 빈칸에는 ③ powerlessness가 가장 적절하다.

［어 휘］ lug 끌다, 무겁게 움직이다 resentment 분노, 화 compensate 보상하다 instill 서서히 스며들게 하다 reclaim 교정하다, 교화하다 vengefulness 복수심에 불탐 indebtedness 은혜를 입음, 빚을 짐 guiltlessness 죄 없음, 무고함 unforgetfulness 용서할 수 없음

08 ⑤ 당신이 마지막으로 보았던 영화에서, 당신은 주인공이 마시고 있던 음료수가 무엇인지 알아챘는가?, 또는 여배우가 운전하던 차는 어떤가? 텔레비전 쇼와 영화에 나오는 배우들은 항상 음료를 마시거나 차를 운전해 왔다. 하지만 이제는 그 음료수 캔의 이름과 자동차의 마크가 더 (A) 유명하다. 되었다. 광고주들은 그들의 상품을 텔레비전이나 영화에 출연시킴으로써 더욱 많이 노출시킬 수 있다는 사실을 알았다. 영화 제작사도 그들이 이른바 '끼워 팔기'라고 말하는 이러한 방법을 통해서 돈을 벌 수 있다는 사실을 알았다. 그런데 그래서 어쩌란 말인가? 다음번에 당신이 음료수를 Y 대신에 X를 선택하게 된다면, 생각해봐라, 당신이 마지막으로 봤던 영화가 X가 나오는 영화였는지, 아니면 Y가 나오는 것이었는지. 당신은 영화 제작자와 광고주들에게 (B) 조종당해 왔는가?

	(A)		(B)
①	은밀한	……	단념하다
②	은밀한	……	속다
③	잠재의식의	……	조종당하다
④	유명한	……	단념하다
⑤	유명한	……	조종당하다

［주 제］ 영화와 텔레비전의 상품 끼워 팔기

［정답 해설］ (A) 음료수 캔의 이름이나 자동차의 상징물이 많이 노출되어 더욱 유명해졌다는 내용이 자연스러우므로 빈칸에는 prominent가 적절하다. (B) 광고주들이 영화에 상품을 노출시켜서 더 많은 돈을 번다는 내용으로 미루어 볼 때 빈칸에는 manipulated가 적절하다.

［어 휘］ emblem 상징, 상표 feature (TV, 영화 등에) 출연시키다 embed 끼워 넣다 covert 은밀한, 비밀리의, 은신처 dissuade

~을 단념시키다 **subliminal** 잠재의식의 **manipulate** 조작하다
prominent 유명한, 뛰어난

09 ① 대부분의 남성들은 자신들이 평균적인 외모라고 생각한다. 평균적이라는 것은 그들을 불편하게 하지 않는다. 남성들에게 평균은 괜찮은 것이다. 이것이 바로 남성들이 남에게 자신이 어떻게 보이는가에 대해서 절대로 묻지 않는 이유이다. 미용에 대한 그들의 주요 형태는 면도를 하는 것인데, 본질적으로 그들이 잔디에 제공하는 미용과 동일한 형태로 자신을 면도하는 것이다. 여성들은 자신들에 대해 이렇게 생각하지 않는다. 만약 내가 여성들이 생각하는 외모에 대해 세 단어로만 표현해야 한다면, 그 단어는 아마도 "충분하지 않아."가 될 것이다. 그녀는 다른 사람들에게 매력적으로 보이더라도 그녀 자신이 거울 속 자신의 모습을 바라볼 때 '우웩'이라고 생각한다. 왜 여성들은 이렇게 낮은 자존감을 갖고 있는 것일까? 거기에는 바비 인형으로 빗대어 말할 수 있는 많은 복잡한 정신적, 사회적인 이유가 있다. 여자 아이들은 만약 인간이라면, 7피트 정도의 키에, 81파운드 몸무게인 그런 균형 잡힌 인형을 가지고 놀면서 성장한다.

① 낮은 자존감   ② 여성다움
③ 높은 자부심   ④ 숙고
⑤ 외모

〔주 제〕 여성의 외모 불만족 성향
〔정답 해설〕 남성들에 비해 여성들은 스스로 자신의 외모가 부족하다고 생각한다는 내용이므로 빈칸에는 낮은 자존감을 의미하는 ① low self-esteem이 적절하다.

〔어 휘〕 **femininity** 여성성, 여자다움 **reflection** 반사, 숙고 **woof** 개가 크게 짖는 소리 **proportion** 비, 비율, 균형 잡히게 하다

10 ① 과학과 기술이 우리의 세상을 변화시키는 것을 막지 못한다는 것을 우리가 받아들인다면 우리는 최소한 그것들이 만드는 변화들이 반드시 올바른 방향을 향하도록 노력은 할 수 있다. 민주주의 사회에서 이것은 대중들이 과학에 대한 기초적인 이해를 할 필요가 있으며, 그래서 그들이 잘 알고 결정을 내리고 그 결정을 전문가의 손에 맡기지 않도록 하는 것을 의미한다. 현재 대중은 과학에 대해 다소 양면적인 태도를 가지고 있다. 그들은 과학과 기술이 계속해서 가져올 새로운 발전에 의해 삶의 질은 지속적으로 향상될 것이라 기대하지만 과학에 대한 명확한 이해가 없기 때문에 과학을 불신하기도 한다.

① 양면적인   ② 적대적인
③ 동정적인   ④ 수륙 양용의
⑤ 무정형의

〔주 제〕 과학을 보는 대중의 양면적 태도
〔정답 해설〕 빈칸 뒤로 바로 이어지는 내용이 대중이 과학 기술에 대해 가지고 있는 서로 상반되는 태도에 대해 언급하고 있으므로, 빈칸에는 '양면적인, 상반되는 감정을 가진'을 의미하는 ① ambivalent가 들어가는 것이 가장 적절하다.

〔어 휘〕 **make an informed decision** 잘 알고 결정을 하다 **ambivalent** 상반되는 감정을 가진, 양면적인 **amphibious** 양서류의, 수륙 양용의 **amorphous** 무정형의, 특성이 없는

11 ② 독서는 복잡한 정신적인 통제를 요구하기 때문에 독자는 텔레비전 시청자보다 훨씬 더 많이 집중할 것을 요구받는다. 한 오디오 전문가는 "전자 매체에서 중요한 것은 개방성이다. 개방성은 시각, 청각적 자극들이 보다 직접적으로 뇌에 전달될 수 있도록 한다."고 강조한다. 누군가를 어설픈 TV 시청자로 만드는 것은 아마도 그의 독서 경험을 통해 습득된 (A) 집중 성향일 것이다. 그러나 반대되는 상황이 존재할 가능성은 훨씬 더 많은 것 같다. 수십 년 간의 TV 시청을 통해 획득한 (B) 개방성에 대한 성향은 집중하고 책을 읽고 쓰는 시청자의 능력에 부정적인 영향을 미쳤다.

	(A)		(B)
①	집중	……	참여
②	집중	……	개방성
③	조작	……	참여
④	조작	……	근사
⑤	자극	……	개방성

〔주 제〕 TV 시청의 개방 성향과 독서의 집중 성향
〔정답 해설〕 (A) 앞부분에서 독서는 집중을 요구한다는 내용이 언급되었다. 또한 개방성이 중요한 TV 시청에 있어서 한 사람을 어설프게 만드는 것은 독서 경험을 통해 습득된 집중 성향이라는 내용이 문맥상 자연스럽다. 따라서 빈칸에는 concentration이 적절하다. (B) 집중을 요구하는 책을 읽고 쓰는 일에 부정적인 영향을 미치는 것으로는 TV 시청을 통해 획득한 개방성이라는 내용이 문맥상 자연스럽다. 따라서 빈칸에는 openness가 적절하다.

〔어 휘〕 **manipulation** 교묘한 처리, 조작 **auditory** 청각의 **stimuli** 자극제, 자극(stimulus의 복수형) **predisposition** 경향, 성질 **adversely** 거스르는, 반대의

12 ② 많은 사람들, 아이들이나 어른들 모두 동시에 여러 작업을 하는 것이 짧은 시간 안에 많은 것을 할 수 있는 가장 최적의 방법이라고 생각한다. 그러나 과학적인 증거는 그것이 사실이 아님을 밝히고 있다. Michigan 대학의 두뇌, 인지, 행동 연구소를 맡고 있는 David E. Meyer는 "사람들이 두 가지 이상의 연관된 일을 동시에 하거나 또는 매우 짧은 시간 사이에 그것들을 번갈아가면서 할 때, 그들은 두 가지 일 모두 제대로 하지 못했다."고 말했다. 그리고 "그들은 더 많은 실수를 했고 그들이 (A) 순차적으로 일을 했을 때보다 더 오랜 시간을 소비했다"고 말했다. 만약 숙제를 하면서 동시에 또 다른 일을 하려고 한다면 400퍼센트 더 시간을 소비할 수도 있다고 그는 말한다. 왜 그럴까? 인간의 뇌는 한 번에 한 가지 이상의 일을 할 수 있도록 구조화되어 있지 않다. 대신 뇌가 하는 일은 임무의 (B) 우선순위를 매기는 것이다. 따라서 만약 당신이 음악을 들으며 책을 읽는다면 뇌는 음악에 우선 집중할 것이고 그것이 끝났을 때 책으로부터 받을 수 있는 정보에 집중하게 될 것이다. "그러나 당신의 뇌가 각각의 업무에 새롭게 적응하도록 하는 것은 막대한 정신적 에너지를 필요로 한다."라고 Meyer는 말한다. 결과는 어떤 일도 효율적으로 되지 않는다는 것이다.

	(A)		(B)
①	동시에	……	우선순위를 매기다
②	순차적으로	……	우선순위를 매기다
③	순차적으로	……	수행하다
④	무작위로	……	소원하게 만들다
⑤	무작위로	……	수행하다

[주 제] 작업 우선순위를 매기는 뇌

[정답 해설] (A) 숙제를 하면서 동시에 또 다른 일을 할 때 시간을 400퍼센트 더 소비할 수도 있다는 뒷부분의 내용으로 미루어 볼 때 빈칸에는 '순차적으로'라는 뜻의 sequentially가 적절하다. (B) 음악을 들으며 책을 읽을 때 뇌는 음악에 우선 집중하고 그것이 끝났을 때 책의 정보에 집중하게 된다는 뒷부분의 내용으로 미루어 볼 때 빈칸에는 '우선순위를 매기다'라는 뜻의 prioritize가 적절하다.

[어 휘] simultaneously 동시에 prioritize 우선순위를 매기다 sequentially 연속적으로, 연달아 alienate 소외시키다, 소원하게 만들다, 멀리하다 back and forth 왔다갔다, 앞뒤로 cognition 인식, 인지 reorient 새로이 순응시키다, 방향을 재설정하다

13 ④ 텔레비전이 가족생활에 끼친 기여도는 애매모호하다. 왜냐하면 그것은 실제로 가족 구성원들을 (A) 흩어지지 않게는 했지만 그들을 결속시키는 데에 기여하지 않았기 때문이다. 텔레비전이 가족들끼리 함께 보내는 시간 대부분을 지배하면서 한 가족을 다른 가족과 구별하는 특성, 가족이 하는 일들, 어떤 특별한 의식, 게임, 반복되는 농담, 익숙한 노래 및 가족들 간에 축적된 공통된 행동에 좌우되는 특성들을 없애버렸다. 그러나 부모들은 텔레비전의 지배를 받는 가족생활을 온전히 받아들여 매체가 그들이 가지고 있을 수 있는 문제들에 어떤 영향을 끼치는지 모른다. 심지어 가족들이 텔레비전을 통제하려는 노력을 할 때에도 너무 자주 텔레비전의 존재 자체가 가족 생활의 좋은 특성들을 (B) 상쇄한다.

	(A)		(B)
①	모이지	……	유지하다
②	수집하지	……	상쇄하다
③	흩어지지	……	강화하다
④	흩어지지	……	상쇄하다
⑤	흔들리지	……	강화하다

[주 제] 텔레비전이 가족생활에 끼친 영향

[정답 해설] (A) 가족들끼리 모이는 시간의 대부분을 텔레비전이 차지하고 이 때 다양한 공통 행동에 의해 좌우되는 가족의 특성이 없어졌다는 내용으로 미루어 볼 때 가족들을 흩어지지 않게 했지만 결속시키는 데에는 실패했다는 내용이 문맥상 자연스럽다, 따라서 빈칸에는 dispersing이 적절하다. (B) 텔레비전이 가족에게 미치는 부정적인 영향이 글의 소재라는 점을 고려할 때 빈칸에는 '상쇄하다'라는 뜻의 counterbalances가 적절하다.

[어 휘] equivocal 애매모호한, 다의적인 to a great extent 대부분은, 크게 recurrent 되풀이되는 counterbalance 균형을 맞추다, 상쇄하다 disperse 해산하다, 흩어지다 wavering 흔들리는, 떨리는, 망설이는

14 ① 화학 폐기물들은 종종 하천에 방류되거나 드럼통에 넣어져서 땅에 묻히거나, 거대한 화학 물질 "처리장"에 버려져 왔다. 때때로 화학 폐기물들은 사람이 없는 길에서 밸브를 열어 화학 물질들이 천천히 흘러 나가게 해놓은 빠르게 달리는 "불법 트럭들"에 의해서 길가에 뿌려지기도 한다. 종종 이러한 불법 투기는 화학 폐기물들을 생산하는 대기업들에 의해 고용된 작은 회사들에 의해서 이루어진다. 여기에는 어떠한 의문도 없다. 대기업의 경영진들은 더 조금 알수록 더 좋다. 하지만 무지가 더 이상 그들의 보호막이 되어줄 수 없다. 의회는 지금 모든 관련자가 책임지도록 만들고, 화학 폐기물들을 '요람에서 무덤까지' 추적하도록 보장하는 법률을 제정하려 하고 있다.

① 책임 있는   ② 독립적인
③ 결백한   ④ 준비된
⑤ 나누어진

주 제 화학 폐기물 책임 범위 확대의 필요성

정답 해설 대기업에 의해 고용된 작은 회사들의 화학 폐기물 처리 방식에 대해 대기업들이 몰랐다는 이유로 처벌받지 않았음을 유추해 볼 수 있다. 따라서 새로 개정되는 법률은 폐기물 관련 모든 parties가 각자의 과정에 대한 '책임'을 지도록 한다는 내용이 문맥상 자연스러우므로 ① responsible이 적절하다.

어 휘 dump 버리다, 털썩 내려놓다   bury 묻다, 매장하다 outlaw 법과 무관한, 탈법적인   valve 밸브(파이프의 개폐 장치)   spill 흘리다, 엎지르다

15 ① 첫 번째 소설은 작가가 지인들과 인생에 대한 것들을 소설 안에 넣는다는 점에서 보통 자전적이라고 한다. 하지만 심지어 스무 번째 소설이라 할지라도 그것은 또한 어느 정도는 개인적인 글이다. 소설가는 여전히 그의 개인적인 경험으로부터 쓰고 있기 때문이다. 소설가는 그의 소설 속 인물들이 순수한 상상의 산물이라 주장하겠지만, 이것은 그저 소설 속 인물들이 그 자신의 상상과, 사람들에 대한 그 스스로의 생각하는 방식과 그들에 대한 그만의 이해에서 나왔다는 것을 의미할 뿐이다. 완벽하게 숨을 수 있는 소설가는 아무도 없다.

① 숨은   ② 미화된
③ 경쟁자가 없는   ④ 통제 아래의
⑤ 비판을 넘어

주 제 소설에 나타나는 작가의 모습

정답 해설 문맥상 소설 속의 인물들은 작가의 개인적인 사고방식에 기인한다고 하였으므로 작가가 소설에 투영된다는 의미로 보는 것이 적절하다. 즉, 소설가는 숨을 수 없는 존재이므로 빈칸에는 ① hidden이 알맞다.

어 휘 autobiographical 자전적인, 자서전 형식의   assert 단언하다

16 ① 격식이 없는 일상 대화를 듣고 있으면 사람들이 사용하는 다양한 농담의 규칙들을 구분할 수 있다. 즉, 정상적인 언어활동으로부터 아주 익숙한 언어의 영역 내에서만 적절히 벗어나는 것이다. 또한 일반적으로 한

번에 한 가지 일탈만 발생한다. 만약 우리가 소리로 장난을 친다면, 문법과 어휘는 그대로 남아있는 경향이 있다. 만약 우리가 어휘나 문법 구조로 장난을 할 경우에는 발음은 온전하게 둔다. 이런 것들이 없을 때 언어가 이해할 수 없을 정도로 해체될 수 있고 장난의 모든 목적이 없어지기 때문에 이러한 제약은 중요하다.

① 온전한   ② 멸종된, 사라진
③ 조용한   ④ 소리가 큰
⑤ 부드러운

주 제 농담이 성립하기 위한 제약

정답 해설 농담을 할 때에 우리가 일반적으로 쓰는 말에서 일탈이 일어나는데, 그러한 일탈은 한 번에 한 가지만 발생한다고 하였으므로 '어휘'나 '문법'에 일탈을 주었다면 발음은 그대로 두어야 한다. 따라서 빈칸에는 ① intact가 적절하다. 문법을 바꾸고 싶으면 어휘는 그대로, 혹은 어휘를 바꾸고 싶으면 문법을 그대로 두어야 상대방이 장난으로 받아들이게 된다.

어 휘 namely 즉, 다시 말하자면   stable 안정적인, 견고한   intact 본래대로의, 때 묻지 않은   discern 분별하다, 구분하다 territory 영토, 토지   deviate 정상 궤도에서 벗어나다, 일탈하다 constraint 강제, 압박, 구속

17 ⑤ 전통적인 경제에서 가치는 희소성에 기인한다. 다이아몬드와 금과 같은 전통적인 부의 상징은 소중한데 그 이유는 그것들이 희귀하기 때문이다. 80-90년대 석유가 그랬듯이 희귀했던 것이 풍부해지면 그 가치를 잃게 된다. 그러나 네트워크의 논리는 이와 정반대이다. 힘과 가치는 이제 풍부함에서 나온다. 당신의 소프트웨어를 더 많이 복제해 내고, 더 많은 사람들을 당신의 네트워크에 포함시킬수록 그것은 더욱 더 강력해진다. 이러한 점이 이메일이 그토록 강력해진 이유이다. 그것은 이러한 종류의 개인 네트워크를 쉽게 만들어내는 궁극적인 도구이다.

① 경쟁   ② 디자인
③ 광고   ④ 요구, 수요
⑤ 결핍, 희소성

주 제 힘과 가치가 풍부함에서 나오는 네트워크

정답 해설 다이아몬드와 금이 귀한 이유는 그것들이 희귀하기 때문이라고 했으므로 전통적인 경제에서 가치는 희소성에서 나온다고 할 수 있다. 따라서 빈칸에는 ⑤ scarctity가 적절하다.

어 휘 icon 우상, 상징   abundance 풍부함, 많음

18 ⑤ 1942년 내가 12살 소년이었을 때, 나는 더운 여름 밤에 하는 프로 야구 경기의 약속으로 흥분해 있었다. 나의 아버지는 일주일에 6일 동안 힘들게 일하는 노동자였는데 그날은 나를 경기에 데려갈 수 있도록 서둘러 일을 끝마치셨다. 우리가 경기장에 도착했을 때, 땅을 고르는 거대한 기계가 들어갈 수 있도록 우익수 쪽 외야석 넓은 출입구가 열렸다. 수많은 팬들이 그 입구 쪽으로 몰려갔고 몇몇 사람들은 큰소리로 공짜 경기에 대해 이야기했다. 그날 밤은 우리의 행운의 밤이라고 생각하며, 내가 열린 출입구 쪽으로 향했지만 아버지는 나를 단단히 붙잡고 돌려세워 표를 끊기 위해 서있던 줄로 돌아갔다. 경기 내용이나 승자는 오래 전에 잊었지만 다정하고도 엄격한 아버지로부터 받았던 정직이라는 무언의 메시지는 잊지 않았다.

① 조화　　　　　② 호기심
③ 열정　　　　　④ 희망
⑤ 정직

〔주 제〕 아버지께 배운 정직의 미덕

〔정답 해설〕 이 글은 편법으로 이득을 취하려던 화자에게 아버지가 정당한 대가를 지불하도록 가르침을 주었다는 내용이다. 그러므로 빈칸에는 ⑤ honesty가 알맞다.

〔어 휘〕 road scraper 바닥을 평평하게 다지는 기계 grip 꽉 쥠, 손잡이 bleacher 표백 업자, 표백제, 야구장의 외야석 angle 각, 각도, ~로 향하다

More Practice

01 ②　　02 ②　　03 ②　　04 ①

01 ② 국제적으로도 국내적으로도 관광은 보다 더 부유한, 선진화된 나라나 지역에서 덜 개발되고 보다 더 빈곤한 지역으로 부와 투자를 이전하는 효과적인 수단으로 간주된다. 이와 같은 부의 (A) 재분배는, 이론적으로, 관광지에서 관광객 지출과 보다 더 부유하고 관광객을 창출하는 국가들의 관광 시설에 대한 투자의 결과로 일어난다. 후자의 경우, 선진국은 원칙적으로 관광에 투자함으로써 후진국의 경제 성장과 개발을 지원하고 있다. 하지만 관광객 지출의 순수 보유액은 여행 목적지에 따라 상당히 차이가 있고, 관광 시설에 대한 해외 투자는 자주 (B)착취와 의존으로 이어질 수 있다고 오랫동안 인식되어 왔다. 이것은 소득을 종종 후진국으로부터 빼돌리는 것에서 볼 수 있고, 그들을

투자하는 국가와 기업에 잠재적으로 종속되게 한다.

	(A)		(B)
①	집중	……	착취와 의존
②	재분배	……	착취와 의존
③	불균형	……	번영과 안전
④	재분배	……	번영과 안전
⑤	불균형	……	협업과 개발

〔주 제〕 후진국에서 행해지는 선진국의 관광산업

〔정답 해설〕 (A) 앞부분에서 선진국의 부와 투자가 후진국으로 옮겨진다고 하였으므로 빈칸에는 '재분배'를 뜻하는 redistribution이 적합하다. (B) 뒷부분에서 선진국이 이익을 가로채서 후진국이 선진국에 종속되는 상태가 되는 상황을 설명하고 있다. 따라서 빈칸에는 '착취와 의존상태'를 뜻하는 exploitation and dependency가 적절하다.

〔어 휘〕 domestically 가정적으로; 국내적으로, 국내(실정)에 알맞게 expenditure 지출 retention 보유, 보존 more often than not 자주, 종종 overseas 해외(로부터)의, 외국의, 해외로 가는(향한) divert (딴 데로) 돌리다, (물길 따위를) 전환하다

02 ② 농작물을 사서 어떤 재료를 사용하고 어디에서 그것을 얻을지에 대하여 융통성을 가지고 있기 때문에, 가공식품 생산자들은 농부들에 비해 이점을 가진다. 예를 들면, 가공식품은 감미료를 필요로 하지만, 필수적으로 사탕수수에서 나온 설탕이어야 하는 것은 아니다. 그것은 기름을 필요로 하지만, 반드시 옥수수 기름이어야 하는 것은 아니다. 그것은 전분을 필요로 하지만, 이는 감자나 밀 또는 수많은 다른 곡물에서도 얻을 수 있다. 감자 칩의 생산은 이러한 대체 효과의 좋은 예가 된다. 생산자들은 감자를 어떤 기름이든지 생산 당시에 가장 저렴한 기름에 튀길 수 있다. 이것은 왜 농부들이 자주 농산물 시스템에서 불리한 위치에 처하는지를 보여준다.

① 통합　　　　　② 대체
③ 보존　　　　　④ 단순화
⑤ 과소비

〔주 제〕 농산물 시스템에서 대체물 효과

〔정답 해설〕 빈칸 앞에서 가공식품에는 일반 재료를 대신하여 다양한 재료가 활용될 수 있다는 것에 대한 예시를 들고 있으므로, 빈칸에는 ② substitution이 가장 적절하다.

〔어 휘〕 flexibility 융통성 necessarily 반드시 sugarcane 사탕수수 starch 전분 illustrate 설명하다 disadvantaged 불리한 agrofood 농산품

03 ② 이 현대 세계에서, 사람들은 불편함과 사는 것에 익숙하지 않다. 우리는 즉각적인 결과와 만족을 기대한다. 우리는 답이 도착할 수 있는 것 보다 빠르길 원한다. 24시간 수리, 24시간 쇼핑이 있다. 전자레인지 저녁식사부터 밤새 운영하는 식료품점과 식당까지, 배가 고프면 언제나 이용할 수 있는 음식이 있다. 사람들은 더 이상 기다리는 법을, 혹은 기다림의 의미조차도 알지 못한다. 당신이 원하는 것을 원할 때 가질 수 있다는 것은 좋은 일이지만, 만족을 미루는 능력은 중요하다. <u>인내</u>는 분명 중요한 덕목이지만, 많은 사람들이 "빨리!"라고 생각하며 자신의 전자레인지 앞에 서 있다.

① 야망
② 인내
③ 정직
④ 겸손
⑤ 근면

주 제) 불편함을 견디지 못하는 현대인

정답 해설) 현대인들이 빠르고 편리한 생활에 익숙해져 기다림을 견디지 못하는 점을 지적하는 글이므로, 중요한 덕목이 제시되는 빈칸에는 ② Patience가 가장 적절하다.

어 휘) be used to ~ing ~하는 데 익숙하다 discomfort 불편 immediate 즉각적인 delay 미루다, 연기하다 virtue 덕목, 미덕

04 ① 당신의 저녁 식사를 먹은 후 15분에서 30분 사이에 당신이 무엇을 하는가가 당신의 물질대사에 강력한 신호를 보낸다. 식사 후에 활동적인 상태를 유지한다면 당신은 체중 감량의 이점과 더불어 저녁 시간 동안 더 많은 활력을 위한 바탕을 마련할 것이다. 가능한 많은 활동 중에서, 걷기는 식사 후 몇 분간 운동을 하는 가장 쉬운 방법 중 하나이다. 사실, 연구는 당신이 식사 후에 걷는다면 당신이 빈속에 같은 시간과 거리를 같은 강도로 걸을 때보다 15퍼센트 많은 칼로리를 태울 수 있음을 보여준다.

① 활동적인
② 혼자서
③ 가득 찬
④ 만족한
⑤ 조용한

주 제) 식후 운동의 이점

정답 해설) 빈칸의 뒤에 활동적인 운동 중의 한 예로 걷기가 소개 되고 있으므로, 빈칸에는 ① active가 가장 적절하다.

어 휘) metabolism 물질대사 set the stage 준비하다 vigor 활력 intensity 강도, 세기

UNIT **10** 빈칸 II

Example
답 ③

코요테는 회색 늑대 가죽에 덮여 있고, 언제나 축 늘어지고 웬만큼 털 많은 꼬리와, 교활하고 사악한 눈, 길고 뾰족한 얼굴, 살짝 올라간 입과 돌출된 이빨을 가지고 있는, 길쭉하고 날씬하면서도 병들고 초라한 뼈만 남은 동물이다. 그는 전체적으로 살금살금 걷는 모습이다. 코요테는 살아 있는, 숨쉬는 <u>결핍의 상징</u>이다. 그는 항상 배고프다. 그는 항상 초라하고 운이 없고 친구가 없다. 가장 비열한 생명체들이 그를 경멸하고 심지어 벼룩들도 눈 깜짝할 사이에 그를 버릴 것이다.

① 분노의 전형
② 가학성의 유추
③ 결핍의 상징
④ 효율성의 상징
⑤ 지배의 은유

주 제) 코요테의 외형 묘사

Practice

01 ③	02 ⑤	03 ②	04 ①	05 ①
06 ⑤	07 ①	08 ②	09 ④	10 ①
11 ④	12 ②	13 ③	14 ①	15 ①
16 ②	17 ①	18 ⑤	19 ④	20 ③
21 ⑤	22 ⑤	23 ④	24 ④	25 ③
26 ④	27 ⑤	28 ④	29 ②	30 ②

01 ③ 공무원들이 대중에게 말하든 서로 간에 말하든 간에 모호한 말이 정부에 넘쳐난다. 토지 관리부는 1986년에 기자 회견을 가졌다. "법에 명시된 요구사항을 준수하는 것에 대한 행정적 절차를 추가하고자 하는 움직임으로, 오늘 토지 관리부(BLM)의 내부 부서는 연방 정부 석탄 차지인 자격에 대한 규칙제정을 출간합니다." 이 모호한 말은 BLM이 석탄 계약을 엄중히 단속할 것임을 의미한다. 임금 인상을 요구했던 상무부의 한 공직자는 "정부의 기준에 병치하여 당신의 직위의 생산성이 끊임없이 변동하는 경향 때문에, 임금 인상을 지지하는 것은 재정적으로 부적절하다."라고 들었다. 다시 말해, <u>임금 인상 없음</u>.

① 해고 통지서
② 모든 탄원서의 유예
③ 임금 인상 없음

④ 새로운 개장 없음
⑤ 조기 은퇴

정부가 사용하는 모호한 말

정답 해설 정부에서 볼 수 있는 모호한 말에 대한 글이다. 길게 늘어서 쓴 말도 간단히 요점만 짚을 수 있다고 말하고 있다. 빈칸에는 '임금 인상을 지지하는 것은 재정적으로 부적절하다'라는 내용을 줄인 말이 들어가야 내용상 자연스럽다. 따라서 ③ '임금 인상 없음'이 가장 적절하다.

어 휘 doublespeak 모호한 말 compliance 준수 statutory 법에 명시된 leasee 차지인 fluctuational 변동하는 predisposition 성향 juxtaposed 병치된 monetarily 금전상으로 injudicious 부적절한 increment 인상 pink slip 해고 통지서 petition 진정, 탄원 pay raise 임금 인상

---

02 ⑤ 인간의 욕구가 생산의 요구로 희생되는 자본주의의 철창처럼, 현대 사회의 과학 또한 마음의 감옥이 되었다는 인식이 있다. 제도화된 과학과 이론적인 학문의 영역에서, 창의성과 혁신은 다양한 전문적 훈련을 관리하는 전문화된 성취 기준에 따라 조정되어야 한다.

① 지성의 길을 비추는 횃불
② 관료적 요구에서 해방된
③ 어떤 공격에도 확고한 요새
④ 당면한 도덕적 문제에 취약한
⑤ 마음의 감옥

주 제 현대 과학에 대한 비판

정답 해설 빈칸에는 '자본주의의 철창'에 상응하는 표현이 문맥상 자연스럽다. 따라서 ⑤ '마음의 감옥'이 적절하다.

어 휘 exigency 긴급 사태, 긴급 필요, (보통 -cies) 요구 institutionalized 제도화된 domain 영역 accommodate 수용하다 torchlight 횃불 avenue 길, 방안 emancipate 해방시키다 bureaucratic 관료의 impregnable 확고한

---

03 ② 예를 들어 나는 그랜드캐니언에 가서 경치를 보고 큰 즐거움을 느끼고 나의 좋은 친구인 너에게 엽서로 간단한 메시지를 쓴다. "네가 여기 있었으면." 이러한 친근한 말로 나는 무엇을 의미하는가? 그랜드캐니언을 바라보는 즐거움을 너와 함께 나누었더라면 그것이 더 컸을 것이라는 것을 의미한다. 나는 혼자서도 그랜드캐니언은 그 자체로서 좋다는 것을 느끼지만, 그 경험을 너와 함께 나눈다면 훨씬 더 좋을 것이라는 것을 느낀다. 달리 말하면 나의 엽서는 그랜드캐니언을 함께 보는 우리의 즐거움의 합이 너와 내가 각각 다른 날에 협곡을 보는 즐거움의 합보다 더 크다는 점에서 친구들이 특별한 의미의 공동의 즐거움을 나눈다는 것을 말한다.

① ~로 나누어질 수 있다
② ~의 합보다 더 크다
③ ~의 합한 양과 같다
④ 보다 기억 속에 더 오래 머무를 수 있다
⑤ 고려할 필요가 없다

주 제 함께 하는 즐거움

정답 해설 그랜드캐니언을 바라볼 때의 즐거움을 친구와 나누면 각자 느끼게 되는 즐거움의 합보다 감정이 더 커진다는 내용이므로 빈칸에는 ②가 가장 적절하다.

어 휘 take into consideration 고려하다

---

04 ① 내가 어렸을 때 어떻게 식품 제조업자들이 온전한 호두를 유리병에 채울 수 있었는가 하는 것은 매우 인상 깊었다. 어찌됐든 그들은 열매는 그대로 남겨둔 채 껍데기를 깰 수 있었다. 나는 가까스로 열 번에 한 번 정도 전체 열매를 꺼낼 수 있었고 내가 시도했던 대부분의 경우에 껍데기와 열매가 섞인 부스러기들을 얻게 되었다. 그러나 이후에 비록 제조업자들이 나보다 성공률이 높기는 했지만, 나는 그들도 껍데기와 열매 부스러기들을 만든다는 사실을 알게 되었다. 그러나 나는 또한 그들이 다른 무언가를 한다는 것을 알게 되었다. 그들은 그들의 결과물을 선별했다. 그들이 성공적이었을 경우에는 그들은 전체 호두를 "통호두"라고 이름 붙인 병에 집어넣었다. 다른 경우에는 그들은 껍데기로부터 열매 조각을 분리하여 "호두 알갱이"라고 붙은 병에 집어넣었다.

① 그들의 결과물을 선별했다
② 특별한 종류의 견과류를 재배했다
③ 새로운 브랜드의 장비를 사용했다
④ 판매를 위해 열매를 섞었다.
⑤ 고생하면서 그 교훈을 배웠다

주 제 통호두와 호두 부스러기 분류하기

정답 해설 열매를 그대로 남겨둔 채 껍데기를 깼을 경우 '통호두'라고 이름 붙인 병에 호두를 집어넣고 그렇지 않을 경우 껍데기로부터 열매 조각을 분리하여 '호두 알갱이'라고 붙은 병에

집어넣었다는 내용과 문맥상 일치하는 보기로는 ① '그들의 결과물을 선별했다'가 적절하다.

어 휘 crack 부수다 intact 본래대로의, 전혀 다치지 않은

05 ① 우리는 자신에 대해서 다른 사람들이 어떻게 생각하는지에 마음을 빼앗길 정도로 사회적인 동물이다. 거의 모든 성공은 실제로 다른 사람들이 어떻게 생각하는지에 대해서 결정되기 때문에, 집단에 순응하고자 하는 압박은 집단에 의해 가치를 인정받는 것을 포함한다. 유명인 위주의 현대사회와 특히 최근에 뜨고 있는, 다른 사람들에게 인정을 받기 위해 상당한 시간과 노력을 투자하는 소셜 네트워크가 이러한 선입관에 대한 자명한 예시이다. 이 지구상에서 17억 이상의 사람들이 다른 사람들에게 인정을 받고 나누기 위해 인터넷상에서 소셜 네트워크를 이용하고 있다. 유명한 공연예술학교 뮤지컬 시리즈의 등장인물이었던 Rachel Berry는 "요즘 세상은 무명이 가난보다 더 비참하다."라고 얘기했다. 그녀는 현대 사람들의 유명함에 대한 강박과, 비록 대부분이 모르는 사람이거나 면식만 있는 사람들일지라도 많은 사람들이 자신을 좋아해 주었으면 하는 열망에 대해 그대로 말을 해주었다.

① 다른 사람들에게 인정을 받기 위해
② 그들 자신의 친구 관계를 늘리기 위해
③ 전문가들의 상당한 비판에도 불구하고
④ 대중들 사이에서 오해를 일으키는
⑤ 권위자들에 의한 한계를 넘어서

주 제 소셜 네트워크에서 나타나는 인정 욕구
정답 해설 사람들은 다른 사람들이 자신에 대해 내리는 평가에 상당히 신경 쓰며 그들에게 인정받으려고 노력한다는 내용의 글이다. 소셜 네트워크는 이러한 현상을 보여주는 사례가 된다. 따라서 빈칸에는 ① '다른 사람들에게 인정을 받기 위해'가 가장 적절하다.

어 휘 preoccupy (생각, 걱정이) 뇌리를 사로잡다, 마음을 빼앗다 pressure 압박, 압력 conform 따르다, ~에 일치하다 define 정의하다 evident 분명한, 눈에 띄는 celebrity 유명인사 validation 확인 anonymous 익명의 obsession 집착, 강박관념 acquaintance 면식, (약간의) 친분

06 ⑤ 예술의 심오한 지식과 아름다운 멜로디를 창작한 가장 적절한 재능을 결합해 보고, 그런 후 모차르트의 음악적 천재성을 가장 충실하게 그린 그림을 얻기 위

해서 이 두 가지를 가장 위대한 독창성과도 연결해 보자. 그의 작품 중 어떤 부분에서도 누군가 어디서 들은 적이 있다는 느낌을 받지 않는다. 심지어 그의 반주들 역시 항상 새로웠다. 한 곡은 마치 하나의 관념에서 다른 관념으로 끊임없이 이어져 나오는 듯 했기에 새로운 작품에 대한 찬사가 기존의 것을 거듭 집어삼켰으며, 심지어 한 사람의 모든 힘을 다 쏟아부어서 만든 작품을 듣는 사람들은 그들 앞에 주어진 모든 아름다움을 다 흡수할 수조차 없다. 만약 모차르트의 작업에서 어떠한 실수를 찾을 수 있다면, 이것 하나뿐이라고 확신할 수 있다. 넘치는 아름다움은 오히려 정신을 힘들게 하고 가끔은 몽롱하게 만든다. 하지만 음악가의 유일한 실수가 과한 완벽함이라는 것은 행복이다.

① 과도한 신념
② 황폐해진 영혼
③ 구령, 명령
④ 불필요한 멜로디
⑤ 넘치는 아름다움

주 제 모차르트의 음악적 독창성
정답 해설 모차르트의 음악은 새로움과 사람들이 다 흡수할 수조차 없는 아름다움을 지니고 있다고 언급하고 있다. 모차르트의 음악에 대해 찬사하는 글이므로 문맥상 빈칸에는 ⑤ '넘치는 아름다움'이 가장 적절하다.

어 휘 profound 엄청난 originality 독창성 faithful 충실한 accompaniment (노래나 다른 악기를 지원하는) 반주 incessantly 그칠 새 없이 admiration 감탄, 존경 strain 모든 걸 짜내는, 압박감 scarcely 거의 ~ 않다 obscure 이해하기 힘든, 모호한

07 ① 한 장의 사진이 수천 단어의 가치가 있을 수 있지만, 수 세기 동안 언어가 법적 영역을 지배했다. 언어를 사용한 예술인 웅변술은 항상 변호사들의 트레이드마크였고, 특히 관습법에서 재판은 언어의 전쟁으로 폭넓게 이해되었다. 하지만 모든 영광은 슬프게도 운명을 다하고, 19세기 후반 새로운 방법의 설득법이 지배적으로 증가했는데, 이러한 방법은 우리가 사용하는 언어들을 조금 더 낮은 수준의 전달 실제로 바꾸도록 위협하는 기계로 만들어진 증거들의 새로운 계층에 의해 비롯되었다. 언제나 작동 중이지만 손이 가는 일은 없는 현미경, 망원경, 초고속 카메라, 그리고 엑스레이 튜브 같은 기계들은 더 풍부하고, 더 좋고, 더 사실에 가까운, 종종 사람들이 접근하기 어려운 증거들을 전달하려는 취지를 갖고 있었다. 기계적 객관성의 이러한 새로운 유형의 상징은 시각적 근거였다. "자연이 스스로 이야기하게 하라"는 좌우명이 되었고, 자연 언어는 그러한 사진들과 기계적으로 만들어진 그래프들인 것으로 보인다.

① 시각적 근거　　　　② 구두 증언
③ 합법적 용어　　　　④ 언어학적 웅변
⑤ 주관적 표현

주 제 기계를 이용한 시각적 근거

정답 해설 현미경, 망원경, 초고속 카메라, 엑스레이 튜브 등의 도구들 덕분에 사진이나 그래프와 같은 시각적인 자료들을 근거로 사용할 수 있게 되었다는 내용의 글이다. 따라서 빈칸에는 ① '시각적 근거'가 가장 적절하다.

어 휘 domain (지식, 활동의) 영역, 범위 rhetoric 수사법 doom ~을 운명짓다 persuasion 설득 testimony 증거 threaten 협박하다, 위협하다 inferior 하위의, 더 낮은 microscope 현미경 telescope 망원경 inaccessible 접근하기 어려운 objectivity 객관성 watchword 좌우명

08 ② 현대 서구 사회에서, 종교가 본래 가진 설명적인 역할은 과학에 의해 점점 빼앗기고 있다. 우리가 아는 우주의 근원은 빅뱅과 그 이후의 물리적 법칙의 작용에 의한 결과로 보인다. 현대 언어의 다양성은 더 이상 바벨탑이나 New Guinea의 경질 수목을 감싸고 있는 덩굴 식물의 끊어짐과 같은 기원 신화로 설명되지 않지만, 대신 언어 변화의 관찰된 역사적 과정들을 통해 충분히 설명된다고 여겨진다. 일몰, 일출 그리고 밀물과 썰물의 설명은 천문학자들에게, 바람과 비에 대한 설명은 기상학자들에게 남겨진다. 새의 지저귐은 생태학자에 의해 설명되고 인간을 포함한 식물과 동물 종의 기원은 생물진화론자들에 의해 해석되도록 남겨졌다.

① 과학적 근거의 기반을 제공한다
② 과학에 의해 점점 빼앗기고 있다
③ 우주 만물에 대해 가장 잘 설명할 수 있는 방법으로 떠올랐다
④ 과학의 타당성에 대해서 논쟁을 일으켰다
⑤ 창조론자와 진화론자에 의해 강화되었다

주 제 자연 현상 설명에서 과학의 역할 증가

정답 해설 자연을 설명하는 종교의 역할이 과학의 기술 발달 및 발견으로 인해 줄어들고 있음을 서술하고 있다. 따라서 빈칸에는 ②가 가장 적절하다.

어 휘 explanatory 이유를 밝히는 attribute to (~의) 결과로 보다 subsequent 차후의 physics 물리학 diversity 다양성, 포괄성 myth 신화 snap 덥석 물다, 딱 부러지다 adequately 어울리는, 적당한 tide 조수 meteorologist 기상학자 ethology 행동학 interpret ~의 뜻을 해석하다 usurp 빼앗다

09 ④ 봉급 인상은, 조합의 일원이 아니거나, 봉급에 대해 항의하는 파업에 뛰어들지 않은 노동자들도, 조합의 일원이나 파업을 실행한 노동자들과 동등한 처우를 받을 수 있다는 점에서 공공의 이익이다. 이것은 개인이 집단 구성원이 수반할 수도 있는 다양한 비용을 초래하지 않고도 개인이 수익을 얻는 무임승차자가 될 수 있는 기회를 제공한다. 그것은 공통의 이익이 있다는 것이 조직의 구조를 더욱 발전된 상태로 이끌 수 있고, 또는 그 이익을 지켜낼 수도 있다는 것에 대한 어떠한 보장도 없다는 것을 의미하고 있기 때문에 이러한 분석은 매우 중요하다. 따라서 모든 집단은 저마다 정치적인 견해를 갖고 있다는 다원주의적인 가설은 매우 미심쩍은 것이다. 또한 집단 정치는 종종 큰 집단의 희생을 통해 작은 집단에 권한을 부여하고 있는 것일지도 모른다는 주장이 있다. 각각의 개인들은 그들이 집단에 참여하는 데 실패하더라도 집단 전체의 효율성에는 거의 손해를 끼치지 않게 되리라고 계산할 것이기 때문에, 더욱 큰 집단은 무임승차를 장려하게 될 것이다.

① 이론으로 발전된다
② 비평받지 않을 것이다
③ 약한 경쟁에 직면할 것이다
④ 매우 미심쩍다
⑤ 더 견고한 기반을 얻을 것이다

주 제 조직 내부 무임승차 문제

정답 해설 집단행동에 참여하지 않고도 이익을 얻는 개인이 많고, 집단이 클수록 이러한 무임승차자를 양성할 것이라는 내용의 글이다. 따라서 모든 집단은 정치적인 견해를 갖고 있다는 다원주의적 가설은 의문의 여지가 있다는 내용이 문맥상 적절하다. 따라서 빈칸에는 ④가 적절하다.

어 휘 public good 공익 in furtherance of ~이 일어나도록, ~을 촉진하기 위해 entail 수반하다 pluralist 다원적인, 다원론적인 empower 권한을 부여하다 at the expense of ~을 희생하여, ~을 대가로 하여 impair 악화시키다, 손상시키다

10 ① 놀랍지도 않게, 많은 사람들이 미국은 열등감과 함께 탄생했다고 주장한다. 미국의 이야기들은 유럽으로부터 전해져 온 것이다. 미국의 전설은 고유한 것이 아니다. 미국 사람들이 누구인지에 대해 이야기하기 위해서는 유럽 사람들이 필요했다. 미국 정부의 형태도 유럽의 것을 차용해 왔다. 위대한 자본가들이 그들의 입지를 확고히 다지기 전까지는, 미국인들은 왕도 왕비도 그리고 성도 갖지 못했다. 어떤 부와 권력도 이러한 공허함을 지울 수는 없었기에, 해마다 여름이면 수많은 미국인들이 탁월한 품격을 직

접 느끼고 음미하기 위해 유럽으로 여행을 떠난다. (괴상하게도 그 반대도 사실이다. 즉 해마다 여름이면 마지막 개척지를 보고, 유럽인이 그들에게 주었던 유산을 가지고 미국인이 무엇을 했는지를 보기 위해 수많은 유럽인들이 미국으로 여행을 한다.) 미국은 미국인들과 유럽인들이 '어떤 이유에서건 그들이 보도록 길들여진 것'을 발견하기를 바라면서 지속적으로 들여다보는 거울이다.

① 열등감
② 개척자 윤리학
③ 완벽주의자 정신
④ 현실주의자 정신
⑤ 은수저

주제) 미국 문화의 고유성 결여

정답 해설) 글의 중반부까지 미국은 문화적으로나 인적으로 유럽에서 기인하였기 때문에 자생적이거나 독창적인 부분이 부족하다는 논지를 전개하고 있다. 중반부에 voidness와 같은 어휘를 사용한 것으로 보아 확실히 알 수 있다. 따라서 빈칸에는 ① '열등감'이 가장 적절하다.

어휘) inferiority complex 열등감, 열등의식 pragmatist 실용주의자 silver spoon (상속 받은) 부, 재산 voidness 공허함 touch of class 탁월함, 품격, 격조 perversely 삐딱하게, 괴상하게 obverse 반대되는 것 condition 영향을 끼치다, 길들이다

11 ④ 명상 속에서 수련하는 것을 통해, 전체적인 인식 체계는 자신, 즉 육체의 행동을 통제하고, 무엇을 할 것인지에 대해 결정하는, 관념상의 '자기 자신'에 대해 덜 집중된 형태를 구축하도록 다듬어진다. 환상에 불과한 이 자아가 서서히 사라져 버림에 따라, 세상은 더욱 선명하게 드러나고 그것의 요구에 따라 덜 왜곡되어 보인다. 여러 가지 감정이 생겨나고, 사라지게 된다. 생각이 형성되고 사라져 버린다. 그러한 형태가 된다는 것은 흘러가는 듯 자유를 느끼고, 우리 스스로 만들어낸 환상에 의한 어리석은 행동들에 대해 미소 지을 수 있을 것처럼 생각하는 것이다. 그것은 우리 대부분이 지금까지 대부분의 시간 동안 그래왔었던 것과 같이, 자기 자신과 매우 밀접하게 연결되어 있고 고수해오던 자기 자신의 형태와는 매우 다른 존재이다.

① 그것을 함에 따라 성공하다
② 되고 싶어 하다
③ 가는 것을 허락받다
④ 대부분의 시간 동안 그러하다
⑤ 서로에게 달려있다

주제) 명상 수련이 주는 효과

정답 해설) 명상을 하면 환상에 불과한 자아가 사라지고 세상이 덜 왜곡되어 보인다는 내용의 글이다. 명상의 결과는 과거의 모습과는 다른 형태라는 뒷부분의 내용으로 미루어 볼 때 이 과거는 대부분의 시간 동안 유지되어 온 것이라는 내용이 문맥상 자연스럽다. 따라서 빈칸에는 ④가 적절하다.

어휘) cognitive 인식의, 인지의 illusory 환상에 불과한, 현실이 아닌 distorted 왜곡된 folly 어리석은 행동

12 ② 다른 모든 장르와 마찬가지로 예술도 그것에 대해 무엇인가 알고 있을 때 훨씬 더 즐길 수 있게 된다. 당신은 뛰어난 작품들에 대해 예찬하며 몇 시간이고 루브르 박물관을 거닐 수도 있겠지만, 만약 누군가 잘 알고 있는 사람이 당신과 함께 해준다면 그 경험은 훨씬 더 흥미로운 것이 될 것이다. 멀티미디어 문서는 당신이 집에 있든지 박물관에 있든지 상관없이 안내인의 역할을 해줄 수 있다. 그것은 당신이 예술 작품에 대한 저명한 학자의 강의의 일부분을 듣게 해줄 수 있다. 그것은 당신이 동일한 작가의 다른 작품이나, 동시대의 작품들을 참고하게 해줄 수 있다. 심지어 당신은 자세한 관찰을 위해 확대해 볼 수도 있다. 만약 멀티미디어를 통한 사본과 시연이 예술을 훨씬 더 접근 가능하고, 가까이 다가갈 수 있게 만들어 준다면 그 사본을 본 사람들은 원본을 보고 싶어 하게 될 것이다. 사본을 공개하는 것은 실제 예술 작품에 대한 경외감을 떨어뜨리기는커녕 오히려 증대시키고 더욱 더 많은 사람들이 박물관이나 전시관을 찾게 만들 가능성이 높다.

① 더 창의적으로 된다.
② 원본을 보고 싶어 한다.
③ 미술의 정교함을 떨어트린다.
④ 멀티미디어 작품을 자세히 설명한다.
⑤ 고급 미술품에 대한 갈망을 약화시킨다.

주제) 멀티미디어 자료가 예술에 대한 관심에 끼치는 역할

정답 해설) 마지막 문장에서 '사본을 공개하는 것이 사람들이 실제 예술에 대한 경외감을 증진시키고 더 많은 사람들을 박물관과 전시장으로 이끌 것이다.'라고 하였으므로, 인과관계상, '사본을 본 사람들은 진본을 보고 싶어 할 것이다.'라는 내용이 빈칸에 들어가는 것이 가장 자연스럽다. 따라서 빈칸에는 ②가 적절하다.

어휘) knowledgeable 많이 아는, 아는 것이 많은 refer A to B A가 B를 참고하도록 하다 preeminent 탁월한, 훌륭한 reproduction (예술 작품의) 복사, 복제품 reverence for (~에 대한) 존경, 숭배, 경외

13 ③ 텔레비전 뉴스(그리고 이른바 다른 정보성 쇼)를 특징짓는 점 중 하나는 바로 드라마와는 다르게 그것이 우리의 존재나 모습을 숨기려고 하지 않는다는 점이다. 우리는 언제나 직접적으로 그리고 개방적으로 발표된 것들을 통해 인정받게 된다. 우리가 텔레비전에 나오는 앵커를 볼 때, 그들은 누군가 고양이와 함께 해보았을지도 모르는 눈싸움을 하는 것과 같은 모습으로 우리를 똑바로 바라본다. 그러나 이런 시합에서는 지루함 때문에, 혹은 더 그럴듯하게 어떤 TV 프로그램도, 심지어 뉴스조차도 계속되는 전기의, 그리고 정보를 전달하는 간헐적인 흐름에 불과하기 때문에 언제나 먼저 눈을 감거나 다른 곳을 보는 것은 우리들이다. 우리는 다른 곳을 보지만 앵커는 절대로 그렇게 하지 않는다. 왜냐하면 그것이 그들의 하루와 존재의 핵심이기 때문이다. 우리는 우리가 그들을 지켜본다고 생각하지만, 그들이 우리를 바라보고 있는 것이거나 또는 훨씬 더 힘들게 가상의 우리를 지켜보고 있는 것이다.

① 시청자, 우리에 대한 시선을 고정하다.
② 시청자의 관심을 하찮은 것으로 돌리다.
③ 우리의 존재와 시선을 숨기다.
④ 우리의 존재, 우리가 볼 것을 예상하다.
⑤ 시청자 수에 대한 정보를 얻다.

[주 제] 텔레비전 뉴스에서 앵커의 시선
[정답 해설] 드라마와 달리 뉴스는 시청자가 화면 앞에 존재하고 있다고 전제하고 제작된다는 내용의 글이다. 따라서 빈칸에는 '우리의 존재나 모습을 숨기려고 하지 않는다'는 ③의 내용이 가장 적절하다.

[어 휘] disguise 숨기다, 가장하다, 위장하다 look back at ~을 돌아보다, 회고하다 intermittently 간헐적으로, 가끔, 간간히

14 ① 돌이켜 생각해보면 Massachusetts가 1994년에 명망과 경제적 가치가 가장 높았고, Harvard와 제휴가 된 Massachusetts General Hospital과 Brigham & Women's Hospital을 Partners HealthCare라는 하나의 의료 시스템으로 합병시킨 것은, (A) 심각한 실수였던 것으로 보인다. 보험 회사로부터 제공되는 치료에 대한 질적 수준 또는 치료의 복잡함과는 관련이 없는 높은 배상금을 요구하게 됨으로써 그 합병은 보스턴 지역의 거대한 의료 시장의 건강관리 비용을 상승시키는 영향을 끼쳤다는 조사 결과가 입증되었다. 오늘날 뒤늦게 법무장관 Martha Coakley는 비록 일시적인 것이겠지만, 적어도 동반자로 생각하는 범위 내에서 비용의 인상 속도를 늦추고, 그것이 닥치는 대로 해치우는 진료 행위의 건수에도 제한을 두게 될 협의된 합의점을 통해 병원을 (B) 제재하기 위해 노력하고 있다. Massachusetts에서의 경험은 다른 주들에게 대형 병원들의 합병의 위험성에 대한 경고의 메시지를 전해주고 있다.

	(A)		(B)
①	심각한 실수	……	제재하다
②	심각한 실수	……	그만두다
③	커다란 기여	……	제재하다
④	커다란 기여	……	목을 조르다
⑤	눈에 띄는 발전	……	그만두다

[주 제] 대형 병원 합병이 가져온 부작용
[정답 해설] (A) 병원을 합병한 결과, 비용이 상승했고, 그로 인해 전체적인 건강관리 비용이 높아졌다고 했기 때문에 합병을 부정적으로 언급하고 있다는 것을 알 수 있다. 특히 이러한 뉘앙스는 마지막 문장에서 더욱 확실하게 알 수 있다. 따라서 '두 병원을 합병하여 대형 병원을 만든 것은 심각한 실수였다.'라는 내용이 자연스럽다. 따라서 빈칸에는 a serious mistake가 적절하다. (B) 법무장관이 제시하려는 협상안이 가격 인상을 늦추고 병원들의 진료 건수를 제한하자는 내용이므로, 병원의 횡포를 억제하거나 제재하려고 한다고 보는 것이 타당하다. 따라서 빈칸에는 rein in이 가장 적절하다.

[어 휘] in retrospect 돌이켜 생각해 보면 costly 값비싼, 비용이 많이 드는 affiliate 제휴하다, 연계하다 prestigious 명망 있는 merger 합병 leverage 영향력, 지렛대 reimbursement 변제, 상환, 배상 insurer 보험사, 보험회사 rein in 억제하다, 말의 고삐를 당기다 belatedly 뒤늦게 gobble up 게걸스럽게 먹어 치우다 albeit 비록 ~일지라도 physician practice 진료, 진료행위 cautionary 충고의, 경고의 choke up (감정에 복받쳐) 목이 메다

15 ① 아마도 인류를 대상으로 만들어진 것 중에 가장 큰 함정은 "모든 것을 다 갖기"라는 말을 만들어낸 일이었을 것이다. 이 세 단어는 각종 연설과, 신문 헤드라인, 그리고 기사들에 의해 널리 퍼뜨려지는 중에, 이 문구는 성공 지향적으로 의도되었지만 오히려 사람들이 스스로 부족하다고 느끼도록 만들고 말았다. 나는 지금까지 단 한번도 "그렇다, 나는 모든 것을 다 가지고 있다."라고 힘주어 말하는 사람을 본 적이 없다. 왜냐하면 우리가 무엇을 갖고 있는지와는 상관없이, 누구도 전부를 다 가질 수는 없기 때문이다. "모든 것을 다 갖기"라는 오래된 문구는 모든 경제적인 관계의 기본을 무시하고 있다. 그것은 바로 '교환의 개념'이다. 우리 모두는 직업, 자녀, 관계의 변수를 기초로 해서 우리의 수단을 최대화하기 위해 노력하고 시간의 자원을 할당하기 위해 최선을 다하여 삶이라는 제한된 최적화를 위해

노력한다. 자원의 부족 때문에, 그러므로 그 누구도 "전부 다 갖는 것"은 불가능하다. 그리고 다 가졌다고 주장하는 사람은 대부분 거짓말을 하고 있는 것일 가능성이 높다.

① 교환의 개념　　　　② 행복의 추구
③ 절대적 부의 개념　　④ 동등 분배의 믿음
⑤ 공급과 수요의 법칙

주 제　자원 부족에 따른 소유의 한계

정답 해설　빈칸 뒤에는 사람들은 누구나 모두 다 가질 수는 없기 때문에 제한된 자원 내에서 누리고자 하는 것들을 최대한 효율적으로 활용하기 위해 노력한다는 내용이 이어진다. 이와 가장 관련성이 있는 내용은 ①의 'the idea of trade-offs'이다.

어 휘　coin of a phrase 새로운 말을 만들어 내다 bandy about (소문 등을) 퍼뜨리고 다니다, 토론하다 fall shot 부족해지다 aspirational 야망에 찬, 출세지향적인 antiquate 낡아 빠진, 시대에 뒤쳐진 rhetoric 수사, 화려한 문체, 웅변 disregard 무시하다, 경시하다 trade-off 교환 constrain 강요하다, 강제하다 optimization 최적화, 최대의 활용 parameter 변수 scarcity 부족, 결핍

---

16 ②　생태학적 지속 가능성에 대한 논쟁은 대개 온실가스배출, 생물학적 다양성, 그리고 여타 자연계에 대한 측정치에 대해 초점을 맞추고 있다. 그것은 생산량과 인구수에 대한 경제적이고 사회적인 동향도 포함한다. 하지만 그들은 시간 사용은 좀처럼 다루지 않는다. 하지만 사람이 시간을 사용하는 방식은 생태학적인 결과에 있어 핵심적인 요소이다. 사람들은 그들의 일상적인 삶과 활동들을 수행하기 위해 시간과 돈, 그리고 천연 자원들을 결합시킨다. 회사들은 상품을 만들어내기 위해 시간과 물적 자본, 그리고 천연 자본을 결합한다. 대개 시간과 천연자원들은 서로를 대체하기 마련이다. 어떤 일을 더 빠른 속도로 진행하면 보통 지구에 더 큰 피해를 입히기 마련이다. 따라서 시간에 대해 스트레스를 받는 가정과 사회는 더욱 더 무거운 생태학적 결과를 남기게 되고, 1인당 더 많은 에너지를 사용하게 된다.

① 시간과 돈에 대한 오해
② 시간에 대해 스트레스를 받는 가정과 사회
③ 자원 개발에 대한 일시적 제약
④ 지속가능한 자연에 대한 전통적인 개념
⑤ 재활용 자원들이 더 많은 시간을 차지하는 사례들

주 제　빠른 속도가 야기하는 자원 소모

정답 해설　빠른 속도로 일을 진행할수록 많은 자원을 사용하게 되어 자연에 더 큰 피해를 입히게 된다는 내용의 글이다. 따라

서 시간에 대해 스트레스를 받는 가정과 사회는 더욱 더 무거운 생태학적 결과를 남기게 된다는 내용이 문맥상 적절하다. 따라서 빈칸에는 ②가 적절하다.

어 휘　sustainability 유지(지속) 가능성 feature 특색을 묘사하다, 다루다 to a great extent 대부분은, 대개 per capita 1인당

---

17 ③　나는 빠르게 달리는 것을 굉장히 좋아한다. 나는 마치 중력의 구속에서 탈출한 것처럼, 활강하거나 회전하면서 아래로 내려가는 것을 정말 좋아한다. 사진 속에서의 나는 자전거 경주 선수와 닮았을지도 모르지만, 나는 보통의 미토콘드리아를 가진 사람이다. 하지만 그 사실이 내가 가끔씩 내가 할 수 있는 한 가장 빠르게 달리려고 노력하는 것을 막지는 못한다. 나는 내 자신을 그렇게 힘든 상황에 처하게 했을 때 내 자신에 대한 중요한 무엇인가를 깨닫게 된다. 나는 마찬가지로 천천히 달리는 것 역시 매우 좋아한다. 자전거에 똑바로 앉아 빙글빙글 돌 때, 나는 세상을 보게 되고, 에너지가 충만해짐과 나의 공동체와 연결되어 있음을 느낀다. 나는 청바지를 입고 농부의 시장으로 페달을 밟을 때나 꼬부랑 시골길로 페달을 밟을 때, 마치 사이클 선수가 된 것처럼 충만한 기분을 느낀다. 나는 정말로 내 안장과 사랑에 빠졌다.

① 경주자가 되어가는 과정에 있다
② 내 몸에 감동받았다
③ 내 안장과 사랑에 빠졌다
④ 내 영역에 확신이 있다
⑤ 내가 이야기하는 것에 어려움이 없다

주 제　자전거를 좋아하는 이유

정답 해설　글의 전체적인 내용을 통해 화자가 자전거를 매우 좋아하는 사람이라는 사실을 알 수 있다. 이와 관련이 있는 답지는 ①과 ③인데 본문에서 빠르게 달리는 것도 좋지만 천천히 달리는 것도 좋아한다고 하였으므로 ①은 적절하지 않다. 따라서 빈칸에는 ③이 가장 적절하다.

어 휘　adore 굉장히 좋아하다 mitochondria 미토콘드리아 energize 에너지를 주입하다, 기운 나게 하다 meander 꼬부랑길 saddle 안장

---

18 ⑤　열차표는 인간의 삶이라는 세상에서 가장 위대한 쇼의 맨 앞줄 관람석을 가져다준다. 비행으로 인한 시차나 운전으로 인한 피곤함을 겪지 않으면서도 승객은 흔들리는 열차 속에서 잠시나마 시간이 그를 위해 멈춘 것

같은, 어떤 요구도 받지 않는 특별한 나그네가 된다. 그는 창밖의 생생한 광경을 지나는 인생의 목격자이다. 그는 하루를 이루는 작은 순간들을 관통하여 미끄러져 나간다. 뒤뜰, 아름다운 나무들, 도시의 광장, 어떤 것도 시야에서 벗어나지 않는다. 만약 그가 선택한다면, 그는 길가에 있는 어떤 역에서나 내려서 그가 관찰하던 것 속으로 들어갈 수도 있다. 한밤중 밝게 빛나는, 세관 직원이 담배를 피우고 있고 우유 통이 실린 짐마차가 옆을 지나가는 외국의 어떤 역에 도착하게 되는 이와 같은 모험은 어디에도 없다.

① 풍경의 아름다움을 해친다
② 운전자의 피로에 더해진다
③ 그로 하여금 과거를 떠올리게 한다
④ 편의시설의 질을 향상시킨다
⑤ 시야에서 벗어나다

주 제 열차를 타는 묘미
정답 해설 전체적인 글의 주제가, 기차 여행을 통해 아름다운 광경을 볼 수 있고, 원하면 그 광경 어디로든 여행할 수 있다는 것이므로 빈칸에는 창밖의 광경과 관련있는 ⑤가 가장 적절하다.
어 휘 privilege 특권, 특전, 특권을 주다 pilgrim 순례자, 나그네, 방랑자 rock 바위, 암석, 흔들다, 흔들리다 vivid 생생한 glide 미끄러지다, 미끄러짐 light-lit-lit 빛을 밝히다 stack 짐을 쌓다 roll by 옆을 지나가다

19 ④ "우리의 조각상이나 조형물들 중 적어도 80퍼센트는 산성비에서부터 기술적인 손상에 이르는 다양한 공격들에 의해 좋지 못한 상태입니다." 문화부의 보존 담당 책임자가 말했다. "우리의 도로는 마차를 위해 설계되었고, 이제는 자동차들이 후진해서 조각상들을 치고 있습니다." 환경부에서는 더욱 잘 보존된 조각상들이 관광객들로부터 경제적인 수익을 거둘 수 있을 거란 신념으로 복구 예산을 증액시켜 주었다. 하지만 복구 작가인 Mr. Branda나 그의 동료들에게 있어서 이 일은 관광객들을 위한 장식적인 작업이라기보다는 그 도시의 정신을 지켜나가고자 하는 열정이다. 때로는 그 열정은 그들이 엄청난 시간 동안 일하도록 만들었다. 수많은 밤 자정이 지나서도 Branda씨와 그의 동료들은 바람이 몰아치는 St. Salvator Church의 지붕 위에 올랐고, 12사도를 조각한 17세기 석상을 포장하고 고정시키기 위해 Charles Bridge의 기둥에 올랐다. 그리고 어둠 속에서 작업장에 안전하게 보관하고 수리하기 위해 크레인은 그 석상을 뜯어냈다.

① 돈을 벌기 위하여 더 많이 수리하는
② 단지 유명해지기 위한 욕망이라기보다는

③ 건축물에 대하여 더 많이 조사하는
④ 관광객들을 위한 장식적인 작업이라기보다는
⑤ 봉사활동이라기보다는

주 제 조각상 보존 작업
정답 해설 역접의 접속사 however 뒤에 이어지는 내용이므로 앞 문단의 내용과 반대되는 내용이 이어져야 한다. 또한 후반부에는 기술자들이 업무 시간 외에도 헌신적으로 작업을 한다는 내용이 이어지므로, 빈칸에는 단순히 경제적인 이득 이상의 것을 추구한다는 내용이 들어가는 것이 적절하다. 따라서 ④가 가장 적절한 표현이다.
어 휘 statue 상, 조상 sculpture 조각, 조소 assault 공격, 습격, 공격하다 ranging from A to B A에서 B에 이르는, 걸치는 carriage 마차 back into (자동차 등이) ~로 후진하다 past night 자정이 지난 뒤 clamber 기어오르다, 등반 windswept 바람이 몰아치는 disciple 제자, 문하생, 12사도 crane 기중기, 두루미 pluck 잡아 뽑다, 뜯어내다 cosmetic 미용의, 장식적인

20 ③ 누군가는 고전 작가들의 위대한 명성이 어째서 지속되는지 궁금해할지도 모른다. 그 이유는 바로 고전 작가들의 명성이 대다수의 사람들로부터 어떤 영향도 받지 않기 때문이다. 만약 Shakespeare의 명성이 길거리의 어떤 사람에게 좌우되었다면, 그것은 2주일이라도 살아남았을 것이라 생각하는가? 고전 작가들의 명성은 열정적인 소수에 의해 최초로 형성되고, 계속 이어진다. 심지어 일류의 작가들이 그들의 생전에 엄청난 성공을 거둘 때조차도, 대다수의 사람들은 그들을 이류 작가로 평가할 정도로 진정으로 그 가치를 알지 못했다. 그(고전 작가)는 언제나 열렬한 소수의 열정으로 힘을 얻어왔다. 그리고 사망 후에 명성을 얻은 작가들의 경우에, 그 행복한 결과는 그들 소수의 완고한 인내 덕분에 생기는 것이다.

① 상급 독자들에 의해서 실력이 부족한 작가들과 동등한 취급을 받는다
② 그의 명성은 거리의 사람들의 덕이다
③ 열렬한 소수의 열정으로 힘을 얻어왔다
④ 아류의 사람들과 저절로 구별되었다
⑤ 대중의 상당한 존경에 고무되어 왔다

주 제 열렬한 소수의 지지로 지속되는 고전 작가의 명성
정답 해설 앞부분에서 고전 작가의 명성은 평범한 사람들이 아닌, 열정적인 소수에 의해 유지된다고 언급하고 있다. 따라서 빈칸에도 비슷한 취지의 표현이 와야 문맥상 자연스럽다. 따라서 빈칸에는 ③이 가장 적절하다.
어 휘 fortnight 2주간, 짧은 기간 sequel 결과, 귀추, 결말

obstinate 완고한, 완강한 perseverance 인내 indebt ~에게 빚을 지우다, ~에게 은혜를 입히다 reinforce ~의 힘을 북돋우다, 강화하다 admiration 감탄, 칭찬

---

21 ⑤ 만약 당신이 영혼이 담긴 사진을 찍을 수 있다면, 그 사진은 아마도 남북전쟁 당시의 어떤 노예들과 군인들을 담은 흑백의 사진과 비슷하게 보일지도 모른다. 그들은 스스로를 바라보거나 그들의 외모에 대해서 걱정할 만한 시간을 갖지 못한 사람들이었고, 사진들은 그것을 보여준다. 그들의 얼굴은 그들의 열정과 경험을 보여주며, 절대로 그들의 성격과 다르지 않다. 어떤 사진은 커다란 체구의 남자가 사나워 보이는 뾰족한 수염을 기른 채 강하게 응시하는 것을 보여준다. 또 다른 사진에서는, 한 어머니의 눈 밑 다크서클에서 그녀의 지혜가 엿보인다. 아이의 작고 팽팽한 입에서 회의적인 태도가 엿보인다. 어쨌든, 그들의 상황은 그들의 정신이 세속적인 부와 자기 점검에 더럽혀지지 않은 그대로 얼굴에서 보이도록 했다.

---

① 서로의 고통과 절망을 반영하면서
② 그들의 따뜻한 영혼으로 보충되어서
③ 영원히 내적 평화를 찾아다니면서
④ 현대 사람과의 신체와는 다르게
⑤ 세속적인 부와 자기 점검에 더럽혀지지 않은

주 제 꾸밈없는 사람의 정신을 보여주는 사진
정답 해설 사진 속의 얼굴이 인물의 성격을 여과나 과장 없이 있는 그대로 보여준다는 내용이다. 따라서 내용을 정리하는 마지막 문장에는 ⑤가 가장 적절하다.
어 휘 transmit 전달하다, 보내다 betray 배신하다, (감정·무지·약점을) 무심코 드러내다 spiky 뾰족뾰족한 fierceness 흉포함, 사나움 skepticism 의심스럽게 생각함, 회의론 mirror 거울, 비추다, 반사하다 agony 고뇌, 고통 complement 보충, 보충하다 untainted 순수한, 더럽혀지지 않은

---

22 ⑤ 아버지는 학기 중에 동네 식료품점에서 시간제 근무를 하기로 한 나의 결정에 대해 격렬하게 반대하셨다. 아버지는 내가 너무 무리하지 말고 일은 나중에 하기를 바라셨다. 나도 일을 그만두는 것에 분명하게 이점이 있음을 동의했지만 일하는 것에 대한 단점을 능가하는 다른 장점이 있다는 것 또한 알고 있었다. 예를 들어, 나는 비록 적지만 내 자신의 수입을 통해 독립된 생활을 하는 것이 좋다. 아버지가 이러한 점을 인정하지 않는 것에 화가 났지만 나는 그의 반대 내용을 잘 들어왔고 우리는 또다시 합의점

에 도달할 수 있었다. 나는 내가 너무 무리하고 있다거나 학업성적이 너무 나빠지면 바로 그만두기로 동의했다. 결과적으로 아버지와 나의 불화는 효과적으로 해결되었다.

---

① 나의 독립에 간섭하는
② 나의 학업에 크게 기여하는
③ 처음부터 우리의 관계를 굳히는
④ 결국 나의 견해에 반대하는
⑤ 단점을 능가하는

주 제 일하기 위해 아버지를 설득한 필자
정답 해설 필자는 시간제 근무의 단점과 아버지의 반대에도 불구하고 일하고 싶어 했고 이에 대해 아버지와 합의점을 이끌어냈다. 따라서 일하지 않을 때의 이점과 일할 때의 장점이 자연스럽게 연결되려면 빈칸에는 ⑤가 가장 적절하다.
어 휘 vehemently 격렬하게, 맹렬하게 compromise 타협, 절충 dissolve 녹다, 사라지다, 끝내다

---

23 ⑤ 우선, 그들의 이해할 수 없고 전적으로 통제할 수 없었던 운명을 'holocaust'라고 이름 붙인 것은 나치의 불운한 희생자들이 아니다. 나치의 유럽 유대인들에 대한 실험에 이 인공적이며 매우 전문적인 단어를 적용한 것은 미국 사람들이었다. 그러나 그것이 단순히 '가장 끔찍한 대량 학살'이라고 이름 붙여질 때 그 사건이 가장 즉각적이며, 가장 강력한 혐오감을 떠올리게 하는 반면에, 그 단어가 흔하지 않은 전문 용어로 이름 붙여질 때 우리는 우리 마음속에서 가장 먼저 그것을 감정적으로 의미 있는 언어로 다시 번역해야 한다. 일상적으로 사용하는 어휘 대신 특별히 창안된 전문적인 어휘를 사용하는 것은 감정적인 경험에서 지적인 것을 분리하는 가장 잘 알려진, 그리고 가장 광범위하게 사용되는 거리 두기 장치이다. 'holocaust'에 대해 말하는 것은 평범한 명칭을 부여받은 노골적인 사실들이 우리를 정서적으로 압도하는 경우에 우리가 그 사건을 지적으로 다룰 수 있게 해준다. 왜냐하면 그것은 이해할 수 없으며, 우리의 상상력의 한계를 넘어서는 충격적인 참사였기 때문이다.

---

① 지적 용어에서 기술적인 것을 분리하는
② 이해할 수 없는 용어에서 기술적인 것을 분리하는
③ 이해할 수 있는 용어에서 기술적인 것을 분리하는
④ 지적 경험에서 통상적인 것을 분리하는
⑤ 감정적인 경험에서 지적인 것을 분리하는

주 제 holocaust라는 용어의 역할
정답 해설 holocaust에 대해 말하는 것이 우리를 정서적으로

압도하는 사건들을 지적으로 다룰 수 있게 해준다는 빈칸 뒷부분의 내용으로 미루어 볼 때 빈칸에는 ⑤가 가장 적절하다.

어 휘 hapless 불운한, 불행한 incomprehensible 이해할 수 없는 extermination 절멸, 몰살 foul 더러운, 잘못된 evoke (감정, 기억 등을) 떠올리게 하다 revulsion 혐오감, 역겨움 overwhelm 압도하다 intellectual 지적인, 지능의

24 ④

한 나라와 그 문화를 제대로 이해하기 위해서는 그것의 일부가 되어야 한다. 그것이 바로 KAB에서 우리가 다른 어떤 곳들보다 더 많이 외국 현지 은행을 두고 있는 이유이다. 세계 각지에 있는 우리의 지점들은 모두 현지인들을 채용한다. 그들의 식견으로 우리는 외부 사람들에게는 보이지 않는 재무상의 기회를 제공받는다. 하지만 이러한 기회들이 지역 고객들에게게만 이익만 되는 것은 아니다. 혁신과 좋은 생각들은 KAB 네트워크에 의해서 공유되고, 이를 통해 우리와 은행 업무를 하는 모든 사람들이 이익을 볼 수 있다. 이것들을 세계를 포괄하는 지역 정보라고 생각해 보라.

① 도시 지역을 노린
② 다음 10년을 이끌
③ 세계화를 멈추는
④ 세계를 포괄하는
⑤ 고국으로 돌아오는

주 제 KAB 네트워크를 통해 공유되는 정보의 효용
정답 해설 KAB 네트워크를 통해 공유된 정보를 통해 전 세계의 사람들이 이익을 얻는다는 본문의 내용으로 미루어 볼 때 지역 정보는 세계를 포괄한다는 내용이 문맥상 자연스럽다. 따라서 빈칸에는 ④가 가장 적절하다.

어 휘 outsider 외부인 insight 통찰력

25 ③

지금까지 오직 철학자들에 의해서만 연구되어진 윤리학의 확장은 사실 생태학적인 진화의 한 과정이다. 일련의 과정들은 철학적인 용어뿐만 아니라 생태학적 용어로도 묘사될 수 있다. 생태학적으로 윤리는 생존 경쟁에 있어서 행위의 자유를 제한하는 역할을 한다. 철학적으로 윤리는 반사회적인 행위로부터 사회적인 행위를 구분하는 기준이 된다. 이것이 하나에 대한 두 가지 정의이다. 그것은 협력의 방식을 진전시키려는 상호 의존적 개인들이나 그룹들의 경향에서 그 기원을 갖는다. 생태학자들은 그것을 공생이라고 부른다. 정치학과 경제학은 초기 무한 경쟁 체제가 윤리적인 내용을 지닌 상호 협력체제에 의해 부분적으로 대

체된 발전된 공생의 형태이다.

① 경쟁 활동의 새 모습
② 적응 경쟁의 최근 경향
③ 윤리적 내용을 지닌 상호 협력 체제
④ 전체 그룹으로부터 각각의 회원의 독립성
⑤ 생태 윤리와 철학 윤리의 두드러진 유사점

주 제 생태학에서 윤리를 바라보는 입장
정답 해설 문맥상 '무한 경쟁 체제'가 '발전된 공생의 형태'가 되어야 하므로 빈칸에는 '오늘날의 발전된 공생의 형태'와 상통하는 내용인 ③ '윤리적 내용을 지닌 상호 협력 체제'가 적절하다.

어 휘 extension 확장 so far 지금까지는 philosophically 철학적으로 symbiosis 공생, 공존, 공생하는

26 ④

우리 시골 지역에 대한 정밀 조사가 이루어지면 멀리 버려져 있는 것, 수천의 쓸모없는 냉장고, "일회용" 용기, 고장난 토스터기, 믹서, 전자레인지뿐만 아니라 규제받지 않은 음식물 쓰레기가 드러난다. 쓰레기 문제의 대부분은 우리가 중독되어 버린 노동 절약기 및 기기의 재활용이 불가능한 의도적 훼손으로 설명할 수 있다. 결국 현재 우리나라를 손상시키는 많은 쓰레기들은 꽤 직접적으로, 사용이 가능한 제품들을 버리는 대부분의 사람들의 부주의한 행동으로 인해서 야기된 것이라고 말할 수 있다. 우리는 식량 생산과 음식의 요리에 최소한 참여하는 사회적 이상을 만들었다. 그럼에도 불구하고, 우리가 음식과 조리 기구에 의존하게 될수록 더 많은 폐기물을 생산할 것이다. 우리를 둘러싼 이 혼란은 더 크고 심각한 문제의 증상으로 이해되어야 한다. 우리 경제의 중앙 집중화, 생산 재산과 권력의 수집, 그리고 가정, 이웃, 지역 사회로 구성된 지역 경제의 결과적인 파괴와 같은 가볍지 않은 증상으로 이해되어야 한다.

① 자신의 제품을 재활용하려는 식품 산업의 시도
② 천연 자원을 파괴하는 과도한 소비
③ 식품 경제에 관련된 수많은 지역의 부엌
④ 사용 가능한 제품을 버리는 대부분의 사람들의 부주의한 행동
⑤ 식품 경제에 적극적인 참여에 대한 대부분의 배제

주 제 식량 관련 제품 쓰레기 문제
정답 해설 이 글에서 쓰레기 문제는 재활용이 불가능한 의도적 훼손 때문이라고 설명하고 있다. 따라서 이와 상통하는 의미의 보기인 ④가 적절하다.

27 ⑤

우리 대부분은 올림픽에서 선수들이 동메달보다 은메달을 땄을 때 더욱 행복할 것이라고 생각한다. 하지만 동메달을 딴 선수들이 은메달을 딴 선수들보다 더 행복하다는 연구 결과가 나왔다. 이는 선수들이 자신들의 경기 내용을 생각하는 방식에 그 이유가 있다. 은메달리스트들은 자신들이 약간만 더 잘했더라면 금메달을 땄을 것이라는 생각에 초점을 맞춘다. 반면에 동메달리스트들은 자신들이 약간만 더 못했더라면 아무 것도 얻지 못했을 거라는 생각에 초점을 맞춘다. 심리학자들은 실제로 일어났던 일보다는 <u>일어났을지도 모를</u> 일을 상상하는 것을 '반현실적 사고'라고 부른다.

① 일어나고 있는　　　　② 일어났던
③ 일어났었던　　　　　④ 일어나려 하는
⑤ 일어났을지도 모를

주 제 은메달리스트가 동메달리스트보다 불행한 이유
정답 해설 상상하는 비현실적 사고와 연결되는 것이기 때문에 '일어났을지도 모르는'이라고 해야 한다. 따라서 ⑤ might have happened가 적절하다.
어 휘 factual 사실의, 실제의

28 ④

세종대왕이 발명한 한글은 한자의 장방형에, 몽골이나 티베트 문자의 글자 구성 원리에 영향 받았음이 분명하다. 물론 세종대왕은 한글의 글자 모양과 철자들의 조합, 비슷한 철자의 사용, 조음 기관 위치를 묘사하는 자음의 형태를 포함한 몇몇 독특한 특징들을 발명했다. 그러나 한글의 발명은 독자적인 발명이라기보다는 <u>아이디어의 전파</u> 덕분이라고 자신있게 말할 수 있다.

① 개인의 발명　　　　② 과학적 시스템
③ 우연한 일　　　　　④ 아이디어의 전파
⑤ 순수한 독창성

주 제 다른 문자가 한글에 미친 영향
정답 해설 한글이 세종대왕의 독특한 발명인 것은 사실이지만 however를 사용해 글을 반전시켜 이웃 나라의 문자에 많은 영향을 받았다고 말하고 있다. 그러므로 독특한 개인의 발명이나

우연이 아닌 ④ '아이디어의 전파'가 가장 적절하다.
어 휘 consonant 자음(문자) devise 궁리하다, 고안하다 articulator 발성 기관, 소리를 만드는 기관 diffusion 확산, 전파

29 ②

선생님은 한 소녀에게 cliché라는 단어를 문장 안에서 사용해 보라고 시켰다. 소녀는 이렇게 대답했다. "그 소년은 시험을 보고 나서 진부한 표정으로 집에 돌아왔다." 선생님이 소녀에게 이유를 묻자 소녀는 사전에서 "<u>진부한 표현[지친 표정]</u>"이라는 cliché의 정의를 가리켰다.

① 독창적인 관용어구
② 진부한 표현
③ 신조어 표현
④ 알기 쉬운 합성어
⑤ 얼굴의 표정

주 제 cliché의 뜻을 착각한 소녀
정답 해설 cliché는 '진부하거나 상투적인 표현'을 일컫는 단어이다. 그런데 이 글에서 소녀는 사전상의 'worn out expression(진부한 표현)'이라는 설명을 expression for worn out situation 즉 '지친 상황에서 지을 수 있는 표정'으로 오해한 것이다.
어 휘 statement 말, 진술, 구술 worn out 지친, 다 떨어진, 오래된, 진부한 cliché 진부한 표현, 상투적인 표현

30 ②

20년 전, 심리학은 정신의 완전하고 창의적인 이용에 관심이 있었던 사람들에게는 다소 멀게 느껴지는 불모지였던 듯하다. 그 당시에 그 분야에는 학술 심리학, 정신 분석, 행동주의라는 비인기 학과 삼총사가 머물고 있었다. 학술적 심리학은 시각적 환상의 인지나 이상한 음절의 긴 목록을 암기하는 연구를 하기 위한 부자연스러운 실험 도구를 사용하는 것을 특징으로 한다. 그러한 연구 방식들이 인간의 사고와 관련이 있다는 증거는 거의 없다.

> 정신 분석의 설명과 단점

쥐와 비둘기를 이용하는 접근 방법으로 행동주의가 있다. 행동주의자들은 우리가 그렇게 행동하도록 강제되어 그렇게 행동하는 것이라고 주장했고, 외적 활동에 초점을 맞춰 이 분야의 학자들은 내면의 삶을 부정했다. 즉, 사고도 없고 상상도 없고 열망도 없다는 것이다.

① 정신 분석이 사라진 이유
② 정신 분석의 설명과 단점
③ 정신 분석의 강점과 영향력

④ 정신 분석이 오늘날까지 유명해진 방법
⑤ 정신 분석과 학문적 심리학의 비교

[주 제] 학술 심리 · 정신 분석 · 행동주의의 특징
[정답 해설] 이 글은 심리학의 세 분야를 말한 뒤 각각 그 분야에 대한 단점을 말하고 있다. 그런데 두 번째 분야인 '정신 분석'에 대한 내용이 없으므로 빈칸에 적절한 내용은 ② '정신 분석의 설명과 단점'이다.

[어 휘] harbor 정박하다, 머물다 psychoanalysis 정신 분석학 behaviorism 행동주의 contrived 억지로 꾸민 듯한 부자연스러운 sterile 메마른, 불모의 apparatus 장치, 기계, 도구 syllable 한마디, 음절, 똑똑히 말하다 aspiration 열망, 포부, 야망

More Practice

01 ①   02 ④   03 ④   04 ④   05 ①
06 ③

01 ① Theodore Berger는 쥐의 해마상 융기의 손상된 부분을 대체하기 위해 이식된 칩을 사용하면서 장기 기억 재생에서 성공을 거두었다. University of Southern California의 Berger와 그의 팀은 이 동물들의 해마상 융기에 오랜 시간 저장된 기억을 기록하고 컴퓨터 코드로 전환하는 데 성공했다. 그들은 쥐들에게 기억 임무를 수행하도록 했다. 그리고 그들은 그 임무의 기억을 다운로드해 디지털 코드로 전환했다. 그 후에, 그들은 이러한 기억을 운반하는 해마상 융기의 부분을 제거하고 뇌의 일부를 특수한 컴퓨터 칩과 교체했는데, 그들은 그것에 인공적으로 저장된 기억을 다시 장착하였다. 그들은 이러한 기술을 사용하여 쥐들의 기억이 완전히 재생될 수 있다는 점을 발견했다.

① 장기 기억 재생
② 기억 능력 증대
③ 기억의 선별적 왜곡
④ 정신적 외상 기억의 제거
⑤ 기억 이전 속도 향상

[주 제] 칩을 이용한 장기 기억력 재생
[정답 해설] 기억을 운반하는 해마상 융기의 부분을 제거하고 뇌의 일부를 인공적으로 저장된 기억이 담긴 특수한 칩과 교체하여 쥐들의 기억을 완전히 재생시켰다는 내용의 글이다. 따라서 빈칸에는 ①이 가장 적절하다.
[어 휘] reload 재장착하다 artificially 인공적으로 regeneration 재생 selective 선별적인 distortion 왜곡 traumatic 외상의, 상처 깊은

02 ④ 시간은 세상과 그 속의 우리의 위치에 대한 이해에 중요하고 필수적인 차원을 더해준다. 시간이 부재할 때 우리가 경험한 세상이 어떠할지 상상하는 것은 거의 불가능해 보인다. 결국 사건들은 시간 안에서 일어난다. 이것은 물리학자들로 하여금 시간을 공간과 더불어 이론적이고 실제적인 근원으로 취급하도록 했다. 시간이 우주의 물리적인 구조를 어느 정도 구성한다는, 그리고 그와 같은 것이 실제라는 관점은, 시간의 흔한 관점이라고 내가 칭할 것과 일치한다. 대다수의 사람들이 시간에 관한 이 관점, 즉 진정한 시간, 물리적인 의미에서 실제로 존재하는 시간을 믿는다. 이런 이유로 시간은 우리가 거주하는 환경을 지배하는 물리적 법칙에 반영되어 외부 세계에 객관적으로 내장되어 있다(존재한다). 시간 자체는 "감지할 수 없"을 수 있는 반면, 그것은 그럼에도 불구하고 가시적인 결과들을 나타내면서 실재한다. 시간의 "경과" 없이는 연속성도, 그러므로 지속의 경험도 없다.

① 자체 구동력으로 전달하다.
② 물리적으로 인식될 수 없다.
③ 물리학 분야에서 취급되지 않다.
④ 외부 세계에 객관적으로 내장되어 있다(존재한다).
⑤ 인간의 경험으로 만든 가상의 구조이다.

[주 제] 시간의 실재성
[정답 해설] 제시문에서 글쓴이는 '시간'에 대하여 '눈에는 보이지 않지만 물리적인 실체'라면서 '시간이 없는 세상은 인간이 이해할 수 없다.'고 말하고 있다. 또한 빈칸 다음 문장에서는 '시간이 가시적인 결과들을 나타내면서 실재한다.'고 언급하고 있으므로 빈칸에 가장 적절한 보기는 ④이다.
[어 휘] dimension 차원 conceive 상상하다 empirical 경험적 primitive 근원 fabric 구조 tangible 가시적인, 만질 수 있는 succession 연속 duration 지속

03 ④ Walt Whitman이 'Leaves of Grass'를 쓰기 오래전에, 시인들은 명성에 주의를 기울였다. Horace, Petrarch, Shakespeare, Milton, 그리고 Keats는 모두 시의 위대함이 자신들에게 일종의 세속적 불멸을 부여해주기를 바랐다. Whitman도 세상이 수 세기동안 자신의 시를 가치 있게 여길 것이라는 비슷한 믿음을 갖고 있었다. 그러나 지면 위에서 영원히 살아남고자 하는 이 고대의 열망에다 그는 새로운 명성의 의미를 추가했다. 독자들이 단순히 시인의 작품에만 주목하는 것이 아니라, 그들은 그의 인격적인 위대함에도 이끌릴 것이었다. 그들은 그의 시에서 고동치는 문화적 공연, 즉 엄청난 카리스마와 호소력으로 책에

서 솟구쳐 나오는 한 개인을 보게 될 것이었다. Jackson주의 미국을 특징지었던 정치 집회와 선거 행진에서 Whitman은 군중과 관련하여 시적 명성을 정의했다. 다른 시인들은 시의 여신으로부터 자신들의 영감을 찾았을지도 모른다. Whitman의 시인은 <u>자신의 동시대인의 인정</u>을 추구했다. 미국 민주주의의 불안정 속에 명성은 인기도, 즉 사람들이 그 시인과 그의 작품으로 기뻐하는 정도에 좌우될 것이었다.

① 대중의 관심으로부터의 도피
② 정치적 혼돈으로부터의 시적 순수성
③ 문학 그 자체 속에서의 불멸성
④ 자신의 동시대인의 인정
⑤ 정치적 유명인사와의 명성

주제 인기도 시인의 명성이라 생각했던 Walt Whitman
정답 해설 Whitman은 시인의 명성이 시의 훌륭함뿐만 아니라 대중으로부터의 인기도에 의해서도 좌우된다고 생각했으므로 빈칸에는 ④ '자신의 동시대인으로부터의 인정'이 가장 적절하다.
어휘 address oneself to ~에 주의를 기울이다 grant 부여하다, 주다 earthly 세속적인, 현세의 attend to ~에 주의하다 vibrant 고동치는, 활력이 넘치는 spring 솟구치다, 튀어 오르다 tremendous 엄청난 appeal 호소력, 매력 rally 집회, 모임 electoral 선거의 mark 특징짓다 inspiration 영감 instability 불안정 celebrity 인기도, 명성 rejoice 기뻐하다

04 ④ 누군가가 개에 대해서 "음, 그는 매우 성공적이고 아름다운 집에 살지만, 그다지 행복하지는 않아"라고 말하는 것을 들어본 적 있는가? 대부분의 개가 대부분의 사람보다 훨씬 행복한 한 가지 이유는 개들이 우리가 처한 외적 상황에 영향을 받지 않는다는 점이다. 나는 바깥에 비가 억수로 쏟아질 때에도, 내 개 Blue와 Celeste는 여전히 산책 갈 생각에 신이 난다는 것을 알고 있다. 내가 바깥을 보기 위해 앞문을 열자마자 그들은 모험을 준비하고 순식간에 내 곁에 와, 기대에 차 서있다. 나는 보통 폭우가 잠잠해지길 기다렸다가 다함께 뛰쳐나간다. 땅이 젖고 지면에 점점이 진흙 웅덩이가 있다는 사실은 <u>그 개들에게 아무 문제도 되지 않는다</u>. 내가 신중하게 전은 곳을 피해 길을 찾는 동안, 개들은 그것을 즐겁게 첨벙거리며 가로지른다. 그들은 자신의 발이 더러워지는 것을 겁내지 않는다.

① 우리가 더 짧게 산책할 동기를 부여한다
② 나를 매우 신나게 한다
③ 개들을 곤경에 처하게 한다
④ 그 개들에게 아무 문제도 되지 않는다

⑤ 내가 여기저기 돌아다니고 싶게 만든다

주제 외적 상황에 영향을 받지 않는 개의 행복
정답 해설 나는 비가 온 이후의 땅과 웅덩이를 피해서 걷지만 개들은 그냥 즐겁게 첨벙거린다는 말에서 개들에게 젖은 땅과 진흙 웅덩이는 아무런 문제가 되지 않는다는 것을 알 수 있으므로, 빈칸에는 ④ '그 개들에게 아무 문제도 되지 않는다'가 가장 적절하다.
어휘 affect 영향을 끼치다 external 외부의 in a flash 순식간에 dash out 급히 뛰쳐나가다 puddle 웅덩이 splash 첨벙거리다

05 ① 나의 친구는 과학적인 발전이 전쟁과 기아를 없앰으로써 세상의 불행을 치유하지 못했다는 것, 엄청난 인간 불평등이 아직도 널리 퍼져 있다는 것, 행복이 보편적이지 않다는 것에 실망했다. 내 친구는 흔한 실수, 즉 지식의 본질에 있어서 기본적인 오해를 했다. 지식은 도덕과 관계가 없고, 비도덕적인 것은 아니지만 도덕 중립적이다. 그것은 어떤 목적으로든 사용될 수 있지만, 많은 사람은 그것이 사회에 대한 그들이 선호하는 희망을 증진하는 데 사용될 것이라고 가정하는데, 이것이 근본적인 잘못이다. 세상의 지식은 별개의 것이다. 이것의 사용은 분리된 문제를 일으킨다. 이해에 있어서의 진보가 세계의 사회적인 불행을 치유하지 못해왔다는 것에 실망하는 것은 타당한 견해이지만, 이것을 <u>지식의 진보와 혼동하는 것</u>은 터무니없다. 아프리카나 중동의 갈등 때문에 지식이 진보하지 않는다고 주장하는 것은 요점에서 벗어난다. 지식에는 그 어떤 구체적인 사회적 또는 도덕적 적용을 좌우하는 내재된 것이 없다.

① 지식의 진보와 혼동하는 것은 터무니없다
② 지식의 특성을 아는 것은 그것의 도덕적 가치를 실행하는 것이다
③ 사회적 불평등을 제거하는 것은 지식의 내재적 목적이다
④ 지식을 축적하는 것은 그것의 사회적 적용을 향상시키는 것이다
⑤ 과학을 발전하게 하는 것은 그것이 사회적 불행을 치유하게 하는 것이다

주제 지식의 도덕적 중립성
정답 해설 과학적 발전이나 지식의 발전이 반드시 세계의 사회적인 불행을 치유해 주는 것이 아니며 지식의 발전과 지식의 이용은 서로 별개의 문제라는 내용의 글이므로 빈칸에는 ① '지식의 진보와 혼동하는 것은 터무니없다'가 가장 적절하다.
어휘 amoral 도덕과 관계없는, 도덕관념이 없는 assume 가

정하다 **further** 증진하다 **flaw** 결함 **remedy** 치유하다, 치료하다 **legitimate** 타당한, 정당한 **inherent** 내재적인, 타고난 **dictate** 좌우하다, 지시하다

06 ③ 좋음과 나쁨에 대한 몇 가지 분별은 생명 작용 안에 타고난 것이다. 유아는 고통을 나쁜 것으로 달콤함을 (어느 정도는) 좋은 것으로 반응하도록 준비되어 세상에 들어선다. 그러나 다양한 상황에서, 좋고 나쁨의 경계는 시간에 따라 변하고 즉각적인 상황에 좌우되는 판단 기준이다. 당신이 시골의 추운 밤, 폭우에 부적절하게 차려입고 옷은 푹 젖은 채 야외에 있다고 상상해 보라. 찌르는 듯한 찬바람이 당신의 비참함을 완성할 것이다. 당신은 여기저기 돌아다니다가, 격렬한 비바람으로부터 약간의 피난처를 제공할 커다란 바위를 찾는다. 생물학자 Michel Cabanac은, 기쁨이 보통 그러하듯, <u>생물학적으로 중대한 상황 개선</u>의 방향을 보여주는 기능을 하기 때문에, 그 순간의 경험을 극도로 기뻐할 만하다고 말할 것이다. 물론 기쁜 안도는 오래 가지 않을 것이고, 당신은 곧 바위 뒤에서 다시 떨면서, 당신의 새로운 괴로움으로 말미암아 더 나은 피난처를 찾게 될 것이다.

① 상황적 요구에 대한 영구적 정서 적응
② 신체적 고통을 통한 자의식 강화
③ 생물학적으로 중대한 상황 개선
④ 바람직한 상황과 바람직하지 못한 상황을 공정하게 판단하기
⑤ 정서 안정을 위해 정신적으로 예정된 성향

주제 좋고 나쁨에 대한 기준의 유동성

정답 해설 문맥상 빈칸에는 추위를 피할 피난처를 찾은 경험의 기능이 무엇인지가 들어가야 하는데, 이어지는 내용으로 볼 때 피난처의 발견은 현재의 괴로움을 감소시키는 개선의 계기라고 추측할 수 있으므로, 빈칸에는 ③ '생물학적으로 중대한 상황 개선'이 가장 적절하다.

어휘 **distinction** 구별 **hardwired** 타고난, 굳어진 **biology** 생명 활동[작용], 생물학 **boundary** 경계 **reference point** (판단·비교)기준 **immediate** 당면한, 즉각적인 **inadequately** 부적절하게 **soak** 흠뻑 적시다 **stinging** 찌르는 듯한 **elements** 비바람, 폭풍우 **misery** 고통, 빈곤 **shelter** 피난처, 안식처 **fury** (전쟁·폭풍우 등의) 격렬, 맹위 **intensely** 대단히, 강렬하게 **indicate** 보여주다, 가리키다 **direction** 방향, 지도 **relief** 안도, 안심 **renewed** 새로워진 **suffering** 고통 **adjustment** 적응, 조정 **enhance** 강화하다 **impartially** 공정하게

UNIT **11** 빈칸 Ⅲ

Example 답 ③

자극이나 부분적 강화 형태의 사회적 학습은, 많은 사회적 종의 인지 발달 과정에서와 같이 인간 발달에서도 필수불가결한 역할을 한다. 그러나 몇몇의 사례에서 인류는 서로에게 질적으로 다른 방식으로 배운다. 인류는 때때로 우리가 문화적 학습이라 부르는 것에 관여한다. 문화적 학습에서 학습자들은 단지 다른 사람의 행동의 위치에만 그들의 주의를 집중하지 않는다. 그보다는 <u>그들은 다른 사람이 바라보는 방식으로 상황을 보려고 시도한다.</u> 학습자가 다른 사람에게서 배우려고 시도하는 것이 아니라 다른 사람을 통해서 배우려고 하는 것이 바로 학습이다.

① 그들은 다른 사람들을 이해하는 데 그들의 통찰력에 의존한다
② 그들은 전반적인 문화적 유연성을 광범위하게 강화한다
③ 그들은 다른 사람이 보는 방식으로 상황을 보려고 시도한다
④ 그들은 다른 사람들의 숨겨진 의제를 미리 짐작하는 것을 배운다
⑤ 그들은 스스로에게 자율적인 학습에 참여하도록 권한을 부여한다

주제 문화적 학습의 특징

Practice

01 ③	02 ①	03 ①	04 ②	05 ①
06 ①	07 ②	08 ①	09 ①	10 ①
11 ②	12 ②	13 ①		

01 ③ <u>추론 불능의 예시는 매우 풍부하다.</u> 분석가가 사실과 추정을 구별하는 것에 실패하거나 추정이 사실이라는 가정하에 작업하는 것을 보는 것은 드문 일이 아니다. 귀납적으로 도출된 일반화가 논리적 증명인 것은 아님에도 불구하고 분석가가 그의 결론은 단서에서 '논리적으로' 도출되었다고 말하는 것을 듣는 것은 특이한 일이 아니다. 다른 종류의 질문은 다른 종류의 '증명'을 필요로 한다는 것은 많은 연구자들에게는 낯선 생각이다. 그리고 추론과 암시의 일반적인 오용은 용어학적 지식 부족뿐만 아니라 논리의 근본적인 개념에도 익숙지 않음을 반영한다.

① 용어상의 혼란은 논리의 오류를 심화시키기까지 한다

② 논리적인 사고는 과학적 연구의 선도자이다
③ 추론 불능의 예시는 매우 풍부하다
④ 일반화는 철저한 테스트의 대상이다
⑤ 귀납적인 논리는 학계에 만연하다

주 제 추론할 수 없는 경우들

정답 해설 빈칸 뒤에서 언급된 사실과 추정 구별의 실패, 추정이 사실이라는 가정하에 이루어지는 작업, 귀납적으로 도출된 결론이 논리적으로 도출되었다고 주장하는 것 등은 모두 추론 불능의 예시이다. 따라서 빈칸에는 ③이 가장 적절하다.

어 휘 inference 추정 inductively 귀납적으로 alien 생경한, 이상한 underlying 근본적인 terminological 용어상의 aggravate 악화시키다 precursor 선도자 abound 풍부하다 rigorous 철저한

02 ① 시간을 되돌려라. 우리는 늙은 쥐의 근육을 젊게 하는 호르몬을 발견했다. 뼈에서 분비되는 호르몬인 오스테오칼신은 연료를 태우고 에너지를 생산하는 근육의 능력을 증가시킨다고 컬럼비아 대학교의 연구자들이 밝혀냈다. 연구팀이 그 호르몬을 늙은 쥐에게 투여했을 때 쥐들은 쥐의 나이로는 오랜 시간인 일 년 정도가 더 늙었음에도 불구하고 그들의 젊은 상대 쥐만큼 멀리 달릴 수 있었다. 호르몬을 투여받지 않은 늙은 쥐들은 반 정도밖에 달리지 못했다. 쥐와 사람 모두 나이가 들면서 오스테오칼신 수준이 감소하므로, 연구팀은 사람에게도 이 호르몬이 근육 기능을 개선시켜 줄 수 있는지 실험을 할 계획을 세웠다.

① 시간을 되돌려라
② 문제를 즉각 처리하면 일이 훨씬 수월해진다
③ 시간은 사람을 기다려주지 않는다
④ 노인들에게 그들이 마땅히 받아야하는 것을 주어라
⑤ 시간을 빨리 가게 하라

주 제 근육을 젊게 만드는 호르몬

정답 해설 주어진 글은 쥐 실험을 통해 오스테오칼신이라는 호르몬이 에너지를 생산하는 근육 기능을 증가시킨다는 것을 밝혀냈다는 내용이다. 따라서 빈칸에는 ① '시간을 되돌려라'가 가장 적절하다.

어 휘 rejuvenate 활기를 되찾게 하다 due 마땅히 받아야 할 것 sand of time 시간

03 ① Hobbes의 특별한 표현 중에 "자연권"은 우리가 이미 자연 상태에서 가지고 있는 것, 우리의 생명

유지에 필수적인 운동을 보호하는 것은 무엇이든지 할 수 있는 권리를 말한다. Hobbes는 자연 상태에서 죽음의 공포로부터 자연의 제1법칙을 도출한다. 그는 제2법칙을 제1법칙에서 도출한다. 나는 당신이 나에 대한 전쟁을 수행하는 당신의 자연권을 호혜적으로 기꺼이 포기하는 한, 당신에 대항하여 전쟁을 수행하는 나의 자연권을 기꺼이 포기할 것이다. 이러한 상호 무장해제는 각자의 자기 이익 안에 있다. 전쟁에 대한 권리를 포기하는 것에 동의할 때 각자 개인적으로 "자신에게 좋은 어떤 것"을 추구하며, 이러한 좋은 것은 "한 사람의 자기보전에 지나지 않는다."

① 이러한 상호 무장해제는 각자의 자기 이익 안에 있다
② 이렇게 공유된 무관심은 사회의 평화를 증진한다
③ 권리의 상호 양도는 원한을 키우는 것을 의미한다
④ 이러한 사회적 합의는 자연법을 강화하는 데 도움이 된다
⑤ 전쟁 수행에 대한 이러한 억제 수단은 당사자들 중 더 약한 자에게 좋다

주 제 자연권의 의미

정답 해설 전쟁에 대한 권리를 포기하는 것에 동의할 때 각자 개인적으로 '자신에게 좋은 어떤 것'을 추구하며, 이러한 좋은 것은 '한 사람의 자기 보전에 지나지 않는다'는 내용과 문맥상 일치하는 보기는 ① '이러한 상호 무장해제는 각자의 자기 이익 안에 있다'이다.

어 휘 natural rights 자연권 derive 도출하다 wage (전쟁을) 수행하다 to the extent that ~라는 한, ~의 범위에서 reciprocally 호혜적으로, 상호적으로 surrender 포기하다 disarming 무장해제 conducive to ~에 도움이 되는 restraint 억제 수단

04 ② 소비자 심리학저널(the Journal of Consumer Psychology)에서 이뤄진 한 연구는 반복의 힘을 연구하기 위해 1958년부터 2012년까지 90위 밑으로 절대 내려가지 않은 Billboard Hot 100 목록 위의 모든 1위 노래들을 비교했다. 연구자들은 노래의 가사들이 더 단순하고 더 반복될수록 높은 순위에 올라갈 확률이 더 높다는 걸 발견했다. 이러한 노래들은 반복 부분이 더 적은 노래들보다 차트 순위에 더 빠르게 진입했다. 이런 결과들은 유창성 처리 이론을 지지하는 근거가 되는데, (유창성 처리 이론이란) 전달되는 메시지가 이해하기 쉬울수록 사람들이 더 긍정적으로 반응한다는 것이다. 이것은 단순히 음악가들 사이의 비밀이 아니다. 비슷한 전략이 광고에서 광고를 포화시키는 슬로건을 통해 사용된다. 심지어는 코미디에서도 사용되는데 스탠드업 코미디는 공연 내내 같은 펀치 라인(급소를 찌르는 말)을 반복한다.

① 뇌는 더 많은 노력을 발휘해야 한다.
② 사람들이 더 긍정적으로 반응한다.
③ 메시지를 더 정교하게 다듬을 가능성이 높아진다.
④ 노래를 들은 후에 사람들이 따라 부를 기회가 낮아진다.
⑤ 사람들이 숨겨진 메시지를 이해할 가능성이 낮아진다.

주제　메시지 반복의 효과

정답 해설　지문에서 노래가 단순하고 반복하는 부분이 많을수록 더 쉽게 Billboard 차트에 올라가서 오랫동안 유지된다는 점을 보았을 때, 사람들이 쉽고 단순한 노래는 듣기 좋아하는 다는 점을 유추할 수 있다. 따라서 '전달되는 메시지가 더 쉬울수록 사람들이 더 긍정적으로 반응하는 유창성 처리이론'이 문맥상 자연스럽다. 따라서 빈칸에는 ②가 적절하다.

어휘　psychology 심리학 repetition 반복 lyric 노래의 fluency 유창성 digest 소화하다 saturate 포화시키다 punch line 급소를 찌르는 말

05　①　만약 Caesar가 징후와 징조들을 믿었다면, 그는 아마 더 오래 살았을지도 모른다. 전설에 따르면 그의 죽음에 앞서 여러 가지 안 좋은 징조들이 있었으며, 그 중에는, Plutarch의 말에 따르면, "하늘의 빛, 한밤중에 들리는 시끄러운 소리들, 그리고 광장에 앉아 쉬고 있는 야생 조류들."도 있었다. 그리고 잘 알려져 있듯이, 그 독재자는 점쟁이로부터 "3월 15일을 조심하시오."라는 경고를 받았었다. 그의 생에 마지막 날 아침 그의 아내인 Calpurnia는 그에게 그녀가 밤중에 끔찍한 악몽을 꿨다고 말했다. 그녀는 눈물을 흘리며 그에게 원로원에 가지 말 것을 애원했다. Plutarch가 다음과 같이 언급하듯 Caesar는 두려워졌다. "왜냐하면 이전에는 한 번도 Calpurnia로부터 여자들이 믿기 좋아하는 미신에 대한 것은 찾아볼 수 없었기 때문이다." 그는 그녀의 경고에 따라 주의를 기울이기로 했지만, 그에 대한 공모자 중 한 명인 Decimus Brutus가 그날 원로원이 그를 이탈리아를 포함한 전체 로마 지역의 왕으로 선포하려는 계획을 갖고 있다고 조언을 해주자 마음을 바꾸게 되었다.

① Caesar가 징후와 징조를 믿었더라면
② Calpurnia가 예언을 들으러 가지 않았더라면
③ Caesar가 Calpurnia의 여자 특유의 미신을 무시했다면
④ Caesar가 점쟁이의 말을 듣지 않았더라면
⑤ 원로원이 Caesar를 모든 로마 속주의 왕으로 공표했더라면

주제　징조와 징후를 믿지 않은 Caesar

정답 해설　바로 뒤에 이어지는 내용으로 보아, Caesar가 오래 살았을지도 모르는 원인이 되는 내용이 빈칸에 오는 것이 적절할 것이다. 문맥상 여러 가지 징조, 특히 아내의 꿈을 믿었더라면 그날 죽음을 당하지 않았을 것이라는 내용이 가장 자연스럽다.

어휘　portent (불길한) 징조, 전조 perch (새가) 나뭇가지에 앉아 있다 forum (고대 로마의) 광장 famously 유명하게 ides (고대 로마의) 1달 중 가운데 날(15일) Senate (고대 로마의) 원로원 heed 주의를 기울이다 conspirator 공모자, 음모를 꾸미는 사람

06　①　플라톤은 그의 저서인 「국가」에서 시인들이 젊은 이들을 타락시킨다고 비판했다. 또한 그는 이상적인 국가는 시와 연극을 통제하는 것보다 훨씬 더 강하게 음악을 통제한다고 말했다. 플라톤은 음악적인 리듬이 "그들 자신을 영혼의 가장 깊숙한 곳에 스며들게 하는" 엄청난 능력이 있다고 말했다. 이따금 연무장에서 지나치게 거칠어진 시민들의 기질을 완화시킬 때와 비슷한 경우에 음악은 좋은 목적을 위해 사용되는 것이다. 하지만 다른 어떤 때에는, 음악을 즐기는 것은 우리가 정신세계에서 추구해야 할 절제를 방해하고, 사나운 성질에 불을 지핀다. 국가가 어린 시민들을 훌륭히 키워내고자 한다면 미학은 반드시 정치적 견해를 따라야 한다.

① 미학은 반드시 정치적 견해를 따라야 한다
② 체육은 시학과 동반되어야 한다
③ 절제는 군사적 잔인함에 굴복해야 한다
④ 공동의 선보다 개인의 취향이 우세해야 한다
⑤ 시민들은 한 가지 음악에 만족해서는 안 된다

주제　음악에 대한 플라톤의 주장

정답 해설　음악적 리듬이 정신에 큰 영향을 주므로, 이상적 공화국은 특히 음악을 통제해야 한다는 플라톤의 주장에 대한 글이다. 따라서 마지막 문장의 빈칸에는 정치에 따라 미학이 결정되어야 한다는 내용의 ①이 가장 적절하다.

어휘　insinuate (사상 등을) 스며들게 하다 disposition 성향, 성격, 기질 moderation 완화, 절제, 온건함 ferocity 사나움, 잔인성, 만행 aesthetics 미학 defer to ~을 따르다 indulge 만족시키다, 충족시키다

07　②　유전자가 선천적인 행동의 발현 가능성을 정확히 어떻게 높이는가는 복잡한 문제이다. 일부 유전자들은 뇌의 화학 물질들을 통제하지만, 다른 것들은 간접적으로 행동에 영향을 끼친다. 너의 유전자들이 너를 아주 특별히 매력적인 사람으로 만들었다고 가정해 보자. 결과적으로 낯선 사람들도 너를 향해 미소 지을 것이며, 많은 사람들

이 너에 대해 알고 싶어할 것이다. 너의 외모에 대한 그들의 반응은 너의 성격을 바꾸어 놓을지도 모른다. 그리고 그렇게 된다면, 그 유전자들은 너의 환경을 바꾸어 놓음으로써 너의 행동을 바꾼다. 다른 예를 들면, 평균보다 훨씬 더 신장을 크게 하고 더 빠른 달리기 속도와 운동 능력까지 뛰어나게 만드는 유전자를 갖고 태어난 아이가 있다고 상상해 보자. 그 아이는 이른 나이에 농구에서 뛰어난 모습을 보여줄 것이고 곧이어 점점 더 많은 시간을 농구를 하며 보내게 될 것이다. 이에 따라 그 아이는 다른 취미활동들, 예를 들면 텔레비전 시청, 체스, 또는 우표 수집 등과 같은 일들에는 시간을 덜 쓰게 될 것이다. 따라서 많은 행동들의 측정된 유전력은 다리 근육에 영향을 주는 유전자에 따라 부분적으로 좌우되는 것인지도 모른다. 이것은 가상의 예에 불과하지만, 이것은 다음과 같은 요점을 명확히 설명해준다. 유전자는 간접적인 방법들을 통해 행동에 영향을 끼친다.

① 성공은 유전적 형식에 크게 좌우된다
② 유전자는 간접적인 방법들을 통해 행동에 영향을 끼친다
③ 성격은 유전자와 행동에 좌우된다
④ 환경에의 적응은 진화의 핵심이다
⑤ 자연적 선택은 행동 신호에 자극받는다

주 제 유전자가 행동에 미치는 간접적 영향
정답 해설 글의 전반부는 유전자 중 간접적으로 행동에 영향을 끼치는 것이 있다고 언급하며 사람의 매력, 신장, 운동 능력을 결정하는 유전자가 행동에 영향을 끼치는 과정을 예로 들고 있다. 마지막에 이 글의 주제를 한 번 더 강조하는 문장이 위치하는 것이 자연스러우므로 빈칸에는 ②가 적절하다.

어 휘 coordination (신체 동작의) 조정력 pursuits 취미 활동 heritability 유전율, 유전력, 상속 가능성 hypothetical 가설의, 가정의, 가상적인 roundabout (말이나 행동 등이) 완곡한

08 ① 잘 알려진 극작가이자 17세기 John Donne과 동시대를 살았던 Ben Jonson은 "Donne는 어떤 면에서는 세계 최초의 시인이지만 그럼에도 불구하고 운율을 지키지 않았기 때문에 교수형 감이다."라고 기록했다. Donne의 세대는 그의 깊은 감성은 경외했지만 빈번히 불규칙한 리듬과 애매모호한 언급에 대해서는 당혹스러워했다. 20세기가 되고 감정과 암시를 찬미하는 현대적인 사조가 생긴 뒤에야 Donne은 진가를 인정받기 시작했다. T. S. Eliot 이나 W. B. Yeats와 같은 작가들은 한 때는 그의 부인과의 세속적인 유희를 뽐냈었고, 그 이후에는 신에게 "당신의 힘을 부려서, 나를 부수고, 날려버리고, 태워서 나를 새롭게 만들어 주소서."라고 처절하게 애원했던 그의 심리학적인 심오함을 존경했다.

① Donne은 진가를 인정받기 시작했다
② 잊혀진 Donne의 작품이 다시 쓰이게 되었다
③ Jonson은 그가 Donne을 잘못 판단했다고 인정했다
④ Donne의 불명확한 기준이 더 모호해졌다
⑤ 시의 운율이 더 일반적으로 쓰이게 되었다

주 제 시인 Donne에 대한 평가의 변화
정답 해설 문맥상 감성과 암시가 찬양 받는 20세기의 현대 문학 시대에 이르러서야 Donne이 비로소 제대로 인정을 받았다는 내용이므로 빈칸에는 ①이 가장 적절하다.

어 휘 contemporary 동시대의, 동시대의 사람 hanging 매달림, 교수형 rhythm 리듬, 운율 allusion 암시, 인유법 intricacy 복잡함, 복잡한 것 flaunt 자랑하다, 과시하다 earthly 세상에, 지구상에 dalliance 빈둥거림, 놀이, 희롱 wretched 불쌍한, 초라한, 비열한

09 ① 다중지능이론은 지능에 대한 전통적인 학설에 이의를 제기한다. 그것은 또한 지능 검사의 가치에 대해서도 의문을 제기한다. 다중지능 연구자들은 전통적인 가르침이나 평가가 인간이 소유하고 있는 7가지 지능 중 오직 2가지, 언어 능력과 논리적 능력에만 초점을 맞추고 있다고 지적한다. 따라서 언어와 논리에 의존하는 방법으로 배우지 않는 아이들은 부족한 것으로 평가된다. 그러나 Seven Kinds of Smart의 저자인 Thomas Armstrong은 아이들은 훌륭하지만 교육 방법이 부적절하다고 말한다. "전통적인 교육에서 우리들은 학생들을 우리와 같은 방식으로 가르치려고 노력해왔다. 하지만 이와는 대조적으로 우리는 그것이 학생들에게 들어맞을 수 있도록 교수방법을 새롭게 정립할 필요가 있다."고 말했다. "우리는 서로 다른 아이들은 다양한 방법으로 배운다는 것과 어떤 교육 방법도 괜찮다는 사실을 인정해야만 한다. 그러면 우리는 진정한 교육을 하게 될 것이다."라고 그는 말을 더했다.

① 그것이 학생들에게 들어맞을 수 있도록
② 그들이 질문에 더 나은 대답을 할 수 있도록
③ 우리가 우리 자신의 교육 방법을 선택할 수 있도록
④ 그들이 언어와 논리 능력을 개발할 수 있도록
⑤ 학습 이론이 교육에 기여할 수 있도록

주 제 전통적 교육에 대한 다중지능이론의 비판
정답 해설 빈칸이 있는 문장 앞머리에 'on the contrary'가 쓰인 것으로 보아 앞문장과는 대조되는 내용이 나올 것임을 유추할 수 있다. 따라서 빈칸에는 학생들에게 잘 맞는다는 내용이 포함된 ①이 가장 적절하다.

어 휘 multiple intelligences 다중 지능 inadequate 부적
당한, 불충분한

10 ①　나를 사주기를 바랐던 회색 눈의 남자가 있었다.
나는 그가 나를 다루는 방식 덕에 그가 말에 익숙
한 사람이라는 것을 알게 되었다. 그는 나를 사기 위해 흥정
을 했지만 액수가 너무 적어서 거절당했다. 매우 험악하고 시
끄러운 목소리의 남자가 그 다음으로 다가왔고, 그 사람이 더
높은 가격을 제시해서 나를 가지게 되는 것이 몹시 무서웠다.
하지만 그 회색 눈의 남자가 나를 두드리며 말했다. "음, 나는
우리가 서로 잘 맞을 거라고 생각한다." 그리고 <u>그는 더 높은
가격을 제시했다</u>. 판매인은 "되었네."라고 말했다.

① 그는 더 높은 가격을 제시했다
② 그는 목소리를 낮췄다
③ 그는 제안을 취소했다
④ 나는 자비를 구했다
⑤ 나는 다른 거래를 제안했다

주 제 흥정 중 일어난 생각과 감정
정답 해설 낮은 가격 때문에 거절당했던 회색 눈의 남자가 다
시 말을 구매했다는 내용이므로 '더 높은 가격을 제시했다'라는
①의 내용이 오는 것이 적절하다.
어 휘 bid 입찰, 입찰 가격, 명령하다 dreadfully 몹시, 무시무
시하게

11 ②　오늘날 교외 지역은 놀랄 만큼 다양해졌다. 많은
교외의 통근자 주거 지역들이 교외의 노동자 주
거 지역과 임대주택 지역, 산업 단지 지역과 함께 해왔다. 역
사적으로 교외 지역은 '부차적'인 것으로 여겨졌는데 <u>그들은
경제적으로 자립하지 못했기</u> 때문이다. 교외 거주자들은 생
계를 위해 도시 중심지로 통근을 해야 했다. 하지만 그런 사
실들은 더 이상은 유효하지 않다. 교외 지역은 증가하는 고
용의 중심지가 되어가고 있다. 15개의 수도권 지역에서, 교
외 지역에 사는 72%의 노동자들은 교외 지역에서 일하고 있
다는 1970년의 인구 조사 수치가 이를 잘 보여준다. 우리의
교외 지역에 대한 이미지는 현실을 정확히 반영하지 못했다.

① 그들은 노동자 거주민들로 이루어졌다
② 그들은 경제적으로 자립하지 못했다
③ 그들은 여가를 즐길 충분한 시설이 없었다
④ 대다수의 사람들이 그곳에서 돈을 쓰고 싶어 하지 않았다

⑤ 그곳의 풍경은 도시 중심지와 달랐다

주 제 교외 지역의 위상 변화
정답 해설 후반부에서 교외 지역이 실질적인 고용의 중심지가
됨으로서 우리가 갖고 있던 이미지는 유효하지 않게 되었다고
하였으므로 교외 지역이 부차적으로 여겨진 이유는 '경제적인
자립도가 부족했기 때문'으로 보는 것이 적절하다. 따라서 빈칸
에는 ②가 가장 적절하다.

어 휘 diverse 다양한 catch up with ~의 수준을 갖추다, 따
라잡다 suburbia 교외 거주자, 교외 사람 condominium 공동 주
택, 빌라 census 인구 조사, 인구 조사를 하다

12 ②　역사가 스스로가 끊임없이 활동하고 있는 그 연
속선에서 역사는 과거와 미래를 잇고자 한다. 우
리가 과거든 미래든 역사에서 어떤 절대적인 판단도 추출하
기를 기대하지 말아야 하는 것은 분명하다. 이러한 판단은
그 본질이 줄 수 있는 것이 아니다. 모든 인간의 판단은, 모
든 인간의 행동처럼, 결정론과 자유 의지의 논리적 딜레마에
빠져있다. 인간은 매우 먼 과거에 이르는 인과관계의 사슬에
의하여 그의 행동과 판단에 불가분하게 종속되어 있다. 하지
만 인간은 주어진 시점 ― 현재에서 ― <u>그 사슬을 끊는 데 적
격인 힘을 가지고 있고 미래를 변경할 수 있다</u>.

① 그는 사슬을 다시 조일 것으로 예상된다.
② 그는 그 사슬을 끊는 데 적격인 힘을 가지고 있다.
③ 새로운 사슬을 성형하는 것은 그의 타고난 능력을 넘어
선다.
④ 사슬의 제한을 푸는 것은 사실상 불가능하다.
⑤ 그는 강한 사슬을 멀리 유지할 도덕적인 책임이 있다

주 제 인간의 종속성과 자유의지
정답 해설 빈칸이 포함된 yet 이후 내용은 인간이 인과관계의
사슬에 의하여 행동과 판단이 종속되었다는 앞부분의 내용과
상반되어야 한다. 따라서 '그 사슬을 끊는 데 적격인 힘을 가지
고 있고 미래를 변경할 수 있다'라는 내용이 문맥상 자연스러우
므로 빈칸에는 ②가 가장 적절하다.

어 휘 historian 역사학자, 역사가 constantly 꾸준하게
extract 뽑아내다, 추출하다 dilemma 딜레마, 선택하기 곤란한 상황
determinism 결정론 indissolubly 불가분하게, 용해할 수 없게, 풀
수 없게, 영원하게 bind-bound 속박하다 causation 원인, 인과관계

13 ①　St. Louis 신문의 1면 기사는 두 남자가 주먹다짐
뒤에 입원을 한 사건을 보도했다. 어떤 사건이 일

어났다면, 자동차 운전자가 교차로에서 빨간 불에 정차했다. 인도에 있던 한 남자가 "이봐요, 자동차 왼쪽 앞바퀴에서 바람이 새고 있어요."라고 소리쳤다. 운전자가 내려서 타이어를 보고는 친절을 베푼 남자에게 "고맙습니다. 당신은 착한 사마리아 사람 같군요!"라고 말했다. 이에 그 보행자는 인도에서 뛰어나와 "당신은 나를 그런 더러운 호칭으로 부를 수 없어!"라고 외치며 주먹으로 운전자를 마구 때렸다. 황당한 운전자도 맞받아쳤고 그 결과 두 사람 모두 병원에 실려 온 것이었다. 모든 것은 한 사람이 <u>사마리아인이란 말을 욕이라고 생각했기 때문이다.</u>

---

① 사마리아인이란 말은 욕이다
② 다른 이가 그를 'mister'라고 불렀다
③ 보행자가 그에게 의도적으로 거짓말을 했다
④ 운전자가 그의 친절에 감사하지 않았다
⑤ 운전자가 버스를 깨끗이 유지하지 않았다

(주 제) '사마리아인'의 의미를 오해하여 생긴 다툼

(정답 해설) 이 글은 보행자가 운전자의 '착한 사마리아인'이라는 말을 듣고 이를 욕으로 오해했다는 내용이다. 성경에서 사마리아인은 유대인의 경멸의 대상이지만 '착한 사마리아인'은 어려움에 처한 유대인을 도와주었던 훌륭한 사람이다. 글에 나온 보행자가 '착한 사마리아인'이라는 운전자의 말을 전부 듣지 못하고 오해했기 때문에 사건이 일어난 것이다. 따라서 빈칸에는 ①이 가장 적절하다.

(어 휘) fistfight 주먹다짐 flat 평평한, 완전히 curb (말의) 재갈, 고삐, (인도의) 연석 strike back 되받아 치다 hospitalize 입원시키다 Samaritan 사마리아인 pound 사정없이 때리다, 타격, 연타

More Practice

| 01 ① | 02 ② | 03 ① | 04 ② |

01 ① 원시인들의 생존은 음식에 대한 끊임없는 탐색에 지배되었기 때문에 그들의 삶은 보통 냉혹하다고 여겨진다. 사실 몇몇 원시인들은 일을 많이 하지 않는다. 현대의 기준과 비교해 보면, 우리는 그들을 게으르다고 판단할 수 있다. 파푸아뉴기니의 Kapauka들은 하루 일을 하면 다음날에는 일을 하지 않는다. Kung Bushmen들은 일주일에 이틀 반, 하루에 6시간만 일을 한다. 하와이의 Sandwich 섬 거주민들은 오직 하루 4시간만 일을 한다. 그들은 왜 우리들처럼 더 많은 것을 얻으려고 더 많은 일을 하지 않는가에 대한 이해의 핵심은 <u>제한된 욕구를 가지고 있는 것</u>이라 할 수

있다. 바라는 것과 가지고 있는 것 사이의 밀고 당기기에서 그들은 욕구 수준을 높이지 않았고, 이렇게 하여 그들 나름의 충족을 보장받아 왔다. 현재 기준에서 보면 그들은 물질적으로 가난하지만 적어도 한 가지 측면, 즉 시간에서는 우리는 그들을 더 부자로 여겨야 한다.

---

① 그들은 제한된 욕구를 가지고 있다
② 그들은 물질적으로 매우 풍요하게 산다
③ 그들의 생산성은 비교적[상대적으로] 낮다
④ 그들은 시간 개념이 없다
⑤ 그들은 재화를 서로 교환한다

(주 제) 물질의 풍요보다는 시간의 여유를 누리는 원시 부족의 삶

(정답 해설) 빈칸 바로 뒤에서 원하는 것과 소유하는 것 사이의 밀고 당기는 과정에서 그들이 욕구 수준을 계속 낮추었으며 그렇게 하여 그들 나름의 충족을 보장받는다고 언급하고 있다. 따라서 빈칸에는 ①이 가장 적절하다.

(어 휘) harsh 고된 incessant 부단한 quest 탐구, 탐색 put in 투입하다 ensure 보증[보장]하다 count 여기다

02 ② 오케스트라에서 금관악기 연주자들은 종종 <u>다른 연주자보다 더 일찍 연주해야 한다</u>는 얘기를 듣는다. 금관악기들은 몇 야드의 둥근 관으로 만들어지며, 뱀과 같이 감겨있다. 예를 들어, 만약 당신이 전형적인 프렌치 호른의 모든 관을 푼다면 그 길이는 17피트가 될 것이다. 그것은 평균 키의 성인 세 명이 서로의 어깨에 올라가 있는 높이만큼이나 긴 것이다! 금관악기를 불 때 그 공기가 관 속으로 들어가서 굽이치며 그 길이를 모두 지난 다음에, 그 악기 안에 약간의 침을 남기고 다른 쪽 끝에서 소리로 나온다. 이것은 시간이 좀 걸린다. 소리가 조금 늦게 나는 것은 당연하다. 가끔 뛰어난 금관악기 연주자들은 다른 음악가들보다 뒤처져서 연주하는 것을 피하기 위해서는 이러한 시차를 보완해야 할 필요가 있다고 생각한다.

---

① 그들의 악기가 더 자주 교체되어야 한다.
② 그들이 다른 연주자들보다 더 일찍 연주를 해야 한다.
③ 그들의 악기가 동물의 형태와 닮아야 한다.
④ 그들이 다른 연주자들을 피해야 한다.
⑤ 그들이 비싼 금관악기를 구입해야 한다.

(주 제) 다른 연주자보다 조금 일찍 연주를 시작해야 하는 금관악기

(정답 해설) 금관악기는 내부의 관이 길어서 연주자가 악기를 분

후 관의 다른 끝에서 소리를 내기까지 시차가 있으므로 다른 연주자들보다 뒤처지지 않기 위해 조금 일찍 연주해야 한다는 내용의 글이다. 따라서 빈칸에는 ②가 가장 적절하다.

어휘 brass 금관악기 tubing 배관 coiled up 감긴 unroll 펼치다 deposit (특정한 곳에) 두다 spit 침 be bound to ~하지 않을 수 없다 compensate for ~에 대해 보상하다, 보충하다

03 ① 의사소통에서 거의 이해가 되지 않는 역설들 중의 하나는 단어가 어려우면 어려울수록 설명은 더 간결해진다는 것이다. 한 단어에 더 많은 의미를 집어넣는 것이 가능할수록 그 생각을 이해시키는 데 더 적은 단어가 필요하게 된다. 어려운 말은 그 말을 이해하지 못하는 사람들을 화나게 하고, 물론 그 말은 매우 자주 명료하게 하기보다는 혼란스럽고 관심을 끌려고 사용된다. 그러나 이것은 언어의 잘못이 아니다. 그것은 의사소통 도구를 잘못 사용하는 사람의 오만이다. 풍부한 어휘를 습득하는 가장 좋은 이유는 <u>그것으로 인해 당신이 장황해지지 않게 된다는 것이다.</u> 성실하게 교육을 받은 사람은 간결하고 깔끔하게 자신을 표현할 수 있다. 예를 들어, 만약 당신이 'imbricate'라는 단어를 모르거나 사용하지 않는다면, 당신은 누군가에게 '지붕 위의 기와나 물고기의 비늘 혹은 식물의 꽃받침처럼 규칙적인 배열로 겹쳐진 모서리가 있는'이라고 말해야 한다. 한 단어로 말해질 수 있는 것을 말하기 위해 스무 개가 넘는 단어를 사용하게 되는 것이다.

① 그것으로 인해 당신이 장황해지지 않게 된다
② 당신은 심각한 오해를 피할 수 있다
③ 그것으로 인해 당신의 진정한 의도를 감출 수 있다
④ 그것으로 인해 당신 자신을 더 인상적으로 표현할 수 있다
⑤ 당신은 어려운 단어보다 쉬운 단어를 사용할 수 있다

주제 풍부한 어휘 습득의 이점
정답 해설 imbricate라는 단어를 모르면 그 의미를 전달하기 위해 스무 개가 넘는 단어를 사용하게 된다는 예시를 통해, 풍부한 어휘를 습득하면 간결하게 표현할 수 있다는 것을 알 수 있다. 따라서 빈칸에는 '그것으로 인해 당신이 장황해지지 않게 된다'라는 뜻의 ①이 들어가는 것이 가장 적절하다.

어휘 paradox 역설, 패러독스 get the idea across 생각을 이해시키다 big words 허풍, 어려운 말 impress 깊은 인상을 주다, 관심을 끌다 clarify 분명하게 하다 arrogance 오만, 거만 misuse 남용하다, 오용하다 long-winded 길고 지루한, 장황한 genuinely 진정으로, 성실하게 tersely 간결하게 trimly 깔끔하게 imbricate 비늘 모양으로 겹친 overlap 겹쳐지다, 포개지다 sepal 꽃받침

04 ② 흥미롭게도, 사람들은 자신들이 결과에 대한 통제력을 지니고 있다고 느낄 때 더 자신만만한데, 이는 사실이 명백히 그렇지 않을 때조차도 그러하다. 예를 들면, 동전 던지기에서 앞면이 나올 것인지 뒷면이 나올 것인지에 대해 내기를 하도록 요청을 받으면 대부분의 사람들이 동전이 아직 던져지지 않았을 때 더 많은 금액을 거는 것으로 기록되어 있다. 동전이 던져졌고 그 결과가 감춰진 경우에는 내기를 하라는 요청을 받았을 때 사람들은 더 적은 금액을 걸려 한다. 사람들은 마치 <u>그들의 관여가 동전 던지기 결과에 어떻게든 영향을 미칠 것처럼</u> 행동한다. 이 경우 결과에 대한 통제력은 명백한 착각이다. 이러한 인식은 투자에서도 또한 나타난다. 심지어 아무런 정보 없이도 사람들은 자신들이 소유한 주식이 자신들이 소유하지 않은 주식들보다 더 좋은 성과를 올리게 될 것이라고 믿는다. 그러나 주식의 보유는 그 주식의 성과에 대한 통제력을 지니고 있다는 착각을 제공할 뿐이다.

① 내기에 거는 돈의 양이 결과에 영향을 미칠 것이다
② 그들의 관여가 동전 던지기 결과에 어떻게든 영향을 미칠 것이다
③ 동전 던지기와 주식 투자 간에 유사점이 있다
④ 심지어 동전이 던져진 이후에도 그들의 착각은 사라지지 않을 것이다
⑤ 그들은 신뢰할 만한 정보로 결과를 예측할 수 있다

주제 결과를 통제할 수 있다는 착각으로 인한 사람들의 행동
정답 해설 사람들은 동전 던지기 내기에서 동전이 던져지기 전에는 더 많은 금액을 걸지만 동전이 던져진 후 그 결과가 드러나지 않은 상태에서 내기를 걸 때는 더 적은 금액을 건다. 즉 사람들은, 돈을 건 후에 동전이 던져지면 그 결과가 자기가 원하는 쪽으로 나올 수 있을 것처럼 행동하고 있다는 설명이다. 그러므로 빈칸에는 ② '그들의 관여가 동전 던지기 결과에 어떻게든 영향을 미칠 것처럼'이 가장 적절하다.

어휘 overconfident 자신만만한 outcome 결과 the case 실정, 사실 coin toss 동전 던지기 heads 동전의 앞면 tails 동전의 뒷면 conceal 숨기다, 비밀로 하다 perception 지각, 인식 stock 주식 credible 믿을 수 있는

Example 답 ①

어떤 경우에는 연구자가 단순히 자연의 동물을 각기 다른 시간, 다른 계절, 식이 변화에 따라 관찰한다. 이러한 절차는 윤리적인 문제를 야기하지 않는다. 그러나 다른 연구에서는 동물이 뇌 손상, 전극 삽입, 약물이나 호르몬 주사, 그리고 분명히 그들의 이익을 위하지 않는 다른 절차의 대상이 된다. 양심이 있는 사람은 (과학자를 포함하여) 이 사실에 괴로움을 느낀다. 그럼에도 불구하고 동물 실험은 소아마비, 당뇨병, 홍역, 천연두, 방대한 화상, 심장 질환 및 기타 심각한 상태의 예방 또는 치료 방법으로 이어진 의학 연구에 중요하다. 생리학이나 의학 분야의 노벨상은 대부분 비인간 동물에 수행된 연구에 수여되었다. AIDS, 알츠하이머 병, 뇌졸중 및 기타 여러 질환을 치료하거나 예방하는 방법을 찾는 희망은 주로 동물 연구에 달려 있다. 의학과 생물 심리학의 많은 영역에서 연구는 동물 없이는 느리게 진행되거나 전혀 진행되지 않는다.

↓

동물에 수행되는 (A) 실험적인 연구는 간단한 관찰 연구와 달리, 윤리적 문제를 제기하지만 다양한 의료 분야에서 진전을 이루는 데 (B) 도움이 된다.

	(A)		(B)
①	실험적인	……	도움이 되는
②	통계적인	……	성공한
③	분야	……	중대한
④	개발상의	……	그럴듯한
⑤	실험실	……	하찮은

주 제 동물 실험의 윤리적 문제와 의학적 효용

Practice

01 ③	02 ①	03 ②	04 ⑤	05 ⑤
06 ⑤	07 ④	08 ③	09 ③	10 ②

01 ③ 특정 상표의 상품들이 특히 효과가 있다고 그저 생각하는 것에는 일종의 위약효과가 있다는 것을 연구자들이 밝혀냈다. 일련의 연구에서 참가자들은, 골프와 수학 기량 시험에서 거의 동일한 도구를 받았다. 단 하나의 차이점은 다음과 같다. 시험 응시자들에게 주어진 귀마개의 절반은 3M에 의해 제조되었다고 알려진 반면, 퍼터의 절반이 나이키 상표를 붙이고 있었다. 나이키 퍼터를 사용하고 있다고 생각한 사람들은 평균적으로 공을 넣는 데 정말 더 적은 퍼트를 필요로 했고, 3M 귀마개를 가지고 있다고 생각한 참가자들은 수학 시험 중 문제에 더 정확하게 답했다. 그들의 능력에 대해 초기에 가장 낮은 자신감을 보인 사람들은 그 사소한 업그레이드로부터 가장 많은 것을 얻은 것으로 보였다는 것 또한 밝혀졌다.

↓

연구는 평균적으로 시험 참가자들의 성과가 그들이 보다 (B) 저명한 브랜드를 사용하고 있다고 믿을 때 (A) 향상되었다는 것을 보여주었다.

	(A)		(B)
①	향상된	……	포괄적인
②	향상된	……	운동 경기의
③	향상된	……	저명한
④	감소된	……	인기 있는
⑤	감소된	……	평범한

주 제 유명 상표 제품의 위약 효과

정답 해설 이 글의 요지는 사람들이 저명한 브랜드를 사용하고 있다고 믿을 때, 능력을 더욱 잘 발휘할 수 있다는 것이다. 따라서 (A)에는 enhanced가, (B)에는 prominent가 적절하다.

어 휘 placebo effect 위약 효과 generic 일반적인, 포괄적인

02 ① 평균 기대 수명은 수십 년간 서서히 늘었고, 흡연과 태양의 노출로 인한 암을 제외하고는, 암으로 인한 사망률도 감소하거나 상대적으로 과거와 비슷하게 유지되고 있다. 하지만 설문 조사들은 사람들은 이보다 더 심한 적이 없을 정도로 건강에 대해 걱정하고 있음을 반복적으로 보여준다. 자연적으로 생긴 살충제가 사람들이 인위적으로 만든 살충제보다 약 10000배는 더 흔하다고 제일 처음 언급한 Bruce Ames는 "사람들이 마치 어디로 가든 대재앙을 마주하게 될 것처럼 행동한다."라고 말했다. "물론 중대한 위험은 당연히 있다. 하지만 사람들은 걱정을 덜고 여유를 가질 필요가 있다." 때로는 이러한 마음가짐을 갖는 것이 힘들 것이다. 과도한 콜레스테롤 수치, 비타민 A 부족, 운동량 부족으로 인해 오는 문제점과 자극적인 경고들은 미국인들의 삶에 태피스트리처럼 일부분이 되었다. 몇몇 사람들에게는, 암세포가 모든 식단에 숨겨져 있다고 믿어질 것이다.

↓

비록 미국인들은 그 어느 때보다도 (A) 더 건강해졌지만, 그들은 건강에 대해 상당한 (B) 걱정을 하고 있는 것처럼 보인다.

	(A)		(B)
①	더 건강한	……	걱정
②	더 유행에 민감한	……	걱정
③	더 건강한	……	소망
④	더 유행에 민감한	……	염려
⑤	더 마른	……	염려

주 제) 미국인의 건강에 대한 걱정

정답 해설) 지문에서는 사람들의 수명이 늘고 과거에 비해 암 사망률도 감소하거나 비슷하게 유지됨에도 불구하고, 여전히 건강에 대해 과도할 정도로 걱정하는 사람이 많다는 점을 서술하고 있다. 이 글을 통해서 한 문장으로 요약할 때 (A)에는 healthier, (B)에는 anxiety가 적절하다.

어 휘) life expectancy 기대 수명 steadily 꾸준히 exposure 노출 stable 안정된 fretful 초조한 apocalypse 묵시, 세상의 종말 pesticide 농약 tapestry 태피스트리(여러 가지 색실로 그림을 짜 넣은 직물) anxiety 걱정

03 ② 시공간적인 매체로서 영화가 갖는 지위는 그것에 기술적으로 인정받은 기능들과 관련된 역사적인 배경 덕분이다. 19세기 말에 처음 등장하여, 그 움직이는 그림은 시간과 공간에 대한 전통적인 경계를 무너뜨리는 기술적인 능력을 극대화시키는 일련의 발명품 중의 정점으로 우뚝 서게 되었다. 영화는 (상당한 거리에 의해 서로 떨어져 있는 두 공간에서 이루어지는 의사소통을 가능하게 만들었던) 전보나 전화로부터 (승객들이 이전과는 비교할 수 없는 속도로 많은 지역들을 횡단하는 것을 가능하게 해 준, 따라서 여행의 시간을 무너뜨렸던) 기차와 자동차, 그리고 (광전자의 처리 과정을 통해 실제 세계의 소리와 이미지를 각각 사로잡음으로써 시간을 멈춰버리는) 축음기와 사진에 이르기까지 확장된 연장선상의 일부분으로서 작용했다. 영화는 시간과 공간을 표현하고 개념화하는 전통적인 감각을 확장시킨 최신 발명품이었다.

⬇

역사적으로 영화의 (A) 출현은 시간과 공간의 경계를 (B) 초월하는 것을 돕는 기술적 발전의 최고조를 보여준다.

	(A)		(B)
①	출현	……	압축하다
②	출현	……	초월하다
③	줄어듦	……	압축하다
④	줄어듦	……	초월하다
⑤	부활	……	붕괴하다

주 제) 영화 발명의 의의

정답 해설) 주어진 글의 마지막 문장이 이 글의 주제를 나타낸다. '영화는 시간과 공간을 표현하고 개념화하는 전통적인 감각을 확장시킨 최신 발명품이었다'는 내용의 마지막 문장은 '영화의 출현 혹은 등장은 시간과 공간의 경계를 초월하는 것을 돕는 기술적 발전의 최고조를 보여준다'라고 쓸 수 있다. 따라서 (A)에는 '도래, 출현'을 뜻하는 advent가, (B)에는 '(범위, 한계 등을) 초월하다'라는 뜻의 surpass가 적절하다.

어 휘) spatiotemporal 시간과 공간상의, 시공간적인 as to ~과 관련된 culmination 정점, 최고조 continuum 연속체, 계속되는 것 locomotive 기관차 phonograph 축음기, 레코드플레이어 photoelectric 광전자를 이용한 traverse 가로지르다, 횡단하다 via ~을 거쳐 conceptualize 개념화하다, 개념을 정립하다 condense 응축하다, 응결되다

04 ⑤ 유럽에서는 수백 년에 걸쳐서 종교 예술만이 거의 유일하게 존재하는 예술이었다. 교회와 종교 관련 건물들은 성경책에 나오는 사람들과 이야기를 묘사하는 그림들로 가득 채워졌다. 비록 대부분의 사람들이 글을 읽을 수 없었지만, 그들도 교회 벽에 있는 그림들에 나오는 성경의 이야기는 이해할 수 있었다. 이와는 대조적으로 중동 지방의 예술은 사람과 동물의 형상이 나타나지 않는 것이 주요한 특징 중 하나이다. 이슬람 율법에 따라서, 예술가들은 깔개나, 그릇들과 같이 일상에서 자주 사용하는 작은 물품들을 제외하고는 인간이나 동물의 형상을 옮겨 넣는 것이 허용되지 않았다. 따라서 궁전이나 사원, 또는 다른 건물들에서 이슬람 예술가들은 독특하게 원, 직사각형, 삼각형 등의 모양을 이용해 만든 매우 아름다운 장식인 아라베스크 무늬를 창조해냈다.

⬇

유럽의 미술과 중동의 미술은 전자는 (A) 성경의 이미지를 이용하고, 후자는 (B) 기하학적 패턴을 이용한다는 점에서 다르다.

	(A)		(B)
①	신성한	……	동물적
②	세속적인	……	비세속적
③	종교의	……	순환의
④	분명한	……	절묘한
⑤	성경의	……	기하학적

주 제) 유럽 미술과 중동 미술의 차이점

정답 해설) 서두에서 중세 유럽의 예술은 성경의 내용과 인물에 대한 그림이 많았다고 언급했다. 그리고 중간 부분에서는 중

동의 예술은 이와 대조적으로 사람이나 동물의 이미지를 사용하는 것이 제한되고 있기 때문에 삼각형이나 직사각형, 원 등의 이미지를 이용한 아라베스크 무늬가 발달되었다고 서술하고 있다. 따라서 (A)에는 '성경의'라는 뜻의 biblical이, (B)에는 '기하학적'이라는 뜻의 geometric이 적절하다.

[어 휘] biblical 성경의, 성경에 대한 mosque 이슬람 사원 exclusive 독점적인, 배타적인 geometric 기하학의, 기하학적인 secular 세속적인, 일반인다운 exquisite 매우 아름다운, 절묘한, 정교한

05 ⑤ 아마도 당신은 함께 있기 위해 텔레비전에 의존하는 수많은 사람들 중 한명이거나 또는 실제로 자기의 컴퓨터에게 이야기하는 자신의 모습을 발견했을지도 모른다. 하지만 당신의 기계들과의 모든 관계는 연애 관계는 아닐 것이다. 당신은 또한 스스로의 생각을 가지고 있는 컴퓨터나 시동이 걸리지 않는 자동차, 항상 빵을 태우는 토스터기 그리고 당신의 돈을 가로채는 자판기 등의 기계들은 싫어할지도 모른다. 비록 기계들은 보통 당신의 삶을 편하게 해주기 위해 설계되지만 그것들 또한, 역시 때로는 당신의 삶을 비참하지는 않더라도 불만스럽게 만들 수도 있다. 기계들은 확실히 우리의 삶에서 안 좋은 많은 부분에 기여한다. 총은 높은 범죄율의 원인이고, 자동차들은 공기 오염을 증가시켰고, 사고를 초래한다. 그리고 대개의 기계들은 사람들을 일터에서 내쫓았다. 하지만 어느 누구도 기계의 도움 없이 일하고 싶어 하지 않는다. 기계들과 그들이 주는 편리함과 즐거움, 자극에 익숙해졌기 때문에 사람들은 기계들이 많은 역할을 해주지 않는 삶은 상상할 수도 없게 되었다.

↓

기계는 자주 골치 아프고, 실망시키고 (A) <u>해롭기</u>까지 할 수 있다. 그러나 일단 기계가 주는 장점에 익숙해지면, 너는 그것이 너의 일상생활에 (B) <u>필수 불가결</u>하다고 느낄 것이다.

	(A)		(B)
①	중독성 있는	……	과잉의
②	실망스러운	……	중요하지 않은
③	해로운	……	과잉의
④	중독성 있는	……	필수 불가결한
⑤	해로운	……	필수 불가결한

[주 제] 기계의 양면성

[정답 해설] 본문은 기계들이 어느 정도 문제가 있고 나쁜 영향을 끼치는 것도 사실이지만 현대인들이 기계가 주는 편리함에 익숙해져서 생활에 필수적인 요소가 되었다는 것을 설명하고

있다. 따라서 (A)에는 '해로운'이라는 뜻의 harmful이, (B)에는 '필수 불가결한'이라는 뜻의 indispensable이 적절하다.

[어 휘] keep company 어울리다. 함께 있다. stimulation 자극 troublesome 골치 아픈, 문제가 되는 accustomed 익숙해진 addictive 중독성 있는 superfluous 과잉의, 여분의, 남는 indispensable 필수 불가결한, 절대 필요한

06 ⑤ 문학 작품의 언어가 매우 간단하고 단순한 경우에 그것은 도움이 될 수 있지만 외국어 학습을 위한 문학 작품을 선택하는 가장 중요한 척도는 그 자체에 있지 않다. 관심, 매력, 관련성이 더 중요하다. 외국어로 된 문학 작품을 이해하는 독자들에게 의심할 여지없이 필요한 추가적인 시간과 노력을 정당화하려면, 즐거움과 서스펜스, 그리고 신선한 통찰력 등과 같이 사람들의 관심의 핵심에 가깝게 느껴지는 새로운 동기가 있어야만 한다. 이러한 요인들은 이런 것들을 덜 포함한 문학 작품에서는 너무 크게 느껴질 언어적 장애를 독자들이 열정적으로 극복할 수 있도록 이끄는 장려책이다.

↓

외국어 학습을 위한 문학 작품을 선택하는 중요한 요소는 언어의 수준이 아니라 그 작품이 <u>성취 동기를 제공함으로써 독자들의 참여를 촉진하는지</u>에 대한 것이다.

① 독자들이 언어적 장애를 극복하는 것을 배우는 데 도움을 주는지
② 기본적인 인간의 문제에 대해 독자에게 무언가를 말하는지
③ 그것을 읽는 데 다 써버린 독자의 시간과 노력에 정당성을 부여하는지
④ 외국어 학습에 새로운 통찰력을 제공하는지
⑤ 성취 동기를 제공함으로써 독자의 참여를 촉진하는지

[주 제] 외국어 학습을 위한 문학 작품의 요건

[정답 해설] 이 글은 문학 작품을 통해 외국어를 학습할 때 독자가 문학 작품에 대해 느끼는 관심, 매력, 관련성, 즐거움 등의 가치가 중요하다고 말하고 있다. 따라서 빈칸에는 ⑤ '성취 동기를 제공함으로써 독자들에게 참여를 촉진하는지'가 가장 적절하다.

[어 휘] straightforward 똑바른, 곧은 yardstick 표준, 척도 suspense 걱정, 불안, 긴장 obstacle 장애, 방해물

07 ④ 전자메일은 Ralph와의 우정을 더욱 깊어지게 해주었다. 비록 그의 사무실은 내 사무실 옆에 있었지만 그가 수줍어해서 우리는 긴 대화를 거의 하지 않았다.

서로 얼굴을 마주하면 그는 말을 중얼거렸고, 나는 그의 말을 거의 이해할 수 없었다. 하지만 우리가 둘 다 전자메일을 시작했을 때, 나는 그의 길고 사적인 감정을 드러내는 메시지를 받기 시작했다. 우리는 마음껏 서로의 진실한 마음을 드러냈다. 어떤 친구는 전자메일이 그녀의 아버지와의 소통을 열어주었다는 것을 알았다. 그는 휴대 전화로 말을 많이 하지 않을 것이다. 하지만 그들이 모두 온라인으로 연결된 이후 그들은 가까워졌다. 나는 궁금했다. 왜 어떤 사람들은 전자메일을 통해서 마음 여는 것을 쉽다고 생각할까? 이것은 기술과, 쓰여진 글의 완곡함의 조합으로, 마치 많은 이들이 운전을 하거나 무언가 다른 일을 할 때 얼굴을 맞대고 앉아서 절대 이야기를 할 수 없는 감정들을 조금씩 드러내는 것과 같다.

↓

전자 메일 의사소통에서 그것이 편지를 쓰는 대상들과의 간접적인 접촉을 보장하기 때문에 사람들은 더 자유롭다고 느낀다.

① 주제 선택의 자유
② 긴 일상적 만남
③ 적은 책임감
④ 편지를 쓰는 대상들과의 간접적인 접촉
⑤ 메시지를 보내는 사람들의 명확한 정체

주 제) 전자 메일을 이용한 의사소통의 장점

정답 해설) 전자메일을 쓸 때 사람들은 얼굴을 직접 맞대고 말하지 않아도 되기 때문에 더 자유롭게 감정을 드러낼 수 있다는 내용의 글이다. 따라서 빈칸에는 ④ '편지를 쓰는 대상들과의 간접적인 접촉'이 가장 적절하다.

어 휘) mumble 중얼거리다, 웅얼거리다 obliqueness 완곡함, 완곡한 표현 in drips and drabs 조금씩

08 ③ 천 년 이상 일본은 그들의 시와 설화에 붉은 왕관을 쓴 두루미 'tancho'에 대해 표현해 왔다. 그들은 그것의 그림과 조각상을 만들었다. 그들은 그것을 긴 수명과 행복 그리고 행운의 상징으로 숭배해왔다. 그것의 생활 습관에서 그들은 자신의 행동을 설명하는 문구와 은유를 끌어냈다. 그들은 그것을 모방하여 그것들이 춤추듯 춤을 추었다. 무엇보다도 그들은 그것을 아이콘으로 만들어 모든 곳에 그것의 이미지를 넣었다. 그래서 아이러니하게도 매우 희귀한 이 조류는 일본 전역을 통해 찻잔이나 쟁반, 선풍기, 가로등의 기둥, 청첩장, 1000엔짜리 노트의 뒤, 전투기의 꼬리 날개 등에서도 볼 수 있다.

↓

일본인들은 붉은 왕관을 쓴 두루미 tancho를 (A) 소중히 여기는 오랜 전통을 가지고 있으며, 그것을 대하는 태도는 그들의 (B) 일상적인 생활에 널리 반영된다.

	(A)		(B)
①	양육하는	……	일상적인
②	양육하는	……	종교적인
③	소중히 여기는	……	일상적인
④	소중히 여기는	……	전통적인
⑤	감탄하는	……	전통적인

주 제) tancho에 대한 일본인의 태도

정답 해설) 일본인들이 대대로 tancho를 장수와 행복, 행운의 상징으로 여겨 신봉했다는 내용의 글로 tancho의 이미지를 일상생활에 사용한 다양한 사례를 보여주고 있다. 따라서 요약문의 (A)에는 '소중히 여기는'이라는 의미의 cherishing이, (B)에는 '일상적인'이라는 의미의 everyday가 적절하다.

어 휘) crane 학, 두루미 folktale 민간 설화, 전래 동화 sculpture 조각(품) revere 숭배하다 phrase 어구 reflect 반영하다 fin 작은 날개, 지느러미 metaphor 은유, 은유법

09 ③ 우리가 평면적인 '종이를 오려놓은 것 같은' 이집트 벽화나 중세 거장인 Cimabue의 부자연스러운 성모자 목상을 볼 때, 우리는 도식적이고 비현실적인 예술 작품에 직면하게 된다. 그 후 르네상스 시대가 도래와 함께 Giotto의 성모상과 같은 명확한 반대의 성질과 마주하게 된다. 사실주의를 퍼뜨리려는 행진이 시작되었고, 이는 15세기부터 19세기까지 계속되었다. 영국 화가 John Constable이 'Wivenhoe Park'를 그린 19세기 초기에 이르러서야 관객들은 사실주의 묘사에서 사진과 견줄만한 정도의 풍경과 장면을 만나게 되었다.

↓

예술의 (A) 역사를 훑어보면 지난 3천 년간 (B) 사실주의로의 엄청난 발전이 있었음이 드러난다.

	(A)		(B)
①	재료	……	우수
②	박물관	……	정밀도
③	역사	……	사실주의
④	책	……	복사
⑤	기법	……	모방

주 제) 사실주의 예술의 발전

정답 해설 고대 이집트의 벽화부터 19세기에 이르기까지 미술의 사실주의 화풍의 발전을 설명하고 있다. 따라서 요약문의 (A)에는 역사를 의미하는 history가, (B)에는 사실주의를 뜻하는 realism이 적절하다.

어 휘 flatten 평평하게 만들다 Madonna 성모마리아 stilted 부자연스러운, 지나치게 격식적인 schematic 개략적인, 개요, 요약도 exemplify 예를 들어 설명하다, 예증하다

10 ② 기본적인 심리의 이해는 많은 측면에서 사람에게 도움을 줄 수 있으나 심리가 당신들에게 줄 수 있는 도움에는 한계가 있다. 그 중 하나는 무례하고 반사회적인 행동의 원인을 이해하는 것이고 다른 하나는 그것을 너그럽게 봐 주는 것이다. 당신의 화를 잘 내는 성격이 부분적으로는 불우한 어린 시절 때문임을 안다는 것은 가족들에게 소리를 지르는 것에 대한 허락이 아니다. 또한 과학적인 중립이 사회가 합법적으로나 도덕적으로 중립적이어야 한다는 것을 의미하지는 않는다. 아이를 때리는 이유를 더 잘 이해하는 것은 아동 학대를 줄이거나 가해자를 치료하는 데 도움을 줄 수 있을지도 모르지만 우리는 여전히 아동을 때리는 사람에게 그 행동에 대한 책임을 물을 수 있다.

↓

비록 (A) 심리에 대한 지식이 어떤 행동에 대해 이해하는 데 도움을 줄 수 있지만, 이것이 우리가 한 행동에 대해 (B) 책임을 지지 않게 하는 것은 아니다.

	(A)		(B)
①	심리	……	도덕
②	심리	……	책임
③	인성	……	도덕
④	인성	……	무례함
⑤	심리	……	무례함

주 제 기본적 심리 이해의 이점과 한계
정답 해설 심리를 이해하는 것이 반사회적이고 무례한 행동을 이해하는 데는 도움을 줄 수 있겠지만 한계가 있다고 언급하고 있다. 또한 불우한 어린 시절을 보냈다고 해도 아이를 때리는 행동을 했을 때 그 행동에 대한 책임을 져야 한다고 말하고 있다. 따라서 (A)에는 psychology가 (B)에는 responsibility가 들어가는 것이 적절하다.

어 휘 offensive 불쾌한, 무례한 antisocial 반사회적인 temper 기질 green light 허락 yell 소리 지르다 neutrality 중립 abuse 남용하다 offender 범죄자, 위반자 accountable 책임이 있는, 설명할 의무가 있는

More Practice

01 ①	02 ①	03 ①	04 ②

01 ① 한 심리학 연구에서 연구자들은 두 그룹의 학생들에게 설문지를 나누어주고 이메일로 응답하도록 요청했다. 모든 질문은 은행 계좌를 개설하는 것과 같은 일상적인 업무와 관련이 있었다. 그러나 두 그룹은 질문에 대답을 하는 데 있어 다른 지시를 받았다. 첫 번째 그룹의 학생들은 개인의 특징과 같은 어떤 실체가 없는 정보에 대해 그 활동이 무엇을 암시하는지 쓰게 되었는데 예를 들자면 어떤 유형의 사람이 은행 계좌를 가졌는가와 같은 것이었다. 두 번째 그룹은 과정의 특정 단계, 즉 예를 들어 은행원과 말하고, 양식을 쓰고, 초기 입금을 하는 것 등에 대해 간단하게 기록했다. 두 그룹의 응답 시간 사이에는 상당한 차이가 있음이 입증되었다. 첫 번째 그룹의 학생들은 연기하는 경향이 있었으며 실제로 일부는 그 일을 전혀 완료하지 못했다. 반면에, 일의 방법, 시기 및 장소에 초점을 맞춘 두 번째 그룹의 학생들은 첫 번째 그룹보다 빨리 과제를 완료했다.

한 연구에서, 좀 더 (A) 추상적인 관점에서 사고할 필요가 있는 과제를 받은 첫 번째 그룹의 학생들은 다른 그룹의 학생들보다 훨씬 더 많이 답변을 (B) 연기하는 것으로 밝혀졌다.

	(A)		(B)
①	추상적인	……	연기하다
②	추상적인	……	강조하다
③	양적인	……	연기하다
④	실용적인	……	과장하다
⑤	실용적인	……	강조하다

주 제 추상적인 사고의 지연
정답 해설 두 집단에서 행했던 심리학 연구 결과에 대해 이야기하고 있다. 실체가 없는 정보에 대해 생각해야 했던 집단이 과제를 연기하거나 회피하는 경향이 있었다고 말한다. 따라서 요약문의 빈칸 (A)와 (B)에는 각각 '추상적인'과 '연기하다'를 뜻하는 abstract와 postpone이 들어가는 것이 적절하다.

어 휘 have (something) to do with ~와 관련이 있다 intangible 실체가 없는, 무형의 quantitative 양적인

02 ① 많은 10대들은 학교 식당에 있는 모든 사람들처럼 되고 싶어 한다. 원숭이의 행동을 연구한 Erica van de Waal은 "우리는 우리가 생각하는 것처럼 특별하지 않다. 우리는 동물들에게서 우리 행동의 근원을 찾

을 수 있다."라고 말한다. 그녀의 연구팀은 야생에서 무리지어 사는 버빗원숭이 109마리에게 분홍색이나 파란색으로 물들인 음식을 주었다. 각 그룹의 한 색깔은 맛을 없게 하려고 알로에로 오염되었지만, 처음 몇 번만의 식사를 위한 것이었다. 나중에 맛이 정상으로 돌아와도 원숭이들은 그들이 나쁘다고 생각한 색깔은 먹지 않았다. 그러자 몇몇 파란색을 먹는 원숭이들은 분홍색을 먹는 무리로 갔고 몇몇 분홍색을 먹는 원숭이들은 파란색을 먹는 무리로 갔다. 이것이 연구자들이 행동에서의 동료 압박을 목격한 때이다. 분홍 음식 섭취자들로 가득한 지역으로 이동한 파란 음식 섭취자들은 그들이 분홍 음식을 과거에 피했음에도 불구하고 바뀌었다. 분홍색 섭취자들 또한 그들이 파란 음식 지역으로 이동했을 때 변했다. 그들은 다른 모두가 먹는 것을 먹었다.

⬇

버빗원숭이의 (A) 음식 바꿈 행동은 새로운 그룹에서의 (B) 사회적 순응의 결과인 것으로 생각된다.

	(A)		(B)
①	음식 바꿈	……	사회적 순응
②	음식 바꿈	……	식품 풍부
③	식사 거부	……	권력 투쟁
④	식사 거부	……	식품 풍부
⑤	접촉 거부	……	사회적 순응

주제 동물을 통해 알아낸 인간 행동 양식

정답 해설 원래 먹지 않던 것임에도 동료들의 압박에 의해 먹던 음식의 취향을 바꾸는 버빗원숭이들의 행동을 통해 새 그룹에서 살아가기 위해 그 그룹의 사회에 순응하는 동물들의 행동을 엿볼 수 있다. 따라서 (A)에는 switching food가 (B)에는 social conformity가 적절하다.

어 휘 conduct 시행하다 tint ~에 색을 칠하다 taint 오염시키다 conformity 순응

시터, 사냥터 및 기타 휴양지에 지나치게 몰리거나 교통과 보행의 혼잡을 초래할지도 모른다는 우려를 표한다. 몇 가지 연구들은 환경 훼손과 관광산업의 관계에 대해 주민들이 가지는 생각의 차이가 관광산업의 유형, 주민들이 자연환경이 보호될 필요가 있다고 느끼는 정도, 그리고 주민들이 관광 명소에서 떨어져 사는 거리와 연관이 있음을 보여 준다.

⬇

주민들은 관광산업의 환경에 대한 영향을 동일하게 (A) 평가하지 않는데, 왜냐하면 그들이 관광산업의 유형, 보호 정도에 관한 의견, 그리고 관광 명소로부터의 거리와 같은 요인을 근거로 (B) 다른 태도를 취하기 때문이다.

	(A)		(B)
①	평가하다	……	다른
②	평가하다	……	공통의
③	평가하다	……	균형 잡힌
④	통제하다	……	호의적인
⑤	통제하다	……	상반되는

주제 주민들의 가치관과 생활 조건에 따라 달라지는 관광산업에 대한 입장

정답 해설 주민들은 관광산업의 유형, 자신들의 가치관, 거주 지역에 따라 판단하는 태도가 달라져 그 환경적 영향을 다르게 평가한다는 내용의 글이다. 따라서 (A)에는 '평가하다'라는 뜻을 가진 weigh가, (B)에는 '다른'이라는 뜻의 dissimilar가 가장 적절하다.

어 휘 evident 명확한 mixed (의견, 생각 등이) 엇갈린 contribute to ~의 원인이 되다, ~에 기여하다 ecological 생태계의, 생태학적인 decline 쇠퇴, 감소 resident 주민, 거주자 attribute A to B A를 B의 탓으로 돌리다 sociocultural 사회문화적인 disturbance 방해 alternatively 그 대신에 pedestrian 보행자(의) variation 차이, 변화

03 ① 관광산업이 환경에 미치는 영향은 과학자들에게는 명확하지만, 모든 주민들이 환경 훼손을 관광산업의 탓으로 돌리지는 않는다. 주민들은 대개 관광산업이 삶의 질에 미치는 경제적이고 몇 가지 사회문화적인 영향에 대해 긍정적인 견해를 가지고 있지만, 환경적 영향에 대한 그들의 반응은 엇갈린다. 몇몇 주민들은 관광산업이 더 많은 공원과 휴양지를 제공하고, 도로와 공공시설의 질을 개선하며, 생태계 쇠퇴의 원인이 되지는 않는다고 생각한다. 많은 이들이 교통 문제, 초만원인 야외 오락 활동이나 공원의 평화로움과 고요함을 방해하는 것에 대해 관광산업을 탓하지는 않는다. 그 대신에 몇몇 주민들은 관광객들이 현지의 낚

04 ② 업무 수행은 개인의 통제 범위를 벗어난 업무 수행에 대한 영향보다는 평가를 받는 개인의 통제 하에 있는 것의 측면에서 판단되어야 한다. 심사 받는 모든 사람의 업무 수행을 억제하는 광범위하고 영향력 있으며 때로 경제적 성격을 띠는 요인이 있을 수 있다. 한 예는 매출액에 관한 것이다. 경제에 일반적인 경기 침체가 있어서 상품이나 서비스가 전년도와 동일한 빈도로 구매되지 않고 있다면, 매출액이 예를 들어 평균 15%만큼 감소될 수 있다. 그렇다면 이 15%(사실은 −15%) 수치는 "평균" 업무 수행을 나타낼 것이다. 아마도 그 해의 가장 우수한 영업사원은 전년도에 비해 매출액이 3%만 감소했을 것이다. 따라서 이러

한 상황에서 '훌륭한' 업무수행이란 어떤 평균 혹은 기준 집단과 비교했을 때 더 적은 양의 감소를 말한다.

⬇

성과 평가에 있어서, 우리는 수치에만 (B) 의존하기보다는 개인의 업무 수행에 영향을 미치는 (A) 상황적 요인들을 고려해야 한다.

	(A)		(B)
①	상황적인	……	제쳐놓다
②	상황적인	……	의존하다
③	통제할 수 있는	……	제쳐놓다
④	긍정적인	……	무시하다
⑤	긍정적인	……	의존하다

주 제] 성과 평가에 상황적 요인을 고려할 필요성

정답 해설] 개인의 업무 수행 실적을 평가할 때에는 경과적인 수치를 보는 동시에 업무를 수행할 당시의 상황을 고려하여 평가해야 한다는 내용의 글이다. 따라서 (A)에는 '상황적인'이라는 뜻의 contextual이 (B)에는 '의존하다'라는 뜻의 rely on이 가장 적절하다.

어 휘] **in terms of** ~의 면에서 **downturn** (경기) 침체 **norm group** 기준 집단, 준거 집단

UNIT 13 무관한 문장

Example ────────────────── 답 ③

예술적으로 멋을 낸 그레인 볼부터 인기 있는 천천히 우린 사골국까지, 메시지는 분명하다. 아름다움과 건강은 영양에 사로잡혔다. ① 오늘날, 정갈하게 먹는 것은 단지 군살 없는 몸을 유지하는 수단이 아니다. 그것은 점점 빽빽하고 바쁜 삶에 맞게 몸을 튼튼히 하는 중요한 단계이다. ② 그러나 점심에 곁들여 메일이 오는, 이 멀티태스킹의 시대에, 모든 사람은 너무 자주, 그들의 접시에 실속 있는 식사를 뺀 많은 것들을 올린다. ③ 이러한 지역 식품에서 얻는 적절한 영양의 결여는 바로 좌식 생활 습관 때문에 악화된다. ④ 전국적인 요구에 대한 대답은 집집마다 찾아가는 편리함과 건강에 좋은 식사를 결합시켜 사업을 시작하는 젊은 요리사와 기술적 선구자들의 물결이다. ⑤ 지난해가 해독주스로 성황이었다면, 지금은 고급 음식 배달의 해가 되어가고 있다.

[주 제] 건강 음식에 대한 관심 증가

Practice

01 ③	02 ②	03 ⑤	04 ④	05 ③
06 ④	07 ②	08 ①	09 ④	10 ②
11 ②	12 ③	13 ④	14 ④	15 ④
16 ④				

01 ③ 원칙적으로 의사가 환자의 최선의 이익을 위해 행동할 때 이타적인 것으로 간주되어서는 안 된다. 그들은 우리가 일상적으로 이타주의와 관련짓는 행동에 대한 선택이 없기 때문이다. 의사는 선택의 차원에서 퇴원시킬 수 없는 환자에 대한 직업적 의무가 있다. 의사가 되어 환자와 전문적인 관계를 맺는 것은 물론 선택적인 행동이다. ① 그러나 의사가 이 관계에 들어서면, 그 또는 그녀는 의무를 선택할 수 없다. ② 의사는 특정 상황에서 특정 환자를 치료하는 것이 인격적이고 직업적인 무결성을 훼손하는 경우에 치료하지 않는 것을 선택할 수 있다. ③ 그러므로 환자를 치료가 필요한 개인으로 보는 의사에게는 잠재적인 갈등이 발생한다. ④ 그러나 의사는 환자의 진료가 다른 의사에게 이송되도록 해야 한다. ⑤ 일단 의사가 되면, 의사는 그의 환자의 의학적 이익을 극대화할 것을 약속한다. 이것은 선택 사항이 아닌 의무 사항이다.

[주 제] 의사의 직업상 의무
[정답 해설] 환자에 대한 의사의 행위는 이타적인 것이기보다는 직업상의 의무라고 말하는 글이다. 따라서 의사가 특정 상황에서 특정 환자를 치료하지 않기로 선택할 수 있다는 내용 다음에는 진료가 다른 의사에게 이송되도록 해야 한다는 내용이 이어지는 것이 문맥상 자연스럽다. 따라서 글의 흐름을 방해하는 문장은 ③이다.
[어 휘] altruistic 이타적인 obligation 의무 compromise 타협하다, (원칙을) 굽히다, 위태롭게 하다 integrity 진실성

02 ② 다른 기후 문제와 달리 해수면 상승의 과학은 매우 간단하다. ① 모든 다양한 상태에서, 해수면은 주로 열이 물에 미치는 영향으로 인해 상승한다. ② 해수면 상승을 막기 위해 물의 분자 구조를 이해하는 것이 가장 중요하다. ③ 대기 온도가 상승함에 따라 대기 중 추가 열의 대부분인 약 90퍼센트가 바다에 가라앉는다. ④ 물이 따뜻해지면 온도계의 수은처럼 팽창한다. ⑤ 이 열팽창은 해수면 상승의 3분의 1을 차지한다. 나머지 3분의 2는 그린란드와 남극의 산악 빙하와 빙상이 녹는 것에서 나온다.

[주 제] 해수면의 상승 원리
[정답 해설] 대기의 열이 해수면 상승의 중요한 원인이라고 설명하는 글이다. 따라서 해수면 상승을 막기 위해 물의 분자 구조를 이해하는 것이 가장 중요하다는 ②는 문맥의 흐름을 방해한다.
[어 휘] combat 싸우다 account for ~의 이유가 되다

03 ⑤ 파스타의 민족적 기원은 오랫동안 논쟁이 되어왔다. ① 많은 이론이 제시되었고, 어떤 것은 특히 억지스러웠다. ② 파스타가 중국에서 이탈리아로 전파되었다는, 13세기 탐험가 마르코 폴로의 저술에 기반을 둔 오래 지속되는 신화는 폴로의 책 Travels의 유명한 구절을 잘못 해석한 데서 비롯되었다. ③ 그것에서 폴로는 파스타와 비슷한 것의 재료가 되는 나무를 언급한다. ④ 그것은 아마도 사고야자 나무였는데, 이것은 파스타와 비슷하지만 파스타는 아닌 녹말 음식을 만들어 낸다. ⑤ 아시아가 본국인 이 나무는 파스타가 중국에서 유래한다는 부정할 수 없는 단서를 제공했다.

[주 제] 파스타의 전파에 대한 논란

정답 해설 파스타가 아시아에서 기원하지 않았다는 점을 설명하는 글이다. 따라서 파스타가 중국에서 유래했다는 ⑤의 내용은 이와 반대된다.

어 휘 ethnic 민족적 far-fetched 억지스러운 enduring 지속하는 misinterpretation 오해 sago 사고 열매 undeniable 부정할 수 없는 originate 기원하다

04 ④

정의의 관념에 대한 또 다른 차이는 법이 무엇인지에 대한 다양한 사회들의 생각에 있다. 서양에서는 사람들은 "법"이 "관습"과는 꽤 다른 것이라 여긴다. "죄악"(종교적인 법을 어기는 것)과 "범죄"(정부의 법을 어기는 것) 간에도 극명한 차이가 있다. ① 그러나 많은 비서구 문화에서는 관습, 법, 그리고 종교적 신념 사이에 차이가 거의 없다. 다른 문화에서 이러한 세 가지는 서로 분리되어 있지만, 여전히 서양의 그것들과는 많이 다르다. ② 이러한 이유들로 인해 어떠한 행동이 한 국가에서는 범죄로 여겨질 수 있지만, 다른 국가에서는 사회적으로 용인될 수 있다. ③ 예를 들면 도둑은 세계 대부분에서는 범죄자로 여겨지지만, 상당한 수준의 공유 생활과 물건을 공유하는 작은 마을에서는, 도둑이라는 단어는 아무 의미가 없을지도 모른다. ④ 작은 마을에서 모든 사람들은 어떤 의미에서는 판사가 되고, 그러한 사회에서 사람의 행동에 대한 사회적인 비난은 강력한 처벌과 범죄에 대한 강력한 억제 수단으로 작용한다. ⑤ 물어보지 않고 무언가를 가져가는 누군가는 단순히 무례한 사람으로 여겨진다.

주 제 사회별 법의 차이

정답 해설 한 지역에서 범죄로 여겨질 수 있는 행동이 다른 지역에서는 사회적으로 용인될 수 있다는 내용의 글이다. 그 예로 생활과 물건을 공유하는 작은 마을에서는 '도둑'이라는 개념이 없을 수도 있다고 언급하고 있다. 따라서 ④는 문맥에 어긋난다.

어 휘 justice 정의 communal 공유의

05 ③

겉으로 보기에, 산업화된 농업은 세계의 굶주림이라는 풀리지 않을 문제에 대한 가장 환영받는 해답으로 여겨졌다. ① 하지만 소위 해답으로 불리는 몇 가지 것들은, 작가이자 농부였던 Wendell Berry가 관찰한 결과, 새로운 문제점을 일으킨다. ② 그리고 지난 수십 년 동안, 산업화된 농업이 사람들의 건강과 지구에 영향을 끼치는 문제를 만드는 주요 원인이 된 것은 점차 분명해졌다. ③ 그래서 새로운 기술을 통해 생긴 기회를 인지한 회사들과 정부는 산업화된 농업의 신속한 발전을 장려했다. ④ 한 예로, 비료와 살

충제의 사용은 암의 더 높은 발병률과 토지, 강줄기 그리고 지하수의 오염을 발생시켰다. ⑤ 단일농업은 생물의 다양성을 감소시켰고, 생태계의 안정성과 생산성을 파괴시켰다.

주 제 산업화된 농업의 문제점

정답 해설 산업화된 농업이 굶주림을 해결할 것으로 여겨졌으나 차차 문제점이 나타났다는 내용의 글이다. 산업화된 농업이 사람들의 건강과 지구에 영향을 끼치는 문제를 만드는 주요 원인이 되었다는 내용 다음 산업화 농업의 발전을 장려했다는 내용이 언급되는 것은 문맥상 부자연스럽다. 따라서 ③은 글의 흐름에 어긋난다.

어 휘 ramify 작게 구분되다 indeed 실로, 참으로 impact 영향 recognize 알아보다, 인지하다 foster 기르다, 양육하다 fertilizer 거름 pesticide 농약 contamination 오염, 더러움 monoculture 단일경작

06 ④

CT 방사선에 대한 새로운 안전 기준을 확실하게 설정하기 위해, 연구자들은 CT 촬영을 받았던 환자들 중 암에 걸린 환자들의 수를 직접 조사하기 시작하는 중이다. ① 향후 몇 년간 십여 건에 해당하는 그러한 연구가 서로 다른 국가에서 발표될 것이다. ② 한편 그러는 사이에 다른 연구자들은 일반적인 CT 촬영에 의해 생성되는 방사선의 양보다 더 적은 양의 방사선으로 선명한 이미지를 만들어 낼 수 있는지 시험해보기 시작했다. ③ Mass 종합 병원의 방사선 전문의들은 그러한 연구를 수행하는 특별한 방법을 가지고 있다. ④ 한 번의 CT 촬영은 사람의 몸에 전통적인 X-ray에 비해서 150~1100배에 달하는 방사선에 노출되게 한다. ⑤ 이러한 방법을 통해 그들은 사람들을 병들게 할 것에 대한 걱정 없이 몇 번이고 인체에 대한 정밀 촬영을 하고 있으며, 그 촬영 결과가 의학적인 문제점을 정확히 발견하였는지 확인하기 위한 부검을 수행하고 있다. 그 연구를 위해 살아있고 숨을 쉬는 지원자들을 고용하는 것보다, 그들은 시체를 통해 연구를 진행한다.

주 제 방사선 사용량을 줄인 인체 촬영법 연구

정답 해설 Mass 종합 병원의 방사선 전문의들이 적은 양의 방사선을 이용하여 선명한 이미지를 만들 수 있는지 연구하는 특별한 방법을 가지고 있다는 내용 다음 CT 촬영시 방사선에 노출되는 정도를 언급하는 것은 문맥상 자연스럽지 않다. 따라서 정답으로는 ④가 적절하다.

어 휘 conclusively 확정적으로 CT computed tomography 의 약자, 컴퓨터 단층 촬영 in the mean time 그러는 동안에, 그 사이에 radiologist 방사선 전문의 subject A to B A가 B를 겪게 하다, 당하게 하다 autopsy 사체 부검, (사후) 정밀 검사 identify 찾다, 발견하다 cadaver (해부용) 시체

07 ②

외국어를 배우는 사람들은 같은 맥락에서 원어민과는 약간 다른 식으로 말하게 되거나, 또는 그 대신에 아예 어떤 말도 하지 않는 것을 선택할지도 모른다. 이것의 가장 좋은 사례들은 화자가 자신이 할 말이나 행동을 어느 정도 유연하게 결정할 수 있는 실제의 대화와 역할극에서 나온다. 학업 지도 시간에도, 원어민들과 유학생들은 서로 다른 말하기 방식을 선호한다. ① 원어민들은 더 많은 제안을 내놓는 반면에, 유학생들은 학업 지도 시간마다 원어민들에 비해 더 많은 거절을 한다. ② 게다가, 조언에 대해 말해주는 행위 자체가 존재하지 않는 것은 학업 조언자에게 있어서 더욱 두드러진다. ③ 제안과 거절이라는 두 가지 말하기 방식은 통제라는 똑같은 기능을 하고 있는 것처럼 보인다. ④ 원어민들은 제안을 제시함으로써 자신의 학사 일정을 통제하려는 권한을 행사한다. 이와 대조적으로 유학생들은 조언을 해주는 사람들이 제시하는 내용을 거부하는 것, 즉 거절을 통해 그렇게 하려고 한다. ⑤ 비록 두 집단 모두 그들이 궁극적으로 수행하게 될 학업 과정에 대한 결정 과정에 참여하게 되는 것이긴 하지만, 면담 과정을 통해 발생되는 조화를 이루는 느낌은 조언자들에게는 매우 다르게 받아들여진다.

주 제 원어민과 유학생 간 제안 및 거절 빈도 차이와 그 역할

정답 해설 원어민과 유학생들의 제안과 거절의 빈도 차이에 대해 언급한 다음, 제안과 거절의 역할을 설명하고 있는 글이다. 따라서 학업 조언자에게 있어서 조언을 말해 주는 행위가 존재하지 않는다는 내용은 문맥상 어울리지 않는다. 따라서 정답으로는 ②가 적절하다.

어 휘 elect 선택하다, 선출하다 alternatively 그 대신, 대안으로 authentic 실제의, 진짜인 per ~을 통해서, ~에 의해서, 마다 salient 현저한, 두드러지는 exert (권한, 영향력 등을) 행사하다

08 ①

세포 배양기술의 발달 덕택에, 연구자들은 진짜에 가깝고 먹을 수 있는 고기를 실험실에서 길러내는 일에 다른 어느 때보다 더욱 가까이 다가섰다. 미국에서 해마다 식량을 위해 도축되는 90억 마리의 동물을 기른다는 윤리적 문제 이상으로 기업 형태의 농장들은 어마어마한 양의 쓰레기를 생산해 낸다. ① 과학자들은 이 쓰레기들을 재활용하는 효율적인 방법을 개발하기 위해 노력하고 있다. ② 그 2조 파운드에 달하는 동물 부산물 쓰레기들은 공기와 물을 오염시킨다. ③ 환경오염 문제 외에도, 고기에 대한 전 세계적인 수요는 2050년에는 지금보다 60% 향상될 것으로 전망되고 있는데, 전체 농경지와 그 닭들과 돼지들, 그리고 소들을 먹이는 데 필요할 곡식들은 아마도 부족하게 될 것이다. ④ 하지만 동물의 세포에서 배양되고 실험실에서 자라게

되는 근육조직인 '시험관 고기'를 생산하는 방식은 이러한 고민을 해결해준다. ⑤ 실제로 그것은 다른 존재하는 고기 생산 방식과 비교했을 때 45% 더 적은 에너지와 99% 더 적은 대지를 사용하고도 군침 돌 만큼 효율적이다.

주 제 세포 배양기술을 이용한 시험관 고기

정답 해설 전체적으로 시험관에서 배양하는 인조 고기에 대한 긍정적인 점들을 설명하고 있는 글이다. 따라서 기업형 농장에서 배출하는 쓰레기를 재활용하는 방법을 개발한다는 내용인 ①은 문맥에 어긋난다.

어 휘 (in) vitro 시험관 hang-up 콤플렉스, 고민, 곤란 mouthwateringly 군침이 돌게, 맛있게

09 ④

유아가 아주 뛰어난 대화 능력을 갖지 못한다는 사실은 우리 모두가 의사소통할 수 있는 능력을 갖고 태어났다는 사실을 이해할 수 없게 만들지도 모른다. ① 언어에 대한 능력은 우리의 눈과 귀, 팔과 다리, 그리고 장기들에 걸쳐서, 우리가 분만실에 있을 때의 작고 소리내어 우는 몸 속에 존재한다. ② 그 능력들은 자극을 받아야만 한다. 우리는 스스로 말을 만들어 내기 위해서 다른 사람들이 하는 말을 들을 필요가 있다. 하지만 우리는 몹시 말을 하고 싶어 하는 존재이다. ③ 신생아들은 참을성 있게 다음과 같은 질문들에 대한 답을 기다리고 있다. "나를 둘러싸고 있는 저 물체들을 나는 뭐라고 불러야 할까? 나는 긍정적이거나 부정적인 문장들을 어떻게 만들까? 나는 어떻게 사물이나 사람들에 대한 감정을 표현할 수 있을까?" ④ 아이들이 그러한 질문에 대한 대답을 명확히 표현할 수 있을 때가 되어서야 부모들은 의사소통을 시작한다. ⑤ 아이들의 두뇌는 이러한 질문들에 대해 본능적으로 대답을 탐색한 다음 마치 스펀지처럼 그것들을 흡수해낸다.

주 제 유아의 언어 습득

정답 해설 유아의 언어 습득 능력에 대한 글이다. 따라서 부모가 의사소통을 시작하는 시기를 언급한 ④는 문맥에 어긋난다.

어 휘 sparkling 반짝이는, 아주 뛰어난 obscure 모호하게 하다, 이해하기 어렵게 하다 articulate (생각, 감정 등을) 분명히 표현하다 instinctively 본능적으로, 반사적으로

10 ②

내 근처에서 작업을 했던 남자들 몇 명은 나를 보고는 웃곤 했다. ① 나이가 많은 두세 명의 남자들이 나에게 바르게 삽질하는 방법을 가르쳐주는 수고를 자청했다. "자네는 지금 잘못 하고 있네." 한 남자가 잔소리를 해댔다. ② 매일 아침 7시쯤 시작했기 때문에, 나는 내 몸이

첫 삽을 뜨지 않으려고 저항하는 것처럼 느끼곤 했다. "등을 너무 무리해서 사용하지 말게." 그가 가르쳤다. ③ 나는 조바심을 내며 듣고 건성으로 쳐다보며 서 있었다. 그러다 나는 작업을 통해 두꺼워진 그의 손가락들이 삽을 움켜잡고 있는 것을 알아챘다. 나는 짜증이 났고 내가 잘못된 방식으로 삽질하는 것을 즐기고 있다고 그에게 말하고 싶었다. 나는 막 그러려고 했지만, 결과적으로 나는 아무 말도 하지 않았다. ④ 오히려 그 순간 나는 내가 단 몇 주 간의 일을 통해 진짜 일꾼의 세계로 들어서는 자격을 얻기를 기대한다면 스스로를 바보로 만드는 일이라는 사실을 깨달았다. 나는 부모님이 "진짜 일"이라는 말을 통해 의미하신 바를 석 달 안에 배우지는 못할 것이다. 나에게 있어서 노력과 피로에서 느껴지는 기분은 음미할 수 있는 것이었다. ⑤ 우리 부모님이 나와 같은 나이였을 때, 나와 비슷한 일을 하셨다면 그러한 기분은 두려운 것이었을 것이다. 피로는 그들의 몸과 마음에 다른 대가를 취했다.

주 제) 삽질하는 방법을 배우며 알게 된 교훈
정답 해설) 본문의 장면은 한 남자가 '나'에게 잘못된 삽질을 지적하고 고쳐주는 장면이다. ②의 앞, 뒤에 나오는 남자의 지적과 몸이 삽질을 하지 않으려고 저항하는 것 같다는 '나'의 느낌은 관련이 없다.

어 휘) vaguely 막연하게, 공허하게, 애매하게 clutch 움켜잡다, 사로잡다 take toll on 나쁜 영향을 끼치다, 대가를 받다.

---

11 ② "당신의 혈액형은 무엇인가?"라는 질문은 서양인들의 관점에서는 익숙하지 않은 질문이다. 한국인과 일본인의 관점에서 볼 때 그러한 질문은 꽤 일반적이다. ① 이 문화권의 사람들은 특수한 성격적 특성이 혈액형과 관련되어 있다고 믿는다. ② 하지만 오늘날에는 더욱더 많은 서양인들이 이러한 겉보기에는 연관이 없을 것 같은 두 가지 특징 사이의 관계에 대해 받아들이고 있다. ③ 이러한 믿음은 서양인들의 점성학과 별자리에 대한 관념과 매우 비슷하다. ④ 대부분의 서양인들은 혈액형과 성격 사이의 관계에 대한 개념을 모르고 있기 때문에 그러한 질문에 굉장히 놀라워한다. ⑤ 실제로 수많은 서양인들은 심지어 그들 자신의 혈액형조차 알지 못한다.

주 제) 혈액형과 성격의 관계에 대한 동서양의 차이
정답 해설) 혈액형과 성격이 관련이 있다고 믿는 것이 동양에서는 익숙하지만 서양에서는 그런 생각이 익숙하지 않다는 내용의 글이다. 따라서 오늘날 더 많은 서양인들이 혈액형과 성격이 관련 있다는 생각을 믿고 있다는 ②는 문맥상 적절하지 않다.

어 휘) perspective 관점, 시각 buy into ~을 믿다. ~을 따르다. astrology 점성학 zodiac 12궁도, 12별자리

---

12 ③ 5월 18일 아침 8시 32분에, St. Helens 산은 말 그대로, 그 산 정상을 날려버렸다. 갑자기 그 산은 이전보다 1,300피트 낮아졌다. 같은 순간에, 리히터 규모 5 강도의 지진이 기록되었다. ① 그것은 뜨거운 바위, 눈과 얼음이 섞인 눈사태를 초래했다. ② 엄청나게 뜨거운 화산 가스와 암석 파편의 물결은 화산의 측면에서 시간당 200 마일의 속도로 뿜어져 나왔다. ③ St. Helens 산의 화산 활동이 우리의 기후에 영향을 미쳤음은 의심할 여지가 없는 일이다. ④ 밀려 내려오는 얼음과 눈이 녹으면서 진흙과 화산 분출물로 뒤섞인 파괴적인 급류를 촉발시켰으며, 이는 경로에 있는 모든 생명을 파괴시켰다. ⑤ 분쇄된 바위는 대기에 먼지 구름으로 올라갔다. 마지막으로, 화산재와 가스 구름과 함께 용암은 화산의 새로운 분화구와 측면의 균열에서 솟아올랐다.

주 제) St. Helens 산의 화산 활동
정답 해설) St. Helens 산의 화산 활동 상황을 자세히 묘사한 글이다. 따라서 St. Helens 산의 화산 활동이 기후에 영향을 미친다는 내용의 ③은 글의 흐름에 어긋난다.

어 휘) literally 말 그대로, 문자 그대로 on the Richer scale 리히터 척도로 flank 옆구리, 측면 avalanche 눈사태 scorching 그을리는, 몹시 뜨거운 touch off 폭발을 일으키다, 점화하다 torrent 급류 pulverize 분쇄하다, 가루로 만들다 well out 뿜어져 나오다 crater 분화구, 패인 구멍

---

13 ④ Giganotosaurus의 유해는 가죽을 포함하지 않기 때문에 과학자들은 그들의 색에 대한 가설을 세워야만 한다. ① 그들은 공룡의 가죽의 색에 대하여 근거가 있는 가설을 세우고자 노력했다. ② Giganotosaurus는 작은 먹잇감을 포획했기 때문에 그것의 피부 생김새는 위장을 위하여 주위 환경에 잘 뒤섞이게 했을 가능성이 높다. ③ Giganotosaurus는 현재는 아르헨티나인 아프리카 사바나와 유사한 환경의 잔디 습지에서 살았다. ④ 그것은 초식 공룡들에 비해 훨씬 더 큰 치아를 가지고 있었다. ⑤ 따라서 이 공룡은 아마도 그 주변의 초목과 밀접하게 어울리는 피부색을 가졌을 것이다.

주 제) Giganotosaurus의 피부색 추정
정답 해설) Giganotosaurus의 가죽 색에 대한 추측성 내용이 주를 이룬다. 따라서 Giganotosaurus가 다른 초식 공룡보다 큰 이빨을 가지고 있다는 ④의 내용은 글의 흐름에 어긋난다.

어 휘) skeletal 해골의, 뼈의 theorize 이론을 세우다 camouflage 위장, 위장하다 vegetation 식물, 초목

14 ④ 만약 달이 바다를 움직이게 할 수 있다면 인간의 피도 그렇게 할 수 없을까? 우리 몸은 결국 60% 이상의 물로 되어있다. 아마도 혈액 내의 조수가 우리의 감정과 자기 통제의 밀물과 썰물을 야기할지도 모른다. ① 셰익스피어는 '달이 사람을 미치게 한다.'는 이러한 사실을 어느 정도 감지했다. ② 그리고 실제로 그것은 Robert Louis Stevenson의 소설인 Strange Case of Dr Jekyll and Mr Hyde(지킬 박사와 미스터 하이드)에서 Mr. Hyde의 모델의 역할을 한 사람의 주장이었다. 그는 자신의 범죄를 달에 의한 광기 탓으로 돌렸다. ③ 폭력 범죄 증가가 보름달 아래에서 더 증가한다는 일부 관측 결과가 그러한 생각을 뒷받침한다. 달이 차츰 커지면, 아이스하키 선수들은 페널티 박스에서 더 많은 시간을 보내고, 선수 부상자 부서는 늘어난 사고로 바쁜 시간을 보낸다고 한다. ④ 그리고 하늘에 나타나는 달의 규칙적인 출현은 — 초승달에서 다음 초승달까지 정확히 29일 12시간 44분이 걸리는 — 위안을 주는 상수이다. ⑤ 그럼에도 불구하고, 우리의 일부가 달 아래에서 느끼는 불안 — 갑자기 산을 오르고 싶은 욕망, 그림자 속에 겁쟁이처럼 웅크리거나 또는 뒷다리로 서서 울부짖고 싶은 그러한 욕구는 누구도 부정할 수 없다.

〔주제〕 달이 인간의 감정에 끼치는 영향

〔정답 해설〕 이 글은 달이 인간의 감정 변화에 많은 영향을 주고 있다고 주장하며 달의 변화 주기가 인간의 불안 심리 내지는 광기를 유발한다고 말한다. 그러나 ④번은 달의 주기에 대한 과학적인 내용으로 글의 흐름과 무관하다.

〔어휘〕 ebb 썰물 flow 밀물 sense 감지하다 charge 비난하다 induce ~을 야기하다, 유발하다, 초래하다 lunacy 정신 이상, 광기, 미친 짓 observation 관찰 notion 개념 wax (달이) 차다(↔ wane) casualty department 응급병동 constant 불변의 것 casualty 불의의 사고, 재난, 사상자, 피해자 restlessness 침착하지 못함, 들떠있음

15 ④ 우리가 행하는 모든 의도적인 행동들은 일정한 허용범위를 누린다. ① 우리의 의도는 하나의 규칙으로서 '어떻게 할 것인지' 보다는 '무엇을 할 것인지'에 유일하게 적용된다. ② 내가 전화의 수화기를 들기를 원하든지 자물쇠에 열쇠를 넣기를 원하든지 간에 항상 감사하며 내 눈에 의지한다. 목표물에 손을 안내하고 내가 더듬는 수고도 절약해 준다. 왜냐하면 잘못된 움직임도 시각적인 조정으로 바로 수정되기 때문이다. ③ 엔지니어들의 언어에서 이러한 종류의 상호 작용은 피드백으로 알려져 있다. ④ 엔지니어들의 언어는 어떤 혼동도 없이 아이디어를 전달하기 위하여 항상 간결하고 정확하다. ⑤ 대체적으로 우리는 의도가

'무엇을' 결정하고 피드백이 '어떻게'를 결정한다고 말할 수 있다. 그것은 사람들이 환경을 효율적으로 다룰 수 있도록 하는 상호작용의 특징이다.

〔주제〕 의도와 피드백의 역할 차이

〔정답 해설〕 이 글은 인간의 의도된 행동에 대한 내용이다. 따라서 엔지니어들이 사용하는 어휘의 특성에 대한 내용을 언급하고 있는 ④는 이 글의 흐름과 무관하다.

〔어휘〕 intention 목적, 의지, 의도 concise 간결한, 간단한 latitude 위도, (선택·행동 방식의) 자유 rely on 의존하다 grope 더듬다, 더듬기 interaction 상호작용 feedback 반응 concise 간결한 precise 정밀한 confusion 혼돈 determine 결정하다 enable 가능하게하다 deal with 다루다

16 ④ 불확실성의 회피는 한 문화가 모호함에 의해 위협받는 정도이다. 불확실성에 대한 회피가 "약한" 문화에서는 불확실성을 좀 더 받아들이며, 하루하루 살아가고, 스트레스의 수치가 낮으며, 다른 의견을 받아들이고, 사회적 일탈을 두려워하지 않으며, 좀 더 위험을 감수하고, 젊음을 지향하며, 시간은 공짜라고 믿으며, 여러 가지 규율을 좋아하지 않는다. 불확실성에 대한 회피가 강한 문화에서는 ① 불확실성을 지속되는 위협으로 간주하고, ② 더 큰 스트레스를 경험하며, ③ 서로 다른 의견보다는 합의를 장려하고, ④ 일탈을 바람직한 것으로 여기고 ⑤ 안전 의식이 강하며, 젊은이들을 신뢰하지 않고, 시간은 돈이라 믿으며 여러 가지 규율을 선호한다..

〔주제〕 불확실성의 수용 정도에 따른 문화별 특성

〔정답 해설〕 ①~⑤에는 불확실성에 대한 회피가 약한 문화와 대조되는 불확실성에 대한 회피가 강한 문화의 특징이 언급되는 것이 문맥상 자연스럽다. ④는 불확실성에 대한 회피가 약한 문화의 특징으로 글의 흐름에 어긋난다.

〔어휘〕 distrustful 의심 많은, 의심스러운 ambiguity 애매모호함, 불분명함 dissent 의견을 달리하다

More Practice

01 ④	02 ④	03 ④	04 ②

01 ④ 기원전 776년에 최초의 올림픽 승리자가 기록되었을 때, 로마는 전투 부족에 둘러싸인 한낱 농업 사회에 불과했다. ① 기원전 500년쯤에는, 올림피아에서 운동 경기 프로그램이 확고하고 예측 가능한 양식으로 안착되

었을 때 로마인들은 북쪽에 있는 적대적 이웃 국가인 에트루리아의 지배에 대한 반대 운동을 일으켰다. ② 2세기 이내에, 로마의 군사력, 행정 관료, 언어와 문화가 이탈리아 전역을 지배했다. ③ 그 후에 시칠리아, 카르타고와 그리스에 대한 그들의 제국적 정복이 시작되었다. ④ 게다가, 그리스의 스포츠와 경기는 너무 개인적이었고, 관객에게 어필하기보다는 참여자들에게 너무 맞춰져 있었다. ⑤ 기원전 1세기말 무렵에, 로마 제국은 지중해의 온 가장자리에 이르러, 북쪽으로는 영국, 유럽에서는 다뉴브 강, 동쪽으로는 카스피해까지 뻗었다.

[주 제] 로마의 확대 과정
[정답 해설] 전체적인 글의 내용은 로마가 힘을 키워 점차적으로 지중해까지 세력을 확장했다는 것이다. ④번 문장은 그리스의 스포츠에 대한 이야기이기 때문에 문맥의 흐름을 방해한다.
[어 휘] mere 단지 athletic (운동) 경기의 administrative 행정상의 imperial 제국의 conquest 정복 gear to ~에 맞게 하다 spectator 관중 appeal 매력 rim 가장자리

02 ④ 한 연구는 5947명의 노인 남성 중 매일 (섭취하는) 종합 비타민의 인지 감퇴 예방의 효능을 평가했다. ① 12년의 후속 연구 후에, 전반적인 인지 능력과 언어 기억력에 있어서 종합 비타민과 위약효과 그룹 사이의 차이는 없었다. ② 연구자들은 영양 섭취를 충분히 하는 노년층에서는 종합 비타민 보충이 인지 감퇴를 예방하지 않았다고 결론지었다. ③ 이러한 결론은 종합 비타민, 비타민 B, 비타민 E, C와 오메가 3 지방산을 경미한 인지기능 손상 또는 경미한 정도에서 중간 정도의 치매가 있는 사람들에게 보충한 것을 평가했던 다른 몇몇 연구의 검토에 의해 더욱 더 뒷받침된다. ④ 모든 비타민이 최적의 건강과 두뇌 기능을 위해 요구되지만, 건강한 두뇌를 위해 필수적이라는 점에서 두드러지는 몇몇 비타민이 있다. ⑤ 종합 비타민 섭취가 치매 치료에 어떠한 영향도 미치지 못한다는 점을 보여주면서 이 보충물 중 어느 것도 인지 기능을 개선하지 못했다.

[주 제] 종합 비타민은 두뇌 기능 개선에 아무런 영향을 미치지 않는다.
[정답 해설] 종합 비타민은 치매 치료에 아무런 영향을 미치지 못한다는 내용의 글이다. 따라서 모든 비타민이 두뇌 기능에 요구되고, 몇몇 비타민이 건강한 두뇌를 위해 필수적이라는 ④는 문맥에 어긋난다.
[어 휘] efficacy 효능 multivitamin 종합 비타민 cognitive 인지의 decline 감퇴 placebo 위약효과 overall 전반적인 verbal 언어의 supplement 보충 well-nourished 영양공급이 잘 된 supplementation 보충 impairment 손상 optimal 최적의

03 ④ 1997년 교토 협상 중 브라질은 그 후 브라질 제안으로 알려진 한 가지 제안을 했다. ① 제안의 요점은 나라들이 그 문제에 대해 역사적으로 얼마나 책임이 있었는가에 따라 이제는 배기가스 감축의 부담을 나누어 가져야 한다는 것이었다. ② 다시 말해서, 우리는 각 나라가 그 동안 어느 정도의 온실가스를 대기로 배출했는지 계산하고 그 수치들을 배기가스 감축량 할당에 사용해야 한다. ③ 예컨대, 이는 대부분의 나라들보다 더 오랫동안 배기가스를 배출해 온 독일과 영국 같은 나라들이 그들의 현재 배출량이 가리키는 것보다 더 큰 몫을 감수하게 될 것을 의미한다. ④ 온실 가스는 열을 우주로 다시 반사해서 돌려보내는 대신 이 열을 흡수하여 대기 중에 계속 유지하는 것으로 알려져 왔다. ⑤ 그것은 또한 호주처럼 보다 최근에 산업을 발전시킨 대규모 배출국들은 더 적은 부담을 받게 될 것을 의미한다.

[주 제] 브라질 제안의 내용
[정답 해설] 브라질 제안에서 온실가스 배출량 감축분을 할당하는 기준에 현재 배출량뿐만 아니라 과거의 배출량도 반영할 것을 주장했다는 내용의 글이므로, 온실가스가 열을 흡수한다는 ④는 글의 흐름과 무관하다.
[어 휘] emission 배출가스 concentration 농도 allocate 할당하다, 배분하다 emit 방출하다 bear 부담하다, 떠맡다

04 ② 매우 자주 여러분은 자신이 하는 일 혹은 자신이 시간을 보내는 일로 스스로를 소개하는 사람들을 발견하거나 만날 것이다. 이러한 사람들은 자기 자신을 판매원이나 간부라고 소개한다. ① 이렇게 하는 것이 죄는 아니지만, 정신적으로 우리는 우리가 믿는 존재가 된다. ② 직장에서 우리가 할 수 있는 것을 밝히는 것은 우리가 하는 직업적 경력의 질을 높이는 데 도움이 된다. ③ 이러한 관행을 따르는 사람들은 자신들의 개성을 잃어버리고 자신들이 하는 일에 의해 인식된다는 개념을 가지고 살기 시작하는 경향이 있다. ④ 그러나 일은 영구적이지 않을지도 모르고, 무수한 이유로 일자리를 잃을 수도 있는데, 그 중 몇 가지는 당신에게 책임이 없을지도 모른다. ⑤ 그러한 경우에 이러한 사람들은 피할 수 없는 사회적, 정신적 외상 때문에 고통을 받고 이것은 감정적 스트레스와 한때 그들의 정체성이었던 것과 자신들이 갑자기 단절되었다는 느낌을 받게 된다.

[주 제] 직업을 자신의 정체성으로 삼는 일의 부작용
[정답 해설] 직업으로 자신의 정체성을 확인하는 사람들은 일자리를 잃게 된 경우에 심한 스트레스를 받을 수 있다는 내용의 글이므로, 자신이 하는 일을 밝힘으로서 직업적 이득을 얻을 수

있다는 ②는 글의 흐름과 무관하다.

어휘 executive 경영 간부 criminal 범죄의 enhance 높이다 individuality 개성, 개인성 inevitable 피할 수 없는 mental trauma 정신적 외상 disassociate 단절하다, 관계를 끊다

Example ────────▶ 답 ④

일반적으로 모형은 목적 달성을 위해 만들어진, 실제의 단순화된 묘사이다. 특정 목적을 위해 무엇이 중요하고 중요하지 않은지에 대한 몇 가지 가정을 토대로 하거나 간혹 정보 또는 취급 용이성에 대한 제약에 기초하여 단순화된다. 예를 들어, 지도는 물리적 세계의 모형이다. 이것은 지도 제작자가 그 목적과 관련이 없다고 생각한 엄청난 양의 정보를 추상화한다. 이것은 관련 정보를 보존하고 때로는 더 간소화한다. 예를 들어, 도로 지도는 도로, 기본 위상 기하학, 이동하려는 장소와의 관계 및 기타 관련 정보를 유지하고 강조 표시한다. 다양한 직업은 건축 설계도, 공학 시제품 등의 잘 알려진 모형 유형을 가지고 있다. 이들 각각은 주요 목적과 관련이 없는 세부 사항은 추상화하고 관련이 있는 사항들은 유지한다.

주제 모형의 의의

Practice

01 ④   02 ②   03 ⑤   04 ⑤   05 ④
06 ②

01 ④ 당신이 다른 사람들과 교류할 때, 당신은 자신이 특정한 방식으로 그들을 모방하는 것을 잘 알게 될 것이다. 예를 들면, 당신은 무의식적으로 당신 친구들의 말하는 방식과 억양에 맞추게 된다. 사회 심리학자들은 이러한 모방 유형을 카멜레온 효과라고 이름 붙였다. 카멜레온은 자동적으로 그들의 환경에 맞추기 위해 그들의 색깔을 바꾼다. 사람들은 또한 주변 사람들과 섞이기 위해 자동적으로 그들의 행동을 조정한다. 이러한 형태의 모방은 "사회적인 결속"의 한 유형으로 기능한다고 추측된다. 사람들은 동일한 움직이는 몸짓을 만들어내면서 자신들을 그들 주변의 다른 사람들과 더욱 비슷하게 만든다.

주제 사람의 모방 현상

정답 해설 사람들이 교류할 때 다른 사람을 모방하게 되는 현상인 카멜레온 효과를 설명하고 있다. 주어진 문장은 '사람들은 또한 주변 사람들과 섞이기 위해 자동적으로 그들의 행동을 조정한다'라는 뜻이다. 이 문장은 카멜레온 효과의 한 예시이다. 그리고 '또한'이라는 뜻의 also로 보아 주어진 문장은 카멜레온 효과의 또 다른 예시 이후에 위치해야 함을 알 수 있다. 덧붙여

④ 다음 문장들은 주변 사람들과 섞이기 위해 조정된 행동의 역할을 설명하고 있다. 따라서 주어진 문장이 들어가기에 가장 적절한 위치는 ④이다.

어휘 adjust 맞추다 blend 섞다 unconsciously 무의식적으로 match 맞추다 mimicry 모방 speculate 생각하다, 추측하다 glue 접착제

02 ②
내 딸들 중 한 명이 최근에 결혼을 해서, 나는 200명의 다양한 연령대의 사람들과 딸의 결혼식을 축하해주는 밤을 보냈다. 그들의 나이는 3살짜리 나의 손녀 딸부터 세계 2차 대전에 참전하고 약 50년 동안 법률 및 회계 관련 회사를 운영한 85세의 삼촌까지 다양했다. 어느 순간, 그는 내 뒤에서 박수로 나를 부르고 내게 말했다: "조카야, 오늘 밤 여기 온 모든 사람들이 너의 집 정문을 들어올 때보다 나갈 때 스스로 더 기분 좋게 느끼도록 모든 사람을 만나보고 이야기를 나눴으면 좋겠구나." 그 충고는 내가 좀 더 정신적으로 날카롭게 결정을 내릴 수 있도록 만들어 주었다. 비록 우리의 배우는 능력과 기억력이 나이를 먹어갈수록 줄어들지만, 우리가 중요한 정보를 구별해내는 능력과 경험은 점점 증가한다는 것에 대한 상당한 증거들이 있다. 이것이 바로 지혜라고 알려져 있는 것이고 과학자들은 이제 막 이 분야에 대해서 연구하기 시작했다. 그것의 대표적인 요소들은 좋은 결정, 심리적 통찰력, 길고 다양한 삶의 경험, 감정 통제, 감정 이입적 이해, 그리고 당연히 지식을 포함하고 있다.

주제 삼촌의 충고로 알게 된 지혜의 필요성
정답해설 주어진 문장은 삼촌이 주인공에게 딸의 결혼식 파티에서 해준 말이다. 주어진 문장은 자신의 조카를 위한 삼촌의 충고의 뉘앙스를 담고 있기 때문에 주인공의 상태 변화나 심적 변화가 들어가는 문장 주변에 위치하는 것이 적절하다. ②번 빈칸의 다음 문장을 보면 그의 충고를 들은 후에 주인공이 정신적으로 이성적인 판단을 할 수 있게 되었다고 언급되어있다. 따라서 문맥의 흐름상 ②에 들어가는 것이 제일 적절하다.

어휘 granddaughter 손녀 wisdom 지혜 judgement 판단력 insight 통찰력 empathetic understanding 감정 이입적 이해

03 ⑤
모든 개구리와 두꺼비는 방어를 위한 액상 물질을 분비하는데 그것 중에 대부분은 항생제로서의 특징을 갖고 있다. 그것이 바로 중국의 민간 치료사들이 염증으로 인해 따갑거나 개에게 물린 곳 등의 상처에 두꺼비 분비물을 바르는 이유이며, 그런 분비물들은 종종 거울을 두려워하는 두꺼비들을 거울로 에워싸서 얻어진다. 비록 그런 방법이 생소하게 들릴지 몰라도, 서양의 국가들에서 사용되는 치료약의 상당 부분이 자연에서 그대로 가져온 것이거나 자연에서 발견된 화학식에 의한 것이다. 스테로이드나 페니실린, 디기탈리스, 모르핀, 그리고 아스피린 등은 아주 적은 예에 불과하다. 약학적인 발견에서 가장 흥미로운 것 중의 하나는 바로 Taxol의 발견인데, Taxol은 유방암이나 난소암에 저항하는 성질이 있고 주목 나무의 껍질에서 추출된다. 또 다른 유망한 것들은 실제로 아직까지는 전통 의학 또는 현대 의학 시스템에 의해서도 건드려진 적 없는 거대한 근원, 즉 바다로부터 오게 될 것이다. 가능한 후보에는 남극의 해저로부터 유래될 항생제와 열대 지방의 원뿔 달팽이의 독에서 추출할 진통제 등이 포함되어 있다.

주제 자연에서 비롯된 의약품
정답해설 Other promising leads로 미루어 볼 때 주어진 문장은 자연에서 추출되는 또 다른 의약품에 대한 내용 다음에 위치하는 것이 문맥상 적절하다. 또한 '바다'에서 추출될 수 있는 다른 의약품들에 대한 예시 이전에 위치하는 것이 문맥상 자연스럽다. 따라서 주어진 문장의 가장 적절한 위치는 ⑤이다.

어휘 toad 두꺼비 property 특성, 특징 secrete 분비하다 sore (염증 등으로 인해) 따끔한 상처 chemical formula 화학식 digitalis 디기탈리스(강심제) ovarian 난소의 yew 주목, 주목나무 promising lead 유망한 것, 훌륭한 단서 seabed 해저 cone snail 원뿔 달팽이

04 ⑤
건강 관리 부분에 있어서 다른 어떤 선진국들보다 더 많은 비용을 쓰기 위해 노력하는 국가치고, 미국은 이상하게도 의사들의 수가 부족한 나라이다. 우리는 인구 100,000명당 30명의 1차 진료가 가능한 의사를 보유하고 있다. 그 수치는 다른 산업화된 나라들에 비해서 꽹장히 적은 것이다. 당신은 뉴스 표제에서 미국의 의사 부족에 대한 문제와 베이비부머 세대가 은퇴하면서 이러한 문제가 얼마나 더 나빠지게 될지에 대한 기사를 읽어 본 적이 있을지도 모른다. 이러한 문제들은 아직 건강 보험에 가입하지 않고 있다가 이제 막 가입을 하려는 수백만의 사람들에 의해 더 나빠지게 될 뿐이다. 이러한 모든 사람들을 누가 나서서 치료해 줄 것인가? 가장 유망한 해결책은 발달되고 체계적인 교육 훈련을 받고, 의사가 하는 일과 많은 부분에서 비슷한 일들을 할 수 있도록 자격을 취득한 간호사들과 다른 종류의 임상의 수를 늘리는 것이다.

주제 미국의 의사 부족 문제
정답해설 주어진 문장은 누가 문제점들을 해결할 수 있느냐는

질문이므로, 질문의 앞에는 여러 가지 문제점들에 대해서, 그리고 뒤에는 그 문제에 대한 해결책이 나와야 한다. 따라서 주어진 문장은 ⑤에 위치하는 것이 가장 적절하다.

[어 휘] outspend ~보다 더 많이 소비하다(사용하다) oddly 특이하게, 이상하게 primary-care 1차 진료 clinician 임상의(직접 환자를 보는 의사)

05 ④ 미래에는 전 세계의 점점 더 많은 사람들이 직업에 더 적은 시간을 보내고, 개인적인 일에는 더 많은 시간을 보내게 될 것이다. 그들의 자유시간이 강요된 것인지, 비자발적인 것인지, 그리고 강요된 시간제 업무나 일시적인 해고, 그리고 실업의 결과인지, 아니면 생산성의 향상, 근무시간 단축과 더 나아진 임금에 의해 가능해진 여가시간에 의한 것일지는 정치권에서 해결할 문제로 남아있다. 만약 역사 속에서 알려지지 않았던 어떤 유형의 대량 실업이 인간의 노동력을 대대적으로 기계로 대체하는 과정에 의해 발생하게 된다면 배려심이 넘치고 서로 돌보는 사회를 발전시키는 기회는 희박해질 것이다. 더 가능성이 높은 경과는, 사회적으로 만연한 격변, 일찍이 겪어 보지 못했던 수준의 폭력, 그리고 가난한 사람들이 서로에게 뿐 아니라 세계 경제를 통제하는 부자 엘리트들에게 폭력을 행사하는 야전 상태가 될 것이다. 만약 대신에 근무자에게 더 짧은 근무 시간과, 적절한 소득을 보장하면서 증가된 생산성으로부터 이득을 얻게 하는 바람직한 과정을 추구한다면, 현대 역사상 그 어떤 시기보다도 더 많은 여가 시간이 존재할 것이다. 그 여가 시간은 사회적인 결속을 새롭게 하고, 민주주의적 관습을 새롭게 정비하는 데 사용될 수 있을 것이다. 새로운 세대는 국가주의의 좁은 한계를 초월하고, 서로에게, 그리고 사회에, 더 나아가서는 생태계 전체에 대한 책임을 공유하는, 인류의 한 구성원으로서 행동하고 생각하게 될지도 모른다.

[주 제] 여가 시간 증가에 따른 미래 삶의 모습
[정답 해설] 주어진 문장 앞부분의 If instead(만약 대신에~)를 참고하여 볼 때 주어진 문장의 앞부분에는 주어진 문장과 반대되는 내용이 나와야 한다. ④의 앞부분에서는 부정적인 원인을 통해 여유시간이 많아지는 경우에 대해 예측하고 있고, 주어진 문장을 포함함 이어지는 내용에서는 긍정적인 원인을 통해 여유시간이 많아지는 경우에 대해 예측하고 있다.

[어 휘] enlighten 계몽하다, 깨우쳐 주다 coerce 강요하다, 강제하다 layoff 일시적 해고 political arena 정치권, 정계 compassionate 자비로운, 온정적인 upheaval 혼란, 격동, 변동 unprecedented 이전에 없던, 겪어보지 못한 lash out 덤벼들다, 달려들다 rejuvenate 젊게 만들다, 활기를 띄게 만들다 legacy 유산, 유물 transcend 초월하다, 능가하다 biosphere 생물계, 생물권

06 ② 한 이야기 속의 사건의 나열들을 '플롯'이라고 부른다. 실제 삶에서의 불규칙적인 사건들과는 달리 이야기 속의 플롯은 화자에 의해 조율되고 연출되어야 한다. "시점"도 그래야만 한다. 시점이란 이야기가 서술되는 상위의 위치를 말한다. 그것은 당신이 경기장에서 미식축구 경기를 보는 것과 TV로 시청하는 것의 차이를 생각한다면 이해하기 어려운 개념은 아니다. 카메라는 화면상에서 당신의 시점을 통제한다. 당신은 오직 카메라가 보여주는 것만 보게 된다. 그러나 관람석에서는 자유롭게 경기장 전체를 훑어볼 수 있고 쿼터백이나 라인을 보거나, 치어리더들에 집중할 수도 있다. 당신의 시점은 오직 당신 눈에 의해 결정되는 것이다.

[주 제] 이야기에서 시점의 의미
[정답 해설] 주어진 문장은 시점도 플롯처럼 조율되고 연출되어야 한다는 뜻이므로 시점에 대한 설명과 역할을 설명한 ② 이후 내용의 도입부로 적절하다. 따라서 주어진 문장은 ②에 위치해야 한다.

[어 휘] sequence 연달아 일어남, 연속 narrator 화자, 해설자 quarterback 쿼터백 vantage 우월함, 유리함

More Practice

01 ⑤　　02 ③　　03 ⑤　　04 ⑤

01 ⑤ 플라밍고, 펭귄, 타조, 기린, 돌고래, 악어와 다른 많은 종들은 잠시 동안 그들의 새끼가 다른 다 자란 동물의 보살핌을 받도록 놔둔다. 이것은 부모에게 커져가는 가족을 위해서 가장 영양가 있는 식량을 찾아낼 자유를 제공한다. 새끼 동물들을 돌보는 대리 부모는 대체 누구일까? 돌보미는 무작위로 차례를 정하는 부모일 수도 있고 부모와 관련된 새끼를 낳지 않은 개체일 수도 있다. 이타주의처럼 보일 수도 있지만, 돌보미는 단지 그들이 돌보고 있는 어린 조카나 형제와 연관된 자신의 유전자를 촉진시키고 있는 것이다. 만약 그들의 목표가 유전자를 증진시키는 것이라면, 당신은 이렇게 질문할 수도 있다. 그들은 왜 자신의 새끼를 낳지 않는 걸까? 안정되고 가득 찬 서식지에서는 주어진 해에 새로운 번식자가 자발적으로 독립하기 위해 이용할 수 있는 둥지나 음식이 충분하지 않을 수 있다. 둥지를 트는 장소에 비집고 들어가기보다는 그들을 더 나은 부모로 만들어 줄 기술들을 그동안 연마하면서 1년을 연기할 수 있다.

주제] 돌보미가 존재하는 이유

정답 해설] 어미가 먹이를 찾아 떠날 때 새끼를 대신하여 돌봐주는 동물들에 대한 이야기이다. 그 돌보미들이 누구인지 왜 자신의 새끼를 낳지 않고 다른 새끼를 돌봐주고 있는지에 대한 설명이 나온다. 주어진 문장의 내용은 돌보미가 새끼를 낳지 않는 이유로 알맞다. 따라서 주어진 문장은 ⑤번 빈칸에 들어가는 것이 문맥상 가장 자연스럽다.

어 휘] altruism 이타주의 marginal 주변의 strike out 독립하다

02 ③ 다른 나라들과 일하는 크고 작은 회사들이 점차 증가하고 있다. 어떤 회사들은 외국의 회사에 판매한다. 다른 회사들은 전 세계에서 제품을 구매하여 그들의 국가들로 수입한다. 그들이 국경을 초월하여 제품을 사든지 팔든지 간에, 이러한 사업들은 모두 글로벌 경제를 가속화하는 국제 무역의 규모에 기여한다. 이론적으로, 국제 무역은 주 사이의 무역, 즉, 캘리포니아와 워싱턴 간 무역처럼 논리적이고 가치 있다. 그러나 국가들은 다양한 이유로 특정 상품의 수입을 제한하는 경향이 있다. 예를 들면, 2000년대 초반, 미국은 국내 신선한 토마토의 가격 수준을 낮춘다는 이유로 멕시코의 신선한 토마토 수입을 제한했다. 그러한 제한에도 불구하고, 국제 무역은 제2차 세계대전 이후로 거의 꾸준하게 증가해왔다. 산업화된 국가들 중 많은 국가들은 국제 사업에서의 문제를 제거하고 저개발국가가 국제 무역에 참여하는 것을 도울 목적으로 하는 무역 협정에 서명했다.

주제] 전 세계적인 무역 증대 현상

정답 해설] ③ 앞부분은 국제무역의 증대 현상을 설명하고 있는데 뒷부분은 수입 제한의 예시로 토마토를 들고 있다. 따라서 역접의 접속사 Yet을 포함하고 국가들이 다양한 이유로 특정 상품의 수입을 제한하는 경향이 있다는 내용의 주어진 문장이 들어갈 위치는 ③이 가장 적절하다.

어 휘] fuel ~에 연료를 공급하다 worthwhile 상당한 undercut 남보다 싼 값으로 팔다, (가격을) 내리다

03 ⑤ 여러분이 어렸고 어른들은 무한한 힘을 가졌다고 상상하던 때를 기억하는가? 분명 자동차를 운전하고, 주스 용기를 열고, 개수대에 손이 닿을 수 있는 사람은 비를 그치게 할 수 있을 것이었다. 나는 그것이 우리의 개와 그들의 냄새 맡는 능력과 관련하여 우리가 가지고 있는 기대와 같다고 생각한다. 그들이 코를 사용하는 능력이 아주 뛰어나기 때문에 우리는 그들이 언제나 무엇이든 냄새를 맡을 수 있다고 상정한다. 그렇지만 개들은 다른 감각도 사용

하고, 인간과 개 모두의 뇌는 한 번에 한 가지 감각을 강화하는 경향이 있다. 많은 주인이 머리 모양을 새로 하거나 새 코트를 입고 집에 돌아왔다가 자신의 개에게 물린 적이 있다. 낯선 윤곽이 집으로 밀고 들어오는 광경에 깜짝 놀라, 이 개들은 코 대신 눈을 사용하고 있었다. 그들의 코가 뛰어날 수 있지만, 항상 켜져 있는 것은 아니다.

주제] 개들의 후각의 한계

정답 해설] 주어진 문장은 코 대신 눈을 사용한 개가 낯선 모습에 놀랐다는 내용이므로, 주인이 새로운 머리 모양이나 새로운 코트를 입고 나타났다가 개에 물리기도 한다는 문장 다음인 ⑤에 들어가는 것이 가장 자연스럽다.

어 휘] remarkable 뛰어난, 놀라운 switch on (스위치를) 켜다 silhouette 검은 윤곽, 실루엣 infinite 무한한 expectation 기대 with respect to ~에 대하여 assume 추정하다, 상정하다 intensify 강화하다 snap at ~에 달려들다, ~을 덥석 물다 hairdo 머리 모양

04 ⑤ 음식과 거처에 필요한 기본적인 최소한의 범위 이상의 돈은 목적을 위한 수단에 불과하다. 하지만 아주 흔히 우리는 수단을 목적과 혼동하여 돈(수단)을 위해서 행복(목적)을 희생한다. 우리 사회에서 아주 흔히 그렇듯이, 물질적 부가 궁극적인 목적의 위치에 올랐을 때에 이렇게 되기 쉽다. 이것은 물질적 부의 축적과 생산이 그것 자체로서 잘못된 것이라고 말하는 것이 아니다. 물질적 번영은 사회뿐만 아니라 개인이 더 높은 수준의 행복을 얻을 수 있도록 도와줄 수 있다. 재정적 안정은 우리가 의미 있다고 생각하지 않는 일과 다음 번 봉급을 걱정해야 하는 일로부터 우리를 해방시켜 줄 수 있다. 더욱이, 돈을 벌고자 하는 욕구는 우리에게 도전 정신을 심어 주고 영감을 줄 수 있다. 그렇다고 하더라도, 가치가 있는 것은 '그 자체로'서의 돈이 아니라 그것이 잠재적으로 더 긍정적인 경험을 낳을 수 있다는 사실이다. 물질적 부가 본질적이고 그 자체적으로 반드시 의미를 만들어 내거나 감정적인 풍요로 이끌어 주는 것은 아니다.

주제] 수단일 때에 긍정적인 돈의 가치

정답 해설] 주어진 문장은 돈이 긍정적 역할을 하는 상황을 경험을 가능하게 하는 경우로 한정짓고 있으므로, 돈이 긍정적으로 작용하는 사례를 보여주는 문장과 물질적 부의 한계를 지적하는 문장 사이인 ⑤에 들어가는 것이 가장 자연스럽다.

어 휘] confuse A with B A를 B와 혼동하다 elevate 들어 올리다 ultimate 궁극적인 accumulation 축적, 쌓음

Example

답 ⑤

당신이 가족, 그리고 친구와 함께 하는 모든 식사들로부터, 당신은 아마도 사람들이 매우 다른 음식 선호도를 가지고 있다는 사실을 알고 있을 것이다.

(C) 예를 들면, 어떤 사람들은 매운 음식을 좋아하는 반면, 다른 사람들은 매운 후추만 생각해도 몸서리를 친다. 몇몇 선호는 사람들이 꽤 어린 시절에 경험한 맛의 차이에 의해서 설명된다.

(B) 사실 어머니가 먹는 음식이 양수의 맛을 바꾸어서 어떤 음식 선호는 자궁에서 결정된다. 그러나 사람들은 또한 그들이 가지고 있는 미뢰의 수에서 놀라운 차이를 보여준다.

(A) 평균보다 상당히 미뢰를 많이 가진 집단의 사람들은 초미각자들로 불린다. 사람들의 혀 위 미뢰의 밀도의 차이는 유전적인 것으로 보인다. 여성들은 남성들에 비해 초미각자가 될 가능성이 훨씬 높다.

주 제 | 미뢰 수가 음식 취향에 미치는 영향

Practice

| 01 ② | 02 ⑤ | 03 ④ | 04 ④ | 05 ② |
| 06 ② | 07 ③ | 08 ③ | 09 ③ | 10 ③ |

01 ②
관습법, 달리 말해 판례법으로도 알려져 있는 것은 특정 경우에 대한 판결(또는 결정)을 통해 판사에 의해 개발된 법이다. 판사는 이론과 선례의 규칙에 따라 인도되는데, 즉 '선례'를 정한 이전 판결에 구속된다는 의미이다.

(B) 이는 본질적으로 과거 결정된 유사한 사례, 특히 최고 법원에서 결정된 판결을 고려해야 한다는 것을 의미한다. 이 판사가 만든 법률의 영역은 의회가 법을 제정하지 않은 상황이 있을 때 그 틈새를 메우는 판사에게 넘어가기 때문에 중요하다.

(A) 마찬가지로, 판사는 의회가 통과시킨 법을 해석해야 한다. 한 예가 1967년의 낙태법과 연관이 있었다. 한 비서는 양심에 따라 낙태에 관여하기를 반대할 권리가 그녀의 거부를 보호한다고 주장하면서 임신 중절 수술을 위한 소개서를 타이핑하는 것을 거부했다.

(C) 판사는 '관여'라는 단어를 검토했고 그녀가 절차에 충분

히 포함되지 않았기 때문에 그 비서가 보호되지 않는다는 결론을 내렸다.

주 제 | 관습법의 의미

정답 해설 | 선례에 구속된다는 판례법의 특징을 언급한 주어진 문장 다음 이 의미를 더 자세하게 설명한 (B)가 이어지는 것이 적절하다. 그 다음 판례법을 따르는 것과 마찬가지로 국회에서 통과시킨 법도 따라야 한다는 (A)가 이어진 후 (A)에서 언급된 비서관의 사례의 결론을 언급한 (C)가 이어지는 것이 자연스럽다. 따라서 (B)-(A)-(C)가 글의 순서로 가장 적절하다.

어 휘 | common law 관습법 ruling 결정 precedent 선례 be bound to ~에 속박되다 take into account 고려하다 conscientiously 양심적으로 enact 제정하다 referral 소개

02 ⑤
로봇 공학이 확산되기 시작하면서 한 국가가 로봇 분야에서 성취 가능한 수준은 부분적으로, 사람들이 자신의 삶에 로봇을 얼마나 쉽게 받아들이는가 하는 문화에 달려있다.

(C) 서양과 동양 문화는 로봇을 보는 방식이 크게 다르다. 일본은 로봇에 대한 경제적 필요와 기술적 노하우를 보유하고 있을 뿐만 아니라 문화적 성향이 있다.

(B) 일본인의 80%가 따르는 고대 신토 종교는 물체와 인간 모두 영혼을 가지고 있다고 믿는 애니미즘에 대한 믿음을 포함한다.

(A) 그 결과, 일본 문화는 로봇을 영혼이 없는 기계로 보는 서양 문화보다 로봇 동반자를 실제 동반자로 더 많이 받아들이는 경향이 있다.

주 제 | 문화별 로봇을 대하는 태도 차이

정답 해설 | 사람들이 로봇을 받아들이는 정도에 따라 로봇 분야의 성취가 결정된다는 주어진 문장 다음에 로봇에 대한 동서양의 시각 차이를 언급하면서 일본에게 로봇에 대한 문화적 성향이 있다고 언급한 (C)가 이어지고 이러한 로봇에 대한 성향을 뒷받침하는 종교적 배경을 언급한 (B)가 이어진 다음, 그 결과 일본이 서양보다 로봇을 실제 동반자로 더 많이 받아들인다는 (A)로 마무리되는 것이 문맥상 자연스럽다. 따라서 (C)-(B)-(A)가 글의 흐름으로 가장 적절하다.

어 휘 | era 시대 in part 어느 정도는 readily 쉽게, 기꺼이 predisposition 성향

03 ④
많은 사람들은 여행가가 되길 원하지 않는다. 그들은 자신들의 삶은 그대로 유지하면서 다른 사

람들의 세계를 잠시 스치는 관광객이 되기를 더 원한다.

(C) 그들이 어디에 가든지 자신의 세계를 가지고 가려 하거나 그들이 떠난 세상을 다시 만들려고 시도한다. 그들은 자신이 알고 있는 것이 변질되는 위험을 원치 않으며 그들의 경험이 사실은 얼마나 작고 사소한 것인지 알고 싶어 하지 않는다.

(A) 하지만 진정한 여행가가 되려면, 당신은 그 순간에 기꺼이 자신을 완전히 맡겨버리고 당신의 세계의 중심에서 벗어나야 한다. 당신은 당신이 스스로 찾은 새로운 세상과 그곳의 사람들의 삶을 무조건적으로 믿어봐야 한다.

(B) 그들의 삶의 일부가 되어라. 당신은 이 세계에서 살아갈 수 있는 삶의 가능성이 얼마나 다양한지 알게 될 것이며, 다양한 언어와 문화 아래에서 우리가 모두 사랑하고 사랑받고자 하는, 슬픔보다는 더 많은 즐거움을 누리는 삶을 사는 같은 꿈을 공유한다는 것을 깨달을 것이다.

주 제 진정한 여행가의 조건

정답 해설 많은 사람들이 여행가이기보다는 관광객이기를 선택한다는 주어진 문장 다음에 그 이유를 언급하는 (C)가 이어진 후, 진정한 여행가가 되기 위한 마음가짐을 언급한 (A)가 이어진 다음, 그러한 마음가짐을 가질 때 얻을 수 있는 깨달음을 언급한 (B)가 이어지는 것이 문맥상 자연스럽다. 따라서 (C)-(A)-(B)가 글의 순서로 가장 적절하다.

어 휘 flit 훨훨 날다, 휙 스치다 fabric 구조, 직물 beneath 아래쪽에 recreate 휴양시키다, 기분 전환시키다 security 보안

04 ④ 당신이 새로운 이웃들이 있는 곳으로 막 이사를 했고 사람들을 만나는 데 어려움이 있어서 약간 우울한 기분을 느끼고 있다고 상상해보자.

(B) 그냥 재미로, 당신은 당신을 위해 예정된 미래에 대해 알아보고자 그 지역의 점쟁이에게 가보기로 결정한다. 그 점쟁이는 수정으로 된 공을 바라보고 웃으면서 미래가 밝아 보인다고 말한다. 그녀는 몇 달 안에 많은 친밀하고 충실한 친구들에게 둘러싸이게 될 것이라고 말한다.

(C) 당신은 점쟁이의 말에 안심하고, (점쟁이에게) 도착했을 때보다 훨씬 더 행복함을 느끼며 떠나게 된다. 이제는 당신이 행복을 느끼고 있으며 미래에 대해 확신을

갖게 되었기 때문에, 더 많이 웃고 자주 바깥에 나가서 더 많은 사람들과 이야기를 나누게 된다.

(A) 몇 주가 지나고 나면 당신은 실제로 당신이 가까운 친구들로부터 둘러싸여 있다는 것을 알게 될 것이다. 사실대로 말하자면, 점쟁이가 미래를 들여다보지 않더라도 그 대신 그런 미래를 실제로 이뤄내도록 도와주는 것은 얼마든지 가능한 일이다.

주 제 소망을 실현시키는 말의 효과

정답 해설 새로운 사람을 만날 때 약간 우울한 기분을 느낀다고 상상하라는 주어진 문장 다음 점쟁이를 찾아가 친구들에게 많이 둘러싸이게 될 것이라는 조언을 듣는다는 내용의 (B)가 이어진 후, 점쟁이의 말에 안심하고 바깥에 나가 더 많은 사람들을 만나게 된다는 내용의 (C)가 이어진 다음, 친구들이 많이 생기게 되었다는 결과와 점쟁이가 미래를 실제로 이루도록 도와주었다는 결론이 나오는 (A)가 이어지는 것이 문맥상 자연스럽다. 따라서 (B)-(C)-(A)가 글의 순서로 가장 적절하다.

어 휘 gaze 응시하다 reassure 안심시키다

05 ② 달을 보고 판단해보니, 나는 내가 눈보라 때문에 갇힌 지도 거의 4주가 지났다는 사실을 알게 되었다. 나는 1월 6일자로 더 이상 날짜를 세는 것을 그만두었다. 왜냐하면 그날 갑자기 전망이 더욱 안 좋아졌기 때문이었다.

(A) 거세게 몰려든 구름이 내가 있던 산비탈을 눈으로 에워싸 버렸고, 금세 태양의 좋은 작품들을 무효로 만들었다. 그럼에도 불구하고 해가 잠깐 나오는 사이를 이용해서 나는 조금 걸어 나왔다.

(C) 나는 내가 눈을 공 모양의 얼음으로 단단히 다져서 햇볕 아래 놓아두면, 마실 수 있는 물이 바닥에 떨어질 것이라는 사실을 알게 되었다. 이 방법은 눈이나 얼음을 내 입속에 직접 넣고 녹이는 것보다 훨씬 더 쉬운 방법이었다. 눈으로 만든 공을 녹이는 일은 내 일상에서 빼놓을 수 없는 일종의 의식이 되었다.

(B) 시원한 물이 내 목을 타고 아래로 흘러가는 느낌은 너무 좋아서 거의 중독이 될 지경이었다. 나는 몇 시간도 더 전부터 그 작은 즐거움에 대해 기대했다.

주 제 갇힌 상황에서 벗어난 기쁨

정답 해설 폭풍우 속에 갇힌 글쓴이가 전망이 더욱 안 좋아져서 날짜 세는 것을 그만두었다는 내용 다음에 구름이 산비탈을 눈으로 에워싸 버린 상황에서 글쓴이가 걸어 나왔다는 내용의 (A)가 이어지고, 쌓여 있던 눈을 입에 넣어 녹였다는 내용의 (A)가

(C)가 이어진 후, 그 눈을 마신 소감을 언급한 (B)가 이어지는 것이 문맥상 자연스럽다. 따라서 (A)-(C)-(B)가 글의 순서로 가장 적절하다.

어 휘 prospect 가망, 예상, 전망 bluster 거세게 불다, 고함치다 engulf 에워싸다, 휩싸다 sunny spells 해가 잠깐 나오는 날씨 make progress 진행하다, 전진하다 compact (단단히) 다지다 trickle (액체가) 흘러가다 anticipate 예상하다, 기대하다 beforehand 사전에, 미리

06 ② 논리는 진실을 장려한다. 하지만 우리는 어떤 말이 그 어휘의 일반적인 의미로 볼 때 사실인지 혹은 거짓인지에 대해 확실히 알지 못하거나 또는 충분히 살펴보지 않고서는 깊이 있는 논리적 전개를 해낼 수 없다. 일반적인 발화에서 우리는 '진실'이라는 단어를 통해 어떤 사실과 부합한다는 것을 의미하고, '거짓'이라는 단어를 통해 그 반대 의미를 표현한다. 이제 사실과 부합한다는 서술은 그 문맥 속에서 논리적 규칙을 어기는 것이고, 사실이 아니라는 서술은 그 문맥 속에서 논리적 규칙을 따르는 것일지도 모른다.

(A) 논리학자는 그 자체로써 사실과 직접적인 연관을 가지고 있지는 않고, 대신 논리적 규칙에 따르는 것에 훨씬 더 많은 관련이 있다. 따라서 논리학자는 논리적 규칙을 따르는 것과 논리적 규칙에 따르지 않는 것을 구분하여 표현하기 위해 '유효한'과 '유효하지 않은'이라는 한 쌍의 기술적인 단어들을 사용한다.

(C) 이러한 용어들의 도움으로 논리학자는 특정 발언들이 사실인지 거짓인지에 대해 고민하지 않고도 사고의 규칙을 설정할 수 있다. '유효한'이라는 용어는 라틴어인 'validus' 즉 'strong(강한)'이라는 단어에서 유래한 것이다.

(B) 유효한 여권도 실제로는 문제를 일으킬 수도 있다. 하지만 만약 정식으로 서명이 된 것이고 기한이 만료되지 않은 것이라면, 그 여권은 제 기능을 다 할 것이고 너를 국경 너머로 데려다 줄 것이다. 하지만 반면에 기한이 만료되어 버렸다면, 그 여권은 주인의 눈동자 색이나 다른 사실적 요소들은 정확히 전달해 주겠지만 제 기능을 다 할 수는 없을 것이다. 그 여권은 유효하지 않은 것이다.

주 제 논리학의 유효성

정답 해설 (A)에서는 논리학자에 대해 언급하였고 그들이 사용하는 용어들에 대해 소개했다. (C)에서는 이에 더해 그 용어들에 대해 구체적으로 설명을 했고 (B)에서는 그것들에 대해

구체적인 예를 들어 보였다. 따라서 (A)-(C)-(B) 순서대로 진행하는 것이 가장 자연스럽다.

어 휘 infringe (법규를) 어기다, (권리를) 침해하다 logician 논리학자 observance 관찰, 관측 respectively 각각의, 각자의 thereto 거기에, 그것에, 게다가, 다시

07 ③ 시각은 우리가 거의 인간으로 지내온 만큼 긴 시간 동안 시각 예술에 의해 도움을 받고 밝혀져 왔다. 백년 조금 넘어, 그것은 또한 카메라에 의해 제공되었다.

(B) 잘 사용하면 카메라는 볼 수 있는 우리의 능력을 개발하고 즐겁게 한다는 점에서 고유하다. 악용되거나 무관심하게 사용된다면 그것은 그 능력을 더럽히거나 파괴하는 힘에 있어 독보적이다. "카메라는 결코 거짓말을 하지 않습니다."라는 말은 이제 대부분의 사람들에게 분명 어리석은 말임이 분명하다.

(C) 하지만 대부분의 사람들이 카메라가 얼마나 특별하게 교활한 거짓말쟁이인지 깨닫고 있느냐는 여전히 의심스럽다. 카메라는 눈과 마음, 정신, 그리고 찍는 사람의 기술 속에 있는 인상적이면서도 대체로 매우 잔인할 정도로 냉혹하게 사실 그대로를 기록하는 단순한 기계일 뿐이다.

(A) 일반적으로 비교적 소수의 조작자들만이, 특히 이러한 면에서 천부적인 기술적 스킬을 부여받았기 때문에, 결과는 대개 실망스럽다. 보수적인 측면에서 지난 10년에서 15년 동안 카메라가 수많은 사람들의 눈을 현혹시켰다고 평가하는 것은 당연한 것으로 보인다.

주 제 카메라의 거짓말

정답 해설 주어진 글은 카메라의 효용에 대해 언급하고 있다. (B)는 카메라의 이점을 언급한 뒤 카메라가 거짓말을 할 수 있다고 말하고 있으므로 주어진 글 다음에 오는 것이 적절하다. (C)는 역접의 접속사로 시작하며 사람들이 카메라가 거짓말을 할 수 있다는 사실을 잘 깨닫고 있지 않다고 언급하므로 (B) 다음에 오는 것이 적절하다. 사람의 의도를 반영하는 카메라의 속성을 언급한 (C)의 뒷부분에 이어서 소수의 기술자들에 의해 카메라가 수많은 사람들을 현혹시켰다고 말하는 (A)가 오는 것이 자연스럽다. 따라서 (B)-(C)-(A)가 글의 순서로 가장 적절하다.

어 휘 ill used 잘못 사용된 defile 더럽히다, 오염시키다 extraordinarily 비상하게 slippery 미끄러운, 교활한 as a rule 대체로, 대개 endow ~에게 주다, 부여하다 dishearten 낙담시키다, 실망시키다 save ~을 제외하고는 It is well on 잘 진행되다, 상당히 진행되다

08 ③ 코끼리들 사이에서 하루 종일 지내보라! 그러면 당신은 혼란스러워질 것이다. 갑작스럽고 조용하고 동시적인 행동 — 명백하지도 들리지도 않은 이유인데도 도망가는 무리, 동시에 귀를 세우고 그 자리에서 움직이지 않는 흩어져 있는 동물의 무리 — 이러한 행동들은 설명이 필요하지만 어떤 설명도 준비되어 있지 않다.

(B) 기억력과 오감을 초월하는 어떤 알려지지 않은 능력이 코끼리에게, 은밀히 그리고 멀리서도, 다른 코끼리들의 행동과 위치에 대해 알려주는 듯하다.

(D) 나는 Oregon에 있는 Portland의 한 동물원에 방문했을 때 이 가능성 있는 수수께끼에 대한 단서를 우연히 마주치게 되었다. 세 마리의 아시아 코끼리 어미와 그들의 새끼들을 관찰하는 동안, 나는 주변에서 먼 거리에서 울리는 천둥처럼 명백한 진동을 거듭 느낄 수 있었다. 하지만 내 주변은 아주 조용했다.

(C) 나중에야 어떤 생각이 떠올랐다. 내가 어린 시절 뉴욕에서 성가대 활동을 할 때 나는 교회의 가장 크고 깊은 오르간 파이프 옆에 서곤 했다. 그 오르간이 바흐 합창의 베이스 라인을 큰 소리로 울릴 때, 교회 전체는 마치 동물원의 코끼리 사육장에서 그랬던 것처럼 진동하곤 했었다.

(A) 알고 보니, 오르간의 파이프처럼, 코끼리가 진동을 일으키는 원인이라고 밝혀졌다. 코끼리는 사람이 듣기에는 너무 낮은 소리를 이용해서 서로 간에 의사소통을 한다.

주 제 코끼리의 의사소통
정답 해설 주어진 글은 설명이 되지 않는 코끼리들의 행동을 언급하고 있다. 따라서 이러한 코끼리들의 행동의 의도가 의사소통이라고 추측한 (B)가 이어지는 것이 적절하다. 그 다음 화자의 추측에 대한 단서가 되는 경험이 이어지는 것이 적절하다. (D)는 이러한 경험의 첫 부분으로 동물원에서 코끼리들을 관찰하면서 느낀 진동을 언급하고 있다. 따라서 (B) 다음에는 (D)가 오는 것이 적절하다. 그 다음 이 진동을 어린 시절 교회 오르간 파이프 옆에서 느꼈던 진동과 비교한 (C)가 오는 것이 자연스럽다. 마지막으로 진동의 원인이 코끼리이며 사람이 듣기에는 매우 낮은 소리로 코끼리들이 의사소통을 한다는 내용의 (A)가 이어지는 것이 적절하다. 따라서 가장 적절한 글의 순서는 (B)-(D)-(C)-(A)이다.

어 휘 synchronous 동시에 발생하는 herd 짐승의 떼, 무리 take a flight 이동(비행)하다 apparent 분명한 audible 청각의 scatter 뿔뿔이 흩어버리다, 해산시키다 whereabouts 소재, 행방 palpable 명백한, 뚜렷한 calves 새끼들(calf의 복수형) chorale 합창곡, 성가 throb 진동하다, 고동치다 pitch 던지다, 음의 높이를 정하다 chapel 채플, 예배당 stumble (우연히) 발견하다 clue 실마

09 ③ 운이 좋은 사람들은 불운한 사람들보다 기회를 더 만들고, 잘 알아차리고 기회에 따라 행동하는 경향이 있다.

(C) 그들은 이것을 다양한 방식으로 실행한다. 그들은 외향적이기 때문에 많은 사람들과 대화를 시작한다.

(A) 그들의 사회적인 흡입력 때문에 더욱 많은 사람들이 그들과 대화하기 시작한다. 그들은 사람들과의 관계를 다루는 것 또한 능숙하다.

(B) 운이 좋은 사람들은 또한 불운한 사람들에 비해 더 여유롭고, 이런 점이 그들로 하여금 삶의 다양한 방면의 예상치 못한 기회들을 더 잘 알아챌 수 있게 한다.

마지막으로 운이 좋은 사람들은 스스로의 삶에 더 많은 변화와 새로운 경험을 들여 오고, 또한 이것은 그들이 얻은 기회를 경험하고 극대화 할 수 있도록 해준다.

주 제 운이 좋은 사람들의 특징
정답 해설 주어진 첫 번째 글은 운이 좋은 사람이 불운한 사람과 구별되는 특징으로 기회를 더 만들고, 잘 알아차리고, 기회에 따라 행동하는 모습을 언급하고 있다. 그 다음 이것을 다양한 방식으로 실행한다고 언급하고 그 사례로 대화를 든 (C)가 이어지는 것이 적절하다. 그리고 대화에 대해 더 자세히 설명한 (A)가 이어지는 것이 자연스럽다. (B)는 운이 좋은 사람의 또 다른 특징인 여유와 그 효용을 언급하고 있으므로 (A) 다음에 이어지는 것이 적절하다. 따라서 (C)-(A)-(B)가 글의 내용으로 가장 적절하다.

어 휘 initiate 시작하다 maximize 극대화하다 extrovert 외향적인, 외향적인 사람 magnetism 자석의 성질, 끌어들이는 힘

10 ③ Gutenberg는 출판계에 두 가지 독창적인 기술적 공헌을 한 것으로 보인다. 그는 새로운 기본 잉크를 개발했다.

(A) 그의 잉크는 종이보다는 동물 가죽으로 만든 피지에 더 적합했으나 종이가 피지를 대체하고 있었기 때문에 이 개선은 그다지 중요한 것은 아니었다.

(D) 반면에 그의 활자 주조 과정 정비는 매우 중요한 발전

이었다. Gutenberg는 활자 도구인 손으로 잡는 작은 주형을 개량하여 액체 금속을 부어 넣을 수 있도록 하였다.

(C) 이는 문장으로 조합하여 인쇄하고 분해하면 재사용이 가능한, 소위 sorts라고 불리는 개별적인 활자를 가능하게 하였다. 활자를 만들어낸 틀도 다시 사용할 수 있어 1분에 활자 4벌을 만들어 낼 수 있었고, 쉽게 분해될 수 있었다.

(B) 본문의 각 페이지마다 많은 활자들이 필요했고 반복해서 사용되어 빨리 닳았으므로 주형은 아주 중요한 발전이었다.

주제 출판계에서 Gutenberg의 공헌

정답 해설 주어진 글은 Gutenberg가 출판계에 두 가지 공헌을 했다고 언급하면서 그 첫째로 새로운 기본 잉크를 개발했다고 말한다. 따라서 개발한 잉크의 특징과 잉크의 개발은 중요한 것은 아니었다고 언급한 (A)가 이어지는 것이 적절하다. 그 다음 또 다른 공헌이자 중요하게 여겨지는 활자 주조 과정 정비에 대한 내용이 시작되는 (D)가 이어지는 것이 적절하다. 그 다음 (D)에서 언급한 주형의 내용을 자세히 설명한 (C)가 이어진 후 (C)에서 자세히 설명된 주형의 가치를 언급한 (B)가 그 다음에 이어지는 것이 자연스럽다. 따라서 (A)-(D)-(C)-(B)가 글의 순서로 적절하다.

어휘 refinement 정제, 정련 reusable 다시 쓸 수 있는 vellum 피지(동물 가죽), 피지에 쓴 문서

More Practice

01 ⑤   02 ④   03 ②   04 ②

01 ⑤ 사람들을 지도하는 것의 가장 가치 있는 성과 중 하나는 지도하는 과정에서 당신 또한 자신을 발전시킨다는 것이다. 우리 자신을 변화시키도록 자극하는 것은 바로 다른 사람들을 성장시키려는 진정한 열정과 의지이다.

(C) 다른 사람들을 발전시키기 위해서는 우선 우리 자신을 발전시켜야 한다. 그리고 다른 사람들을 지속적으로 변화시키기 위해서 우리는 계속해서 자신을 변화시킬 수밖에 없다. 우리가 지도하기 전에, 우리는 배우고, 준비하며, 우리가 어떻게 효과적인 지도자가 될 수 있는지를 생각한다.

(B) 지도하는 동안, 우리는 실습 경험을 쌓고 지도하는 스킬과 테크닉을 연습한다. 지도 후, 우리는 대화 도중에 일어났던 일과 잘된 일, 못한 일, 그리고 다음에 더 잘할 수 있는 일을 생각한다.

(A) 이 학습의 주기는 전체 지도 관계에서 반복된다. 우리가 더 많은 사람들을 지도할수록, 우리는 전문적이고 개인적인 삶의 여러 측면에서 우리를 도울 지도의 지식, 기술 및 역량을 심어준다.

주제 지도의 과정과 가치

정답 해설 주어진 글은 지도의 과정과 가치에 대해 서술하고 있다. 주어진 문장에서 언급된 지도가 지도하는 사람에게 미치는 영향과 일맥상통하는 내용이 (C)에 나온다. 그 다음 (C)의 마지막 부분에 나오는 효과적인 지도자가 되기 위한 고민을 (B)에서 상세하게 설명하고 있다. 마지막으로 (A)에서는 지도 과정이 반복된다면서 앞 내용을 정리하고 있다. 따라서 이 글의 가장 적절한 흐름은 (C)-(B)-(A)가 된다.

어휘 spur 자극하다 cannot help but ~할 수 밖에 없다

02 ④ 어기는 것이 너무나 고통을 주어서 그 가능성을 생각조차 하지 않는 특정한 규칙들이 있다. 우리는 거의 그것들을 깨뜨리지 않는다. 나는 이를 한계 규칙이라고 부른다.

(C) 예를 들면, 내가 만일 "당신이 절대 하지 않을 일이 무엇입니까?"라고 묻는다면, 당신은 한계 규칙을 이야기할 것이다. 당신은 절대 어기지 않을 규칙을 이야기할 것이다. 왜? 당신은 그것을 너무 많은 고통과 연관시키기 때문이다.

(A) 역으로 우리는 우리가 어기고 싶지 않은 몇몇 규칙을 가지고 있다. 나는 이것을 개인적인 기준이라고 부른다. 우리가 그것들을 어기면 기분이 좋지 않지만, 이유에 따라 우리는 잠시 동안 그것들을 기꺼이 어긴다. 이 두 가지 규칙의 차이는 종종 의무와 당위로 표현된다.

(B) 우리는 우리가 해야만 하는 특정의 것들, 우리가 하지 말아야 하는 특정의 것들, 우리가 절대 하지 말아야 할 것들, 그리고 우리가 항상 해야만 하는 것들이 있다. "해야만 하는" 규칙들과 "절대 하지 말아야 하는" 규칙들은 한계 규칙이다. "해야 하"고 "절대 하지 않는" 규칙들은 개인적인 기준들이다. 이 모두는 우리의 삶에 체계를 부여한다.

주제 한계 규칙과 개인적인 기준

정답 해설 주어진 문장은 한계 규칙에 대한 정의이다. 그 다음 한계 규칙에 대해 부연 설명한 (C)가 이어지는 것이 문맥상 자연스럽다. 그 다음 Conversely라는 부사에 이어서 개인적인 기준에 대해 설명한 (A)가 이어진 후 한계 규칙과 개인적인 기준들을 함께 설명하며 정리하는 (B)가 이어지는 것이 적절하다. 따라서 이 글의 가장 적절한 흐름은 (C)-(A)-(B)가 된다.

어휘 certain 특정한 threshold rule 한계 규칙

03 ② 진화는 동물이 남기는 후손들의 수를 최대화하기 위해 작용한다. 동물이 성장함에 따라 어로행위로 죽을 위험이 증가하는 상황에서, 진화는 천천히 성장하고, 더 어린 나이에 그리고 더 작을 때에 성숙해, 더 일찍 번식을 하는 쪽을 선호한다.

(B) 이것은 정확하게 우리가 현재 야생에서 보는 것이다. 캐나다의 St. Lawrence 만에 사는 대구는 현재 네 살쯤 되었을 때 번식을 시작한다. 40년 전에 그것들은 성숙기에 도달하려면 6세 혹은 7세가 될 때까지 기다려야만 했다. 북해의 가자미는 1950년에 그랬던 것에 비해 체중이 절반 정도만 되면 성숙한다.

(A) 분명히 이러한 적응은 과도한 어로행위에 의해 심한 압박을 받는 종들에게는 좋은 소식일까? 꼭 그렇지는 않다. 어린 물고기는 몸집이 큰 동물들보다 훨씬 더 적은 수의 알을 낳으며, 많은 기업형 어업이 현재 너무나도 집중적이어서 성숙기의 연령을 지나서 2년 넘게 살아남는 동물이 거의 없다.

(C) 동시에 이것은 미래 세대를 보장하는 알이나 유충이 더 적어진다는 것을 의미한다. 어떤 경우에는 오늘날 생산되는 어린 동물의 양이 과거보다 백 배 혹은 심지어 천 배까지도 더 적어서, 종의 생존, 그리고 그것들에 의존하는 어업이 심각한 위기에 처해 있다.

주제 남획 때문에 더 어릴 때 번식하도록 진화하는 어류

정답 해설 동물이 더 어릴 때 번식하게 되는 쪽으로 진화하는 상황을 설명한 주어진 글 다음에 대구와 가자미의 사례를 설명하는 (B)가 오고, 그것이 반드시 좋은 것은 아님을 지적하며 이유를 설명하는 (A)로 이어진 뒤, 그 이유를 부연설명 하는 (C)가 오는 것이 가장 자연스럽다. 따라서 이 글의 가장 적절한 흐름은 (B)-(A)-(C)가 된다.

어휘 evolution 진화 descendant 후손 reproduce 번식하다 hard-pressed 심한 압박을 받는 fishery 어업 intensive 집중적인 maturity 성숙 cod 대구 sole 가자미 larvae 유충

04 ② 살면서 의도적인 변화를 거의 하지 않는 사람들이 있다. 물론, 시간이 지나면서 그들은 더 뚱뚱해지고, 주름이 늘고, 그리고 머리가 희끗희끗해질 것이다.

(B) 그러나 그들은 편안하고 예측 가능한 삶이 쉽다는 이유만으로 똑같은 방식의 머리를 하고, 똑같은 상표의 신발을 사고, 똑같은 아침을 먹으며 판에 박힌 일상을 고수한다. 하지만 연구와 현실의 삶이 모두 보여 주듯이, 다른 많은 사람들은 실제로 중요한 변화를 한다.

(A) 그들은 마라톤을 위해 훈련을 하고, 담배를 끊고, 분야를 바꾸고, 희곡을 쓰고, 기타를 배우고, 또는 살면서 전에 한 번도 춤을 춰 본 적이 없다고 해도 탱고를 배운다. 이 두 집단의 사람들 사이에 있는 차이는 무엇인가?

(C) 그것은 그들의 시각이다. 변화하는 사람들은 변화가 가능한지를 묻지 않으며 변화할 수 없는 이유를 찾지 않는다. 그들은 그저 자신이 원하는 변화를 결정하고 그것을 성취하는 데 필요한 것을 한다. 항상 확고한 결심에서 생겨나는 변화는 최우선이 된다.

주제 의도적 변화를 하는 사람과 하지 않는 사람의 차이

정답 해설 의도적 변화를 하지 않는 사람들도 시간이 흐름에 따라 변한다는 주어진 글 다음에, 그럼에도 그들이 변화 없는 삶을 살며 그와는 반대로 삶에 변화를 주는 사람이 있음을 언급하는 (B)가 온 뒤, 의도된 변화의 예를 나열하며 두 집단의 차이를 묻는 (A)가 오고, 두 집단의 차이에 대해 설명하는 (C)로 이어지는 것이 가장 자연스럽다. 따라서 이 글의 가장 적절한 흐름은 (B)-(A)-(C)가 된다.

어휘 intentional 의도적인 switch 바꾸다 take up ~을 배우다, 시작하다 stick to ~을 고수하다 routine 판에 박힌 일상 for no reason other than ~라는 이유만으로 predictable 예측 가능한 accomplish 성취하다 stem from ~에서 생기다 firm 확고한

Example
답 ⑤

당신은 아마, 당신의 대부분의 과거 경험들에 대해 기억을 재구성할 필요가 있다는 것에 동의할 것이다. 예를 들어, 누군가 당신에게 3년 전 당신의 생일을 어떻게 보냈냐고 묻는다면, 당신은 시간을 되짚고 맥락을 재현하려고 노력할 것이다. (A) 그러나 사람들이 그들의 기억이 원래의 사건에 완전히 충실하게 남아있다고 믿는 어떠한 상황들이 있다. 플래시 전구 기억이라고 불리는 이런 유형의 기억은 사람들이 격렬한 감정을 느낀 사건을 경험할 때 일어난다. 사람의 기억은 너무 선명해서 원래 사건의 사진처럼 남아있다. 플래시 전구 기억의 최초의 연구는 대중적인 사건에 대한 사람들의 회상에 초점을 맞췄다. (B) 예를 들어, 연구자들은 참여자들에게 그들이 John F. Kennedy의 암살에 대해 처음에 어떻게 알게 되었는지에 관한 구체적인 기억을 가지고 있는지 물었다. 참가자 80명 중 한명을 제외하고는 모두 선명한 기억을 가지고 있다고 답했다.

	(A)		(B)
①	결과적으로	……	따라서
②	결과적으로	……	예를 들어
③	게다가	……	그러나
④	게다가	……	따라서
⑤	그러나	……	예를 들어

주 제 ┃ 플래시 전구 기억의 선명함

Practice

01 ④	02 ④	03 ⑤	04 ③	05 ③
06 ⑤	07 ②			

01 ④ 국가들을 비교하는 하나의 기본적인 기준은 그들의 경제 발달 수준이다. 경제학자들이 경제 발전을 측정하기 위해 사용하는 가장 일반적인 방식은 국내총생산(GDP)이다. GDP는 한 국가의 1인당 평균소득에 대한 기본적인 척도를 제공한다. (A) 그러나, GDP 통계는 꽤 오해하기 쉽다. 우선 한 가지는, 사람들은 다른 나라보다 어떤 나라에서 훨씬 더 많이 벌지도 모르는데, 그러한 대략적인 수치는 그러한 나라의 상대적인 생계비용에 대한 반영을 하지 않는다. (B) 게다가 국가 통화 간 환율이 오르거나 떨어짐에 따라, 국가는 실제보다 더 부유하거나 가난한 것으로 보일 수도 있다.

	(A)		(B)
①	그에 반해서	……	그러나
②	그에 반해서	……	예를 들어
③	게다가	……	그러므로
④	그러나	……	게다가
⑤	그러나	……	그에 반해서

주 제 ┃ GDP 통계의 한계

정답 해설 ┃ (A) 앞부분에서는 GDP는 국가의 1인당 평균 소득에 대한 기본적인 기준을 제공한다는 내용이 나오고 뒷부분에서는 GDP 통계는 오해하기 쉽다면서 오해의 구체적인 내용을 언급하고 있다. GDP에 대해 대립되는 내용을 연결하려면 However가 적절하다. (B) 앞부분에서는 GDP 통계의 오해 사례 중 하나인 상대적 생계비용 미반영 문제를 언급하고 있다. 뒷부분에서는 또 다른 GDP 통계의 오해 사례인 환율 문제를 언급하고 있다. 따라서 Moreover가 적절하다.

어 휘 ┃ criterion 기준 gross 총계의 benchmark 기준, 척도 per capita 1인당 exchange rate 환율 currency 통화

02 ④ 연쇄반응은 이 세상 어디에서나 발생한다. 화학 공장에서 활성화된 하나의 분자가 이웃한 분자를 자극하여 플라스틱을 만들기 위한 일련의 결합을 촉발할 때에도 연쇄 반응은 일어난다. (A) 게다가 연쇄 반응은 가속화된 원자보다 작은 조각이 무거운 원자와 충돌하여 그것을 쪼개 놓으면서, 이를 반복하여 에너지의 증폭과 함께 이 과정을 확산시키는 더 많은 분자들을 방출하는 원자에서도 흔하게 발생한다. 오늘날 전문가들은 새로운 종류의 위험한 연쇄 반응이 우주에서 진행 중이고, 이는 행성을 벗어나고자 하는 인류의 노력을 제한하는 위협을 한다고 말한다. (B) 예를 들면 그 연쇄 반응은 수십억 달러의 가치가 있는 발전된 통신 시설과, 기상 위성을 파괴될 위험에 처하게 할 수도 있다. 문제는 지구와 가까운 우주 궤도가 작동하거나 멈춘 인공위성들, 분리된 로켓 잔해들과 수많은 부유 파편들을 위한 고물 처리장이 되어버린 것이다.

	(A)		(B)
①	결과적으로	……	그러나
②	게다가	……	그러나
③	대조적으로	……	예를 들어
④	게다가	……	예를 들어
⑤	대조적으로	……	불행히도

주 제 ┃ 연쇄 반응의 사례

정답 해설 ┃ (A)의 뒤에는 연쇄 반응의 또 다른 예가 이어지므로

In addition이, (B)의 뒤에는 앞 문장에 대한 구체적인 설명이 이어지므로 For instance가 적절하다.

어휘 molecule 분자 prompt 신속한, 빠른, 자극하다 cascade 폭포, 폭포처럼 떨어지다 subatomic 원자 내의, 원자보다 작은 particle 미립자, 작은 조각 slam 세게 부딪치다 split 쪼개다 amplify 확대하다, 확장하다 endeavor 노력하다, 애쓰다, 노력 orbit 궤도 junkyard 쓰레기장 whirl 빙빙 돌다, 회전하다 debris 부스러기, 파편

03 ⑤ 19세기의 미국의 철학자인 Henry David Thoreau는 "단순화하라, 단순화하라"라고 말한 것으로 유명하다. 운이 나쁘게도 오늘날의 시류는 "복잡하게 하라, 복잡하게 하라"가 대세이다. 많은 사람들은 어느 때보다도 오랜 시간 일하고, 더 많은 돈을 소비하고 이전보다 더 많은 빚을 지고 있다. 그들은 또한 더 적게 쉬고, 가족이나 친구들과는 더 적은 시간을 보낸다. (A) 하지만 자발적으로 단순함을 지향하는 경향도 있다. 자발적으로 단순화하려는 사람들은 자신의 삶을 더 단순하고, 더 즐겁게 만들기 위한 다양한 조치를 행한다. 어떤 사람들은 매주 더 적은 시간 동안 일한다. 어떤 사람들은 야채 정원 식물을 기르는데, 이는 유기 농산물 뿐만 아니라 그들에게 신선한 공기, 운동, 시간을 제공한다. 어떤 사람들은 덜 구매하려고 노력한다. 그들은 불필요한 상품은 사지 않는다. (B) 요약하자면 이 자발적인 운동을 하는 사람들의 우선순위는 단순화하라는 Thoreau의 제안을 따르는 것이다.

	(A)		(B)
①	더욱이	……	게다가
②	더욱이	……	요약하면
③	따라서	……	게다가
④	하지만	……	유사하게
⑤	하지만	……	요약하면

주제 자발적인 단순함의 추구
정답 해설 (A)를 기준으로 서로 반대되는 내용이 전개되고 있으므로 (A) 뒤에는 역접을 나타내는 however가, (B) 뒤에는 앞에서 주장한 내용을 정리하고 있으므로 in short가 가장 자연스럽다.

어휘 simplicity 단순함 complicate 복잡하게 만들다 priority 우선, 우선순위 organic produce 유기농 제품

04 ③ 1619년 초, 조상들이 미국으로 강제 이주된 흑인 여성들은 너무 끔찍하고 잔인한 환경에서 살았기

에 스스로 재창조를 해야 했다. 그들은 스스로 내면의 안전과 존엄성을 찾아야 했고, 그렇게 하지 않았다면 그 우여곡절이 많은 삶을 견딜 수 없었을 것이다. 그들은 신속하게 자기를 용서하는 방법을 배워야 했다. 왜냐하면 종종 외부의 착취는 그들 내면의 신념과는 반대였기 때문이다. (A) 그럼에도 불구하고 그들은 감염되기 쉽고 아프기 쉬운 환경에서 가능한 한 온전하고 건강하게 생존해야만 했다. 이러한 환경에서 살았던 삶은 말소되거나 꿰뚫을 수 없는 합금으로 벼려진다. (B) 그러므로 초기에 의식적으로, 현실로서의 흑인 여성들은 그들 자신에게만 가능한 것이 되었다. 그들은 다른 사람들에게 추상적인 사람으로, 노동에 있어서는 현실적이었으나 인간성 면에서는 초현실적으로 보여지고 묘사되었다.

	(A)		(B)
①	마찬가지로	……	그러나
②	그럼에도 불구하고	……	게다가
③	그럼에도 불구하고	……	그러므로
④	더욱이	……	게다가
⑤	더욱이	……	그러나

주제 흑인 여성들이 정신적·육체적으로 강해진 배경
정답 해설 (A) 앞부분은 힘든 환경 속에서 내면의 안전과 존엄성을 찾아야 했던 흑인 여성들의 상황에 대한 내용이고 (A) 뒷부분은 육체적으로 힘든 환경 속에서 생존해야 했다는 내용이다. 따라서 (A)에는 Still이 적절하다. (B) 앞 전체 내용은 흑인 여성들이 힘든 환경 속에서 견디면서 정신적, 육체적으로 단단해졌다는 내용이고 (B) 뒷부분은 이를 정리하고 있으므로 (B)에는 Thus가 적절하다.

어휘 cruelty 야만 reinvent 완전히 바꾸다 safety 안전 sanctity 신성, 존엄, 고결 tolerate 인내하다 tortuous 비틀린, 우여곡절이 많은 exterior 외부의 exploit 착취하다, (부당) 이용하다 at odds 차이 나는, 불화한 infectious 전염성의 obliterate 지우다, 없애다 forge 벼리다, 만들다 impenetrable alloy 침투할 수 없는, 불가해한 합금 consciously 의식적으로 abstract 추상적인

05 ③ 우리는 어떤 행동을 하거나 무엇인가를 원하도록 마음이 움직이게 된 것을 나타내기 위해 '동기를 부여하다'라는 단어를 사용한다. 초기의 동기 부여에 대한 설명은 음식, 사회적 지지와 인정과 같은 요소를 얻기 위한 측정 가능한 육체적 '필요'와 '충동'이라고 해석됐다. 하지만 그러한 이론으로는 특정 행동들은 설명이 불가능하다. 왜 누군가는 2년간을 홀로 전 세계를 항해하며 보내려는 것일까? 왜 누군가는 1만 피트 상공에서 목숨을 걸고 비행기에서 낙하하고 싶어 할까? 이러한 예시에서는 필요나 충동이 실제로 작용하는지와 관련된 신체 작용을 확인할 방법이

없다. 필요에 대한 개념이 다양한 행동들에 동기를 부여하는 원인을 설명할 수는 없음에도 불구하고, 사람들이나 개개인의 사이에서 어떤 행동이 계속되는 이유를 설명하기에는 유용한 용어이다.

① 왜냐하면
② 만약
③ 그럼에도 불구하고
④ 고려하여
⑤ ~때

주 제 '필요' 개념의 유용성과 한계
정답 해설 이 글은 '필요'의 개념은 동기부여에 대해서 설명하기에는 부족하지만 '그럼에도 불구하고' 사람들 사이에서 지속되는 행동들을 설명하는 데는 여전히 유용하다고 설명하고 있다. 빈칸의 앞뒤 문장은 서로 상반되는 내용이므로 Although가 적절하다.

어 휘 measurable 측정 가능한 recognition 인식, 인정, 승인 designate 나타내다, 지정하다

06 ⑤ Piaget의 공헌에 대해서는 누구도 이견이 없다. 거의 모든 사회학자들처럼, 나도 그에게 많은 것을 배웠다. 그의 공헌은 비단 학문적인 것뿐만이 아니다. (A) 예를 들면, 아동 중심 학습와 "열린 교육"에 대한 최근의 관심도는 Piaget의 정신 발달과 사고의 본질에 대한 관점으로부터 직접적인 영향을 받은 것이다. (B) 게다가 Piaget가 한계를 의식하지 못했다고 주장하는 것은 Piaget를 잘못 이해하고 있는 것이다. 그가 그의 강력한 지성을 과학적 사고 위에 고정시킴으로써 상상력, 감정 그리고 "살아 낸" 경험의 영역을 무시하기로 선택한 것은 명백한 의도를 가진 것이었다.

	(A)		(B)
①	그러나	……	참으로
②	그러나	……	우연히
③	그래서	……	이처럼
④	즉	……	그렇지 않다면
⑤	예를 들어	……	게다가

주 제 Piaget의 공헌
정답 해설 (A) 뒷부분에서는 Piaget의 관점을 예를 들어 설명하고 있기 때문에 For example이 적절하다. (B) 뒷부분에서는 (B) 앞부분에 이어 Piaget에 대한 설명이 추가되므로 Besides가 자연스럽다.

어 휘 mislead 잘못 이끌다, 오해하게 만들다 oblivious ~을 의식하지 못하는, 안중에 없는 explicit 뚜렷한, 명백한

07 ② 사회과학자들은 취급 효과와 선별 효과로 알려진 두 가지를 구분한다. (A) 예를 들어 해병대는 대체로 취급 효과 기관이다. 해병대는 지원자들을 강인함과 지능에 따라 4가지로 구분하는 대형 입대 사무소가 없다. 해병대의 기본 훈련을 완수한 경험은 당신을 굉장한 군인으로 바꾸어 놓을 것이 확실하다. (B) 반면에 모델 알선업은 선별 효과 기관이다. 에이전시와 계약한다고 당신이 아름다워지는 것이 아니다. 당신이 아름답기 때문에 에이전시와 계약을 할 수 있는 것이다.

	(A)		(B)
①	그래서	……	게다가
②	예를 들어	……	반면에
③	즉	……	반면에
④	그러나	……	그래서
⑤	사실	……	이처럼

주 제 취급 효과와 선별 효과
정답 해설 (A) 뒤에는 해병대에 대한 구체적인 예가 제시되었으므로 for instance가 적절하다. (B) 뒤에는 앞서 언급했던 해병대와는 반대되는 모델 에이전시에 관한 내용이 언급되고 있으므로 by contrast가 적절하다.

어 휘 admission 승인, 입학 허가 marine 바다의, 해양의, 해병대 dimension 치수, 길이, 차원 formidable 상당한, 굉장한, 만만치 않은

More Practice

| 01 ① | 02 ① | 03 ① | 04 ② |

01 ① 우리가 우리의 기억 속에 저장한 일종의 개인 지식은 우리가 좋아하는 것과 싫어하는 것에 대한 지식이다. 이것은 개인적인 취향에 따르는 매우 개인적인 지식이다. (A) 예를 들어, 우리가 당신에게 당신이 좋아하는 수프의 종류가 무엇인지 묻는다면, 당신은 Borscht 또는 Chicken Noodle 또는 Egg Drop이라고 우리에게 말할 것이다. 당신은 전에 많은 종류의 수프를 먹어 보았고, 당신이 가장 좋아하는 것이 무엇인지 기억하고 있기 때문에 알 수

있다. 그 기억을 바탕으로 당신은 아마도 집이나 식당에서 반복해서 그것을 달라고 주문할 것이다. (B) 마찬가지로, 당신은 쉽게 당신의 가장 친한 친구가 누구인지, 가장 좋아하는 가수가 누구인지, 가장 좋아하는 축구팀이 누구인지, 그리고 가장 좋아하는 색상이나 책 또는 TV 프로그램이 무엇인지 쉽게 말할 수 있다. 이러한 모든 것들을 당신이 기억하고 있는 이유는 과거에 이것들과 광범위하고 직접적인 경험을 했고, 어떤 것이 당신에게 가장 큰 즐거움을 주는지 판단하기 위해 다양한 경험을 쉽게 비교하고 대조할 수 있기 때문이다.

	(A)		(B)
①	예를 들어	……	마찬가지로
②	예를 들어	……	그러므로
③	반면에	……	그렇지 않다면
④	반면에	……	그러므로
⑤	다시 말해서	……	그러므로

[주제] 기억에 근거한 선호

[정답 해설] 빈칸 (A) 앞에는 개인의 취향은 기억 속에 저장된 지식에 따른다는 내용이 나오고 (A) 뒤에는 그 예시로 선호하는 수프에 대한 내용이 나온다. 따라서 (A)에는 '예를 들어'를 의미하는 for example이 적절하다. 빈칸 (B) 뒷부분은 수프뿐만 아니라 다른 영역에서도 과거의 직접적인 경험을 바탕으로 무엇을 선호하는지 묻는 여러 질문에 답할 수 있다는 내용이므로 (B)에는 '마찬가지로'를 뜻하는 Similarly가 가장 적절하다.

[어휘] ask for ~을 청구하다; ~을 달라고 부탁하다; 은 없느냐고 묻다 over and over again 몇 번이고 되풀이하여

02 ① 화석 연료의 부족이 대체 에너지로의 전환의 동기가 될 수는 없다. 수십 년 동안, 에너지 생산자들은 새로운 화석 연료 보유고를 부단히 확인해 왔고, 이전에 접근하기가 너무 어렵다고 여겼던 매장층으로부터 경제적으로 석유와 가스를 끌어내기 위하여 기술을 발전시켜 왔다. (A) 예를 들어, 일본은 최근 바다 속 수산화물 매장층에서 메탄을 추출할 수 있다고 발표하였는데, 이는 지구상의 화석 연료를 다 합친 것보다 두 배 이상 많은 탄소를 함유하고 있는 것으로 보인다. 이것은 인류가 지금까지 화석 연료의 극히 일부만을 사용해 왔음을 의미한다. 비록 우리가 그렇게 적은 양의 화석 연료를 이용해 왔음에도 불구하고 지구는 이미 심각한 온난화 문제를 겪고 있다. 만약 우리가 에너지 공급을 위하여 계속 화석 연료에 크게 의존한다면, 화석 연료 공급의 실질적인 압박을 받기 훨씬 전에, 이미 기후 변화와 관련된 피해가 매우 심각해질 것이다. (B) 그러므로 대체 에너지를 위한 운동은 기후를 계속 살 만하고 건강에

좋게 하려는 일치된 노력에 의해 추진되어야 한다.

	(A)		(B)
①	예를 들어	……	그러므로
②	반면에	……	그럼에도 불구하고
③	예를 들어	……	반대로
④	반면에	……	그러므로
⑤	같은 방법으로	……	그럼에도 불구하고

[주제] 화석 연료와 대체 에너지

[정답 해설] (A) 앞 문장에서 화석 연료 매장층 가운데 경제적으로 석유와 가스를 끌어내기 위한 기술을 발전시켜 왔다고 언급했고, 뒤에서는 일본이 바다에서 메탄 추출이 가능하다고 발표했다고 했으므로 빈칸에는 '예를 들어'를 뜻하는 For example이 적절하다. (B) 앞 문장에서 계속 화석 연료에 의존하게 되면 공급 자체에 대한 압박 이전에 그와 관련된 피해가 매우 심각해질 것이라 언급했으므로, 대체 에너지 개발에 힘을 모아야 한다는 내용과 자연스럽게 이어지려면 빈칸에는 '그러므로'라는 뜻의 Therefore가 적절하다.

[어휘] transition 이행 reserve 비축(량) deposit 매장층 deem 여기다 extract 추출하다 hydrate 수산화물 to date 지금까지 fraction 일부; 분수 concerted 합심한, 일치된

03 ① 뉴미디어란 동시에 네 가지 특징으로 정의될 수 있다. 그것들은 통합적이고 쌍방향이며 기술적 수단으로 디지털 코드와 하이퍼텍스트를 사용하는, 20세기와 21세기의 전환기의 매체이다. 그렇기에 그것들의 가장 일반적인 다른 이름이 다중 매체, 쌍방향 매체, 디지털 매체라는 이야기가 된다. 이 정의를 사용하면 매체가 구식인지 신식인지를 구별하는 것이 쉽다. (A) 예를 들어, 전통적인 텔레비전은 그것이 이미지, 소리, 글을 포함하고 있기 때문에, 통합적이지만, 쌍방향이 아니며 디지털 코드에 기반을 두고 있지도 않다. 평범한 구식 전화는 쌍방향이었지만, 그것은 오로지 말과 소리만 전송하기 때문에 통합적이지 않았으며, 디지털 코드로 작동하지 않았다. 대조적으로, 쌍방향의 텔레비전이라는 뉴미디어는 쌍방향성과 디지털 코드를 더한다. (B) 게다가, 새로운 세대의 이동식 또는 고정식 전화 통신은 글, 그림 또는 영상을 추가하고 인터넷과 연결되기 때문에 완전히 디지털화되고 통합적이다.

	(A)		(B)
①	예를 들어	……	게다가
②	그럼에도	……	다시 말해
③	그러므로	……	게다가

④ 예를 들어 …… 다시 말해
⑤ 그럼에도 …… 그 결과

주제 뉴미디어의 특징

정답 해설 (A) 빈칸 앞에는 뉴미디어의 정의를 이용하여 뉴미디어와 구식 매체를 구별할 수 있다는 내용이 나오고 빈칸 뒤에서 양자를 구별하는 예를 보여주고 있으므로, 빈칸에는 For example이 적절하다. (B) 새로운 매체의 예를 추가로 제시하고 있으므로, 빈칸에는 Additionally가 적절하다.

어휘 integrated 통합적인, 통합된 interactive 쌍방향의, 상호작용하는 hypertext 하이퍼텍스트(문장 중의 어구나 그것에 붙은 표제, 표제를 모은 목차 등이 서로 연결된 문자 데이터 파일) transmit 전송하다

04 ②

석유와 가스 자원은 수백만 년이 걸리는 과정에 의한 결과로 생성되어 지질학적으로 묻혀있는 것이므로 기후 변화에 영향을 받지 않을 것이다. (A) 반면에, 기후 변화는 석유가스 생산 지역들을 폐쇄시킬 뿐만 아니라, 덮여 있는 얼음의 양을 감소시킴으로써 북극 지역의 탐사 가능성을 높여 줄 수도 있다. 따라서 기후 변화가 이러한 자원들에 영향을 미치지는 않겠지만, 기후 변화는 이러한 자원들에 대한 접근성에 영향을 미치므로 석유 및 가스 매장량과 알려진 혹은 발견 가능성이 있는 자원은 새로운 기후 조건에 영향을 받을 수 있다. (B) 예컨대, 시베리아에서 실제적인 탐사의 어려운 문제는 1월 기온이 영하 20°C에서 영하 35°C에 이르는 극한의 환경 조건 하에서 석유에 접근하여, 생산하고, 배송하는 데 필요한 시간이다. 온난화는 극한의 환경 조건을 완화하여, 생산 한계 지역을 넓혀 줄 수도 있다.

	(A)		(B)
①	반면에	……	하지만
②	반면에	……	예컨대
③	결과적으로	……	예컨대
④	결과적으로	……	하지만
⑤	다시 말해	……	그러므로

주제 기후 변화가 매장 자원의 발견에 미치는 영향

정답 해설 (A) 빈칸 앞에는 자원 그 자체는 기후 변화의 영향을 받지 않는다는 내용이 나오고 빈칸 뒤에서는 기후 변화가 자원 탐사 가능성에 영향을 준다는 내용이 나오므로, 빈칸에는 On the other hand가 가장 적절하다. (B) 빈칸 앞에서 기후 조건이 자원에 대한 접근성에 미치는 영향을 설명하고 빈칸 뒤에서 시베리아의 기후 조건이 석유 자원에 대한 접근성에 미치는 영향을 예시하고 있으므로, 빈칸에는 for instance가 가장

적절하다.

어휘 impact 영향을 주다 geologically 지질학적으로 shutting down 폐쇄 exploration 탐사 reserves 매장량 potential 가능성 있는 frontier 경계, 한계

PART 05 정보 파악하기

UNIT 17 세부 정보

Example 답 ⑤

Yellowstone National Park는 간헐천 지대를 보호하기 위해 1872년에 조성되었다. 그러나 2백만 에이커의 공원은 정부를 야생 동물 사업에 들여놓았고 안타깝게도 과학적인 야생 동물 관리는 반세기 이후까지도 시작되지 않았다. 공원이 조성되었을 당시의 동물의 개체수와 식습관의 구체적인 기록은 존재하지 않는다. 초기의 공원 관리원들은 소에게 먹이를 주듯이 엘크와 들소들에게 먹이를 주었고 늑대들을 죽이기 시작했다. 1926년쯤에 연방 정부의 명령에 따라 마지막 늑대들이 제거되었다. 그리고 엘크는 공원에서 잔디, 풀, 그리고 그들이 닿을 수 있는 나무의 모든 부분들을 먹으면서 과밀해졌다. 그래서 1934년 공원 관리자들은 그것들도 사냥하기 시작했다. 1962년 한 해에만 4,619마리의 엘크들이 죽었다는 기록이 있다. 1967년에 여론이 공원으로 하여금 사냥을 중지시켰다. 하지만 공원은 회복되지 않았다.

① 1900년대부터 야생 동물이 과학적으로 관리되었다.
② 1872년의 정확한 동물 개체수는 알 수 없다.
③ 엘크는 그들의 자연적 천적의 제거 이후에 잘 자랐다.
④ 총 4,619 마리의 엘크는 1962년에 도살당했다.
⑤ 여론이 늑대 사냥을 중지시켰다.

[주 제] Yellowstone National Park의 야생동물 관리

Practice

01 ④	02 ②	03 ⑤	04 ⑤	05 ⑤
06 ①	07 ③	08 ⑤	09 ⑤	10 ④
11 ⑤	12 ②	13 ②	14 ④	15 ⑤
16 ④	17 ③	18 ⑤	19 ③	20 ②
21 ⑤	22 ②	23 ②	24 ④	25 ②
26 ②	27 ③	28 ④	29 ⑤	30 ③
31 ②				

01 ④ 게르라고 알려진, 몽골 전역에서 볼 수 있는 커다란 하얀 텐트는 아마도 이 나라의 가장 특징적인 상징일 것이다. ('yurt'라는 단어는 러시아인들에 의해 서양에 알려진 튀르크 단어이다. 몽골인들의 민족주의적 감수성을 상하게 하고 싶지 않다면, 'ger'라는 단어를 사용하라.) 대부분의 몽골인들은 여전히 게르에 살며 울란바토르의 교외 지역에 있는 몽골인들조차 게르에 살고 있다. 그 이유를 이해하는 것은 어렵지 않다. 나무와 벽돌은 특히나 스텝 지대에서 드물고 비싸지만 동물 가죽은 값이 싸고 손쉽게 구할 수 있기 때문이다. 유목민들은 확실히 유동적이고 이동적이어야 하며 게르는 옮기기 쉽다. 크기에 따라 1시간에서 3시간이면 게르를 조립할 수 있다. 만약 기회가 생긴다면, 게르에 방문하거나 머물라는 초대를 놓쳐서는 안 될 것이다

① 대부분의 몽골인들은 'yurt'라고 부른다.
② 울란바토르의 도시 지역에서만 게르를 볼 수 있다.
③ 나무와 벽돌로 만들어져 있다.
④ 3시간 또는 그보다 적은 시간 안에 세워질 수 있다.
⑤ 현대의 여행자에게는 추천하지 않는다.

[주 제] 게르의 특징
[정답 해설] 게르는 크기에 따라 1~3시간 안에 세워진다고 언급했으므로 ④가 정답이다.

[어 휘] identifiable 알아볼 수 있는 scarce 드문 steppe 스텝 지대 nomadic 유목민의 assemble 조립하다 urban 도시의

02 ② 의학 박사인 Walter Reed은 1901년에 황열병이 특정 모기 종류에 의해 전염될 수 있다는 것을 발견한 미군 내과 의사였다. 그는 버지니아에서 태어나 버지니아 대학에서 1869년에 의학박사 학위를 취득했다. Reed는 그의 두 번째 박사학위를 1870년에 뉴욕대학교 Bellevue 의과대학에서 취득했다. Reed는 의학박사로서 군대에 입대하였다. 그리고 그는 1876년에 결혼했다. 부부는 아들과 딸을 낳았고, 미국 원주민 여자 아이를 이후에 입양했다. 그는 또한 군대 의학 박물관에서 큐레이터를 역임하였는데, 이 박물관은 이후에 국립 보건 의학 박물관이 되었다. 그는 수천 명의 군인을 사망케 한 황열병을 연구하기 위해 쿠바에 배치되었다. 다른 의사들의 도움으로, Reed는 그 질병이 모기에 의해 전염된다는 것을 확인했다. 이 발견은 수많은 생명을 구했다. 그의 업적을 기념하기 위해 많은 미국의 병원들은 Reed를 따라 이름이 지어졌다.

[주 제] 황열병을 연구한 의사 Walter Reed
[정답 해설] 1869, 1870년에 각각 의학박사 학위를 취득하였다고 서술되어 있다. 따라서 정답은 ②이다.

[어 휘] physician 내과 의사 curator 큐레이터(박물관 · 미술관 등의 전시 책임자) station ~을 배치하다 commemorate 기념하다

03 ⑤ 1803년에 미국 정부는 프랑스로부터 Louisiana 전 영역을 사들였다. 영토는 Mississippi 강부터 Rocky 산맥 중앙에 이르렀지만, 누구도 Mississippi 강이 어디서 시작하는지 또는 정확히 Rocky 산맥이 어디 위치하는지 확신하지 못했다. Thomas Jefferson 대통령은 이 지역에 원정대를 파견했다. 그 부대는 Meriwether Lewis 대위와 William Clark 소위의 지휘 아래 미군 자원자들로 선별된 그룹으로 구성되었다. 그들의 위험한 여정은 1804년 5월부터 1806년 9월까지 계속되었다. 그들의 주요한 목표는 탐험하면서 새롭게 획득한 영토의 지도를 만들고, 대륙의 서쪽 절반을 가로지르는 실질적인 경로를 찾는 것이었다. Lewis와 Clark은 43명의 남성과 2년 치 군수품을 가지고 출발하였다. 그들은 새 여성(Bird Woman)이라는 의미의 Sacajawea라는 이름을 가진 16살의 미국 원주민 여성과 알게 되었다. 그녀의 도움으로 Lewis와 Clark는 인디언으로부터 말을 얻어 큰 어려움 없이 인디언 영토를 지나갔다.

[주 제] Louisiana 원정대의 여정
[정답 해설] 본문에서 새 여성(Bird Woman)이라는 의미의 Sacajawea라는 이름을 가진 16살의 미국 원주민 여성의 도움으로 Lewis와 Clark는 인디언으로부터 말을 얻어 큰 어려움 없이 인디언 영토를 지나갔다고 서술하고 있으므로 정답은 ⑤이다.
[어 휘] territory 영토 commission 임명하다, 파견하다 expedition 원정대 Second Lieutenant 소위 perilous 위험한

---

04 ⑤ Halibut은 북대서양과 북태평양의 오른눈박이 넙치과의 두 넙치에 주로 적용되는 일반적인 이름이다. Halibut은 배 아래쪽은 황백색이고, 윗부분은 암갈색이며 피부에는 육안으로는 안 보이는 매우 작은 비늘이 박혀 있다. 태어날 때 그것은 머리의 양쪽에 눈을 갖고 있다. 6개월 후에는 한쪽 눈이 다른 쪽으로 이동한다. Halibut은 신선할 때 종종 삶거나 기름에 튀기거나 구워진다. 낮은 지방 함유량으로 인해서 Halibut은 연어보다 훈제하기 어렵다. 현재 대서양에서 남획으로 인해 개체수가 고갈되어 멸종위기에 처한 종으로 공표될지도 모른다.

[주 제] Halibut의 특징
[정답 해설] 태평양이 아닌 대서양 지역에서 멸종위기에 처한 종으로 공표될 수 있다고 서술되어 있으므로 정답은 ⑤이다.
[어 휘] flatfish 넙치 flounder 넙치 off-white 황백색 underbelly 하복부 scale 비늘 embedded 박힌 smoking 훈제

---

05 ⑤ 생태학자들은 일반적으로 외래종을 사람들이 무심결에 혹은 일부러 새로운 지역으로 옮겨 놓는 것이라고 정의한다. "적은 비율의 외부의 종만이 그들의 새로운 서식지에서 문제를 일으킨다."라고 생태학과 진화생물학 교수가 말한다. 그러나 겉모습은 생태학자들의 주의를 속일 수 있고, 이들 외부의 종 중 많은 것들이 단지 아무도 그들의 해로운 효과를 기록하지 않았다는 이유만으로 수용 가능한 것으로 여겨질 수 있다. 더욱이 비토착 종들은 수십 년 동안 무해한 것으로 보이다가 해로운 것이 될 수 있다. 그러한 불확실성에 직면하여 많은 생태학자들은 강력한 조치가 취해져야 한다고 주장한다. 그들의 방식은 외부의 종을 자연 생태 시스템에서 제거해야 한다는 것이다. 그러나 많은 전문가들은 생태 시스템을 그들이 더욱 자연적이었던 시절로 끌어내리는 과학적인 지식에 대해 의문을 던진다. 심지어 생태 시스템에서 모든 외부 종을 제거하고자 하는 많은 생태학자들도 그 목표가 비현실적이라는 점을 인정한다. 더욱이 애리조나 대학의 Rosenzweig 교수는 침투적인 외부의 종이 생물 다양성을 감소시킨다는 만연한 관점에 대해서 반박한다. 외부의 종들은 그 환경에서의 종의 수를 증가시킨다. 비록 외부의 종이 멸종을 일으키더라도 멸종 단계는 결국 끝날 것이고 새로운 종이 진화하기 시작할 것이라고 그는 설명한다.

[주 제] 외래종 제거에 대한 비판
[정답 해설] 본문의 마지막 부분에 외부의 종이 멸종을 일으키더라도 멸종 단계는 결국 끝날 것이며 새로운 종이 진화하기 시작할 것이라는 설명이 나오므로 정답은 ⑤이다.
[어 휘] inadvertently 무심결에 deliberately 고의적으로 innocuous 무해한 prevailing 만연한

---

06 ① 신경학자, 가축, 그리고 패스트푸드점이 갖는 공통점이 무엇인가? 이것들은 모두 자폐를 갖고 태어난 한 저명한 여성 동물과학자 Temple Grandin에게 큰 빛을 지고 있다. 비록 그녀는 4번째 생일까지 단어 하나 말하지 못했지만, 1995년 유명한 신경학자 Oliver Sacks 덕분에 대중의 인식을 사로잡았다. 하지만 많은 심리적 장애처럼, 자폐증은 (넓은) 범위이고 그녀는 한 극단에 서 있었다. 이 모험적인 삶을 사는 것은 그녀에게 많은 자폐성 아이들을 위한 대단한 영감의 원천이 되는 것을 허락했다. 그녀는 또한 '소'라는 다른 포유동물의 희망이 되었다. 다른 동물들의 심리를 보는 그녀만의 특별한 창을 사용해서, 그녀는 스트레스를 줄임으로써 가축들의 삶을 향상시키는 목장을 발달시켰다. 그리고 비록 패스트푸드 산업이 지속적으로 소로 패티를 만들지만, 이 산업은 Grandin 버거의 윤리와 동정심을 감사하게 여겼다.

【주 제】 동물과학자 Temple Grandin의 업적

【정답 해설】 지문의 '자폐를 갖고 태어난 한 저명한 여성 동물과학자 Temple Grandin에게 큰 빚을 지고 있다'라는 문장을 통해 ①이 정답이라는 것을 알 수 있다.

【어 휘】 neurologist 신경학자 autism 자폐증 utter 말하다 renowned 명성 있는 spectrum 범위 edge 가장자리 extraordinary 대단한, 비상한 inspiration 영감 mammal 포유동물 compassion 동정심

07 ③ 지금은 보이지만, 이제는 보이지 않는다. 가느다란 쥐치는 적으로부터 완벽하게 도망치는 교묘한 방법을 가지고 있다. 그것은 거의 보이지 않도록 하는 능력을 발달시켰다. 브라운 대학교의 Justine Allen은 카리브 해에서 이들을 봤을 때 이 물고기들이 스스로 얼마나 빨리 위장하는지에 대해 놀랐다. 이것은 바다 산호들 혹은 부채뿔 산호들의 색깔과 단 2초 만에 일치시키고, 헤엄쳐 지나간다. 어떻게 이런 일을 해낼까? 이 물체가 무엇인지 보기 위해, 당신은 배경과 약간 차이가 나는 이것의 테두리들을 감지할 수 있어야 한다. Allen은 쥐치가 "거짓 테두리들"을 만들기 위해 보호색을 바꾼다는 걸 발견했다. 예로 들어, 쥐치는 진짜 테두리처럼 보이기 위해 어두운 세로 줄무늬를 자신의 몸에 만들어 낼 수 있다. 눈은 이 거짓 테두리를 보기 때문에, 이 물고기의 진짜 모습을 놓치게 된다.

【주 제】 쥐치의 위장에 대한 연구

【정답 해설】 지문에서 쥐치들은 2초 만에 바다 산호 혹은 부채 뿔 산호들의 색깔과 몸 색깔을 일치시켜 위험에서 빠져나간다고 했기 때문에 ③ '2초 만에 몸의 색을 바꿀 수 있다.'가 정답이다.

【어 휘】 filefish 쥐치 camouflage 위장 sea fan 바다 산호 gorgonian 부채뿔 산호 perceive 감지하다 longitudinal stripe 세로 줄무늬

08 ⑤ 실망에 이르게 하는 혼란과 오해의 근원은 주로 보험계약에서의 복잡하고 애매모호한 언어이다. Katrina의 거대한 폭풍 해일이 수천의 집들과 사업체들을 파괴하거나 부쉈을 때, Mississippi의 Gulf Coast 상에서 초래된 수십 억 달러의 피해가 발생했다. 그들의 보험 회사들이 물이 아닌 바람에 의한 피해만 보상한다는 걸 알았을 때, 격노한 주택 거주자들은 그들의 주(州) 정부에 보험 회사를 상대로 소송을 걸기 위해 단체를 만들었다. 그들은 그들의 보험이 물에 의한 피해는 보상하지 않는다 해도, Katrina의 날카로운 바람이 물벼락을 가져와 그들의 재산에 피해를 줬기 때문에 (보험은) 이에 대해 지불해야 한다고 주장했다.

주택 소유자들은 소송에서 졌지만, 보험업계는 상당한 신용을 잃었고 사람들은 그들의 보험이 종이에 적힌 것보다 배상범위가 훨씬 좁다는 것에 대해 더욱 걱정하게 되었다.

【주 제】 보험계약상 모호한 언어와 배상 축소

【정답 해설】 '주택 소유자들은 소송에서 졌지만, 보험사는 상당한 신용을 잃었고, 사람들은 그들의 보험이 종이에 적힌 것보다 배상 범위가 훨씬 좁다는 것에 대해 더욱 걱정하게 되었다.'라는 부분을 통해 소유자들이 보험사에 패소했다는 걸 알 수 있다. 그렇기 때문에 ⑤ '주택 소유자들은 보험회사를 상대로 한 소송에서 승소했다.'는 글의 내용과 일치하지 않는다.

【어 휘】 misunderstanding 오해 disappointment 실망 ambiguous 애매모호한 wrought (work의 과거, 과거분사형을 나타내는 고어) 초래하다 insurance contract 보험계약서 storm surge 폭풍 해일 infuriate 극도로 화나게 만들다 credibility 신용

09 ⑤ 100미터 달리기에서 11초는 성인 여성부와 여학생 부문을 나누는 기준점이다. 지난주 토요일, Seattle에서 열린 Brooks PR Invitational에서 16세의 Candace Hill이 10.98초라는 무서운 기록으로 상위권 그룹에 참가해 우승하면서, 미국 여고생 최초로 11초의 벽, 미국 주니어 그리고 17세 이하 세계 신기록을 동시에 깨는 명예를 안게 되었다. 지난 달 Georgia의 RockDale County 고등학교에서 2학년을 마친 Candace는 5번의 미국 내 챔피언 그리고 Georgia 주(州)의 100미터와 200미터 기록을 보유하고 있다. 그녀가 기록한 성적은 만약 올해 NCAA 대회에 나갔다면 3등을 차지했을 것이며, 이번 시즌 세계 10위와 동점을 이루는 기록이다.

【주 제】 Candice Hill의 달리기 기록

【정답 해설】 Candace Hill이 NCAA 대회에 나갔다면 3등을 차지했을 것이라고 언급된 것으로 미루어 볼 때 그녀는 NCAA 대회에 나간 적이 없다고 유추할 수 있다. 그렇기 때문에 ⑤ '올해 NCAA 대회에서 3등을 차지했다.'는 본문의 내용과 일치하지 않는다.

【어 휘】 benchmark 기준 scorch 전력 질주하다 tie 동률

10 ④ Garth Brooks는 아주 훌륭하고 긴 은퇴 기간을 누렸다. 하지만 이제는 그것은 끝이 난 것으로 보인다. 화요일 Nashville에서 있을 기자회견에서는 52세의 Brooks가, 세계 순회공연에 대한 계획이 포함되어 있을 가능성이 높은 그의 컴백의 구체적인 사안을 발표할 것으로 예정되어 있다. 미국 음반 판매 순위에서 오직 The Beatles

와 Elvis Presley에게만 뒤졌던 전국적인 슈퍼스타인 그는, 2001년 3명의 딸을 양육하기 위해 음악계를 등졌다. 그 이후로 그는 드물게 음반을 내고 공연을 했을 뿐이었다. Brooks의 가장 어린 딸인 Allie가 가을에 대학에 들어감으로써, 그의 복귀를 위한 무대가 준비되었다. 그는 기대감을 불러일으키는 것에 아주 능숙하다. 지난주에 그의 웹사이트는 그가 진짜 발표를 하게 될 날에 대해 언급하며 애가 닳게 했다. 그가 그 자리에서 그의 원대한 계획 중 일부분만을 공개하는 것도 얼마든지 가능하다. 아니면 순회공연 역시 그가 발표할 내용 중 일부분에 불과할지도 모른다. Brooks는 그 외에 또 어떤 것들에 대해 이야기 하려고 준비하고 있을까?

11 ⑤ 이번 여름이 시작될 무렵, 홍콩 정부는 200,000명의 젊은이들에게 저작권이 보호되는 노래와 영화의 불법 복제본에 대해 인터넷 토론 사이트를 검색하고 그 결과를 관련 기관에 보고하도록 하는 계획을 수립했다. 그 캠페인은 연예 사업 분야를 만족시켰지만, 시민의 자유를 옹호하는 사람들 사이에서는 의혹을 유발시켰다. 이른바 청년 대사 캠페인은 수요일에 체육관에서 홍콩의 대표적인 영화계와 가요계의 스타들, 그리고 몇몇 정부 관료들 앞에서 다짐하는 1,600명의 청년들과 함께 시작 될 것이다. 청년 대사란 인터넷상의 질서를 지키려는 청년들의 새로운 의존 관계를 의미한다. 9세에서 25세에 이르는 보이스카우트와 걸 가이드, 그리고 9종류의 서로 다른 유니폼을 입는 청소년 단체의 모든 멤버들이 참가할 것으로 예정되어 있다.

12 ② Utah는 Interconnect Adventure Tour와 함께 다섯 군데의 세계적 수준의 리조트에서 하루 동안 스키를 탈 수 있는 기회를 상급 스키어들에게 제공한다. 미국 국립 산림청으로부터 특별 사용 허가를 받은 Ski Utah에 의해 기획 된 이번 여행은, 눈사태 상황에서의 안전과 관리에 대해 훈련을 거친 숙련된 산악 가이드들에 의해 진행된다. 여행을 신청하는 스키어들은 반드시 신체적으로 좋은 컨디션을 유지하고 있어야 하며, 다양한 상태의 눈에서 스키를 타본 경험을 갖고 있어야만 한다. 각각의 참가자들의 실력은 여행을 출발하기 전에 점검 받게 된다. 일요일, 월요일, 수요일 그리고 금요일에 이루어지는 여행은 Park City에서 시작되며, Park City, Brighton, Solitude, Alta 그리고 Snowbird를 포함한다. 전체를 마치는 데는 점심을 위한 휴게 시간 포함 8시간이 소요된다. 화요일과 목요일, 토요일에 이루어지는 여행은 Snowbird에서 시작하며 Snowbird, Alta, Brighton, 그리고 Solitude가 포함되어 있다.

13 ② 이제 막 시작한 그의 유기농산물을 집으로 배달해주는 벤처 사업을 위해 창고로 활용하던 차고 안에서 그가 골판지 박스를 분리하고 있었을 때도, David Gersenson은 스스로에게 직감을 통해 Door to Door Organics가 반드시 크게 성장하게 될 것이라고 말했다. "내가 상자들을 분해할 때, 이 일이 언젠가는 반드시 도약할 것이라는 사실을 알고 있었다." 그는 그가 그의 회사의 미래를 내다보았던 1997년의 그 순간을 회상한다. Pennsylvania의 Upper Bucks County에서 700달러로 시작된 그의 사업은, 그가 20대 초반에 인도 여행을 하면서 유기농산물을 먹은 뒤에 품게 된 아이디어를 기반으로 하고 있다. 비록 Gersenson의 식견은 미래를 내다본 것으로 판명되었지만, 그가 사업을 진행하는 것에 있어서 Door to Door Organics를 오늘날과 같이 급속도로 미국 전역에 확장되는 회사가 되도록 전환시켰던 전략적인 결정의 결과가 어떻게 될지는 거의 예상할 수 없었다. 자연적이고 유기농인 상품을 판매하는 온라인 식료품점은 전국적으로 5개의 대형 마켓에서 200명 이상의 사람들의 고용을 창출했고, 2013년에는 2,600만 달러의 수익을 기록했으며, 올해는 4,000만 달러 이상으로 성장할 것으로 전망이 되고 있다.

그는 20대 초반에 인도 여행을 준비하면서가 아니라 인도 여행을 하면서 사업을 착안하였다. 따라서 ②의 내용은 본문과 일치하지 않는다.

take off 도약하다, 성공하다, 빛을 발하다 hatch (사상 관념 등을) 품게 되다 disassemble 분해하다, 분리하다 cardboard 골판지 gut 직감, 본능 (복수로도 사용 가능), 배짱 while (문장 첫머리에서) ~임에도 불구하고, ~이긴 하지만 Pa. (Pennsylvania) 펜실베이니아 (미국 지명) prophetic 예언의, 예언적인 bustle 바삐 움직이다, 서두르다 multistate 여러 주에 걸쳐 있는 revenue 수익

---

14 ④ 　27살의 변호사인 Kevin Han은 검소하다. 아침 식사는 5위안(82센트) 어치의 두유 한 잔과 삶은 계란 한 개이다. 점심은 베이징에 있는 그의 직장 구내식당에서 20위안 어치의 쌀밥과 약간의 고기가 섞인 야채를 먹는다. 그는 저녁 식사를 위해서도 같은 금액만 사용한다. 그는 옷을 사는 거래도 온라인을 통해서 하고 있고, 저렴한 임대아파트에서 살고 있으며, 직장까지는 지하철을 이용한다 (왕복 4위안). 그가 자신만의 공간을 마련하려면 절약하는 것은 반드시 필요한 일이다. 그는 한 달에 13,000위안을 벌고 절반가량을 저축한다. "나의 아버지는 부자가 아니다. 따라서 나는 스스로 모든 것들을 모아야만 한다."

변호사 Kevin Han의 돈 씀씀이
그는 한 달에 13,000위안을 벌고, 절반 정도를 저축한다고 했으므로 ④의 6,500 yuan을 저축한다는 말은 적절하다.

frugal 검소한 scrimp (지나치게) 절약하다, 인색하게 굴다

---

15 ⑤ 　Ed Sheeran은 그의 라디오 시티 뮤직 홀 쇼에서 매진을 기록한 관객들에게 노래를 들려준 뒤에 "나는 집에 가서 텔레비전을 볼 거야."라고 말했다. 그 그래미상 후보로 오른 22살의 싱어송라이터는 현재의 자기 자신, 즉 당신의 부모님들이 실제로 들을 만한 포크-팝 래퍼를 제외하고는 다른 어떤 존재가 되는 것에도 관심을 갖지 않는다. 그리고 지금에 이르기까지 이러한 참신한 접근이 그를 위치에 오르게 한 것으로 보인다. 믿을 수 없다고? 650만 명 이상의 트위터 팔로워들과 그저 그를 보기 위해서 수없이 많은 공연장에 나타나는 함성을 지르는 수천의 소녀들에게 물어보라. 누군가는 Ed가 하룻밤 사이에 음악적 돌풍을 일으킨 것이라고 말한다. 하지만 England의 Halifax 출신인 그는 그의 음악에 대한 사랑이 어릴 때부터 길러진, 예술적인 집안에서 성장했다.

인기 싱어송라이터 Ed Sheeran
마지막 문장에서 그는 England 출신이고 예술적인 집안에서 자랐다고 했으므로, ⑤는 글의 내용과 일치한다.

serenade 사랑 노래, 사랑 노래를 들려주다 folk-pop 포크송의 멜로디와 가사를 채용한 대중음악 overnight 밤을 새는, 하룻밤(일시적으로)만 유효한 nurture 기르다, 영양분을 주다

---

16 ④ 　5년 전 35세의 Pete Bodharamik은 엄청난 도전을 하고 있었다. 그는 그 때 그의 아버지가 1982년에 창업했던 통신지주 회사인 Jasmine International을 막 물려받았다. 회사는 그의 아버지가 1990년대에 빌린 돈으로 사업을 다각화 한 이후 법원의 파산 관리를 벗어나는 과정에서 어려운 시기를 보내고 있었다. 그리고 Pete가 상황을 회복시킬 수 있는 사람이라는 기대 역시 그렇게 높지 않았다. 하지만 Pete는 새로운 형태의 대중매체를 위한 콘텐츠에 대해 탐구하고, 대중문화와 연예에 대한 그의 사랑을 추구하면서 시간을 보냈다. 그는 경쟁자가 거의 없던 방콕의 외곽 지역에서 Jasmine의 제한적인 광대역 통신망을 확장하기 위한 대대적인 투자를 감행했다. 그는 그 거대한 파이프를 영화, 텔레비전 쇼, 뮤직비디오, 게임, 그리고 다른 풍부한 콘텐츠들로 채워 넣었고, 때때로는 그가 설립했던 미디어 회사에서 만든 내용도 포함시켰다.

자사 통신망을 통해 대중매체 컨텐츠를 제공한 Pete
Pete Bodharamik은 방콕 시내 지역이 아닌 외곽지역에 대대적인 투자를 감행했다. 따라서 방콕 시내 지역에 투자를 집중했다는 내용의 ④는 글의 내용과 일치하지 않는다.

holding (회사의) 보유 주식 수, 자산 take over 이어 받다, 인수하다 turn ~ around (상황을) 호전시키다, 돌려 세우다 delve into ~을 탐구하다, ~을 캐다 broadband 광대역의 province 지방, 지역 pipe 관, 관 모양의 물체

---

17 ③ 　John Philip Sousa는 그의 음악 교육을 6살 때 바이올린을 연주하는 것으로 시작했다. 그가 13살이 되었을 때, 해병대 악단의 트롬본 연주자였던 그의 아버지는 Sousa를 미국 해군에 견습생으로 등록시켰다. 수습 과정을 이수한 뒤 몇 년이 지나고, Sousa는 그가 지휘하는 방법을 배운 극장 관현악단의 일원이 된다. 행진용 베이스 금관악기나 수자폰(sousaphone)과 같은 악기들은 디자인에 대한 Sousa의 몇몇 조언들을 참고해서 1893년에 필라델피아의 악기 장인인 J. W. Pepper에 의해 탄생하게 되었다. 그는 해병대 악단을 떠난 해에 Sousa 악단을 조직했다. 그 악단은 미국과 파리 세계 박람회를 포함한 전 세계 곳곳에

서 연주를 했다. 그는 펜실베이니아에서 심장마비로 77세에 생을 마감했다. 그 전날 그는 Ringgold 악단과 함께 "The Stars and Stripes Forever"라는 공연의 리허설을 지휘하고 있었다. 그의 사망 후 1976년에는 위대한 미국인으로서의 명예의 전당에 오르게 되었다.

주 제 음악가 Sousa의 일생과 업적
정답 해설 J. W. Pepper의 제안으로 만든 게 아니라 Sousa의 조언을 참고하여 J. W. Pepper가 sousaphone을 만들었다. 따라서 반대로 설명하고 있는 ③은 글의 내용과 일치하지 않는다.
어 휘 apprentice 견습생 apprenticeship 수습 기간 theatrical 극장의, 극단의 orchestra 관현악단 sousaphone 수자폰(tuba 종류의 관악기) brass 놋쇠, 황동, 금관악기 bass (음악의) 베이스, 낮은 음 부분 exposition 엑스포, 박람회, 전람회 posthumously 사후에, 죽은 뒤의 enshrine (고인을) 안치하다, 소중히 간직하다

18 ⑤ Los Angeles의 북쪽 경계를 따라 늘어선 언덕 위에 있는 Hollywood의 표지판은 전 세계적으로 알려져 있는 굉장히 유명한 랜드마크이다. 흰색으로 칠해진, 50피트 높이의 얇은 금속 글자들은 엄청나게 거리가 먼 Los Angeles 분지를 가로질러서도 보인다. 하지만 이 표지판은 누군가 그렇게 생각하는 것처럼, 영화 산업에 종사하는 사람들에 의해 Hollywood가 갖는 중요성을 보여주기 위한 수단으로 세워진 것은 아니다. 대신에 그 표지판은 1923년에 "Hollywoodland"라고 불리던 Los Angeles의 한 지역의 500에이커에 달하는 주거 지구에서 주택을 팔기 위한 광고의 수단으로 처음 건설되었다. 물론 그 표지판은 그 당시에는 "Hollywoodland"로 건설되었다. 시간이 흐르고, 사람들은 그 지역을 축약된 형태인 "Hollywood"로 부르기 시작했다. 그리고 그 표지판과 지역 일대가 1945년에 Los Angeles로 기증된 이후에는 마지막 네 글자는 철거되었다. 그 표지판은 오랜 시간에 걸쳐 낡게 되었고, 1973년에는 한 글자당 27000달러의 비용을 들여 완전히 교체되었다. Alice Cooper 등을 포함한 수많은 유명 인사들은 필요한 금액을 모금하는 데 도움이 되었다.

주 제 Hollywood 표지판의 변천사
정답 해설 글의 마지막 부분에 Alice Cooper를 포함한 많은 유명 인사들이 교체 비용을 모금하는 데에 도움을 주었다고 나와 있다. 따라서 ⑤의 내용은 적절하다.
어 휘 landmark 대표적인 지형지물 sheet 얇은 물건 (이불, 종이, 석판 등) celebrate 축하하다, 찬양하다 subdivision 일부 지역 celebrity 유명 인사 instrumental 도움이 되는, 도구를 쓰는

19 ③ 인도는 아시아 부속 대륙의 일부이며 10억 명 이상의 사람들의 고국이다. 유일하게 중국만이 더 많은 인구를 가지고 있다. 국토의 절반보다 조금 더 많은 면적이 농경에 적합하지만 국민의 65퍼센트 정도가 농부이거나 농장 노동자이다. 그들은 쌀과 밀, 면, 소, 양, 물소 등을 기른다. 생산량을 늘리기 위해 정부는 관개 사업과 농지 개간 사업을 실시했다. 새로운 종류의 곡식과 비료 역시 시도되었다. 인도는 또한 녹색 혁명을 통해 이익을 내는 나라 중 하나이다. 하지만 불행하게도 녹색 혁명에 대한 인도의 초기 높은 기대는 씨앗과 비료의 높은 비율과 살충제의 과도한 사용으로 일어난 환경 문제 때문에 헛된 것으로 밝혀졌다.

주 제 인도 농업의 특징
정답 해설 인도의 농부들이 물소를 기른다는 내용은 있지만 물소를 숭배한다는 내용은 나와 있지 않다. 따라서 ③은 글의 내용과 일치하지 않는다.
어 휘 subcontinent 부속 대륙, 아대륙 institute (제도 등을) 실시하다, 개설하다 irrigation 관개 시설 reclamation 개간 illusory 환영의, 가상의 pesticide 농약

20 ② Thoreau는 그의 친구들, 학교에 다니는 아이들, 특별히 목적이 없는 여행객들, 그리고 몇몇 부유한 방문객들보다 훨씬 흥미로운 지역 구호소의 가난한 사람들까지 포함해서 "많은 여행객들이 나를 보기 위해 멀리까지 찾아온다."고 기록했다. Thoreau는 소란스럽게 재잘거리는 소리는 참지 못했지만 그에게 꽃이나, 잡초, 죽은 동물 등을 가져오는 아이들에게는 관심을 보였다. 대체적으로 아이들은 "알 수 없는 어른 손님들"과는 달리 그들 스스로 즐거워했다. 그리고 그보다도 훨씬 더 파렴치한 사람들은, Thoreau의 추측이지만, 그가 숲 속을 산책할 때 찾아와서 그의 서랍이나 수납장을 뒤져놓고 가기도 했다. 대부분의 손님들은 근처의 Concord와 Lincoln, 또는 Boston에서 찾아왔다. "소년과 소녀들 그리고 젊은 여성들은 숲 속에서 기뻐하는 듯 보였다." Thoreau는 다음과 같이 기록했다. "그들은 연못 속과 꽃들을 바라봤으며, 그들의 시간을 더 좋게 만들었다. 하지만 사업가나, 심지어는 농부조차도 고독과 일, 그리고 내가 사는 곳이 어떤 것, 혹은 다른 것으로부터 떨어진 먼 거리만을 생각했다. 그럼에도 불구하고 그들은 때때로 숲 속에서의 산책을 좋아한다고 말했다. 그들이 산책을 좋아하지 않는다는 것은 분명했다."

주 제 사람들에 대한 Thoreau의 기록
정답 해설 Thoreau는 그에게 꽃, 잡초 그리고 죽은 동물을 가

져오는 어린이들에게 흥미를 보였다. 따라서 ② '죽은 동물을 가져오는 어린이들에게 화를 내기도 했다.'는 글의 내용과 일치하지 않는다.

어 휘 **come out of one's way** 일부러 ~하는 수고를 하다 **almshouse** 빈민 구호 시설 **affluent** 풍부한, 많은 **drop in** 방문객 **tolerance** 인내, 참을성 **babble** 재잘거리다, 비밀을 누설하다 **on the whole** 전체적으로, 대체로 **unreckoned** 세어지지 않는, 포함되지 않는 **root** 뿌리, 정착하다, 샅샅이 뒤지다 **dwell-dwelt-dwelt** 살다, 거주하다 **ramble** 꼬부랑길, 산책하다

21 ⑤ Whistling Swan은 검정색 부리와 발을 제외하고는 온전히 하얀, 우아하고 아름다운 새이다. 그 Whistling Swan이라는 이름은 그 새의 낮고 아름다운 울음소리를 빗댄 것이 아니고 그 새가 날 때 힘찬 움직임이 만들어내는 소리를 빗댄 것이다. 이 백조의 이동은 놀랍게도 왕복 3725마일이나 된다. 이 동물들은 이동 중에 무리를 짓는 반면, 그들은 연못 또는 물살이 약한 강 근처를 골라 혼자 둥지를 트는 새들이다. 둥지를 틀기에 최적인 장소는 동일한 새들에게 해마다 사용된다. 암컷은 2~4개의 알을 낳고 수컷의 도움을 조금 받아 약 한 달 동안 알들을 품는다. 알이 부화하면 부모들은 새끼들을 돌보며 그들을 먹이로 이끈다. 새끼들은 약 두세 달이 지나면 날 수 있지만 거의 첫 번째 겨울은 부모와 함께 난다.

주 제 Whistling Swan의 생태
정답 해설 마지막 부분에 새끼들은 약 2~3달이 지나면 날 수 있다고 언급되므로 ⑤는 글의 내용과 일치한다.

어 휘 **melodic** 음률이 아름다운 **whistling** 휘파람, 휘파람을 부는 **migration** 이동, 이주 **flock** 떼지어가다 **solitary** 혼자 하는 **nester** 둥지를 트는 새 **incubate** 알을 부화하다, 새끼를 품다 **tend** 돌보다

22 ③ "우리는 전쟁을 하지 않아야 합니다."라고 말을 하는 것만으로는 충분하지 않다. 평화를 사랑하고 그것을 위해 희생하는 것도 필요하다. 우리는 전쟁의 근절만이 아니라 평화의 확언에도 집중해야 한다. 그리스 문학에서는 율리시스와 사이렌에 대한 매혹적인 이야기가 보존되어 전해 내려온다. 사이렌은 노래를 달콤하게 부르는 능력이 있어서 선원들은 그의 섬으로 향하지 않을 수 없었다. 많은 배는 암초로 유혹 당했고, 그들은 죽음으로 인도하는 사이렌의 팔에 안기기 위해 바다에 자신을 던지면서 집의 의무와 명예를 잊어 버렸다. 사이렌들의 유혹에 절대 넘어가지 않겠다고 결심한 율리시스는 첫 번째로 그의 몸을 돛대

에 단단히 묶었고, 그의 선원들은 그의 귀를 왁스로 가득 채워 막았다. 하지만 결국 그와 그의 대원은 자신을 구하기 위해 더 나은 방법을 배웠다. 그들은 배에 사이렌의 노래보다 선율이 달콤한 아름다운 가수 오르페우스를 태웠다. 오르페우스가 노래를 할 때, 누가 사이렌의 노래를 듣겠는가? 이와 같이 우리는 평화가 더 감미로운 음악, 전쟁의 불화보다 훨씬 뛰어난 우주의 멜로디를 나타내는 것임을 볼 수 있어야 한다. 어떻게든 우리는 세계의 모든 민족을 위한 평화와 번영을 실현하기 위한 목적으로, 누구도 승자일 수 없는 핵 군비 경쟁에서 세계 권력 투쟁의 역학을 인간의 천재성을 활용하는 창조적인 대회로 변환해야 한다.

주 제 전쟁 근절을 넘어선 평화의 필요성
정답 해설 글의 중간 부분의 '사이렌의 노래보다 선율이 달콤한 아름다운 가수 오르페우스를 태웠다. 오르페우스가 노래를 할 때 누가 사이렌의 노래를 듣겠는가?'라는 내용으로 미루어 볼 때 ③은 글의 내용과 일치한다.

어 휘 **wage a war** 전쟁을 일으키다 **eradication** 박멸, 뿌리 뽑음 **affirmation** 단언, 확언 **fling-flung-flung** 던지다, 내던지다 **succumb** 굴복하다, 압도되다 **stuff** 채워 넣다 **cosmic** 우주의 **discord** 불화, 불일치 **transform A into B** A를 B로 변형시키다 **harness** 이용하다 **prosperity** 번영, 번성, 부

23 ② Messier 45라고도 알려진 Pleiades 성운은 아주 옛날부터 알려진 것들 중 하나이다. Kenneth Glyn Jones에 따르면 이 성운에 관한 최초의 언급은 Homer가 (대략 기원전 750년경에 쓴) 그의 저서 Iliad와 (기원전 720년경에 쓴) Odyssey에서 한 언급들이다. Pleiades 성운에 있는 별들은 1억 년 전에 형성된 것으로 보이며, 이는 태양 나이의 50분의 1에 해당한다. 비록 그 별들은 425광년 떨어진 곳에 있지만 적어도 6개의 별은 육안으로 볼 수 있는 반면, 맑은 밤하늘에서는 12개 이상 볼 수 있다. 현대 관측 방법은 적어도 약 500 개의 대부분 희미한 별이 2도 정도의 필드(달 지름의 4배)에 걸쳐있는 Pleiades 성단에 속한 것을 밝혀냈다. 이들의 밀도는 다른 산개 성단에 비해 매우 낮다. 이것은 Pleiades 성운의 삶이 매우 짧은 이유 중의 하나이다.

주 제 Pleiades 성운의 특징
정답 해설 본문에 의하면 Pleiades 성단 별들의 나이는 태양의 50분의 1에 불과하다. 즉 Pleiades 성단의 별들이 태양보다 훨씬 나중에 생성되었으므로 ②는 글의 내용과 일치하지 않는다.

어 휘 **cluster** (과일) 송이, 사람들의 무리, 성단 **naked eye** 육안 **diameter** 지름 **density** 밀도

24 ④ 내가 남성들이 공인되지 않은 특권을 기반으로 일을 하는 정도를 깨달은 후, 나는 그들의 억압의 대부분은 무의식임을 이해했다. 그 후 나는 유색 여성들이 자신들과 맞닥뜨리는 백인 여성들이 억압적이라고 비난하는 것을 기억해냈다. 나는 우리가 우리 자신을 그렇게 보지 않을 때에도 왜 당연하게 억압적으로 보이는지에 대해서 이해하기 시작했다. 나는 내가 노력 없이 선천적으로 주어진 피부색의 특권을 즐기고, 그것의 존재에 대해서는 망각한 상태였음을 인정하기 시작했다. 나의 학교 교육은 나 자신을 억압자, 부당하게 혜택받은 사람으로, 또는 잘못된 문화의 참가자로서 보는 것에 대해 나에게 어떤 훈련도 시켜주지 않았다. 나는 내 자신을 스스로의 개인적 도덕 의지에 따라 도덕적 수준이 좌우되는 개인으로 보도록 배웠다. 나의 학교 교육은 나의 동료인 Elisabeth Minnich가 지적한 방식을 따르고 있었다. 백인들은 그들의 삶을 도덕적으로 중립적이고, 표준적이며 평범하고 또한 이상적인 것으로 배운다. 그래서 우리가 다른 사람을 돕기 위해 일을 할 때, 그 일은 "그들"이 더욱 "우리"처럼 되도록 허락하는 것으로 보인다.

(주 제) 선천적 · 제도적 특권을 당연시하는 사회
(정답 해설) '나는 내 자신을 스스로의 개인적 도덕 의지에 따라 도덕적 수준이 좌우되는 개인으로 보도록 배웠다.'라는 본문의 내용으로 미루어 볼 때 ④는 글의 내용과 일치하지 않는다.
(어 휘) privilege 특권 oppressiveness 가혹함, 억압 women of color 유색인 여성 justly 바르게, 공정하게, 당연하게 unearned 일하지 않고 얻은 oblivion 망각, 기억에서 사라짐 skin privilege 피부색에서 오는 특권 normative 기준이 되는, 표준이 되는

25 ③ 상호 교대는 정치적 또는 사회적 차이를 인정하면서 합의를 도출하려고 시도하고 모든 사람들이 참여하도록 권한다. 상호 교대 접근법은 더 많이 지지하는 사람들에게 더 많은 기회를 주지만 그것은 또한, 소수자에 의해서만 공유되는 견해를 가진 사람들까지도 포함하는 개개인의 관점으로부터 도출된 결과도 타당한 것으로 정당화한다. 나는 민주주의가 권력 있는 사람들, 심지어 권력이 있는 다수에 의한 통치라도 독려해서는 안 된다고 생각한다. 대신, 민주주의의 아이디어는 우리 공동의 열망을 달성하는 방법에 대한 스스로 정의된 동등한 사람들 사이의 공정한 토론을 약속한다. 그 약속을 이행하기 위해 우리는 우리의 대의제 개념의 중심에 상호 교대 개념을 적용할 필요가 있다. 특히 우리가 더욱 다각적인 시민으로서 21세기로 이동할 때, 투표 및 의회제도가 다수가 지배하되 압제하지 않는 시스템을 장려하는 데 있어서 성공 혹은 실패하는 상황들을

고려하는 것은 중요하다.

① 획일적인 다수의 아이디어는 권장되지 않아야 한다.
② 지배하지만 위압하지 않는 다수가 바람직하다.
③ 다수는 가변적이기보다 효과성을 위해 고정되어야 한다.
④ 소수는 상호 교대 시스템 아래에서 적극적인 참여를 보여줄 것이다.
⑤ 전제 정치는 왕 혹은 영주 뿐만 아니라 다수의 사람들로부터도 나온다.

(주 제) 상호 교대 개념의 특징과 필요성
(정답 해설) 주어진 글은 상호 교대를 강조하고 있으므로 다수가 효과성을 위해 확고해야 한다는 ③의 내용은 글의 내용에서 추론하기 어렵다.
(어 휘) taking turns 서로 번갈아 하기 consensus 합의, 여론 legitimate 합법적인, 적법한 perspective 견해 aspiration 열망, 포부 redeem 되찾다, 회복하다 citizenry 시민 tyrannical 폭군의, 압제하는 despotism 폭정

26 ② 타조는 다른 조류들과 달리, 다양한 고급스러운 상품을 생성한다. 고기부터 말하자면, 애호가들은 타조 고기를 소고기의 안심 맛에 비유한다. 파운드당 약 20달러로, 평균 400파운드의 새에서 많은 덩어리를 자를 수 있다. 타조 고기는 또한 건강에도 좋다. 소고기의 절반의 칼로리와 1/7에 불과한 지방 그리고 콜레스테롤도 훨씬 더 적다. 심지어는 같은 범주에 있는 닭고기와 칠면조 고기를 능가한다. "처음에 우리 고객들은 우리가 농담하는 줄 알았어요. 타조라고요?"라고 레스토랑 매니저가 말한다. "그러나 그들은 그것에 의해 매료되었어요." 식사하는 4명 중 1명은 레스토랑에서 살코기를 주문한다. 비록 타조는 높은 수준의 요리가 되지 않더라도, 투자자들은 그 큰 새가 'sesame street'(방송 프로그램)의 자리보다 더 큰 명성을 얻기를 바라고 있다. 타조 속눈썹은 브러시의 딱딱한 털로 쓰이고, 깃털은 청소 도구나 모자, 코트로 사용된다. 그리고 두께가 두껍고 질긴 가죽은 카우보이 부츠에서 소파에 이르기까지 매우 소중하게 사용된다.

(주 제) 상품에서 타조의 쓰임새
(정답 해설) 주어진 글은 타조 고기가 건강에 좋다고 언급하면서 타조 고기가 소고기의 절반의 칼로리를 가지고 있음을 근거로 들었다. 따라서 ②는 글의 내용과 일치한다.
(어 휘) avian 조류의 peer 동료 aficionados 애호가 liken 비유하다 tenderloin 안심고기 fascinated 매료된 lean meat 살코기 eyelash 속눈썹 bristle 강모 hide 가죽 prize 높이 평가하다

27 ③ 오래 전 멀리 떨어진 서태평양의 작은 섬 'Nauru'에서 행복한 사람들이 살고 있었다. 그리고 그들은 그곳에서 그들에게 필요한 것, 즉, 식량과 음료를 위한 코코넛 나무와 풍부한 새, 물고기로 가득 찬 바다 등을 모두 소유하고 있었다. 그리고 Nauru의 원주민들은 세계에서 인산염(우라늄 채취 원석이 되는 화석의 일종) 바위의 가장 부유한 더미에서 살고 있었다. 그러다 100년 전에 기념품으로 호주 Nauru에서 반출된 한 조각의 화석(인산염)이 화학자들의 눈을 사로잡는 일이 일어났다. 그는 그것을 조사하고는 그것이 매우 가치 있는 것이라는 사실을 발견했다. 수백만 톤의 인산염은 호주와 뉴질랜드로 옮겨져 20세기의 대부분 기간 동안 그곳의 들판과 농장을 비옥하게 만들었다. 1968년 Nauru 섬의 독립 후, 인산염 광산은 국유화 되었고 세계에서 가장 작은 공화국의 시민들은 가장 부유한 삶의 반열에 합류했다. 그러나 오늘날, 한때 자급자족했던 이 사람들은 암울한 동화에 붙들려 있다. 인산염은 거의 다 고갈되고 돈의 대부분 역시 사라졌다. 섬의 심장의 4/5가 파헤쳐져 있다.

주 제) 인산염이 가져온 Nauru 섬의 변화
정답 해설) 주어진 글에서 수백만 톤의 인산염은 호주와 뉴질랜드로 옮겨져 20세기의 대부분 기간 동안 그곳의 들판과 농장을 비옥하게 만들었다고 했으므로 ③은 글의 내용과 일치한다.
어 휘) chemist 화학자 souvenir 기념품, 선물 fertilize 땅을 기름지게 만들다, 풍요롭게 만들다 phosphate 인산염, 인산광물 independence 독립 nationalize 국유화하다 grim 암울한 fossilize 화석화 하다, 화석으로 만들다

28 ④ 사냥과 채집방법을 포기한 최초의 인류가 밀과 보리를 키우기 위해 지중해 동부 연안에 정착했고, 고기와 우유를 얻기 위해 양과 염소를 사육했다고 대부분의 고고학자들은 믿고 있다. 그러나 터키의 10,000년 된 마을의 유적은 다른 상황을 보여준다. 둥근 돌집의 거주자들은 최초라고 알려진 사육된 양과 염소 이전 아마도 오백년 전쯤 야생 양과 염소를 사냥했고, 견과류와 콩류를 먹었고 동시에 돼지를 사육하여 먹었다. Delaware 대학의 Michael Rosenberg가 이끄는 발굴 작업이 수백 년 가량 지속되어 온 그 지역의 공동체를 밝혀냈다. 마을 사람들이 돼지를 사육한다는 증거는 일반적으로 야생의 돼지들의 이빨보다 작은 이빨을 포함한다. 돼지 뼈의 대부분은 수컷에서 왔다. 암컷들은 번식을 위해 아껴두는 경향이 있었다. Rosenberg는 돼지를 사육하면서 배운 방법이 나중에 야생 염소와 양들을 키우는 데 적용되었다고 믿는다.

주 제) 터키에서 발견된 돼지 사육 증거
정답 해설) 주어진 글은 마을 사람들이 돼지를 사육한다는 증거로 '일반적으로 야생의 돼지들의 이빨보다 작은 이빨'을 들었다. 따라서 ④는 글의 내용과 일치하지 않는다.
어 휘) mediterranean 지중해의 tame 길들이다, 조련하다 archaeologist 고고학자 excavation 굴착, 땅굴 파기 domesticate 길들이다, 교화시키다 legume 콩과 식물 breeding 사육 apply 적용하다

29 ⑤ 앞으로 몇 년 동안, 항공 우주국 (NASA)과 다른 우주관련 정부 기관은 태양계 안의 생명체에 대한 탐색을 강화할 것이다. 하지만 탐색 작업은 근본적인 의문에 의해 더욱 복잡해진다. 도대체 생명체란 무엇인가? NASA는 '생명체란 다윈의 진화론을 계속해 진행할 수 있는 자기 유지적 화학 시스템이다.'라는 간단한 기본적인 정의를 이용해왔다. 다른 과학자들은 "생명체란 자가 촉매작용을 통해서 스스로를 복제할 수 있고, 서서히 촉매작용의 효율을 증가시키는 실수를 할 수 있는 화학적 시스템이다."와 같은 자신의 정의를 퍼뜨려왔다. 생명체는 하나의 정의에 의해 사로잡히는 것을 피하는 경향이 있다. 어쩌면 생명체는, 예를 들면 진화할 필요가 없을지도 모른다. DNA와 같은 정보를 가진 분자를 하나도 함유하고 있지 않은 생물을 상상해 보라. 그들은 번식할 수는 있지만 복제는 하지 못할 수 있다. 부모는 아이에게 생물학적으로 완전히 낯선 사람에 지나지 않을 것이다.

① 생명의 정의는 태양계에서의 생명에 대한 탐색을 복잡하게 한다.
② 다윈의 진화론의 개념은 항공 우주국 (NASA)의 생명의 정의에 반영되어 있다.
③ 많은 과학자들은 NASA와는 다른 그들 자신만의 생명의 정의가 있다.
④ 생명의 본질에서 하나의 정의만을 포착해 내는 것은 어렵다.
⑤ 유기체가 복제를 할 경우, 그 아이는 부모와 생물학적으로 관련이 없다.

주 제) 생명체에 대한 정의
정답 해설) 마지막 부분에서 '생명체가 복제를 하지 못한다면 부모와 아이의 생물학적 밀접성은 이방인과 아이의 생물학적 밀접성과 다를 바가 없다'고 말하고 있다. 하지만 생명체가 복제를 할 경우, 부모와 아이의 생물학적 밀접성에 관한 내용은 본문에 언급되지 않았다. 따라서 ⑤의 내용은 본문과 일치하지 않는다.

어휘 intensify 강화하다 complicate 복잡하게하다 fundamental 근본적인 definition 정의 self-sustained 자립한 replicate 복제하다, 사본을 만들다 autocatalysis 자가 촉매작용 elude 교묘하게 피하다, 회피하다 molecule 분자 reproduce번식 하다 replicate 복제하다

---

30 ③ 당신은 20대에 가장 총명할 것이다. 그리고 30대 즈음에 당신의 기억력이, 특히 수학적인 계산을 하는 능력이 감소하기 시작한다. 하지만 다른 일을 위한 당신의 IQ는 향상된다. 예를 들어 45세의 어휘는 대학을 졸업할 때보다 거의 3배만큼 많다. 60세에 당신의 뇌는 21세 때보다 거의 4배나 많은 정보를 보유하고 있다. 대부분의 분야에서 정점이 일찍 온다지만 — 대부분의 노벨상 수상자들은 20대 후반이나 30대에 그들의 최고의 연구를 했고, 위대한 음악의 대부분은 33세에서 39세 사이에 쓰여졌다. — 어떤 사람들은 삶 전체에 걸쳐 우수한 작품을 계속 생산해낸다. 71세에 Tolstoi는 '부활'을 완성했고, Voltaire는 그의 놀라운 풍자 문학인 Candide를 64세에 집필했다. Will Durant는 69세 때 5권 분량의 기념비적인 'History of a Civilization'의 집필을 시작했다.

① 기억력의 상실은 건강한 신체에 영향을 주지 않는다.
② 나이 든 여성이 나이 든 남성보다 산수에 더 나은 경향이 있다.
③ 인생에는 특정한 성취 패턴이 있지만, 약간의 예외도 있다.
④ 사람들에게 인생의 전성기는 단 한 번이기 때문에, 그것을 놓치면 안 된다.
⑤ 손실과 이득 사이의 균형이 파괴되는 때가 있다.

주제 연령별 능력의 차이
정답 해설 이 글의 내용은 대부분의 사람들이 일반적으로 20~30대에 최고의 기량을 발휘하고 있지만 예외도 있다는 것이다. 그러므로 추론할 수 있는 내용은 ③이다.
어휘 decline 감퇴하다 sharp 날카로운, 예리한 computation 계산, 계산 결과 resurrection 부활, 소생 marvelous 놀라운 satire 풍자, 풍자문학 monumental 기념이 되는, 기념비적인

---

31 ② 번개의 순간적인 번쩍임과 나뭇가지가 뚝하고 부러지는 소리는 극도로 짧은 시간 동안의 자극을 나타내지만, 그럼에도 불구하고 그것들은 몇 가지 반응을 필요로 하는 중요한 정보를 제공할지도 모른다. 그러한 자극들은 최초에, 그리고 아주 짧은 순간, 세상이 우리에게 주는 정보의 첫 번째 저장소 '감각 기억' 속에 저장된다. 사실 "감각 기억"

이라는 용어는 각각 다른 감각 정보원에 관련된 몇 종류의 감각 기억을 포함한다. 시각 체계를 통한 정보를 반영하는 영상 기억이 있고, 귀로부터 수집된 정보를 저장하는 음향 기억이 있으며, 나머지 감각들에 해당하는 각각의 기억들이 있다. 개별적인 하위 유형과는 무관하게 감각 기억은 일반적으로 아주 짧은 시간 동안만 정보를 저장할 수 있고, 만약 자료가 다른 형태의 기억으로 전환되지 않는다면 그 정보는 영원히 사라진다.

① 찰나의 시간에 일어나는 자극도 몇 가지 반응을 필요로 한다.
② 감각 기억의 몇몇 하위 유형들은 정보를 오랫동안 저장한다.
③ 감각 기억에는 두 개 이상의 종류가 있다.
④ 우리가 노출된 정보는 처음에 감각 기억에 저장된다.
⑤ 영상·음향 기억들은 각각 시각과 청각의 정보를 저장한다.

주제 감각 기억의 특징
정답 해설 마지막 문장에서 '감각 기억'은 일시적으로만 존재하며 다른 형태의 기억으로 전환되지 않을 경우 영원히 사라지게 된다고 설명하고 있다. 그러므로 ② '감각 기억의 몇몇 하위 유형들은 정보를 오랫동안 저장한다.'가 이 글과 내용이 일치한다.
어휘 momentary 순간의, 순간적인 flash 번쩍이다, 번쩍임 lightning 번개, 번개가 치다 snap 덥석 물다, 찰칵 소리가 나다 branch 가지, 가지가 뻗어나가다 duration 계속됨, 지속됨, 내구성 nonetheless ~에도 불구하고 sensory 감각의, 감각기관의 exceedingly 대단히, 매우, 몹시 encompass 둘러싸다, 포함하다 iconic 모양의, 형상의 echoic 반향을 일으키는, 의성의, 음성의

More Practice

01 ④   02 ③   03 ⑤   04 ⑤

---

01 ④ 1967년에 앤디 워홀은 다양한 대학에서 강연을 요청받았다. 그는 말하는 것을 싫어했는데, 특히 그 자신의 예술에 관해서 그러했다. "무언가 말할 것이 적을수록 그것은 더 완벽하다"고 그는 느꼈다. 그러나 돈벌이가 좋았기 때문에, 늘 그는 거절하기가 어려웠다. 그의 해결책은 간단했다. 배우 Allen Midgette에게 그인 척 가장을 해달라고 요청했다. Midgette은 진한 머리에 피부가 햇볕에 탄 반 체로키 인디언이었다. 그는 워홀과 조금도 닮지 않았다. 그러나 워홀과 그의 친구들은 그의 얼굴을 파우더로 칠하고, 그의 갈색 머리에 은색으로 스프레이를 뿌렸고, 그에게 짙은 안경을 주었고, 그에게 워홀의 옷을 입혔다.

Midgette은 예술에 대해 아무 것도 알지 못했기 때문에, 학생들의 질문에 대한 그의 답변은 워홀 자신의 것처럼 짧고 수수께끼 같은 경향이 있었다. 분장은 효과가 있었다. 워홀은 아이콘이었을지 모르지만, 누구도 그를 진정으로 알지 못했고, 그는 짙은 색의 안경을 자주 착용했기 때문에, 심지어 그의 얼굴도 상세하게 알려지지 않았다.

주 제 가짜 앤디 워홀

정답 해설 앤디 워홀로 분장한 Midgette은 예술에 대해 아무것도 알지 못했다는 내용이 본문에 나와 있으므로 정답은 ④이다.

어 휘 impersonate ~(다른 사람을) 흉내내다, 가장하다

02 ③ 그것(러시아 소설과 희곡의 작품 목록)이 적절한 영어 번역 가운데 존재했던 그 세기 동안, 러시아 소설과 희곡의 작품 목록은 명성과 확고한 "분위기"를 얻었다. 그것은 진지하고(즉, 비극적이거나 부조리하지만 좀처럼 편한 마음으로는 즐길 수 없고 절대 사소하지 않고) 다소 설교하는 듯하고, 정치적으로 야당권이며, 대개 느닷없거나 기이한 시작과 마무리를 가진 혼란스러운 장르로 만들어졌다. 소설들은 특히나 너무 길고 형이상학적인 생각들로 넘치며 독자들이 단지 즐기면서 읽는 것이 아니라 교훈을 배우는 것을 분명하게 열망한다. 이 책들은 그런 허세들을 풍자하면서도 선과 악에 대해 깊이 고찰한다. 만약 희곡이 있었다면, 결말 직전에 당신의 피를 얼릴 반전이 존재한다. 러시아 문학의 등장인물들은 돈, 경력, 그들을 위한 사회적 성공, 트로피 아내나 남편, 교외의 집들을 추구하지 않고 그 대신에 도달하기 어려운 다른 것을 갈망했다.

주 제 영어로 번역된 러시아 작품들의 특성

정답 해설 러시아 문학은 진지했고, 설교하는 듯하고, 정치적으로 반동스러웠으며 러시아 문학의 인물들은 사회가 말하는 돈과 경력, 성공과 트로피 아내나 남편, 교외의 집들을 좇지 않고 다른 도달하기 어려운 것을 열망했다는 내용으로 미루어 볼 때 '소설은 도덕적 교훈을 배제하고 즐거움을 추구한다.'라는 ③의 내용은 주어진 글과 일치하지 않는다.

어 휘 adequate 적절한 absurd 우스꽝스러운, 부조리한 preacherly 설교하는 듯한 oppositionist 야당(반대자) mystify 혼란스럽게 하다 metaphysical 형이상학적 manifestly 분명하게 trophy wife/husband 남들에게 과시하기 위한 아내/남편 crave 갈망하다

03 ⑤ Great Salt Lake는 서반구에서 가장 큰 염수호이다. 그 호수는 Bear강, Weber강, 그리고

Jordan강에서 유입되지만 배출구는 없다. 빙하기가 끝났을 때 그 전 지역은 빙하가 녹은 물로 된 호수 밑으로 잠겼고, 그 호수로부터 넘쳐흐른 물은 Snake강과 Columbia강을 통해 태평양으로 빠져나갔다. 그 호수가 겪은 심한 기후 변화와 담수의 유입량을 초과한 계속된 증발로 인해 호수의 크기가 이전의 20분의 1로 줄어들었다. Great Salt Lake에 있는 대부분의 소금은 모든 담수에 존재하는 용해된 소금의 잔존물이다. 물이 증발하면서 미량의 용해된 소금이 줄어드는 호수에 서서히 농축되었다.

주 제 Great Salt Lake의 형성 과정

정답 해설 호수의 소금은 대부분 호수에 유입된 담수에 녹아있던 것이므로 ⑤는 글의 내용과 일치하지 않는다.

어 휘 hemisphere 반구 outlet 배출구, 하구 close 끝, 종결 submerge 물에 잠그다, 물속에 넣다[가라앉히다] meltwater 빙하가 녹은 물 overflow 넘쳐흐른 물, 범람, 홍수 the Pacific Ocean 태평양 undergo 겪다, 경험하다 evaporation 증발, (수분의) 발산 exceed 초과하다 inflow 유입, 유입량 fresh water 담수, 민물 remnant 잔존물, 나머지 dissolve 용해시키다, 녹이다 trace 미량, 극소량 gradually 서서히, 점차 concentrate 농축하다 shrink 줄어들다

04 ⑤ Jean Baptiste Joseph Fourier는 프랑스의 수학자이자 물리학자였다. 그가 여덟 살때 그의 아버지가 사망했고, 이러한 비극이 있은 지 일 년도 안 되어 그를 고아로 남겨 둔 채 그의 어머니가 돌아가셨다. 한 자비로운 여인은 그가 지역의 군사학교에 다니도록 도와주었다. 그는 장교가 되고 싶었지만 그가 재단사의 아들이라는 이유 때문에 허용되지 않았다. 1795년 그는 파리 École Normale의 교사가 되었다. 혁명 후 광란의 기간 동안 그는 단두대의 사용을 반대한다는 의견을 밝혔는데, 그것 때문에 그는 거의 목숨을 잃을 뻔하였다. 나폴레옹이 1798년 이집트를 침공했을 때, Fourier와 다른 학자들은 그 원정에 함께했다. 프랑스에 돌아왔을 때 Fourier는 열전도에 대한 그의 연구를 시작했다. 열전도에 대한 그의 수학적 이론은 그에게 지속적인 명성을 가져다주었다. 이집트에 머무는 동안 그는 이상한 질병에 걸려서 그 병 때문에 남은 생애동안 난방이 잘된 방 안에 갇혀 살아야만 했다. 1830년 5월 16일 Fourier는 파리에서 사망했다.

주 제 Jean Baptiste Joseph Fourier의 일생

정답 해설 이집트에 머무는 동안 이상한 질병에 걸렸으므로 ⑤는 글의 내용과 일치하지 않는다.

어 휘 mathematician 수학자 physicist 물리학자 tragedy 비극 pass away 돌아가시다, 사망하다 orphan 고아

charitable 자비로운 tailor 재단사 frenzy 광란, 발작 invade 침공하다 accompany 동반하다, 동행하다 expedition 원정, 탐험 heat conduction 열전도 contract (병에) 걸리다 confine 가두다, 감금하다

UNIT 18 도표

Example

답 ④

매년 미국 식품 소비 평균(1970~2000)

(파운드)
150
201.7 야채

126.8 과일

100
66.5 붉은 고기
64.4 가금류

50
29.8 치즈
15.2 어류

1970 1980 1990 2000 (년)

위의 그래프는 1970년부터 2000년까지 이르는 기간 동안 여러 음식들에 대한 소비량의 변화를 나타낸다. ① 채소와 과일의 소비량은 30년의 기간 동안 20% 이상 증가하였다. ② 육류와 가금류 소비량의 차이는 2000년도에 최소화되었다. ③ 30년 동안 수산물 소비는 거의 일정했던 것에 비해 치즈의 소비는 지속적으로 증가하였다. ④ 같은 기간 동안 소비율의 하락을 보인 음식은 없다. ⑤ 2000년도에 평균적인 미국인들에 의해 소비된 과일과 채소의 총량은 그 해에 다른 모든 식품들의 합계보다 더 많다.

주 제) 미국인의 식품별 연간 소비량 변화 추이

Practice

01 ④   02 ②

01 ④

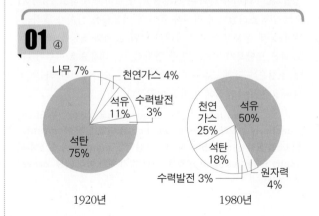

1920년   1980년

가까운 미래에 발생 가능한 에너지원 부족 현상 해결책을 찾기 위해 에너지원이 20세기 동안 어떻게 변했는지 연구해 보는 것은 충분히 가치 있다. 위의 그래프는 1920년과 1980

년 사이 미국에서 에너지원의 변화 추이에 대해 보여준다. ① 석탄은 1920년경에는 도표에서 가장 많은 부분을 표시하고 있으며 정확히 전체 에너지 공급량의 3/4을 구성하고 있었다. ② 하지만 1980년대에 공급의 18%를 구성하고 3번째로 많은 양에 불과했다. ③ 석유 사용의 비율은 1920년과 1980년 사이에 4배 이상 증가하였으며 1980년대에 가장 큰 에너지원이 되었다. ④ 천연 가스는 1980년에 다섯 번째에서 두 번째 에너지원으로 강화되었으며, 전체 에너지 공급의 정확히 1/4을 차지했다. ⑤ 1980년, 나무는 도표에서 없어졌고 수력이 그와 같은 비율을 유지하였으며 원자력이 새롭게 포함되었다.

주제 1920년과 1980년 사이 미국 에너지원 변화 추이
정답 해설 도표를 살펴보면 1920년대에 천연가스는 4번째로 많이 사용되는 에너지원이고, 1980년대에는 2번째로 많이 사용되는 에너지원이었다. 따라서 ④는 도표와 일치하지 않는다.
어휘 be worth ~ing ~할 가치 있다 shortage 부족 consist of ~구성되다 constitute 구성하다 quadruple 4배가 되다 hydropower 수력 maintain 유지하다

02 ②

미국의 종교 선호도

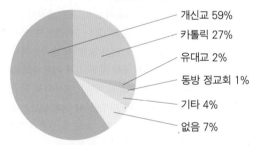

개신교 59%
카톨릭 27%
유대교 2%
동방 정교회 1%
기타 4%
없음 7%

미국의 매우 다양한 인종적 배경은 종교적 다원주의를 형성해왔다. ① 전체 미국인의 93%가 종교를 가지고 있다고 대답했다. ② 오직 11%만이 종교적인 선호도나 믿음을 가지고 있지 않다고 답했다. ③ 미국인의 약 87%가 기독교이고, 2%가 유대교, 그리고 나머지 4%가 이슬람교, 불교, 힌두교 등과 같은 종교였다. ④ 87%를 차지하는 기독교에는 개신교와 가톨릭, 동방 정교회가 포함된다. ⑤ 비록 개신교도는 59%에 불과하지만 그들은 미국에서 가장 큰 종교 집단이다.

주제 미국의 종교 선호도
정답 해설 도표에 따르면 종교가 없다고 말한 사람의 비율은 7%이므로 ②는 도표와 일치하지 않는다.
어휘 Christian 기독교도 Moslem 무슬림 Protestant 개신교도 Catholic 가톨릭 Eastern Orthodox 동방정교

More Practice

01 ③   02 ④   03 ⑤   04 ③

01 ③

세대별 여가 미디어 소비

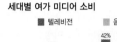

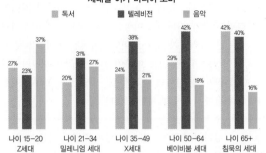

독서   텔레비전   음악

| | 나이 15-20 Z세대 | 나이 21-34 밀레니엄 세대 | 나이 35-49 X세대 | 나이 50-64 베이비붐 세대 | 나이 65+ 침묵의 세대 |

위 그래프는 세 가지 대중적인 여가 미디어 활동에 대한 세대별 참여 비율을 보여준다. ① 세 가지 여가 활동 중에, 독서가 침묵의 세대에서 가장 인기 있는 반면에, 음악은 Z세대에서 가장 인기 있는 여가 활동이다. ② 독서를 하면서 여가를 보내는 밀레니엄 세대의 비율은 다른 세대들에 비해 눈에 띄게 적다. ③ 텔레비전은, 1/4 미만이 선호하는 여가 활동이라고 선택한 Z세대를 제외하고 모든 세대에 가장 인기 있는 여가 활동이다. ④ X세대, 베이비붐 세대, 침묵의 세대 사이에서 음악은 독서보다 인기가 적다. ⑤ 가장 젊은 세대보다 독서를 많이 하는 두 세대는 베이비붐 세대와 침묵의 세대이다.

주제 세대 간 여가 미디어 활동 비교
정답 해설 침묵의 세대에서는 TV(40%)보다 독서(42%)가 더 인기가 높으므로 ③은 도표의 내용과 일치하지 않는다.
어휘 generational 세대의, 세대 간의 millennial 천년의 counterpart 대응물

02 ④

사업상 여행: 차량 또는 비행기 이용

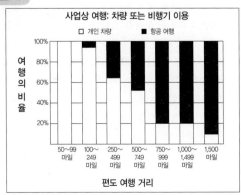

개인 차량   항공 여행

여행의 비율

| 50~99 마일 | 100~ 249 마일 | 250~ 499 마일 | 500~ 749 마일 | 750~ 999 마일 | 1,000~ 1,499 마일 | 1,500 마일 |

편도 여행 거리

위의 그래프는 편도로 여행하는 장거리 출장에서 개인 차량과 항공 여행의 비율을 보여 준다. (이 그래프는 다른 운송 수단은 반영하고 있지 않다.) ① 목적지까지 개인 차량을 탈 것인지 혹은 비행기로 갈 것인지에 대한 결정은 여행 거리에 따라 달라진다. 거리가 멀면 멀수록 항공을 이용한 출장의 비율이 더 커진다. ② 100~249마일의 출장에서 개인 차량은 몇 안 되는 다른 유형의 운송 수단과 함께 우세한 운송 수단이다. ③ 만일 목적지가 250~499마일 떨어진 곳이라면 출장의 60퍼센트 이상이 개인 차량으로 이루어진다. ④ <u>반면, 목적지가 500~749마일 떨어진 곳이라면 출장의 2/3 이상이 항공편으로 이루어진다.</u> ⑤ 750~999마일과 1,000~1,499마일 사이의 출장에서는 항공을 선호하는 여행자들의 비율에서 뚜렷한 차이가 없다.

주 제 장거리 출장에서 개인 차량과 비행기 이용 비율
정답 해설 그래프에 따르면 목적지가 500~749마일 떨어진 곳은 출장의 절반 정도가 항공편으로 이루어지므로 ④는 도표와 일치하지 않는다.

어 휘 business trip 출장 share 몫, 비율 one-way 편도 destination 목적지 dominant 지배적인, 우세한

03 ⑤

한국 연구원의 수

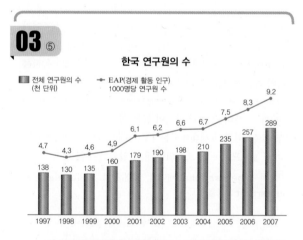

위의 그래프는 1997년부터 2007년까지 전체 연구원의 수와 한국의 경제 활동 인구 (EAP) 1,000명당 연구원의 수를 보여준다. ① 이전 해와 비교했을 때, 매년 기록된 두 수치는 모두 1998년에 기록된 수치를 제외하고 증가되는 현상을 보여주었다. ② 경제 활동 인구 1,000명당 연구원의 수에서 보이는 가장 큰 연간 증가는 2000년과 2001년 사이에 기록되었다. ③ 2004년부터 2007년까지 한국에는 매년 200,000명 이상의 연구원이 있었는데, ④ 2007년에 가장 많은 수를 기록했다. 2007년 경제 활동 인구 1,000명당 연구원의 수는 1999년 경제 활동 인구 1,000명당 연구원의 수의 2배였다. ⑤ <u>전체 연구원 수의 연간 증가는 1998년과 1999년 사이에 가장 컸다.</u>

주 제 한국의 연구원 수 변화
정답 해설 전체 연구원 수의 연간 증가폭은 2006년과 2007년 사이에 32,000명으로 조사 기간 중 가장 크다. 따라서 ⑤는 도표와 일치하지 않는다.

어 휘 researcher 연구원 economically 경제적으로 active 활동 중인, 활동적인 population 인구 be compared to ~과 비교하다 previous 이전의 annual 1년의, 연간의 growth 증가, 성장

04 ③

검색 엔진을 이용하여 찾은 정보의 정확도와 신뢰도

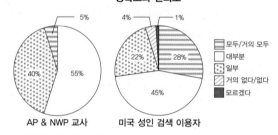

- AP: 대학 과목 선이수제 과정
- NWP: 전국 글쓰기 프로젝트

위의 두 원 그래프는 2012년에 두 응답자 집단(AP & NWP 교사와 미국의 성인 검색 이용자)이 검색 엔진을 이용해 찾은 정보를 얼마나 정확하거나 신뢰도 있다고 생각하는지를 보여준다. ① AP & NWP 교사의 경우, 5퍼센트가 검색 엔진을 이용해 찾은 정보의 "모두/거의 모두"가 정확하거나 신뢰할 수 있다고 한 반면에, 미국의 성인 검색 이용자의 28퍼센트가 같은 대답을 한다. ② AP & NWP 교사와 미국 성인 검색 이용자 모두에서 정보의 "대부분"이 정확하고 신뢰할 수 있다는 응답의 비중이 가장 크다. ③ <u>또한, AP & NWP 교사의 40퍼센트가 정보의 "일부"가 정확하거나 신뢰할 수 있다고 하며, 미국 성인 검색 이용자의 30퍼센트가 넘는 사람이 같은 대답을 한다.</u> ④ 검색 엔진을 이용해 찾은 정보 중 정확하거나 신뢰할 수 있는 것이 "매우 약간/없다"라고 한 미국 성인 검색 이용자는 5퍼센트 미만을 차지한다. ⑤ "모르겠다"라고 대답한 미국 성인 검색 이용자는 1퍼센트에 불과하다.

주 제 검색 엔진을 이용해 찾은 정보의 정확성 및 신뢰도
정답 해설 정보의 "일부"가 정확하거나 신뢰할 수 있다고 말한 미국 성인 검색 이용자의 비율은 22퍼센트로 30퍼센트에 못 미친다. 따라서 ③은 도표와 일치하지 않는다.

어 휘 pie chart 원 그래프 accurate 정확한 trustworthy 신뢰할 수 있는 respondent 응답자 account for ~을 차지하다

Example 답 ④

그날은 농장에서의 여느 겨울날처럼 그렇게 시작되었다. 하지만 오후 무렵에는 큰 소란이 일어났다. 돼지우리의 지붕에 쌓였던 눈이 너무 무거웠던 것으로 드러났다. 지붕은 휘어서 내려앉았고, 무거운 나무 기둥이 새끼 돼지를 덮쳤다. 그 기둥은 ① 그것을 못 움직이도록 누르고 있었고, 그것은 움직일 수 없었다. 내가 그 현장에 도착했을 때, ② 그것은 고통 속에 비명을 지르고 있었다. 나는 ③ 그것으로부터 그 기둥을 치워버리려고 시도해 보았지만 예상치 못했던 문제에 봉착하게 되었다. 어미 돼지가 그 새끼 돼지를 보호하고 있었다. 그것은 새끼의 근처로 누구도 가까이 오지 못하도록 하려고 했다. ④ 그것은 내가 도우려고 노력하는 사실을 거의 이해하지 못하고 있었다. 농장의 다른 일꾼이 밧줄을 이용해 어미 돼지를 붙잡고 나서야 나는 새끼 돼지에게 접근할 수 있었고, ⑤ 그것을 풀어줄 수 있었다.

주 제 어느 겨울 농장의 새끼 돼지 구출

Practice

01 ④　　02 ②　　03 ④

01 ④ 날아다니는 차를 만드는 것은 사실 그렇게 어려운 일이 아니다. 첫 제품 모델은 1947년에 시작되었다. 실현 가능한 ① 날아다니는 차를 만드는 것은 진정한 도전으로 밝혀졌다. Tesla와 SpaceX의 최고 경영자인 Elon Musk는 왜 그의 두 회사가 합작해서 ② 로켓 차를 만들 수 없냐고 지속적으로 질문을 받았다. 그는 최근 트위터에 연달아 답글을 올렸는데, "③ 날아다니는 차의 장점: 3D에서 빠르게 이동할 수 있다. 단점: ④ 두 방향으로 달리는 차(길을 따라 달리는 차)보다 정면으로 떨어지는 사고의 위험이 더 높다"라는 답변을 포함했다. 그리고 유명한 투자자, Peter Thiel은 "우리는 ⑤ 진짜 날아다니는 차를 원했지만 고물을 얻었다."고 말했다.

주 제 비행 자동차 제작

정답 해설 지문상에서 나머지 보기들은 날아다니는 차에 대해서 언급하고 있지만 ④ '두 방향으로 달리는 차'는 날아다니는 차가 아닌 길을 따라 달리는 차를 의미한다.

어 휘 pro 이로운 점 con 단점 vector 방향, 진로 investor 투자자 junk 고물, 쓰레기

02 ② Eton에는 이른바 'capping'이라고 알려져 있는 ① 전통이 있었다. 학생들은 거리에서 그들의 손가락 끝 머리에 가리키는 행동을 통해 교사들에게 경의를 표하곤 했는데, 그것은 이른바 간소화시킨 모자 벗기였고 교사들에 의해서 다시 화답을 받았다. 최근에는, 정부가 ② 그것이 기쁘게 '존경'이라 부르는 것의 증진 노력을 함에도 불구하고 ③ 이러한 전통은 점차 사라져 간다. 나는 그것이 너무 많은 시간과 노력을 필요로 하고, 또 지나치게 과도한 경외감을 보여준다고 생각한다. 따라서 다른 많은 유사한 관습처럼, ④ 그것 역시 현대 사회의 영국에서는 사라질 운명에 처해있다. 공평하게 말하자면, 위의 내용을 기록한 직후에도, 나는 TV에 나오는 골프 선수들이 관중에게 경의를 표하기 위해 ⑤ 그 오래된 관습을 여전히 따르고 있다는 것에 주목하며 용기를 얻었다.

주 제 사라질 운명에 처한 Eton의 capping 전통

정답 해설 ②는 바로 앞에 나오는 government를 가리키는 지시 대명사이고, 나머지 선지는 모두 교사들을 향해 경의를 표하는 Eton의 전통을 가리키고 있다.

어 휘 beak (영국 학생 속어) 교사, 교장 capping 모자 쓰기 salute 경의를 표하다, 경례를 하다 abbreviated 축약된, 축소된 doff (경의를 표하며) 모자를 벗다 reciprocate (받은 것과 같은 감정이나 행동으로) 화답하다 drive for ~을 위해 노력하다, ~을 노리다 doom (죽음 등) 불행한 운명을 맞다 in fairness 공정하게 말하자면, 공평하게 말하자면 deference 존중, 경의

03 ④ 우리 중 대다수는 너무 좋아해서 차마 버릴 수 없는 물건이 있다. ① 그것은 아마도 좋아하는 영화 배우의 친필서명이 적힌 오래된 누더기 티셔츠일 수도 있다. 그리고 ② 그것은 오래 돼서 잉크는 다 떨어져 버렸지만 믿음직한 동료로써 수많은 시험을 함께 해온 행운의 펜일 수도 있다. 어떤 사람들에게는 ③ 그것은 이미 오래 전부터 빛을 잃은 녹슨 은반지일수도 있다. 비록 그 반지는 더 이상 장신구로서의 목적을 수행할 수는 없지만 ④ 그것은 돌아가신 할머니와 같은 사랑하는 사람들에 대한 기억을 떠올리게 할 수 있다. 어떤 물건이 되었든지, 그 물건을 간직하는 진짜 이유는 그 물건의 표면적인 가치가 아니라 ⑤ 그것이 우리의 과거의 일부분, 즉 우리 마음에 소중히 간직하는 기억을 나타내기 때문이다.

주 제 추억이 담긴 물건 간직하기

정답 해설 ④의 it이 가리키는 것은 앞 문장의 tarnished silver ring이다. 나머지가 가리키는 것은 an item of endearment이다.

어휘 endearment 사랑스러움, 좋아함 tatter 해지다, 넝마, 누더기 sidekick 조수, 단짝 tarnish 녹슬게 하다, 빛을 잃게 만들다 adornment 장신구, 장식 conjure up (생각, 마법, 기억 등을) 불러일으키다

More Practice

01 ⑤	02 ③	03 ②	04 ④

01 ⑤ J. R. Kline은 다른 수학자들에 관한 이야기를 하는 것을 좋아했다. Norbert Wiener에 관한 이야기는 그가 좋아하는 것이었다: 어느 여름날, Kline 부부와 Wiener 부부는 New Hampshire의 호숫가에 오두막을 서로 가까이 두고 있었다. Wiener는 ① 그의 부두에서 호수 근처 작은 섬까지 수영하는 습관이 있었다. 수영을 할 때, Kline은 옆에서 배의 노를 저으며 Wiener의 곁에서 따라가곤 했고, 그들은 Wiener가 ② 그의 목표를 향해 확고부동하게 나아가는 동안 대화를 나누곤 했다. Wiener는, 심지어 ③ 그가 숨을 내뱉고 헐떡거리며 작은 섬으로 향하는 동안에도 항상 대화의 주도권을 유지하고자 노력했다. 그러던 어느 날, 수영이 다 끝날 때쯤 ④ 그는 "Kline, 현존하는 5대 수학자가 누구야?"라고 힘없는 소리로 말했다. Kline은 조용히 대답했다. "재미있는 질문이네. 어디 보자." ⑤ 그는 재빠르게 네 명의 이름을 댔다("Wiener"는 제외하고). "그래, 그래, 계속해봐." Wiener가 식식거리며 말했다. 섬세한 유머로, Kline은 5번째 이름을 대는 것을 피했다.

주제 수학자 Wiener에 대한 일화

정답 해설 본문의 주요 등장인물은 Kline과 Wiener이다. ⑤는 Kline을 가리키고 나머지는 Wiener를 가리킨다.

어휘 adjacent 인접한 paddle 노를 젓다 rowboat 노를 젓는 배 steadfastly 확고부동하게 puff (숨을)훅훅 불다 gasp 헐떡거리다 bleat 우는 소리를 내다, 힘없는 소리로 말하다 tick off 예를 들다 splutter 식식거리며 말하다

02 ③ Misty May-Treanor와 Kerri Walsh는 대단한 운동선수고, 대단한 사람들이다. 2008 베이징 올림픽 비치발리볼 준결승에서 ① 그들은 뛰어난 브라질 팀을 이겼다. 그 후에 그들은 브라질 팀원들과 악수하며 "고맙다."고 말했다. 그러고 나서 ② 그들은 공을 회수하거나 모래를 긁어모으는 등의 일을 한 아주 많은 봉사자들과 악수했다. 저널리스트인 Mike Celizic는 쓰기를, "③ 그들이 그들

의 노력에 대한 감사함을 알지 못한 채 사라져 주기를 원하지 않았고, 그들은 그들이 코트를 떠날 때 뒤에 있던 몇몇 봉사자들을 문자 그대로 쫓아 다녔다."라며 경외하였다. ④ 그들은 또한 팬들을 향해 손을 흔들고 필수 약물 검사 후에 팬들에게 돌아오기로 약속했다. 그들은 돌아왔고, 사진과 사인을 아주 많은 팬들에게 해 주기 위해 자세를 잡았다. 그리고 팬들은 정말 고마워하며 ⑤ 그들과 악수했다.

주제 어느 운동선수들의 존경할 만한 인성

정답 해설 ③ them은 자원봉사자들을 의미하고 나머지는 모두 Misty May-Treanor와 Kerrie Walsh를 의미한다.

어휘 defeat 이기다 retrieve 회수하다 rake 긁어모으다 awe 경외심 wave to ~을 향해 손을 흔들다 mandatory 의무적인

03 ② 인간이 발명한 최초의 진정한 운동 장비 품목은 공이었다. 고대 이집트에서는 돌을 던지는 것이 아이들이 좋아하는 놀이였지만, 잘못 던진 돌이 아이를 다치게 할 수 있었다. 그래서 이집트인들은 보다 덜 위험한 던질 것을 찾게 되었다. 그리고 ① 그들은 어쩌면 최초의 공일 수도 있는 것을 개발했다. ② 그것들은 처음에 풀이나 잎을 끈으로 묶어서 만들었고 나중에는 동물의 가죽 조각을 실로 꿰매어 붙이고 그 안에 깃털이나 건초를 채워서 만들었다. 이집트인들은 호전적이었지만, ③ 그들은 평화로운 경기를 하는 시간도 가졌다. 곧 ④ 그들은 많은 구기 종목을 고안했다. 아마 ⑤ 그들은 재미보다는 교육을 위해서 공놀이를 했을 것이다. 공놀이는 주로 젊은이들에게 전쟁에 필요한 속도와 기술을 가르치는 한 가지 수단으로 생각되었다.

주제 이집트에서 발명된 공과 구기 종목

정답 해설 ②는 the first balls를 가리키고 나머지는 모두 Egyptians를 가리킨다.

어휘 equipment 장비 string 줄, 끈 sew 꿰매다 stuff 채워 넣다 warlike 호전적인 instruction 교육, 가르침 think of A as B A를 B로 생각하다

04 ④ Nancy는 ① 그녀의 십대 딸아이가 자신의 생활과 능력에 대한 부정적인 관점을 겪고 있을 때, 긍정적인 면을 찾아보려고 애쓰고 있었다. 의도적으로 부모 역할을 제대로 하고자 하는 바람에서, ② 그녀는 딸의 방에 들어갔고 그녀가 목격했던 한 가지 긍정적인 성과물을 적어 두었다. "나는 네가 최근에 힘든 시간을 보내고 있고 네 삶에 대해 정말로 좋거나 긍정적으로 느끼지 않고 있다는 것을

안단다. 그런데 너는 오늘 네 방 청소를 훌륭하게 해냈고, ③ 나는 그 일이 틀림없이 네게 큰 노력이 필요했을 거라는 것을 안다." 다음 날, Nancy로서는 놀랍게도, 그 십대 소녀는 다소 기분이 좋아보였다. 지나가는 말로 ④ 그녀는 "엄마, 어제 저에 관한 긍정적인 점을 말씀해 주셔서 감사해요. 저는 마음이 너무나 울적했고 저 자신에 대해 어떤 좋은 점도 생각할 수가 없었어요. ⑤ 엄마가 그 긍정적인 점을 말씀하신 후, 그것은 제가 저 자신에게서 한 가지 좋은 자질을 보는 것을 도와주었고, 저는 그 말씀을 계속 붙들고(생각하고) 있어요."라고 말했다.

주제 딸에게 힘이 된 Nancy의 메모

정답 해설 ④는 Nancy의 딸을 가리키고 나머지는 모두 Nancy를 가리킨다.

어휘 perspective 관점, 시각 in passing 지나가는 말로 hold onto 꼭 잡다, 매달리다

Example

답 ②

사람들은 종종 그렇게 하는 것이 자신의 세계관에 대한 인식과 충돌함에도 불구하고 이것을 보여준다. 이것에 대한 주요 원인 중 하나는 다른 사람들의 인정을 얻거나 반감을 피하기 위해서다. 우리는 종종 다른 사람들이 우리를 받아들여주고, 우리를 좋아해주며 우리를 잘 대접해주기를 바란다. 자라면서 사람들은 다른 사람들과 잘 지내는 좋은 방법은 그 집단의 기준을 따르는 것이라는 것을 배우게 된다. 졸업반 무도회를 위해 어떤 옷을 입을지 결정할 때에 우리는 (무도회에) 잘 어울리거나, 좋은 인상을 주고 반감을 피하기 위해서 적당한 옷을 선택하려고 한다. 우리는 실제로 정장 입는 것을 좋아하지 않을지도 모르지만, 어쨌든 그러한 상황에서는 그것이 사회적으로 적절하기 때문에 그렇게 한다. 체중에 민감한 친구들과 함께 할 때 우리가 좋아하지 않음에도 불구하고 샐러드나 건강식품을 먹게 될지도 모른다. 혼자 있을 때 우리는 햄버거나 튀김을 먹는 등 개인적인 선호를 따를 가능성이 훨씬 높다. 그런 상황에서 이것은 사회적 행동에 대한 외적인 변화를 초래하지만, 꼭 개인의 사적인 성향까지 변화시키는 것은 아니다.

① 권한   ② 순응
③ 고집   ④ 독립
⑤ 지배

주제 사람들이 주변에 순응하는 이유

Practice

01 ①   02 ④   03 ③   04 ③   05 ②
06 ⑤   07 ①

01 ① 이것은 일의 성공과 실패에 대해 예측하는 데에도 영향을 줄 뿐만 아니라 목표 설정을 통한 성취 동기에도 영향을 준다. 우리가 만약 외국어 학습 등과 같은 분야에서 이것의 감각이 높은 상태라면, 우리는 더 높은 목표를 설정하고 실패에 대해서는 덜 두려워하며, 어려운 상황을 만났을 때 더 오랜 시간 존속할 수 있을 것이다. 그러나 만약 우리가 이것이 부족하다면 우리는 일 자체를 피하려 할 것이고 문제가 생겼을 때 쉽게 포기하려 들 것이다. 이것

은 또한 책임 전가에도 영향을 끼치는 듯하다. 주어진 업무에 대해서 이 감각이 강한 사람들은 그들이 실패한 원인을 부족한 노력이라 생각한다. 하지만 이것이 부족한 사람들은 그들의 실패를 능력의 부족 때문이라고 생각하는 경향이 있다. 알다시피 실패의 원인을 능력 부족의 탓이라고 할 때 일을 하고자 하는 성취동기는 사라지고 만다.

① 자기 효능감 ② 비율, 균형
③ 공감 ④ 자의식
⑤ 흥미

주 제 자기 효능감의 역할

정답 해설 성취동기에도 영향을 끼치고, 일의 성공과 실패에도 영향을 끼치며 일이 실패했을 때 이 감각이 부족한 사람들은 스스로 능력이 부족하다고 생각을 하고 이 감각이 충만한 사람들은 노력이 부족했다고 느낀다는 점에서 it이 의미하는 것으로는 ① self-efficacy가 적합하다.

어 휘 persist 고집하다, 지속하다 attribution 원인 등을 남에게 돌림 proportion 비율, 균형 empathy 공감, 감정 이입

02 ④ 공간적인 관계의 사회적 관습은 신체 접촉의 사회적 관습과 밀접하게 연관되어 있다. 인류학자들은 우리 개개인들이 "개인적인 공간의 방울들"을 맴돌고 있다고 말한다. 그 방울의 크기는 우리의 개인의 영역, 세력이 미치는 영역, 또는 "개인적인 완충 지역"을 상징한다. 우리는 다른 누군가가 우리의 bubbles 안에 침범할 때 그것을 좋아하지도 않고 참지도 않는다. 우리는 확실히 불편해진다. 그러나 우리가 여행을 할 때, 우리는 어떤 문화적인 방울들은 다른 것보다 넓거나 좁다는 것을 배우게 된다.

① 불편함을 느끼는 것
② 방울들 내부로 걸어가는 것
③ 방울들의 크기
④ 누군가 우리의 방울들에 침범하는 것
⑤ 우리의 개인적인 영역

주 제 침해받고 싶지 않은 개인의 영역

정답 해설 밑줄 친 it은 바로 다음에 이어지는 'someone invades our bubbles'라는 내용을 가리킨다. 즉 it은 문맥상 다른 사람이 자신의 방울을 침범하는 것을 의미한다.

어 휘 societal 사회의, 사회활동의 spatial 공간의, 공간적인 anthropologist 인류학자 territorial imperative 세력권 의식, 텃세 buffer 완충기, 완충장치 distinctly 별개로, 구분되게

03 ③ 10월 말에 나는 연극 연습을 시작했다. 처음에는 연극 연습 일정이 그렇게 엄격하지 않았고 내 생활을 좌우하지도 않았다. 하지만 악마는 내가 걱정해야 할 것은 아무것도 없다고 안심하라고 했다. 1월인 기한은 아직 멀었기 때문에 나는 그 말에 설득당했다. 다른 작은 기한들이 다가와 그 못생긴 얼굴을 치켜세운 것은 리허설이 시작된 지 얼마 되지 않은 때였고, 시험과 과제의 연속은 나를 무자비하게 몰아세웠다. 크리스마스가 다 되었을 무렵이었고, 악마가 실제 기한을 맞추는 일은 매우 고통스러운 일이 될 것을 알고 낄낄대는 동안, 쇼핑의 책임은 나의 학업적 의무들과 합쳐져서 나를 몸부림치게 만들었다. 나는 최종 기한이 닥칠 때까지, 매일 나 자신 스스로 불행을 증가시키는 호된 시련을 시작했다. 나는 처음에 큰 소리로 그 악마를 저주했다. 그러나 내가 해야 할 일은 최종 기한을 포착하고 결코 악마가 다시 나를 잡으러 오지 않게 해야 한다는 것임을 경험에서 배웠다.

① 경쟁력 ② 강박 관념
③ 지연, 미루는 버릇 ④ 불안
⑤ 까다로움

주 제 미루는 버릇 때문에 생긴 고통스러운 경험

정답 해설 이 글은 처음에는 최종 기한까지 시간이 많이 남아 있다고 생각했지만 결국 최종 기한에 쫓겨 힘든 시간을 보냈다는 내용이다. 이로 미루어 볼 때 demon의 의미로는 ③ procrastination이 가장 적절하다.

어 휘 rigorous 준엄한, 혹독한, 엄격한 a long way off 멀리 떨어진 곳에 creep 기어 오다, 살금살금 다가오다 rear 슬그머니 고개를 들다 obligation 책임, 책무, 의무 thrash 채찍질하다, 상대를 패배시키다 chuckle 낄낄거리며 웃다 ordeal 호된 시련 obsession 사로잡힘, 강박 관념 procrastination 지연, 꾸물거림 agitation 동요, 흥분, 불안 fastidiousness 까다로움

04 ③ "물질의 가장 기본적인 구조가 무엇인가?"에 대한 것은 고대 그리스인들이 가장 관심 있어 했던 문제 중 하나였다. 그들이 생각했던 하나의 물체를 작은 조각으로 쪼개고, 각각의 조각을 더 작은 조각으로 계속해서 쪼개는 것을 우리가 직접 실행하는 상상을 해보자. 누군가 그것을 영원히 계속할 수 있을까, 아니면 누군가는 최종적으로 더 이상 쪼개질 수 없고 모든 물질을 이루는 최종 단계의 작은 조각에 도달할 수 있을까? 더 이상 쪼개질 수 없는 최종 단계의 그 조각은 이것이라 불린다. 과학자들은 이것의 매우 작은 크기에 대해 만약 물 한 방울이 지구의 크기로 확대된다면 이것들은 크리켓 공 정도의 크기가 될 것이라는

잘 알려진 예와 같이, 생생한 묘사를 제공하는 경향이 있다.

① 세포   ② 단위
③ 원자   ④ 세균
⑤ 기초

주 제 물질의 기본 구조인 원자

정답 해설 these는 문맥상 물질의 가장 기본 단위인 원자를 묘사하고 있으므로 ③의 atoms가 적절하다.

어 휘 cricket 귀뚜라미, 크리켓(구기 종목 중 하나) brick 벽돌 magnify 확장하다

05 ② 그것은 행정의 주 분야들 중 하나이며, 업무를 효율적으로 잘 마칠 수 있게 하는 지식과 기술을 사용하여 직원들을 돕는 것과 관련이 있다. 그것은 Dr. Towle에 의해 이를 "직원들의 발전에 공헌하는 것을 목표로 삼는 행정 절차"로 정의되었다. 그에 덧붙여 Towle는 다른 직원들의 업무에 대해 책임을 지고 있는 직원들은 직무 능력의 발전을 이끄는 리더십을 발휘할 의무가 있다고 설명했다. 그것은 다른 사람들이 지식을 얻는 것을 돕고 그것을 실제에 적용하는 연습에 초점을 맞추고 있다. 그것은 행정적인 것뿐만 아니라 교육적인 하나의 배우고 가르치는 상황이다.

① 선택   ② 감독
③ 승진   ④ 분배
⑤ 소개

주 제 직원 감독의 역할

정답 해설 '다른 직원들의 업무에 대해 책임을 지고 있는 직원들은 직무 능력의 발전을 이끄는 리더십을 발휘할 의무가 있다.'는 내용을 비롯한 주어진 글의 it에 대한 설명으로 미루어 볼 때 it의 의미로는 '감독'을 의미하는 ② supervision이 가장 적절하다.

어 휘 obligation 의무, 책임 competence 능력, 경쟁력

06 ⑤ 투우에서 황소는 종종 영광을 얻고, 투우사는 절망에 빠지곤 한다. 황소는 절대 죽도록 내버려지지 않는다. 그러나 공개된 장소에서 그의 용기와 붉은 천 조각을 제외하고는 자신을 방어할 것이 아무것도 없는, 두 발로 선 남자와 아슬아슬한 접촉을 통해 죽임을 당한다. 그러나 투우는 우리에게 뭔가를 알려 준다. 그것은 강력한 개인

주의자의 경주에서 모순의 사랑에 대해 우리에게 잘 말해 준다. 그것은 용기와 스타일이라는 이상을 목표로 하고 지루함과 불결함에 빠진다. 라틴 사람들이 바라보는 것처럼 그것(투우)은 축소된 삶의 한 이미지이다. 즉 삶 자체의 매우 많고 터무니없는 무질서에 의해 좌절되는 고결한 로맨스에 대한 도전인 것이다. 이것은 이 예의바르고, 열정적이며, 기사도적인 사람들이 가장 소중하게 여기는 가치들을 고립시키고, 서로 대립하게 하는 교훈극이다. 이 자질들은 내가 갖고 싶은 것으로, 용기, 예의, 폭력적인 죽음에 대한 즉각적인 예상보다 인류에게 도움이 되는 것은 없다는 반대의 암시에 따라 스스로 조심하는 자부심이다.

주 제 투우의 의미

정답 해설 morality plays는 '권선징악 극, 교훈극'을 의미한다. 그리고 그러한 의미의 morality plays가 투우를 의미하며 투우가 보여주는 외적인 모습과 모순되는 성질이 있음을 언급하고 있다. 그러므로 이러한 상반된 내용을 잘 보여 주는 ⑤가 문제의 답으로 가장 적절하다.

어 휘 honor 예우하다 bravery 용기, 용맹 dullness 우둔함, 무딤 miniature 모형, 축소판 courteous 예의바른, 정중한 hairsbreadth 아슬아슬한 contradiction 부인, 부정, 모순 squalor 불결함, 비열함, 야비함 fatuous 어리석은, 얼빠진 morality 죽을 운명 isolate 격리시키다 courteous 정중한 chivalrous 예의바른, 관대한 caution 경고하다

07 ① 1921년 1월 독일에서 일간 신문 1부 가격은 0.3마르크였다. 채 2년이 지나기도 전인 1922년 11월에 똑같은 신문의 가격은 7천만 마르크가 되었다. 다른 모든 경제 분야의 가격도 비슷한 정도로 상승했다. 이 일례는 역사상 가장 볼만한 이것의 예시 중 하나이다. 미국은 1920년대의 독일에 가까운 정도로 이것을 겪어 본 적은 없었지만, 이것은 때때로 경제 문제가 되곤 했다. 예를 들어 1970년대에 전체적인 물가는 두 배가 올랐고 Gerald Ford 대통령은 이것을 '제 1의 공공의 적'이라고 불렀다.

① 인플레이션   ② 세금
③ 실업   ④ 적자
⑤ 불황

주 제 독일과 미국의 인플레이션 현상

정답 해설 이 글은 가격이 비정상적으로 상승하는 현상을 설명하고 있다. 따라서 '이것'은 ① '인플레이션'을 의미한다.

어 휘 spectacular 구경거리의, 볼만한 inflation 물가 상승, 팽창

More Practice

01 ①   02 ⑤

01 ① 나는 이 외국에서 5년째 살고 있다. 내 집 근처에는 수다스럽고 나이가 많은 두 여자가 운영하는 작은 세탁소가 있다. 그들은 60대인 듯한데, 완전히 많은 나이는 아니지만 그들의 서비스는 "영원히 걸린다."고 할 수 있을 정도로 느리다. 때로 그들은 내 인내를 시험한다. 한번은 내가 물건 두 개를 찾으러 5번을 돌아가기도 했다. "아이고, 바쁘군요." 그들은 쾌활하게 말한다. "우리가 어찌나 느린지! 우리는 끔찍하군!" 그 느린 서비스에도 불구하고, 그들의 가게는 끊임없이 손님으로 차 있고 그들의 카운터에는 옷이 높이 쌓여 있다. 이것을 나는 전혀 이해할 수 없다.

[주 제] 느린데도 불구하고 항상 붐비는 세탁소

[정답 해설] '나'가 이용하고 있는 세탁소는 '나'가 몇 번씩이나 맡긴 것을 찾으러 되돌아가야 할 정도로 일이 느리고, 세탁소를 운영하는 두 주인은 그것을 심각하게 여기지도 않는다는 것이 글 전반부의 내용이고, 마지막 부분의 내용은 그럼에도 불구하고 세탁소에 일이 끊이지 않는다는 것이다. 따라서 이 글의 내용 전체를 가리키는 '이것'이 가리키는 것으로 가장 적절한 것은 ① '세탁물 처리가 느려도 영업이 잘 되는 것'이다.

[어 휘] chatty 수다스러운 constantly 끊임없이, 거듭

02 ⑤ 오랫동안, 이것은 나를 매우 화나게 했다. 한번은 내가 가장 좋아하는 코미디언 중 하나인 Mike Myers를 인터뷰할 기회를 얻었다. 우리의 시간이 끝나고, 그는 나를 놀리며 말하기를, "와, 당신은 11살처럼 보여요." 그 때 나는 26살이었다. 그것은 난처한 일이었는데, 내가 좋아했던 사람이 내가 초등학생인 것처럼 보였다고 말했기 때문이다. 나는 이제 그 문제를 가지고 있지 않다. 나는 최근에 내 운전면허를 갱신했고, 내게 마주 웃고 있는 사진이 꼭 32살 된 여성 같아 보이는 걸 발견하고 기뻤다. 오랜 시간이 걸렸지만, 나는 마침내 내 나이로 보인다.

[주 제] 어려 보이는 얼굴 때문에 겪었던 고충

[정답 해설] '나'는 나이보다 어려보이는 외모 때문에 좋아하는 사람에게서 초등학생 같아 보인다는 말을 듣는 일을 겪어 왔다. 따라서 '이것'이 가리키는 것으로 가장 적절한 것은 ⑤ '나이보다 어려 보이는 것'이다.

[어 휘] irritate 짜증나게 하다, 화나게 하다 tease 놀리다 embarrassing 난처한, 창피한 renew 재개하다, 갱신하다 look one's age 제 나이대로 보이다

UNIT **21** 어조 · 분위기 · 심경

Example   답 ②

엘리베이터가 하강을 시작했을 때, David의 얼굴에 큰 웃음이 번졌다. 현기증과 멀미는 가셨다. 그의 가슴에 대한 압박도 사라졌다. 그는 그것을 하고 있었다. 그는 직장을 떠나서 악몽과 작별인사를 나누고 있었다. 그는 그 우울한 아침으로부터 벗어날 용기를 얻었다. 그는 씩 웃으면서 층 번호가 빨간 숫자로 내려가는 것을 보면서 텅 빈 엘리베이터에 서 있었다. 엘리베이터는 건물의 중앙을 거치면서 살짝 흔들렸다. 그것이 멈추었을 때, 그는 내려서 하강하는 에스컬레이터에 돌진했다. 누군가 소리쳤다. "이봐, David, 어디 가는 거야?" David는 마치 모든 것이 통제 하에 있는 것처럼 웃으면서 목소리가 들리는 방향으로 손을 흔들었다. 그는 밖으로 나갔고 이전에 축축하고 황량했던 공기는 이제 새로운 시작의 약속을 머금고 있었다.

① 슬프고 흥분한
② 편안하고 희망찬
③ 지루하고 무관심한
④ 초조하고 혼란스러운
⑤ 공허하고 자포자기한

[주 제] 퇴사 후 심경

Practice

01 ②   02 ②   03 ⑤   04 ②   05 ①
06 ①   07 ③   08 ④

01 ② 심호흡을 하고, 팔을 몇 번 젓는지 세며, 스스로에게 천 번의 팔 젓기가 끝날 때까지 물 위로 나오지 않을 것이라고 다짐하면서 나는 다시 한 번 전속력으로 나가기 시작했다. 나는 천천히 한 피트를 갔고 몇 백 야드를 갔다. 이제 나는 영국 해협이 수영의 에베레스트 산인 이유를 깨달았다. 모든 사람의 목표는 정상에 도달하는 것이지만, 정상은 공기가 점점 더 옅어지고 모든 것이 어려워지는 곳이다. 5백 번 팔을 젓기 전까지 고개를 들지 마라. 네가 할 수 있는 한 빨리 가라. 밀어라. 네가 가지고 있는 모든 것을 가지고 팔을 당겨라. 발로 차라. 그래. 다리를 차라. 깊게 당겨라. 빨리. 어서. 당겨라.

---

① 절망적이지만 회복력 있는
② 단호하고 끈질긴
③ 겁먹고 실망한
④ 놀랍지만 명랑한
⑤ 압도되고 낙담한

스스로를 독려하며 영국 해협 수영하기

글쓴이는 수영을 하고 있는 상태로 보인다. 끈기를 가지고 정상, 즉 목표를 향해 나아감을 알 수 있다. 스스로 정한 횟수의 팔 젓기가 끝나기 전에 고개를 들지 말라는 내용을 포함하여 자신에게 명령하는 말로 미루어 볼 때 글쓴이의 단호함과 끈질긴 면모를 알 수 있다. 따라서 글쓴이의 심경으로는 ② '단호하고 끈질긴'이 가장 적절하다.

resilient 회복력 있는 daunt 겁먹게 하다 exhilarated 명랑한

---

02 ② Dave는 정확히 무슨 일이 일어났는지 알지 못했다. 그가 단지 알고 있는 건 그가 깜짝 놀라며 깨어난 기분에 뒤섞여 침대에서 내동댕이쳐지고, 끔찍한 폭발만이 있었다는 것뿐이었다. 잠시동안 그는 아무런 생각 없이 방바닥에 누워서, 다시 감각을 되찾으려고 애썼다. 그리고서서히 그는 그가 배에 타고나서부터 익숙해지는 데 일주일이 걸린 엔진의 진동이 갑자기 멈췄다는 것을 느꼈다. 무슨 일이 생긴 거지? 그는 일어난 뒤 느낌으로 전등 스위치를 찾아서 떨리는 손으로 켰다. 아무런 일도 일어나지 않았고, 그는 다시 시도해봤다. 불은 들어오지 않았다.

① 어수선하고 화난
② 혼란스럽고 긴장된
③ 매우 기쁘고 자랑스러운
④ 관심 없고 지겨운
⑤ 짜증나고 흥분한

엔진이 멈춘 배 안 Dave의 행동

지문에서 주인공은 잠을 자던 상태에 갑자기 폭발로 인해 침대에서 내동댕이쳐진 상태이다. 또한 지문을 통해 주인공은 배에서 생활을 하고 있는데 배 엔진의 진동이 멈추는 것을 느꼈다는 내용으로 미루어 볼 때 Dave가 긴장감을 느꼈을 것이라고 추측할 수 있다. 따라서 Dave의 심경으로는 ② '혼란스럽고 긴장된'이 가장 적절하다.

hurl 집어던지다 mingle with ~와 섞다 startle 깜짝 놀라게 하다 deck 갑판 steady 안정된, 확고한 throb (엔진 등의) 진동, 떨림 abruptly 돌연한, 갑작스러운 cease 멈추다 tremble 떨다

---

03 ⑤ 낮 동안 공기는 뜨겁고 건조하며, 미세한 먼지들로 가득 차있었다. 더 서늘해지는 밤에는, 각다귀나 모기들이 숲속에서 그들의 부재를 오히려 더 감사하게 만들곤 한다. 사냥터에 있는, 나의 집의 10배 크기에 달하는 나의 오두막집은 밀폐되어 있고 답답한 것처럼 느껴진다. 그리고 내가 잠자리에 누울 때면 나는 거대한 거미들, 특히 어떤 것들은 폭이 몇 인치나 달하는 그런 거미들이 지붕 위의 낙엽들 속에서 기어가는 소리를 들을 수 있었다. 때때로 어떤 거미는 둔탁한 소리를 내며 내 침대 위로 떨어졌고, 거기에서 자리를 뜨기 전까지 한참 동안을 머물렀다. 처음엔 나는 그것들을 해결하기 위해 몇 가지 조치를 취해보았다. 하지만 소용이 없었고, 모기장은 견딜 수 없을 만큼 더웠을 것이다. 익숙한 밤중의 숲속에서 들렸던 소리들은, 이제는 근처의 호텔에서 댄스파티를 마치고 집으로 돌아오는 취객들의 시끄러운 소리로 바뀌었다.

① 우울하고 초연한
② 슬프지만 호기심이 드는
③ 움찔하게 하지만 기대하게 하는
④ 유쾌하고 활력이 넘치는
⑤ 회상하게 하면서 불쾌한

오두막 사냥터의 분위기

마지막 부분을 통해 현재 화자는 도시에 있는 집으로 돌아왔다는 사실을 알 수 있다. 따라서 글 전체적으로 묘사하고 있는 내용은 과거에 대한 회상이라는 것을 알 수 있고, 전반적으로 썩 유쾌하지 않았던 일에 대해 언급하고 있으므로, 글쓴이의 심경으로는 ⑤ '회상하게 하면서 불쾌한'이 가장 적절하다.

fine 미세한 gnat 각다귀, (사람을 무는) 작은 벌레 all the more 더욱 더 stalk away 성큼성큼 걸어가다 detached 분리된, 고립된 daunted 겁먹은, 기죽은 exhilarated 기분이 들뜬, 신나는

---

04 ② 여름의 매우 무더운 날이었다. 태양은 밝게 내리쬐고 있었지만, Jake는 뒷마당에 있는 그늘에서 편안히 쉬고 있었다. 그는 오른손에는 아이스티 잔을 들고 있었고 왼손에는 훌륭한 읽을거리를 쥐고 있었다. Jake는 어떤 걱정도 없었다. 오늘 그는 해가 질 때까지 빈둥거리며 하는 일 없이 지낼 예정이었다. 그의 장난기 많은 강아지는 공을 가지고 놀고 있었다. 그 강아지는 마치 Jake에게 공을 물어오는 놀이를 함께 하자고 초대하는 것처럼 쳐다보았다. 하지만 오늘 그는 그 강아지가 원하는 대로 해주지 않을 것이다. 오직 리히터 규모 10 이상의 지진만이 그를 그의 아늑한 둥지에서 끌어낼 수 있을 것이다.

① 지루한　　　　　　　　② 느긋한
③ 긴장한　　　　　　　　④ 놀란
⑤ 쾌활한

주 제 여름 어느 날의 한가로움
정답 해설 Jake는 무더운 날 뒷마당 그늘에서 아이스티를 마시며 쉬고 있다. 또한 어떤 걱정도 없이 해가 질 때까지 하는 일 없이 지낼 예정이다. 따라서 글의 분위기로는 ② '느긋한'이 가장 적절하다.
어 휘 dog day 무더위, 아주 더운 날 vegetate (하는 일 없이) 지내다 playful 장난기 많은, 놀기 좋아하는 fetch (어디를 가서) 가지고 오다 snug 포근한, 아늑한

05 ① 태양은 매력적인 그림자를 보낼 만큼 서쪽 하늘의 충분히 먼 곳에 있었다. 작은 초원의 한 가운데, 그곳에 있는 짚더미의 그림자 속에서 한 소녀가 잠을 자며 누워 있었다. 그녀가 부드러운 산들바람에 깨어났을 때 그녀는 오랫동안 깊은 잠을 잔 뒤였다. 그녀는 눈을 뜨고 잠시 동안 푸르고 하얀 하늘을 올려다봤다. 그녀는 하품을 하고 천천히 그녀의 길고 갈색인 팔과 다리를 쭉 뻗었다. 그리고 그녀는 그녀의 검은 머리와 붉은 스웨터 그리고 발목까지는 닿지 않는 파란 면 치마에 붙은 짚 풀 조각은 신경 쓰지 않은 채 일어섰다. 그 소녀는 멍하게 그녀의 머리 위를 천천히 지나가는 구름을 바라보며 어떤 동물과 가장 닮았는지 정해 보려 했다.

① 차분하고 나른한　　　　② 활기차고 흥미진진한
③ 재밌고 유쾌한　　　　　④ 슬프고 끔찍한
⑤ 긴급하고 절박한

주 제 초원에서 낮잠을 깬 소녀의 모습
정답 해설 소녀가 늦은 오후 들판에서 한가롭게 낮잠을 즐기다 깨어나는 모습을 묘사한 주어진 글의 분위기로 가장 적절한 것은 ① '차분하고 나른한'이다.
어 휘 haystack 짚더미, 건초 더미 breeze 산들바람 yawn 하품하다 stretch 기지개를 펴다 absentmindedly 멍하게, 넋 나간 채로

06 ① 10년 전, Dallas 남부의 Jefferson Boulevard는 빈 상점들로 가득했던 죽어가는 도심 내부의 상업 지역이었다. 오늘날에는 거의 800개의 가게들이 그곳과 주변 거리에 들어서 있고, 그것들 중 4분의 3가량은 대부분

1세대 혹은 2세대인 라틴계 아메리카 이민자가 소유하고 있다. "그들은 자신의 비즈니스를 시작할 만큼 충분히 배가 고팠다."라고 Jefferson 지역 연합체의 수장인 Leonel Ramos가 말했다. 사회학자인 Kasarda는 "사회 전반에 걸쳐 전체 상승효과가 있었다."고 말했다. 이주민들은 현대의 서비스 경제 체계가 굴러가도록 저임금 일자리를 채워줄 성실한 노동력을 제공했다. 많은 도시에서 호텔, 식당 그리고 탁아 산업은 이주 노동자들의 노동력이 없다면 난관에 봉착할 것이다.

① 높이 평가하는　　　　　② 부정적인
③ 무관심한　　　　　　　④ 거만한
⑤ 기피하는

주 제 Jefferson 지역 서비스 경제 활성화에 끼친 이주민들의 공로
정답 해설 이주 노동자들이 저임금 노동력을 제공함으로써 산업이 활성화되고, 호텔과 레스토랑과 탁아 시설 등이 원활히 운영될 수 있다는 등, 이주 노동자들의 경제적 활동이 사회에 미치는 영향에 대해 언급하고 있다. 따라서 이주 노동자에 대한 필자의 태도로는 ① '높이 평가하는'이 가장 적절하다.
어 휘 storefront 점포, 상점 hispanic 라틴 아메리카계 immigrant 이민자 multiplier effect 상승효과 hardpressed 곤경에 처한, 쪼들리는

07 ③ 이것은 1943년, 전쟁이 한창 진행 중이던 때 일어난 일이었고, 그 당시에는 어디에서도 새 자전거를 찾아볼 수가 없었다. 그 시절 나는 자전거를 꼭 가져야만 했다. 나는 아빠에게 두 바퀴가 달린 것이면 어떤 종류든 상관없다며 애원했던 것을 기억할 수 있다. 아빠는 내게 매우 참을성 있게 대해 주셨고 그 해에는 불가능할 것이라고 설명해 주셨다. 마음으로는 이해했지만 조금 더 졸라보는 것도 나쁠 것은 없을 것이라 생각하여 계속 떼를 썼다. 마침내 크리스마스 이브가 되었고 나는 사방을 살펴봤지만 집에는 자전거가 보이지 않았다. 하지만 다음날 아침 내가 아래층으로 내려왔을 때, 나는 눈이 튀어나올 정도로 놀랐다. 크리스마스 트리 바로 옆에는 내가 보았던 것 중에 가장 크고 멋진 빨갛고 은색인 자전거가 서 있었다. 나는 이 기적 같은 광경을 확인하기 위해 두발이 바닥에 닿을 새도 없이 달려 내려갔다.

① 당혹스러운　　　　　　② 질투하는
③ 기쁜　　　　　　　　　④ 헷갈리는
⑤ 실망스러운

주 제 갖고 싶던 자전거를 선물 받은 기쁨

정답 해설 평소에 바라던 자전거를 선물로 받은 상황이므로 글쓴이의 심정으로는 ③ '기쁜'이 가장 적절하다.

어 휘 wheel 수레바퀴, 핸들 dash 돌진하다 pop out 튀어나오다 plead 애원하다 persist 고집하다, 주장하다

08 ④ 만약 모든 사람들이 평균적인 중국인이나 인도인처럼 살아간다면 당신은 지구 온난화에 대한 기사는 읽지 않게 될 것이다. 1인 기준으로 보면 중국과 인도는 에너지 효율이 높은 일본, 환경적으로 철저한 스웨덴, 특히 연료를 마구 쓰는 미국에 비해 훨씬 적은 온실 가스를 배출한다. 예를 들어 미국인은 평균적으로 인도인의 평균에 비해 연간 20배나 더 많은 이산화탄소 배출에 대한 책임이 있다. 문제는 단 하나다. 중국과 인도에는 24억 명이 살고 있고, 그 중 많은 수가 많은 에너지가 필요한 미국식 생활방식을 꿈꾼다는 것이다. 그리고 두 나라의 빠른 경제 성장 덕분에 조만간 그곳(그러한 생활 방식)에 도달할 것이고, 잠재적으로 세계 기후에 참담한 결과를 가져올 것이다.

① 찬성하는　　　　　② 무관심한
③ 만족해 하는　　　　④ 걱정하는
⑤ 회의적인

주 제 중국과 인도 경제 성장이 가져올 기후 문제

정답 해설 중국과 인도의 경제가 성장할 경우에 발생 가능한 기후 문제를 걱정하는 내용의 글이므로, 이 글에서 찾을 수 있는 필자의 태도로는 ④의 '걱정하는'이 가장 적절하다.

어 휘 potentially 잠재적으로, 어쩌면 per capita 1인당 scrupulous 세심한, 꼼꼼한, 철저한 guzzle 게걸스레 먹고 마시다, 술이나 돈 등을 써버리다

More Practice

01 ①　　　02 ①

01 ① 저녁식사 후에 그는 불을 피우고, 차고 옆에 쌓아둔 나무를 가지러 바람을 무릅쓰고 밖에 나갔다. 그의 얼굴에 닿는 공기는 맑고 차가웠으며, 차량진입로에 쌓인 눈은 이미 그의 무릎 절반 높이였다. 그는 장작들을 모아, 그 위에 덮인 부드럽고 하얀 눈을 털어내고 안으로 가지고 들어왔다. 그는 벽난로 앞에 다리를 꼬고 앉아 장작을 넣고 따뜻한 불꽃을 응시하면서 잠시 시간을 보냈다. 밖에서는,

가로등 옆으로 떨어지는 빛의 원뿔 안으로, 소리 없이 계속 눈이 내리고 있었다. 그가 일어나 창밖을 내다보았을 때, 그의 차는 길가의 부드럽고 하얀 언덕이 되어 있었다.

① 차분하고 평온한
② 활기차고 축제 같은
③ 우습고 즐거운
④ 흥미롭고 소름 돋는
⑤ 전망 있고 희망적인

주 제 눈이 많이 내린 겨울밤

정답 해설 바깥에는 고요히 눈이 계속 내리고, 인물은 벽난로를 피워 따뜻한 집 안에서 바깥의 정적인 풍경을 내다보고 있다. 따라서 글의 분위기로는 ⑤ '차분하고 평온한'이 가장 적절하다.

어 휘 go into the weather 악천후를 무릅쓰고 나가다 driveway 차량진입로 shake off 털어내다 cross-legged 다리를 포갠 gaze at ~을 응시하다 cone 원뿔모양 by the time 그때까지, ~할 때(까지도)

02 ① 나는 마침내 내일 아침 일찍 떠날 것이다! 나는 항상 미지의 신비로운 세계인 아마존을 탐험하고 싶었다. 이 시각이면, 멋진 Emerald Amazon Explorer가 나의 승선을 기다리면서 항구에 와 있을 것이다. 민물돌고래가 즐거운 강에서 나를 호위할 것이며, 500종의 새들, 6종의 원숭이들, 그리고 수많은 화려한 나비들이 나를 맞이해 그들의 왕국으로 데려갈 것이다. 야생에서 야영을 하면서 모기, 뱀, 그리고 거미들과 함께 즐길 수 있다면 좋겠다. 나는 세계에서 가장 큰 열대우림을 집으로 만들고 싶다. 내 가슴은 나의 불룩한 가방만큼 많이 부풀어 오르지만, 길고 힘든 여행을 앞두고 있으니 잠을 좀 자는 편이 낫겠다.

① 흥분된　　　　　② 지친
③ 절망한　　　　　④ 무관심한
⑤ 안심한

주 제 아마존 여행을 앞두고 흥분된 심경

정답 해설 다음날 아침이면 Emerald Amazon Explorer에 승선해 아마존을 탐험하게 될 필자는 탐험 여행에 대한 기대에 차 있다. 따라서 필자의 심경으로는 ① '흥분된'이 가장 적절하다.

어 휘 get on board (배에) 승선하다 freshwater 민물 escort 호위하다 swell 부풀다 chubby 불룩한, 통통한 tough 힘든

UNIT 22 장문 독해 I

Example
답 01 ④ 02 ③

우리는 미국으로 돌아왔지만 Julie의 마음은 여전히 이탈리아에 있었다. 그녀는 더 많은 피자를 원한다. 그녀는 나를 부주방장으로 두고 그녀가 직접 만들기로 결정한다.

나는 가지와 주키니를 썬다. 우리는 둘 다 말이 없고 우리의 일에 집중한다. 다음은 양파 깎기다. 나는 양파를 껍질을 벗기고 싱크대에 가져가서 수도꼭지를 틀고 흐르는 물에서 양파를 자르기 시작한다.

"뭐하는 거야?"

"나는 물속에서 양파를 자르고 있어."

"왜?"

"그렇게 하면 눈물이 멈춘다고 백과사전에 나와 있어."

드물게 유용한 것들 중 하나로 백과사전에 나와 있는 Heloise 스타일의 조언이었고 나는 그것을 실제로 해 볼 생각에 꽤 들떠 있었다.

"안 돼, 너무 위험해."

"하지만 백과사전에 나와 있어."

"안 돼, 내가 총주방장이야. 너는 부주방장이고."

이때 나는 백과사전이냐 내 아내냐 하는 불행한 상황에 직면해 있다. 권위의 두 큰 근원. 어느 것을 선택할까? 음, 백과사전은 꽤 믿음직스럽다. 그러나 내가 아는 한 그것은 내 아이를 낳거나 며칠 동안 나를 무시하거나 그것이 싫어하는 티셔츠를 버릴 수 없다.

그래서 나는 Julie가 이번에는 이긴 것이라고 결정했다. 양파는 물 없이 썰릴 것이고 나는 울 것이다.

주제 피자를 만들면서 드러난 Julie의 주도권

01 ① 눈물을 막기 위해 수중에서 양파 껍질을 벗겨라
② 무승부로 끝난 젠더 싸움
③ 이탈리아 요리법의 여파
④ 우리 집의 진정한 대장
⑤ 백과사전에서의 부주방장

02 ① 일하는 여성이 얼마나 강한지 입증하는 것
② 수정을 요청하기 위해 Britannica에 전화해야 할지도 모른다
③ 양파는 물 없이 썰릴 것이고 나는 울 것이다
④ 다음 며칠 간 나는 그녀를 무시할 것이다
⑤ 하지만 내일은 내가 총주방장이 될 것이다

Practice

01 ①	02 ⑤	03 ⑤	04 ①	05 ③
06 ①	07 ④	08 ②	09 ③	10 ③
11 ②	12 ①	13 ②	14 ⑤	15 ④
16 ①	17 ⑤	18 ②	19 ③	20 ⑤
21 ②	22 ①	23 ④	24 ⑤	25 ④
26 ④	27 ①	28 ②	29 ④	30 ②
31 ④	32 ④	33 ④	34 ④	35 ①
36 ④	37 ③	38 ④		

01 ①
02 ⑤

우리는 까마귀가 바보가 아니란 것을 오래 전부터 알고 있다. 그들이 나중을 위해 음식을 은닉하고 매달린 음식을 잡아당기기 위해 끈을 모으고 심지어는 서로 속이려고 하는 것이 관찰되었다. 오늘 사이언스지에 발표된 한 연구는 특히 인상적인 반전을 추가한다. 그것은 까마귀는 자연에서 결코 마주치지 않는 미래의 필요를 위해 계획할 수 있다는 것이다.

이 새로운 연구는 스웨덴의 인지 동물학자들에 의해 주도되었는데 이들은 이전에 유인원의 계획 능력을 시험하기 위해 사용된 일련의 실험을, 이번에는 까마귀를 이용하여 반복했다. 까마귀들은 먼저 돌을 사용하여 미로 상자에서 음식 알갱이가 나오도록 두드리는 것을 배웠다. 그 다음 날, 상자가 없는 상태에서 새들은 돌 도구와 도구로 쓰이기에는 너무 가볍거나 부피가 큰 장난감과 같은 '방해되는' 물체 사이에서 선택을 제안받았다. 상자는 선택 이후 15분이 지나서 다시 가져왔다. 지연에도 불구하고 까마귀는 거의 80퍼센트 올바른 도구를 선택했고 86퍼센트의 확률로 그들의 선택한 도구를 성공적으로 사용했다. 새들은 또한 한 조각의 음식과 교환하기 위해 실험자에게 병뚜껑을 주어야 했을 때도 거의 비슷하게 수행했다. 물물교환을 위해 15분을 기다려야 할지라도 새들은 거의 항상 방해물보다 병뚜껑을 골랐다. 곧 유용해진 물건에 대한 선호도는 까마귀가 도구나 물물교환의 징표를 위해 더 작은 선물을 사양해야 할 때, 그리고 각각의 물건들이 17시간의 지연 후에만 사용할 수 있을 때조차도 계속되었다.

주제 까마귀의 계획 능력 실험

어휘 birdbrain 멍청이, 바보 cache 은닉하다 pellet 작은 알갱이 barter 물물교환하다 in favor of ~을 위하여

01 정답 해설 (a) 유인원의 계획 능력을 시험하기 위해 사용된 일련의 실험이라는 의미가 문맥상 자연스럽다. experiments 뒤에 나오는 구문은 '주격관계대명사+be used to 동사원형'의 형태에서 주격관계대명사와 be 동사가 생략된 것이다. 따라서 testing은 동사인 test로 수정되는 것이 적절하다.

02 정답 해설 빈칸 뒤에 이어지는 내용은 스웨덴 동물학자의 까마귀 실험에 대한 이야기이다. 까마귀가 도구를 사용하는 법을 배운 후 당장 눈에 보이는 보상이 없음에도 불구하고 도구를 선택하고 기다렸다가 그것을 사용했다는 내용이다. 이것은 까마귀가 미래에 대비하고 있음을 보여준다. 따라서 빈칸에는 ⑤가 가장 적절하다.

① 긴급 상황을 위한 기구를 보존하다
② 사태에 대해 단체로 행동하다
③ 앞으로 일어날 일을 예측하다
④ 잠재적 경쟁자를 속이다
⑤ 미래의 필요성을 위해 계획하다

---

03 04

나는 가기로 결심했으며 갈 것이고, 나는 어머니의 생일까지 거기에 도착해야만 했다. 이것은 매우 중요했다. 만약 어머니를 집에 다시 모셔올 기회가 생긴다면 그녀의 생일에 그렇게 될 것이라고 믿었다. 아버지나 조부모님께 소리 내어 이렇게 말한다면, 그들은 마치 내가 공중에서 물고기를 잡으려고 할 수도 있을 거라고 말했을 것이다. 그래서 나는 소리 내어 말하지 않았다. 그러나 나는 그것을 믿었다. <u>때때로 나는 늙은 당나귀처럼 성미가 고약하고 고집이 세다.</u> 아버지는 내가 언젠가 부러진 갈대에 누워 얼굴은 늪의 진흙투성이가 될 것이라고 말했다.

마침내 Gram과 Gramps Hiddle 그리고 내가 여행을 떠나던 첫날, 나는 처음 30분을 꼬박 기도했다. 나는 우리가 사고를 당하지 않을 것을 기도했고 (나는 자동차와 버스가 무서웠다) 우리가 그곳에 앞으로 7일 남은 어머니의 생일까지 도착해서 어머니를 집으로 데리고 오기를 기도했다. 몇 번이고 나는 같은 것을 기도했다. 나는 나무들에게 기도했다. 이것은 하나님께 직접 기도하는 것보다 쉬웠다. 거의 항상 나무가 근처에 있었다. 신의 창조물 중에서 가장 평평하고 가장 곧은길인 Ohio 유료 도로에 우리가 차를 세웠을 때, Gram은 나의 기도에 끼어들었다. "Salamanca-"

나는 즉시 나의 진짜 이름이 Salamanca Tree Hiddle이라고 설명해 주어야겠다. 부모님의 생각에 Salamanca는 고조모가 속한 인디언 부족의 이름이었다. 부모님이 실수하셨다. 부족의 이름은 Seneca였지만, 부모님은 내가 태어난 후에서야 이 실수를 발견했고 그 때쯤에는 내 이름이 그들에게 익숙해졌기 때문에 이름이 Salamanca로 남았다. 나의 중간 이름, Tree는 당신이 알고 있는 나무에서 비롯된 것으로, 나무는 어머니에게 아름다운 것이어서 그녀는 그것을 내 이름의 일부로 만들었다. 그녀는 더 구체적이고 싶어 했고 어머니가 가장 좋아하는 Sugar Maple Tree를 사용하고 싶었지

만 Salamanca Sugar Maple Tree Hiddle은 그녀에게조차 좀 너무했다. 어머니는 나를 Salamanca라고 부르곤 했지만 그녀가 떠난 후, 조부모님 Hiddle만이 나를 Salamanca라고 불렀다(그들이 나를 chickabiddy라고 부르지 않았을 때). 대부분의 다른 사람들에게, 나는 Sal이었고, 특히 재미있다고 생각하는 몇 소년들에게 나는 Salamander였다.

주제 어머니를 모시러 가는 여행길

어휘 reed 갈대 swamp 늪 solid 줄곧 salamander 도롱뇽 accompany 동반하다

03 정답 해설 ⑤ 대부분의 사람들은 그녀를 Sal이라고 부른다고 언급했다.

① 그녀 여행의 목적은 그녀의 어머니를 집으로 데려오는 것이다.
② 그녀의 조부모님은 그녀의 여행에 동반했다.
③ 그녀는 신보다 나무에게 기도하는 것이 쉽다고 느꼈다.
④ 그녀의 부모님이 그녀의 이름을 지을 때 오해가 있었다.
⑤ 대부분의 사람들은 그녀를 Salamanca 또는 Salamander라고 불렀다.

04 정답 해설 글쓴이 자신이 때로는 고집이 세고 완고하다는 주어진 문장은 아버지와 조부모가 터무니없는 일이라고 말하여도 자신의 믿음을 져버리지 않는다는 내용 다음에 이어지는 것이 문맥상 자연스럽다. 따라서 주어진 문장은 ①에 위치하는 것이 적절하다.

---

05 06

새로운 기술 가치로의 집단적 전환은 매우 효과적이었어서, 심지어 1929년 대공황이 강타하였을 때도 미국인들은 기술적인 비전을 계속해서 옹호했다. 대신 그들은 그들의 분노와 두려움을, 그들의 생각 속에서 국가의 새로운 영웅들인 기술자들의 높은 목적과 목표를 해치고 훼방 놓는 욕심 많은 사업가들에 대항해서 표출하기로 선택했다. 꽤 많은 미국인들은 경제학자이자 사회 이론가인 Thorstein Veblen의 초기의 비판에 동의했다. 그는 1921년에 국가의 경제를 금전적이고 편협한 관심을 초월한 고상한 기준을 가진 전문적인 기술자들에게 위임하는 것만이 경제가 구제되고 국가가 새로운 에덴동산으로 변화하게 할 수 있다고 주장했다. 그러나 기술주의 정치의 성공은 수명이 짧았다. 지도자들 간의 내부적인 분쟁은 운동의 분파를 적대적인 당파로 만들었다. 그때 또한 히틀러의 권력으로의 급속한 부상과 기술적인 효율성에 대한 독일의 제3 제국의 광적인 집착이 사회 사상가들로 하여금 미국에서 기술 관료들의 기술적인 독재에 대한 요청에 대해 재고하게 만들었다. 기술적인 세계의 관점은 미국 비행기가

1945년 일본의 도시에 원자폭탄을 투하했을 때 훨씬 더욱 치명적인 좌절을 겪게 되었다. 전 세계는 뜻밖에도 기술 유토피아적인 관점의 어두운 이면을 보도록 강요받았다. 전후 세대는 현대 기술이 미래를 창조해내는 것뿐만 아니라 파괴하는 놀라운 위력에 대해서도 끊임없이 상기하면서 살아가는 첫 세대였다.

주 제 기술주의적 정치 관념과 그 몰락

어 휘 conversion 전환 depression 경제공황 vent 배출하다 undermine 해치다 thwart 훼방 놓다 lofty 높은 entrust 위임하다 pecuniary 금전적인 parochial 편협한 technocracy 기술주의 정치 bickering 분쟁 splinter 분리되다 warring 적대적인 faction 당파 meteoric 급속한 fanatical 광적인 technocrat 기술관료 dictatorship 독재 setback 좌절 abruptly 뜻밖에 downfall 몰락 belligerent 호전적인

05 정답 해설 주어진 문장에 but이 포함되므로, 글의 흐름이 전환되는 지점을 찾아야 한다. ③ 앞에서는 기술자 중심 사회를 주장하는 내용이 서술되고 있는데, 그 이후에는 기술 중심 사회의 부작용에 대해 서술하고 있으므로 이 사이에 주어진 문장이 들어가서 논의의 방향을 전환해 주는 것이 자연스럽다. 따라서 주어진 문장이 들어갈 위치로는 ③이 가장 적절하다.

06 정답 해설 본문의 내용은 미국 사회에서 기술 중심적인 가치관이 어떻게 생겨났고 이것이 어떻게 몰락하게 되었는지에 대해 서술하고 있으므로 주제로는 ①이 가장 적절하다.
① 기술주의적 정치 관점과 그것의 몰락
② 민주주의와 기술의 짧은 협조 관계
③ 기술적인 세계관의 불가피한 도래
④ 더 나은 사회를 위한 기술 관료들의 호전적인 접근 방식
⑤ 기술주의 정치의 밝은 면과 어두운 면의 불균형

07 ④
08 ② 폭력의 피해자와 그 가족으로부터 가해자들을 잡아서 처벌하는 책임을 인계받을 국가나 다른 조직화된 공동체가 있기도 전에, 보복 과정의 일부를 경감하는 관습들이 발달한다. 이들 중에는 응보의 원칙, 즉 눈에는 눈이라는, 잘못에 대한 정확한 보복이라는 것이 있다. 현대의 함축적인 표현으로 피에 굶주리기보다는, 징벌은 불화를 만들어 낼 가능성이 있는 과잉반응(내 눈에 대한 대가로 당신의 생명)의 가능성을 낮춰준다. 또 다른 (A) 경감의 원칙은 "합의금"(희생에 대한 돈)인데, 이는 가해자의 책임을 면제주면서 희생자나 희생자의 가족들에게 부상에 대한 보상의 지불을 받도록 요구하거나 최소한 장려하는 것이다. 금전이나 물질로의 전환은 전체적으로 폭력 행위보다 사회에 비용이 덜 들고, 이 폭력 행위는 사회적

순손실을 가한다는 것 이외에 단지 부를 한 사람에게서 다른 사람에게로 이전하기보다는 더 심한 폭력을 불러올 지도 모른다. 다른 (B) 경감하는 제도는 양쪽 친족에 대한 것이다. 아이슬란드 사람들은 아버지와 어머니 양쪽 모두를 친족으로 합산한다(많은 사회에서 아버지 쪽만 친족으로 생각하고 일부만 어머니 쪽을 친족으로 생각한다). 이는 가족을 강화하여 공격에 대한 억제책으로서의 복수에 대한 신뢰를 증대할 뿐 아니라 분쟁자가 분쟁의 양쪽에 친족을 가지게 한다. 일리아드는 동정과 공감이 복수의 잔인함을 제한할 수 있다는 데 대한 더 큰 가능성을 암시하고 있다.

주 제 보복 과정 경감 제도

어 휘 aggression 공격, 가해 aggressor 가해자 alleviate 경감하다 retribution 응징, 징벌 retaliation 보복 an eye for an eye 눈에는 눈 bloodthirsty 피에 굶주린 connotation 함축 composition 합금 liability 책임 inflict 가하다 bilateral 쌍방의 kinship 친족 reckon 합산하다 deterrent 억제수단 disputant 분쟁자 empathy 공감 savagery 잔인함

07 정답 해설 본문은 가해자에 대한 복수를 경감하는 방안을 설명하고 있으므로 빈칸에는 ④ moderating이 가장 적절하다.
① 수정하는
② 처벌하는
③ 갈등하는
④ 경감하는
⑤ 매혹적인

08 정답 해설 '눈에는 눈'의 원칙이 아니라 징벌의 방식이 피해자의 과잉 대응의 가능성을 줄여준다고 언급했으므로 ②는 본문의 내용과 일치하지 않는다.

09 ③
10 ③ 2008년 이후부터 Zsófia Virányi와 그녀의 동료들은 오스트리아의 늑대 과학센터에서 개와 늑대들을 키우며 무엇이 각각 개와 늑대의 특성을 형성시키는지 연구했다. "만약 당신이 테이블 위에 고기 한 조각을 올려놓고 우리 개들 중 한 마리에게 '안 돼!'라고 얘기한다면 먹지 않을 것이다." Virányi가 말했다. "하지만 늑대들은 당신을 무시할 것이다. 그들은 당신의 눈을 쳐다보면서 고기를 물어갈 것이다." 그리고 이런 일이 일어날 때, 그녀는 그럼에도 어떻게 늑대가 (A) 길들여진 개가 되었는지 다시 궁금해한다. "당신은 당신을 무시하는 거대한 육식동물과는 같이 살 수 없을 것이다."라고 그녀는 말했다. "당신은 '안 돼!'라고 외쳤을 때 명령을 듣는 개와 같은 동물을 원할 것이다."
'안 돼.'라는 명령을 절대적으로 받아들이는 강아지들의 인식은 늑대와 같이 동등하지 않고 독재적인 서열을 유지하는 (B) 그들의 구성관계와 관련이 있다는 것을 센터의 과

학자들이 발견했다. 늑대들은 먹이를 같이 먹을 수 있다고 Virányi는 기록했다. 심지어 서열이 높은 늑대가 이빨을 드러내고 낮은 서열에게 으르렁거리려도, (C) 낮은 서열의 동료는 물러서지 않는다. 개들의 구조에서 이러한 일은 일어날 수 없다. "서열이 낮은 개가 높은 개와 먹이를 같이 먹는 일은 드물다."라고 그녀는 말했다. "그들은 시도하려 하지도 않는다." 그들의 연구는 또한 개들이 사람들과 함께 어떠한 일을 같이 하기보다는, 무엇을 해야 하는지 명령을 받는 것을 더 원한다고 주장한다.

독립적이고, 절대적인 서열에 복종하지 않는 늑대를 (D) 복종적이고 명령을 기다리는 애완동물로 만들기 위해 고대의 사람들이 했던 본성을 방해하는 역할을 Virányi가 했다. 늑대의 본성을 바꾸는 일은 그녀 혼자만의 일이 아니었다. 연구가들은 성공적으로 시간과 장소 그리고 양에서 소, 닭 그리고 기니피그까지 거의 모든 다른 가축들까지 밝혀냈지만 그들은 우리들의 (E) 가장 친한 친구인 갯과 동물들을 위해 지속적으로 이러한 질문에 대해 토론하고 있다.

(주 제) 개와 늑대의 서열 차이

(어 휘) colleague 동료 ignore 무시하다 wonder 궁금해 하다 domesticate 길들이다 egalitarian 평등주의의 dictatorial 독재적인 growl 으르렁거리는 소리 subordinate 하위, 종속하는 cooperate 협동하다 Canis familiaris 갯과 동물

09 (정답 해설) 지문에서는 늑대와 개의 특성이 어떻게 다른지에 대한 연구가 서술되어 있다. 지문상의 (A) '길들여진 개', (B) '그들', (D) '복종적이고 명령을 기다리는 애완동물', (E) '가장 친한 친구'는 모두 개를 뜻하지만, (C) '낮은 서열의 동료'는 늑대를 뜻한다.

10 (정답 해설) 개와는 다르게 늑대의 무리의 경우 서열이 낮은 늑대는 서열이 높은 늑대가 먹이를 먹는 중에 이빨을 드러내며 위협해도 끝까지 눈치를 보며 먹이를 같이 먹는다고 서술되어 있다. 따라서 ③ '무리 중 강한 늑대가 약한 늑대에게 으르렁대면 약한 늑대는 먹이로부터 물러난다.'는 글의 내용과 일치하지 않는다.

11 ②
12 ①

왜 사람들은 이용 가능한 모든 정보를 사용해서 그들의 기대와 미래에 대한 최상의 예측을 <u>일치</u>하게 만들려고 할까? 이를 위한 가장 단순한 설명은 사람들이 그렇게 하지 않으면 비용이 많이 들기 때문이다. 통근자 Joe는 회사를 가는 시간을 가능한 한 가장 정확한 예측을 하려는 강한 동기가 있다. 만약 자신의 출근시간을 제대로 예측하지 못한다면, 그는 자주 회사에 늦

을 것이고 해고 당할 위험도 부담해야 한다. 하지만 과하게 추측하게 되면 그는 대체로 너무 이른 시간에 회사에 출근하고, 잠이나 개인 시간을 불필요하게 포기하게 될 것이다. 정확한 추측은 바람직하고, 그 보상은 강력해서 사람들이 모든 이용 가능한 정보를 사용함으로 최적화된 예보를 해서 동일한 보상을 얻기 위해 노력하도록 한다.

이러한 원리는 사업에서도 적용된다. 어떤 제품 생산 회사가 금리의 변동이 제품 판매에 중요하다는 것을 안다고 가정해 보자. 만약 회사가 금리에 대한 잘못된 예측을 한다면, 회사는 너무 많거나 적은 제품을 생산할 수 있기 때문에, 회사는 낮은 이익을 취하게 될 것이다. 회사가 금리를 예측하기 위한 모든 이용가능한 정보를 얻고, 이 정보를 미래의 금리에 대한 가능한 가장 정확한 추측을 하기 위해 사용하려는 동기는 상당히 강하다. 특히 금융시장에서는 최적화된 예측을 이용하려는 동기가 강하다. 이러한 시장에서, 더 정확한 예측을 하는 사람들이 돈을 벌어들인다.

(주 제) 사람들이 최상의 예측을 하려고 노력하는 이유

(어 휘) expectation 예상, 기대 underpredict 실제 결과보다 덜 예측하다 overpredict 실제 결과보다 과하게 예측하다 incentive 격려, 동기, 보상 forecast 예상, 예측 optimal 최적의 manufacturer 제조업자 interest rate 이자율 appliance 제품 acquire 손에 넣다, 획득하다

11 (정답 해설) 사람들이 최적화된 예측을 해야 하는 이유를 예시들과 함께 설명하고 있다. 최적화된 예측을 하면 개인으로서도 여러 이득을 볼 수 있지만, 크게는 회사부터 금융시장에서도 상당한 이익을 취할 수 있다. 따라서 ② '최적화된 예측으로 보상을 취해라'가 글의 제목으로 가장 적절하다.
① 너의 목표를 최대한 높게 잡아라
② 최적화된 예측으로 보상을 취해라
③ 금리를 조종해서 이익을 최대화하라
④ 사업상의 실전과 이론의 차이
⑤ 출퇴근 거리가 생산성에 어떻게 영향을 끼치는가?

12 (정답 해설) 빈칸이 포함된 질문 다음에 언급된 두 사례는 각각 회사에 가는 데 걸리는 시간을 최대한 정확하게 예측하려는 이유, 금리 예측을 정확하게 하려는 이유이다. 따라서 '왜 사람들은 이용 가능한 모든 정보를 사용해서 그들의 기대와 미래에 대한 최상의 예측을 일치하게 만들려고 할까?'가 첫문장으로 가장 적절하다. 따라서 빈칸에는 '일치하다'라는 뜻의 ① match가 가장 적절하다.
① 일치하다
② 초과하다
③ 무효화하다
④ 변형시키다
⑤ 과소평가하다

13 ② **14** ⑤

Delhi 지방에 있는 Indian Institue of Technology (IIT)의 Balak 교수는 시각 장애인에게 일반적으로 사용되는 흰 지팡이를 기반으로 인도의 복잡한 거리에서 초음파를 사용하여 시각적으로 장애가 있는 사람들을 안내해주는 새로운 도구인 Smartcane™에 대해 연구하는 팀을 이끌고 있다. "시각 장애인을 위한 흰 지팡이는 아주 훌륭한 도구이고, 사용자에게 많은 정보를 제공해 줍니다." 그는 이렇게 말했다. "하지만 그것은 허리 높이 위에 있거나, 지면에서 건드릴 수 있는 부분이 없는 장애물들, 예를 들면 보도 위쪽으로 뻗어져 나온 나뭇가지와 같은 것들을 감지해내는 데는 매우 취약합니다." Smartcane™을 연구하는 팀은 주위로 음파를 내뿜고 주위에 있는 물체들에 의해 방향을 바꾸어 그들에게 다시 반사되어 돌아오는 울림을 이용하는 박쥐와 같은 동물들의 기술을 모방하는 것으로써 이러한 문제점에 대응했다. 스마트 기술이 적용된 버전에서는 대신에 보통의 시각 장애인용 흰 지팡이에 부착된 장치를 통하여 초음파를 방출한다. 초음파는 다시 돌아오는 중에 사물에 대해 감지하고, 사용자에게 전방에 장애물이 있음을 알리기 위해 진동을 이용한다. 그 장비가 정말 좋은 점은, 무릎 위 45도 각도에 해당하는 범위까지 초음파가 검색을 통해 일반적인 지팡이로서는 절대 알려줄 수 없는 정보를 제공해 준다는 것에 있다. 사람들이 보행 중에 지팡이를 왼쪽에서 오른쪽으로 움직였을 때 만약 한쪽에서만 진동이 느껴진다면, 그것은 그들이 반대 방향으로 이동해야만 한다는 것을 의미한다. 진동의 패턴과 강도의 차이는 3미터 한도 내에서 그들을 가로막고 있는 물체와의 거리를 사용자들에게 가르쳐준다.

주 제) 초음파를 이용한 Smartcane™

어 휘) ultrasound 초음파 impaired 손상된, 악화된 white cane 시각장애인들이 사용하는 흰 지팡이 sonar 음파 divert 방향을 바꾸다 span 폭, 너비 intensity 강도, 강렬함

13 정답 해설) 주어진 문장의 this challenge에 해당되는 내용으로는 (B) 바로 앞의 '허리 높이 위에 있거나 지면에서 건드릴 수 있는 부분이 없는 장애물들을 감지해내는 데 취약함'이 적절하다. 또한 박쥐가 음파를 내뿜는 내용을 응용한 것이 (B) 바로 다음 문장의 초음파를 방출하는 시각 장애인용 흰 지팡이이다. 따라서 주어진 문장이 들어가기에 가장 적절한 위치는 (B)이다.

14 정답 해설) 지문에서는 사람들이 허리 위나 지면에서 나오는 물체가 아닐 경우 시각 장애인들이 인식하기 힘들어하는 문제를 해결하기 위해서 초음파를 보내 장애물을 만나면 돌아오게 하는 기술을 사용한다고 서술하였다. 그렇기 때문에 ⑤ '진동의 패턴으로 장애물의 높이를 식별한다.'는 지문의 내용과 일치하지 않는다.

15 ④ **16** ①

아주 오래 전, 한 때, 나는 North Carolina 지역의 Fort Bragg에서 82 공수 사단의 젊은 중위였고, 위치와 관련된 사항을 정확하게 파악하기 위해 노력하고 있었다. 내가 지도를 읽으며 서 있을 때, 많은 하급 병사들의 고참인 내 소대의 병장이 다가왔다. "중위님, 우리가 어디에 있는지 알아내셨습니까?" 그가 물었다. "음, 지도에서는 저쪽에 언덕이 있어야 된다고 하는데, 나는 잘 안 보인다." 내가 대답했다. "알겠습니다." 그가 말했다. "만약 지도가 지형과 일치하지 않는다면, 그건 지도가 잘못된 것입니다." 심지어 그때도, 나는 내가 아주 깊은 신뢰가 담긴 말을 들었다는 것을 알고 있었다.

나는 사람들의 이야기, 특히 일이 엉망이 될 수 있는 모든 방식들을 들으면서 오랜 시간을 보냈다. 나는 우리가 삶을 살아가는 과정이 우리의 마음속에서 실제 우리가 걷게 될 지형에 맞춰진 지도를 얻기 위한 노력으로 이루어져 있다는 것을 배웠다. 이상적으로, 이러한 과정은 우리가 성장하면서 일어나게 된다. 우리의 부모님들은 그들이 배웠던 것을 예로 들어 우리를 가르친다. 애석하게도 우리가 그 교훈을 전적으로 받아들이는 경우는 드물다. 그리고 종종 우리의 부모님들의 삶은 우리에게 그것들이 전달할 가치가 거의 없고, 따라서 우리가 알고 있는 많은 것들은 빈번히 발생하는 시행착오에 의한 고통스러운 과정을 통해 우리에게 오게 된다고 생각하게 만든다.

주 제) 삶에서 개인 경험의 중요성

어 휘) lieutenant 중위 Airborne Division 공수 부대 사단 orient oneself 정확하게 파악하다, 태도를 분명히 하다 platoon 소대 sergeant 병장 awry 빗나간, 엉망이 된 conform 따르다, 순응하다 all the way 내내, 시종일관, 완전히 receptive 수용하는, 받아들이는 conducive (어떤 일이 발생하는 데) 도움이 되는

15 정답 해설) 마지막 부분에서 우리가 아는 많은 것들이 빈번히 발생하는 시행착오에 의한 고통스러운 과정을 통해 우리에게 온다고 생각하게 된다는 것, 즉 우리는 경험적으로 알게 되는 내용이 많다는 내용으로 미루어 볼 때 ④ '삶에서의 개인 경험의 중요성'이 이 글의 주제로 가장 적절하다.

① 지도를 보는 방법을 학생들에게 가르치는 이유
② 리더십을 복종으로 바꾸는 것의 어려움
③ 우리 마음에 그려진 지도의 가치
④ 삶에서의 개인 경험의 중요성
⑤ 아이들을 직접적 경험에 노출시키는 방법

16 정답 해설) 부모님이 전해주시는 지식을 전적으로 받아들이기 힘들다는 내용이 문맥상 자연스러우므로 빈칸에는 '받아들이는'이라는 뜻의 ① receptive가 적절하다.

① 받아들이는
② 부적절한

③ 제한된
④ 중독된
⑤ 도움이 되는

17 ⑤
18 ②

'지구 접근 천체들(NEO)'은 지구의 공전 궤도를 주기적으로 가로지르고, 그렇게 함으로써 우리의 행성에 가까이 다가오는 거대한 물체들을 이르는 현대적인 용어이다. 그것들에는 소행성과 유성, 그리고 혜성이 포함된다. 거의 대부분의 소행성은 화성과 목성 사이에 위치하고 있는 소행성 지대에 한정되어 존재하고 있다. 적어도 약 1마일 폭으로 천 개 이상의 소행성들이 존재하는 것으로 추정된다. 아마도 그 중 십여 개는 3마일이나 그 이상의 폭으로 존재할 것이다. 소행성은 작게는 아주 작은 돌 조각이나 먼지 입자까지도 포함하므로 크기에 있어서 최소한의 제한은 없지만, 그 어떤 소행성도 대기를 지닐 만큼 충분히 크지는 않다. 소행성은 어떻게 생겨나게 된 것일까? Isaac Asimov는, 소행성이 작은 행성에 사는 사람들이 핵에너지를 발견해 그들이 사는 세계를 아주 작은 파편 조각으로 날려버린 것의 잔해라고 하는, 한때 인기 있던 공상 과학 소설의 아이디어를 제기했다. 하지만 심지어는 핵폭발이라 할지라도 소행성 지대를 형성할 만큼 충분한 에너지는 되지 못한다. 가장 우세한 과학적 견해는 소행성이 행성으로 결합하는 데 실패한 물질이라는 것이다. NEO가 최근에 대량으로 출현했던 사례 중 하나는 1908년에 시베리아에 충돌했던 것이다. 그것은 주위 수 마일에 걸쳐서 나무들을 평평하게 밀어버렸고, 순록 떼를 죽음에 이르게 했다. 지구는 비슷한 충격을 증명해주는 관찰 가능한 수많은 분화구들과 함께 관측된다. 보편적으로, 거대한 NEO의 충격으로 인해 6천 5백만 년 전에 공룡을 포함한 수많은 생물들이 멸종했다고 믿어지고 있다.

[주 제] NEO의 개념과 출현

[어 휘] contemporary 동시대의, 현대의 asteroid 소행성 meteoroid 유성 comet 혜성 situate 위치시키다, 두다 confine 제한하다, 국한시키다 remnant 남은 부분, 잔해 scientific 과학의 reindeer 순록 be spotted with (~으로 인해) 얼룩덜룩하다 testify 증명하다, 진술하다

17 [정답 해설] 주어진 문장은 거대한 폭발이나 충격에 대한 결과를 설명한 부분이다. 따라서 문맥상 바로 앞에 폭발이나 충격이 일어났다는 내용이 나오는 것이 자연스럽다. 따라서 주어진 문장은 (E)에 위치하는 것이 가장 적절하다.

18 [정답 해설] 작은 행성에 살던 사람들이 핵에너지를 발견해 그들이 사는 세계를 날려버렸고 asteroids가 그 잔해라는 내용

은 한때 인기 있던 공상 과학 소설의 아이디어라고 언급되었다. 따라서 ②가 글의 내용과 일치한다.

19 ③
20 ⑤

두 가지의 역사적인 사실들이 컴퓨터 보안 분야에서 논의되어야 할 필요성이 있는 근원적인 문제점에 대해 주목하도록 만들고 있다. 첫 번째로, 모든 복잡한 소프트웨어 시스템은 종국에 가서는 지속적인 수정을 필요로 하는 결점이나 오류를 드러낸다. 두 번째로, 다양한 보안 공격에 취약하지 않은 컴퓨터의 하드웨어나 소프트웨어 시스템을 구축하는 것은 굉장히 어려운 일이다. 1990년대에 마이크로소프트 사에 의해 소개되었던 윈도 NT 운영체제는 이러한 어려움들에 대해 설명해준다. 윈도 NT는 아주 높은 수준의 보안이 보장되었다. 슬프게도, 윈도 NT는 이 약속을 지킬 수 없었다. 이 OS와 그 이후에 나온 윈도 시리즈들은 광범위한 보안 취약성 때문에 만성적인 어려움을 겪어 왔다.

강력한 컴퓨터 보안을 제공하는 것과 관련된 문제는 설계와 실행 두 가지를 포함하고 있다. 어떤 하드웨어나 소프트웨어 모듈을 설계할 때 그 설계가 실제로도 의도했던 수준의 보안을 확실히 제공해 준다고 보장되기는 어렵다. 이러한 어려움은 예상치 못한 다양한 보안 취약성을 낳는다. 비록 설계 자체는 어느 정도 정확할지 몰라도, 그 설계를 실수나 오류 없이 실행하는 것은 불가능하지는 않지만 어려운 일이다. 그 설계는 여전히 또 다른 취약한 부분을 많이 만들어 낼 것이다.

[주 제] 안전한 컴퓨터 시스템 제작의 어려움

[어 휘] highlight (사람들이 관심을 더 갖도록) 강조하다 vulnerable 취약한, 연약한 chronically 만성적으로, 지속적으로 plague with ~으로 괴롭히다 to do with ~과 관계가 있는 implementation 이행, 실행 software module (독립되어 있는) 프로그램 단위 stabilize 안정되다, 안정시키다 unduly 지나치게, 과도하게 erroneously 잘못되게, 그릇되게

19 [정답 해설] 전체적으로 컴퓨터에 대한 보안 시스템을 설계하고 실행하는 것이 얼마나 어려운 일인지에 대해 자세하게 설명하고 있다. 따라서 ③이 주제로 가장 적절하다.
① 설계와 실행에 대한 문제의 해결책 찾기
② 안전한 컴퓨터 프로그래밍 회사 세우기
③ 안전한 컴퓨터 시스템을 만드는 것의 어려움
④ 결점 없는 소프트웨어 개발자들의 책임감
⑤ 새로운 하드웨어 시스템을 설치하는 것에의 요구사항

20 [정답 해설] 다양한 보안 공격에 취약하지 않은 컴퓨터의 하드웨어나 소프트웨어 시스템을 구축하는 것은 굉장히 어려운 일이라고 설명하고 있으므로 빈칸에는 ⑤번이 들어가는 것이

가장 적절하다.
① 수많은 시도와 오류 후에 최근에 안정되었다
② 그들의 선행자를 능가하기 위해 지속적으로 업데이트 했다
③ 과도하게 홍보하여 천만이 넘는 소비자에게 팔았다
④ 소프트웨어 개발자들이 가장 강력하다고 잘못 알았다
⑤ 광범위한 보안 취약성 때문에 만성적인 어려움을 겪어 왔다

21 ②
22 ①

이 정도는 알려져 있다. 28번 뉴런이 전기적인 신호를 발사하고, 28번 뉴런의 축색돌기가 29번 뉴런의 수상돌기와 닿아있는 부분인 시냅스 안에서 발생한 어떤 화학적인 변화가 29번 뉴런 안에서의 전기적 신호를 유발한다고 하자. 그 신호는 30번 뉴런에까지 전달되고 이러한 과정이 계속해서 반복된다. 만약 28번과 29번 사이의 연결이 빈번하게 발생한다면 두 뉴런 사이의 결합은 더욱 더 강해진다. 이 대단한 결합 과정은 기억이 만들어지는 근간이 되는 듯하다. 우리 몸에 있는 기타 세포들과는 달리, 뉴런은 분열하지 않는다. 사람이 65세에서 70세에 이를 때쯤이면 28번 뉴런과 그 주변의 뉴런들은 사멸하거나 또는 너무 약해져서 더 이상은 전기 신호를 효율적으로 전달하지 못한다.

하지만 여전히 수십억의 뉴런이 더 존재하고 있다. 그리고 비록 뇌가 새로운 뉴런을 만들어 낼 수는 없을 지라도 뉴런은 대개 다른 시냅스가 자라나게 할 수 있고, 따라서 서로 새로운 연결 관계를 형성할 수 있다. 어떤 연구원은 우리 안의 실험용 쥐에게 매일매일 새로운 장난감을 제공해 주고 미끄럼틀이나 터널 등의 구조를 바꿔 주었다. 이 쥐들의 뇌를 해부해 봤을 때 그는 장난감이 없거나 새로운 장치가 없는 쥐들에 비해 훨씬 더 많은 수의 시냅스를 발견할 수 있었다. 이것은 사람의 두뇌 역시 보다 자극적이고 도전이 요구될 때 훨씬 더 많은 시냅스를 만들어 낼 수 있다는 좋은 추측의 근거가 된다. 그러므로 뇌는, 심지어는 축소되고 있는 중에도, 기억을 저장해 놓기 위한 훨씬 더 많은 새로운 길을 새길 수 있을지도 모른다. 만약 28번 뉴런의 연결부가 더 이상 쉽게 통하지 않게 되더라도, 대체할 수 있는 길의 수는 사실상 무한할 것이다. 비결은 뇌에게 새로운 경로를 만들도록 지시하는 것이다.

[주 제] 기억력 쇠퇴를 극복하기 위한 뉴런의 구조

[어 휘] neuron 신경 단위, 뉴런 synapse 시냅스, 신경 전달 부위 trigger 방아쇠, 시발점, 시작하게 만들다 transmit 전달하다, 보내다 sprout 자라나게 하다, 싹이 트다, 발아하다 thereby 그것에 의하여, 그것으로 인해 lab rats 실험용 쥐 chute 활강로, 미끄럼틀 decor 장식품, 장식 blaze 길을 만들다, 불길을 일으키다

21 [정답 해설] 글 전반부에서는 기억이 형성되는 과정에 대해

설명했고, 중반부 이후부터는 나이가 들어서 뉴런이 제 기능을 못하게 되더라도 또 다른 시냅스를 만들어 냄으로써 이를 극복할 수 있다고 설명하고 있다. 마지막 부분에서는 심지어 뇌가 축소되고 있는 과정 중에서도 여전히 기억을 위해 새로운 저장 장소를 만들 수 있다고 언급하고 있다. 따라서 전체적인 주제로 ②가 가장 적절하다.
① 새로운 기억을 형성하는 데 있어서 뉴런의 중요한 역할
② 기억력 쇠퇴를 극복하기 위한 뉴런의 구조
③ 기억의 기능에서의 인간과 쥐의 뇌의 유사성
④ 전기 신호를 보내고 촉발시키는 데에서의 뇌 세포의 기능
⑤ 자신의 번식을 위한 뇌 세포의 자극과 도전의 요구

22 [정답 해설] 두 번째 문단의 앞부분의 내용을 참고하면, 새로운 뉴런을 만들 수는 없지만 새로운 시냅스를 만들어서 다른 연결 통로를 만들 수 있다고 언급하고 있다. 따라서 빈칸에는 ①이 들어가는 것이 가장 적절하다.
① 대체할 수 있는 길의 수는 사실상 무한할 것이다
② 누군가의 뇌의 기억 기능이 일시적으로 멈출 것이다
③ 뉴런의 자신의 채널을 더 강하게 만들 것이다
④ 뇌는 그것을 늘임으로서 다시 삶에 가져오려고 노력한다
⑤ 뇌는 전기 신호를 전달하기 위해 새로운 뉴런을 만든다

23 ④
24 ⑤

지난 몇 십 년간, 'The other'라는 용어는 차이, 다양성, 편견, 인종 차별에 대한 논의에서 점점 더 일반화되고 있다. 그것은 가끔 이상한 소리가 나는 동사로 사용된다. 당신은 "othered" 될 수 있다. 즉, 당신은 일반적으로 의미 있는 뭔가 이상으로 분류되기보다 무언가 이하인 "other"가 될 수 있다. 대부분의 경우, 소수 집단 또는 비주류 문화에 속한 사람들이 이 방법으로 "othered" 되지만 그 아이디어는 편견 또는 선입견을 반영하는 방식으로 대우받는 어느 사용자나 그룹에도 적용할 수 있다. 우리 모두 아마 'The Other'였던 상황에 처해 본 적이 있지만, 일부 그룹이 오랫동안 손상과 불안감을 주는 체계적인 방법으로 'Other'로 분류되어온 것은 분명하다. 우리가 서로의 정체성에 어떻게 반응하는지에 대해 'The other'라는 개념이 무엇을 말하는지 생각할 가치가 있다. 인종, 성별, 민족성, 종교, 문화 등의 일에 근거한 불평등한 토론에서 이 용어는 특별한 의미를 갖는다. 그것은 편견 이상의 어떤 것을 제시한다. 편견을 가지는 것은 누군가 또는 무언가를 싫어하거나 그것에 대해 부정적인 감정을 가지는 것이다. 반대로, 우리는 무언가를 선호할 때도 편견을 가질 수 있다. 예를 들어, 스포츠 팬은 좋아하는 팀에 대한 편향이 생길 수 있다. 그러나 누군가를 'Other'로 간주하는 것은, 그 사람을 우리 자신과 분리된 범주에 두는 것이며, 더욱 중요하게는 왠

지 자신보다 <u>열등한</u> 범주에 두는 것이다. 이는 그 사람의 정체성을 어떻게 해서든 탐탁하지 않은 것으로 여기는 것이다.

주 제 Other라는 용어의 차별적 의미

어 휘 categorize 분류하다 injustice 불공평 ethnicity 민족성 in some way 어떻게 해서든 odd-sounding 이상하게 들리는 minority group 소수집단 non-mainstream 비주류 damaging 피해를 주는 disturbing 불안감을 주는 conversely 정반대로

23 정답 해설 어떤 점에서 '이하'라고 여겨질 때 'other'가 될 수 있다는 점, 누군가를 'other'로 간주하는 것은 어떻게 해서든 탐탁하지 않은 것으로 여긴다는 것이라는 내용으로 미루어 볼 때 누군가를 'other'로 간주하는 것은 그 사람을 우리 자신과 분리된 범주에 두는 것이라는 내용이 문맥상 자연스럽다. 따라서 빈칸에는 ④ inferior to가 가정 적절하다.

① 특정한 　　　　　　② 다른
③ 동등한 　　　　　　④ 열등한
⑤ 이상의

24 정답 해설 주어진 글은 타자화의 부정적인 의미에 대해서만 언급하고 있으므로 ⑤는 글의 내용과 일치하지 않는다.

25④
26② 직장에서 생물학적 무능력과 자연적 선호는 (A) <u>그것들</u>이 이론적으로는 어떻든 간에, 차별의 혐의 제기에 대해 방어하는 데 사용되는 반작용이다. 하버드 대학의 Larry Summers 총장은 경쟁이 차별을 비합리적으로 만든다고 주장한다. 그렇지만 한 분야 전체가 차별이 팽배하다면, 그곳에 여자가 속하지 않는다는 합의가 있다면, 또한 여성 후보들이 모든 잠재적인 고용주들에게 더 가혹하게 평가받는다면, 그것은 적용되지 않을 것이다. 또한 그것은 경쟁의 위협들이 매우 신뢰할 수 없는 경우에는 효과가 없다. Ivies(아이비리그 대학들)가 (B) <u>그들</u>이 어리석게 놓쳐 버린 일류 여성들을 채용함으로써 인지도를 높인 Northwestern 대학들의 열기를 느끼기까지는 오랜 시간이 걸릴 것이다. 직장에서 여성과 소수 민족의 역사는 반차별 법의 활발한 집행이 발전을 추진시키는 원동력임을 보여준다. 또한, 경쟁 논쟁은 Summers에게 등을 돌릴 수 있다. 명성과 부를 고려할 때, 하버드는 여성을 위해 지구상의 어느 대학과도 경쟁할 수 있다. 그런데 왜 그렇게 하지 않는 것일까?

주 제 여성 고용 차별

어 휘 biological 생물학의 incapacity 무능력, 부적당 natural preference 자연적 선호 accusation 비난, 혐의 제기 discrimination 차별 irrational 비이성적인 pervade with ~이 만연

하다 profile 옆모습, 인지도 antidiscrimination 인종 차별 반대

25 정답 해설 유명 대학들이 일류 여성들을 어리석게도 놓쳤을 때 Northwestern 대학은 그 여성들을 고용하면서 인지도를 높였다는 글의 내용으로 볼 때 ④는 글쓴이의 의견과 일치하지 않는다.

26 정답 해설 (A)는 바로 뒤에 이어지는 문장의 주어가 가리키는 내용과 같고, (B)는 before가 이끄는 절의 주어와 동일하다고 보는 것이 적절하다. (A) 밑줄 친 they는 바로 뒤에 이어지는 문장의 주어인 biological incapacity and natural preference를 가리킨다. (B) Northwestern 대학은 최고의 여성들을 고용해 인지도를 높였다. 하지만 어리석게 유능한 그녀들을 놓쳐버린 they는 Ivies를 가리킴을 알 수 있다.

① (A) : 생물학적 무능력과 자연적 선호
　(B) : 아이비리그와 노스웨스턴
② (A) : 생물학적 무능력과 자연적 선호
　(B) : 아이비리그
③ (A) : 반작용
　(B) : 아이비리그와 노스웨스턴
④ (A) : 혐의 제기
　(B) : 아이비리그
⑤ (A) : 혐의 제기
　(B) : 아이비리그와 노스웨스턴

27①
28④ (A) "한 국가, 여러 민족들 : 문화 상호 의존의 선언"이라는 최근 보고서에서 학자와 교사 위원회는 공립학교가 다문화 교육을 제공하는 것이 좋다고 한다. 이 보고서에 따르면, 이것은 미국이 다양한 민족적 배경의 사람들에 의해 형성되었고, 그 역사는 계속 과거의 발견과 해석의 진행 과정이라는 것과, 그리고 세상을 보는 하나 이상의 방법이 있다는 것을 인식하는 것을 의미한다.

(E) 따라서, 백인 미국인의 서부 이민은 단순히 길들여지지 않은 야생의 영웅적 정착일 뿐만 아니라 토착민의 정복이기도 하다. 이민자들 중에는 단지 백인만이 아니라 아시아인들도 있었다. 흑인들 역시 북쪽의 백인들에 의해 해방된 소극적인 노예가 아니라 그들 자신의 자유를 위해 적극적으로 투쟁한 투사였다.

(C) 특히, 보고서에 따르면, 교과 과정은 아이들이 "미국과 사회 현실의 이상 사이의 불일치에 대한 이유를 비판적으로 평가하고, 그들이 현실을 이상에 더 가깝게 하는데 공헌할 수 있도록" 도와야 한다. 다시 말해서 아이들에게 실제로 무슨 일이 발생했는지 보여주고 그들의 나라를 발전시킬 수 있는 기술을 제공해 주는 것이다. 무엇이 이보다 더

애국적일 수 있겠는가?

(B) 반대 의견을 가진 몇몇 위원들은 이 다문화 교육 과정이 채택되면 미국은 민족의 파편들로 쪼개질 것을 공공연하게 우려하고 있다. 그들은 위원회의 보고서가 국가 통합을 희생하면서 민족성에 초점을 두고 있다고 주장한다.

(D) 그러나 민족성을 경시하는 것은 국가의 단결을 강화하지 않을 것이다. 미국의 역사는 어떻게, 왜 전 세계의 사람들이 미국으로 모여들었는지 그리고 그들의 삶을 더 윤택하게 하려는 분투 속에서 어떻게 그들이 서로를 변화시키고, 국가를 변화시키고, 그들 스스로 미국인이라 부르게 되었는지에 대한 이야기이다.

[주 제] 공립학교의 다문화 교육 제공 필요성

[어 휘] indigenous 토착의, 고유한 inconsistency 불일치, 모순 patriotic 애국적인, 애국의 dissent 반대하다, 의견을 달리하다 splinter 조각, 파편 fragment 조각 at the expense of ~를 잃어가며, ~을 훼손시켜가며 assess 평가하다 inconsistency 불일치 downplay 경시하다, 무시하다 bolster 북돋우다, 강화하다

27 [정답 해설] (A)는 공립학교가 다문화 교육을 제공하는 것이 좋다는 보고서의 내용을 언급하면서 이것은 세상을 보는 하나 이상의 방법이 있음을 인식하는 것이라고 말한다. 따라서 역사에서 백인과 흑인에 대한 상반되는 관점을 언급한 (E)가 그 다음에 이어지는 것이 자연스럽다. 그 다음 보고서가 언급한 또 다른 내용, 즉 실제로 어떤 일이 발생했는지 보여주고 나라를 발전시킬 수 있는 기술을 제공한다는 내용을 언급한 (C)가 이어진 후 보고서에 대한 반대 의견을 제시한 (B)가 이어지는 것이 자연스럽다. 마지막으로 (B)에 등장한 반대 의견에 대해 다시 반박하는 내용이 이어지는 것이 문맥상 가장 적절하다. 따라서 (A)에 이어지는 적절한 글의 순서는 (E)-(C)-(B)-(D)이다.

28 [정답 해설] (E)의 첫 부분에서 백인의 영웅적인 서부 이주와 정착의 이면에는 원주민에 대한 정복이 있었다고 언급된다. 따라서 ④가 글의 내용과 일치한다.

리에서 발생하는 먼지에 대한 편견과 주민들에게 더 중요한 순수한 공기와 햇빛을 고려하면 석탄의 불완전 연소로 인해 발생되는 다른 종류의 먼지들도 역시 같은 시설로 쉽게 없앨 수 있다. 비록 우리는 위험과 먼지로 인한 불편을 최소화 할 수는 있지만 전적으로 그것을 없앨 수는 없다. 그리고 <u>우리가 그렇게 할 수 없다는 것이 참으로 다행스럽다</u>. 왜냐하면 우리가 살고 있는 이 지구의 아름다움과 거주 가능성 자체도 바로 먼지의 존재 덕분이라는 사실이 밝혀졌기 때문이다. 먼지가 없다면, 우리는 대기 뿐만 아니라 수평선 근처의 구름에서도 푸른 하늘과 일몰과 일출의 환상적인 빛깔들을 보며 감탄할 수 없다.

[주 제] 먼지의 유용성

[어 휘] majority 다수 reply 응답하다 nuisance 성가신 것, 방해 blindness 시력상실 injurious 유해한, 해가 되는 abolish 폐지하다, 없애다 get rid of 제거하다, 없애다 horizon 수평선 gorgeous 멋진, 매력적인 habitability 거주 가능성, 살기에 적합한 환경 admire 감탄하며 바라보다, 존경하다 tint 색조 atmosphere 대기

29 [정답 해설] 빈칸 앞부분의 먼지를 완전히 없앨 수 없다는 내용과 빈칸은 '그리고'로 연결되어 있다. 또한 빈칸 뒷부분은 먼지의 이점을 언급하고 있다. 이때 빈칸에는 우리가 먼지를 완전히 없앨 수 없다는 것은 참으로 다행스럽다는 내용이 오는 것이 문맥상 자연스럽다. 따라서 빈칸에는 ④가 가장 적절하다.
① 우리는 그렇게 할 방법을 찾느라 매우 바쁘다
② 우리는 그렇게 한 것을 쉽게 잊어버릴 것이다
③ 그렇게 해야 하는 것은 우리의 가장 큰 임무 중의 하나이다
④ 우리가 그렇게 할 수 없다는 것은 참으로 다행스럽다
⑤ 아무도 그렇게 하는 것을 피하는 방법을 모른다

30 [정답 해설] 글의 앞부분에서 먼지가 심각한 질병과 실명의 원인이 되기도 한다고 언급되었으므로 ②는 글의 내용과 일치한다.

29 ④
30 ②

대부분의 사람들은, 먼지의 유용성에 대해 질문을 받았다면, 그것들이 어떤 쓸모가 있는지는 모르겠으나 굉장히 귀찮은 존재라는 사실만을 확신한다고 대답할 것이다. 먼지는 우리 도시에서, 그리고 우리 집에서 종종 귀찮은 존재일 뿐만 아니라 심각한 질병과 실명의 원인이 되기도 한다. 하지만 먼지는 잘못된 장소에서만 문제일 뿐, 그것이 만들어내는 해롭고 불쾌한 효과가 무엇이든 그것은 우리 자신이 자연을 대하는 행동에서 기인한다. 우리가 완전히 기계적인 이동 수단을 채택한다면 우리는 거리에서 질병을 유발하는 먼지들을 완전히 제거할 수 있다. 거

31 ③
32 ④

나는 8살의 말괄량이였다. 나는 모두 빨간 색인 카우보이 모자와 카우보이 부츠, 체크무늬 셔츠와 바지를 가지고 있었다. 나의 놀이 친구는 두 살과 네 살 이상 많은 오빠들이었다. 내 부모님은 오빠들에게 총을 사주기로 결정했다. 그것들은 물론 "진짜" 총은 아니었다. 그것들은 오빠가 새를 죽일 수 있다고 말했던 구리 총알인 "비비탄"을 쏘았다. 내가 여자였기 때문에 나는 총을 소유하지는 않았다. 바로 나는 인디언 역할로 물러났다. 이제 우리 사이에는 큰 거리가 생겼다. 오빠들은 그들의 새로 산 총으로 모든 것을 쏘았다. 나는 나의 활과 화살로 따라잡기 위해 노력했다. 난 내 오른쪽 눈에 믿을 수 없는

타격을 느꼈다. 내가 오빠가 총을 내리는지 보기 위해 바깥을 내다보던 그 때였다. 나는 그 사건을 지금도 기억한다. 나는 처음으로, 의식적으로 수년 전 의사의 말의 의미에 직면한다. "눈은 서로 교감합니다. 만약 한 쪽 눈이 안 보이게 되면 다른 한쪽도 그렇게 될 가능성이 있습니다." 나는 내가 빛의 사라짐에 맞서 이것도 보고 저것도 보고 미친 듯이 세계를 질주하면서 이미지를 저장해왔음을 깨달았다. 그 후, 내가 25년 이상 시력을 유지하고 있다는 사실에 감사의 마음은 문자 그대로 나를 무릎 꿇게 만든다. 말이 끊임없이 이어진다. 어쩌면 이것은 누군가가 기도하는 방식이다.

주 제 시력을 유지한 것에 대한 감사함

어 휘 regretful 후회하는 reserved 말수가 적은, 내성적인 absent-minded 멍한 relegate 지위를 떨어뜨리다, 좌천시키다 pellet 총알 incredible 엄청난 lower 내리다 confront 대결하다 consciously 의식적으로 sympathetic 공감하는, 동정하는 fading 희미함 gratitude 감사 maintain 유지하다 literally 말 그대로, 완전히

31 정답 해설 내가 시력을 잃은 것은 오빠가 쏜 총 때문이다. 따라서 ③은 글의 내용과 다르다.

32 정답 해설 필자는 오빠들이 쏜 총을 맞고 실명할 수 있다는 의사의 진단을 받은 후 25년 이상 시력을 유지해 온 것에 대해 감사하고 있다. 따라서 필자의 현재 심경으로는 ④ '감사하는'이 가장 적절하다.
① 미안해하는
② 후회하는
③ 내성적인
④ 감사하는
⑤ 다른 데 정신이 팔린

33 ④
34 ④
몇 달 전 버지니아의 실버타운에서 한 남자가 사망한 뒤, 가족들이 그의 속세의 물건을 가져가기 위해 찾아왔다. 그의 집은 바닥에서 천장에 이르기까지 식기, 모조 장신구, 침구와 세제가 수십 개씩, (a) 그가 가졌는지 알지도 못했던 물건들로 가득 차 있었다. (b) 그는 이 모든 것들을 일주일 내내 24시간 텔레비전에서 나와 거실로 통하는 홈쇼핑 네트워크를 통해 사들였다. 그는 거의 매일 상품들을 주문했다. (c) 그는 도착한 물건 중 일부는 남에게 주어버렸다. 대부분의 것들은 그저 쌓아둔 채 사용하지 않았다. 무엇이 그로 하여금 벽을 따라 홈쇼핑 물건들을 늘어놓게 하였을까? 그것은 바로 교제였다. 홈쇼핑 호스트들은 단지 물건을 판 것이 아니다. 그들은 그에게 말을 걸어 준 것이다. 실버타운의 한 직원이 떠올리길,

(d) 그(실버타운 직원)는 그(사망한 남자)가 혼자 많은 시간을 보내던 모습을 봤었다. 그는 외로워지는 것에 대해 말하곤 했다. 하지만 그가 물건을 살 때 (e) 그는 상담원들이 30분 동안 그에게 이야기하게 했다고 말했다. 그는 낮과 잠이 오지 않는 밤을 보낼 방법을 찾은 것이다. 그의 발견에서 그는 혼자가 아니었다. 홈쇼핑 채널을 따라 흘러간 시간과는 달리, 구매자들의 알 수 없는 목소리들은 화려한 귀금속 증명서 위를 떠돈다. 그 목소리의 대부분은 여성들이다. 목소리의 다수는 나이가 들어 갈라지기 시작한다.

주 제 홈쇼핑으로 외로움을 달랜 어느 노인의 죽음

어 휘 worldly 이 세상의, 속세의 possession 소유, 소유물, 재산 gadget 간단한 장치, 도구 linen 린넨(천의 종류) pile up 쌓다 companionship 친구 사귀기, 교제, 우정 sparkle 불꽃이 튀다, 번뜩이다 cram 잔뜩 들어가다, 억지로 채워 넣다, 벼락치기 공부

33 정답 해설 밑줄 친 내용은 '그'가 혼자가 아니었다는 것인데, 이는 홈쇼핑을 하는 동안은 판매원과 이야기를 나눌 수 있으므로 외롭지 않았다는 것이다. 그러므로 ④ '많은 사람들이 홈쇼핑에서 교제를 찾는다.'가 밑줄 친 부분의 의미로 알맞다.
① 실버타운에는 많은 사람들이 있다.
② 버지니아 실버타운에서 그는 외로웠다.
③ 그는 홈쇼핑에서 산 모든 물건들을 보관했다.
④ 많은 사람들이 홈쇼핑에서 교제를 찾는다.
⑤ 그는 홈쇼핑 채널에서 물건을 찾는 것에 외로움을 느끼지 않았다.

34 정답 해설 (a), (b), (c), (e)는 모두 혼자 살다 사망한 노인을 가리키고, (d)는 그 사망한 노인이 혼자 오랜 시간을 보낸 것을 떠올린 실버타운 직원을 가리킨다.

35 ①
36 ④
요즘에는 정치인들이나 전문가들로부터 미국이 가난한 나라들에게 일을 빼앗기고 있다는 말 외의 것들을 듣기 힘들다. 즉 생산업은 중국에게, 사무 지원은 인도에게, 그냥 거의 모든 일은 남미에게 빼앗기고 있다는 말이다. 이러한 한탄은 더 많은 미국인에게 좋은 직장을 마련하려는 더 큰 도전에 집중하는 것을 방해한다.
미국의 제조업 분야의 고용이 수년 간 하락한 것은 사실이지만, 그것이 그 자리를 차지한 외국인들에게 주로 책임이 있는 것은 아니다. 공장의 일자리는 전 세계적으로 없어지고 있다. 나는 최근에 직원 2명과 400대의 전산화된 로봇들이 있는 미국 공장에 방문했다. 두 사람은 컴퓨터 화면 앞에 앉아 로봇들을 조종했다. 계량기를 검침하러 오는 가스 검침원처럼 로봇을 수리하고 업그레이드하는 기술자들이 가끔씩

방문하는 것을 제외한다면 몇 년 내에 이 공장에는 단 한 사람도 상주하고 있지 않을 것이다.

제조업은 농업과 같은 추세를 따르고 있다. 생산성이 향상되는 것과는 달리, 필요한 인력이 줄어들기 때문에 고용은 하락한다. 1910년에 미국인의 3분의 1이 농장에서 일했다. 현재는 3% 미만만이 농장에서 일을 한다. 1995년 이래로, 전 세계적인 제조업 고용이 하락했을 때, 전 세계 생산량은 30% 이상 상승해 왔다. 무엇인가를 원망하고 싶은가? 지금 거의 모든 일상 업무를 가능하게 만든 전자 기계와 소프트웨어를 발명한 신지식을 탓하라. 이것은 공장의 작업장 범위를 넘어 확장되고 있다.

(주 제) 제조업이 사라지는 이유

(어 휘) vanish 사라지다 instruct 가르치다, 지시하다 pundit 학자, 박식한 사람, 전문가 lament 슬퍼하다, 애도하다 distract 주의를 산만하게 만들다

35 (정답 해설) 이 글은 제조업의 일자리가 감소한 근원적인 이유가 기술의 발전 때문이라는 사실을 설명하고 있다. 그러므로 이 글의 주제로는 ① '제조업종이 왜 사라지는가?'가 적절하다.
① 제조업종이 왜 사라지는가?
② 자유무역이 왜 국내 직종을 파괴하는가?
③ 국제 경쟁을 타파하는 방법
④ 사라지는 제조업종에 대처하는 방법
⑤ 제조업종을 지키는 방법

36 (정답 해설) 빈칸 앞 Blame이라는 단어로 미루어 볼 때 빈칸에는 제조업종이 사라지게 된 원인이 올 것이다. 빈칸 뒷부분을 보면 빈칸에 들어갈 원인이 전자 기계와 소프트웨어를 발명했다는 것을 알 수 있다. 따라서 보기 중 빈칸에 가장 적절한 것은 ④ '신지식'이다.
① 가난한 나라   ② 국제 무역
③ 낮은 고용률   ④ 신지식
⑤ 무역 적자

37 ③
38 ④
한 기업의 대표가 인디언 보호 지역 근처를 자신의 회사의 공공 교류 프로그램의 일환으로 방문했다. 그는 모여 있는 부족민들에게 이렇게 말했다. "저희가 이 지역에 5년간 위치해 있었음에도 불구하고 인디언들을 전혀 고용하지 않고 있다는 사실을 깨달았습니다. 하지만 우리는 그 문제를 매우 심각하게 검토하고 있는 중입니다." 그러자 "Hora, Hora"라고 몇몇 인디언들이 말했다. "우리는 회사 전체 인력의 5% 정도를 이 보호구역에서 채용하고자 합니다."라고 그가 말했다. 그러자 더 많은 인디언들이 "Hora, Hora"라고 외쳤다. 그들의 열

광에 고무되어 기업 대표는 향후 2년 안으로 회사가 고용을 실현할 수 있기를 바란다고 말하며 짧은 연설을 끝맺었다. "Hora, Hora, Hora"라며 이번에는 모든 사람들이 외쳐댔다. 사장은 만족하며 홀을 떠났고 보호 지역 내를 관광했다. 들판에 잠시 들러 그곳에서 풀을 뜯어 먹는 몇 마리의 말들에 감탄하며, 그 사장은 그 동물 근처에 가까이 갈 수 있는지를 물었다. "그럼요. 하지만 Hora를 밟지 않도록 주의하세요."라고 인디언 운전사가 대답했다.

(주 제) 인디언들의 야유를 찬사로 착각한 기업 대표

(어 휘) tribesman 부족민 reservation 보류, 예약, 인디언 보호구역

37 (정답 해설) 마지막 택시 기사의 말로 유추해 볼 때 Hora라는 것은 '바닥에 있는 밟으면 안 되는 것'이라 볼 수 있다. 즉 하찮거나 더러운 것으로 생각해 볼 수 있다. 따라서 기업 대표의 연설에 마을 사람들이 Hora라고 외친 것은 긍정적인 의미가 아니라 부정적인 의미의 '야유'라고 볼 수 있다. 그러므로 ③ '인디언들은 사장의 연설을 믿지 않았다.'가 알맞다.
① 사장은 인디언들이 고용될 자격이 있다고 생각했다.
② 회사는 인디언을 고용하지 않는 정책을 고수했었다.
③ 인디언들은 사장의 연설을 믿지 않았다.
④ 회사는 인디언들에게 그 지역에 공장을 짓는 것을 제안했다.
⑤ 사장은 인디언 고용이 회사에 좋지 않을 것으로 생각했다.

38 (정답 해설) 기업 대표는 자신의 연설에 대한 인디언들의 Hora라고 반응하자, 이를 만족하였다는 것으로 알아 매우 만족스러워 했다. 그러므로 빈칸에 들어갈 말로는 ④가 적절하다.
① 그럼에도 불구하고
② 알지 못한 채
③ 진정하며
④ 고무되어
⑤ 우울해하며

More Practice

01 ③   02 ④   03 ④   04 ⑤   05 ①
06 ②   07 ④   08 ③

01 ③
02 ④
제2차 세계 대전 중, 작곡가 Dmitry Shostakovich와 그의 동료 몇 명이 러시아의 통치자 Joseph Stalin과의 만남에 초대되었는데, 스탈린은 그들(Dmitry Shostakovich와 그 동료들)에게 새로운 애국가를 쓸 것을 의뢰했다. Shostakovich는 Stalin과의

만남은 (A) 무섭다고 들었는데, 한 번의 실수가 매우 어두운 골목으로 이어질 수 있다는 것이었다. Stalin는 목이 죄는 느낌이 들 때까지 당신을 응시할 것이다. 그리고 Stalin과의 만남이 종종 그러했듯이 이번 만남도 나쁜 방향으로 흘러갔다. 그 통치자는 애국가를 형편없이 편곡했다며 작곡가 중 한 명을 비판하기 시작했다. 너무 무서워서, 그는 일을 형편없이 한 편곡자에게 일을 맡겼음을 인정했다. 여기에서 그는 몇 개의 무덤을 파고 있었다. 분명히 그 서툰 편곡자는 책임을 추궁당할 수 있다. 작곡가는 그 (B) 고용에 책임이 있었고, 그 역시, 실수에 대한 대가를 지불할 수 있었다. Shostakovich를 포함한 다른 작곡가들은 어떠한가? Stalin은 일단 상대가 두려움을 느낀다는 것을 알면 가차 없었다. Shostakovich는 더 이상 참을 수가 없었다. 그는 주로 명령을 따르는 편곡자를 탓하는 것은 멍청한 것이라고 말했다. 그러고 나서 다른 주제, 즉, 작곡가가 자신의 음악을 직접 편곡해야 하는지에 대한 것으로 교묘히 전환했다. 이 문제에 대해 Stalin은 어떻게 생각했을까? 항상 자신의 전문성을 증명하기를 열망하던 그는 미끼를 물었다. 위험한 순간이 지나갔다. Shostakovich는 여러 방법으로 그의 침착함을 유지했다. 첫째, Stalin이 그를 협박하게 두는 대신에, 그는 스스로가 키작고 뚱뚱하고 못생긴 상상력이 부족한 남자로서 Stalin의 본 모습을 보게 했다. 따라서 독재자의 유명한 날카로운 시선은 그저 자신의 (C) 불안감을 나타내는 속임수였을 뿐이다. 둘째, Shostakovich는 Stalin을 마주하여 평범하고 직설적으로 이야기했다. 그의 행동과 목소리의 톤으로 그는 겁을 먹지 않았음을 보여주었다.

주 제 Shostakovich가 Stalin 앞에서 침착함을 유지한 방법
어 휘 composer 작곡가 anthem 애국가 misstep 실수 orchestration 관현악 편곡 bait 미끼 intimidate 위협하다 piercing 날카로운 gaze 응시

01 정답 해설 (A) 한 번의 실수로 무서운 일을 당할 수 있고 Stalin은 상대가 목이 조이는 느낌이 들 정도로 뚫어지게 응시할 것이라는 언급으로 보아 빈칸에는 '무서운'을 의미하는 terrifying이 적절하다. (B) 앞에서 작곡가가 편곡자에게 일을 맡겼다는 내용이 나오고, 다음 문단에서 편곡자는 주로 지시를 따르는 사람이라고 언급된 것으로 보아 작곡가가 편곡자를 '고용'했다는 내용이 흐름상 알맞다. 따라서 hire가 들어가는 것이 적절하다. (C) 앞에서 Stalin의 볼품없는 외모를 언급하고 그가 날카롭게 응시하는 것은 속임수라고 말하고 있다. 따라서 Stalin의 태도는 자신의 불안감을 숨긴다는 신호라고 보는 것이 적절하다. 따라서 insecurity가 알맞다.

	(A)	(B)	(C)
①	매력적인	…… 고용	…… 창의성
②	매력적인	…… 해고	…… 불안감

③　무서운　……　고용　……　불안감
④　무서운　……　해고　……　불안감
⑤　무서운　……　고용　……　창의성

02 정답 해설 'Always eager to prove his expertise'에서 언급된 것처럼 Stalin은 자신의 전문성을 입증하는 것을 좋아했기 때문에 ④번 문장은 이 글의 내용과 일치하지 않는다.

03 ④
04 ⑤

(A) Don은 25살 때 동남아시아로 배낭여행을 갔다. 여행 중 3주 동안 인도네시아 여행을 했는데 Bukittinggi라는 아름다운 마을에 들르기도 했다. 그의 게스트 하우스에서 스웨덴 출신의 Stephen이라는 멋진 친구를 만났는데, (a) 그는 휴화산의 꼭대기에 있는 가까운 호수를 탐험하라고 추천했다. .

(D) (e) 그의 조언에 따라, Don은 그곳에 가는 버스를 찾았다. 그곳은 그리 가깝지는 않았고 차를 타고 4시간을 가야했고, 가파르고 바람이 강한 다소 위험한 길이었다. 정상에서 보는 경치가 굉장했기 때문에 그만한 가치가 있었다. 한때는 화산의 분출구였던 산 정상에는 굉장히 장엄한 호수가 있었다. 그것은 아름다운 산책길로 둘러싸여 있었는데, Stephen에 의하면 주변을 걷는 데 약 2시간이 걸릴 것이었다.

(B) 호수 주변에서 (b) 그의 트레킹을 시작하면서, Don은 산에서 내려가는 마지막 버스가 오후 5시에 출발한다는 것을 알았고, 그때까지 반드시 버스 정류장으로 돌아가야 했다. 오후 1시가 되자 그는 호수 전체를 한 바퀴 돌고 산에서 내려가는 마지막 버스를 타기까지의 시간이 엄청 많이 남았다고 생각했다. 그것은 굉장한 하이킹이었다. 그러나 오후 4시경에 그는 (c) 그가 호수 주변 절반 근처에도 있지 않다는 것을 깨달았다.

(C) 그는 그가 온 길을 되돌아가기로 결심했다. 그는 버스 정류장에 가까이 갔을 때 마지막 버스가 (d) 그 없이 떠나가는 것을 보았다. 너무 놀라서, 그는 산을 걸어 내려갈 수밖에 없었고 어떤 친절한 사람이 자신을 데리고 가기를 바랐다. 그는 차 한 대를 만나기 전에 몇 시간을 걸었다. 다행히 결국 멋진 인도네시아 신사가 멈춰서 도움을 주었다. 그는 Don의 상황에 매우 호의적이었고 Don을 그의 게스트하우스까지 태워다 주었다. Don은 말할 수 없이 감사한 마음을 가졌다.

주 제 하이킹을 간 Don
어 휘 sympathetic 동정적인; 호의적인 grateful 고마워하는 turn out ~이 되다; ~인 것으로 드러나다 majestic 장엄한

03 정답 해설 (A)는 배낭여행을 간 Don이 Stephen에게 휴화산 근처 호수를 추천받았다는 내용이다. (D)에는 Stephen의 조언에 따라 Don은 호수에 갔고 주변을 산책하기로 했다는 내용과 호수 주변 산책로에 대한 묘사가 나온다. (B)에는 Don이 하산하는 마지막 버스의 출발 시각까지 시간이 넉넉하다고 생각하고 트래킹에 나섰지만 호수의 반도 둘러보지 못했다는 이야기가 나온다. (C)에서는 Don이 호수를 다 둘러보지 않고 되돌아갔으나 버스를 놓쳤다는 이야기와 행인에게 도움을 받았다는 이야기가 나온다. 따라서 이 글의 가장 자연스러운 흐름은 (D)-(B)-(C)가 된다.

04 정답 해설 (a)~(d)는 주인공인 Don이고 (e)는 게스트하우스에서 만난 스웨덴 사람인 Stephen이다.

05 ①
06 ②
우리는 알려진 실용적 가치가 없는 과학을 기초 과학 혹은 기초 연구라고 설명할 수 있다. 목성과 같은 세계에 대한 우리의 탐사는 기초 과학으로 불릴 것이며, 기초 과학은 알려진 실용적 용도가 없으므로 노력과 비용을 들일만한 가치가 없다고 주장하기 쉽다. 물론, 문제는 우리에게, 우리가 어떤 지식을 얻을 때까지는 그 지식이 쓸모가 있을 것인지를 알아낼 방법이 없다는 것이다. 19세기 중반에 Victoria 여왕이 물리학자인 Michael Faraday에게 전기와 자성에 관한 그의 실험이 무슨 도움이 되느냐고 물었다고 한다. 그는 대답하기를, "여왕님, 아기는 무슨 도움이 됩니까?"라고 했다. 물론 Faraday의 실험은 전자 시대의 시작이었다. 우리의 세상을 채우고 있는 많은 과학적 지식의 실용적 사용 — 트랜지스터, 백신, 플라스틱 — 은 기초 연구로 시작되었다. 기초 과학적 연구는 기술과 공학에서 문제점을 해결하기 위해서 사용하는 원료를 제공한다. 기초 과학 연구는 또 다른 한 가지 중요한 쓰임을 지니고 있는데, 그것은 매우 중요한 것이어서 그것을 단순히 기능적인 것으로 언급하는 것은 모욕적인 말처럼 들린다. 과학은 자연의 연구이며, 우리가 자연이 어떻게 작용하는지에 대해 더 많이 학습함에 따라 우리는 이 우주 안에서의 우리의 존재가 우리에게 무엇을 의미하는지에 대해 더 많은 것을 알게 된다. 외부 세계에 대한 우주탐사기로부터 우리가 얻는 비현실적인 지식으로 보이는 것이 우리의 행성에 대해 우리에게 알려주고 자연의 체계 안에서의 우리 자신의 역할에 대해 알려준다. 과학은 우리가 어디에 있으며 우리가 무엇인지 우리에게 말해주며, 그러한 지식은 가치를 넘어서는 것이다.

주 제) 기초 과학의 실용적, 철학적 가치

어 휘) physicist 물리학자 magnetism 자성, 자력 engineering

공학 scheme 체계, 계획

05 정답 해설 기초 과학과 기초 연구가 우리에게 필요한 이유와 어떤 도움이 되는지에 대해 쓴 글이므로, 제목으로 가장 적절한 것은 ① '기초 과학이 우리에게 무엇을 가져다주는가?'이 가장 적절하다.
① 기초 과학이 우리에게 무엇을 가져다주는가?
② 기초 과학 연구자들의 위기
③ 과학과 기술의 공동 목표
④ 기술: 기초 과학의 궁극적인 목표
⑤ Michael Faraday, 전자 시대의 개척자!

06 정답 해설 외부 세계에 대한 우주탐사기로부터의 지식이 '비현실적인' 것으로 보일 수 있지만 그것이 우주 안에서의 인간 존재의 의미와 자연 체계 내에서의 인간의 역할 등에 대해 말해준다고 하는 것이 자연스러우므로 빈칸에 들어갈 말로는 ② '비현실적인'이 가장 적절하다.
① 적용되는
② 비현실적인
③ 부정확한
④ 값을 매길 수 없는
⑤ 지략이 풍부한

07 ④
08 ③
당신이 원하는 것을 얻는 것과 당신이 원한다고 생각하는 것을 얻는 것은 다르다. 기술은 우리가 생각하기에 우리가 원하는 것을 점점 더 많이 부여한다. 오늘날, 사교적인 로봇과 디지털화 된 친구를 보면, 누군가는 우리가 만나는 것이 누구이고 무엇인지에 상관없이, 우리가 원하는 것이 항상 손닿는 곳에 있고 절대 혼자가 되지 않을 거라 여길지도 모른다. 누군가는 우리가 원하는 것이 수많은, 온라인 관계를 지지하는 비공식적 연결망인, 약한 유대라고 여길지도 모른다. 하지만 만약 우리가, 우리가 원한다고 생각하는 것들의 진짜 결과에 관심을 기울인다면, 우리는 우리가 정말로 원하는 것을 발견할지도 모른다. 우리는 얼마간의 고요와 고독을 원할지도 모른다. 예전에 한 미국인 작가가 썼듯, 우리는 덜 '빽빽하게' 살고, 더 드물지만 의미 있는 면대면 만남을 기다리고 싶을지도 모른다. 우리의 많은 시간을 모든 손가락 또는 엄지손가락만으로 자판을 두드리는 데 할애하면서, 우리는 우리가 인간의 목소리를 그린다는 것을 발견할지도 모른다. 우리는 로봇과 체스를 두는 것은 괜찮다고 결정할 수 있지만, 그 로봇은 가족이나 친구에 관한 대화에는 전혀 적합하지 않다. 로봇은 욕구를 가질 수 있지만, 욕망을 이해하기 위해서는 언어와 육체가 필요하다. 이러한 대화를 위해서, 우리는 먼저,

태어나고, 부모와 가족을 가지고, 사랑과 어쩌면 아이를 소망하고, 죽음을 기다린다는 일이 무엇을 의미하는지를 아는 사람을 가져야 한다고 결정할지도 모른다. 그리고 물론, 전기가 끊어지는 것으로 사라지지 않는 현실 세계로부터 가상의 것이 우리를 데려가지 않도록 해야 한다.

주 제 | 가상의 관계로 채울 수 없는 인간적 관계에 대한 욕구

어 휘 | underpin 지지하다 acquaintanceship 지인, 아는 사이(관계) thickly 두껍게, 빽빽하게 unfit 부적당한, 어울리지 않는 flesh 육체, 인간성 outage (정전으로 인한) 기계의 운전 정지 supernatural 초자연의

07 정답 해설 | 인간은 기술이 제공하는 약한 관계와 네트워크를 원한다고 생각할 수도 있지만, 사실은 인간적인 사건들을 이해하고 그것에 대해 대화할 수 있는 인간과의 관계를 원한다는 내용으로 가상세계에서 맺은 관계의 한계를 이야기하는 글이므로, 제목으로는 ④ '가상세계에서 이어졌지만 분리되다'가 가장 적절하다.
① 전원을 꽂고 접속하기: 외로움과의 작별
② 온라인 커뮤니티의 윤리적 문제
③ 인간과 로봇: 친구인가, 적인가?
④ 가상세계에서 이어졌지만 분리되다
⑤ 연결망을 탐험하고, 현실을 넘어서라

08 정답 해설 | 가상세계에서 로봇이나 온라인의 상대와 맺게 되는 무수한 가벼운 연결과는 반대로 드물고 유의미한 만남을 원하며 실제의 인간을 그리워한다는 내용이 이어지고 있으므로, 빈칸에는 ③이 가장 적절하다.
① 모험으로 가득한 시도
② 기술적 급팽창
③ 대면하는 만남
④ 사교적인 로봇과의 대화
⑤ 초자연적 개입

Example   답 01 ② 02 ③ 03 ④

나는 항상 마술의 기법에 흥미를 가져왔다. 내가 열 살 무렵에 나는 손수건이 사라지게 할 수 있었고, 순서를 변경하지 않고 카드 한 벌을 완전히 섞을 수 있었다. 십대 초반에 나는 런던에 있는 세계에서 가장 유명한 마술 협회 중 하나에 가입했다. 20대 초반에는 나는 미국에 초청되어 저명한 쇼에서 몇 번 공연을 했다.

매혹적인 속임수와 환상의 세계에 대한 나의 사랑은 우연한 기회에 시작되었다. 내가 여덟 살 때 나는 체스의 역사에 관한 학교 과제를 해야 했다. 나는 부지런한 어린 학생이었기 때문에 그 주제에 관한 책을 찾기 위해 지역 도서관에 갔다. 나는 잘못된 책장으로 안내받았고 우연히 마술에 관한 책을 몇 권 보게 되었다. 나는 호기심이 생겨서 마술사들이 불가능한 것들을 해내는 데 사용하는 모든 비밀에 관해 읽기 시작했다. 내가 제대로 책장을 찾아가서 체스 책을 찾았다면 무슨 일이 벌어졌을지 모르겠다.

많은 사람들은 우연한 만남과 계획에 없던 낯선 사람들과의 만남이 진로 방향에서 어떻게 중요한 변화를 이끌어내는지에 대해 이야기해왔다. 우리 각자는 결정적이고 계획되지 않은 사건들이 어떻게 주요한 직업적 영향을 끼치는지, 그리고 알려지지 않은 수천 개의 사소한 계획되지 않은 사건들이 어떻게 최소한 작은 영향을 미치는지에 관해 이야기할 수 있을 것이다. 영향력 있는 계획되지 않은 사건들은 흔치 않은 일이 아니다. 그것들은 매일 일어나는 것들이다. 우연한 사건은 우연한 것이 아니다. 우연한 것은 어디에나 있다.

Joseph Pulitzer를 예로 들어보자. 그는 헝가리에서 태어났다. 젊었을 때 Pulitzer는 건강이 좋지 않고 시력이 매우 나빠서 고통스러웠다. 그가 17세가 되었을 때, 좀 더 나은 삶을 위해 미국으로 갔다. 그러나 그는 거기서 직업을 구할 수 없었다. Pulitzer는 지역 도서관에서 체스를 하며 매우 많은 시간을 보냈다. 도서관을 방문한 어느 날 그는 지역 신문 편집자를 우연히 만났다. 이러한 예상치 못한 만남은 Pulitzer가 신입 기자직을 제안받는 결과를 낳았다. 그는 신문 기자직에서 꽤 성공했고, 편집장이 되었고 결국 그의 생애에 두 개의 가장 유명한 신문사의 소유주가 되었다.

주 제 | 우연한 일이 가져오는 기회

01 ① 근면함에는 항상 보답이 있다
② 우연한 일들이 좋은 기회이다
③ Joseph Pulitzer: 알려지지 않은 일화
④ 명성과 당신의 직업적 선택
⑤ 오래 기억되는 마술의 순간들

02 ① 예상된다

② 환영받지 못한다

③ 드물지 않다

④ 미래를 예언할 수 있다

⑤ 그들의 영향력을 잃을 수 있다

Practice

01 ③	02 ③	03 ③	04 ②	05 ④
06 ②	07 ②	08 ②	09 ③	10 ④
11 ④	12 ④	13 ③	14 ②	15 ⑤
16 ④	17 ④	18 ①	19 ①	20 ⑤
21 ④	22 ⑤	23 ③	24 ①	25 ②
26 ①	27 ②	28 ④	29 ②	30 ③
31 ③	32 ③	33 ⑤	34 ⑤	35 ②
36 ⑤	37 ⑤	38 ②	39 ③	

01 ③
02 ③
03 ③

암스테르담의 Schipol 공항에서 내려 터미널 안쪽으로 몇 걸음만 가면 도착장, 출구 및 환승 데스크로 가는 길을 보여주는, 천장에 매달려 있는 표지판 모양을 보고 나는 놀랐다. 그것은 높이 1미터, 폭 2미터의 단순한 디자인의 밝은 노란색 표지판으로 케이블과 에어컨 덕트의 망으로 복잡하게 덮인 천장에서 나온 철제 버팀대에 매달린, 조명이 달린 알루미늄 상자 안에 있다. 그것의 단순함, 심지어 평범함에도 불구하고, 이 표지판은 나에게 흔치 않지만 '이국적'이라는 형용사가 어울리는 듯한 즐거움을 준다. 이국적임은 Aankomst의 a 한 쌍, Uitgang의 u와 i의 인접, 영어 자막의 사용, '책상'이라는 단어, balies, Frutiger 또는 Univers라는 실용적이고 현대적인 글꼴의 선택 같은 특정 영역에 있다.

표지판이 나에게 진정한 즐거움을 불러일으킨다면 그것은 어느 정도는 내가 다른 곳에 도착했다는 첫 번째 결정적인 증거가 되기 때문이다. 그것은 해외에 있다는 상징이다. 얼핏 봐서는 유별나 보이지 않을 수도 있지만, 우리나라에서는 절대로 정확하게 이 형태로는 존재하지 않을 것이다. 거기에서 그것은 덜 노랗고 서체는 더 부드럽고 더 향수를 불러일으킬 것이다. 외국인의 혼란에 대한 무관심으로 인해 자막은 없을 것이고, 언어는 내가 당황하며 다른 역사와 사고방식의 존재를 느끼는 반복인 두 개의 a를 포함하지 않을 것이다.

각기 다른 장소에서 기호가 다를 수 있다는 것은 간단하지만 유쾌한 아이디어의 증거이다. 국가는 다양하고 관례는 국경을 초월하는 변수이다. 그러나 차이만으로는 즐거움을 충분히 또는 오랫동안 이끌어내지 못한다. 그 차이는 우리나라가 할 수 있는 것에 대한 개선처럼 보여야 한다. 내가

Schipol 표지판을 이국적이라고 한다면, (그건) 그것이 모호하지만 강렬하게, 그것을 만들고 uitgang 너머에 있는 나라가 나의 기질과 관심사에 있어 내 자신보다도 더 결정적인 방식으로 잘 맞음을 증명할 수 있다고 암시하는 데 성공했기 때문이다. 표지판은 행복의 약속이다.

주 제 표지판이 주는 즐거움

어 휘 fascia 간판 strut 버팀대 mundanity 속세, 세속적임, 평범함 provoke 유발하다 indifference 무관심 subtitle 자막 elicit 끌어내다 congenial 마음이 맞는 nostalgic 향수를 불러일으키는 esoteric 난해한 bewilderment 어리둥절함

01 정답 해설 표지판이 이국적인 느낌을 불러일으키고 다른 나라에 와 있음을 상기시키는 즐거움을 준다는 내용의 글이다. 따라서 이 글의 제목으로는 ③이 가장 적절하다.

① 이국적인 동시에 향수를 불러일으킨다

② 너무 난해한 표지판은 호기심을 없앤다

③ 행복한 어리둥절함: 나는 다른 곳에 있는가?

④ 같은 접시의 다양한 언어들

⑤ 국경을 넘어서: 선구적인 여행가

02 정답 해설 암스테르담의 Schipol 공항에서 본 표지판의 특징이 나온 앞 문단의 내용과 비교하여 빈칸이 포함된 문단에서는 글쓴이의 나라의 표지판을 설명하고 있다. 앞 문단에서 Schipol 공항의 표지판에는 영어 자막이 있었다고 언급했지만 글쓴이의 나라 표지판에는 자막이 없다고 말했다. 자막이 없는 이유로는 외국인이 겪을 법한 '혼란'에 대한 무관심을 드는 것이 문맥상 자연스럽다. 따라서 빈칸에는 ③ confusion이 적절하다.

① 재주　　　　　　　　② 흥분

③ 혼란　　　　　　　　④ 친밀감

⑤ 숫자

03 정답 해설 ③ 표지판의 단순함이 이국적임의 주요 이유라는 언급은 없다. 단순하지만 이국적인 즐거움을 준다고만 언급했다.

① 그것의 길이는 높이의 두 배이다.

② 그것은 두 개의 언어로 쓰여 있다.

③ 그것의 이국적임의 주요 이유는 단순함이다.

④ 그것은 다른 나라에 도착했다는 것을 증명한다.

⑤ 글쓴이는 이것과 같은 표지판을 자신의 나라에서 찾을 수 없다.

04 ②
05 ④
06 ②

(A) 많은 국가에서는 개인에게 오토바이를 탈 때 헬멧을 착용하도록 하는 법을 가지고 있다. 이러한 법률은 그것의 유일한 목적이 운전자들을 부상으로부터 보호해주기 위한 것이라는 것을 근거로 자주 어겨진다.

(B) 대학 시절 나는 헬멧 착용하기를 확고하게 거부하는 오토바이를 타는 친구가 있었다. 그는 우리들로부터 그의 명청함 때문에 자주 놀림을 받았기 때문에 (a) 그는 다음과 같이 다소 유창한 방어 논리를 전개했다. "이봐, 나는 이러한 부르주아 생활에 지쳤어. 나는 모험을 좀 하고 싶어. 그게 내가 오토바이를 타는 첫 번째 이유야. 나는 위험하길 원해. 스릴은 위험부담을 지는 거야. 그리고 내가 더 위험부담을 가질수록 스릴이 더 커져."

(D) 헬멧 없이 타기로 한 내 친구의 결정이 단지 그 자신에게만 영향을 미쳤는가? 돌이나 다른 물체가 (d) 그를 다른 사람에게 빗나가게 하면서 도로에서 날아갈지도 모른다. 심지어 그 혼자만 부상을 입더라도, 그러한 부상은 헬멧을 찼으면 피했을 수 있는 머리 부상을 동반할 수 있다. 내 친구는 그렇게 되면 혼자 남겨지는 것이 아니라 앰뷸런스 운전자와 의사들과 구급 의료진들의 도움을 받는 것을 기대하게 될 것이다. 귀중한 시간과 돈은 그의 스릴을 추구하는 것을 보조하는 데 쓰이게 된다. 의사들은 (e) 그의 깨진 두개골에 뇌 세포 조직을 다시 넣느라 바빠서 다른 피해자들에게 제 시간에 가지 못하게 될지도 모른다. 병원 공간과 자원 또한 세금이 붙을 것이고, 의사들이 불려가게 될 것이고, 의료 보험과 자동차 보험료가 우리 모두에게 인상될 것이다.

(C) 그 일화로부터 보면, 헬멧을 안 쓰는 오토바이 운전자들은 결국 다른 사람들과 관련된 행동에 연관되어 있는 것처럼 보인다. 대중이 관심을 갖는 것은 오토바이 운전자에게 무슨 일이 일어나는지가 아니다. 우리는 무모한 행동에서 비롯되는 나머지 우리에게 드는 비용에 관심이 있다. 모든 사람의 생활 방식이 (b) 그가 공공 자원에 내는 부담이나 세금의 차원에서 같은 것은 아니다. 나의 무모한 친구는 (c) 그를 홀로 남겨두라는 것뿐 아니라 대중들에게 그의 선택을 지원해달라고 요청하는 이기주의자의 특별히 극단적인 예로 보인다.

주 제) 다른 사람의 희생을 대가로 한 자유

어 휘) on the grounds that ~를 이유로 steadfastly 확고하게 eloquent 유창한, 웅변의 bourgeois 부르주아 daredevil 무모한 in terms of ~의 차원에서 reckless 무모한 subsidize 보조금을 주다 stuff 채우다 skull 두개골 psyche 마음 recipe 비법 at the expense of ~을 희생하여

04 정답 해설) 오토바이를 탈 때 헬멧을 착용하는 법이 위반되고 있다는 (A)의 내용에 이어 대학 시절 오토바이를 타면서 헬멧을 착용하기를 거부했던 친구에 대해 언급한 (B)가 이어진 후 헬멧을 착용하지 않을 경우 당사자와 다른 사람들에게 미칠 피해를 언급한 (D)가 이어지고 오토바이를 탈 때 헬멧을 쓰지 않는 행위가 초래하는 사회적 비용에 대해 언급한 (C)로 마무리되는 것이 문맥상 자연스럽다. 따라서 (A)에 이어지는 글의

순서로는 (B)-(D)-(C)가 가장 적절하다.

05 정답 해설) 오토바이를 탈 때 헬멧을 착용하지 않는 친구의 일화를 통해서 자신의 자유를 위해 다른 사람들의 희생을 대가로 하는 행동에 대해 비판하고 있다. 따라서 글의 주제로는 ④가 가장 적절하다.
① 헬멧을 쓰지 않는 오토바이 운전자들의 마음
② 사고 없는 사회를 위한 비법
③ 위험 부담을 지는 사람들과 위험 부담을 지지 않는 사람들의 생활방식
④ 다른 사람의 희생을 대가로 한 개인의 자유
⑤ 교통 법규 위반자들에 대한 논란의 소지가 있는 규제

06 정답 해설) (b)는 일반적인 개인을 가리키고, 나머지 (a), (c), (d), (e)는 필자의 친구를 가리킨다.

07 ②
08 ②
09 ③

동기 이득은 공동 작업에서 그룹 내 구성원들이 쏟는 노력을 증가시키는 상황을 말한다. 능력이 상대적으로 떨어지는 팀 내의 구성원이 더욱 더 노력을 하는 동기 이득을 갖게 되는 것을 Köhler 효과라고 한다. 몇몇의 연구에서, 운동선수들은 도르래에 연결된 막대기를 지칠 때까지 당겼다. 처음에 그들은 혼자, 그 다음에는 두 명이 한 팀이 되어 당겼다. 동기 이득은 각각의 운동선수가 각각 적당한 차이의 힘을 가지고 있었을 때 발생했다. (A) 반대로, 운동선수들이 동등하거나 아니면 너무 차이가 나는 능력을 가지고 있을 때 동기 이득은 발생하지 않았다. 이러한 동기 이득은 그룹의 상대적으로 능력이 떨어지는 구성원의 책임이다. Köhler 효과의 심리 기제는 사회적 비교(특히 어떠한 팀 내의 한 사람이 그의 팀 구성원들이 더 능력이 좋다고 생각할 때)와 팀을 위한 한 사람의 노력이 필수적이라고 생각할 때를 기반으로 발생했다. 그룹의 구성원들은 그들이 개인적으로 가치있다고 여기는 결과물을 만드는 데 자신의 노력이 필요하다고 느낄 때 더욱 더 팀을 위해 기꺼이 기여한다. 더군다나, 특히 가장 능력이 낮은 사람은 모든 사람들이 팀 내에서 적절한 시기에 피드백을 받을 때면 더욱 노력하는 경향이 있다.

그룹에서 (Köhler 효과보다) 더 흔하게 볼 수 있는 것은 동기 상실인데, 이는 사회적 태만이라고도 한다. 프랑스의 농업기사 Max Ringelmann은 말, 소, 기계 그리고 일꾼에 의해 공급되는 농장 노동력의 상대적 효율성에 대해 관심을 가졌다. 특히, 그는 그들이 마치 줄다리기처럼 평평한 바닥에서 줄을 당기는 상대적인 능력에 대해 궁금증을 가졌다. 그의 실험들 중 하나에서, 14명의 사람들이 짐을 당겼

고 그들이 만들어낸 힘의 양을 측정했다. 또한 각각의 사람이 혼자 줄을 당길 때 낼 수 있는 힘도 측정했다. 줄을 당기는 사람들의 인원수가 늘어날 때마다 한 사람이 평균적으로 줄을 당기는 힘은 지속적으로 줄어들었다. 한 사람이 혼자 줄을 당길 때 평균적으로 63kg의 힘을 발휘했다. (B) 하지만, 세 명이 줄을 당길 때 각자가 내는 힘은 53kg으로 줄어들었고, 8명이 줄을 당길 때는 각자가 낼 수 있는 힘의 절반도 안 되는 31kg으로 급격히 줄어들었다. 이러한 연구 결과는 팀워크의 근본적인 법칙을 드러냈다. 사람들은 같이 일할 때 혼자 있을 때만큼 열심히 일하지 않는다.

주 제) 팀워크에서 동기의 영향

어 휘) motivation gain 동기 이득 circumstance 상황, 환경 capable 역량 있는, 유능한 investigation 연구, 조사 exhaustion 소모, 고갈 indispensible 필수 불가결한 efficiency 능률, 능력 tug-of-war 줄다리기 measure 재다 plummet 수직으로 떨어지다, 갑자기 내려가다 exert 발휘하다, 쓰다 reveal 드러내다, 누설하다 fundamental 근본적인, 기본의

07 정답 해설) 지문의 전반부에서는 팀 내에서 자신의 능력이 상대적으로 낮다고 여겨질 때 사람들이 더 열심히 노력하려는 동기를 가지게 되는 Köhler 효과를 설명하고 있다. 후반부에서는 사람들이 많아질수록 더욱 더 개인이 노력을 덜 하게 되는 Ringelmann 효과에 대해서 설명하고 있다. 따라서 ② '팀워크에서 동기의 영향'이 제목으로 가장 적절하다.
① 줄다리기의 작용 원리
② 팀워크에서 동기의 영향
③ 일의 효율성을 측정하는 방법
④ 개인 업무의 동기를 끌어올리는 방법
⑤ Ringelmann의 효과 뒤에 숨겨진 심리학

08 정답 해설) 지문에서 운동선수들을 상대로 행한 연구 중에 선수들의 능력이 동등하거나 너무 심하게 차이가 날 경우 동기 이득은 발생하지 않았다고 서술했기 때문에 ② '같은 능력의 사람들과 같이 일할 때 동기 이득이 생길 가능성이 더 높다.'는 글의 내용과 일치하지 않는다.
① 그룹 내의 능력이 부족한 사람이 더욱 더 열심히 노력하는 것을 Köhler 효과라고 한다.
② 같은 능력의 사람들과 같이 일할 때 동기 이득이 생길 가능성이 더 높다.
③ 적절한 시기에 피드백을 주게 되면 가장 능력이 낮은 사람은 더욱 더 노력하게 된다.
④ Max Ringelmann은 다른 그룹들의 노동의 효율성에 대해서 연구했다.
⑤ Max Ringelmann은 사람들이 다 같이 일할 때 효율성이 더 떨어진다는 것을 알아냈다.

09 정답 해설) (A) 앞부분은 운동선수들의 능력 차이가 적

당할 경우 동기 이득이 발생한다고 언급한다. 반면 (A) 뒷부분은 운동선수들의 능력 차이가 심할 경우 동기 이득이 발생하지 않는다고 언급한다. 따라서 (A)에는 '반대로'라는 뜻의 Conversely가 적절하다. (B) 앞부분은 한 사람이 혼자 줄을 당길 때에는 평균적으로 64kg의 힘을 발휘했다고 언급한다. 반면 (B) 뒷부분은 여러 사람이 줄을 당길수록 한 사람이 혼자 줄을 당길 때 내는 평균 힘보다 작은 힘을 발휘한다고 언급한다. 따라서 (B)에는 '하지만'이라는 뜻의 However가 적절하다.

	(A)		(B)
①	마찬가지로	……	하지만
②	대신에	……	그 동안
③	반대로	……	하지만
④	반대로	……	결과적으로
⑤	마찬가지로	……	그 동안

10 ④
11 ④
12 ④

Carnegie Mellon University의 심리학자 Sheldon Cohen은 의도적으로 100명의 사람에게 감기를 감염시켰다. 신중하게 통제된 환경에서, 그는 감기를 일으키는 라이노 바이러스에 체계적으로 지원자들을 노출시켰다. 전체 실험자의 약 3분의 1이 감기의 많은 증상을 보였고, 나머지는 훌쩍거림 하나 없었다.

실험 첫째 날, Cohen의 실험 지원자들은 바이러스에 노출되기에 앞서 그들이 다른 곳에서 감기에 걸리는 걸 막기 위해 24시간 동안 격리된다. 그 후 5일 간 실험자들은 각각 특별한 그룹으로 나뉘어, 서로 감기를 옮기지 않기 위해 다른 사람으로부터 적어도 3피트(약 1m)에서 생활하였다. 이 5일 동안, 그들의 코 분비물은 감기와 라이노 바이러스를 인지하는 기계를 통해 측정되며(그들의 콧물의 양을 측정하는 등), 특정 라이노 바이러스의 존재와 그들의 혈액 샘플 또한 항체를 위해 테스트 되었다.

우리는 비타민 C 부족, 흡연 그리고 수면 부족이 감염의 확률을 더 높인다는 것을 알고 있다. 여기서 의문점이 있다. 부정적인 인간관계 역시도 포함될 수 있을까? Cohen은 당연하다고 대답했다. Cohen은 다른 사람은 건강을 유지하는 동안 또 다른 사람들을 감기에 걸리게 하는 원인들에 대해 정확한 수치를 부여한다. 진행중인 개인적 갈등을 가지고 있는 사람들은 그렇지 않은 사람들보다 약 2.5배 감기에 걸릴 확률이 높았으며, 불안정한 이성 관계를 유지하는 사람은 비타민 C와 수면 부족으로 인한 민감성과 유사했다. 한 달이나 그 이상 지속된 갈등은 감기에 걸릴 확률을 증대시켰지만, 가끔 생기는 언쟁은 건강 문제를 야기하지 않았다. 번번

한 논쟁은 우리의 건강에 해롭지만, 자신을 고립시키는 것은 더 해롭다. 인터넷상에서 많은 친분 관계를 유지하고 있는 사람과 비교했을 때, 그렇지 않은 사람은 약 4.2배 더 감기에 걸릴 확률이 높았다.

우리가 사람들과 더 많이 어울릴수록, 감기에 걸릴 확률은 더 낮았다. 이러한 발상은 직관에 어긋나 보인다. 많은 사람들에게 노출된다면 감기에 걸릴 확률이 더 높지 않을까? 그렇다. 하지만 활기찬 인간관계는 스트레스 상태에서 코티졸을 억제하고 면역성을 향상시키면서 좋은 기분을 북돋우고 부정적인 기분은 제한시킨다. 즉 사람들과의 관계 그 자체는 바로 그것이 주는 감기바이러스에 노출될 위험으로부터 우리를 지켜주는 것처럼 보인다.

주 제   활기찬 인간관계가 주는 면역력 증가

어 휘   psychologist 심리학자 intentionally 계획적인, 고의의 systematically 계획적인, 체계적인 expose 노출시키다 rhinovirus 코감기 바이러스 panoply 모음 symptom 징후, 조짐 nary ~없는 sniffle 코를 훌쩍이다 quarantine 격리하다 secretion 분비물 antibody 항체 conflict 마찰, 충돌 deficiency 결핍, 부족 susceptibility 민감한 counterintuitive 직관에 반(反)한 vibrant 활기찬 suppress 억제하다, 가라앉히다

10 정답 해설   지문에서는 감기 실험을 하던 중 얻어낸 연구 결과에 대해서 서술하고 있다. 심리학자 Cohen의 연구에 따르면 비타민 부족이나 흡연, 수면 부족뿐만 아니라 인간관계도 감기의 원인이 될 수 있다. 따라서 ④ '평범한 감기 실험으로 얻어낸 평범하지 않은 연구 결과'가 제목으로 가장 적절하다.
① 인체 항생 신진대사의 특성
② 코감기(라이노) 바이러스에의 노출: 가장 정확한 방법론
③ 더 많은 인간관계를 맺을수록, 더 심한 감기에 걸리게 된다.
④ 평범한 감기 실험으로 얻어낸 평범하지 않은 연구 결과
⑤ 사이버 공간에서 찾아낸 새로운 건강 위험

11 정답 해설   기분 좋은 인간관계는 스트레스를 줄여주고 면역력을 강화시켜 주므로 빈칸이 포함된 문장은 '사람들과의 관계 자체는 바로 그것이 주는 감기바이러스에 노출될 위험으로부터 우리를 지켜주는 것처럼 보인다.'라고 해석되는 것이 문맥상 자연스럽다. 따라서 빈칸에는 ④ protect us from이 가장 적절하다.
① ~에 의해 수정되다
② 그들을 ~하도록 밀다
③ ~에 의해 약해지다
④ ~로부터 우리를 지켜내다
⑤ 점차적으로 증가하다

12 정답 해설   지문에서는 심리학자 Cohen이 코감기(라이노) 바이러스에 노출된 사람들의 바이러스 감염 여부를 위해 코 분비물을 검사했다고 서술되어 있다.

13 ③
14 ②
15 ⑤

수렵 채집인들은 약 5만 년 전에 호주에 도착했다. 원시적인 도구로 무장한 그들은 새롭게 이주한 곳의 환경에 큰 영향을 줄 수 있었다. 화석으로 남아있는 기록들은 호주에서 수많은 대형 포유류들이 갑자기 멸종했다는 사실을 보여주는데, 그것은 사람들의 정착지에서도 동시에 일어났던 것으로 보인다. 하지만 그 원인과 결과에 대한 근거는 (A) 확실하지 않다. 그러한 멸종이 사람들의 활동에 의한 것인지 아니면 많은 종들이 적응 (B) 할 수 있을(→ 할 수 없을) 만큼 갑작스러운 기후 변화가 있었던 시기에 의한 것인지에 대해서는 다소 논쟁이 발생하고 있다. 홍적세기 후기에 인류가 호주에 도착했고, (무게가 44kg 이상이 나가는) 큰 유대목 동물과 새들의 85% 이상이 멸종을 당했다. 이러한 사건은 그저 우연의 일치에 불과한 것일까? David Miller 박사는 에뮤와 가까운 미히룽(크고 날지 못했던 새)이 멸종한 원인에 대한 근거에 대해 검증해 보았다. 멸종 시기는 오직 온화한 기후로 바뀌는 시기와 일치하고 있었고 그는 인간이 이 새의 서식지에 끼친 영향이 가장 유력한 (C) 원인이라는 결론을 내린다. 하지만 Susan Bowman 박사는 이에 대해서, 호주의 원주민들의 인구수가 오늘날보다 (D) 더 밀집되지 않는 한 인간의 수렵이 그렇게 많은 수의 호주의 거대 동물들의 사멸에 대한 직접적인 원인이라고 볼 수 있을 만한 설득력 있는 근거는 없다고 반박한다. 더 그럴듯한 예측은 초기 원주민들이 불을 사용한 영향으로 자연을 너무 심하게 바꾼 나머지 많은 동물들이 살아남지 못했다는 것이다. 원주민들의 대지를 불태우는 행위는, 유럽 사람들이 호주에 도착하기 이전에 일반적인 호주의 초지 식물 군락지를 (E) 형성하는 데 핵심적인 역할을 했다. 그 결과, 풀을 뜯는 데 알맞게 적응한 종들에게는 적합하지만, 키가 작은 나무에 의존해서 그 잎을 뜯어먹기 쉽게 적응한 많은 동물들에게는 적대적인 서식 환경이 조성되었다. 나뭇잎을 뜯어먹는 것은, 당시 멸종한 많은 종들의 공통적인 특징이었다.

주 제   초기 호주 정착민들이 동물 멸종에 미친 영향

어 휘   hunter-gatherer 수렵 채집인 colonize (식민지로서) 개척하다, 이주시키다 have impact on ~에게 영향을 주다, 영향을 끼치다 fossil record 화석으로 남아있는 기록 equivocal 애매한, 모호한 Pleistocene 홍적세기 (빙하기가 끝나고 인류가 출현했던 시기) marsupial 유대목 동물 (주머니가 있는 포유동물, 캥거루 등) coincidence 우연의 일치 emu 에뮤(오스트레일리아의 큰 새) megafauna 거대 동물 aboriginal 오스트레일리아 원주민의 browse (나무의 잎 등을) 뜯어먹다 play a role 역할을 하다, 역할을 맡다 grassland plant (초원) 초지 식물 community (식물의) 군락지, 서식지 reliant on ~에 의지하는, 의존하는 scrubby vegetation 키가 작은 나무

13 정답 해설   인류가 호주에 도착한 이후 호주에서 많은 동물이 멸종했다는 것이 주된 내용이므로, 이 글의 제목으로는 ③

'인간의 도착이 호주에 남긴 흔적'이 가장 적절하다.
① 불태움이 대지에 가져온 것
② 인간 활동이 기후 변화에 영향을 미치는 정도
③ 인간의 도착이 호주에 남긴 흔적
④ 호주인들이 자연을 정복한 방법
⑤ 동물들의 서식지가 없어지면서 나타난 영향

14 정답 해설 동물들이 멸종한 이유에 대해 두 가지 견해가 대립되고 있다. 하나는 인간의 등장이고, 다른 하나는 기후 변화이다. 따라서 만약에 기후 변화에 의해 멸종한 것이라면 동물들이 기후 변화에 적응하지 못해서 멸종했다는 내용이 문맥상 자연스러우므로 (B)에는 able이 아니라 적응하지 못했다는 뜻을 만드는 unable이 적당하다.

15 정답 해설 호주의 원시인들이 대지를 불태워 군락지를 만든 일이 작은 나무의 어린잎을 먹는 동물들에게는 부적합한 환경을 만들었으므로 ⑤는 글의 내용과 일치하지 않는다.
① 갑자기 사라진 몇몇 호주의 큰 포유동물들은 화석으로 입증할 수 있다.
② Miller 박사는 호주에 사람들이 오게 된 것과 많은 새들이 후기 홍적세 중에 멸종하게 된 것은 우연이 아니라고 믿고 있다.
③ Bowman 박사는 사람들의 사냥이 호주의 많은 동물들이 대량으로 멸종된 원인이라 할 수 없다고 말했다.
④ 미히룽은 온화한 기후의 변화 시기에 멸종했다.
⑤ 목초지 사회는 풀을 뜯어먹는 동물과 어린잎을 먹는 동물들에게 새로운 서식지를 제공했다.

16 ④
17 ④
18 ①

(가) 당신이 두 개의 빵 조각 사이에 고기를 탁 하고 놓게 되면, 당신은 샌드위치를 갖게 된다. 적어도 고기와 가금류에 대한 정보를 표시하고, 안전성을 지키도록 규제하는 미국 농림부에 의하면 그런 것이다. USDA(미국 농림부)의 식품 안전 부서에서 근무하는 Mark Wheeler는 "우리는 전통적인 한 쪽 면이 가려진 샌드위치에 대해서만 이야기하고 있습니다."라고 말했다. "샌드위치란 두 개의 얇은 빵이나 번, 혹은 비스킷 사이에 고기나 가금류 등을 채워 넣은 것입니다." 여기에 부리토나 랩 샌드위치 또는 핫도그와 같은 상품들은 포함되지 않는다.

(라) 하지만 USDA가 샌드위치에 대해서 정의를 내려야만 하는 유일한 기관인 것은 아니다. 주로 점검과 세금 부과에 대한 전국에 걸친 사법권에 있어서도 그것은 중요한 일이다. 컴퓨터 개발자인 Noah Veltman은 괴상한

취미를 가지고 있는데, 그것은 잘 알려져 있지 않은 정부의 기록들을 열람하는 것이다. 그는 다음과 같이 말했다. "나의 새로운 보금자리인 뉴욕은 샌드위치의 범주에 속하는 것들에 특별세를 부과하고 있습니다. 그래서 그들은 샌드위치라는 것이 클럽 샌드위치와 BLT 샌드위치, 핫도그와 부리토를 포함하고 있다는 것을 설명하기 위한 기록물을 발행했습니다. 그렇다면 당신은 궁금해 할 것입니다. 부리토는 진짜 샌드위치가 맞나요?" 뉴욕은 그렇다고 말하고, USDA는 아니라고 말한다. 그리고 이러한 것들은 검열 시기가 되면 분명한 차이를 보이게 된다.

(나) 2006년도에는 그것에 대한 논쟁이 굉장히 뜨거워져서, Qdoba Mexican Grill의 부리토가 샌드위치로서의 조건을 충족시키는지의 여부와 관련된 계약상의 분쟁이 재판까지 가게 되었다. 요리사와 음식 관련 비평가들을 포함하는 전문적인 증인들이 법정에서 증언을 했다. 충분한 심사숙고가 이루어졌고, 그리고 마침내 고등 법원의 판사인 Jeffrey Locke은 부리토는 샌드위치가 아닌 것으로 판결했다. 그 재판은 Massachusetts에서의 그 문제를 종식시켰다. 하지만 어디에서든, 어떤 확고한 정의에서도 당신은 (A) 구분 짓기 어려운 경우를 찾을 수 있다. 연방 정부의 직원에 따르면 아이스크림 샌드위치는 진짜 샌드위치는 아니다. 하지만 우리는 그것을 그렇게 부른다. New York에서 타코는 샌드위치가 아니지만, 어째서인지 부리토는 샌드위치가 맞다. 하지만 New York 주는 그 이유가 무엇인지에 대해서는 설명하지 않는다. 적어도 아직까지는 그렇다.

(다) 이 모든 것들이 말해주는 바는 무엇일까? 얇게 잘려진 빵은 우리에게 샌드위치를 가져다 주었다. 하지만 그것들은 계속 변화하고 있다. 음식의 유행은 순식간에 지나간다. 그리고 (B) 단속 기관이 새롭게 혁신된 모든 것들에 대해 뒤처지지 않으려 하는 것은 불가능한 것이다. 그것이 샌드위치가 되었든 스마트폰이 되었든, 정부는 대중을 보호하기 위해 이러한 상품들을 분류하기 위해 노력한다. 하지만 혁신은 기준이 변화 가능한 것보다 훨씬 더 빨리 변화한다. 그것이 바로 Veltman이 수없이 지켜보는 팽팽한 대치 관계이다. "이러한 기록을 남겼던 사람들은 분류할 수 없는 성질의 것들을 분류하려고 노력하는 일을 하고 있습니다. 사람들의 행동은 무궁무진하게 다양한 것입니다. 당신들은 그 일에 대해서 모든 사물에 실제로 완벽하게 부합하는 방법은 절대로 생각해 낼 수 없을 것입니다."라고 Veltman은 말한다.

주 제 혁신 속도에 뒤처지는 규정

어 휘 slap (탁, 철썩 소리를 내며) 놓다 closed-face 한쪽 면

이 가려진 **bun** 번 (빵의 한 종류) **jurisdiction** 사법권, 관할권 **club sandwich** 클럽 샌드위치(세 조각의 빵 사이에 내용물을 채워 넣은 샌드위치) **BLT** 비엘티 샌드위치(베이컨, 상추, 토마토를 넣은 샌드위치) **testify** (법정에서) 증언하다 **deliberation** 심사숙고 **settle** 논쟁, 논란 등을 해결하다 **fed** 연방 정부 직원 (federation의 축약어) **flash** 순식간에 지나가다 **edge case** 이쪽인지 저쪽인지 구분 짓기 어려운 사건 **lucid** 명백한, 명료한

16 정답 해설 (가)에서는 USDA가 정의하고 있는 샌드위치에 대한 설명이 나왔으며, (라)의 바로 앞에서는 비단 USDA만이 정의 기관은 아니라고 하였으므로 (가)와 (라)는 자연스럽게 연결된다. (라)의 마지막 부분에서는 부리토가 진짜 샌드위치가 맞는지에 대해서 의견의 차이가 있다고 하였고, (나)의 앞에서는 이러한 논쟁이 더욱 뜨거워졌다고 하였으므로 (나)는 (라) 다음에 자연스럽게 연결이 된다. (다)는 의미상으로 앞에 언급했던 모든 내용들을 정리하고 있으므로 마지막에 오는 것이 자연스럽다. 따라서 (가)에 이어지는 글의 순서로는 (라)-(나)-(다)가 가장 적절하다.

17 정답 해설 새롭게 변화하는 혁신과, 규제 사이의 관계를 샌드위치를 예로 들어 설명하고 있으므로 ④가 제목으로 가장 적절하다.
① 두 세력 사이에 샌드위치처럼 끼인 고등 법원
② 부리토를 샌드위치라고 부르는 때는 언제가 가장 적절한가?
③ 뉴욕과 USDA 사이의 긴장: 그 숨겨진 이야기
④ 샌드위치 정의하기: 규제과 혁신에 대한 교훈
⑤ 현지 음식이 언제나 이긴다: 부리토와 샌드위치의 사례

18 정답 해설 (A) 정답에 해당하는 an edge case는 이쪽인지 저쪽인지 구분 짓기 어려운 경우를 뜻하는 말인데, (A)의 바로 앞에서는 부리토가 샌드위치에 해당하는지 아닌지에 대한 법정 공방을 벌였고, 그 자체가 구분 짓기 굉장히 모호하다고 했으므로 an edge case가 가장 적절한 답이다. (B) 바로 뒤에는 정부 기관이 대중을 보호하기 위해 새로운 상품들을 분류하려고 노력하지만 혁신은 기준보다 더 빨리 변화한다고 언급했다. 따라서 (B)에는 새롭게 혁신되는 모든 것에 뒤처지는 주체, 즉 정부 기관 등장하는 것이 적절하다. 따라서 보기 중에서는 regulators가 가장 적절하다.

	(A)		(B)
①	구분 짓기 어려운 경우	……	단속 기관
②	구분 짓기 어려운 경우	……	요리사와 음식 비평가
③	명료한 사례	……	소프트웨어 개발자
④	명료한 사례	……	요리사와 음식 비평가
⑤	명료한 사례	……	단속 기관

19 ①
20 ⑤
21 ④

수많은 이야기들에서와 같이, Bell Witch가 정확히 누구인지, 또는 무엇인지에 대한 자세한 내용은 버전마다 각각 다르다. 이에 대한 가장 일반적인 설명은, 그것이 John Bell이라는 사람의 이웃으로, 아주 늙고 교활했던 Kate Batts라는 여성의 (A) 귀신이라는 것이다. Batts는 토지 거래에 관해 Bell이 자신을 속였다고 믿었고, 임종 시에는 스스로 귀신이 되어 John Bell과 그의 가족들을 괴롭히겠노라고 맹세했다. 이 버전의 이야기는 1933년에 출판된 테네시 주의 안내 책자에 나와 있다.

"물론 Bell과 그 가족들은 수년에 걸쳐서 그 늙은 Kate Batts의 악령으로부터 괴롭힘을 당했다. John bell과 그의 딸인 Betsy가 주 대상이었다. 다른 가족 구성원들에게는 그 마녀는 무관심하거나 혹은 Mrs. Bell에게 하듯이 친근하게 대했다. 누구도 (B) 그녀를 본 적은 없지만 벨의 집에 방문했던 모든 사람들은 너무도 분명하게 그녀의 소리를 들을 수 있었다. 그 늙은 Kate의 영혼은 John과 Betsy Bell을 이리저리 끌고 다니며 괴롭혔다. 그녀는 가구나 접시 등을 그들에게 던졌다. 그녀는 그들의 코를 당기거나, 머리채를 확 잡아 당겼고, 바늘로 그들을 찔렀다. 그녀는 그들이 잠을 자지 못하게 하기 위해 밤새 소리를 질러댔고, 식사 중에는 입에서 음식을 잡아채가기도 했다."

Bell Witch에 대한 소식은 빠르게 퍼져 나갔다. 귀신의 출몰에 대한 이야기가 Nashville에 이르렀을 무렵, 그곳에서 가장 유명한 사람 중 한명인 Andrew Jackson 장군은 친구들을 모아서 그것에 대해 조사해보기로 결심했다. 장래 미국의 대통령이 될 그 사람은 그것이 거짓말이라는 사실을 밝혀내거나 또는 (C) 그 영혼을 멀리 쫓아버리기를 바랐다. Jackson과 그의 동료들이 여행을 하고 있던 중에 마차가 갑자기 멈추어 섰다. 사내들은 계속해서 밀어보았지만 마차는 조금도 움직여지지 않았다. 바로 그때 다음과 같이 말하는 목소리가 숲속에서 들려왔다. "좋아 장군, 그 마차를 움직여 보아라, 나는 오늘 밤 너를 만날 것이다." 놀란 사내들은 그 목소리가 어디서부터 들려 왔는지 찾을 수 없었다. 바로 그 때 갑자기 말들은 다시 가던 길을 가기 시작했고, 마차는 다시 움직였다. Jackson은 실제로 그날 밤에 (D) 그 마녀와 맞닥뜨렸고 다음 날 아침 일찍, Bell Witch와 싸우느니 차라리 영국과 싸우는 것이 낫겠다고 소리 지르며 떠나버렸다.

세월이 흘러가면서 Bell Witch에 대한 현상들에 대해서도 몇 가지 설명들이 나왔다. 그 중 하나는 귀신의 출몰이 Betsy Bell과 그녀가 사랑했던 Joshua Gardner라는 소년의 학교 선생님이었던 Richard Powell에 의해 날조된 거짓 현상들이었다는 것이다. Powell은 Betsy를 깊이 사랑했고, Gardner와 (E) 그녀의 관계를 깨기 위해서라면 무엇이든지 하려고 했었을 것이다. Gardner를 겁을 주어 멀리 쫓

아버리기 위해서 Powell이 다양한 속임수를 통해 귀신같은 효과를 만들어 냈다고 생각된다. 실제로 Gardner는 결국 Betsy와의 관계를 정리하고 그 지역을 떠났다. 그러나 이것은 Powell이 어떻게 해서 그 모든 귀신 효과들을 낼 수 있었는지에 대해서는 만족할 만한 설명이 되지 못한다. 하지만 Powell은 승리자가 되었다. 결국에 그는 Betsy Bell과 결혼했다.

[주 제] Bell Witch의 뒷이야기

[어 휘] deathbed 임종, 임종의 자리 malicious 악의적인 torment 괴롭히다, 고통을 주다 lead A on a merry chase A를 이리저리 끌고 다니다 yank 확 잡아당기다 poke 쿡 찌르다, 쑥 내밀다 snatch 잡아채다 hoax 거짓말 scare away 겁을 주어 쫓아버리다

19 [정답 해설] 전체적으로 미국의 유명한 귀신 이야기인 Bell Witch의 유래와 숨겨진 이야기에 대해서 설명하고 있는 글이므로 ①이 제목으로 가장 적절하다.
① Bell Witch의 뒷이야기
② 마녀의 요술을 조심하라
③ 마녀와 사랑에 빠지지 마라
④ Jackson 장관의 성공적이지 못한 마녀 사냥
⑤ 미국 남부에서의 마법의 발명

20 [정답 해설] (A)~(D)는 문맥상 Bell Witch를 가리키고 (E)는 Betsy Bell을 가리킨다.

21 [정답 해설] Andrew Jackson 장군이 남부에서 전투를 중지했다는 내용은 어디에도 언급되어 있지 않다.

22 ⑤
23 ③
24 ①

(가) 내가 처음 베란다 해변에 대해서 들었던 것은 내가 13살이었을 무렵 여름, 할아버지 댁의 현관에서였다. 느긋한 밤은 언덕이 뿌연 푸른빛을 내게 하고 있었고, 공기는 비 냄새로 다소 무거웠다. 대화가 앞으로 다가올 여름을 향할 무렵 마지막 남아있던 그림자는 석양 속으로 녹아들고 있었다.

(라) "어떤 계획이 있냐?" 할아버지께서 물으셨다. 의자의 등판을 두드리며, 나의 아버지가 대답했다. "베란다 해변이면 되죠." 그들은 모두 껄껄거리며 웃었다. 나의 심장은 매우 요동쳤다. 베란다 해변? 그곳은 어디에 있지? 우리는 언제 가는 건가? "왜? 너 이미 그곳에 도착해 있는데." 아버지께서 나를 놀렸다. 그들이 나에게 이 끔찍한 진실을 말해줬을 때 웃음소리가 부드럽게 울려 퍼졌다. 베란다 해변은 정문에 있는 현관을 의미하는

것이었다. 우리는 아무 곳에도 가지 않을 예정이었다. 내 사춘기의 영혼은 (B) 곤두박질쳤다. 그들은 그렇게 지루해 빠진 현관에서 도대체 무엇을 봤던 것일까? 그들은 정말로 좀 더 멀리 떨어져 있는 곳이 당연히 훨씬 더 좋다는 사실을 몰랐던 것일까?

(나) 물론 여름은 지나갔고, 나이를 먹어감에 따라 지혜도 갖게 되었다. 나는 정문 앞의 현관은 모험해야 할 장애물이 아니라는 사실을 깨달았다. 그곳은 세상을 보는 창문이었으며, 세상이 어떻게 돌아가는지에 대해서 배우는 장소였다. 게다가 오래된 교훈에 새로운 교훈을 더해가며, 그곳에 대한 애정은 오늘날까지 계속되고 있다. 우리 가족의 현관에서, 나는 삶과 사랑, 희망과 꿈, 그리고 약속과 신뢰에 대해 배웠다. 어떤 날은 그곳은 Tara로 향하는 문이었고, 나의 여동생과 나는 지독한 남부 억양을 연기하며 Rhett Butler를 찾기 위해 수평선을 돌아다녔다. 그리고 그 다음날 그곳은 성이자 요새였고, 또는 바다 위의 배가 되기도 했다. 어른들에게는 가벼운 마음으로 농담을 주고받는 것과 체스 게임이 (A) 장려되었다. 세금이나 수표책에 대한 이야기는 그렇지 않았다. 현관은 작은 것들을 즐기는 장소였다. 그곳에서 인생은 훨씬 느리게 흘러갔다.

(다) 이후로 몇 번의 현관을 더 거친 뒤, 이제 나는 현관에 대한 전문가가 되었다. 올 여름 나는 현관의 난간 위에 앉아서 내 아이들과 여러 가지 이야기를 주고받으며 시간을 보내고 있다. 새로운 세대의 아이들이 레모네이드가 담긴 주전자에 서린 물기에 자신들의 이름을 쓰는 것을 지켜보며, 나는 그들 또한 베란다 해변에서의 교훈을 배우길 바란다. 바람에 대항해 더욱 강해져라. 틀에 박히지 않은 방법으로 자라나 다채롭고 창의적인 사람이 되어라. 별똥별을 기다려라. 그 모든 것들에 우선해서, 때로는 가야만 하는 장소보다는 진정한 자신으로 존재할 수 있는 장소를 갖는 것이 훨씬 더 바람직하다는 사실을 알아라.

[주 제] 베란다 해변의 추억

[어 휘] pound 마구 두드리다 plunge 급락하다, 곤두박질치다 love affair 연애, 사랑, 열광 assume 추정하다, 흉내 내다 scout 정찰하다, (무엇을 찾아) 돌아다니다 lighthearted 편한 마음의, 근심 없는 banter 정감 어린 농담, 농담을 주고받다 connoisseur 감식가, 전문가 perch (새가 나뭇가지 등에) 앉아 있다. 쉬다 pitcher 물 주전자 colourful 다채로운, 화려한 droop 축 처지다, 의기소침해지다

22 [정답 해설] 13살 여름, 할아버지 댁 현관에서 처음 베란다 해변에 들어섰다는 (가)의 내용에 이어서 당시 할아버지와의 대화 내용을 언급한 (라)가 이어진 후, 그 여름이 지나고 나이가 들면서 현관이 주는 교훈을 깨닫고 현관을 다양하게 활용하게 되었다는 내용의 (나)가 이어진 다음, 독자들도 자신이 베란

다 해변에서 얻은 교훈을 배우기를 당부하는 (다)로 마무리되는 것이 문맥상 가장 자연스럽다. 따라서 (가)에 이어질 글의 순서로는 (라)-(나)-(다)가 가장 적절하다.

23 정답 해설 글의 마지막 문장, 즉, '때로는 가야만 하는 장소보다 진정한 자신으로 존재할 수 있는 장소를 갖는 것이 훨씬 더 바람직하다'라는 내용이 이 글의 주제이다. 따라서 글의 제목으로는 ③이 가장 적절하다.
① 베란다 앞쪽에서의 부드러운 코러스
② 내 앞마당의 잔디가 더 푸르다(내 것이 더 좋다)
③ 베란다 해변: 자기 자신으로 존재할 수 있는 곳
④ 결코 쉽게 사라지지 않을 기억
⑤ 삶에 대한 교훈: 나이가 들수록 현명해져야 함

24 정답 해설 (A) 현관은 작은 것들을 즐기는 장소라는 언급으로 미루어 볼 때 농담을 주고받는 것이나 체스 게임은 장려되었다는 내용이 문맥상 자연스럽다. 따라서 encouraged가 적절하다. (B) 아버지가 계획한 베란다 해변이 할아버지 댁의 정문 현관이라는 말을 글쓴이는 끔찍하다고 여겼다. 그러므로 '내 사춘기의 영혼은 곤두박질쳤다.'는 내용이 문맥상 자연스럽다. 따라서 plunged가 적절하다.

	(A)		(B)
①	장려된	……	곤두박질쳤다
②	신용이 떨어진	……	곤두박질쳤다
③	탐구된	……	일으켰다
④	선호된	……	일으켰다
⑤	대체된	……	의기소침해졌다

<table>
<tr><td>**25** ②</td><td rowspan="3">(A) 보통의 젊은 성인들이 그들이 학교에서 배운 것이 매우 적다는 것을 깨달았을 때, 그들은 대개 그들이 다녔던 학교에 무엇인가 문제가 있거나 그들이 그곳에서 시간을 보냈던 방법에 문제가 있는 것은 아닐까 추측한다. 하지만 사실은, 가능한 최고의 학교를 졸업한 가능한 최고의 졸업자도 장래에 계속해서 공부를 해야만 한다는 것이다.</td></tr>
<tr><td>**26** ①</td></tr>
<tr><td>**27** ③</td></tr>
</table>

(C) 그들은 그것에 어떤 방식으로 접근해야만 하는 것일까? 작년에 출판된 책에서 나는 그 질문에 대답하기를 시도했다. "모든 학과 과정을 마친 뒤에도 스스로 계속해서 학습을 수행하기를 바라는 사람들은 어떤 과정을 밟아야만 하는 것일까?" 이 중요한 질문에 대한 간결하고 간단한 대답은 바로 '읽고 토론하라'이다.

(B) 하지만 그저 단순히 읽어서는 안 된다. 왜냐하면 같은 책을 읽었던 사람과의 토론이 없는 독서는 그렇게 도움

을 주지는 못하기 때문이다. 그리고 토론이 없이 읽기만 하는 것은 추구해야 하는 수준의 충분한 이해를 유도해 내는 데 실패할 수 있는 것과 마찬가지로, 훌륭하고 위대한 책들이 제시해 주는 본질적인 내용이 없는 토론은 <u>피상적인 의견들</u>의 교환 정도로 수준이 낮아져 버린다.

(D) 이 조언을 진지하게 받아들인 사람들은, 만약 그들의 지난 학교 교육이 그들에게 지적인 훈련을 해주었고 그들이 그것을 수행해 나가는 데 필요한 기술들을 제공해 주었다면, 당연히 더 좋은 결과를 얻을 것이다. 하지만 심지어는 깊이 있는 토론이 수반되는 광범위한 독서를 마친 뒤에 학교 또는 대학을 마칠 만큼 운이 좋은 사람이라 할지라도, 그 또는 그녀가 진정으로 교양 있는 사람이 되기에 앞서 걸어야 할 긴 여정이 남아있을 것이다.

주제 지속적인 학습에서 독서와 토론의 중요성

어휘 continuation 계속하기, 지속 insightful 깊이 있는, 통찰력 있는 schooling 학과 과정, 학교 교육

25 정답 해설 (A)에서 졸업 후에도 지속적으로 학습이 필요함에 대해 언급했으므로 (C)에서 그 구체적인 방법으로 읽기와 토론을 제시하고 (B)에서는 읽기와 토론에 대한 구체적인 주의사항에 대해 언급한 뒤에 (D)에서 위에 언급한 조언을 따랐을 경우에 대해 예측하는 것이 자연스럽다. 따라서 (A)에 이어질 글의 순서로는 (C)-(B)-(D)가 가장 적절하다.

26 정답 해설 글 전체에 걸쳐서 지속적인 학습을 하기 위해서는 독서와 토론의 과정이 필요하다고 언급하고 있으므로 글의 주제로는 ①이 가장 적절하다.
① 지속적인 학습에서의 독서와 토론의 중요성
② 일생의 학습에 대한 학교 교육의 기여
③ 젊은 어른들에 있어서 학교 교육의 문제
④ 젊은 어른들의 폭넓은 독서의 필요성
⑤ 학교 교육을 통한 독서와 토론에 영향을 주는 요인들

27 정답 해설 (B) 앞부분에 '단순히 읽어서는 안 된다'는 내용, 빈칸 앞부분의 '토론이 없이 읽기만 하는 것은 추구해야 하는 수준의 충분한 이해를 유도해 내는 데 실패할 수 있는 것과 마찬가지로'라는 내용으로 미루어 볼 때 빈칸이 포함된 부분은 훌륭하고 위대한 책들이 제시해 주는 본질적인 내용이 없는 토론은 피상적인 의견들의 교환 정도로 수준이 낮아져 버린다는 내용이 될 때 문맥상 자연스럽다. 따라서 빈칸에 가장 적절한 것은 ③ superficial opinions이다.
① 비판적인 질문들
② 심오한 학교 교육
③ 피상적인 의견들
④ 통찰력 있는 이해
⑤ 지적인 훈육

28 ④
29 ②
30 ③

(A) 이것은 보트를 타고 바다로 나간 어부가 막 그물을 던지려고 하던 참에, 그의 바로 앞에서 막 익사하기 직전의 상황에 있는 한 남자를 보았을 때 일어났다. 그는 용감하면서도 동시에 민첩한 남자였기 때문에, 배에 있는 갈고리를 움켜 쥔 채 뛰어올랐고 그것을 물에 빠진 남자의 얼굴을 향해 찔렀다. 그 갈고리는 그 남자의 눈에 걸렸고 눈을 관통했다. 그 어부는 그 남자를 배 위로 끌어 올렸고 그물도 치지 않은 채 해변으로 향했다. 그는 그 남자를 자신의 집으로 데리고 가서 환자가 스스로의 시련을 극복해낼 때까지 최선을 다해 보살피고 치료해 주었다.

(D) 오랜 시간 동안 그 남자는 자신이 눈을 잃어버린 것을 굉장히 불행한 일이라 여기며 그 일에 대해 생각했다. "그 비열한 녀석이 내 눈을 뽑아버렸지만 나는 그에게 어떠한 해도 끼치지 않았다고. 나는 가서 그를 고소해 버릴 거야 — 왜냐하면, 그 녀석에게 어려운 상황을 만들어 버릴거니까." 그런 이유로, 그는 가서 지방 법관에게 불평을 토로했고, 그 법관은 심리를 위한 일정을 잡았다. 그 둘은 모두 그날이 임박할 때까지 기다렸고 그날이 되자 법정으로 갔다. 순서에 따라, 눈을 잃어버린 그 남자가 먼저 말했다. "여러분." 그는 말했다. "저는 여기 있는, 어느 날 야만스럽게 그의 갈고리로 저를 때리고 제 눈알을 뽑아버린 잘못 밖에 없는 훌륭한 분에 대한 불만을 가지고 왔습니다. 이제 저는 장애인입니다. 저에게 정의를 보여주십시오. 제가 원하는 것은 그것 뿐입니다. 저는 더 이상은 할 말이 없습니다."

(B) 나머지 한 사람도 즉시 큰 소리로 말했다. "여러분, 저는 제가 그의 눈을 뽑은 것에 대해 부정할 수는 없습니다. 하지만 만약 제가 했던 일이 잘못이라면, 저는 그 일이 어떻게 일어나게 된 것인지에 대해 설명하고 싶습니다. 이 남자는 그때 바다에서 죽을 수밖에 없는 위험에 빠져 있었습니다. 실제로 그는 익사하기 직전의 상황에 있었고 저는 그를 도우러 갔었습니다. 저는 제가 저의 갈고리로 그를 때린 것에 대해서는 부인하지 않겠습니다. 하지만 저는 그를 위해서 그런 행동을 했던 것입니다. 저는 그 상황에서 그의 목숨을 구했습니다. 저는 더 이상 할 수 있는 얘기가 생각나지 않습니다. 제발, 저에게 정의로운 판단을 해주십시오."

(C) 판결을 내릴 때가 되었을 때 그 법원은 아주 당혹스러워했다. 하지만 그 자리에 있었던 한 명의 바보가 그들에게 말했다. "왜 머뭇거리죠? 첫 번째로 말했던 그 남자를 두 번째 남자가 얼굴을 때렸던 바다 위에 그 장소로 데려가세요. 그리고 만약 그 남자가 이번에도 물 밖으로 빠져 나온다면 피고는 그 남자가 눈을 잃어버린 것에 대해서 보상해 주어야만 해요. 이것이 제가 생각한

공평한 판결이죠." 그러자 그 장소에 있던 모든 사람들이 한 사람처럼 동시에 외쳤다. "네 말이 확실히 옳다! 그것이야말로 바로 우리가 해야 할 일이구나!" 이 결과에 대한 판결이 공표되었다. 그가 일전에 차가운 물과 사투를 벌였던 바로 그 바다에 다시 빠뜨려지게 될 것이라는 얘기를 전해 들었을 때 그는 어떤 일이 있더라도 그곳에는 다시 가고 싶지 않았다. 그는 그 선한 남자를 책임으로부터 자유롭게 해 주었고, 그때까지의 그의 태도는 많은 비난을 받게 되었다.

[주 제] 목숨을 구해준 은혜를 저버린 사람의 최후

[어 휘] **on the point of** 막 ~ 할 때 **stout** 굳건한, 단단한 **agile** 기민한, 민첩한 **boathook** 배의 갈고리 **thrust** 밀어 넣다, 찌르다 **pierce** 관통하다 **promptly** 즉시, 신속하게 **for God's sake** 제발, 부디 **compensate** 보상하다, 갚다 **lodge a complaint** 고소하다, 고발하다 **magistrate** 법관, 지방관 **humanely** 자비롭게, 친절하게 **one after another** 차례로, 이어서

28 [정답 해설] 어부가 물에 빠진 남자를 구하려다가 갈고리로 그 남자의 눈을 찔렀고, 어부는 그 남자를 보살피고 치료해주었다는 내용의 (A) 다음에 그 남자가 눈을 잃은 것을 불행하게 여기고 이것에 대해 어부와 법정에 섰다는 (D)가 이어지는 것이 문맥상 자연스럽다. (D)에는 눈을 잃은 남자의 변론이 등장하므로 어부의 변론이 등장하는 (B)가 (D) 다음에 이어지는 것이 적절하다. 그리고 두 남자의 변론에 대해 법원이 당혹스러워할 때 바보의 말 덕분에 판결이 내려졌다는 (C)로 마무리되는 것이 자연스럽다. 따라서 (A)에 이어지는 글의 순서로는 (D)-(B)-(C)가 가장 적절하다.

29 [정답 해설] 어부 덕분에 생명을 구한 남자는 눈을 잃은 것에 대해 어부를 고발했다가 피해를 보상받으려면 바다에 다시 빠져야 한다는 판결을 받았다. 따라서 주어진 글이 시사하는 바를 가장 잘 표현한 보기로는 ②가 가장 적절하다.
① 이미 지나간 일이다.
② 먹이 주는 사람의 손을 물지 마라(배은망덕하게 굴지 마라).
③ 제 눈에 안경이다.
④ 겉모습으로 판단하지 마라.
⑤ 남의 떡이 더 커 보인다.

30 [정답 해설] 밑줄 친 as one man은 '한 사람인 것처럼'이라는 의미이므로 '만장일치'라는 뜻의 ③ unanimously와 바꿔 쓸 수 있다.
① 독특하게
② 자비롭게
③ 만장일치로
④ 그가 믿었던 것처럼
⑤ 잇따라서

31 ③
32 ③
33 ⑤

나는 원래 시골에서 태어난 사람은 아니었다. 하지만 옛날에, 아주 오래 전에, 시골에 살지 않을 수 없게 되었다. 1942년에 우리는 내 고향이었던 Cardiff로부터 15마일 정도 떨어진 농장으로 피난하게 되었다. 우리는 Cardiff 항구로 향하는 폭격기가 시골 하늘을 휩쓸어 버리는 것을 지켜보았다. 우리는 거의 6개월 동안을 그 농장 안에서 버텨냈고, 그 시절 나는 급격한 변화를 겪었다. 모든 것이 내가 학교를 가기 위해 집을 나서려고 했던 어느 날 아침에 일어났다. 나의 어머니가 먼 들판 너머로 천천히 걷고 있는 한 마리 소를 바라보며 창가에 서 있었다. "나는 저 소가 어디로 가고 있는지 궁금하구나." 그녀가 말했다. "그리고 그 소가 언제 그곳에 도착하게 될지도 말이야." 나의 어머니는 굉장히 현실적인 사람이었다. 그리고 나는 이 시골의 영향으로 그녀의 정신이 마침내 이상해진 것은 아닌가 하고 잠시 두려운 생각이 들었다.

그날 아침에 나는 꾸물거리며 기차역으로 갔기 때문에 학교로 가는 기차를 놓쳐버렸다. 어머니가 궁금해 했던 그 내용들은 나를 당황스럽게 만들었다. 나는 다음 열차를 탔다. 하지만 하루 종일 나는 집중할 수 없었고, 학교가 끝난 뒤 역으로 가는 길에서 나는 울타리 나무에 피어 있는 꽃들을 면밀히 관찰하며 그 꽃들을 찾아낸 것에 대해서 기뻐하고 있는 내 자신을 발견했다. 내가 농장으로 돌아갔을 때, 나는 말했다, "저는 오늘 울타리에서 굉장히 예쁜 꽃들을 보았어요. 저는 그 꽃들의 이름을 알고 싶어요."

그 이후로 나의 어머니와 나는 함께 매일 산책을 했다. 처음에는 우리가 도시에서 가졌던 습관처럼 거의 서로 말을 하지 않았다. 그것은 왜냐하면 도시에서의 주제들 즉, 방치된 숙제, 정리되지 않은 서랍장, 연습하지 않은 피아노 등은 (A) 침묵으로 잔뜩 도배되어 있었기 때문이다. 시간이 지남에 따라 우리는 울타리에 핀 각각의 꽃들을 구분할 수 있게 되었다. 우리는 또한 새들을 지켜보았고, 새롭게 알아낸 새들의 이름을 감상했다. 게다가 밤에 폭격이 끝나고 나면, 우리는 별을 바라보며 오리온 별자리와 북두칠성, 그리고 곰 별자리(큰곰자리, 작은곰자리)에 대해 속삭였다.

우리가 다시 Cardiff로 돌아왔을 때, 우리는 다시 도시의 (B) 침묵 속으로, 각종 시험들과, 깨끗하게 정리된 서랍장이 갖는 의미 없는 우선순위로 돌아가게 되었다. 하지만 우리는 종종 시골에서 겪었던 마법과, 모든 것들의 적당하고 알맞은 장소를 두드려 주었던 온전한 지팡이를 떠올리며 서로 웃음 짓곤 했다. 그리고 수많은 시간이 지난 뒤에, 도시가 내 준 어려운 문제에 빠져 사는 지금, 나는 여전히 붐비는 거리에서 헤매는 개를 볼 수 있고, 그 개가 어디로 갈지에 대해 궁금해 할 수 있다.

주 제) 시골 생활이 주는 여유와 기쁨

어 휘) by nature 원래, 천성적으로 evacuate 탈출시키다 comb 빗, 빗질하다, 휩쓸다 dock 선창, 부둣가 lone 혼자 있는, 외로운 amble 천천히 걷다 round the bend 제정신이 아닌 dawdle 꾸물거리다, 어슬렁거리다 unnerve 불안하게 만들다 hedgerow 산울타리 hedges 산울타리, 산울타리 나무 savour(savor) 맛, 풍미, 음미하다, 즐기다 disenchant 마법에서 깨어나다, 꿈에서 깨어나다 amidst ~의 한 가운데서, ~의 중간에 imprisonment 투옥, 수감, 구속 unwithering 시들지 않는, 언제나 싱싱한, 죽지 않는

31 정답 해설) '나'는 'hedgerow flowers'의 이름을 알고 싶어서 매일 엄마와 산책하기 시작했으므로 ③은 '나'에 관한 글의 내용과 일치한다.

32 정답 해설) 필자가 원치 않았던 시골 생활을 통해 이전에는 알지 못했던 생활 속의 여유와 자연이 주는 기쁨에 대해 알게 되었다는 것이 주된 내용이므로 ③ '시골의 마법: 세계에 눈을 뜨다'가 가장 적절하다.
① 시골의 풍경에 환멸을 느끼다
② 전쟁 중의 위험한 취미
③ 시골의 마법: 새로운 세계에 눈을 뜨다
④ 시골의 감금에서의 예상치 못한 탈출
⑤ 전쟁에서 살아남기: 시들지 않는 산울타리 꽃

33 정답 해설) 방치된 숙제, 서랍장, 피아노, 각종 시험 등은 대화가 필요하지 않고 혼자 하는 일들이다. 또한 (A) 앞부분에서 '처음에 우리가 도시에서 가졌던 습관처럼 거의 서로 말을 하지 않았다.'는 내용으로 미루어 볼 때 (A)와 (B)에 가장 적절한 단어는 ⑤ silence이다.
① 웅변   ② 바쁨
③ 멜로디, 선율   ④ 수수께끼
⑤ 침묵

34 ⑤
35 ②
36 ⑤

(A) 호주의 해안에서 큰돌고래의 행동을 수천 시간 동안 관찰해온 연구원은 수컷 돌고래들이 인간을 제외하고 다른 동물에서 볼 수 있는 것보다 훨씬 더 정교하고 복잡한 사회적 동맹을 서로 형성한 것을 발견했다.

(D) 그들은 수컷 돌고래의 한 무리가 제삼의 무리에게 맞서기 위해 수컷의 또 다른 무리의 도움을 구하는 것을 발견했다. 과학자들에 의하면 이러한 종류의 전술 계획은 상당한 정신적인 계산력을 필요로 한다. 하지만 이런 수컷 돌고래들의 복잡한 사회적 동맹의 목적이 항상 놀이와 관련된 것은 아니다. 수컷들은 경쟁하는 돌고래 무리로부터 출산 가능한 암컷을 빼앗는 수단으로써 동료들과 결탁한다.

(C) 그리고 그들은 암컷 탈취에 성공한 후, 수컷들은 암컷이 계속 머물도록 설득하기 위하여 화려하고도 위협적인 재주를 부리며 결속된 집단 안에 계속 머문다. 두세 마리의 수컷들은 서로 완벽히 동시에 뛰어오르거나, 물 위를 박차고 오르거나, 공중제비를 돌면서 암컷 주위를 둘러쌀 것이다.

(B) 만약 암컷이 수컷에게 매력을 느끼지 못하고 도망간다면, 그 수컷들은 암컷을 쫓아서 물고 지느러미로 때리거나 몸통으로 세게 들이받을 것이다. 과학자들은 수컷의 암컷을 통제하려는 이러한 노력을 '떼짓기'라고 부르지만 그들도 그 단어가 그런 행동의 폭력성을 전달하지 않는다는 것을 인정한다.

[주 제] 동맹을 이용하여 구애하는 돌고래

[어 휘] bottlenose dolphin 큰돌고래 courtship 구애, 구혼 sportive 장난의, 밝고 명랑한 collude 공모하다, 결탁하다 spirit away 납치하다 belly flop 배로 수면을 치며 다이빙하기 somersault 공중제비, 공중제비를 돌다 synchrony 동시, 일치 collude with ~와 한통속이 되다 coalition 연합, 합동

34 [정답 해설] 호주 연구원들이 수컷 큰돌고래들이 정교하고 복잡한 사회적 동맹을 형성한다는 내용의 (A)에 이어서 그 동맹의 목적과 성격을 언급한 (D)가 이어지는 것이 적절하다. 그리고 (D)의 뒷부분에 암컷을 빼앗는 수단으로써 동료들과 결탁한다는 내용에 이어 암컷 탈취에 성공한 후 암컷을 붙잡아 두기 위한 수컷 돌고래들의 행동을 설명한 (C)가 이어지는 것이 자연스럽다. 그리고 이러한 수컷 돌고래의 행동에도 불구하고 암컷이 매력을 느끼지 못하고 도망갈 경우 수컷 돌고래의 행동을 설명한 (B)가 그 다음에 이어지는 것이 적절하다. 따라서 (A) 다음에 이어지는 글의 순서로 가장 적절한 것은 (D)-(C)-(B)이다.

35 [정답 해설] 이 글은 수컷 돌고래들이 암컷과 짝짓기를 하기 위해서 지능적으로 계산하고 행동한다는 특성을 구체적으로 설명하고 있다. 그러므로 이 글의 제목으로는 ②가 알맞다.
① 암수 돌고래의 공생
② 돌고래의 구애의 기묘한 모습
③ 돌고래의 성별 차이
④ 수컷 돌고래들의 암컷 상대에 대한 위협
⑤ 멸종 위기 종의 놀라운 행동

36 [정답 해설] 빈칸에는 '한 무리가 다른 무리에 맞서기 위해 수컷의 또 다른 무리의 도움을 구하는 것'과 '출산 가능한 암컷을 빼앗는 수단으로써 동료들과 결탁하는 것'을 설명할 수 있는 내용이 들어가야 한다. 따라서 빈칸에는 ⑤ '사회적 동맹'이 들어가는 것이 가장 적절하다.
① 이타적인 연합
② 매력적인 기술
③ 연령 그룹

④ 관계에 대한 간섭
⑤ 사회적 동맹

37 ⑤
38 ②
39 ③

(A) 실업자를 위해 일자리를 제공하는 종합적인 고용 및 교육법(CETA)과 같은 정부 프로그램은 더 야심차게 만들어져야 한다. 정부는 최후 수단의 고용주 역할을 할 수 있다. 즉, 정부가 일을 원하지만 민간 부문에서 찾을 수 없는 모든 사람들을 위해 일자리를 제공할 준비를 하는 것이다.

(D) 비록 정부는 민간 기업에서 거부당한 사람들을 위해 일자리를 제공해야만 하는 의무는 없지만, 1976년에 초안이 마련된 Humphery - Hawkins 법안에는 이와 밀접한 관련 제안이 포함되었다. 그 법안은 실업률을 연간 3%라는 목표까지 감소시키기 위해 정부가 필요한 어떤 일자리든 제공하겠다고 약속했다.

(C) 정부를 최후의 수단으로 만들려는 제안은 논쟁의 여지가 있다. (이 반대 때문에 대립되는 정치 세력들에 의해 그 조항들은 Humphrey-Hawkins 법안의 이후 버전에서는 제외되었다. 그리고 Reagan 대통령은 CETA를 1983년 말까지 제거할 것을 제안했다.) 긍정적인 측면에서, 정부의 프로젝트를 수행하는 데 실업자들에게 뭔가 줄 수 있는 유용한 것을 제공할 수 있었다. 예를 들어, 실업자는 도시의 유지 보수작업을 하고, 1930년대 Roosevelt 대통령의 회복 프로그램과 유사한 공공 프로젝트를 수행할 수 있었다.

(B) 반면에 반대자들은 그런 프로그램의 비용이 많이 든다고 반대한다. 얼마나 많은 비용이 드는지는 1977~1978년 사이 나타나는데, 이때, 새로운 Carter 정부가 84억 달러 비용으로 공공 서비스 근로 사업에서 725,000개의 일자리로 고용을 2배 이상 늘렸다. 그것은 직업당 11,500달러에 해당한다. 평균적으로 노동자는 상당히 적은 돈을 받았다. 대략 7,200달러이다. 일부는 관리 및 지원 서비스에 들어갔다.

[주 제] 정부의 실업 정책에 대한 논쟁

[어 휘] comprehensive 포괄적인, 이해력 있는 employment 고용 provide 제공하다 unemployed 실업인 ambitious 야망이 있는, 야심찬 opponent 반대편 controversial 논란이 있는 provision 조항 eliminate 제거하다 maintenance 관리 similar 유사한 commitment 위탁, 전념, 약속, 의무 draft 초안 commit 언질을 주다, 약속하다

37 [정답 해설] 정부가 민간에서 고용되지 못한 실업자를 위해 일자리를 제공해야 한다고 주장하는 (A)에 이어 이 주장의 근

거로 Humphery - Hawkins 법안의 제안을 든 (B)가 이어진 후 이 주장에 대한 논쟁의 여지가 있음을 소개하고 찬성 측의 근거를 든 (C)가 오는 것이 적절하다. 그 다음 이 주장에 대한 반대 측의 근거를 보여주는 (B)가 오는 것이 문맥상 자연스럽다. 따라서 (A)에 이어지는 글의 순서로 가장 적절한 것은 (D)-(C)-(B)이다.

38 정답 해설 개인적으로 민간부분에서 일자리를 구하지 못한 실업자들에게 정부가 최후로 일자리를 제공해 주어야 한다는 의미에서 빈칸에는 ② last resort가 가장 적절하다.
① 국공채
② 최후의 수단
③ 최적의 조건
④ 부족한 공급
⑤ 보안 검색

39 정답 해설 정부가 정책적으로 실업자들에게 일자리를 제공해 주어야 하는가에 대한 찬반 입장이 대조적으로 드러나 있다.
① 오늘날의 힘든 취업 시장 상황
② 완전 고용에 필요한 조건
③ 논란이 많은 정부의 실업자 정책
④ 정부 고용에 대한 공식 가이드라인
⑤ 고용 관련 입법의 역사

More Practice

01 ③	02 ⑤	03 ⑤	04 ⑤	05 ②
06 ⑤				

01 ③
02 ⑤
03 ⑤

(A) 행복해지려면 얼마만큼의 공간이 필요한가? 일부 미국인들은 넓을수록 더 좋으며, 주택 구매자에게 저렴한 신용대출과 세금 우대 조치가 있다면 더 큰 집을 짓거나 구입하려고 자금조달을 늘리고 싶은 마음이 생길 것이라고 이야기한다. 나의 할아버지 Otto는 다른 길을 선택했다. (a) 그는 단지 더 넓은 공간과 그 공간을 채울 물건들을 위한 비용을 지불하기 위해서 자신이 점점 더 오랜 시간 동안 일하는 것을 보고 싶어 하지 않았다. 그는 농촌 지역의 대가족 속에서 성장했기 때문에, 소박하게 사는 것이 삶의 철학에서 절대적이었다.

(C) 1950년대, 아버지가 작은 소년이었을 때, 할아버지는 600제곱 피트의 집을 지었다. (c) 그는 Pleasant Hill에 있는 작은 구획의 땅에 가로 세로 20피트와 30피트

의 건축물을 지었다. 아버지는 "재사용과 재활용이 필수였단다. 본래 (d) 그는 집이 '근사해지기' 전에 재활용을 하고 있었단다."라고 말씀하셨다. 할아버지는 자신이 일하고 있었던 Oakland 부두에서 그의 자그마한 집을 위한 대부분의 자재를 구했다. 그 자그마한 집을 짓는데 4년이 걸렸으며, 그들이 이사했을 때 아직도 지붕이 없었다!

(D) 아버지는 12살 아이였을 때 잠들기 전에 지붕이 없는 집에서 별을 봤던 것을 기억했다. 아버지는 완성되지 않은 집에서 사는 것에 신경을 쓰지 않았다. (e) 그는 Pleasant Hill을 "훤히 트여있으며 눈에 띄지 않고, 모든 집들이 10에이커 위에 있는 것처럼 느껴졌다고" 말했다. 여러 해 동안, 아버지와 할아버지는 자신들이 살고 있는 지역 사회의 급격한 변화를 알아차렸다. 매년 더 많은 농경지가 쇼핑센터와 더 커진 집들이 들어선 주택 지구를 건립하느라 소실됐다. 부동산 가격이 오르면서, 많은 이웃들이 자신들의 집과 땅을 팔아버렸다. 이윽고 할아버지는 그 구획에서 유일하게 남은 작은 집에 살게 되었고, 자신이 사는 집의 네 배 크기의 많은 집들의 바다에 둘러싸이게 되었다.

(B) 그렇지만 할아버지는 자신의 작은 집을 좋아했고 그가 소유한 것에 만족했다. 집이 작기는 했지만, 답답하지는 않았다. 아버지가 말한 것처럼, "모두가 행복하고 만족했다. 집의 크기는 중요하지 않았다." 할아버지는 내게 소박하게 사는 것이 스스로 궁핍해지는 것은 아니라는 것을 가르쳐 주었다. 그 대신에, 그것은 스스로에게 자신의 꿈을 추구할 시간과 자유, 그리고 돈을 제공하는 것이었다. 여러 가지 면에서, 나는 할아버지의 삶을 나의 삶의 모델로 삼았다. 나는 (b) 그에게서 소박함이 금욕적인 생활은 아니라는 것을 배웠다. 그것은 개인적인 성장에 있어서 혁명이다.

주제 할아버지의 소박한 삶이 주는 교훈

어휘 credit 신용대출 tax break 세금 우대 (조치) integral 절대 필요한, 완전한 cramped 비좁은, 답답한 deprivation 궁핍, 박탈 pursue 추구하다, 뒤쫓다 austerity 내핍[금욕적인] 생활 revolution 혁명, 변혁 plot 작은 구획의 땅 devour 게걸스럽게 먹다, 삼켜버리다

01 정답 해설 주어진 글 (A)에서 할아버지의 성장 배경과 생활 철학을 설명한 다음, 1950년대로 거슬러 올라가 할아버지가 4년에 걸쳐 집을 지었으나 이사 갈 때까지도 지붕이 완성되지 않았다는 (C)가 오고, 필자의 아버지가 지붕이 없는 집에서 잠을 잤다고 시작되어 시간이 지남에 따라 할아버지의 집이 인근에서 가장 작은 집이 되었다는 (D)가 이어지고, 환경의 변화에도 불구하고 변화하지 않은 할아버지와 그의 삶이 주는 교훈에 대한 (B)로 마무리되는 것이 자연스럽다.

02 (정답 해설) ⑤는 아버지를 가리키고, 나머지는 할아버지를 가리킨다.

03 (정답 해설) ⑤ 아버지와 할아버지는 여러 해에 걸쳐 자신들이 살고 있는 지역 사회의 급격한 변화를 알아차렸다.

---

04 ⑤
05 ②
06 ⑤

(A) 한낮의 태양은 빛났다. 고등학교 운동장은 화려한 드레스와 정장을 입고 쾌활한 사진사들에게 포즈를 취하는, 옷을 잘 차려입은 사람들로 가득 찼다. 축하, 포옹, 그리고 웃음이 전파되었다. Hannah는 지난 몇 년 동안 (a) 그녀의 삶의 일부였던 모든 친숙한 얼굴들을 바라보았다. 곧 그녀의 어머니가 그들과 합류할 것이었다. 그녀는 불안해하는 많은 신입생들의 한가운데에서 자신이 그 똑같은 곳에 서 있었던 학교에서의 첫날을 기억해 냈는데, 그들 중 몇 명은 그녀의 가장 친한 친구들이 되었다.

(D) 그날은 마치 불가사의한 뭔가가 앞에 있는 것처럼 평소와 달리 안개가 자욱했다. Hannah는 초조했고 떨고 있었다. 교장 선생님은 고등학교 생활의 도전과 스릴에 대해 이야기하면서 그들에게 힘차게 말씀하고 있었지만, 그녀는 집중할 수가 없었다. 후에 키가 크고 엄격해 보이는 남자가 자기 자신을 (e) 그녀의 담임선생님으로 소개했다. 교실은 낡았지만, 정돈되어 있었고 마음을 끌어 당겼다. Hannah는 창가 자리를 원했지만 복도 쪽 다섯 번째 줄에 앉았다. 고등학교 생활은 교장 선생님이 예측했던 대로 도전적이라는 것이 곧 드러났다.

(C) Hannah는 그 많은 수업 시간, 끝없는 과제, 그리고 시험과 씨름했다. 하지만, 운동회 날과 학교 축제처럼 신나는 사건도 있었다. (c) 그녀가 어떻게 자신의 두 번째 해를 잊을 수 있겠는가! 선풍적인 공연의 일환으로 그녀는 축제에서 친구들과 함께 노래를 부르고 춤을 추었다. 그 후에 그녀는 자신감이 더 생기고 활동적이 되었다. 그녀의 생각이 떠도는 사이에 Hannah는 어렴풋이 자신의 어머니의 목소리를 들었다. "여기 있구나!" 그녀의 어머니가 서둘러 다가와 (d) 그녀에게 백합과 장미 한 다발을 주고 강한 포옹을 해 주었다.

(B) "Hannah야, 너 아주 심각해 보여. 무엇에 대해 생각하고 있니?" "아, 엄마, 그저, 아시잖아요." 그녀의 어머니는 미소를 지었다. "넌 이곳을 그리워할 거야, 그렇지 않니?" Hannah는 고개를 끄덕였다. "빨리, 저쪽으로 서서... 그리고 미소를 지으렴, Hannah야. 넌 아주 예쁜 미소를 짓잖아."라고 그녀의 어머니가 말했다. (b) 그녀는 자신의 휴대전화를 서둘러 꺼내, 줌 렌즈로 자신의

딸을 확대하고서, 자신이 한 어린 숙녀를 바라보고 있다는 것을 갑자기 깨달았다. "넌 다 컸구나."라고 그녀는 속삭였다. Hannah는 학교 정원에서 선생님들과 사진을 더 찍었다. 그녀는 모든 추억이 자신의 마음속에 영원히 머물기를 바랐다.

(주 제) Hannah의 고등학교 졸업식

(어 휘) bundle 다발, 묶음 tremble 떨다 energetically 힘차게 neat 정돈된 hallway 복도 predict 예측하다 glorious 빛나는 fancy 화려한 contagious 전파하는 recall 기억해 내다 anxious 불안한 zoom in on (줌 렌즈로) ~을 서서히 확대하다 sensational 선풍적인 performance 공연 confident 자신감 있는 wander (정처 없이) 떠돌다 vaguely 어렴풋이

04 (정답 해설) 마지막 부분에서 Hannah가 자신의 학교 첫날을 떠올리고 있는 주어진 글 (A)의 다음에, 첫날의 일들에 대해 이야기 한 뒤 고등학교 생활이 고되었음을 암시하는 (D)가 오고, 고등학교 생활을 하며 겪었던 일들을 되새기는 도중에 어머니가 등장한 (C)가 온 뒤, Hannah와 어머니의 대화가 나오는 (B)로 이어지는 것이 자연스럽다.

05 (정답 해설) ② (b)는 Hannah의 어머니를 가리키고 나머지는 모두 Hannah를 가리킨다.

06 (정답 해설) ⑤ Hannah는 창가 자리에 앉기를 원했지만 복도 쪽 다섯 번째 줄에 앉았다.

MEMO

MEMO